Ford Focus
Owners Workshop Manual

Martynn Randall

Models covered

(4785 - 7AR2 - 288)

Hatchback, Saloon & Estate models with 4-cylinder petrol engines
1.4 litre (1388cc), 1.6 litre (1596cc), 1.8 litre (1798cc) and 2.0 litre (1999cc)

Does not cover 2.5 litre 5-cylinder engine, FlexFuel, CVT or Powershift transmission
Does not cover features specific to C-Max or CC (Convertible) models

© J H Haynes & Co. Ltd. 2013

ABCDE
FGHIJ
KLMNO
PQRS
2

A book in the **Haynes Owners Workshop Manual Series**

All rights reserved. No part of this book may be reproduced or transmitted in any form or by any means, electronic or mechanical, including photocopying, recording or by any information storage or retrieval system, without permission in writing from the copyright holder.

Printed in Malaysia

J H Haynes & Co. Ltd.
Sparkford, Yeovil, Somerset BA22 7JJ, England

ISBN 978 0 85733 870 9

British Library Cataloguing in Publication Data
A catalogue record for this book is available from the British Library.

Haynes North America, Inc
859 Lawrence Drive, Newbury Park, California 91320, USA

Printed using NORBRITE BOOK 48.8gsm (CODE: 40N6533) from NORPAC; procurement system certified under Sustainable Forestry Initiative standard. Paper produced is certified to the SFI Certified Fiber Sourcing Standard (CERT - 0094271)

Disclaimer

There are risks associated with automotive repairs. The ability to make repairs depends on the individual's skill, experience and proper tools. Individuals should act with due care and acknowledge and assume the risk of performing automotive repairs.

The purpose of this manual is to provide comprehensive, useful and accessible automotive repair information, to help you get the best value from your vehicle. However, this manual is not a substitute for a professional certified technician or mechanic.

This repair manual is produced by a third party and is not associated with an individual vehicle manufacturer. If there is any doubt or discrepancy between this manual and the owner's manual or the factory service manual, please refer to the factory service manual or seek assistance from a professional certified technician or mechanic.

Even though we have prepared this manual with extreme care and every attempt is made to ensure that the information in this manual is correct, neither the publisher nor the author can accept responsibility for loss, damage or injury caused by any errors in, or omissions from, the information given.

Contents

LIVING WITH YOUR FORD FOCUS
Introduction	Page 0•4
Safety first!	Page 0•5

Roadside repairs
If your car won't start	Page 0•6
Jump starting	Page 0•7
Wheel changing	Page 0•8
Identifying leaks	Page 0•9
Towing	Page 0•9

Weekly checks
Introduction	Page 0•10
Underbonnet check points	Page 0•10
Engine oil level	Page 0•11
Coolant level	Page 0•11
Brake and clutch fluid level	Page 0•12
Power steering fluid level	Page 0•12
Tyre condition and pressure	Page 0•13
Washer fluid level	Page 0•14
Wiper blades	Page 0•14
Battery	Page 0•15
Bulbs and fuses	Page 0•16

Lubricants and fluids
Page 0•17

Tyre pressures
Page 0•17

MAINTENANCE

Routine maintenance and servicing
Routine maintenance and servicing	Page 1•1
Servicing specifications	Page 1•2
Maintenance schedule	Page 1•3
Maintenance procedures	Page 1•5

Illegal Copying

It is the policy of J H Haynes & Co. Ltd. to actively protect its Copyrights and Trade Marks. Legal action will be taken against anyone who unlawfully copies the cover or contents of this Manual. This includes all forms of unauthorised copying including digital, mechanical, and electronic in any form. Authorisation from J H Haynes & Co. Ltd. will only be provided expressly and in writing. Illegal copying will also be reported to the appropriate statutory authorities.

Contents

REPAIRS & OVERHAUL

Engine and associated systems
1.4 & 1.6 litre engines (Duratec 16V) in-car repair procedures	Page **2A•1**
1.8 & 2.0 litre engines (Duratec HE) in-car repair procedures	Page **2B•1**
Engine removal and overhaul procedures	Page **2C•1**
Cooling, heating and air conditioning systems	Page **3•1**
Fuel and exhaust systems	Page **4A•1**
Emission control systems	Page **4B•1**
Starting and charging systems	Page **5A•1**
Ignition system	Page **5B•1**

Transmission
Clutch	Page **6•1**
Manual transmission	Page **7A•1**
Automatic transmission	Page **7B•1**
Driveshafts	Page **8•1**

Brakes and suspension
Braking system	Page **9•1**
Suspension and steering	Page **10•1**

Body equipment
Bodywork and fittings	Page **11•1**
Body electrical systems	Page **12•1**

Wiring diagrams
	Page **12•24**

REFERENCE
Dimensions and weights	Page **REF•1**
Fuel economy	Page **REF•2**
Conversion factors	Page **REF•6**
Buying spare parts	Page **REF•7**
Vehicle identification numbers	Page **REF•7**
General repair procedures	Page **REF•8**
Jacking and vehicle support	Page **REF•9**
Tools and working facilities	Page **REF•10**
MOT test checks	Page **REF•12**
Fault finding	Page **REF•16**
Glossary of technical terms	Page **REF•23**

Index
	Page **REF•27**

Introduction

The original Focus model range was introduced to the UK in 1998. It was hailed as being innovative and stylish with excellent roadholding. The new range of Focus covered by this manual shares the attributes of its ancestor, but with improved refinement and performance, coupled with lower emissions. This new Focus shares a platform with other models from Ford's stable, most noticeably the Volvo S40 and V50 range.

Initially only available as a Hatchback or Estate, the range was expanded later by the addition of a 4-door Saloon model. Safety features include door side impact bars, airbags for the driver and front seat passenger, side airbags, head airbags, whiplash protection system (front seats), and an advanced seat belt system with pretensioners and load limiters. Vehicle security is enhanced, with an engine immobiliser, shielded locks, and security-coded audio equipment being fitted as standard, as well as double-locking doors on most models.

The 16-valve DOHC (double overhead camshaft) four-cylinder petrol engines are available in 1.4, 1.6, 1.8 and 2.0 litre capacities, and are based on the familiar Ford range of engines. The engines are controlled by a sophisticated engine management system, which combines multipoint sequential fuel injection and distributorless ignition systems with evaporative emissions control, exhaust gas recirculation, variable intake geometry and a three-way regulated catalytic converter to ensure compliance with increasingly stringent emissions control standards, while providing the expected levels of performance and fuel economy. The 1.6 litre engine is also available with variable valve timing for the intake and exhaust camshafts, further improving the engine's output, driveability and emissions.

The transversely-mounted engines drive the front roadwheels through either a five- or six-speed manual transmission with a hydraulically-operated clutch, or through an electronically-controlled four-speed automatic transmission.

The fully-independent suspension is by MacPherson struts and transverse lower arms at the front, with multilink independent suspension at the rear; anti-roll bars are fitted at front and rear.

The vacuum servo-assisted brakes are disc at the front, and either disc or drum at the rear. An electronically-controlled Anti-lock Braking System (ABS) is fitted on all models, with Dynamic Stability and Traction Control System (DSTC) also available.

Power-assisted steering is standard on all models. Air conditioning is available, and all models have an ergonomically-designed passenger cabin with high levels of safety and comfort for all passengers.

Provided that regular servicing is carried out in accordance with the manufacturer's recommendations, the Focus should prove a reliable and economical car. The engine compartment is well-designed, and most of the items needing frequent attention are easily accessible.

Your Ford Focus manual

The aim of this manual is to help you get the best value from your vehicle. It can do so in several ways. It can help you decide what work must be done (even should you choose to get it done by a garage). It will also provide information on routine maintenance and servicing, and give a logical course of action and diagnosis when random faults occur. However, it is hoped that you will use the manual by tackling the work yourself. On simpler jobs it may even be quicker than booking the car into a garage and going there twice, to leave and collect it. Perhaps most important, a lot of money can be saved by avoiding the costs a garage must charge to cover its labour and overheads.

The manual has drawings and descriptions to show the function of the various components so that their layout can be understood. Tasks are described and photographed in a clear step-by-step sequence. The illustrations are numbered by the Section number and paragraph number to which they relate – if there is more than one illustration per paragraph, the sequence is denoted alphabetically.

References to the 'left' or 'right' of the vehicle are in the sense of a person in the driver's seat, facing forwards.

Acknowledgements

Thanks are due to Draper Tools Limited, who provided some of the workshop tools, and to all those people at Sparkford who helped in the production of this manual.

We take great pride in the accuracy of information given in this manual, but vehicle manufacturers make alterations and design changes during the production run of a particular vehicle of which they do not inform us. No liability can be accepted by the authors or publishers for loss, damage or injury caused by any errors in, or omissions from, the information given.

Safety First! 0•5

Working on your car can be dangerous. This page shows just some of the potential risks and hazards, with the aim of creating a safety-conscious attitude.

General hazards

Scalding
• Don't remove the radiator or expansion tank cap while the engine is hot.
• Engine oil, automatic transmission fluid or power steering fluid may also be dangerously hot if the engine has recently been running.

Burning
• Beware of burns from the exhaust system and from any part of the engine. Brake discs and drums can also be extremely hot immediately after use.

Crushing
• When working under or near a raised vehicle, always supplement the jack with axle stands, or use drive-on ramps. *Never venture under a car which is only supported by a jack.*

• Take care if loosening or tightening high-torque nuts when the vehicle is on stands. Initial loosening and final tightening should be done with the wheels on the ground.

Fire
• Fuel is highly flammable; fuel vapour is explosive.
• Don't let fuel spill onto a hot engine.
• Do not smoke or allow naked lights (including pilot lights) anywhere near a vehicle being worked on. Also beware of creating sparks (electrically or by use of tools).
• Fuel vapour is heavier than air, so don't work on the fuel system with the vehicle over an inspection pit.
• Another cause of fire is an electrical overload or short-circuit. Take care when repairing or modifying the vehicle wiring.
• Keep a fire extinguisher handy, of a type suitable for use on fuel and electrical fires.

Electric shock
• Ignition HT voltage can be dangerous, especially to people with heart problems or a pacemaker. Don't work on or near the ignition system with the engine running or the ignition switched on.

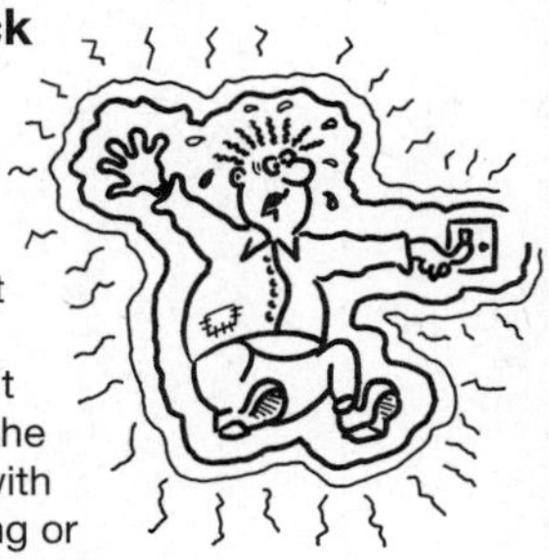

• Mains voltage is also dangerous. Make sure that any mains-operated equipment is correctly earthed. Mains power points should be protected by a residual current device (RCD) circuit breaker.

Fume or gas intoxication
• Exhaust fumes are poisonous; they often contain carbon monoxide, which is rapidly fatal if inhaled. Never run the engine in a confined space such as a garage with the doors shut.

• Fuel vapour is also poisonous, as are the vapours from some cleaning solvents and paint thinners.

Poisonous or irritant substances
• Avoid skin contact with battery acid and with any fuel, fluid or lubricant, especially antifreeze, brake hydraulic fluid and Diesel fuel. Don't syphon them by mouth. If such a substance is swallowed or gets into the eyes, seek medical advice.
• Prolonged contact with used engine oil can cause skin cancer. Wear gloves or use a barrier cream if necessary. Change out of oil-soaked clothes and do not keep oily rags in your pocket.
• Air conditioning refrigerant forms a poisonous gas if exposed to a naked flame (including a cigarette). It can also cause skin burns on contact.

Asbestos
• Asbestos dust can cause cancer if inhaled or swallowed. Asbestos may be found in gaskets and in brake and clutch linings. When dealing with such components it is safest to assume that they contain asbestos.

Special hazards

Hydrofluoric acid
• This extremely corrosive acid is formed when certain types of synthetic rubber, found in some O-rings, oil seals, fuel hoses etc, are exposed to temperatures above 400°C. The rubber changes into a charred or sticky substance containing the acid. *Once formed, the acid remains dangerous for years. If it gets onto the skin, it may be necessary to amputate the limb concerned.*
• When dealing with a vehicle which has suffered a fire, or with components salvaged from such a vehicle, wear protective gloves and discard them after use.

The battery
• Batteries contain sulphuric acid, which attacks clothing, eyes and skin. Take care when topping-up or carrying the battery.
• The hydrogen gas given off by the battery is highly explosive. Never cause a spark or allow a naked light nearby. Be careful when connecting and disconnecting battery chargers or jump leads.

Air bags
• Air bags can cause injury if they go off accidentally. Take care when removing the steering wheel and/or facia. Special storage instructions may apply.

Diesel injection equipment
• Diesel injection pumps supply fuel at very high pressure. Take care when working on the fuel injectors and fuel pipes.

⚠️ *Warning: Never expose the hands, face or any other part of the body to injector spray; the fuel can penetrate the skin with potentially fatal results.*

Remember...

DO
• Do use eye protection when using power tools, and when working under the vehicle.

• Do wear gloves or use barrier cream to protect your hands when necessary.

• Do get someone to check periodically that all is well when working alone on the vehicle.

• Do keep loose clothing and long hair well out of the way of moving mechanical parts.

• Do remove rings, wristwatch etc, before working on the vehicle – especially the electrical system.

• Do ensure that any lifting or jacking equipment has a safe working load rating adequate for the job.

DON'T
• Don't attempt to lift a heavy component which may be beyond your capability – get assistance.

• Don't rush to finish a job, or take unverified short cuts.

• Don't use ill-fitting tools which may slip and cause injury.

• Don't leave tools or parts lying around where someone can trip over them. Mop up oil and fuel spills at once.

• Don't allow children or pets to play in or near a vehicle being worked on.

0•6 Roadside repairs

The following pages are intended to help in dealing with common roadside emergencies and breakdowns. You will find more detailed fault finding information at the back of the manual, and repair information in the main chapters.

If your car won't start and the starter motor doesn't turn

- [ ] If it's a model with automatic transmission, make sure the selector is in P or N.
- [ ] Open the bonnet and make sure that the battery terminals are clean and tight (unclip the battery cover for access).
- [ ] Switch on the headlights and try to start the engine. If the headlights go very dim when you're trying to start, the battery is probably flat. Get out of trouble by jump starting (see next page) using a friend's car.

If your car won't start even though the starter motor turns as normal

- [ ] Is there fuel in the tank?
- [ ] Has the engine immobiliser been deactivated? This should happen automatically, on inserting the ignition key. However, if a replacement key has been obtained (other than from a Ford dealer), it may not contain the transponder chip necessary to deactivate the system. Even 'proper' replacement keys have to be coded to work properly – a procedure for this is outlined in the vehicle handbook.
- [ ] Is there moisture on electrical components under the bonnet? Switch off the ignition, then wipe off any obvious dampness with a dry cloth. Remove the plastic cover on the top of the engine (where applicable). Spray a water-repellent aerosol product (WD-40 or equivalent) on ignition and fuel system electrical connectors like those shown in the photos. Pay special attention to the ignition coil wiring connector and HT leads (where applicable).

A Check the security and condition of the battery connections – unclip and lift the battery cover for access.

B Check the mass airflow sensor wiring plug.

C Check that none of the engine compartment fuses have blown.

Check that all electrical connections are secure (with the ignition switched off). Spray the connector plugs with a water-dispersant spray like WD-40 if you suspect a problem due to damp.

Roadside repairs

Jump starting

When jump-starting a car using a booster battery, observe the following precautions:

✔ Before connecting the booster battery, make sure that the ignition is switched off.

✔ Ensure that all electrical equipment (lights, heater, wipers, etc) is switched off.

✔ Take note of any special precautions printed on the battery case.

✔ Make sure that the booster battery is the same voltage as the discharged one in the vehicle.

✔ If the battery is being jump-started from the battery in another vehicle, the two vehicles MUST NOT TOUCH each other.

✔ Make sure that the transmission is in neutral (or PARK, in the case of automatic transmission).

HAYNES HiNT *Jump starting will get you out of trouble, but you must correct whatever made the battery go flat in the first place. There are three possibilities:*

1 The battery has been drained by repeated attempts to start, or by leaving the lights on.

2 The charging system is not working properly (alternator drivebelt slack or broken, alternator wiring fault or alternator itself faulty).

3 The battery itself is at fault (electrolyte low, or battery worn out).

1 Connect one end of the red jump lead to the positive (+) terminal of the flat battery

2 Connect the other end of the red lead to the positive (+) terminal of the booster battery.

3 Connect one end of the black jump lead to the negative (-) terminal of the booster battery

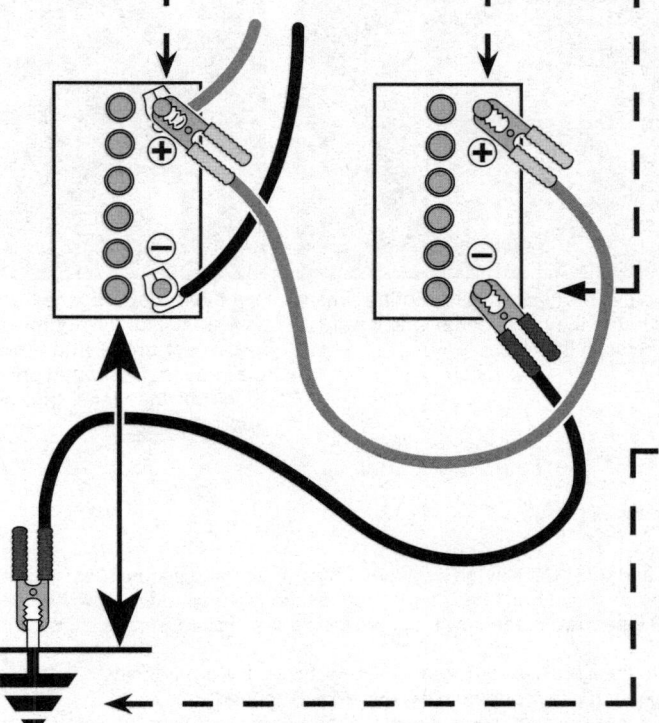

4 Connect the other end of the black lead to the to the earth terminal on the left-hand front suspension turret in the engine compartment.

5 Make sure that the jump leads will not come into contact with the fan, drive-belts or other moving parts of the engine.

6 Start the engine, then with the engine running at fast idle speed disconnect the jump leads in the reverse order of connection.

0•8 Roadside repairs

Wheel changing

 Warning: *Do not change a wheel in a situation where you risk being hit by other traffic. On busy roads, try to stop in a lay-by or a gateway. Be wary of passing traffic while changing the wheel – it is easy to become distracted by the job in hand.*

Preparation

- When a puncture occurs, stop as soon as it is safe to do so.
- Park on firm level ground, if possible, and well out of the way of other traffic.
- Use hazard warning lights if necessary.
- If you have one, use a warning triangle to alert other drivers of your presence.
- Apply the handbrake and engage first or reverse gear (or P on models with automatic transmission).
- Chock the wheel diagonally opposite the one being removed – a couple of large stones will do for this.
- If the ground is soft, use a flat piece of wood to spread the load under the jack.

Changing the wheel

1 The spare wheel and tools are stored under the floor in the luggage compartment. Lift up the cover panel. Unscrew the retaining bolt, and lift the spare wheel out. The jack and wheel brace are located beneath the spare wheel. The screw-in towing eye is located alongside the spare wheel.

2 Where applicable, using the flat end of the wheel brace, prise off the wheel trim or centre cover for access to the wheel nuts. Models with alloy wheels may have special locking nuts – these are removed with a special tool, which should be provided with the wheel brace (or it may be in the glovebox).

3 Slacken each wheel nut by a half turn, using the wheel brace. If the nuts are too tight, DON'T stand on the wheel brace to undo them – call for assistance from one of the motoring organisations.

4 Two jacking points are provided on each side – use the one nearest the punctured wheel. Locate the jack head in the groove at the jacking point in the lower sill flange (don't jack the vehicle at any other point of the sill, nor on a plastic panel). Turn the jack handle clockwise until the wheel is raised clear of the ground.

5 Unscrew the wheel nuts, noting which way round they fit (tapered side inwards), and remove the wheel.

6 Fit the spare wheel, and screw on the nuts. Lightly tighten the nuts with the wheel brace, then lower the vehicle to the ground. Securely tighten the wheel nuts, then refit the wheel trim or centre cover, as applicable.

Finally . . .

- Remove the wheel chocks. Stow the punctured wheel and tools back in the luggage compartment, and secure them in position.
- Check the tyre pressure on the tyre just fitted. If it is low, or if you don't have a pressure gauge with you, drive slowly to the next garage and inflate the tyre to the correct pressure. In the case of the narrow 'space-saver' spare wheel this pressure is much higher than for a normal tyre.
- The wheel nuts should be slackened and retightened to the specified torque at the earliest possible opportunity.
- Have the punctured wheel repaired as soon as possible, or another puncture will leave you stranded.

Note: *Some models are supplied with a special lightweight 'space-saver' spare wheel, the tyre being narrower than standard. The 'space-saver' spare wheel is intended only for temporary use, and must be replaced with a standard wheel as soon as possible. Drive with particular care with this wheel fitted, especially through corners and when braking; do not exceed 50 mph.*

Roadside repairs

Identifying leaks

Puddles on the garage floor or drive, or obvious wetness under the bonnet or underneath the car, suggest a leak that needs investigating. It can sometimes be difficult to decide where the leak is coming from, especially if the engine bay is very dirty already. Leaking oil or fluid can also be blown rearwards by the passage of air under the car, giving a false impression of where the problem lies.

 Warning: Most automotive oils and fluids are poisonous. Wash them off skin, and change out of contaminated clothing, without delay.

 **HAYNES HiNT** *The smell of a fluid leaking from the car may provide a clue to what's leaking. Some fluids are distinctively coloured. It may help to clean the car carefully and to park it over some clean paper overnight as an aid to locating the source of the leak. Remember that some leaks may only occur while the engine is running.*

Sump oil

Engine oil may leak from the drain plug...

Oil from filter
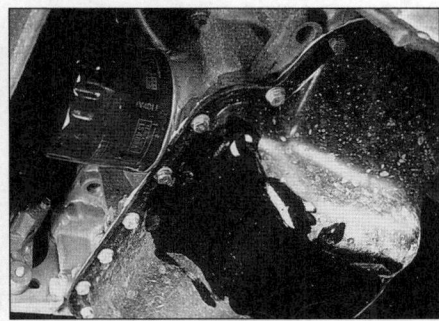
...or from the base of the oil filter.

Gearbox oil
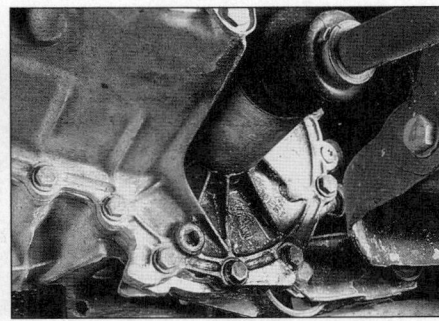
Gearbox oil can leak from the seals at the inboard ends of the driveshafts.

Antifreeze

Leaking antifreeze often leaves a crystalline deposit like this.

Brake fluid

A leak occurring at a wheel is almost certainly brake fluid.

Power steering fluid
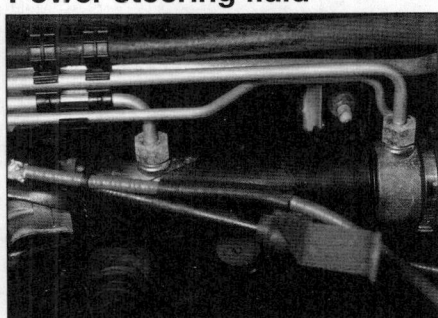
Power steering fluid may leak from the pipe connectors on the steering rack.

Towing

When all else fails, you may find yourself having to get a tow home – or of course you may be helping somebody else. Long-distance recovery should only be done by a garage or breakdown service. For shorter distances, DIY towing using another car is easy enough, but observe the following points:

☐ Use a proper tow-rope – they are not expensive. The vehicle being towed must display an ON TOW sign in its rear window.
☐ Always turn the ignition key to the 'On' position when the vehicle is being towed, so that the steering lock is released, and the direction indicator and brake lights work.
☐ The towing eye is of the screw-in type, and is found in the spare wheel well. The towing eye screws into a threaded hole, accessible after prising out a cover on the right-hand side of the front or rear bumper – later models have a circular cover **(see illustration)**. **Note:** *The towing eye has a left-hand thread – rotate it anti-clockwise to install it.*
☐ Before being towed, release the handbrake and make sure the transmission is in neutral. On models with automatic transmission, special precautions apply – do not exceed 30 mph or travel further than 30 miles, and the wheels must always roll forwards.
☐ Note that greater-than-usual pedal pressure will be required to operate the brakes, since the vacuum servo unit is only operational with the engine running.
☐ The driver of the car being towed must keep the tow-rope taut at all times to avoid snatching.
☐ Make sure that both drivers know the route before setting off.
☐ Only drive at moderate speeds and keep the distance towed to a minimum. Drive smoothly and allow plenty of time for slowing down at junctions.

0•10 Weekly checks

Introduction

There are some very simple checks which need only take a few minutes to carry out, but which could save you a lot of inconvenience and expense.

These *Weekly checks* require no great skill or special tools, and the small amount of time they take to perform could prove to be very well spent, for example:

☐ Keeping an eye on tyre condition and pressures, will not only help to stop them wearing out prematurely, but could also save your life.

☐ Many breakdowns are caused by electrical problems. Battery-related faults are particularly common, and a quick check on a regular basis will often prevent the majority of these.

☐ If your car develops a brake fluid leak, the first time you might know about it is when your brakes don't work properly. Checking the level regularly will give advance warning of this kind of problem.

☐ If the oil or coolant levels run low, the cost of repairing any engine damage will be far greater than fixing the leak, for example.

Underbonnet check points

◀ 1.6 litre engine

A Engine oil level dipstick
B Engine oil filler cap
C Coolant expansion tank
D Brake and clutch fluid reservoir
E Power steering fluid reservoir
F Screen washer fluid reservoir
G Battery

◀ 1.8 litre engine

A Engine oil level dipstick
B Engine oil filler cap
C Coolant expansion tank
D Brake and clutch fluid reservoir
E Power steering fluid reservoir (underneath the headlight
F Screen washer fluid reservoir
G Battery

Weekly checks 0•11

Engine oil level

Before you start
✔ Make sure that the car is on level ground.
✔ Check the oil level before the car is driven, or at least 5 minutes after the engine has been switched off.

 **If the oil is checked immediately after driving the vehicle, some of the oil will remain in the upper engine components, resulting in an inaccurate reading on the dipstick.**

The correct oil
Modern engines place great demands on their oil. It is very important that the correct oil for your car is used (see *Lubricants and fluids*).

Car care
● If you have to add oil frequently, you should check whether you have any oil leaks. Place some clean paper under the car overnight, and check for stains in the morning. If there are no leaks, then the engine may be burning oil.
● Always maintain the level between the upper and lower dipstick marks (see photo 2). If the level is too low, severe engine damage may occur. Oil seal failure may result if the engine is overfilled by adding too much oil.

1 The dipstick is located at the front of the engine (see *Underbonnet check points* for exact location). Withdraw the dipstick. Using a clean rag or paper towel, remove all oil from the dipstick.

3 Oil is added through the filler cap. Unscrew the filler cap and top-up the level; a funnel may be useful in reducing spillage.

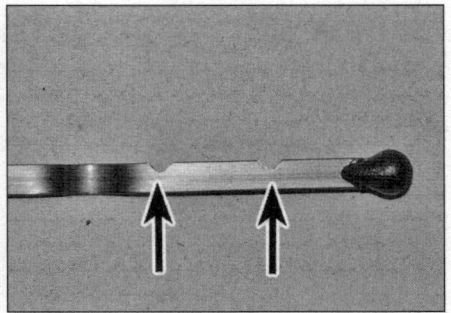
2 Insert the clean dipstick into the tube as far as it will go, then withdraw it again. Note the oil level on the end of the dipstick, which should be between the MAX and MIN marks. If the oil level is only just above, or below, the MIN mark, topping-up is required.

4 Add the oil slowly, checking the level on the dipstick often, and allowing time for the oil to run to the sump. Add oil until the level is just up to the MAX mark on the dipstick – don't overfill (see *Car care*)

Coolant level

 Warning: Do not attempt to remove the expansion tank pressure cap when the engine is hot, as there is a very great risk of scalding. Do not leave open containers of coolant about, as it is poisonous.

Car care
● With a sealed-type cooling system, adding coolant should not be necessary on a regular basis. If frequent topping-up is required, it is likely there is a leak. Check the radiator, all hoses and joint faces for signs of staining or wetness, and rectify as necessary.

● It is important that antifreeze is used in the cooling system all year round, not just during the winter months. Don't top up with water alone, as the antifreeze will become diluted.

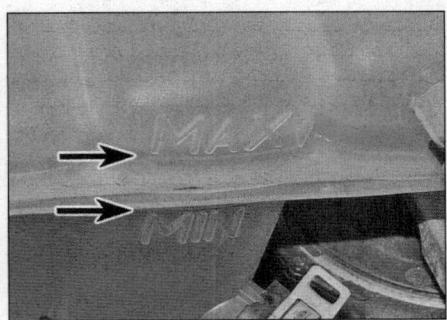
1 The coolant level varies with the temperature of the engine, and is visible through the expansion tank. When the engine is cold, the coolant level should be between the MAX and MIN marks on the front of the reservoir. When the engine is hot, the level may rise slightly above the MAX mark.

2 If topping-up is necessary, **wait until the engine is cold**. Slowly unscrew the expansion tank cap, to release any pressure present in the cooling system, and remove it.

3 Add a mixture of water and antifreeze to the expansion tank until the coolant level is halfway between the level marks. Use only the specified antifreeze – if using Ford antifreeze, make sure it is the same type and colour as that already in the system. Refit the cap and tighten it securely.

0•12 Weekly checks

Brake and clutch fluid level

Note: *All manual transmission models have a hydraulically-operated clutch, which uses the same fluid as the braking system.*

Warning:
• *Brake fluid can harm your eyes and damage painted surfaces, so use extreme caution when handling and pouring it.*
• *Do not use fluid that has been standing open for some time, as it absorbs moisture from the air, which can cause a dangerous loss of braking effectiveness.*

 • *Make sure that your car is on level ground.*
• *The fluid level in the reservoir will drop slightly as the brake pads wear down, but the fluid level must never be allowed to drop below the DANGER mark.*

Safety first!
● If the reservoir requires repeated topping-up this is an indication of a fluid leak somewhere in the system, which should be investigated immediately.
● If a leak is suspected, the car should not be driven until the braking system has been checked. Never take any risks where brakes are concerned

1 The brake fluid reservoir is located on the right-hand side of the engine compartment.

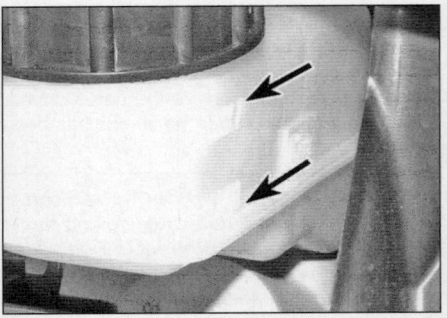
2 The MAX and MIN marks are indicated on the front of the reservoir. The fluid level must be kept between the marks at all times.

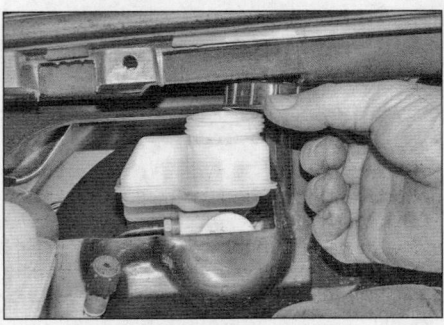
3 If topping-up is necessary, first wipe clean the area around the filler cap to prevent dirt entering the hydraulic system. Unscrew the reservoir cap and carefully lift it out of position, holding the wiring connector plug and taking care not to damage the level sender float. Inspect the reservoir; if the fluid is dirty, the hydraulic system should be drained and refilled (see Chapter 1).

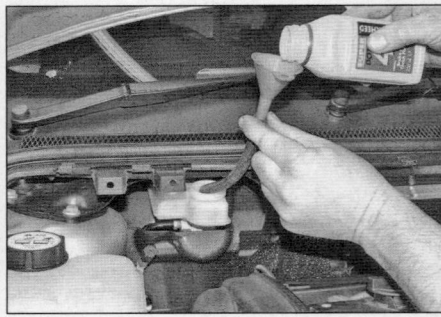
4 Carefully add fluid, taking care not to spill it onto the surrounding components. Use only the specified fluid; mixing different types can cause damage to the system. After topping-up to the correct level, securely refit the cap and wipe off any spilt fluid.

Power steering fluid level

Note: *1.8 and 2.0 litre models are equipped with Electro-Hydraulic power steering (EHPS). According to Ford, there is no requirement to check the fluid level. However, it may be prudent to check the level every few months or so.*

Before you start
✔ Park the vehicle on level ground.
✔ Set the steering wheel straight-ahead.
✔ The engine should be turned off.

 *For the check to be accurate, the steering must not be turned once the engine has been stopped.*

Safety first!
● The need for frequent topping-up indicates a leak, which should be investigated immediately.

1 The reservoir is mounted at the front right-hand side of the engine compartment. On 1.8 and 2.0 litre models, remove the headlight as described in Chapter 12. The fluid level can be viewed through the reservoir body, and should be between the MIN and MAX marks when the engine is cold. If the level is checked when the engine is running or hot, the level may rise slightly above the MAX mark.

2 If topping-up is necessary, use the specified type of fluid – do not overfill the reservoir. Undo the reservoir cap. Take care not to introduce dirt into the system when topping-up. When the level is correct, securely refit the cap.

Weekly checks 0•13

Tyre condition and pressure

It is very important that tyres are in good condition, and at the correct pressure - having a tyre failure at any speed is highly dangerous. Tyre wear is influenced by driving style - harsh braking and acceleration, or fast cornering, will all produce more rapid tyre wear. As a general rule, the front tyres wear out faster than the rears. Interchanging the tyres from front to rear ("rotating" the tyres) may result in more even wear. However, if this is completely effective, you may have the expense of replacing all four tyres at once!
Remove any nails or stones embedded in the tread before they penetrate the tyre to cause deflation. If removal of a nail does reveal that the tyre has been punctured, refit the nail so that its point of penetration is marked. Then immediately change the wheel, and have the tyre repaired by a tyre dealer.
Regularly check the tyres for damage in the form of cuts or bulges, especially in the sidewalls. Periodically remove the wheels, and clean any dirt or mud from the inside and outside surfaces. Examine the wheel rims for signs of rusting, corrosion or other damage. Light alloy wheels are easily damaged by "kerbing" whilst parking; steel wheels may also become dented or buckled. A new wheel is very often the only way to overcome severe damage.

New tyres should be balanced when they are fitted, but it may become necessary to re-balance them as they wear, or if the balance weights fitted to the wheel rim should fall off. Unbalanced tyres will wear more quickly, as will the steering and suspension components. Wheel imbalance is normally signified by vibration, particularly at a certain speed (typically around 50 mph). If this vibration is felt only through the steering, then it is likely that just the front wheels need balancing. If, however, the vibration is felt through the whole car, the rear wheels could be out of balance. Wheel balancing should be carried out by a tyre dealer or garage.

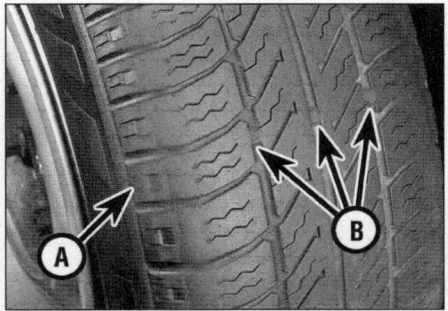

1 Tread Depth - visual check
The original tyres have tread wear safety bands (B), which will appear when the tread depth reaches approximately 1.6 mm. The band positions are indicated by a triangular mark on the tyre sidewall (A).

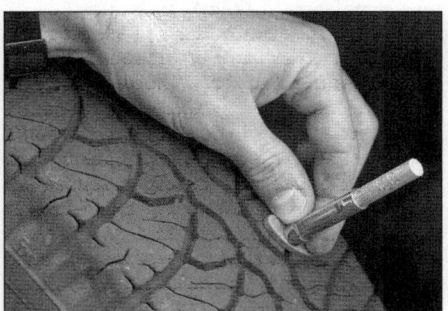

2 Tread Depth - manual check
Alternatively, tread wear can be monitored with a simple, inexpensive device known as a tread depth indicator gauge.

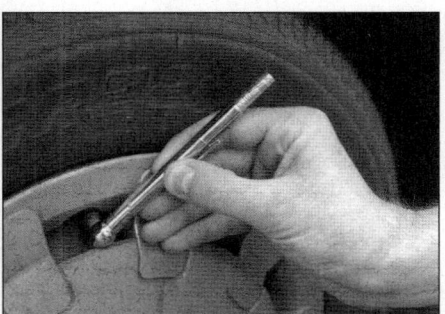

3 Tyre Pressure Check
Check the tyre pressures regularly with the tyres cold. Do not adjust the tyre pressures immediately after the vehicle has been used, or an inaccurate setting will result.

Tyre tread wear patterns

Shoulder Wear

Underinflation (wear on both sides)
Under-inflation will cause overheating of the tyre, because the tyre will flex too much, and the tread will not sit correctly on the road surface. This will cause a loss of grip and excessive wear, not to mention the danger of sudden tyre failure due to heat build-up.
Check and adjust pressures
Incorrect wheel camber (wear on one side)
Repair or renew suspension parts
Hard cornering
Reduce speed!

Centre Wear

Overinflation
Over-inflation will cause rapid wear of the centre part of the tyre tread, coupled with reduced grip, harsher ride, and the danger of shock damage occurring in the tyre casing.
Check and adjust pressures

If you sometimes have to inflate your car's tyres to the higher pressures specified for maximum load or sustained high speed, don't forget to reduce the pressures to normal afterwards.

Uneven Wear

Front tyres may wear unevenly as a result of wheel misalignment. Most tyre dealers and garages can check and adjust the wheel alignment (or "tracking") for a modest charge.
Incorrect camber or castor
Repair or renew suspension parts
Malfunctioning suspension
Repair or renew suspension parts
Unbalanced wheel
Balance tyres
Incorrect toe setting
Adjust front wheel alignment
Note: *The feathered edge of the tread which typifies toe wear is best checked by feel.*

Weekly checks

Washer fluid level

- The windscreen washer reservoir also supplies the tailgate washer jet, where applicable. On models so equipped, the same reservoir also serves the headlight washers.
- Screenwash additives not only keep the windscreen clean during bad weather, they also prevent the washer system freezing in cold weather – which is when you are likely to need it most. Don't top-up using plain water, as the screenwash will become diluted, and will freeze in cold weather.

Caution: On no account use engine coolant antifreeze in the screen washer system – this may damage the paintwork.

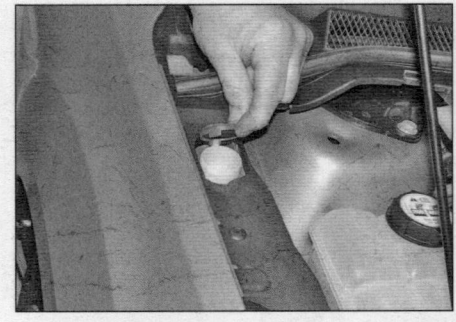

1 The washer fluid reservoir filler neck is located in the right-hand rear corner of the engine compartment. The washer level cannot easily be seen. Remove the filler cap, and look down the filler neck – if fluid is not visible, topping-up may be required.

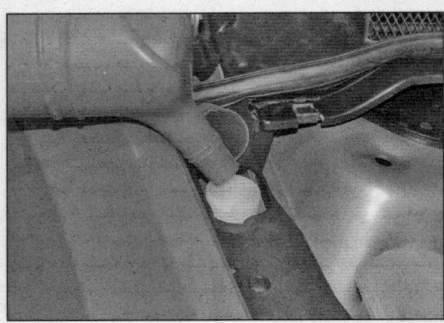

2 When topping-up the reservoir, add a screenwash additive in the quantities recommended on the additive bottle.

Wiper blades

- Only fit good-quality wiper blades.
- When removing an old wiper blade, note how it is fitted. Fitting new blades can be a tricky exercise, and noting how the old blade came off can save time.
- While the wiper blade is removed, take care not to knock the wiper arm from its locked position, or it could strike the glass.
- Offer the new blade into position the same way round as the old one. Ensure that it clicks home securely, otherwise it may come off in use, damaging the glass.

Note: *Fitting details for wiper blades vary according to model, and according to whether genuine Ford wiper blades have been fitted. Use the procedures and illustrations shown as a guide for your car.*

HAYNES HiNT *If smearing is still a problem despite fitting new wiper blades, try cleaning the glass with neat screenwash additive or methylated spirit.*

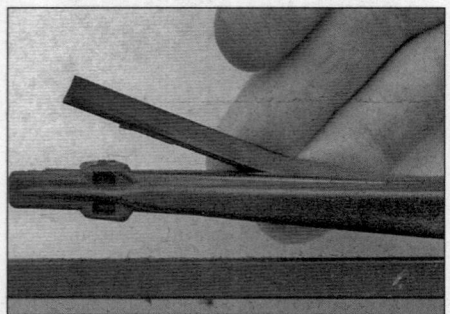

1 Check the condition of the wiper blades; if they are cracked or show any signs of deterioration, or if the glass swept area is smeared, renew them. Wiper blades should be renewed annually, regardless of their apparent condition.

2 To remove a windscreen wiper blade, pull the arm fully away from the glass until it locks. Position the blade at 90° to the arm and lift it from place.

3 To remove the tailgate blade, lift the arm, position the blade at 90° to the arm, and pull the blade from the arm.

Weekly checks 0•15

Battery

Caution: Before carrying out any work on the vehicle battery, read the precautions given in 'Safety first!' at the start of this manual.

✔ Make sure that the battery tray is in good condition, and that the clamp is tight. Any 'white' corrosion on the terminals or surrounding area can be removed with a solution of water and baking soda; thoroughly rinse all cleaned areas with water. Any metal parts damaged by corrosion should be covered with a zinc-based primer, then painted.

✔ Periodically check the charge condition of the battery. On the original-equipment battery, the state of charge is shown by an indicator 'eye' in the top of the battery, which should be green – if the indicator is clear, or red, the battery may need charging or even renewal (see Chapter 5A).

✔ If the battery is flat, and you need to jump start your vehicle, see *Roadside Repairs*.

Battery corrosion can be kept to a minimum by applying a layer of petroleum jelly to the clamps and terminals after they are reconnected.

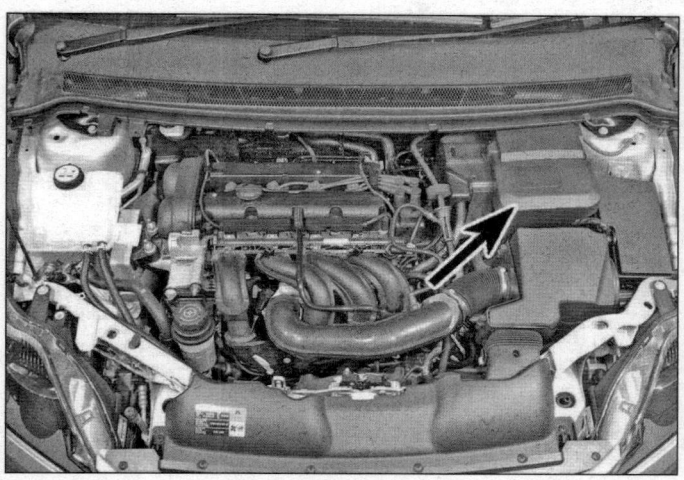

1 The battery is located in the left-hand rear corner of the engine compartment.

2 Unclip and remove the battery cover to gain access. The exterior of the battery should be inspected periodically for damage such as a cracked case or cover.

3 Check the tightness of battery clamps to ensure good electrical connections. You should not be able to move them. Also check each cable for cracks and frayed conductors.

4 If corrosion (white, fluffy deposits) is evident, remove the cables from the battery terminals, clean them with a small wire brush, then refit them. Automotive stores sell a tool for cleaning the battery post . . .

5 . . . as well as the battery cable clamps

Weekly checks

Bulbs and fuses

✔ Check all external lights and the horn. Refer to the appropriate Sections of Chapter 12 for details if any of the circuits are found to be inoperative.

✔ Visually check all accessible wiring connectors, harnesses and retaining clips for security, and for signs of chafing or damage.

 **If you need to check your brake lights and indicators unaided, back up to a wall or garage door and operate the lights. The reflected light should show if they are working properly.**

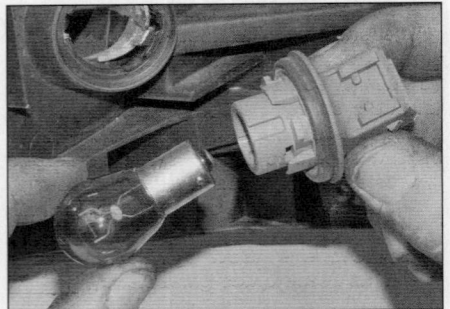

1 If a single indicator light, stop-light or headlight has failed, it is likely that a bulb has blown and will need to be renewed. Refer to Chapter 12 for details. If both stop-lights have failed, it is possible that the switch has failed (see Chapter 9).

2 If more than one indicator light or tail light has failed, it is likely that either a fuse has blown or that there is a fault in the circuit (see Chapter 12). The main fusebox is located below the glovebox on the passenger's side. To access the main fusebox, undo the 2 bolts and pull the trim panel downwards, then undo the two bolts and lower the fusebox from position. Pull the fusebox rearwards and lower it completely. The auxiliary fuse/relay box is located on the left-hand side of the engine compartment – unclip and remove the cover for access.

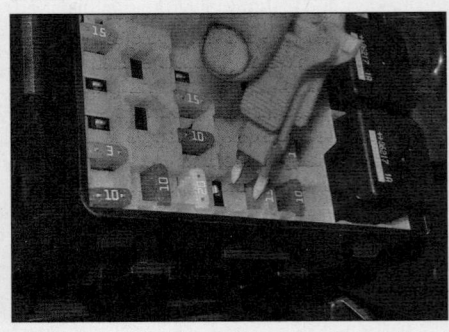

3 To renew a blown fuse, simply pull it out and fit a new fuse of the correct rating (see Chapter 12). Spare fuses, and a fuse removal tool, are provided on the inside of the auxiliary fusebox lid. If the fuse blows again, it is important that you find out why – a complete checking procedure is given in Chapter 12.

Lubricants, fluids and tyre pressures 0•17

Lubricants and fluids

Engine	Multigrade engine oil, viscosity SAE 5W/30 to Ford specification WSS-M2C913-B
Cooling system	Motorcraft SuperPlus pink/red antifreeze to Ford specification WSS-M97B44-D
Manual transmission	SAE 75W/90 gear oil to Ford specification WSD-M2C200-C
Automatic transmission	Automatic transmission fluid to Ford specification WSS-M2C938-A
Brake and clutch hydraulic system	Hydraulic fluid to Ford specification ESD-M6C57-A, Super DOT 4, paraffin-free
Power steering	Ford or Motorcraft power steering fluid to Ford specification WSS-M2C204-A2

Tyre pressures (cold)

The table below gives typical pressures. Check the sticker attached to the driver's door pillar for details specific to your model.

	Normal load		Full load	
Tyre size:	Front	Rear	Front	Rear
195/65 R 15	2.1 bar	2.3 bar	2.4 bar	2.8 bar
205/55 R 16	2.1 bar	2.3 bar	2.4 bar	2.8 bar
205/50 R 17	2.3 bar	2.3 bar	2.5 bar	2.8 bar
225/40 R 18	2.3 bar	2.3 bar	2.5 bar	2.8 bar

Notes

Chapter 1
Routine maintenance & servicing

Contents

	Section number
Air filter element renewal	18
Automatic transmission fluid level check	22
Auxiliary drivebelt check and renewal	21
Brake fluid renewal	24
Brake pads, shoes and discs check	7
Coolant strength check and renewal	16
Driveshaft rubber gaiter and joint check	10
Engine compartment wiring check	6
Engine oil and filter renewal	3
Exhaust system check	8
General information	1
Handbrake check and adjustment	16
Hinge and lock lubrication	12

	Section number
Lights and horn operation check	4
Manual transmission oil level check	23
Pollen filter renewal	15
Regular maintenance	2
Remote control battery renewal	25
Road test	14
Roadwheel nut tightness check	13
Seat belt check	17
Spark plug renewal	19
Steering, suspension and roadwheel check	9
Timing belt renewal	20
Underbody and fuel/brake line check	11
Underbonnet check for fluid leaks and hose condition	5

Degrees of difficulty

| Easy, suitable for novice with little experience | Fairly easy, suitable for beginner with some experience | Fairly difficult, suitable for competent DIY mechanic | Difficult, suitable for experienced DIY mechanic  | Very difficult, suitable for expert DIY or professional  |

Servicing specifications

Lubricants and fluids — Refer to end of *Weekly checks* on page 0•17

Capacities

Engine oil (including filter)
1.4 litre engines	3.8 litres
1.6 litre engines	4.1 litres
1.8 litre engines	4.3 litres
2.0 litre engines	4.3 litres

Cooling system (approximate)
1.4 litre engines:	
With air conditioning	5.5 litres
Without air conditioning	5.2 litres
1.6 litre engines:	
Non-Ti-VCT engines:	
With air conditioning	5.8 litres
Without air conditioning	5.5 litres
Ti-VCT engines	6.0 litres
1.8 litre engines	6.5 litres
2.0 litre engines	6.3 litres

Transmission
Manual transmission:	
1.4, 1.6 and 1.8 litre models	2.3 litres
2.0 litre models	1.9 litres
Automatic transmission (total capacity)	6.7 litres

Washer fluid reservoir
Without headlamp washers	3.3 litres
With headlamp washers	4.5 litres

Fuel tank
All models	55.0 litres

Cooling system
Antifreeze mixture:
50% antifreeze	Protection down to –37°C
55% antifreeze	Protection down to –45°C

Note: *Refer to antifreeze manufacturer for latest recommendations.*

Ignition system
Spark plugs type	Refer to Ford dealer or parts specialist

Brakes
Friction material minimum thickness:
Front or rear brake pads	1.5 mm
Rear brake shoes	1.0 mm

Remote control battery
Type	CR2032, 3V

Torque wrench settings

	Nm	lbf ft
Auxiliary drivebelt idler pulley mounting bolts/nut	25	18
Engine oil drain plug	28	21
Ignition coil retaining bolts	10	7
Manual transmission oil level/filler plug	35	26
Roadwheel nuts:		
Gold nuts for steel wheels	90	60
Silver nuts for steel wheels	130	96
One-piece alloy nuts for alloy wheels and 5-spoke steel wheels	130	96
Two-piece alloy nuts with conical washer	110	81
Spark plugs:		
1.4 and 1.6 litre models	15	11
1.8 and 2.0 litre models	12	9

 Very difficult, suitable for expert DIY or professional
 Difficult, suitable for experienced DIY
 Fairly difficult, suitable for competent DIY mechanic
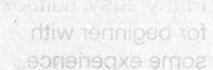 Fairly easy, suitable for beginner with some experience
 Easy, suitable for novice with little experience

Maintenance schedule 1•3

The maintenance intervals in this manual are provided with the assumption that you, not the dealer, will be carrying out the work. These are the minimum maintenance intervals recommended by us for vehicles driven daily. If you wish to keep your vehicle in peak condition at all times, you may wish to perform some of these procedures more often. We encourage frequent maintenance, because it enhances the efficiency, performance and resale value of your vehicle.

If the vehicle is driven in dusty areas, used to tow a trailer, or driven frequently at slow speeds (idling in traffic) or on short journeys, more frequent maintenance intervals are recommended.

When the vehicle is new, it should be serviced by a dealer service department (or other workshop recognised by the vehicle manufacturer as providing the same standard of service) in order to preserve the warranty. The vehicle manufacturer may reject warranty claims if you are unable to prove that servicing has been carried out as and when specified, using only original equipment parts or parts certified to be of equivalent quality.

Every 250 miles or weekly
☐ Refer to *Weekly checks*

Every 6000 miles or 6 months, whichever comes first
☐ Renew the engine oil and filter (Section 3)

Note: *Ford recommend that the engine oil and filter are changed every 12 500 miles or 12 months. However, oil and filter changes are good for the engine and we recommend that the oil and filter are renewed more frequently, especially if the vehicle is used on a lot of short journeys.*

Every 12 500 miles or 12 months, whichever comes first
In addition to the items listed above, carry out the following:
☐ Check the condition of the auxiliary drivebelt (Section 21)
☐ Check the operation of the lights and the horn (Section 4)
☐ Check under the bonnet for fluid leaks and hose condition (Section 5)
☐ Check the condition of the engine compartment wiring (Section 6)
☐ Check the condition of the brake pads, shoes and discs (Section 7)
☐ Check the exhaust system (Section 8)
☐ Check the steering and suspension components for condition and security (Section 9)
☐ Check the condition of the driveshaft joints and gaiters (Section 10)
☐ Check the underbody and all fuel/brake lines (Section 11)
☐ Lubricate all hinges and locks (Section 12)
☐ Roadwheel nuts tightness check (Section 13)
☐ Carry out a road test (Section 14)
☐ Renew the pollen filter (Section 15)*
☐ Check and if necessary adjust the handbrake (Section 16)
☐ Check the condition of the seat belts (Section 17)
☐ Check the antifreeze/inhibitor strength (Section 26)

* **Note:** *If the vehicle is used in dusty conditions, the pollen filter should be renewed more frequently.*

Every 37 500 miles or 3 years, whichever comes first
In addition to the items listed above, carry out the following:
☐ Renew the air filter (Section 18)*
☐ Renew the spark plugs (Section 19)

* **Note:** *If the vehicle is used in dusty conditions, the air filter should be renewed more frequently.*

Every 60 000 miles
In addition to the items listed above, carry out the following:
☐ Renew the timing belt and tensioner – 1.4 and 1.6 litre engines only (Section 20)

Note: *The Ford interval for belt renewal is actually at a much higher mileage than this (100 000 miles or 8 years). It is strongly recommended, however, that the interval is reduced to 60 000 miles, particularly on vehicles which are subjected to intensive use, ie, mainly short journeys or a lot of stop-start driving. The actual belt renewal interval is therefore very much up to the individual owner, but bear in mind that severe engine damage will result if the belt breaks.*

Every 100 000 miles or 8 years, whichever comes first
☐ Renew the auxiliary belt (Section 21)

Every 2 years, regardless of mileage
☐ Check the automatic transmission fluid level (Section 22)
☐ Check the manual transmission oil level (Section 23)
☐ Renew the brake fluid (Section 24)
☐ Renew remote control battery (Section 25)
☐ Renew the coolant (Section 26)*

* **Note:** *If Ford pink/red antifreeze is used, the coolant can then be left indefinitely, providing the strength of the mixture is checked every year. If any antifreeze other than Ford's is to be used, the coolant must be renewed at regular intervals to provide an equivalent degree of protection; the conventional recommendation is to renew the coolant every two years.*

1•4 Maintenance – component location

Underbonnet view of a 1.6 litre model

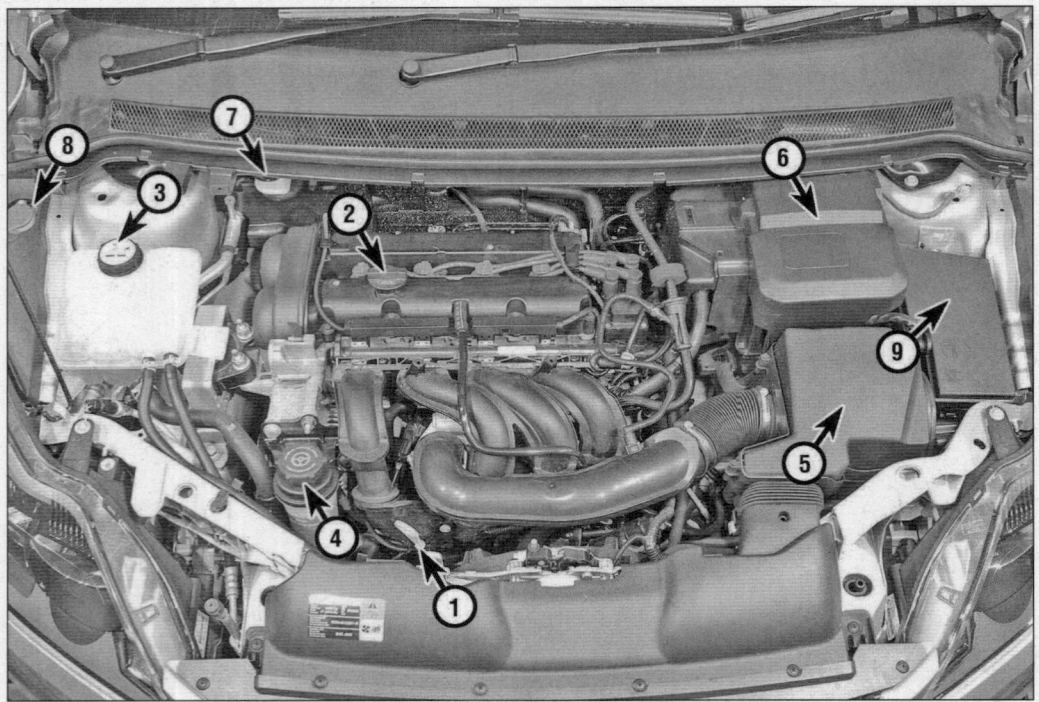

1. Engine oil level dipstick
2. Oil filler cap
3. Coolant expansion tank cap
4. Power steering fluid reservoir
5. Air filter element cover
6. Battery cover
7. Brake/clutch fluid reservoir
8. Washer fluid reservoir cap
9. Fuse/relay box

Front underbody view

1. Oil filter cartridge
2. Engine oil drain plug
3. Suspension control arm
4. Track rod end
5. Right-hand driveshaft
6. Air conditioning compressor
7. Underfloor brace
8. Brake caliper

Maintenance – component location

Rear underbody view

1 Anti-roll bar
2 Carbon canister
3 Fuel tank
4 Silencer
5 Shock absorber
6 Lateral link
7 Lower control arm
8 Tie rod

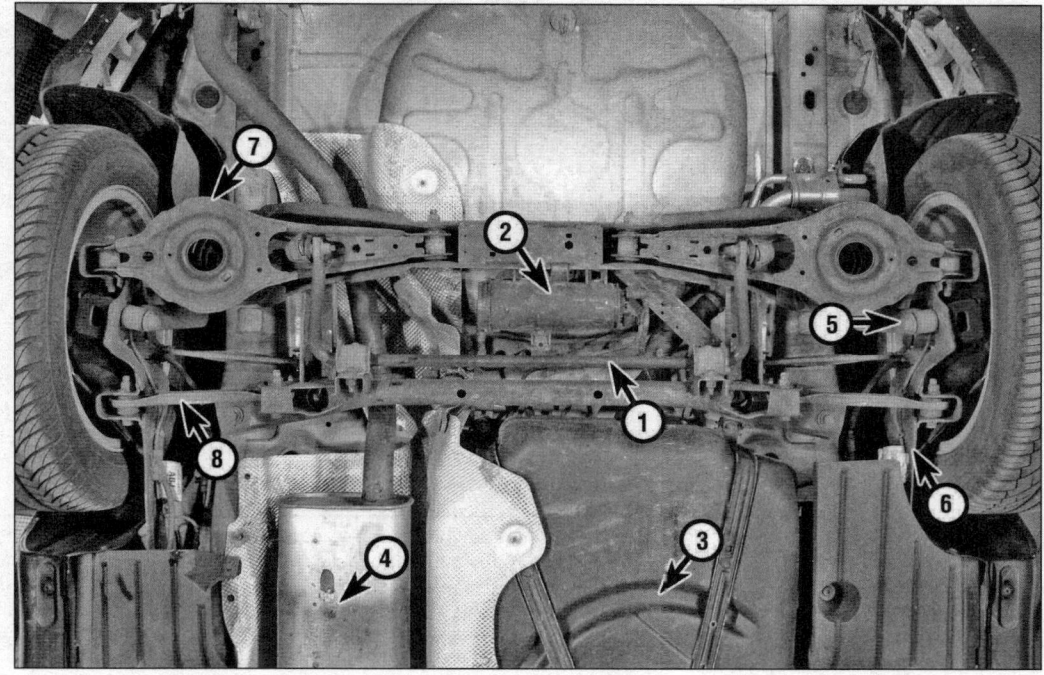

Maintenance procedures

1 General information

1 This Chapter is designed to help the home mechanic maintain his/her vehicle for safety, economy, long life and peak performance.
2 The Chapter contains a master maintenance schedule, followed by Sections dealing specifically with each task in the schedule. Visual checks, adjustments, component renewal and other helpful items are included. Refer to the accompanying illustrations of the engine compartment and the underside of the vehicle for the locations of the various components.
3 Servicing your vehicle in accordance with the mileage/time maintenance schedule and the following Sections will provide a planned maintenance programme, which should result in a long and reliable service life. This is a comprehensive plan, so maintaining some items but not others at the specified service intervals, will not produce the same results.
4 As you service your vehicle, you will discover that many of the procedures can – and should – be grouped together, because of the particular procedure being performed, or because of the proximity of two otherwise-unrelated components to one another. For example, if the vehicle is raised for any reason, the exhaust can be inspected at the same time as the suspension and steering components.

5 The first step in this maintenance programme is to prepare yourself before the actual work begins. Read through all the Sections relevant to the work to be carried out, then make a list and gather all the parts and tools required. If a problem is encountered, seek advice from a parts specialist, or a dealer service department.

2 Regular maintenance

1 If, from the time the vehicle is new, the routine maintenance schedule is followed closely, and frequent checks are made of fluid levels and high-wear items, as suggested throughout this manual, the engine will be kept in relatively good running condition, and the need for additional work will be minimised.
2 It is possible that there will be times when the engine is running poorly due to the lack of regular maintenance. This is even more likely if a used vehicle, which has not received regular and frequent maintenance checks, is purchased. In such cases, additional work may need to be carried out, outside of the regular maintenance intervals.
3 If engine wear is suspected, a compression test (refer to Chapter 2A or 2B, as applicable) will provide valuable information regarding the overall performance of the main internal components. Such a test can be used as a basis to decide on the extent of the work to be carried out. If, for example, a compression test indicates serious internal engine wear, conventional maintenance as described in this Chapter will not greatly improve the performance of the engine, and may prove a waste of time and money, unless extensive overhaul work is carried out first.
4 The following series of operations are those most often required to improve the performance of a generally poor-running engine:

Primary operations

a) Clean, inspect and test the battery (refer to 'Weekly checks').
b) Check all the engine-related fluids (refer to 'Weekly checks').
c) Check the condition and tension of the auxiliary drivebelt (Section 21).
d) Renew the spark plugs (Section 19).
e) Check the condition of the air filter, and renew if necessary (Section 18).
f) Check the condition of all hoses, and check for fluid leaks (Section 5).

5 If the above operations do not prove fully effective, carry out the following secondary operations:

Secondary operations

All items listed under Primary operations, plus the following:
a) Check the charging system (refer to Chapter 5A).
b) Check the ignition system (refer to Chapter 5B).
c) Check the fuel system (refer to Chapter 4A).

1•6 Maintenance procedures

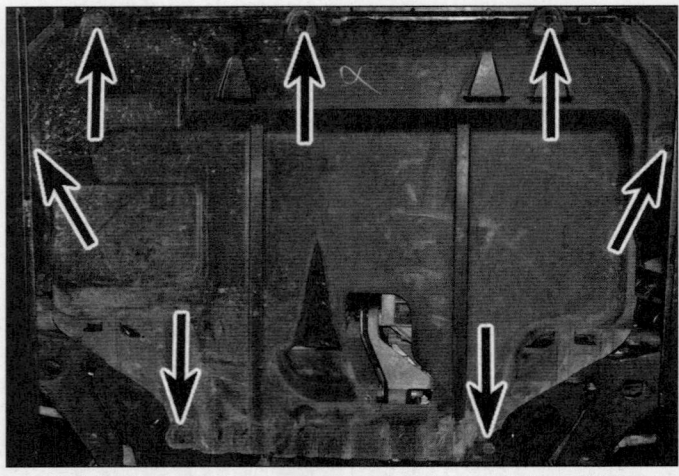

3.4 Undo the fasteners (arrowed) and remove the engine undershield

3.6a Engine oil sump drain plug (arrowed) – 1.4 and 1.6 litre engines

Every 6000 miles or 6 months

3 Engine oil and filter renewal

1 Frequent oil and filter changes are the most important preventative maintenance procedures which can be undertaken by the DIY owner. As engine oil ages, it becomes diluted and contaminated, which leads to premature engine wear.
2 Before starting this procedure, gather together all the necessary tools and materials. Also make sure that you have plenty of clean rags and newspapers handy, to mop-up any spills. Ideally, the engine oil should be warm, as it will drain more easily, and more built-up sludge will be removed with it.
3 Take care not to touch the exhaust (especially the catalytic converter) or any other hot parts of the engine when working under the vehicle. To avoid any possibility of scalding, and to protect yourself from possible skin irritants and other harmful contaminants in used engine oils, it is advisable to wear gloves when carrying out this work.
4 Firmly apply the handbrake, then jack up the front of the vehicle and support it on axle stands (see *Jacking and vehicle support*). Where fitted, release the fasteners and remove the engine undershield **(see illustration)**.
5 Remove the oil filler cap.
6 Using a spanner, or preferably a socket and bar, slacken the sump drain plug about half a turn **(see illustrations)**. Position the draining container under the drain plug, then remove the plug completely.

> **HAYNES HiNT**  *As the plug releases from the threads, move it away sharply, so that the stream of oil from the sump runs into the container, not up your sleeve.*

7 Allow some time for the oil to drain, noting that it may be necessary to reposition the container as the oil flow slows to a trickle.
8 After all the oil has drained, wipe the drain plug with a clean rag. Examine the condition of the drain plug sealing ring, and renew it if it shows signs of flattening or other damage which may prevent an oil-tight seal (it is generally considered good practice to fit a new seal every time. Note that on some models the seal is integral with the drain plug **(see illustration)**. Clean the area around the drain plug opening, and refit the plug complete with the seal and tighten it to the specified torque.
9 Move the container into position under the oil filter, which is located on the front of the cylinder block **(see illustrations)**.
10 Use an oil filter removal tool if necessary to slacken the filter initially, then unscrew it by hand the rest of the way **(see illustration)**. Empty the oil from the old filter into the

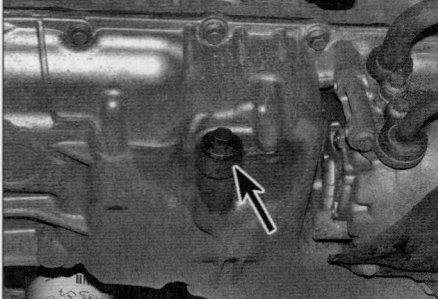

3.6b Engine oil sump drain plug (arrowed) – 1.8 and 2.0 litre engines

3.8 On some drain plugs, the seal is integral with the plug

3.9a Oil filter cartridge (arrowed) – 1.4 and 1.6 litre engines . . .

3.9b . . . 1.8 and 2.0 litre engines

Every 6000 miles

3.10 Using a strap wrench to slacken the filter cartridge

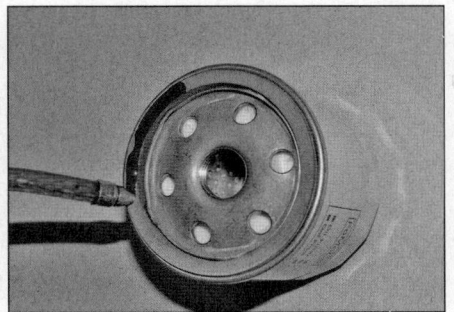

3.12a Apply a light coating of clean engine oil to the sealing ring . . .

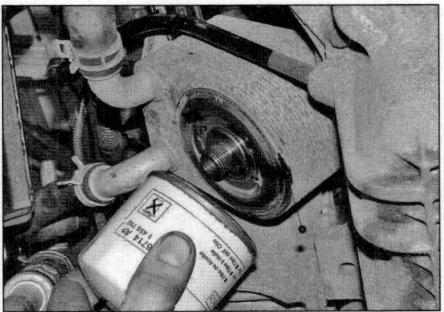

3.12b . . . and screw the cartridge into place by hand

container, then puncture the top of the filter, and allow the remaining oil to drain from the filter into the container.

11 Use a clean rag to remove all oil, dirt and sludge from the filter sealing area on the engine.

12 Apply a light coating of clean engine oil to the sealing ring on the new filter, then screw the filter into position on the engine **(see illustrations)**. Tighten the filter firmly by hand only – **do not** use any tools.

13 Remove the old oil and all tools from under the car, refit the engine undershield (where applicable), then lower the car to the ground.

14 Fill the engine, using the correct grade and type of oil (refer to Weekly checks for details of topping-up). An oil can spout or funnel may help to reduce spillage. Pour in half the specified quantity of oil first, then wait a few minutes for the oil to run to the sump.

15 Continue adding oil a small quantity at a time until the level is up to the MIN mark on the dipstick. Adding around 0.5 litre of oil will now bring the level up to the MAX on the dipstick – do not worry if a little too much goes in, as some of the excess will be taken up in filling the oil filter. Refit the dipstick and the filler cap.

16 Start the engine and run it for a few minutes; check for leaks around the oil filter and the sump drain plug. Note that there may be a few seconds delay before the oil pressure warning light goes out when the engine is started, as the oil circulates through the engine oil galleries and the new oil filter before the pressure builds-up.

17 Switch off the engine, and wait a few minutes for the oil to settle in the sump once more. With the new oil circulated and the filter completely full, recheck the level on the dipstick, and add more oil as necessary.

18 Dispose of the used engine oil and the old oil filter safely, with reference to General repair procedures in the Reference section of this manual. Many local recycling points have containers for waste oil, with oil filter disposal receptacles alongside.

Every 12 500 miles or 12 months

4 Lights and horn operation check

1 With the ignition switched on where necessary, check the operation of all exterior lights.

2 Check the brake lights with the help of an assistant, or by reversing up close to a reflective door. Make sure that all the rear lights are capable of operating independently, without affecting any of the other lights – for example, switch on as many rear lights as possible, then try the brake lights. If any unusual results are found, this is usually due to an earth fault or other poor connection at that rear light unit.

3 Again with the help of an assistant or using a reflective surface, check as far as possible that the headlights work on both main and dipped beam.

4 Renew any defective bulbs with reference to Chapter 12.

HAYNES HiNT *Particularly on older vehicles, bulbs can stop working as a result of corrosion build-up on the bulb or its holder – fitting a new bulb may not cure the problem in this instance. When renewing any bulb, if you find any green or white-coloured powdery deposits, these should be cleaned off using emery cloth.*

5 Check the operation of all interior lights, including the glovebox and luggage area illumination lights. Switch on the ignition, and check that all relevant warning lights come on as expected – the vehicle handbook should give details of these. Now start the engine, and check that the appropriate lights go out. When you are next driving at night, check that all the instrument panel and facia lighting works correctly. If any problems are found, refer to Chapter 12.

6 Finally, choose an appropriate time of day to test the operation of the horn.

5 Underbonnet check for fluid leaks and hose condition

⚠ **Warning:** Renewal of air conditioning hoses must be left to a dealer service department or air conditioning specialist who has the equipment to depressurise the system safely. Never remove air conditioning components or hoses until the system has been depressurised.

General

1 Visually inspect the engine joint faces, gaskets and seals for any signs of water or oil leaks. Pay particular attention to the areas around the cylinder head cover, cylinder head, oil filter and sump joint faces. Bear in mind that, over a period of time, some very slight seepage from these areas is to be expected – what you are really looking for is any indication of a serious leak. Should a leak be

1•8 Every 12 500 miles

5.5 Check the security of the air intake pipes

found, renew the offending gasket or oil seal by referring to the appropriate Chapters in this manual.

2 High temperatures in the engine compartment can cause the deterioration of the rubber and plastic hoses used for engine, accessory and emission systems operation. Periodic inspection should be made for cracks, loose clamps, material hardening and leaks.

3 When checking the hoses, ensure that all the cable-ties or clips used to retain the hoses are in place, and in good condition. Clips which are broken or missing can lead to chafing of the hoses, pipes or wiring, which could cause more serious problems in the future.

4 Carefully check the large top and bottom radiator hoses, along with the other smaller-diameter cooling system hoses and metal pipes; do not forget the heater hoses/pipes which run from the engine to the bulkhead. Inspect each hose along its entire length, replacing any that is cracked, swollen or shows signs of deterioration. Cracks may become more apparent if the hose is squeezed, and may often be apparent at the hose ends.

5 Make sure that all hose connections are tight. If the large-diameter air hoses from the air cleaner are loose, they will leak air, and upset the engine idle quality **(see illustration)**. If the spring clamps that are used to secure some of the hoses appear to be slackening, they should be updated with worm-drive clips to prevent the possibility of leaks.

6 Some other hoses are secured to their fittings with clamps. Where clamps are used, check to be sure they haven't lost their tension, allowing the hose to leak. If clamps aren't used, make sure the hose has not expanded and/or hardened where it slips over the fitting, allowing it to leak.

7 Check all fluid reservoirs, filler caps, drain plugs and fittings, etc, looking for any signs of leakage of oil, transmission and/or brake hydraulic fluid, coolant and power steering fluid. Also check the clutch hydraulic fluid lines which lead from the fluid reservoir and slave cylinder (on the transmission).

8 If the vehicle is regularly parked in the same place, close inspection of the ground underneath it will soon show any leaks; ignore the puddle of water which will be left if the air conditioning system is in use. Place a clean piece of cardboard below the engine, and examine it for signs of contamination after the vehicle has been parked over it overnight – be aware, however, of the fire risk inherent in placing combustible material below the catalytic converter.

9 Remember that some leaks will only occur with the engine running, or when the engine is hot or cold. With the handbrake firmly applied, start the engine from cold, and let the engine idle while you examine the underside of the engine compartment for signs of leakage.

10 If an unusual smell is noticed inside or around the car, especially when the engine is thoroughly hot, this may point to the presence of a leak.

11 As soon as a leak is detected, its source must be traced and rectified. Where oil has been leaking for some time, it is usually necessary to use a steam cleaner, pressure washer or similar, to clean away the accumulated dirt, so that the exact source of the leak can be identified.

Vacuum hoses

12 It's quite common for vacuum hoses, especially those in the emissions system, to be colour-coded, or to be identified by coloured stripes moulded into them. Various systems require hoses with different wall thicknesses, collapse resistance and temperature resistance. When renewing hoses, be sure the new ones are made of the same material.

13 Often the only effective way to check a hose is to remove it completely from the vehicle. If more than one hose is removed, be sure to label the hoses and fittings to ensure correct installation.

14 When checking vacuum hoses, be sure to include any plastic T-fittings in the check. Inspect the fittings for cracks, and check the hose where it fits over the fitting for distortion, which could cause leakage.

15 A small piece of vacuum hose (quarter-inch inside diameter) can be used as a stethoscope to detect vacuum leaks. Hold one end of the hose to your ear, and probe around vacuum hoses and fittings, listening for the 'hissing' sound characteristic of a vacuum leak.

 Warning: When probing with the vacuum hose stethoscope, be very careful not to come into contact with moving engine components such as the auxiliary drivebelt, radiator electric cooling fan, etc.

Fuel hoses

 Warning: There are certain precautions which must be taken when inspecting or servicing fuel system components. Work in a well-ventilated area, and do not allow open flames (cigarettes, appliance pilot lights, etc) or bare light bulbs near the work area. Mop-up any spills immediately, and do not store fuel-soaked rags where they could ignite.

16 Check all fuel hoses for deterioration and chafing. Check especially for cracks in areas where the hose bends, and also just before fittings, such as where a hose attaches to the fuel rail **(see illustration)**.

17 High-quality fuel line, usually identified by the word 'Fluoroelastomer' printed on the hose, should be used for fuel line renewal. Never, under any circumstances, use non-reinforced vacuum line, clear plastic tubing or water hose as a substitute for fuel lines.

18 Spring-type clamps may be used on fuel lines. These clamps often lose their tension over a period of time, and can be 'sprung' during removal. Renew all spring-type clamps with proper petrol pipe clips whenever a hose is renewed.

Metal pipes

19 Sections of metal piping are often used for fuel line between the fuel filter and the engine, and for some power steering and air conditioning applications. Check carefully to be sure the piping has not been bent or crimped, and that cracks have not started in the line; also check for signs of excessive corrosion.

20 If a section of metal fuel line must be renewed, only seamless steel piping should be used, since copper and aluminium piping don't have the strength necessary to withstand normal engine vibration.

21 Check the metal lines where they enter the brake master cylinder, ABS hydraulic unit or clutch master/slave cylinders (as applicable) for cracks in the lines or loose fittings. Any sign of brake fluid leakage calls for an immediate and thorough inspection.

6 Engine compartment wiring check

1 With the vehicle parked on level ground, apply the handbrake firmly and open the bonnet. Using an inspection light or a small electric torch, check all visible wiring within and beneath the engine compartment.

2 What you are looking for is wiring that is obviously damaged by chafing against sharp edges, or against moving suspension/transmission components and/or the auxiliary

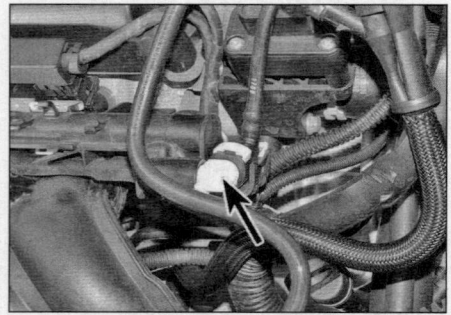

5.16 Check the security of the fuel pipe where it joins the fuel rail (arrowed)

drivebelt, by being trapped or crushed between carelessly-refitted components, or melted by being forced into contact with the hot engine castings, coolant pipes, etc. In almost all cases, damage of this sort is caused in the first instance by incorrect routing on reassembly after previous work has been carried out.

3 Depending on the extent of the problem, damaged wiring may be repaired by rejoining the break or splicing-in a new length of wire, using solder to ensure a good connection, and remaking the insulation with adhesive insulating tape or heat-shrink tubing, as appropriate. If the damage is extensive, given the implications for the vehicle's future reliability, the best long-term answer may well be to renew that entire section of the loom, however expensive this may appear.

4 When the damage has been repaired, ensure that the wiring loom is re-routed correctly, so that it is clear of other components, and not stretched or kinked, and is secured out of harm's way using the plastic clips, guides and ties provided.

5 Check all electrical connectors, ensuring that they are clean, securely fastened, and that each is locked by its plastic tabs or wire clip, as appropriate **(see illustration)**. If any connector shows external signs of corrosion (accumulations of white or green deposits, or streaks of 'rust'), or if any is thought to be dirty, it must be unplugged and cleaned using electrical contact cleaner. If the connector pins are severely corroded, the connector must be renewed; note that this may mean the renewal of that entire section of the loom – see your local Ford dealer for details.

6 If the cleaner completely removes the corrosion to leave the connector in a satisfactory condition, it would be wise to pack the connector with a suitable material which will exclude dirt and moisture, preventing the corrosion from occurring again; a Ford dealer may be able to recommend a suitable product.

7 Check the condition of the battery connections – remake the connections or renew the leads if a fault is found (see Chapter 5A). Use the same techniques to ensure that all earth points in the engine compartment provide good electrical contact through clean, metal-to-metal joints, and that all are securely fastened.

7 Brake pads, shoes and discs check

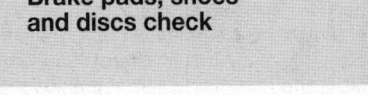

1 The work described in this Section should be carried out at the specified intervals, or whenever a defect is suspected in the braking system. Any of the following symptoms could indicate a potential brake system defect:
a) The vehicle pulls to one side when the brake pedal is depressed.
b) The brakes make squealing, scraping or dragging noises when applied.

6.5 Ensure all electrical connectors are securely clipped together

c) Brake pedal travel is excessive, or pedal feel is poor.
d) The brake fluid requires repeated topping-up. Note that, because the hydraulic clutch shares the same fluid as the braking system (see Chapter 6), this problem could be due to a leak in the clutch system.

Front disc brakes

2 Apply the handbrake, then loosen the front wheel nuts. Jack up the front of the vehicle, and support it on axle stands (see *Jacking and vehicle support*).

3 For better access to the brake calipers, remove the wheels.

4 Look through the inspection window in the caliper, and check that the thickness of the friction lining material on each of the pads is not less than the recommended minimum thickness given in the Specifications **(see illustration)**.

>  **HAYNES HiNT** *Bear in mind that the lining material is normally bonded to a metal backing plate. To differentiate between the metal and the lining material, it is helpful to turn the disc slowly at first – the edge of the disc can then be identified, with the lining material on each pad either side of it, and the backing plates behind.*

5 If it is difficult to determine the exact thickness of the pad linings, or you are at all concerned about the condition of the pads,

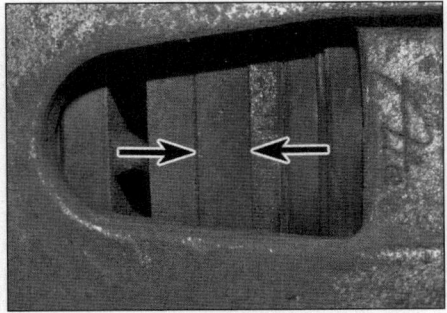

7.4 Measure the thickness of the brake pad friction material (arrowed)

then remove them from the calipers for further inspection (refer to Chapter 9).

6 Check the other caliper in the same way.

7 If any one of the brake pads has worn down to, or below, the specified limit, *all four* pads at that end of the car must be renewed as a set. If the pads on one side are significantly more worn than the other, this may indicate that the caliper pistons have partially seized – refer to the brake pad renewal procedure in Chapter 9, and push the pistons back into the caliper to free them.

8 Measure the thickness of the discs with a micrometer, if available, to make sure that they still have service life remaining. Do not be fooled by the lip of rust which often forms on the outer edge of the disc, which may make the disc appear thicker than it really is – scrape off the loose rust if necessary, without scoring the disc friction (shiny) surface.

9 If any disc is thinner than the specified minimum thickness, renew it (refer to Chapter 9).

10 Check the general condition of the discs. Look for excessive scoring and discolouration caused by overheating. If these conditions exist, remove the relevant disc and have it resurfaced or renewed (refer to Chapter 9).

11 Make sure that the handbrake is firmly applied, then check that the transmission is in neutral. Spin the wheel, and check that the brake is not binding. Some drag is normal with a disc brake, but it should not require any great effort to turn the wheel – also, do not confuse brake drag with resistance from the transmission.

12 Before refitting the wheels, check all brake lines and hoses (refer to Chapter 9). In particular, check the flexible hoses in the vicinity of the calipers, where they are subjected to most movement **(see illustration)**. Bend them between the fingers (but do not actually bend them double, or the casing may be damaged) and check that this does not reveal previously-hidden cracks, cuts or splits.

13 On completion, refit the wheels and lower the car to the ground. Tighten the wheel nuts to the specified torque.

Rear disc brakes

14 Loosen the rear wheel nuts, then chock

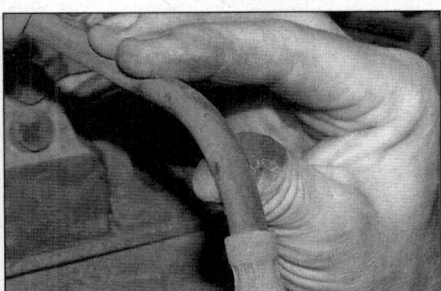

7.12 Check the condition of the rubber brake hoses by bending them slightly and looking for cracks

1•10 Every 12 500 miles

8.2 Check the condition of the exhaust rubber mountings

the front wheels. Jack up the rear of the car, and support it on axle stands. Release the handbrake and remove the rear wheels.
15 The procedure for checking the rear brakes is much the same as described in paragraphs 2 to 13 above. Check that the rear brakes are not binding, noting that transmission resistance is not a factor on the rear wheels. Abnormal effort may indicate that the handbrake needs adjusting – see Chapter 9.

Rear drum brakes

16 Loosen the rear wheel nuts, then chock the front wheels. Jack up the rear of the car, and support on axle stands (see *Jacking and vehicle support*). Release the handbrake and remove the rear wheels.
17 Spin the wheel to check that the brake is not binding. A small amount of resistance from the brake is acceptable, but no great effort should be required to turn the wheel hub. Abnormal effort may indicate that the handbrake needs adjusting – see Chapter 9.
18 To check the brake shoe lining thickness without removing the brake drums, prise the rubber plugs from the backplates, and use an electric torch to inspect the linings of the leading brake shoes. Check that the thickness of the lining material on the brake shoes is not less than the recommendation given in the Specifications.
19 If it is difficult to determine the exact thickness of the brake shoe linings, or if you are at all concerned about the condition of the shoes, then remove the rear drums for a more comprehensive inspection (refer to Chapter 9).
20 With the drum removed, check the shoe return and hold-down springs for correct installation, and check the wheel cylinders for leakage of brake fluid. Apart from fluid being visible, a leaking wheel cylinder may be characterised by an excessive build-up of brake dust (stuck to the fluid which has leaked) at the cylinder seals.
21 Check the friction surface of the brake drums for scoring and discoloration. If excessive, the drum should be resurfaced or renewed.
22 Before refitting the wheels, check all brake lines and hoses (refer to Chapter 9). On completion, apply the handbrake and check that the rear wheels are locked. The handbrake can be adjusted as described in Chapter 9.
23 On completion, refit the wheels and lower the car to the ground. Tighten the wheel nuts to the specified torque.

8 Exhaust system check

1 With the engine cold (at least three hours after the vehicle has been driven), check the complete exhaust system, from its starting point at the engine to the end of the tailpipe. Ideally, this should be done on a hoist, where unrestricted access is available; if a hoist is not available, raise and support the vehicle on axle stands (see *Jacking and vehicle support*).
2 Make sure that all brackets and rubber mountings are in good condition, and tight; if any of the mountings are to be renewed, ensure that the new ones are of the correct type – in the case of the rubber mountings, their colour is a good guide. Those nearest to the catalytic converter are more heat-resistant than the others **(see illustration)**.
3 Check the pipes and connections for evidence of leaks, severe corrosion, or damage. One of the most common points for a leak to develop is around the welded joints between the pipes and silencers. Leakage at any of the joints or in other parts of the system will usually show up as a black sooty stain in the vicinity of the leak. **Note:** *Exhaust sealants should not be used on any part of the exhaust system upstream of the catalytic converter (between the converter and engine) – even if the sealant does not contain additives harmful to the converter, pieces of it may break off and foul the element, causing local overheating.*
4 At the same time, inspect the underside of the body for holes, corrosion, open seams, etc, which may allow exhaust gases to enter the passenger compartment. Seal all body openings with silicone or body putty.
5 Rattles and other noises can often be traced to the exhaust system, especially the rubber mountings. Try to move the system, silencer(s), heat shields and catalytic converter. If any components can touch the body or suspension parts, secure the exhaust system with new mountings.
6 Check the running condition of the engine by inspecting inside the end of the tailpipe; the exhaust deposits here are an indication of the engine's state of tune. The inside of the tailpipe should be dry, and should vary in colour from dark grey to light grey/brown; if it is black and sooty, or coated with white deposits, this may indicate the need for a full fuel system inspection.

9 Steering, suspension and roadwheel check

Front suspension and steering

1 Apply the handbrake, then raise the front of the vehicle and support it on axle stands (see *Jacking and vehicle support*).
2 Visually inspect the balljoint dust covers and the steering rack gaiters for splits, chafing or deterioration **(see illustration)**. Any wear of these components will cause loss of lubricant, together with dirt and water entry, resulting in rapid deterioration of the balljoints or steering gear.
3 Check the power-assisted steering fluid hoses for chafing or deterioration, and the pipe and hose unions for fluid leaks. Also check for signs of fluid leakage under pressure from the steering gear rubber gaiters, which would indicate failed fluid seals within the steering gear.
4 Grasp the roadwheel at the 12 o'clock and 6 o'clock positions, and try to rock it **(see illustration)**. Very slight free play may be felt, but if the movement is appreciable, further investigation is necessary to determine the source. Continue rocking the wheel while an assistant depresses the footbrake. If the movement is now eliminated or significantly reduced, it is likely that the hub bearings are at fault. If the free play is still evident with the footbrake depressed, then there is wear in the suspension joints or mountings.
5 Now grasp the wheel at the 9 o'clock and 3 o'clock positions, and try to rock it as before. Any movement felt now may again be caused by wear in the hub bearings or the steering track rod balljoints. If the outer track rod balljoint is worn, the visual movement will be obvious. If the inner joint is suspect, it can be

9.2 Check the condition of the steering rack gaiters

9.4 Check for wear in the wheel bearing by grasping the wheel and trying to rock it

Every 12 500 miles 1•11

felt by placing a hand over the rack-and-pinion rubber gaiter, and gripping the track rod. If the wheel is now rocked, movement will be felt at the inner joint if wear has taken place.

6 Using a large screwdriver or flat bar, check for wear in the suspension mounting and subframe bushes by levering between the relevant suspension component and its attachment point. Some movement is to be expected as the mountings are made of rubber, but excessive wear should be obvious. Also check the condition of any visible rubber bushes, looking for splits, cracks or contamination of the rubber.

7 With the vehicle standing on its wheels, have an assistant turn the steering wheel back-and-forth, about an eighth of a turn each way. There should be very little, if any, lost movement between the steering wheel and roadwheels. If this is not the case, closely observe the joints and mountings previously described, but in addition, check the steering column joints for wear, and also check the rack-and-pinion steering gear itself.

Rear suspension

8 Chock the front wheels, then raise the rear of the vehicle and support it on axle stands (see *Jacking and vehicle support*).

9 Check the rear hub bearings for wear, using the method described for the front hub bearings (paragraph 4).

10 Using a large screwdriver or flat bar, check for wear in the suspension mounting bushes by levering between the relevant suspension component and its attachment point. Some movement is to be expected as the mountings are made of rubber, but excessive wear should be obvious.

Roadwheel check and balancing

11 Periodically remove the roadwheels, and clean any dirt or mud from the inside and outside surfaces. Examine the wheel rims for signs of rusting, corrosion or other damage. Light alloy wheels are easily damaged by 'kerbing' whilst parking, and similarly, steel wheels may become dented or buckled. Renewal of the wheel is very often the only course of remedial action possible.

12 The balance of each wheel and tyre assembly should be maintained, not only to avoid excessive tyre wear, but also to avoid wear in the steering and suspension components. Wheel imbalance is normally signified by vibration through the vehicle's bodyshell, although in many cases it is particularly noticeable through the steering wheel. Conversely, it should be noted that wear or damage in suspension or steering components may cause excessive tyre wear. Out-of-round or out-of-true tyres, damaged wheels and wheel bearing wear/maladjustment also fall into this category. Balancing will not usually cure vibration caused by such wear.

13 Wheel balancing may be carried out with the wheel either on or off the vehicle. If balanced on the vehicle, ensure that the wheel-to-hub relationship is marked in some way prior to subsequent wheel removal, so that it may be refitted in its original position.

10 Driveshaft rubber gaiter and joint check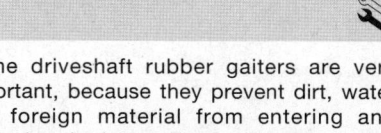

1 The driveshaft rubber gaiters are very important, because they prevent dirt, water and foreign material from entering and damaging the joints. External contamination can cause the gaiter material to deteriorate prematurely, so it's a good idea to wash the gaiters with soap and water occasionally.

2 With the vehicle raised and securely supported on axle stands (see *Jacking and vehicle support*), turn the steering onto full-lock, then slowly rotate each front wheel in turn. Inspect the condition of the outer constant velocity (CV) joint rubber gaiters, squeezing the gaiters to open out the folds. Check for signs of cracking, splits, or deterioration of the rubber, which may allow the escape of grease, and lead to the ingress of water and grit into the joint. Also check the security and condition of the retaining clips. Repeat these checks on the inner tripod joints **(see illustration)**. If any damage or deterioration is found, the gaiters should be renewed as described in Chapter 8.

3 At the same time, check the general condition of the outer CV joints themselves, by first holding the driveshaft and attempting to rotate the wheels. Repeat this check on the inner joints, by holding the inner joint yoke and attempting to rotate the driveshaft.

4 Any appreciable movement in the joint indicates wear in the joint, wear in the driveshaft splines, or a loose driveshaft retaining bolt.

11 Underbody and fuel/brake line check

1 With the vehicle raised and supported on axle stands or over an inspection pit, thoroughly inspect the underbody and wheel arches for signs of damage and corrosion. In particular, examine the bottom of the side sills, and any concealed areas where mud can collect.

2 Where corrosion and rust is evident, press and tap firmly on the panel with a screwdriver, and check for any serious corrosion which would necessitate repairs.

3 If the panel is not seriously corroded, clean away the rust, and apply a new coating of underseal. Refer to Chapter 11 for more details of body repairs.

4 At the same time, inspect the lower body panels for stone damage and general condition.

5 Inspect all of the fuel and brake lines on the underbody for damage, rust, corrosion and leakage. Also make sure that they are correctly

10.2 Squeeze the driveshaft gaiters and check for cracks

supported in their clips **(see illustration)**. Where applicable, check the PVC coating on the lines for damage.

12 Hinge and lock lubrication

1 Work around the vehicle and lubricate the hinges of the bonnet, doors and tailgate with a light machine oil.

2 Check carefully the security and operation of all hinges, latches and locks, adjusting them where required. Check the operation of the central locking system (if fitted).

3 Where applicable, check the condition and operation of the tailgate struts, renewing them if either is leaking or no longer able to support the tailgate securely when raised.

13 Roadwheel nut tightness check

1 Checking the tightness of the wheel nuts is more relevant than you might think. Apart from the obvious safety aspect of ensuring they are sufficiently tight, this check will reveal whether they have been overtightened, as may have happened the last time new tyres were fitted, for example. If the car suffers a puncture, you may find that the wheel nuts cannot be loosened with the wheel brace.

2 Apply the handbrake, chock the wheels, and engage 1st gear (or P).

11.5 Check the fuel and brake pipes under the vehicle body

1•12 Every 12 500 miles

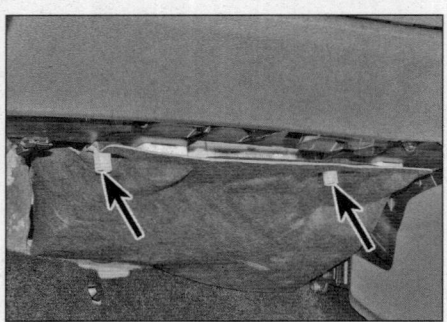

15.1 Squeeze together the sides and remove the two fasteners (arrowed)

3 Remove the wheel cover (or wheel centre cover), using the flat end of the wheel brace supplied in the tool kit.
4 Loosen the first wheel nut, using the wheel brace if possible. If the nut proves stubborn, use a close-fitting socket and a long extension bar.

⚠ **Warning: Do not use makeshift means to loosen the wheel nuts if the proper tools are not available. If extra force is required, make sure that the tools fit properly, and are of good quality. Even so, consider the consequences of the tool slipping or breaking, and take precautions – wearing stout gloves is advisable to protect your hands. Do not be tempted to stand on the tools used – they are not designed for this, and there is a high risk of personal injury if the tool slips or breaks. If the wheel nuts are simply too tight, take the car to a garage equipped with suitable power tools.**

5 Once the nut has been loosened, remove it and check that the wheel stud threads are clean. Use a small wire brush to clean any rust or dirt from the threads, if necessary.
6 Refit the nut, with the tapered side facing inwards. Tighten it fully, using the wheel brace alone – no other tools. This will ensure that the wheel nuts can be loosened using the wheel brace if a puncture occurs. However, if a torque wrench is available, tighten the nut to the specified torque wrench setting.
7 Repeat the procedure for the remaining nuts, then refit the wheel cover or centre cover, as applicable.

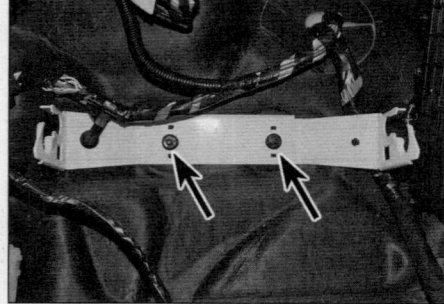

15.4 Undo the 2 nuts (arrowed) securing the bracket

15.3 Rotate the fasteners (arrowed) anti-clockwise and lift the fuse/junction box from the bracket

8 Work around the car, checking and retightening the nuts for all four wheels.

14 Road test

Braking system

1 Make sure that the vehicle does not pull to one side when braking, and that the wheels do not lock when braking hard.
2 Check that there is no vibration through the steering when braking. As all models are equipped with ABS brakes, if vibration is felt through the pedal under heavy braking, this is a normal characteristic of the system operation, and is not a cause for concern.
3 Check that the handbrake operates correctly, without excessive movement of the lever, and that it holds the vehicle stationary on a slope, in both directions (facing up and down a slope).
4 With the engine switched off, test the operation of the brake servo unit as follows. Depress the footbrake four or five times to exhaust the vacuum, then start the engine. As the engine starts, there should be a noticeable 'give' in the brake pedal as vacuum builds-up. Allow the engine to run for at least two minutes, and then switch it off. If the brake pedal is now depressed again, it should be possible to detect a hiss from the servo as the pedal is depressed. After about four or five applications, no further hissing should be heard, and the pedal should feel considerably harder.

Steering and suspension

5 Check for any abnormalities in the steering, suspension, handling or road 'feel'.
6 Drive the vehicle, and check that there are no unusual vibrations or noises.
7 Check that the steering feels positive, with no excessive sloppiness or roughness, and check for any suspension noises when cornering and driving over bumps.

Drivetrain

8 Check the performance of the engine, transmission and driveshafts.

9 Check that the engine starts correctly, both when cold and when hot.
10 Listen for any unusual noises from the engine and transmission.
11 Make sure that the engine runs smoothly when idling, and that there is no hesitation when accelerating.
12 On manual transmission models, check that all gears can be engaged smoothly without noise, and that the gear lever action is smooth and not abnormally vague or 'notchy'.
13 On automatic transmission models, make sure that all gearchanges occur smoothly without snatching, and without an increase in engine speed between changes. Check that all the gear positions can be selected with the vehicle at rest. If any problems are found, they should be referred to a Ford dealer.
14 Listen for a metallic clicking sound from the front of the vehicle as the vehicle is driven slowly in a circle with the steering on full-lock. Carry out this check in both directions. If a clicking noise is heard, this indicates wear in a driveshaft joint, in which case renew the joint if necessary.

Clutch

15 Check that the clutch pedal moves smoothly and easily through its full travel, and that the clutch itself functions correctly, with no trace of slip or drag.
16 If the clutch is slow to release, it is possible that the system requires bleeding (see Chapter 6). Also check the fluid pipes under the bonnet for signs of leakage.
17 Check the clutch as described in Chapter 6.

Instruments and electrical equipment

18 Check the operation of all instruments and electrical equipment.
19 Make sure that all instruments read correctly, and switch on all electrical equipment in turn, to check that it functions properly.

15 Pollen filter renewal

1 Release the 2 fasteners and remove the trim panel above the passenger's side footwell (see illustration).
2 Remove the passenger's glovebox as described in Chapter 11.
3 Undo the 2 fasteners securing the fusebox/central junction box/GEM, then lift it from the mounting bracket on the bulkhead (see illustration). Move the fusebox/module to one side; there is no need to disconnect the wiring plugs.
4 Release the clips securing the wiring harness to the fusebox/module mounting bracket, then undo the 2 nuts and remove the bracket (see illustration).
5 On models with air conditioning, undo the retaining bolt and remove the cool air pipe

Every 12 500 miles 1•13

15.5 Undo the bolt (arrowed) securing the glovebox cooling pipe

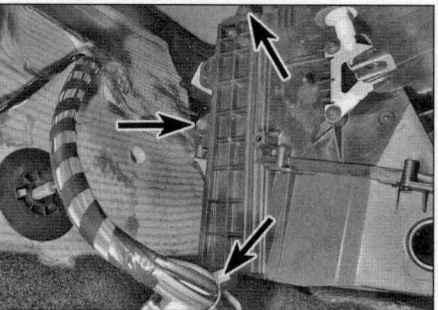

15.7a Undo the 3 bolts (arrowed), remove the cover . . .

15.7b . . . and pull the pollen filter from the housing

from the heater housing to the side of the glovebox (see illustration).
6 Disconnect the wiring plugs from the recirculation flap motor and heater blower motor resistor.
7 Undo the 3 bolts, remove the cover and pull the filter from the housing (see illustrations).
8 Fit the new filter using a reversal of the removal procedure, ensuring that the filter is fitted with the airflow arrows pointing straight back into the cabin.

16 Handbrake check and adjustment

In service, the handbrake should be fully applied within 3 to 5 clicks of the handbrake lever ratchet. Should adjustment be necessary, refer to Chapter 9, Section 22, for the full procedure description.

17 Seat belt check

1 Check the seat belts for satisfactory operation and condition. Inspect the webbing for fraying and cuts. Check that they retract smoothly and without binding into their reels.
2 Check the seat belt mountings, ensuring that all the bolts are securely tightened.

Every 37 500 miles or 3 years

18 Air filter element renewal

Caution: *Never drive the vehicle with the air cleaner filter element removed. Excessive engine wear could result, and backfiring could even cause a fire under the bonnet.*

1.4 and 1.6 litre models

1 The air filter element is located in the air cleaner assembly on the left-hand side of the engine compartment.
2 Remove the four bolts securing the cover to the air cleaner housing (see illustration).
3 The cover can now be lifted, and the filter element removed (see illustrations).
4 If carrying out a routine service, the element must be renewed regardless of its apparent condition.
5 If you are checking the element for any other reason, inspect its lower surface; if it is oily or very dirty, renew the element. If it is only moderately dusty, it can be re-used by blowing it clean from the upper to the lower surface with compressed air. Because it is a pleated-paper type filter, it cannot be washed or re-oiled. If it cannot be cleaned satisfactorily with compressed air, discard and renew it.

 Warning: *Wear eye protection when using compressed air.*

1.8 and 2.0 litre models

6 The air filter element is located in the air cleaner assembly on the left-hand side of the engine compartment.
7 Pull the plastic cover upwards from the top of the engine.
8 Undo the 6 Torx bolts securing the cover to the air cleaner housing (see illustration).
9 The left-hand end of the cover can now be lifted, and the filter element removed (see

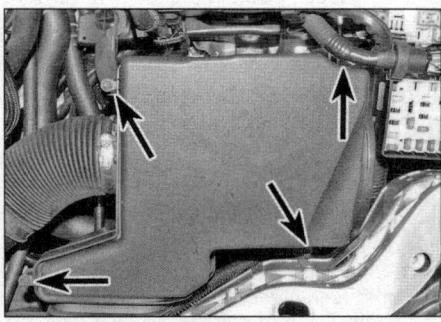

18.2 Undo the air filter cover bolts (arrowed) . . .

18.3a . . . lift up the cover . . .

18.3b . . . and remove the filter element

18.8 Undo the filter cover bolts (arrowed)

1•14 Every 37 500 miles

illustration). If preferred, the cover can be removed completely – this will allow a more thorough cleaning of the filter housing.
10 Loosen the clip and disconnect the air inlet duct from the air cleaner.
11 Withdraw the cover and remove the filter element, noting its direction of fitting.
12 If carrying out a routine service, the element must be renewed regardless of its apparent condition.
13 If you are checking the element for any other reason, inspect its lower surface; if it is oily or very dirty, renew the element. If it is only moderately dusty, it can be re-used by blowing it clean from the upper to the lower surface with compressed air. Because it is a pleated-paper type filter, it cannot be washed or re-oiled. If it cannot be cleaned satisfactorily with compressed air, discard and renew it.

 Warning: Wear eye protection when using compressed air.

All models

14 Where the air cleaner cover was removed, wipe out the inside of the housing. Check that no foreign matter is visible, either in the air inlet or in the air mass meter.
15 Refitting is the reverse of the removal procedure, noting the following points:
 a) Make sure that the filter is fitted the correct way up (observe any direction-of-fitting markings).
 b) Ensure that the element and cover are securely seated, so that unfiltered air cannot enter the engine.
 c) Where removed, secure the cover with the bolts, and ensure that the air inlet duct securing clip is fully tightened.

19 Spark plug renewal

1 The correct functioning of the spark plugs is vital for the correct running and efficiency of the engine. It is essential that the plugs fitted are appropriate for the engine.
2 If the correct type is used and the engine is in good condition, the spark plugs should not need attention between scheduled intervals. Spark plug cleaning is rarely necessary, and

18.9 Lift the cover and pull out the filter element

should not be attempted unless specialised equipment is available, as damage can easily be caused to the firing ends.
3 Spark plug removal and refitting requires a spark plug socket, with an extension which can be turned by a ratchet handle or similar. This socket is lined with a rubber sleeve, to protect the porcelain insulator of the spark plug, and to hold the plug while you insert it into the spark plug hole. You will also need feeler blades, to check and adjust the spark plug electrode gap, and (ideally) a torque wrench to tighten the new plugs to the specified torque.

1.4 and 1.6 litre models

4 To remove the spark plugs, first open the bonnet; the plugs are easily reached at the top of the engine.
5 Note how the spark plug (HT) leads are routed and secured by the clips on the cylinder head cover; unclip the leads as necessary, to provide enough slack in the lead. To prevent the possibility of mixing up spark plug (HT) leads, it is a good idea to try to work on one spark plug at a time.
6 If the marks on the original-equipment spark plug (HT) leads cannot be seen, mark the leads 1 to 4, to correspond to the cylinder the lead serves (No 1 cylinder is at the timing belt end of the engine). Pull the leads from the plugs by gripping the rubber boot sealing the cylinder head cover opening, not the lead, otherwise the lead connection may be fractured **(see illustration)**.
7 It is advisable to soak up any water in the spark plug recesses with a rag, and to remove any dirt from them using a clean brush,

vacuum cleaner or compressed air before removing the plugs, to prevent any dirt or water from dropping into the cylinders.

 Warning: Wear eye protection when using compressed air.

8 Unscrew the spark plugs, ensuring that the socket is kept in alignment with each plug – if the socket is forcibly moved to either side, the porcelain top of the plug may be broken off. Remove the plug from the engine.
9 If any undue difficulty is encountered when unscrewing any of the spark plugs, carefully check the cylinder head threads and sealing surfaces for signs of wear, excessive corrosion or damage; if any of these conditions is found, seek the advice of a Ford dealer as to the best method of repair.
10 As each plug is removed, examine it as follows – this will give a good indication of the condition of the engine:
 a) If the insulator nose of the spark plug is clean and white, with no deposits, this is indicative of a weak mixture.
 b) If the tip and insulator nose are covered with hard black-looking deposits, then this is indicative that the mixture is too rich.
 c) Should the plug be black and oily, then it is likely that the engine is fairly worn, as well as the mixture being too rich.
 d) If the insulator nose is covered with light tan to greyish-brown deposits, then the mixture is correct, and it is likely that the engine is in good condition.
11 If you are renewing the spark plugs, purchase the new plugs, then check each of them first for faults such as cracked insulators or damaged threads.
12 The spark plug electrode gap is of considerable importance as, if it is too large or too small, the size of the spark and its efficiency will be seriously impaired. However, several models covered by this manual use spark plugs with multiple earth electrodes – *unless there is clear information to the contrary, no attempt should be made to adjust the plug gap on a spark plug with more than one earth electrode.*
13 To set the electrode gap on plugs with one earth electrode, measure the gap with a feeler gauge, and then bend open, or closed, the outer plug electrode until the correct gap is achieved **(see illustrations)**. The centre

19.6 Pull the HT lead (arrowed) from the top of the spark plug

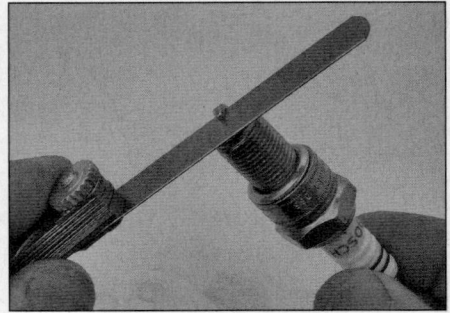
19.13a Check the electrode gap with a set of feeler gauges

19.13b Adjust the electrode gap

Every 37 500 miles 1•15

It is often difficult to insert spark plugs into their holes without cross-threading them. To avoid this possibility, fit a short length of rubber or plastic hose over the end of the spark plug. The flexible hose acts as a universal joint, to help align the plug with the plug hole. Should the plug begin to cross thread, the hose will slip on the spark plug, preventing thread damage to the cylinder head.

19.18 Pull the engine cover upwards

19.19a Undo the coil retaining bolt . . .

19.19b . . . and lift it from place

electrode should never be bent, as this may crack the insulation and cause plug failure, if nothing worse. If the outer electrode is not exactly over the centre electrode, bend it gently to align them.

14 Before fitting the spark plugs, check that the threaded connector sleeves at the top of the plugs are tight (where fitted), and that the plug exterior surfaces and threads are clean. Brown staining on the porcelain, immediately above the metal body, is quite normal, and does not necessarily indicate a leak between the body and insulator.

15 On installing the spark plugs, first check that the cylinder head thread and sealing surface are as clean as possible; use a clean rag wrapped around a paintbrush to wipe clean the sealing surface. Apply a smear of copper-based grease or anti-seize compound to the threads of each plug, and screw them in by hand where possible. Take extra care to enter the plug threads correctly, as the cylinder head is made of aluminium alloy – it's often difficult to insert spark plugs into their holes without cross-threading them **(see Haynes Hint)**.

16 When each spark plug is started correctly on its threads, screw it down until it just seats lightly, then tighten it to the specified torque wrench setting. If a torque wrench is not available – and this is one case where the use of a torque wrench is strongly recommended – tighten each spark plug through *no more than* 1/16th of a turn. *Do not* exceed the specified torque setting, and NEVER overtighten spark plugs.

17 Reconnect the spark plug (HT) leads in their correct order, using a twisting motion on the boot until it is firmly seated on the end of the spark plug and on the cylinder head cover.

1.8 and 2.0 litre models

18 To remove the spark plugs, first open the bonnet; the plugs are easily reached at the top of the engine. Pull the plastic cover on the top of the engine straight up to release its mountings **(see illustration)**.

19 The ignition coils are fitted one per plug, on the top of each spark plug. To aid refitment, use paint (or similar) to identify the ignition coils so they are refitted to their original positions. Undo the retaining bolts and lift each coil from place **(see illustrations)**.

20 Continue as described in paragraphs 7 to 16.

21 Align the coil with the mounting bolt hole, then push it down firmly onto the spark plug. Tighten the retaining bolt to the specified torque.

22 The remainder of refitting is a reversal of removal.

Every 60 000 miles

| 20 Timing belt renewal | The procedure (applicable only to the 1.4 and 1.6 litre engines) is described in Chapter 2A. |

Every 100 000 miles or 8 years

21 Auxiliary drivebelt check and renewal

Drivebelt check

1 Two auxiliary drivebelts maybe fitted – one from the crankshaft pulley to the alternator, power steering pump and coolant pump, and one from the crankshaft pulley to the air conditioning compressor (where applicable). On 1.8 and 2.0 litre engines, an automatic adjuster is fitted to the main auxiliary drivebelt, so checking the drivebelt tension is unnecessary. On 1.4 and 1.6 litre engines, no provision is made to adjust the main auxiliary drivebelt tension. On all models, no provision is made to adjust the air conditioning drivebelt tension.

2 Due to their function and material make-up, drivebelts are prone to failure after a long period of time, and should therefore be inspected regularly.

3 Since the drivebelt is located very close to the right-hand side of the engine compartment, it is possible to gain better access by raising the front of the vehicle and removing the right-hand wheel, then undoing the fasteners and removing the engine undershield (where fitted) **(see illustration 3.4)**.

4 With the engine stopped, inspect the full length of the drivebelt for cracks and separation of the belt plies. It will be necessary to turn the engine (using a spanner or socket and bar on the crankshaft pulley bolt) in order to move the belt from the pulleys so that the

1•16 Every 100 000 miles

21.8 Cut through the drivebelt

21.10a Fit the tool to the crankshaft pulley in the 12 o'clock position . . .

21.10b . . . with the curved side (arrowed) of the tool towards the engine

21.13 Fit the installation tool (arrowed) to the coolant pump pulley

21.16a Rotate the coolant pump pulley/ tool by hand until it catches the belt . . .

21.16b . . . then use a spanner to fully rotate the pulley/tool

belt can be inspected thoroughly. Twist the belt between the pulleys so that both sides can be viewed. Also check for fraying, and glazing which gives the belt a shiny appearance. Check the pulleys for nicks, cracks, distortion and corrosion.

5 Note that it is not unusual for a ribbed belt to exhibit small cracks in the edges of the belt ribs, and unless these are extensive or very deep, belt renewal is not essential.

Renewal – 1.4 & 1.6 litre engines

6 Slacken the right-hand front roadwheel nuts, raise the front of the vehicle and support on axle stands (see *Jacking and vehicle support*). Where fitted – undo the fasteners and remove the engine undershield (see illustration 3.4). Remove the roadwheel.

7 Undo the fasteners, then remove the wheel arch liner and splash shield under the belt(s).

8 Using a sharp knife, cut through the air conditioning compressor drivebelt (where fitted) and the main auxiliary drivebelt, then remove them (see illustration).

9 Ensure the pulley grooves are clean.

10 New auxiliary belts are supplied by Ford with fitting tools included. Fit the main auxiliary drivebelt fitting tool to the crankshaft pulley, with the centre of the tool in the 12 o'clock position, and the curved side towards the engine (see illustrations).

11 Refit the roadwheel, lower the vehicle to the ground and select 1st gear or Park.

12 Position the new auxiliary belt around the crankshaft pulley, power steering pump pulley and coolant pump pulley. Ensure the belt is correctly located in the pulley grooves.

13 Fit the installation tool supplied in the kit to the coolant pump pulley as shown (see illustration). An audible click will be heard when the tool is correctly located on the pulley. If the coolant pump pulley bolts have been previously slackened, take the opportunity to tighten the bolts whilst the tool is fitted.

14 Rotate the coolant pump pulley and installation tool 90° anti-clockwise.

15 Slide the belt from the coolant pump pulley, and fit it around the alternator pulley. Ensure the belt is correctly located in the pulley grooves.

16 Rotate the installation tool and pulley clockwise by hand until the tension on the belt increases, then use a spanner to rotate the tool/pulley clockwise and install the belt on the underside of the pulley (see illustrations). This procedure should be carried out in front of the engine mounting. Use a second spanner to fully rotate the tool/pulley.

17 Release the tool from the coolant pump pulley, then select neutral gear and raise the front of the vehicle again.

18 Rotate the crankshaft pulley approximately 90° using a spanner on the pulley bolt/nut. Remove the installation tool from the crankshaft pulley.

19 Continue to rotate the crankshaft pulley through 2 complete revolutions, and check that the belt is correctly located in the pulley grooves.

20 On models with air conditioning, the new compressor drivebelt is supplied by Ford in a kit with the necessary installation tool. Begin by fitting the installation tool to the crankshaft pulley in the 7 o'clock position (see illustration).

21 Fit the new belt around the compressor pulley, ensuring the belt correctly locates in the pulley grooves, then fit the belt under the crankshaft pulley and around the installation tool (see illustration).

21.20 Fit the compressor drivebelt installation tool in the 7 o'clock position

21.21 Fit the belt around the tool . . .

Every 100 000 miles

21.22 ... then rotate the crankshaft pulley clockwise

21.27 Rotate the tensioner anti-clockwise

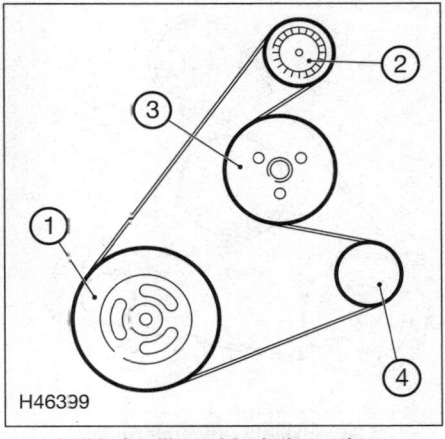

21.29 Auxiliary drivebelt routing – 1.8 and 2.0 litre engines
1 Crankshaft pulley
2 Tensioner pulley
3 Coolant pump pulley
4 Alternator pulley

22 Rotate the installation tool clockwise until the tension increases, holding the belt into the grooves on the underside of the crankshaft pulley, then use a socket on the crankshaft pulley, and rotate the pulley clockwise until the tool is in the 3 o'clock position (see illustration).
23 Remove the installation tool, then rotate the crankshaft pulley 1 complete revolution clockwise and check the belt is correctly located in the pulley grooves.
24 The remainder of refitting is a reversal of removal. Note that when refitting the wheel arch liner, the longest bolt is the rearmost.

Renewal – 1.8 & 2.0 litre engines

25 Slacken the right-hand front roadwheel nuts, raise the front of the vehicle and support on axle stands (see *Jacking and vehicle support*). Where fitted – undo the fasteners and remove the engine undershield (see illustration 3.4). Remove the roadwheel. Undo the fasteners, then remove the wheel arch liner and splash shield under the belt(s).
26 Using a sharp knife, cut through the air conditioning compressor drivebelt (where fitted), and remove it. Unclip the power steering pipe where applicable. Remove the plastic cover from the top of the engine.

Models up to 02/2008

27 Using a spanner on the centre bolt, rotate the main auxiliary drivebelt tensioner anti-clockwise to relieve the tension, and remove the belt (see illustration).
28 Ensure the pulley grooves are clean.
29 Fit the new drivebelt onto the crankshaft, alternator, and coolant pump, then turn the tensioner anti-clockwise and locate the drivebelt on the pulley. Make sure that the drivebelt is correctly seated in all of the pulley grooves, then release the tensioner (see illustration).

Models from 02/2008

30 Undo the 2 bolts and 1 nut securing the auxiliary drivebelt idler pulley to the cylinder head (see illustration).
31 Insert a long bar/rod of suitable diameter into the hole in the top of the idler mounting assembly. Using moderate force only, lever the assembly towards the left-hand side of the vehicle, then pull the assembly forwards a little, and allow the rod/bar to move the right-hand side until the belt can be removed from the pulley (see illustration). Remove the belt from the remaining pulleys.
32 Ensure the pulley grooves are clean.
33 Fit the new drivebelt onto the crankshaft, alternator, and coolant pump, then loop the belt over the idler pulley. At this point the idler pulley mounting assembly should be unbolted, free to pivot on the lower mounting stud with the bar/rod inserted into the top hole.
34 Using moderate force only, pull the rod/bar across the left-hand side of the vehicle, and re-align the idler assembly mounting holes. Insert the bolts, then tighten the nut/bolts to the specified torque. Remove the bar/rod, then make sure that the drivebelt is correctly seated in all of the pulley grooves (see illustration).

All models

35 On models with air conditioning, the new compressor drivebelt is supplied by Ford in a kit with the necessary installation tool. Begin by fitting the installation tool to the crankshaft pulley in the 9 o'clock position (see illustration).

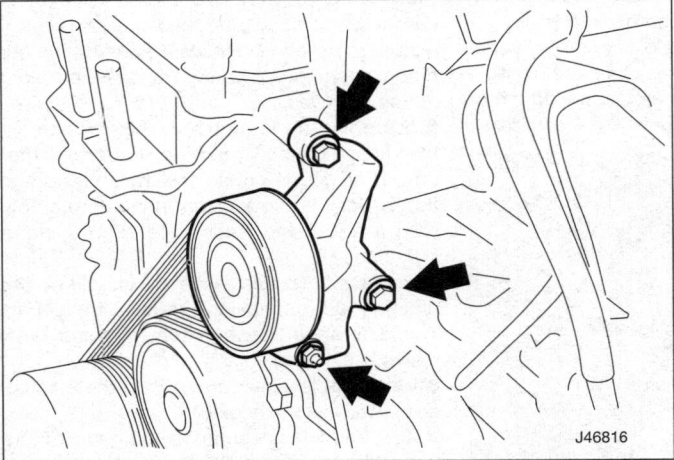

21.30 Undo the auxiliary belt tensioner bolts/nut (arrowed)

21.31 Lever the tensioner to the left, then forwards, then to the right and remove the belt

1•18 Every 100 000 miles

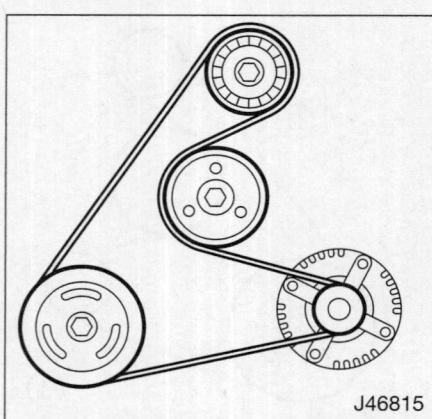

21.34 Auxiliary drivebelt routing – post-02/2008

21.35 Fit the installation tool (arrowed) to the crankshaft in the 9 o'clock position

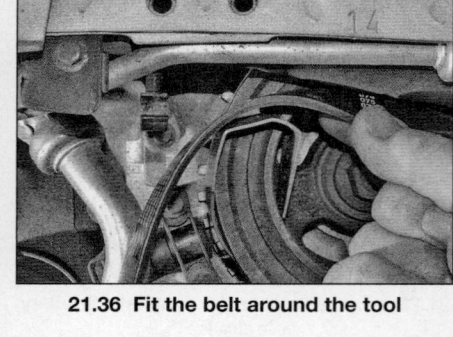

21.36 Fit the belt around the tool

36 Fit the new belt around the compressor pulley, ensuring the belt correctly locates in the pulley grooves, then fit the belt around the installation tool **(see illustration)**.
37 Fit the belt guide tool to the compressor. The curved end of the tool fits around the belt, and the flat end fits between the compressor and the sump **(see illustration)**.
38 Using a spanner on the crankshaft pulley, rotate the pulley clockwise until the installation tool on the pulley is in the 6 o'clock position. Guide the belt onto the pulleys as the crankshaft is rotated **(see illustration)**.
39 Remove the installation tool, then rotate the crankshaft pulley 1 complete revolution clockwise and check the belt is correctly located in the pulley grooves.

21.37 Insert the guide tool between the compressor and the sump – note how the tool fits around the compressor bolt (arrowed)

40 Remove the belt guide tool from the compressor.

21.38 Rotate the crankshaft clockwise until the installation tool is in the 6 o'clock position

41 The remainder of refitting is a reversal of removal.

Every 2 years, regardless of mileage

22 Automatic transmission fluid level check

1 The fluid level **must** be checked with the engine/transmission at operating temperature. This can be achieved by checking the level after a journey of at least 10 miles. If the level is checked when cold, follow this up with a level check when the fluid is hot.

22.5a Pull the automatic transmission fluid level dipstick from place

2 Park the car on level ground, and apply the handbrake very firmly. As an added precaution, chock the front and rear wheels, so that the car cannot move.
3 With the engine idling, apply the footbrake, then move the selector lever gently from position P to position 1 and back to P.
4 The fluid level dipstick is located on the rear of the transmission. Before removing the dipstick, thoroughly clean the area around it – no dirt or debris must be allowed to enter the transmission.

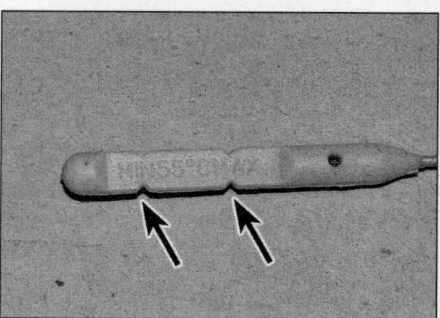

22.5b Dipstick fluid level upper and lower markings (arrowed)

5 Extract the dipstick, and wipe it clean using a clean piece of rag or tissue. Re-insert the dipstick completely, then pull it out once more. The fluid level should be between the reference marks on the side of the dipstick **(see illustrations)**. **Note:** *If the level is checked when cold, the reading obtained will appear to be low – recheck the level when hot before topping-up, as the transmission must not be overfilled.*
6 If topping-up is required, this is done via the dipstick tube. It is most important that no dirt or debris enters the transmission as this is done – use a clean funnel (preferably with a filter) and fresh fluid from a clean container.
7 Pour the fresh fluid a little at a time down the dipstick tube, checking the level frequently. The difference between the MIN and MAX marks is 0.4 litres.
8 When the level is correct, refit the dipstick and switch off the engine.
9 The need for regular topping-up of the transmission fluid indicates a leak, which should be found and rectified without delay.

Every 2 years 1•19

23.3 Filler/level plug (arrowed)

23 Manual transmission oil level check

1 The manual transmission does not have a dipstick. To check the oil level, raise the vehicle and support it securely on axle stands (see *Jacking and vehicle support*), making sure that the vehicle is level. Undo the fasteners and remove the engine undershield (where fitted).
2 Except on 2.0 litre models, to gain access to the filler/level plug, it is first necessary to unclip the plastic cover from the gear selector cables at the front of the transmission.
3 On the lower front side of the transmission housing, you will see the filler/level plug, which has a large Allen key fitting **(see illustration)**. Note it is the plug furthest from the engine; where applicable, do not confuse it with the blanking plug near the bellhousing.
4 Remove all traces of dirt, then unscrew the filler/level plug from the front face of the transmission. Access to the plug is not that easy; use a suitable Allen key or socket, and take care, as the plug will probably be very tight.
5 If the lubricant level is correct, the oil should be up to the lower edge of the hole.
6 If the transmission needs more lubricant (if the level is not up to the hole), use a syringe, or a plastic bottle and tube, to add more.
7 Stop filling the transmission when the oil begins to run out of the hole, then wait until the flow of oil ceases – do not refit the plug immediately, or the transmission may end up being overfilled.
8 When the level is correct, clean and refit the filler level plug and tighten it to the specified torque.
9 Drive the vehicle a short distance, then check for leaks.
10 A need for regular topping-up can only be due to a leak, which should be found and rectified without delay.

24 Brake fluid renewal

Warning: Brake hydraulic fluid can harm your eyes and damage painted surfaces, so use extreme caution when handling and pouring it. Do not use fluid that has been standing open for some time, as it absorbs moisture from the air. Excess moisture can cause a dangerous loss of braking effectiveness. Brake fluid is also highly flammable – treat it with the same respect as petrol.

1 The procedure is similar to that for the bleeding of the hydraulic system as described in Chapter 9.
2 Reduce the fluid level in the reservoir (by syphoning or using a poultry baster), but do not allow the fluid level to drop far enough to allow air into the system.

Warning: Do not syphon the fluid by mouth; it is poisonous.

3 Working as described in Chapter 9, open the first bleed screw in the sequence, and pump the brake pedal gently until nearly all the old fluid has been emptied from the master cylinder reservoir. Top-up to the MAX level with new fluid, and continue pumping until only the new fluid remains in the reservoir, and new fluid can be seen emerging from the bleed screw. Tighten the screw, and top the reservoir level up to the MAX level line. Old hydraulic fluid is invariably much darker in colour than the new, making it easy to distinguish the two.
4 Work through all the remaining bleed screws in the sequence until new fluid can be seen at all of them. Be careful to keep the master cylinder reservoir topped-up to above the MIN level at all times, or air may enter the system and greatly increase the length of the task.
5 When the operation is complete, check that all bleed screws are securely tightened, and that their dust caps are refitted. Wash off all traces of spilt fluid, and recheck the master cylinder reservoir fluid level.
6 Check the operation of the brakes before taking the car on the road.
7 Finally, check the operation of the clutch. Since the clutch shares the same fluid reservoir as the braking system, it may also be necessary to bleed the clutch as described in Chapter 6.

25 Remote control battery renewal

1 Although not in the Ford maintenance schedule, we recommend that the battery is changed every 2 years, regardless of the vehicle's mileage. However, if the door locks repeatedly fail to respond to signals from the remote control at the normal distance, change the battery in the remote control before attempting to troubleshoot any of the vehicle's other systems.

Type 1

2 Press the button to release the key blade. On passive type controls, remove the spare key.
3 On non-passive type controls, insert a small flat-bladed screwdriver into the slot provided, push the screwdriver towards the key blade, and carefully prise the 2 halves of the control apart **(see illustrations)**.
4 On both types of control, insert a screwdriver as shown and separate the two halves **(see illustration)**.
5 Note the fitted position of the battery (positive side down), then prise the battery from place, and insert the new one **(see illustration)**. Avoid touching the battery or the terminals with bare fingers.
6 Snap the 2 halves of the control together.
7 Refit the key blade, and check for correct operation.

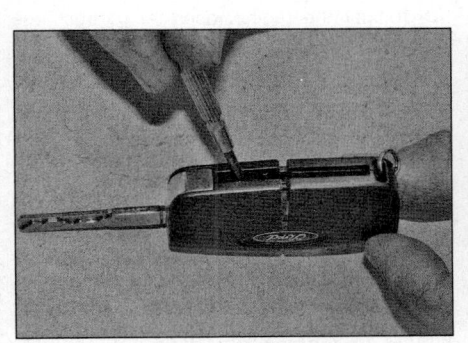

25.3a Insert a screwdriver into the slot . . .

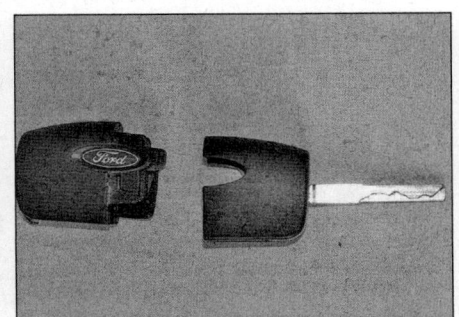

25.3b . . . and prise apart the 2 halves

25.4 Separate the 2 halves

1•20 Every 2 years

25.5 The battery fits positive side down

25.8 Insert a screwdriver into the slot

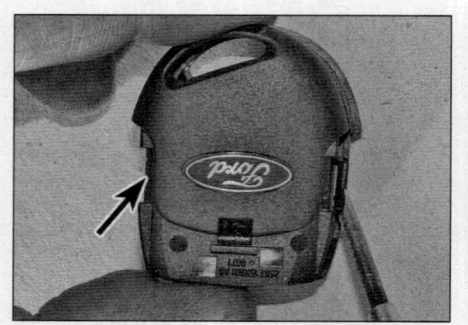

25.9 Release the clip each side (arrowed)

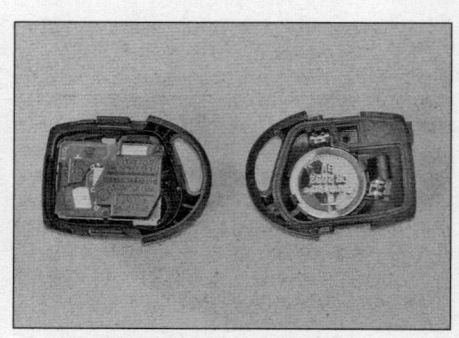

25.10 The battery fits positive side up

Type 2

8 Insert a small flat-bladed screwdriver into the slot provided and slide the transmitter unit from the key **(see illustration)**.
9 Use the screwdriver to release the clip each side and open the transmitter unit **(see illustration)**.
10 Note the fitted position of the battery (positive side up), then prise the battery from place, and insert the new one **(see illustration)**. Avoid touching the battery or the terminals with bare fingers.
11 Snap the 2 halves of the transmitter together, and re-attach it to the key.

26 Coolant strength check and renewal

⚠️ **Warning:** *Do not allow antifreeze to come in contact with your skin or painted surfaces of the vehicle. Flush contaminated areas immediately with plenty of water. Don't store new coolant, or leave old coolant lying around, where it's accessible to children or pets – they're attracted by its sweet smell. Ingestion of even a small amount of coolant can be fatal. Wipe up garage-floor and drip-pan spills immediately. Keep antifreeze containers covered, and repair cooling system leaks as soon as they're noticed.*

⚠️ **Warning:** *Never remove the expansion tank filler cap when the engine is running, or has just been switched off, as the cooling system will be hot, and the consequent escaping steam and scalding coolant could cause serious injury.*

⚠️ **Warning:** *Wait until the engine is cold before starting these procedures.*

Note: *If the pink/red Ford antifreeze is used, the coolant can then be left indefinitely, providing the strength of the mixture is checked every year. If any antifreeze other than Ford's is to be used, the coolant must be renewed at regular intervals to provide an equivalent degree of protection; the conventional recommendation is to renew the coolant every two years.*

Strength check

1 Use a hydrometer to check the strength of the antifreeze. Follow the instructions provided with your hydrometer. The antifreeze strength should be approximately 50%. If it is significantly less than this, drain a little coolant from the radiator (see this Section), add

26.4 Slacken the radiator drain plug

antifreeze to the coolant expansion tank, then recheck the strength.

Coolant draining

2 To drain the system, first remove the expansion tank filler cap.
3 If the additional working clearance is required, raise the front of the vehicle and support it securely on axle stands (see *Jacking and vehicle support*). Where fitted, undo the fasteners and remove the engine undershield **(see illustration 3.4)**.
4 Place a large drain tray underneath, and unscrew the radiator drain plug **(see illustration)**; direct as much of the escaping coolant as possible into the tray.
5 Once the coolant has stopped draining from the radiator, close the drain plug.

System flushing

6 With time, the cooling system may gradually lose its efficiency, as the radiator core becomes choked with rust, scale deposits from the water, and other sediment. To minimise this, as well as using only good-quality antifreeze and clean soft water, the system should be flushed as follows whenever any part of it is disturbed, and/or when the coolant is renewed.
7 With the coolant drained, refit the drain plug and refill the system with fresh water. Refit the expansion tank filler cap, start the engine and warm it up to normal operating temperature, then stop it and (after allowing it to cool down completely) drain the system again. Repeat as necessary until only clean water can be seen to emerge, then refill finally with the specified coolant mixture.
8 If only clean, soft water and good-quality antifreeze (even if not to Ford's specification) has been used, and the coolant has been renewed at the suggested intervals, the above procedure will be sufficient to keep clean the system for a considerable length of time. If, however, the system has been neglected, a more thorough operation will be required, as follows.
9 First drain the coolant, then disconnect the radiator top and bottom hoses. Insert a garden hose into the radiator top hose connection, and allow water to circulate through the radiator until it runs clean from the bottom outlet.
10 To flush the engine, insert the garden hose into the radiator bottom hose, wrap a piece of rag around the garden hose to seal the connection, and allow water to circulate until it runs clear.
11 Try the effect of repeating this procedure in the top hose, although this may not be effective, since the thermostat will probably close and prevent the flow of water.
12 In severe cases of contamination, reverse-flushing of the radiator may be necessary. This may be achieved by inserting the garden hose into the bottom outlet, wrapping a piece of rag around the hose to seal the connection, then flushing the radiator until clear water emerges from the top hose outlet.

Every 2 years

13 If the radiator is suspected of being severely choked, remove the radiator (Chapter 3), turn it upside-down, and repeat the procedure described in paragraph 12.

14 Flushing the heater matrix can be achieved using a similar procedure to that described in paragraph 12, once the heater inlet and outlet hoses have been identified. These two hoses will be of the same diameter, and pass through the engine compartment bulkhead (refer to the heater matrix removal procedure in Chapter 3 for more details).

15 The use of chemical cleaners is not recommended, and should be necessary only as a last resort; the scouring action of some chemical cleaners may lead to other cooling system problems. Normally, regular renewal of the coolant will prevent excessive contamination of the system.

Coolant filling

16 With the cooling system drained and flushed, ensure that all disturbed hose unions are correctly secured, and that the radiator/engine drain plug(s) is securely tightened. Refit the engine undershield (where applicable). If it was raised, lower the vehicle to the ground.

17 Set the heater temperature control to maximum heat, but ensure the blower is turned off.

18 Prepare a sufficient quantity of the specified coolant mixture (see below); allow for a surplus, so as to have a reserve supply for topping-up.

19 Slowly fill the system through the expansion tank. Since the tank is the highest point in the system, all the air in the system should be displaced into the tank by the rising liquid. Slow pouring reduces the possibility of air being trapped and forming airlocks.

20 Continue filling until the coolant level reaches the expansion tank MAX level line (see *Weekly checks*), then cover the filler opening to prevent coolant splashing out.

21 Start the engine and run it at 2500 rpm for 2 minutes. If the level in the expansion tank drops significantly, top-up to the MAX level line, to minimise the amount of air circulating in the system.

22 Fill the expansion tank to the MAX level line, refit the expansion tank cap, and run the engine at 2500 rpm until the thermostat opens and the engine is at normal operating temperature. Check this by feeling the radiator bottom hose – if it's hot, then the thermostat has opened.

23 Briefly run the engine at 4000 rpm, then run it at 2500 rpm for approximately 3 minutes.

24 Stop the engine, wash off any spilt coolant from the engine compartment and bodywork, then leave the car to cool down *completely* (overnight, if possible).

25 With the system cool, open the expansion tank, and top-up the tank to the MAX level line. Refit the filler cap, tightening it securely, and clean up any further spillage.

26 After refilling, always check carefully all components of the system (but especially any unions disturbed during draining and flushing) for signs of coolant leaks. Fresh antifreeze has a searching action, which will rapidly expose any weak points in the system.

Antifreeze type and mixture

Note: *Do not use engine antifreeze in the windscreen/tailgate washer system, as it will damage the vehicle's paintwork. A screenwash additive should be added to the washer system in its maker's recommended quantities.*

27 If the vehicle's history (and therefore the quality of the antifreeze in it) is unknown, owners are advised to drain and thoroughly reverse-flush the system, before refilling with fresh coolant mixture.

28 If the antifreeze used is to Ford's specification, the levels of protection it affords are indicated in the coolant packaging.

29 To give the recommended *standard* mixture ratio for antifreeze, 50% (by volume) of antifreeze must be mixed with 50% of clean, soft water; if you are using any other type of antifreeze, follow its manufacturer's instructions to achieve the correct ratio.

30 You are unlikely to fully drain the system at any one time (unless the engine is being completely stripped), and the capacities quoted in Specifications are therefore slightly academic for routine coolant renewal. As a guide, only two-thirds of the system's total capacity is likely to be needed for coolant renewal.

31 As the drained system will be partially filled with flushing water, in order to establish the recommended mixture ratio, measure out 50% of the system capacity in antifreeze and pour it into the hose/expansion tank as described above, then top-up with water. Any topping-up while refilling the system should be done with water – for *Weekly checks* use a suitable mixture.

32 Before adding antifreeze, the cooling system should be drained, preferably flushed, and all hoses checked for condition and security. As noted earlier, fresh antifreeze will rapidly find any weaknesses in the system.

33 After filling with antifreeze, a label should be attached to the expansion tank, stating the type and concentration of antifreeze used, and the date installed. Any subsequent topping-up should be made with the same type and concentration of antifreeze.

General cooling system checks

34 The engine should be cold for the cooling system checks, so perform the following procedure before driving the vehicle, or after it has been shut off for at least three hours.

35 Remove the expansion tank filler cap, and clean it thoroughly inside and out with a rag. Also clean the filler neck on the expansion tank. The presence of rust or corrosion in the filler neck indicates that the coolant should be changed. The coolant inside the expansion tank should be relatively clean and transparent. If it is rust-coloured, drain and flush the system, and refill with a fresh coolant mixture.

36 Carefully check the radiator hoses and heater hoses along their entire length; renew any hose which is cracked, swollen or deteriorated.

37 Inspect all other cooling system components (joint faces, etc) for leaks. A leak in the cooling system will usually show up as white- or antifreeze-coloured deposits on the area adjoining the leak **(see Haynes Hint)**. Where any problems of this nature are found on system components, renew the component or gasket with reference to Chapter 3.

38 Clean the front of the radiator with a soft brush to remove all insects, leaves, etc, embedded in the radiator fins. Be careful not to damage the radiator fins, or cut your fingers on them. To do a more thorough job, remove the radiator grille as described in Chapter 11.

Airlocks

39 If, after draining and refilling the system, symptoms of overheating are found which did not occur previously, then the fault is almost certainly due to trapped air at some point in the system, causing an airlock and restricting the flow of coolant; usually, the air is trapped because the system was refilled too quickly.

40 If an airlock is suspected, first try gently squeezing all visible coolant hoses. A coolant hose which is full of air feels quite different to one full of coolant when squeezed. After refilling the system, most airlocks will clear once the system has cooled, and been topped-up.

41 While the engine is running at operating temperature, switch on the heater and heater fan, and check for heat output. Provided there is sufficient coolant in the system, lack of heat output could be due to an airlock in the system.

42 Airlocks can have more serious effects than simply reducing heater output – a severe airlock could reduce coolant flow around the engine. Check that the radiator top hose is hot when the engine is at operating temperature – a top hose which stays cold could be the result of an airlock (or a non-opening thermostat).

43 If the problem persists, stop the engine

A leak in the cooling system will usually show up as white- or antifreeze-coloured deposits on the areas adjoining the leak.

1•22 Every 2 years

and allow it to cool down **completely**, before unscrewing the expansion tank filler cap or loosening the hose clips and squeezing the hoses to bleed out the trapped air. In the worst case, the system will have to be at least partially drained (this time, the coolant can be saved for re-use) and flushed to clear the problem. If all else fails, have the system evacuated and vacuum filled by a suitably-equipped garage.

Expansion tank pressure cap check

44 Wait until the engine is completely cold – perform this check before the engine is started for the first time in the day.
45 Place a wad of cloth over the expansion tank cap, then unscrew it slowly and remove it.
46 Examine the condition of the rubber seal on the underside of the cap. If the rubber appears to have hardened, or cracks are visible in the seal edges, a new cap should be fitted.
47 If the car is several years old, or has covered a large mileage, consider renewing the cap regardless of its apparent condition – they are not expensive. If the pressure relief valve built into the cap fails, excess pressure in the system will lead to puzzling failures of hoses and other cooling system components.

Chapter 2 Part A:
1.4 & 1.6 litre engines (Duratec 16V) in-car repair procedures

Contents

	Section number		Section number
Camshaft oil seals – renewal	10	General information	1
Camshafts and tappets – removal, inspection and refitting	11	Oil pressure switch – removal and refitting	15
Compression test – description and interpretation	2	Oil pump – removal, inspection and refitting	14
Crankshaft oil seals – renewal	16	Sump – removal and refitting	13
Crankshaft pulley/vibration damper – removal and refitting	6	Timing belt – removal and refitting	8
Cylinder head – removal, inspection and refitting	12	Timing belt covers – removal and refitting	7
Cylinder head cover – removal and refitting	4	Timing belt tensioner and sprockets – removal, inspection and refitting	9
Engine oil and filter renewal	See Chapter 1	Top Dead Centre (TDC) for No 1 piston – locating	3
Engine oil level check	See Weekly checks	Valve clearances – checking and adjustment	5
Engine/transmission mountings – inspection and renewal	18		
Flywheel/driveplate – removal, inspection and refitting	17		

Degrees of difficulty

Easy, suitable for novice with little experience	Fairly easy, suitable for beginner with some experience	Fairly difficult, suitable for competent DIY mechanic	Difficult, suitable for experienced DIY mechanic	Very difficult, suitable for expert DIY or professional

Specifications

General

Engine type	Four-cylinder, in-line, double overhead camshafts, variable valve timing on Ti-VCT engine only
Designation	Duratec 16V or Duratec 16V Ti-VCT
Engine codes:	
1.4 litre engine	ASDA and ASDB
1.6 litre engine:	
Non-Ti-VCT engine	HWDA, HWDB, SHDA, SHDB and SHDC
Ti-VCT engine	HXDA, HXDB and SIDA
Capacity:	
1.4 litre engine	1388 cc
1.6 litre engines	1596 cc
Bore:	
1.4 litre engine	75.9 mm
1.6 litre engines	79.0 mm
Stroke:	
1.4 litre engine	76.5 mm
1.6 litre engines	81.4 mm
Compression ratio	11.0:1
Output:	
Power:	
1.4 litre engine	59 kW (80 PS)
1.6 litre engine:	
Non-Ti-VCT engine	74 kW (100 PS)
Ti-VCT engine	85 KW (115 PS)
Torque:	
1.4 litre engine	124 Nm
1.6 litre engine:	
Non-Ti-VCT engine	150 Nm
Ti-VCT engine	155 Nm
Firing order	1-3-4-2 (No 1 cylinder at timing belt end)
Direction of crankshaft rotation	Clockwise (seen from right-hand side of car)

Valves

	Inlet	Exhaust
Valve clearances (cold):		
All engines	0.17 to 0.23 mm	0.31 to 0.37 mm

Camshafts

Camshaft bearing journal diameter	Unavailable at time of writing
Camshaft bearing journal-to-cylinder head running clearance	Unavailable at time of writing
Camshaft endfloat (typical)	0.05 to 0.13 mm

Lubrication

Oil pressure (minimum, warm engine):
    Idling (800 rpm) . . . . 1.0 bar
    At 2000 rpm . . . . 2.5 bars
Pressure relief valve opens at . . . . 4.0 bars
Oil pump clearances . . . . Not specified

Torque wrench settings

	Nm	lbf ft
Air conditioning compressor mounting bolts	25	18
Alternator mounting bracket bolts	42	31
Camshaft bearing cap:		
Stage 1	7	5
Stage 2	Angle-tighten a further 45°	
Camshaft position sensor (Ti-VCT engine)	9	7
Camshaft pulley bolt (not Ti-VCT engine)*	60	44
Camshaft sensor ring (Ti-VCT engine)	21	15
Coolant outlet to cylinder head	20	15
Coolant pump pulley bolts (not Ti-VCT engine)	24	17
Crankcase breather to cylinder block	9	7
Crankshaft position sensor	9	7
Crankshaft oil seal carrier	9	7
Crankshaft pulley/vibration damper:*		
Stage 1	40	30
Stage 2	Angle-tighten a further 90°	
Crankshaft sprocket/timing belt retainer plate to cylinder block	9	7
Cross-brace bolts	30	22
Cylinder head bolts:*		
Stage 1	15	11
Stage 2	30	22
Stage 3	Angle-tighten a further 90°	
Cylinder head cover	10	7
Engine mountings:		
Right-hand mounting retaining bolts	90	66
Right-hand mounting bracket-to-engine bolts	56	41
Left-hand mounting nuts	48	35
Left-hand mounting bracket to transmission	80	59
Left-hand mounting centre bolt	148	109
Lower-rear torque rod bolts	80	59
Exhaust flexible section-to-catalytic converter nuts	51	38
Exhaust manifold heat shield bolts	10	7
Exhaust manifold nuts/bolts	54	40
Flywheel/driveplate bolts	85	63
Inlet manifold-to-block bolt	15	11
Oil baffle to cylinder block	9	7
Oil drain plug	28	21
Oil filter connector	45	33
Oil intake pipe to oil baffle	9	7
Oil pressure switch	15	11
Oil pump to cylinder block	9	7
Power steering fluid hose support bracket bolt	25	18
Spark plugs	15	11
Sump bolts:		
Sump-to-block bolts:		
Stage 1	10	7
Stage 2	20	15
Sump-to-transmission bolts	47	35
TDC pin hole blanking plug	20	15
Timing belt cover bolts	9	7
Timing belt tensioner bolts	20	15
Timing belt tensioner central bolt	25	18
Ti-VCT solenoid	8	6
Ti-VCT unit blanking plugs	16	12
Ti-VCT unit retaining bolts:		
Stage 1	25	18
Stage 2	Angle-tighten a further 75°	

Use new fasteners

1 General information

How to use this Chapter

This Part of Chapter 2 is devoted to in-car repair procedures on the 1.4 and 1.6 litre Duratec 16V petrol engine. All procedures concerning engine removal and refitting, and engine block/cylinder head overhaul can be found in Chapter 2C.

Refer to *Vehicle identification numbers* in the Reference Section at the end of this manual for details of engine code locations.

Most of the operations included in this Chapter are based on the assumption that the engine is still installed in the car. Therefore, if this information is being used during a complete engine overhaul, with the engine already removed, many of the steps included here will not apply.

Engine description

The Duratec engine (formerly the Zetec-SE), is a sixteen-valve, double overhead camshaft (DOHC), four-cylinder, in-line unit, mounted transversely at the front of the car, with the transmission on its left-hand end.

Apart from the plastic timing belt covers, plastic cylinder head cover, plastic inlet manifold, and the cast-iron cylinder liners, the main engine components (including the sump) are manufactured entirely of aluminium alloy.

Caution: When tightening bolts into aluminium castings, it is important to adhere to the specified torque wrench settings, to avoid stripping threads.

The crankshaft runs in five main bearings, the centre main bearing's upper half incorporating thrustwashers to control crankshaft endfloat. Due to the very fine bearing clearances and bearing shell tolerances incorporated during manufacture, it is not possible to renew the crankshaft separate to the cylinder block; in fact it is not possible to remove and refit the crankshaft accurately using conventional tooling. This means that if the crankshaft is worn excessively, it must be renewed together with the cylinder block.

Caution: Do not unbolt the main bearing cap/ladder from the cylinder block, as it is not possible to refit it accurately using conventional tooling. Additionally, the manufacturers do not supply torque settings for the main bearing cap/ladder retaining bolts.

The connecting rods rotate on horizontally-split bearing shells at their big-ends, however the big-ends are of unusual design in that the caps are sheared from the rods during manufacture thus making each cap individually matched to its own connecting rod. The big-end bearing shells are also unusual in that they do not have any locating tabs and must be accurately positioned during refitting. The pistons are attached to the connecting rods by gudgeon pins which are an interference fit in the connecting rod small-end eyes. The aluminium alloy pistons are fitted with three piston rings: two compression rings and an oil control ring. After manufacture, the cylinder bores and pistons are measured and classified into three grades, which must be carefully matched together, to ensure the correct piston/cylinder clearance; no oversizes are available to permit reboring.

The inlet and exhaust valves are each closed by coil springs; they operate in guides which are shrink-fitted into the cylinder head, as are the valve seat inserts.

Both camshafts are driven by the same toothed timing belt, each operating eight valves via bucket tappets. Each camshaft rotates in five bearings that are line-bored directly in the cylinder head and the (bolted-on) bearing caps; this means that the bearing caps are not available separately from the cylinder head, and must not be interchanged with caps from another engine.

1.6 litre engines are available with variable valve timing on the both the inlet and exhaust camshafts – this engine is known as the Ti-VCT (Twin Independent Variable Camshaft Timing). Engine oil pressure is used to vary the positions of the camshaft sprocket in relation to the camshafts, thus varying the valves' opening and closing times. Control of the oil flow is achieved using solenoid valves, which in turn are controlled by the engine management electronic control module (ECM). Varying the valve timing is this manner results in improved driveability and output, whist reducing fuel consumption and exhaust emissions.

The coolant pump is bolted to the right-hand end of the cylinder block, beneath the front run of the timing belt, and is driven by the auxiliary drivebelt from the crankshaft pulley.

Lubrication is by means of an eccentric-rotor trochoidal pump, which is mounted on the crankshaft right-hand end, and draws oil through a strainer located in the sump. The pump forces oil through an externally-mounted full-flow cartridge-type filter.

Operations with engine in car

The following work can be carried out with the engine in the car:
a) Cylinder head cover – removal and refitting.
b) Timing belt – renewal.
c) Timing belt tensioner and sprockets – removal and refitting.
d) Camshaft oil seals – renewal.
e) Camshafts, tappets and shims – removal and refitting.
f) Cylinder head – removal and refitting.
g) Sump – removal and refitting.
h) Crankshaft oil seals – renewal.
i) Oil pump – removal and refitting.
j) Flywheel/driveplate – removal and refitting.
k) Engine/transmission mountings – removal and refitting.

Note: *It is possible to remove the pistons and connecting rods (after removing the cylinder head and sump) without removing the engine. However, this is not recommended. Work of this nature is more easily and thoroughly completed with the engine on the bench, as described in Chapter 2C.*

2 Compression test – description and interpretation

1 When engine performance is down, or if misfiring occurs which cannot be attributed to the ignition or fuel systems, a compression test can provide diagnostic clues as to the engine's condition. If the test is performed regularly, it can give warning of trouble before any other symptoms become apparent.

2 The engine must be fully warmed-up to operating temperature, the oil level must be correct and the battery must be fully-charged. The help of an assistant will also be required.

3 Refer to Chapter 12 and remove the fuel pump relay from the engine compartment fusebox. Now start the engine and allow it to run until it stalls.

4 Disable the ignition system by disconnecting the multiplug from the DIS ignition coil. Remove all the spark plugs with reference to Chapter 1.

5 Fit a compression tester to the No 1 cylinder spark plug hole – the type of tester which screws into the spark plug thread is preferable.

6 Arrange for an assistant to hold the accelerator pedal fully depressed to the floor, while at the same time cranking the engine over for several seconds on the starter motor. Observe the compression gauge reading. The compression will build-up fairly quickly in a healthy engine. Low compression on the first stroke, followed by gradually-increasing pressure on successive strokes, indicates worn piston rings. A low compression on the first stroke which does not rise on successive strokes, indicates leaking valves or a blown head gasket (a cracked cylinder head could also be the cause). Deposits on the underside of the valve heads can also cause low compression. Record the highest gauge reading obtained, then repeat the procedure for the remaining cylinders.

7 Due to the variety of testers available, and the fluctuation in starter motor speed when cranking the engine, different readings are often obtained when carrying out the compression test. For this reason, actual compression pressure figures are not quoted by Ford. However, the most important factor is that the compression pressures are uniform in all cylinders, and that is what this test is mainly concerned with.

8 Add some engine oil (about three squirts from a plunger type oil can) to each cylinder through the spark plug holes, and then repeat the test.

3.7a Undo the blanking plug from the right-hand rear corner of the cylinder block . . .

3.7b . . . and screw-in the timing pin

3.9 Locate the home-made camshaft setting tool (arrowed) in the slots

3.14 Undo the nuts/bolts and remove the right-hand engine mounting

9 If the compression increases after the oil is added, the piston rings are probably worn. If the compression does not increase significantly, the leakage is occurring at the valves or the head gasket. Leakage past the valves may be caused by burned valve seats and/or faces, or warped, cracked or bent valves.

10 If two adjacent cylinders have equally low compressions, it is most likely that the head gasket has blown between them. The appearance of coolant in the combustion chambers or on the engine oil dipstick would verify this condition.

11 If one cylinder is about 20 percent lower than the other, and the engine has a slightly rough idle, a worn lobe on the camshaft could be the cause.

12 On completion of the checks, refit the spark plugs and reconnect the HT leads and the DIS ignition coil plug. Refit the fuel pump relay to the fusebox.

3 Top Dead Centre (TDC) for No 1 piston – locating

1 Top dead centre (TDC) is the highest point of the cylinder that each piston reaches as the crankshaft turns. Each piston reaches its TDC position at the end of its compression stroke, and then again at the end of its exhaust stroke. For the purpose of engine timing, TDC on the compression stroke for No 1 piston is used. No 1 cylinder is at the timing belt end of the engine. Proceed as follows.

2 Disconnect the battery negative (earth) lead (see Chapter 5A). Remove the spark plugs as described in Chapter 1.

3 Apply the handbrake, then jack up the front of the vehicle and support it on axle stands (see Jacking and vehicle support). If the engine is to be turned using the right-hand front roadwheel with top gear engaged (manual transmission models only), it is only necessary to raise the right-hand front roadwheel off the ground.

4 Where necessary, undo the fasteners, remove the engine undershield, then remove the wheel arch liner, and auxiliary drivebelt lower cover for access to the crankshaft pulley and bolt.

Non-Ti-VCT engines

5 Remove the cylinder head cover as described in Section 4.

6 The piston of No 1 cylinder must now be positioned just before top dead centre (TDC). To do this, have an assistant turn the crankshaft until the slots in the left-hand ends of the camshafts are parallel with the upper surface of the cylinder head. Note that the slots are slightly offset so make sure that the lower edges of the slots are aligned with the cylinder head. Turn the crankshaft slightly anti-clockwise (viewed from the right-hand end of the engine).

7 Unscrew the blanking plug from the right-hand rear side of the engine cylinder block. A TDC timing pin must now be inserted and tightened into the hole. It is highly recommended that the special Ford timing pin 303-748 is obtained, or alternatively, a timing pin from a reputable tool manufacturer such as Draper **(see illustrations)**. The diameter of the pin is critical as it determines the TDC point where the machined flat on the crankshaft web contacts the *shank* of the tool – note that the web does **not** contact the *end* of the tool.

8 With the timing pin in position, turn the crankshaft *slowly* clockwise until the specially-machined surface on the crank web just touches the timing pin. No 1 piston is now at TDC on its compression stroke. To confirm this, check that the camshaft lobes for No 4 cylinder are 'rocking' (ie, exhaust valves closing and inlet valves opening).

9 It should now be possible to insert the camshaft setting bar into the slots in the left-hand ends of the camshafts. If the Ford setting tool 303-376B is unavailable, a home-made tool can be fabricated out of a length of flat metal bar 5.00 mm thick. The bar must be a good fit in the slots and should be approximately 180 to 230 mm long by 20 to 30 mm wide **(see illustration)**.

10 If the bar cannot be inserted in the slots with the crankshaft at TDC, the valve timing must be adjusted as described in Section 8 of this Chapter.

11 Once the work requiring the TDC setting has been completed, remove the metal bar from the camshaft slots then unscrew the timing pin and refit the blanking plug. Refit the spark plugs (Chapter 1), cylinder head cover (Section 4), auxiliary drivebelt lower cover, and where necessary the engine undershield. Lower the vehicle to the ground and reconnect the battery negative lead (see Chapter 5A).

Ti-VCT engines

12 Remove the upper timing belt cover as described in Section 7.

13 Position a trolley jack under the engine. Use a block of wood on the jack head to prevent damage to the sump. Take the weight of the engine.

14 Make alignment marks between the right-hand engine mounting bracket and the cylinder head bracket/vehicle body, then undo the nuts/bolts and remove the mounting **(see illustration)**. Discard the nuts – new ones must be fitted.

15 Rotate the crankshaft pulley clockwise until the marks (dot on the inlet sprocket, groove on the exhaust sprocket) of the camshaft VCT units are approaching the 11 o'clock position **(see illustrations)**.

16 Undo the blanking plug from the right-hand rear side of the engine cylinder block **(see illustration 3.7a)**. A TDC timing pin must now be inserted and tightened into the hole. It is highly recommended that the Ford timing pin 303-748 is obtained, or alternatively, a timing pin from a reputable tool manufacturer such as Draper **(see illustration 3.7b)**. The diameter of the pin is critical as it determines the TDC point where the machined flat on the crankshaft web contacts the *shank* of the tool – note that the web does **not** contact the *end* of the tool.

1.4 & 1.6 litre engines (Duratec 16V) in-car repair procedures 2A•5

17 With the timing pin in position, turn the crankshaft *slowly* clockwise until the specially machined surface on the crank web just touches the timing pin. No 1 piston is now at TDC on its compression stroke.

18 Now it is necessary to fit Ford special tool 303-1097 over the VCT units on the ends of the camshafts. Note that the tool is marked with a line to indicate the exhaust side, a dot to indicate the inlet side, and an arrow which must point upwards **(see illustrations)**.

19 Once the work requiring the TDC setting has been completed, remove the special tool from the camshaft VCT units then unscrew the timing pin and refit the blanking plug. Refit the spark plugs (Chapter 1), upper timing belt cover, auxiliary drivebelt lower cover, and where necessary the engine undershield. Lower the vehicle to the ground and reconnect the battery negative lead (see Chapter 5A).

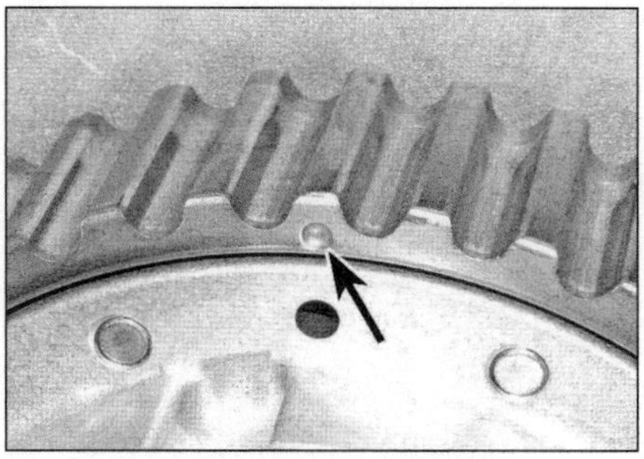

4 Cylinder head cover – removal and refitting

Removal

1 Disconnect the battery negative (earth) lead (see Chapter 5A).
2 Disconnect the breather pipe from the front of the cover **(see illustration)**.
3 Disconnect the HT leads from the spark plugs, unclip them from the cover, and position them to the left-hand side of the engine compartment.
4 On Ti-VCT engines, disconnect the wiring plugs from the camshaft position sensors and VCT solenoids on the cylinder head cover, clean around the area, then undo the retaining bolts and remove both VCT oil control solenoids from the top, right-hand end of the cylinder head **(see illustrations)**. Plug the openings to prevent contamination. Examine the O-ring seals, and renew if necessary.
5 Where fitted, undo the nut and bolt and move the wiring connector bracket at the left-hand rear corner of the cylinder head cover to one side.
6 On all engines, the cylinder head cover is secured by a total of twelve bolts. Note their fitted locations and remove the bolts. On Ti-VCT engines, the bolts are integral with the cover.
7 On non-Ti-VCT engines, remove the centre top bolt from the timing belt upper cover **(see illustration)**. This bolt secures the timing belt cover to the cylinder head cover.

3.15a The inlet camshaft sprocket is marked with a dot (arrowed) . . .

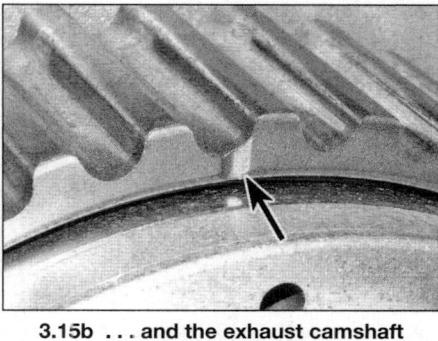

3.15b . . . and the exhaust camshaft sprocket with a groove (arrowed)

3.18a Fit the special tool over the Ti-VCT units

3.18b The tool is marked with a dot (1) for the inlet camshaft, a line (2) for the exhaust camshaft, and an arrow (3) which must point upwards

4.2 Disconnect the breather pipe (arrowed)

4.4a Disconnect the camshaft position sensors wiring plugs

4.4b Disconnect the VCT solenoid wiring plugs (arrowed)

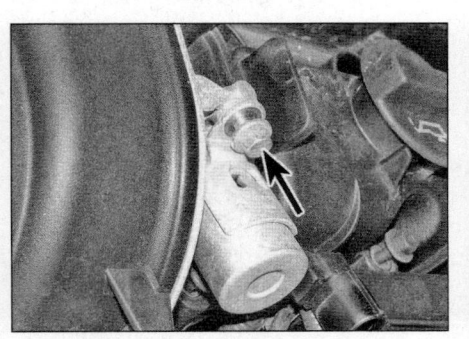

4.4c Then undo the bolt (arrowed) . . .

4.4d . . . and pull the solenoids from place

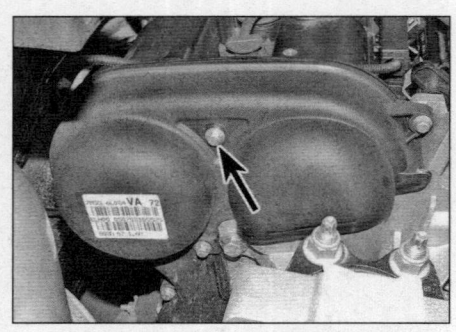

2A•6 1.4 & 1.6 litre engines (Duratec 16V) in-car repair procedures

4.7 Remove the timing belt upper cover centre-top bolt (arrowed)

8 Carefully lift the cover from the top of the cylinder head, unclipping any wiring as necessary. Recover the gasket – this may be re-used if it is not damaged.

Refitting

9 Clean the mating surfaces of the cylinder head and the cover gasket.
10 Lower the cover onto the cylinder head, ensuring that the gasket stays in place.
11 Progressively tighten all bolts to the specified torque.
12 The remainder of refitting is a reversal of removal.

5 Valve clearances – checking and adjustment

1 Remove the cylinder head cover as described in Section 4. *Note: If checking the valve clearances with the timing belt removed (eg, after refitting the camshafts), rotate the crankshaft 90° anti-clockwise back from TDC on No 1 cylinder so the pistons are halfway down the cylinder bores. Verify this by inserting a long screwdriver down the spark plug holes.*
2 Remove the spark plugs (Chapter 1) in order to make turning the engine easier. The engine may be turned using a spanner on the crankshaft pulley bolt or by raising the front right-hand roadwheel clear of the ground, engaging top gear and turning the wheel. If the former method is used, jack up and support the front of the car (see *Jacking and vehicle support*) then unbolt the lower cover for access to the pulley bolt; if the latter method is used, apply the handbrake then jack up the front right-hand side of the car until the roadwheel is clear of the ground and support with an axle stand.
3 Draw the valve positions on a piece of paper, numbering them 1 to 8 inlet and exhaust, from the timing belt (right-hand) end of the engine (ie, 1E, 1I, 2E, 2I and so on). As there are two inlet and two exhaust valves for each cylinder, draw the cylinders as large circles and the four valves as smaller circles. The inlet valves are at the front of the cylinder head, and the exhaust valves are at the rear. As the valve clearances are adjusted, cross them off.
4 Turn the engine in a clockwise direction until both inlet valves of No 1 cylinder are fully shut and the apex of the camshaft lobes are pointing upwards away from the valve positions.
5 Insert a feeler blade of the correct thickness (see *Specifications*) between the heel of the camshaft lobe and the tappet **(see illustration)**. It should be a firm sliding fit. If this is the case, the clearance is correct and the valve position can be crossed off. If the clearance is not correct, use feeler blades to determine the exact clearance and record this on the drawing. From this clearance it will be possible to calculate the thickness of the new tappet to be fitted. Note that no shims are fitted between the camshaft and tappet – the complete tappet must be renewed.
6 Check the clearance of the second inlet valve for No 1 cylinder, and if necessary record the existing clearance on the drawing.
7 Now turn the engine until the inlet valves of

5.5 Insert a feeler gauge between the heel of the camshaft lobe and the tappet

No 2 cylinder are fully shut and the camshaft lobes pointing away from the valve positions. Check the clearances as described previously, and record any that are incorrect.
8 After checking all of the inlet valve clearances, check the exhaust valve clearances in the same way, but note that the clearances are different.
9 Where adjustment is required, the procedure is to remove the camshafts as described in Section 11.
10 If the recorded clearance was too small, a thinner tappet must be fitted, and conversely if the clearance was too large, a thicker tappet must be fitted. To calculate the thickness of the new tappet, first use a micrometer to measure the thickness of the existing tappet (C) and add this to the measured clearance (B) **(see illustrations)**. Deduct the desired clearance (A) to provide the thickness (D) of the new tappet. The thickness of the tappet should be etched on the downward facing surface, however use the micrometer to verify this. The formula is as follows.

New tappet thickness D
= Existing tappet thickness C
+ Measured clearance B
– Desired clearance A

Sample calculation
Desired clearance (A) = 0.20
Measured clearance (B) = 0.15
Existing tappet thickness (C) = 2.725
Tappet thickness required (D) = C+B-A = 2.675

All measurements in mm

11 The tappets are available in varying thicknesses in increments of 0.025 mm.
12 It will be helpful for future adjustment if a record is kept of the thickness of tappet fitted at each position.
13 When all the clearances have been checked and adjusted, refit the lower cover (where removed), lower the car to the ground and refit the cylinder head cover as described in Section 4.

6 Crankshaft pulley/ vibration damper – removal and refitting

Caution: *Removal of the crankshaft pulley effectively loses the valve timing setting, and it will be necessary to reset the timing.*
Note: *The vibration damper retaining bolt may only be used once. Obtain a new bolt for the refitting procedure.*

Removal

1 Remove the auxiliary drivebelt as described in Chapter 1.
2 Set the engine to the top dead centre (TDC) position as described in Section 3.
3 Remove the starter motor as described in Chapter 5A, then use Ford tool 303-393 and 303-393-02 to lock the crankshaft in position.

5.10a Measure the thickness of the tappets with a micrometer

5.10b The thickness of each tappet should be etched on its underside

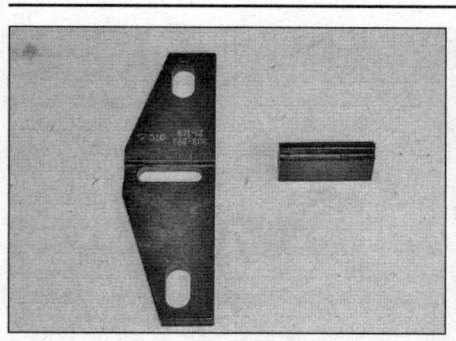

1.4 & 1.6 litre engines (Duratec 16V) in-car repair procedures 2A•7

6.3a Ford tool No 303-393 and 303-393-02

6.3b The assembled tools bolt across the starter motor aperture . . .

6.3c . . . and engages with the teeth on the flywheel ring gear

6.4 Using a home-made tool to hold the crankshaft pulley

6.5a If necessary, use a puller to free the pulley from the crankshaft . . .

6.5b . . . then withdrawn the pulley from the crankshaft

This tool bolts across the starter motor aperture in the transmission bellhousing, and engages with the teeth of the starter ring gear on the flywheel/driveplate **(see illustrations)**.

4 Hold the crankshaft pulley stationary **(see illustration)**. The bolt ends locate in the pulley holes, and an extension bar and socket can then be used to loosen the bolt. Do not allow the crankshaft to rotate, otherwise it will be more difficult to reset the valve timing – also, with the bolt loose, the crankshaft sprocket may not turn with the crankshaft.

5 With the bolt loosened several turns, use a suitable puller to free the pulley from the end of the crankshaft. Fully unscrew the bolt and withdraw the pulley **(see illustrations)**.

6 Clean the end of the crankshaft and the pulley.

Refitting

7 The procedure in this paragraph is necessary in order to be able to set the valve timing after the crankshaft/vibration pulley has been refitted.

Non Ti-VCT engines

8 Unbolt and remove the upper timing cover (see Section 7). While holding each of the camshaft sprockets stationary in turn using the home-made tool described in paragraph 4, loosen the sprocket retaining bolts until they are just finger-tight, to enable the sprockets to turn on the camshafts. Alternatively, the camshafts can be held stationary using a spanner on the special hexagon flats.

9 Locate the pulley on the end of the crankshaft, and press it onto the shaft as far as it will go. This procedure must always be carried out before inserting and tightening the new bolt. Do not simply insert and tighten the new bolt, as in certain circumstances the torque will not be sufficient to press the pulley fully onto the end of the crankshaft. Ford technicians use a special installer which consists of a threaded rod screwed into the crankshaft, together with a spacer which locates on the pulley. In the absence of this tool, use a long bolt or threaded rod together with washers and a nut **(see illustration)**. As a last resort use the removed (old) bolt, however this is not recommended as the threads may be stretched (see Note at the beginning of this Section).

All engines

10 Temporarily remove the crankshaft timing pin.

11 Remove the pulley fitting tool (where applicable), then insert the new bolt and tighten it to the specified Stage 1 torque setting while holding the pulley stationary with the special tool. Note that two different bolts may be fitted: M12 x 29 mm or M12 x 44.5 mm. In order to determine which bolt is required, use a Vernier caliper to measure the depth of the hole in the end of the crankshaft **(see illustrations)**.

6.9 Use a long bolt threaded into the crankshaft to draw the pulley onto the shaft

6.11a Two different length crankshaft pulley bolts may be fitted – see text

6.11b Insert the new crankshaft pulley bolt

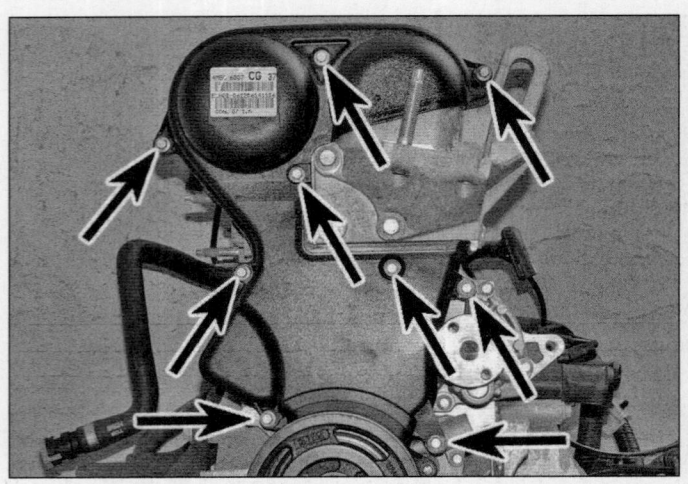

2A•8 1.4 & 1.6 litre engines (Duratec 16V) in-car repair procedures

7.5 Timing belt upper cover bolts (arrowed)

7.9 Timing belt lower cover bolts (arrowed)

A 42 mm depth requires a 29 mm bolt, whereas a 52 mm depth requires a 44.5 mm bolt.

12 Now angle-tighten the bolt through the specified Stage 2 angle. An angle gauge is useful for this, but 90° is a right-angle, which is quite easily judged by eye.

Non Ti-VCT engines

13 The valve timing must now be set and the camshaft sprocket bolts tightened as described in Section 8.
14 Refit the timing belt upper cover.

Ti-VCT engines

15 Remove the crankshaft and camshaft locking tools, then refit the timing belt cover, and engine mounting in the reverse of the procedure described in Section 3.

All engines

16 Fit a new auxiliary drivebelt as described in Chapter 1.

7 Timing belt covers – removal and refitting

Upper cover

Removal

1 Pull the coolant expansion tank upwards and move it to one side.

8.4 Slacken the camshaft sprocket retaining bolts whilst holding the sprockets with a home-made tool

2 Slacken the coolant pump pulley bolts, then remove the auxiliary drivebelt(s) as described in Chapter 1.
3 Unscrew the 4 bolts and remove the coolant pump pulley.
4 On non-Ti-VCT engines, undo the single bolt securing the upper timing belt cover to the cylinder head cover (see illustration 4.7).
5 On all engines, unscrew the timing belt upper cover retaining bolts (see illustration).
6 Manoeuvre the timing cover from the engine compartment.

Refitting

7 Refitting is a reversal of removal. Fit a new auxiliary drivebelt as described in Chapter 1.

Lower cover

Removal

8 The timing belt lower cover is located around the crankshaft. First remove the crankshaft pulley/vibration damper as described in Section 6.
9 Working beneath the right-hand wheel arch, unscrew the retaining bolts and withdraw the timing cover (see illustration).

Refitting

10 Refitting is a reversal of removal.

8 Timing belt – removal and refitting

Caution: The camshaft sprockets are made from a type of plastic. Care must be taken to avoid damage to the sprockets during the following procedure.

Removal

1 Loosen the four bolts securing the coolant pump pulley.
2 Remove the crankshaft pulley/vibration damper as described in Section 6.
3 Remove the coolant pump pulley.

Non-Ti-VCT engines

4 With the camshaft timing bar removed, loosen the camshaft sprocket bolts several turns while holding the sprockets with a suitable tool (see illustration). Bearing in mind the caution at the start of this Section, release the sprockets from the ends of the camshafts so that they are free to rotate.

All engines

5 Remove the timing belt covers as described in Section 7.
6 Where fitted, remove the timing belt guide disc from the end of the crankshaft. Note which way round the disc is fitted – the concave side faces outwards (see illustration).
7 Remove the alternator as described in Chapter 5A.
8 The engine must now be supported, as the right-hand mounting (right as seen from the driver's seat) must be removed. Supporting the engine should ideally be done from above, using an engine crane or a special engine lifting beam. However, in the absence of these tools, the engine can be supported from below, on the cast-aluminium sump, providing a piece of wood is used to spread the load (see illustration).
9 With the engine securely supported, remove the nuts/bolts securing the right-hand mounting, and lift it off (see illustration 3.14).

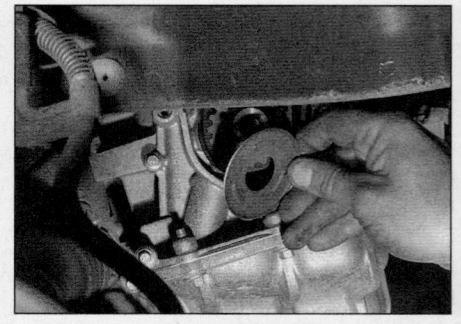

8.6 Remove the timing belt guide disc (where fitted)

1.4 & 1.6 litre engines (Duratec 16V) in-car repair procedures

8.8 Support the engine with a trolley jack and block of wood under the sump

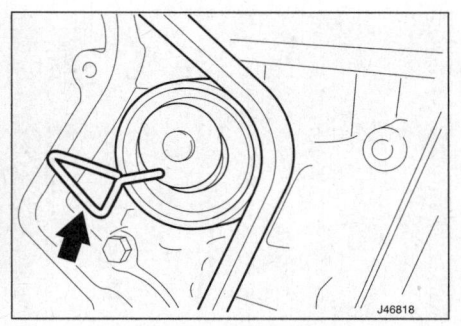

8.11a Insert a 4 mm drill bit or rod (arrowed) into the pulley hub – engines up to 04/2005

8.11b Insert a 4 mm drill bit or rod into the tensioner arms (arrowed)

New nuts should be obtained for refitting the mounting.

10 Unbolt the lower half of the engine right-hand mounting bracket from the engine.
11 Push the timing belt eccentric tensioner pulley rearwards to detension the belt, then insert Ford tool No 303-1054 or a suitable equivalent into the pulley hub (engines up to April 2005) or arm (engines from April 2005) to lock it in position **(see illustrations)**.
12 Undo the bolt(s) and remove the tensioner and bracket assembly. *Note: It is recommended that the tensioner is renewed along with the timing belt.*
13 If the timing belt is to be re-used (this is not recommended), use white paint or similar to mark its direction of rotation, and note from the manufacturer's markings which way round it is fitted. Withdraw the belt from the sprockets and from over the tensioner **(see illustration)**. *Do not* attempt to turn the crankshaft or camshafts until the timing belt is refitted.

Inspection

14 If the belt is being removed for reasons other than routine renewal, check it carefully for any signs of uneven wear, splitting, cracks (especially at the roots of the belt teeth) or contamination with oil or coolant. Renew the belt if there is the slightest doubt about its condition. As a safety measure, the belt should be renewed irrespective of its apparent condition whenever the engine is overhauled.
15 Check the sprockets for signs of wear or damage, and ensure that the tensioner pulley rotates smoothly on its bearings; renew any worn or damaged components. Ford dealers (and many motor factors) now supply 'cambelt kits', consisting of the belt itself and a new tensioner – for peace of mind, it is recommended that one of these is purchased.
16 If signs of oil or coolant contamination are found on the old belt, trace the source of the leak and rectify it, then wash down the engine timing belt area and related components to remove all traces of oil or coolant.

Refitting

Non-Ti-VCT engines

17 Ensure that the engine is still set to TDC. Remove the camshaft sprocket bolts and renew. Only finger-tighten the bolts at this stage, the camshaft sprockets must be free to rotate on their shafts.
18 Locate the timing belt on the crankshaft sprocket, then feed it over the two camshaft sprockets. If the original belt is being refitted, make sure that it is the correct way round as noted during removal **(see illustrations)**. Take care not to rotate the crankshaft.
19 Where applicable, refit the timing belt guide disc on the end of the crankshaft, making sure that the concave side faces outwards.
20 Ensure the tensioner is in the locked position (see paragraph 11), then fit the tensioner/bracket assembly, and tighten the bolt(s) to the specified torque.
21 Remove the locking pin from the tensioner, and allow it to tension the belt.
22 Refit the engine mounting bracket to the cylinder block, and tighten the bolts to the specified torque.
23 Refit the upper engine mounting bracket tighten the new nuts to the specified torque. Remove the jack from under the engine, or remove the hoist from above, as applicable.
24 Refit the timing belt lower cover, and tighten the bolts to the specified torque.
25 Locate the crankshaft pulley/vibration damper on the end of the crankshaft, and press it squarely onto the shaft as far as it will go. Insert the new bolt and tighten it to the specified Stage 1 torque setting while holding the pulley stationary as described in Section 6.
26 Now tighten the crankshaft pulley bolt through the specified angle. The crankshaft sprocket is now effectively clamped to the crankshaft.
27 Moderately tighten the bolts retaining the camshaft sprockets to the camshafts, then remove the camshaft setting bar and crankshaft timing pin and flywheel/driveplate locking tool, then fully-tighten the bolts while holding the sprockets using the tool described in Section 6 or using a spanner on the hexagon flats provided **(see illustrations)**.
28 Rotate the crankshaft clockwise 1¾ turns approximately. Refit the crankshaft TDC timing pin then rotate the crankshaft clockwise until it stops against the timing pin. Check to see whether the setting bar will fit in the camshaft slots. If necessary, loosen the camshaft sprocket bolts, turn the camshafts slightly (without moving the timing belt) so the setting bar can be fitted, then retighten the camshaft

8.13 Note the belt may be marked with direction-of-rotation arrows

8.18a Fit the belt around the camshaft sprockets ...

8.18b ... and the crankshaft sprocket

2A•10 1.4 & 1.6 litre engines (Duratec 16V) in-car repair procedures

8.27a Tighten the camshaft sprocket retaining bolts

8.27b Use an open-ended spanner on the hexagon section of the camshaft

8.30 Timing belt routing

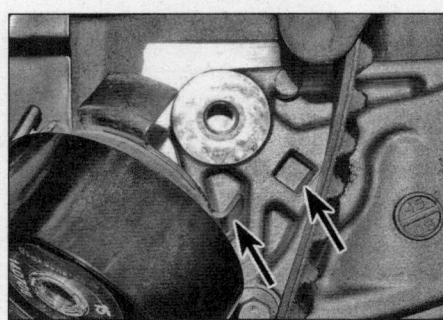

8.31 The lug on the tensioner mounting plate (arrowed) must locate in the square hole (arrowed) in the cylinder block

sprocket bolts. On completion, remove the timing pin and bar and refit the blanking plug.

29 Refit the timing belt upper cover, and the alternator. Refit the coolant pump pulley, and tighten the bolts as far as possible for now – once the auxiliary drivebelt has been fitted it will be easier to tighten the bolts to the specified torque.

Ti-VCT engines

30 Ensure the engine's still set to TDC on No 1 cylinder (Section 3), then working clockwise, locate the timing belt on the camshaft VCT units, then fit the belt over the crankshaft sprocket **(see illustration)**. If the original belt is being refitted, make sure that it is the correct way round as noted during removal. Take care not to rotate the crankshaft.

31 Fit the new tensioner (where applicable). Ensure the tensioner is in the locked position (see paragraph 11), then fit the tensioner assembly, and tighten the bolt to the specified torque **(see illustration)**.

32 Remove the locking pin from the tensioner, and allow it to tension the belt.

33 Refit the lower timing belt cover and tighten the bolts to the specified torque.

34 Locate the crankshaft pulley/vibration damper on the end of the crankshaft, and press it squarely onto the shaft as far as it will go. Insert the new bolt and tighten it to the specified Stage 1 torque setting while holding the pulley stationary as described in Section 6.

35 Now tighten the crankshaft pulley bolt through the specified angle. The crankshaft sprocket is now effectively clamped to the crankshaft.

36 Remove the locking tool from the camshaft VCT units, the crankshaft timing pin, and the flywheel/driveplate locking tool.

37 Rotate the crankshaft clockwise approximately 2 revolutions, until the marks on the camshaft VCT units are in the 11 o'clock position **(see illustration 3.15a and 3.15b)**.

38 Refit the crankshaft timing pin, and rotate the crankshaft clockwise until it stops against the timing pin. Refit the VCT units locking tool to check their positions. If the tool cannot be fitted, remove the belt, and carry out the fitting/tensioning procedure again. If the timing is correct, remove the timing pin and VCT locking tool. Refit the cylinder block blanking plug.

39 Refit the engine mounting, timing belt upper cover, and the alternator. Refit the coolant pump pulley, and tighten the bolts as far as possible for now – once the auxiliary drivebelt has been fitted it will be easier to tighten the bolts to the specified torque.

All engines

40 The remainder of refitting is a reversal of removal.

9 Timing belt tensioner and sprockets – removal, inspection and refitting

Tensioner pulley

1 Removal of the tensioner pulley is described within the timing belt procedure – see Section 8.

Camshaft sprockets

Caution: *The camshaft sprockets are made from a type of plastic. Care must be taken to avoid damage to the sprockets during the following procedure.*

2 Remove the timing belt as described in Section 8.

Non-Ti-VCT engines

3 Unscrew the bolts and remove the sprockets from the camshafts **(see illustrations)**.

Ti-VCT engines

4 Remove the cylinder head cover as described in Section 4.

5 Counterhold the camshafts using an open-ended spanner on the hexagonal sections, then unscrew the blanking plugs from the centre of the VCT units **(see illustration)**.

6 Still counterholding the camshafts, slacken and remove the VCT units' centre Torx bolts **(see illustrations)**. Remove the VCT units from the ends of the camshafts.

All engines

7 Examine the teeth of the sprockets for wear and damage, and renew them if necessary.

Non-Ti-VCT engines

8 Locate the sprockets on the camshafts, and screw in the retaining bolts loosely.

9 Fit the timing belt as described in Section 8.

9.3a Unscrew the bolt . . .

9.3b . . . and remove the camshaft sprocket

1.4 & 1.6 litre engines (Duratec 16V) in-car repair procedures

9.5 Counterhold the camshaft with a spanner on the hexagonal section, then unscrew the blanking plug from the VCT unit

9.6a Unscrew the Torx bolt . . .

9.6b . . . and pull the VCT unit from the camshaft

Ti-VCT engines

10 Insert Ford tool No 303-376B into the slots in the left-hand ends of the camshafts. If the Ford setting tool 303-376B is unavailable, a home-made tool can be fabricated out of a length of flat metal bar 20 mm thick **(see illustrations)**.

11 Locate the VCT units on the ends of the camshafts, but only finger-tighten the retaining bolts at this stage. Ensure the timing marks on the VCT units (dot on the inlet sprocket, groove on the exhaust sprocket) are at the 12 o'clock position **(see illustration)**.

12 Fit the VCT locking tool (No 303-1097) over the units **(see illustrations 3.18a and 3.18b)**. Note how the dots/holes on the VCT units align with the groove/dot on the sprockets **(see illustration)**.

13 Tighten each VCT unit retaining bolt to the specified Stage 1 torque.

14 Remove the camshaft setting bar and the VCT locking tool, then counterhold the camshafts using a spanner on the hexagonal section, and tighten each VCT unit retaining bolt to the specified Stage 2 angle setting. Do not allow the camshafts to rotate.

15 Refit the VCT locking tool, and check the marks on the sprockets align with the marks on the VCT units **(see illustration 9.12)**. If not, repeat the VCT unit refitting procedure.

16 If the timing is correct, counterhold the camshafts using a spanner on the hexagonal section, and fit the each VCT unit blanking plug. Tighten each plug to the specified torque. Renew the plug seal if necessary **(see illustrations)**.

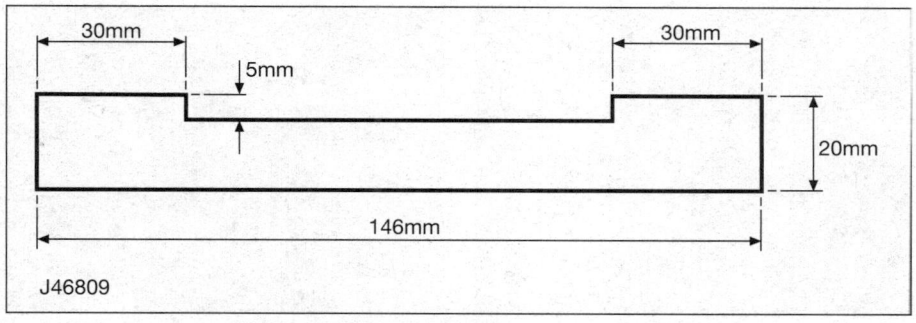

9.10a Camshaft setting tool dimensions
Drawing not to scale

17 Fit the timing belt as described in Section 8, and the cylinder head cover as described in Section 4.

Crankshaft sprocket

18 Remove the timing belt as described in Section 8.

9.10b Fit the setting tool into the slots in the end of the camshafts

9.11 Ensure the groove (1) on the exhaust VCT unit and the dot (2) on the inlet unit are at the 12 o'clock position

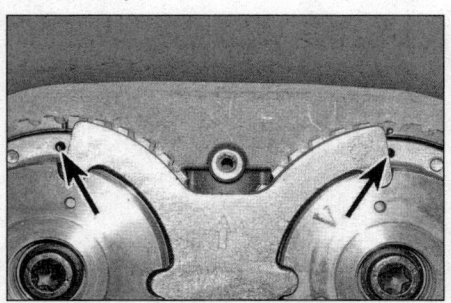

9.12 Note how the dots/holes on the VCT units align with the groove/dot on the sprockets (arrowed)

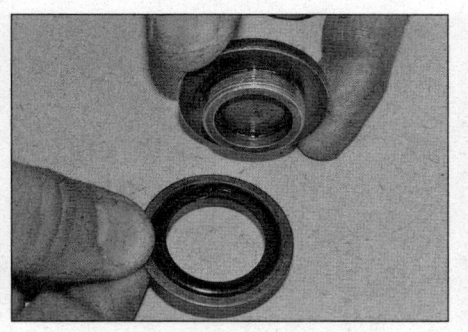

9.16a Renew the seal if necessary . . .

9.16b . . . then refit the plugs to the VCT units

2A•12 1.4 & 1.6 litre engines (Duratec 16V) in-car repair procedures

9.19 Slide the crankshaft sprocket from place

10.3a Drill a small hole and insert a self-tapping screw . . .

10.3b . . . then pull out the oil seal using a pair of pliers

10.5 Locate the new oil seal into the cylinder/camshaft bearing cap

10.6 Drive the new seal into position with a socket

19 Slide the sprocket off the end of the crankshaft **(see illustration)**.
20 Examine the teeth of the sprocket for wear and damage, and renew if necessary.
21 Wipe clean the end of the crankshaft, then slide on the sprocket.
22 Refit the timing belt as described in Section 8.

10 Camshaft oil seals – renewal

1 Remove the camshaft sprockets or VCT units as described in Section 9.
2 Note the fitted depths of the oil seals as a guide for fitting the new ones.
3 Using a screwdriver or similar tool, carefully prise the oil seals from the cylinder head/ camshaft bearing caps. Take care not to damage the oil seal contact surfaces on the ends of the camshafts or the oil seal seatings. An alternative method of removing the seals is to drill a small hole, then insert a self-tapping screw and use pliers to pull out the seal **(see illustrations)**.
4 Wipe clean the oil seal seatings and also the ends of the camshafts.
5 Apply a little clean engine oil to the seal lip, then locate it over the camshaft and into the cylinder head/camshaft bearing cap. Make sure that the closed end of the oil seal faces outwards **(see illustration)**.
6 Using a socket or length of metal tubing, drive the oil seals squarely into position to the previously-noted depths. Wipe away any excess oil **(see illustration)**.
7 Refit the camshaft sprockets as described in Section 9.

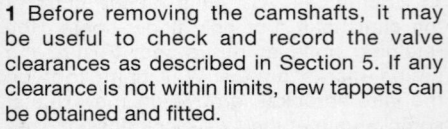

11 Camshafts and tappets – removal, inspection and refitting

Removal

1 Before removing the camshafts, it may be useful to check and record the valve clearances as described in Section 5. If any clearance is not within limits, new tappets can be obtained and fitted.
2 Remove the camshaft oil seals as described in Section 10.
3 The camshaft bearing caps are marked for position – the inlet caps have the letter I and exhaust caps have the letter E. On the project car these were not very clear, and if this is the case, mark them using paint or a marker pen. Make sure they are identified for inlet and exhaust camshafts **(see illustrations)**.
4 Position the crankshaft so that No 1 piston is approximately 25 mm before TDC. This can be done by starting from the TDC position; carefully insert a large screwdriver down No 1 cylinder spark plug hole until the tip touches the top of the piston, and turn the engine anti-clockwise until the screwdriver shaft has descended 25 mm.
5 Position the camshafts so that none of the valves are at full lift (ie, fully-open, being heavily pressed down by the cam lobes). To do this, turn each camshaft using a spanner on the hexagon flats provided.
6 Progressively loosen the camshaft

11.3a No 3 inlet camshaft bearing cap

11.3b No 3 exhaust camshaft bearing cap

11.3c Number the bearing caps with paint if they are not clearly marked

1.4 & 1.6 litre engines (Duratec 16V) in-car repair procedures 2A•13

11.6 Undo the camshaft bearing cap bolts . . .

11.7a . . . withdraw the caps . . .

11.7b . . . then remove the camshafts

bearing cap retaining bolts, working in the **same sequence** shown for tightening (see illustration 11.19). Work only as described to release gradually and evenly the pressure of the valve springs on the caps (see illustration).

7 Withdraw the caps, keeping them in order to aid refitting, then lift the camshafts from the cylinder head and withdraw their oil seals. The exhaust camshaft can be identified by the reference lobe for the camshaft position sensor on non-Ti-VCT engines, therefore, there is no need to mark the camshafts; on Ti-VCT engines, the inlet camshaft is marked 7A and the exhaust marked 3A (see illustrations). **Note:** *On Ti-VCT engines, renew the O-ring between the right-hand bearing cap and the cylinder head* (see illustration).

8 Obtain sixteen small, clean containers, and number them 1 to 8 for both the inlet and exhaust camshafts. Lift the tappets one by one from the cylinder head.

Inspection

9 With the camshafts and tappets removed, check each for signs of obvious wear (scoring, pitting, etc) and for ovality, and renew if necessary.

10 Visually examine the camshaft lobes for score marks, pitting, and evidence of overheating (blue, discoloured areas). Look for flaking away of the hardened surface layer of each lobe. If any such signs are evident, renew the component concerned.

11 Examine the camshaft bearing journals and the cylinder head bearing surfaces for signs of obvious wear or pitting. If any such signs are evident, renew the component concerned.

12 To check camshaft endfloat, remove the tappets, clean the bearing surfaces carefully, and refit the camshafts and bearing caps. Tighten the bearing cap bolts to the specified torque wrench setting, then measure the endfloat using a dial gauge mounted on the cylinder head so that its tip bears on the camshaft right-hand end.

13 Tap the camshaft fully towards the gauge, zero the gauge, then tap the camshaft fully away from the gauge, and note the gauge reading. If the endfloat measured is found to be more than the typical value given, fit a

11.7c The exhaust camshaft is marked 3A (Ti-VCT engines)

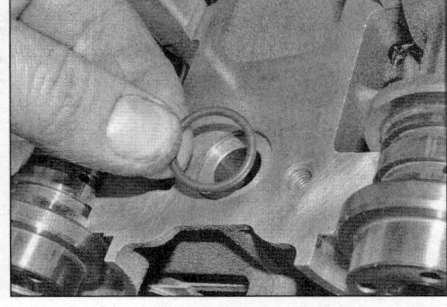

new camshaft and repeat the check; if the clearance is still excessive, the cylinder head must be renewed.

Refitting

14 Lubricate the cylinder head tappet bores and the tappets with engine oil. Carefully refit the tappets to the cylinder head, ensuring each tappet is refitted to its original bore. Some care will be needed to enter the tappets squarely into their bores.

15 Liberally oil the camshaft bearings and lobes. Ensuring that each camshaft is in its original location, refit the camshafts, locating each so that the slot in its left-hand end is approximately parallel to, and just above, the cylinder head mating surface. At this stage, position the camshafts so that none of the

11.15 The slots in the end of the camshafts should be just above, and approximately parallel to the cylinder head upper surface

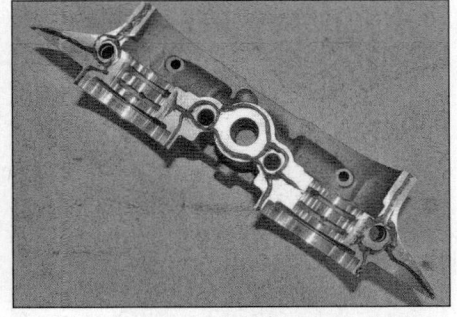

11.7d On Ti-VCT engines, recover the O-ring seal under the right-hand (No 1) bearing cap

valves are at full lift – see paragraph 5 (see illustration).

16 Clean the mating faces of the cylinder head and camshaft bearing caps.

17 Apply a thin smear of suitable sealant (Ford recommend WSK-M2G348-A5 or Loctite 518) to the No 1 camshaft bearing caps at the oil seal ends only (see illustration). On Ti-VCT engines, renew the O-ring seal beneath the No 1 bearing cap (see illustration 11.7d).

18 Oil the bearing surfaces, then locate the camshaft bearing caps on the camshafts and insert the retaining bolts loosely. Make sure that each cap is located in its previously-noted position (see illustration).

19 Ensuring each cap is kept square to the cylinder head as it is tightened down, and working in sequence (see illustration), tighten

11.17 Apply a thin bead of sealant (see text) to the underside of the No 1 bearing cap as shown

2A•14 1.4 & 1.6 litre engines (Duratec 16V) in-car repair procedures

11.18 Oil the camshaft bearing surfaces

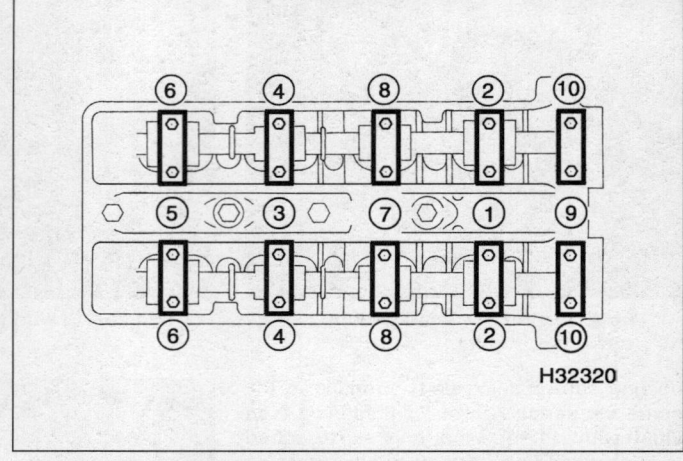

11.19 Camshaft bearing cap bolt slackening and tightening sequence

the camshaft bearing cap bolts slowly and by one turn at a time, until each cap touches the cylinder head. Next, go round again in the same sequence, tightening the bolts to the specified Stage 1 torque wrench setting specified.
20 Finally, still working in the tightening sequence, tightening the bolts further to the Stage 2 angle. It is recommended that an angle gauge is used for this, to ensure accuracy.
21 Wipe off all surplus sealant, and check the valve clearances as described in Section 5.
22 Fit new camshaft oil seals as described in Section 10.

12 Cylinder head – removal, inspection and refitting

Removal

1 Depressurise the fuel system as described in Chapter 4A.
2 Drain the cooling system as described in Chapter 1.
3 Disconnect the battery negative lead as described in Chapter 5A.
4 Remove the inlet manifold and exhaust manifold as described in Chapter 4A.

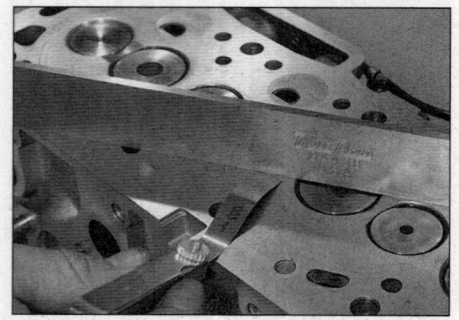

12.18 Check the cylinder head gasket face for distortion using a straight-edge

5 Remove the camshafts and tappets as described in Section 11.
6 Remove the inlet manifold support bolt from the front of the engine at the timing belt end.
7 Lower the car to the ground.
8 Make a note of their fitted locations and the harness routing, then disconnect any wiring plugs attached to components on the cylinder head. Label the plugs if necessary to aid refitting.
9 Unbolt the timing belt rear cover, which is secured by three bolts.
10 Release the spring-type clip and disconnect the coolant pipe from the left-hand rear of the cylinder head.
11 Undo the 4 bolts and detach the coolant housing from the left-hand end of the cylinder head
12 Make a last check round the cylinder head, to ensure that nothing remains connected or attached which would prevent the head from being lifted off. Prepare a clean surface to lay the head down on once it has been removed.
13 Working in the **reverse** of the tightening sequence **(see illustration 12.27a or 12.27b)**, slacken the ten cylinder head bolts progressively and by half a turn at a time; a Torx key (TX 55 size) will be required. Remove all the bolts.
14 Lift the cylinder head away; use assistance if possible, as it is a heavy assembly. Remove the gasket, noting the two dowels. Although the gasket cannot be re-used, it is advisable to retain it for comparison with the new one, to confirm that the right part has been supplied.

Inspection

15 The mating faces of the cylinder head and cylinder block must be perfectly clean before refitting the head. Use a hard plastic or wood scraper to remove all traces of gasket and carbon; also clean the piston crowns. Take particular care during the cleaning operations, as aluminium alloy is easily damaged.
16 Make sure that the carbon is not allowed to enter the oil and coolant passages – this is particularly important for the lubrication system, as carbon could block the oil supply to the engine's components. Using adhesive tape and paper, seal the coolant, oil and bolt holes in the cylinder block. To prevent carbon entering the gap between the pistons and bores, smear a little grease in the gap. After cleaning each piston, use a small brush to remove all traces of grease and carbon from the gap, then wipe away the remainder with a clean rag. Note that Ti-VCT engines have a filter fitted into the oil supply galleries feeding the VCT system. This filter is permanently installed and cannot be removed.
17 Check the mating surfaces of the cylinder block and the cylinder head for nicks, deep scratches and other damage. If slight, they may be removed carefully with a file, but if excessive, renewal is necessary as it is not permissible to machine the surfaces.
18 If warpage of the cylinder head gasket surface is suspected, use a straight-edge to check it for distortion **(see illustration)**. Refer to Part C of this Chapter if necessary.
19 If possible, clean out the bolt holes in the block using compressed air, to ensure no oil or coolant is present. Screwing a bolt into an oil- or coolant-filled hole can (in extreme cases) cause the block to fracture, due to the hydraulic pressure created.
20 Although not essential, if a suitable tap-and-die set is available, it's worth running the correct-size tap down the bolt threads in the cylinder block. This will clean the threads of any debris, and go some way to restoring any damaged threads. Make absolutely sure the tap is the right size and thread pitch, and lightly oil the tap before starting.
21 Ford insist that the cylinder head bolts must be renewed.

Refitting

22 Wipe clean the mating surfaces of the cylinder head and cylinder block, and check

12.24 Locate the new cylinder head gasket over the dowels

that the two locating dowels are in position in the block.

23 Turn the crankshaft anti-clockwise so that pistons 1 and 4 are approximately 25 mm before TDC, in order to avoid the risk of valve/piston contact. Turn the crankshaft using a spanner on the pulley bolt.

24 If the old gasket is still available, check that it is identical to the new one – for instance, there are several different thicknesses of gasket, indicated by the number of small holes on one side. Position the new gasket over the dowels on the cylinder block surface. It can only be fitted one way round – check carefully that the holes in the gasket align with the holes in the block surface, and that none are blocked **(see illustration)**.

25 It is useful when refitting a cylinder head to have an assistant on hand to help guide the head onto the dowels. Take care that the gasket does not get moved as the head is lowered into position. To confirm that the head is aligned correctly, once it is in place, temporarily slide in two or more of the head bolts, and check that they fit into the block holes.

26 Fit the new head bolts carefully, and screw them in by hand only until finger-tight.

27 Working progressively and in sequence, tighten the cylinder head bolts to their Stage 1 torque setting **(see illustrations)**.

28 Next, go around again in the same sequence, and tighten the bolts to the Stage 2 setting.

29 Finally, the bolts should be angle-tightened further, by the specified Stage 3 amount. This means simply that each bolt in the sequence

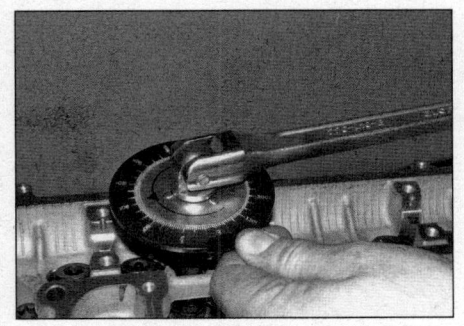

12.29 Use an angle-gauge for the final stage

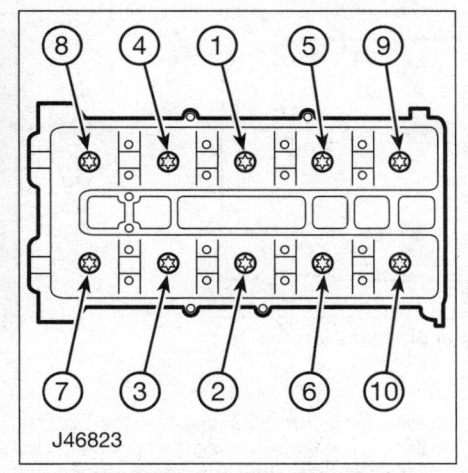

12.27a Cylinder head bolt tightening sequence (non-Ti-VCT engines)

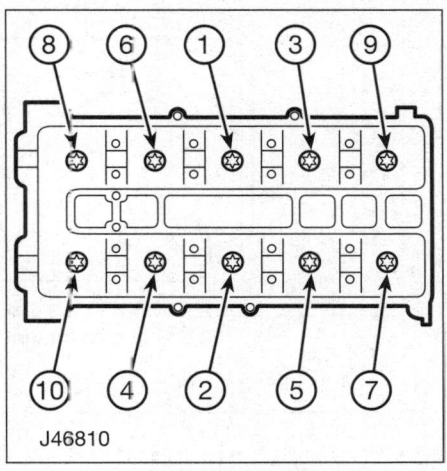

12.27b Cylinder head bolt tightening sequence (Ti-VCT engines)

must be turned through the stated angle. Special 'angle gauges' are available from tool suppliers for measuring this, but since 90° is a right-angle, it is possible to judge reasonably accurately by assessing the start and finish positions of the socket handle **(see illustration)**.

30 The remainder of refitting is a reversal of removal, noting the following points:
a) Refit the camshafts as described in Section 11, and the timing belt as described in Section 8.
b) Tighten all fasteners to the specified torque, where given.
c) Ensure that all hoses and wiring are correctly routed, and that hose clips and wiring connectors are securely refitted.
d) Refill the cooling system as described in Chapter 1.
e) Check all disturbed joints for signs of oil or coolant leakage once the engine has been restarted and warmed-up to normal operating temperature.

13 Sump – removal and refitting

Removal

1 Apply the handbrake, then jack up the front of the car and support it on axle stands (see *Jacking and vehicle support*).

2 Drain the engine oil, then check the drain plug sealing washer and renew if necessary. Clean and refit the engine oil drain plug together with the washer, and tighten it to the specified torque wrench setting. Although not strictly necessary, as the oil is being drained, it makes sense to fit a new oil filter at the same time (see Chapter 1).

3 Release the clip, undo the retaining bolt, and pull the engine oil level dipstick guide tube from the sump. Check the condition of the seal at the base of the tube, and renew it if necessary.

4 Unscrew the bolts securing the transmission to the sump, then progressively unscrew the sump-to-block bolts **(see illustration)**.

5 On these models, a sump gasket is not used, and sealant is used instead. Unfortunately, the use of sealant makes removal of the sump more difficult. If care is taken not to damage the surfaces, the sealant can be cut around using a sharp knife.

6 On no account lever between the mating faces, as this will almost certainly damage them, resulting in leaks when finished. Ford technicians have a tool comprising a metal rod which is inserted through the sump drain hole, and a handle to pull the sump downwards. Providing care is taken not to damage the threads, a large screwdriver could be used in the drain hole to prise down the sump.

7 While the sump is removed, take the opportunity to remove the oil pump pick-up/strainer pipe, and clean it with reference to Section 14.

Refitting

8 Thoroughly clean the contact surfaces of the sump and crankcase. Take care not to damage the oil pump gasket or the crankshaft oil seal, both of which are partially exposed when the sump is removed. If necessary, use a cloth rag to clean inside the sump and crankcase. If the oil pump pick-up/strainer

13.4 Sump viewed from below, showing the engine and transmission bolts

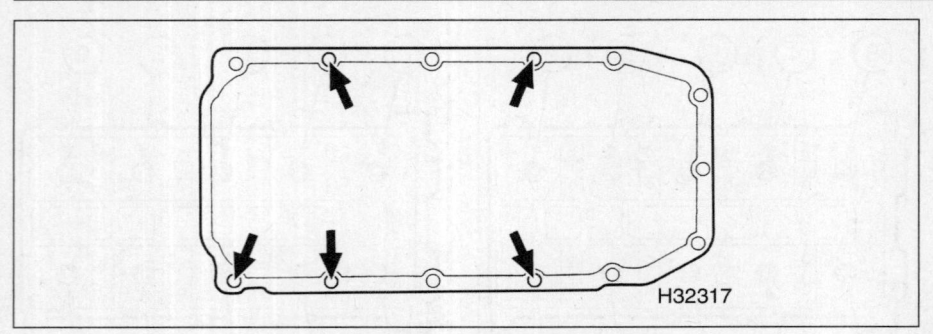

2A•16 1.4 & 1.6 litre engines (Duratec 16V) in-car repair procedures

13.9 Sump alignment stud positions (arrowed)

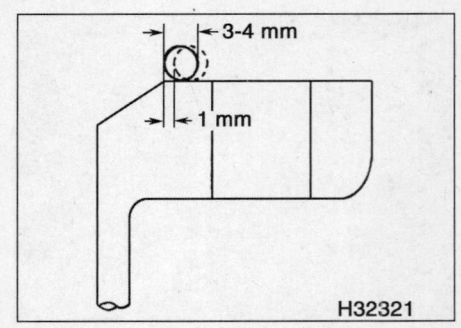

13.10 Apply the bead of sealant to the sump mating surface as shown

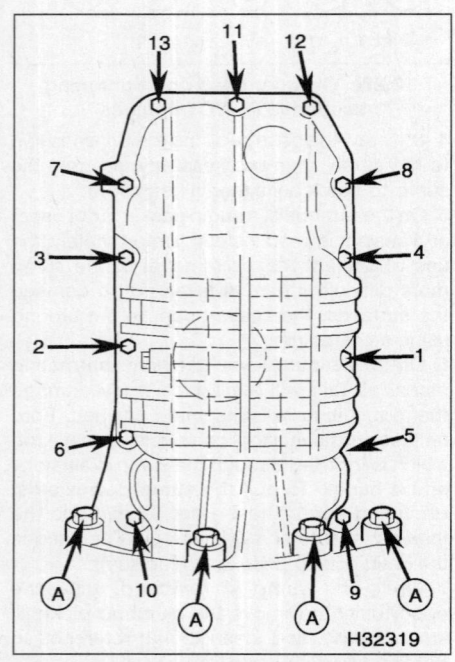

13.13 Sump bolt tightening sequence. Also shows sump-to-transmission bolts (A)

pipe was removed, fit a new O-ring and refit the pipe with reference to Section 14.
9 Ford state that, to refit the sump, five M8x20 studs must be screwed into the base of the engine (see illustration). This not only helps to align the sump, ensuring that the bead of sealant is not displaced as the sump is fitted, but also ensures that the sealant does not enter the blind holes. Cut a slot across the end of each stud, to make removal easier when the sump is in place.
10 Apply a 3 to 4 mm diameter bead of sealant (Ford recommend WSE M4G323-A4, or equivalent) to the sump pan, to the inside of the bolt holes (see illustration). The sump bolts must be fitted and tightened within 10 minutes of applying the sealant.
11 Offer the sump up into position over the studs, and fully refit the remaining bolts by hand. Unscrew the studs, and refit the sump bolts in their place. The sump should be fitted flush with the block at the transmission end.
12 Insert the four sump-to-transmission bolts and tighten them to the specified torque.
13 The sump-to-crankcase bolts are tightened in two stages. Working in sequence (see illustration), tighten all the sump bolts to the specified Stage 1 torque, then go around again in sequence, and tighten them to the Stage 2 setting.
14 Refit the engine oil level dipstick guide tube, with a new seal where necessary, and tighten the retaining bolt securely. Replace the clip.
15 Lower the car to the ground. To be on the safe side, wait a further 30 minutes for the sealant to cure before filling the sump with fresh oil, as described in Chapter 1.
16 Finally start the engine and check for signs of oil leaks.

14 Oil pump – removal, inspection and refitting

Removal

1 Remove the crankshaft right-hand oil seal as described in Section 16.
2 Remove the sump as described in Section 13.
3 Undo the timing belt rear cover lower 2 bolts.
4 On models with air conditioning, remove the four bolts securing the air conditioning compressor, and tie it up clear of the engine without disconnecting any of the hoses.
5 Unscrew the bolts securing the oil pump pick-up/strainer pipe to the baffle plate/main bearing cap.
6 Unscrew the bolt securing the oil pump pick-up/strainer pipe to the oil pump, then withdraw the pipe and recover the sealing O-ring (see illustration). Discard the O-ring.
7 Unscrew the bolts securing the oil pump to the cylinder block/crankcase (see illustration). Withdraw the pump over the nose of the crankshaft.
8 Recover then discard the gasket (see illustration).
9 If necessary, unbolt and remove the baffle plate from the main bearing cap/ladder (see illustration). Thoroughly clean all components, particularly the mating surfaces of the pump, the sump, and the cylinder block/crankcase.

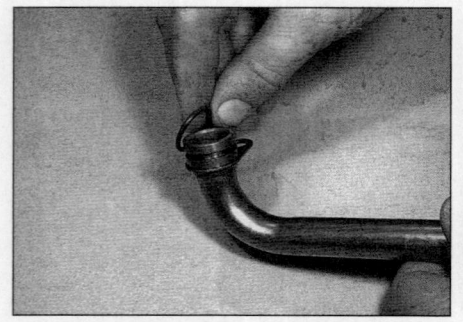

14.6 Remove the O-ring seal from the oil pump pick-up/strainer pipe

14.7 Remove the oil pump-to cylinder block/crankcase bolts

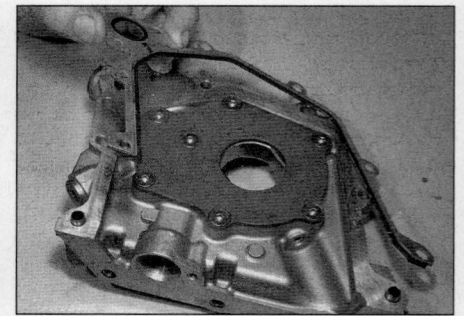

14.8 Remove the oil pump gasket

Inspection

10 It is not possible to obtain individual components of the oil pump, furthermore, there are no torque settings available for tightening the pump cover plate bolts. However, the following procedure is provided for owners wishing to dismantle the oil pump for examination.

11 Take out the bolts, and remove the pump cover plate; noting any identification marks on the rotors, withdraw the rotors.

12 Inspect the rotors for obvious signs of wear or damage, and renew if necessary; if either rotor, the pump body, or its cover plate are scored or damaged, the complete oil pump assembly must be renewed.

13 The oil pressure relief valve can be dismantled as follows.

14 Unscrew the threaded plug, and recover the valve spring and plunger. If the plug's sealing O-ring is worn or damaged, a new one must be obtained, to be fitted on reassembly.

15 Reassembly is the reverse of the dismantling procedure; ensure the spring and valve are refitted the correct way round, and tighten the threaded plug securely.

Refitting

16 If removed, refit the oil baffle plate to the crankcase and tighten the bolts.

17 The oil pump must be primed on installation, by pouring clean engine oil into it and rotating its inner rotor a few turns.

18 Use a little grease to stick the new gasket in place on the cylinder block/crankcase.

19 Offer the oil pump over the nose of the crankshaft, and turn the inner rotor as necessary to align its flats with the flats on the crankshaft. Locate the pump on the dowels, then insert the retaining bolts and progressively tighten them to the specified torque.

20 Locate a new O-ring (dipped in oil) on the pick-up/strainer pipe, then locate the pipe in the oil pump and insert the retaining bolts. Insert the bolts retaining the pipe on the baffle plate/main bearing cap. Tighten the bolts to the specified torque.

21 Where removed, refit the air conditioning compressor, tightening the bolts to the specified torque.

22 Refit the sump as described in Section 13.

23 Fit a new crankshaft oil seal as described in Section 16.

15 Oil pressure switch – removal and refitting

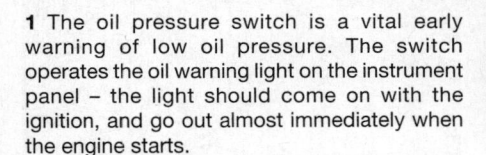

1 The oil pressure switch is a vital early warning of low oil pressure. The switch operates the oil warning light on the instrument panel – the light should come on with the ignition, and go out almost immediately when the engine starts.

2 If the light does not come on, there could be a fault on the instrument panel, the switch wiring, or the switch itself. If the light does not

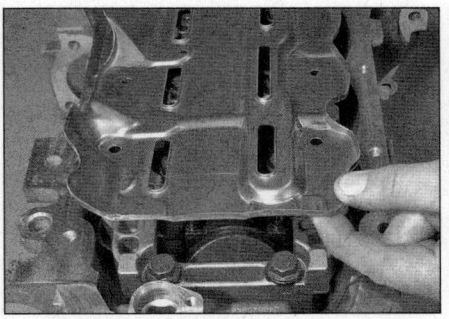

14.9 Unbolt the baffle plate from the main bearing cap/ladder

go out, low oil level, worn oil pump (or sump pick-up blocked), blocked oil filter, or worn main bearings could be to blame – or again, the switch may be faulty.

3 If the light comes on while driving, the best advice is to turn the engine off immediately, and not to drive the car until the problem has been investigated – ignoring the light could mean expensive engine damage.

Removal

4 The oil pressure switch is located on the front face of the engine, above the oil filter **(see illustration)**.

5 Disconnect the wiring plug from the switch.

6 Unscrew the switch from the block, and remove it. There should only be a very slight loss of oil when this is done.

Inspection

7 Examine the switch for signs of cracking or splits. If the top part of the switch is loose, this is an early indication of impending failure.

8 Check that the wiring terminals at the switch are not loose, then trace the wire from the switch connector until it enters the main loom – any wiring defects will give rise to apparent oil pressure problems.

Refitting

9 Refitting is the reverse of the removal procedure, noting the following points:
a) Tighten the switch securely.
b) Reconnect the switch connector, making sure it clicks home properly. Ensure that the wiring is routed away from any hot or moving parts.

16.6 Locate the new right-hand oil seal over the crankshaft

15.4 Oil pressure switch (arrowed)

c) Check the engine oil level and top-up if necessary (see 'Weekly checks').
d) Check for signs of oil leaks once the engine has been restarted and warmed-up to normal operating temperature.

16 Crankshaft oil seals – renewal

Right-hand oil seal

1 Remove the crankshaft sprocket as described in Section 9.

2 As a safety precaution, refit the engine right-hand mounting upper section and mounting bracket, and tighten the mounting bolts/nuts.

3 Note the fitted depth of the oil seal as a guide for fitting the new one.

4 Using a screwdriver, prise the old oil seal from the oil pump housing. Take great care not to damage the seal contact surface on the nose of the crankshaft, or the seating in the housing.

5 Wipe clean the seating and the nose of the crankshaft.

6 Apply a little clean engine oil to the inner lip of the seal, then locate it over the crankshaft and into the oil pump housing. Make sure that the closed end of the oil seal faces outwards **(see illustration)**.

7 Using a socket or length of metal tubing, drive the oil seal squarely into position to the previously-noted depth. The Ford installation tool (303-395) is used together with an old crankshaft pulley bolt to press the oil seal into position. The same idea may be used with metal tubing and a large washer – do not use a new crankshaft pulley bolt, as it is only permissible to use the bolt once. With the oil seal in position, wipe away any excess oil.

8 With the weight of the engine once more supported, unscrew the nuts and bolts and remove the engine right-hand mounting upper section and mounting bracket.

9 Refit the crankshaft sprocket with reference to Section 9.

Left-hand oil seal

10 Remove the flywheel/driveplate as described in Section 17.

16.14 Locate the new oil seal housing (complete with fitting sleeve) over the end of the crankshaft

16.16 With the oil seal housing bolted into position, remove the fitting ring

11 Unscrew the six bolts and withdraw the oil seal carrier from the end of the crankshaft. Note that the seal and carrier are made as one unit – it is not possible to obtain the seal separately.
12 Clean the carrier contact surface on the cylinder block, and the end of the crankshaft.
13 The new oil seal carrier is supplied complete with a fitting sleeve, which ensures that the oil seal lips are correctly located on the crankshaft. Ford state that neither the crankshaft nor the new oil seal should be lubricated before fitting.
14 Locate the oil seal carrier and fitting sleeve over the end of the crankshaft. Press the carrier into position, noting that the centre bolt holes are formed into locating dowels **(see illustration)**.
15 Insert the retaining bolts and progressively tighten them to the specified torque.
16 Remove the fitting sleeve and check that the oil seal lips are correctly located **(see illustration)**.
17 Refit the flywheel/driveplate as described in Section 17.

17 Flywheel/driveplate –
removal, inspection and refitting

Removal

1 Remove the transmission as described in Chapter 7A or 7B, and the clutch as described in Chapter 6.

2 Hold the flywheel/driveplate stationary using one of the following methods:
 a) If an assistant is available, insert one of the transmission mounting bolts into the cylinder block and have the assistant engage a wide-bladed screwdriver with the starter ring gear teeth while the bolts are loosened. Alternatively, a piece of angle-iron can be engaged with the ring gear and located against the transmission mounting bolt.
 b) A further method is to fabricate a piece of flat metal bar with a pointed end to engage the ring gear – fit the tool to the transmission bolt and use washers and packing to align it with the ring gear, then tighten the bolt to hold it in position **(see illustration)**.
3 Unscrew and remove the bolts, then lift the flywheel/driveplate off the locating dowel on the crankshaft **(see illustration)**.

Inspection

4 Clean the flywheel/driveplate to remove grease and oil. Inspect the surface for cracks, rivet grooves, burned areas and score marks. Light scoring can be removed with emery cloth. Check for cracked and broken ring gear teeth. Lay the flywheel/driveplate on a flat surface, and use a straight-edge to check for warpage.
5 Clean and inspect the mating surfaces of the flywheel/driveplate and the crankshaft. If the crankshaft oil seal is leaking, renew it (see Section 16) before refitting the flywheel/driveplate. In fact, given the large amount of work needed to remove the flywheel/driveplate, it's probably worth fitting a new seal anyway, as a precaution.
6 While the flywheel/driveplate is removed, clean carefully its inner face, particularly the recesses which serve as the reference points for the crankshaft speed/position sensor. Clean the sensor's tip, and check that the sensor is securely fastened. The sensor mounting may be removed if necessary by first removing the sensor, then unscrewing the bolt and withdrawing the mounting from the cylinder block **(see illustration)**.

Refitting

7 Make sure that the mating faces of the flywheel/driveplate and crankshaft are clean, then locate the flywheel/driveplate on the crankshaft and engage it with the locating dowel.
8 Insert the retaining bolts finger-tight.
9 Lock the flywheel/driveplate (see paragraph 2), then tighten the bolts in a diagonal sequence to the specified torque.
10 Refit the clutch with reference to Chapter 6, and the transmission as described in Chapter 7A or 7B.

18 Engine/transmission mountings –
inspection and renewal

General

1 The engine/transmission mountings seldom require attention, but broken or deteriorated mountings should be renewed immediately, or the added strain placed on the driveline components may cause damage or wear.
2 While separate mountings may be removed and refitted individually, if more than one is disturbed at a time – such as if the engine/transmission unit is removed from its mountings – they must be reassembled and their fasteners tightened in the position marked on removal.
3 On reassembly, the complete weight of the engine/transmission unit must not be taken by the mountings until all are correctly aligned with the marks made on removal. Tighten the engine/transmission mounting fasteners to their specified torque wrench settings.

17.2 Home-made flywheel locking tool

17.3 Remove the flywheel retaining bolts. Note the dowel (arrowed) in the end of the crankshaft

17.6 Crankshaft position sensor mounting and retaining bolt

Inspection

4 During the check, the engine/transmission unit must be raised slightly, to remove its weight from the mountings.

5 Raise the front of the vehicle, and support it securely on axle stands. Position a jack under the sump, with a large block of wood between the jack head and the sump, then carefully raise the engine/transmission just enough to take the weight off the mountings.

⚠️ **Warning: DO NOT place any part of your body under the engine when it is supported only by a jack.**

6 Check the mountings to see if the rubber is cracked, hardened or separated from the metal components. Sometimes the rubber will split right down the centre.

7 Check for relative movement between each mounting's brackets and the engine/transmission or body (use a large screwdriver or lever to attempt to move the mountings). If movement is noted, lower the engine and check-tighten the mounting fasteners.

Renewal

Note: The following paragraphs assume the engine is supported beneath the sump as described earlier.

Right-hand mounting

8 Lift up the coolant expansion tank and position it to one side. Note there is no need to disconnect the coolant pipes.

9 Mark the position of the mounting on the vehicle, right-hand inner wing panel, undo the nuts securing the upper mounting bracket **(see illustration 3.14)**. Discard the nuts, new ones must be fitted.

10 Undo the two retaining bolts to the vehicle inner wing panel and withdraw the mounting from the vehicle.

11 On refitting, tighten all fasteners to the torque wrench settings specified. Re-align the marks made on removal, then tighten the mounting bracket new retaining nuts.

Left-hand mounting

12 Remove the air cleaner assembly as described in Chapter 4A.

13 Remove the battery as described in Chapter 5A, then undo the 3 bolts and remove the battery tray. Disconnect any wiring as the tray is withdrawn.

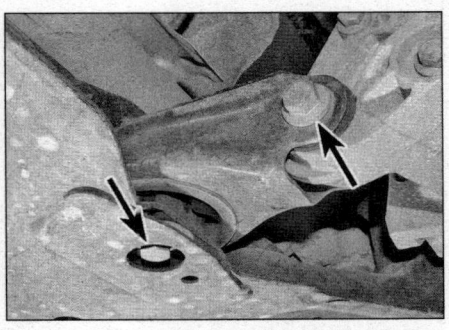

18.14 Left-hand mounting centre bolt (arrowed)

18.17 Rear mounting/roll restrictor bolts (arrowed)

14 With the transmission supported, note the position of the mounting then unscrew the centre retaining bolt to release the mounting from the transmission **(see illustration)**.

15 Unscrew the four outer retaining nuts, and 2 bolts to dismantle the mounting from the mounting bracket.

16 On refitting, renew the self-locking nuts. Re-align the mounting in the position noted on removal, then tighten all fasteners to the specified torque wrench settings.

Rear mounting (roll restrictor)

17 Unbolt the mounting from the subframe and the transmission by unscrewing the mounting's centre bolts **(see illustration)**.

18 On refitting, ensure that the bolts are securely tightened to the specified torque wrench setting.

Notes

Chapter 2 Part B:
1.8 & 2.0 litre engines (Duratec HE) in-car repair procedures

Contents

	Section number		Section number
Camshafts and tappets – removal, inspection and refitting	9	General information	1
Compression test – description and interpretation	2	Oil pressure warning light switch – removal and refitting	14
Crankshaft oil seals – renewal	10	Oil pump – removal, inspection and refitting	13
Crankshaft pulley – removal and refitting	6	Sump – removal and refitting	12
Cylinder head – removal and refitting	11	Timing chain cover – removal and refitting	7
Cylinder head cover – removal and refitting	4	Timing chain, tensioner and guides – removal, inspection and refitting	8
Engine oil and filter change	See Chapter 1		
Engine oil level check	See Weekly checks	Top Dead Centre (TDC) for No 1 piston – locating	3
Engine/transmission mountings – inspection and renewal	16	Valve clearances – checking and adjustment	5
Flywheel/driveplate – removal, inspection and refitting	15		

Degrees of difficulty

Easy, suitable for novice with little experience	Fairly easy, suitable for beginner with some experience	Fairly difficult, suitable for competent DIY mechanic	Difficult, suitable for experienced DIY mechanic	Very difficult, suitable for expert DIY or professional

Specifications

General
Engine type.. Four-cylinder, in-line, chain-driven double overhead camshafts, aluminium alloy cylinder head and engine block

Engine code:
  1.8 litre.. QQDB and Q7DA
  2.0 litre.. AODA
Capacity:
  1.8 litre.. 1798 cc
  2.0 litre.. 1998 cc
Bore:
  1.8 litre.. 83.0 mm
  2.0 litre.. 87.5 mm
Stroke... 83.1 mm
Compression ratio...................................... 10.8:1
Output:
  Power:
    1.8 litre.. 82 kW (125 PS) @ 6000 rpm
    2.0 litre.. 107 kW (145 PS) @ 6000 rpm
  Torque:
    1.8 litre.. 165 Nm @ 4000 rpm
    2.0 litre.. 185 Nm @ 4500 rpm
Firing order... 1-3-4-2 (No 1 cylinder at timing chain end)
Direction of crankshaft rotation....................... Clockwise (seen from right-hand side of vehicle)

Camshafts
Camshaft endfloat...................................... 0.09 to 0.24 mm
Camshaft bearing journal diameter.................. 24.96 to 24.98 mm

Valves
Valve clearances (cold):   **Inlet**   **Exhaust**
  All engines.. 0.22 to 0.28 mm   0.27 to 0.33 mm

Lubrication

Engine oil type/specification	See end of *Weekly checks* on page 0•17
Engine oil capacity	See Chapter 1
Oil pressure (engine at operating temperature):	
At 1500 rpm	1.3 to 2.7 bar
At 3000 rpm	2.3 to 5.2 bar
Oil pressure relief valve opens at	5.0 bar

Torque wrench settings

	Nm	lbf ft
Air conditioning compressor	25	18
Camshaft bearing cap bolts:		
Stage 1	7	5
Stage 2	16	12
Camshaft position sensor	6	4
Camshaft sprocket	72	53
Crankshaft oil seal carrier bolts	10	7
Crankshaft pulley bolt:*		
Stage 1	100	74
Stage 2	Angle-tighten a further 90°	
Cylinder block blanking plug	20	15
Cylinder head bolts:*		
Stage 1	5	4
Stage 2	15	11
Stage 3	45	33
Stage 4	Angle-tighten a further 90°	
Stage 5	Angle-tighten a further 90°	
Cylinder head cover bolts	10	7
Engine mountings:		
Right-hand mounting retaining bolts	90	66
Right-hand mounting bracket-to-engine bolts	56	41
Left-hand mounting nuts	48	35
Left-hand mounting bracket to transmission	80	59
Left-hand mounting centre bolt	148	109
Lower-rear torque rod bolts	80	59
Flywheel/driveplate bolts:*		
Stage 1	30	22
Stage 2	Angle-tighten a further 90°	
Oil pick-up pipe bolts	10	7
Oil pressure switch	15	11
Oil pump chain guide	10	7
Oil pump chain tensioner	10	7
Oil pump sprocket bolt	25	18
Oil pump-to-cylinder block bolts:		
Stage 1	10	7
Stage 2	23	17
Sump drain plug	28	21
Sump pan to lower crankcase	25	18
Sump pan to transmission	50	37
Timing chain covers:		
M6	10	7
M8	48	35
Timing chain guide	10	7
Timing chain tensioner	10	7

* Do not re-use

1 General information

How to use this Chapter

This Part of Chapter 2 is devoted to repair procedures possible while the engine is still installed in the vehicle. Since these procedures are based on the assumption that the engine is installed in the vehicle, if the engine has been removed from the vehicle and mounted on a stand, some of the preliminary dismantling steps outlined will not apply.

Information concerning engine/transmission removal and refitting and engine overhaul can be found in Part C of this Chapter.

Engine description

The engine is of sixteen-valve, double overhead camshaft (DOHC), four-cylinder, in-line type, mounted transversely at the front of the vehicle, with the transmission on its left-hand end. It is available in 1.8 and 2.0 litre versions.

All major engine castings are of aluminium alloy, with cast-iron cylinder liners, and a crankshaft made from forged nodular iron.

The crankshaft runs in five main bearings, the centre main bearing's upper half incorporating thrustwashers to control crankshaft endfloat. The connecting rods rotate on horizontally-split bearing shells at their big-ends. The pistons are attached to the connecting rods by gudgeon pins which are an interference fit in the connecting rod small-end eyes. The aluminium alloy pistons are fitted with three piston rings: two compression rings and an oil control ring. After manufacture, the cylinder bores and piston skirts are measured and classified into three grades, which must be carefully matched together to ensure the correct piston/cylinder clearance; no oversizes are available to permit reboring. Cylinder blocks are supplied complete with crankshafts, pistons and connecting rods assembled. These components are not available separately.

The inlet and exhaust valves are each closed by coil springs; they operate in guides which are shrink-fitted into the cylinder head, as are the valve seat inserts.

The two camshafts are driven by the same timing chain, each operating eight valves via solid tappets (cam followers). The tappets are graded for thickness, and are renewed in order to adjust the valve clearances. Each camshaft rotates in five bearings that are line-bored directly in the cylinder head and the (bolted-on) bearing caps; this means that the bearing caps are not available separately from the cylinder head, and must not be interchanged with caps from another engine.

The coolant pump is bolted to the right-hand end of the cylinder block, and is driven with the alternator by a multi-ribbed auxiliary drivebelt from the crankshaft pulley.

When working on this engine, note that Torx-type (both male and female heads) and hexagon socket (Allen head) fasteners are widely used; a good selection of bits, with the necessary adapters, will be required, so that these can be unscrewed without damage and, on reassembly, tightened to the torque wrench settings specified.

Lubrication system

Lubrication is by means of an eccentric-rotor pump, which is mounted at right-hand end of the cylinder block, and is driven by a chain from a sprocket on the crankshaft, and draws oil through a strainer located in the sump. The pump forces oil through an externally-mounted full-flow cartridge-type filter. From the filter, the oil is pumped into a main gallery in the cylinder block/crankcase, from where it is distributed to the crankshaft (main bearings) and cylinder head.

The big-end bearings are supplied with oil via internal drillings in the crankshaft. Each piston crown is cooled by a spray of oil directed at its underside by a jet. These jets are fed by passages off the crankshaft oil supply galleries, with spring-loaded valves to ensure that the jets open only when there is sufficient pressure to guarantee a good oil supply to the rest of the engine components.

The cylinder head is provided with two oil galleries, one on the inlet side and one on the exhaust, to ensure constant oil supply to the camshaft bearings and tappets. A retaining valve (inserted into the cylinder head's top surface, in the middle, on the inlet side) prevents these galleries from being drained when the engine is switched off. The valve incorporates a ventilation hole in its upper end, to allow air bubbles to escape from the system when the engine is restarted.

While the crankshaft and camshaft bearings receive a pressurised supply, the camshaft lobes and valves are lubricated by splash, as are all other engine components.

Operations with engine in car

The following major repair operations can be accomplished without removing the engine from the vehicle. However, owners should note that any operation involving the removal of the sump requires careful forethought, depending on the level of skill and the tools and facilities available; refer to the relevant text for details.

a) Compression pressure – testing.
b) Cylinder head cover – removal and refitting.
c) Timing chain covers – removal and refitting.
d) Timing chain – renewal.
e) Timing chain tensioner and sprockets – removal and refitting.
f) Camshaft oil seals – renewal.
g) Camshafts and cam tappets – removal and refitting.
h) Cylinder head – removal, overhaul and refitting.
i) Cylinder head and pistons – decarbonising.
j) Sump – removal and refitting.
k) Crankshaft oil seals – renewal.
l) Oil pump – removal and refitting.
m) Flywheel/driveplate – removal and refitting.
n) Engine/transmission mountings – removal and refitting.

Clean the engine compartment and the exterior of the engine with some type of degreaser before any work is done (and/or clean the engine using a steam cleaner). It will make the job easier and will help to keep dirt out of the internal areas of the engine.

Depending on the components involved, it may be helpful to remove the bonnet to improve access to the engine as repairs are performed (refer to Chapter 11 if necessary). Cover the wings to prevent damage to the paint; special covers are available, but an old bedspread or blanket will also work.

2 Compression test – description and interpretation

1 When engine performance is down, or if misfiring occurs which cannot be attributed to the ignition or fuel systems, a compression test can provide diagnostic clues as to the engine's condition. If the test is performed regularly, it can give warning of trouble before any other symptoms become apparent.

2 The engine must be fully warmed-up to normal operating temperature, the oil level must be correct and the battery must be fully-charged. The aid of an assistant will also be required.

3 Referring to Chapter 12, identify and remove the fuel pump relay from the fusebox. Now start the engine and allow it to run until it stalls. If the engine will not start, at least keep it cranking for about 10 seconds. The fuel system should now be depressurised, preventing unburnt fuel from soaking the catalytic converter as the engine is turned over during the test.

4 Disable the ignition system by unplugging the crankshaft speed/position sensor (see Chapter 4A). Remove the spark plugs as described in Chapter 1.

5 Fit a compression tester to the No 1 cylinder spark plug hole – the type of tester which screws into the plug thread is to be preferred.

6 Have the assistant hold the throttle wide open and crank the engine on the starter motor after one or two revolutions, the compression pressure should build-up to a maximum figure and then stabilise. Record the highest reading obtained.

7 The compression will build up fairly quickly in a healthy engine. Low compression on the first stroke, followed by gradually-increasing pressure on successive strokes, indicates worn piston rings. A low compression on the first stroke which does not rise on successive strokes, indicates leaking valves or a blown head gasket (a cracked cylinder head could also be the cause). Deposits on the underside of the valve heads can also cause low compression. Record the highest gauge reading obtained, then repeat the procedure for the remaining cylinders.

8 Due to the variety of testers available, and the fluctuation in starter motor speed when cranking the engine, different readings are often obtained when carrying out the compression test. For this reason, specific compression pressure figures are not quoted by Ford. However, the most important factor is that the compression pressures are uniform in all cylinders, and that is what this test is mainly concerned with.

9 If the pressure in any cylinder is considerably lower than the others, introduce a teaspoonful of clean oil into that cylinder through its spark plug hole and repeat the test.

10 If the addition of oil temporarily improves the compression pressure, this indicates that

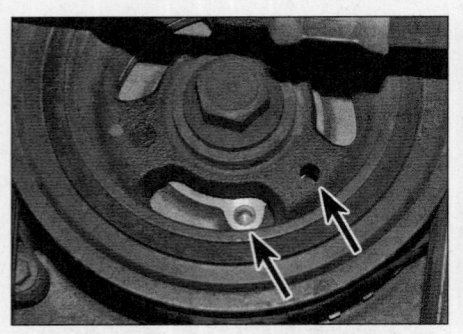

3.8a These 2 holes (arrowed) will align at TDC – so this is about 45° before TDC

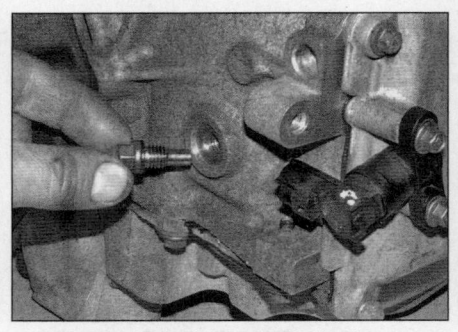

3.8b Remove the timing hole plug . . .

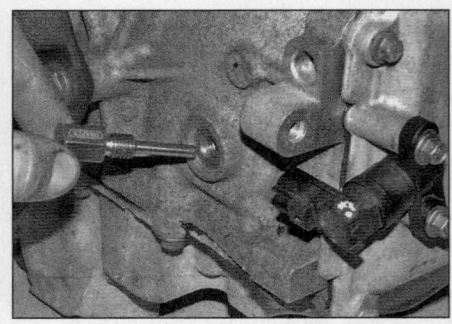

3.8c . . . and insert the timing pin

bore or piston wear is responsible for the pressure loss. No improvement suggests that leaking or burnt valves, or a blown head gasket, may be to blame.

11 A low reading from two adjacent cylinders is almost certainly due to the head gasket having blown between them; the presence of coolant in the engine oil will confirm this.

12 If one cylinder is about 20 percent lower than the others and the engine has a slightly rough idle, a worn camshaft lobe or faulty tappet could be the cause.

13 If the compression is unusually high, the combustion chambers are probably coated with carbon deposits. If this is the case, the cylinder head should be removed and decarbonised.

14 On completion of the test, refit the spark plugs, then reconnect the crankshaft speed/position sensor, and refit the fuel pump fuse. Note that carrying out this test as described, may result in one or more fault codes being stored by the engine management ECM. Have these codes erased by a Ford dealer or suitably-equipped specialist.

3 Top Dead Centre (TDC) for No 1 piston – locating

Note: *Only turn the engine in the normal direction of rotation – clockwise from the right-hand side of the vehicle.*

General

1 Top Dead Centre (TDC) is the highest point in its travel up-and-down its cylinder bore that each piston reaches as the crankshaft rotates. While each piston reaches TDC both at the top of the compression stroke and again at the top of the exhaust stroke, for the purpose of timing the engine, TDC refers to the No 1 piston position at the top of its compression stroke.

2 It is useful for several servicing procedures to be able to position the engine at TDC.

3 No 1 piston and cylinder are at the right-hand (timing chain) end of the engine (right- and left-hand are always quoted as seen from the driver's seat).

Locating TDC

4 Remove all the spark plugs, this will make it easier to turn the engine (Chapter 1).

5 Disconnect the battery negative (earth) lead (refer to Chapter 5A).

6 Apply the handbrake, then jack up the front of the vehicle and support it on axle stands (see *Jacking and vehicle support*). Remove the right-hand front roadwheel.

7 Undo the fasteners, then remove the right-hand front wheel arch liner.

8 There is a timing hole provided on the rear of the cylinder block (behind the TDC sensor) to position the crankshaft at TDC. Using a spanner or socket on the crankshaft pulley bolt, rotate the crankshaft clockwise until it is positioned approximately 45° before TDC **(see illustrations)**. Unscrew the timing hole plug and insert a timing peg (obtainable from Ford dealers (303-507) – or a tool supplier).

9 Rotate the crankshaft clockwise until it stops against the timing peg.

10 There is a bolt hole in the crankshaft pulley which should align with the thread in the timing chain cover, insert a bolt (M6 x 18 mm) to locate the pulley at TDC **(see illustration)**.

11 Number 1 and 4 pistons are now at TDC, one of them on the compression stroke. To determine which cylinder is on the compression stroke the camshaft cover will need to be removed (as described in Section 5).

12 Obtain Ford service tool 303-376A, or fabricate a substitute from a strip of metal 5 mm thick (while the strip's thickness is critical, its length and width are not, but should be approximately 180 to 230 mm by 20 to 30 mm). If number 1 cylinder is on the compression stroke – rest the tool on the cylinder head mating surface, and slide it into the slot in the left-hand end of both camshafts **(see illustration)**. The tool should slip snugly into both slots while resting on the cylinder head mating surface; if one camshaft is only slightly out of alignment, it is permissible to use an open-ended spanner to rotate the camshaft gently and carefully until the tool will fit.

13 If both camshaft slots (they are machined significantly off-centre) are below the level of the cylinder head mating surface, rotate the crankshaft through one full turn clockwise and fit the tool again; it should now fit as described in the previous paragraph. **Note:** *The timing peg and crankshaft pulley locking bolt will have to be removed before turning the engine.*

14 Do not use the locked camshafts to prevent the crankshaft from rotating – use only the locking methods described in Section 6 for removing the crankshaft pulley.

15 Once No 1 cylinder has been positioned at TDC on the compression stroke, TDC for any of the other cylinders can then be located by rotating the crankshaft clockwise 180° at a time and following the firing order (see *Specifications*).

16 Before turning the engine again, make sure that the timing peg and crankshaft pulley locating bolt have been removed.

3.10 Insert an M6 bolt though the pulley into the hole in the casing – TDC position

3.12 Slide the tool/metal bar into the slots in the end of the camshafts

1.8 & 2.0 litre engines (Duratec HE) in-car repair procedures

4.2 Pull the engine cover upwards

4.3 Disconnect the camshaft position sensor wiring plug (arrowed)

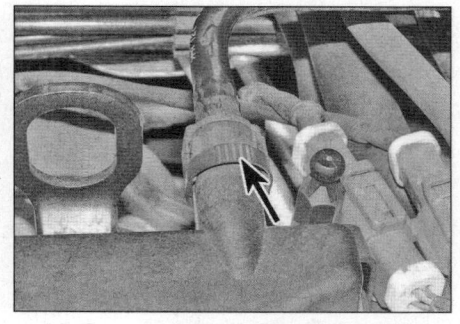

4.5 Squeeze together the sides of the collar (arrowed) and disconnect the breather hose

4 Cylinder head cover – removal and refitting

Removal

1 Disconnect the battery negative (earth) lead (refer to Chapter 5A).
2 Remove the plastic cover on the top of the engine by pulling it straight up from its mountings (see illustration).
3 Disconnect the electrical connector from the camshaft position sensor (see illustration).
4 Detach the wiring harness from the camshaft cover.
5 Disconnect the positive crankcase ventilation (PCV) hose from the left-hand rear corner of the camshaft cover (see illustration).
6 Unscrew the three engine upper plastic cover retaining pegs from the camshaft cover retaining studs, note the position of the retaining studs.
7 Undo the bolt securing the oxygen sensor wiring plugs bracket (see illustration).
8 Carefully undo the retaining bolts and lift out the ignition coils above the spark plugs (see illustration).
9 Working progressively, unscrew the cylinder head cover retaining bolts and withdraw the cover. Note that the bolts are integral with the cover.
10 Check the condition of the cover gasket, and renew it necessary.

Refitting

11 On refitting, clean the cover and cylinder head gasket faces carefully, then fit new gaskets to the cover where necessary, ensuring that they locate correctly in the cover grooves.
12 Apply a little silicone sealant (Ford No WSE-M4G323-A4) to the area where the upper edge of the timing chain cover contacts the cylinder head.
13 Refit the cover to the cylinder head. Start all bolts finger-tight, ensuring that the gasket remains seated in its groove.
14 Working in the sequence shown (see illustration), tighten the cover bolts to the specified torque wrench setting. Refit the three

4.7 Oxygen sensor wiring plugs bracket bolt (arrowed)

engine upper plastic cover retaining pegs to the cover retaining studs noted on removal.
15 The remainder of reassembly is the reverse of the removal procedure.

5 Valve clearances – checking and adjustment

Note: *Only turn the engine in the normal direction of rotation – clockwise viewed from the right-hand side of the vehicle.*

Checking

1 Remove the cylinder head cover as described in Section 4.

4.8 Undo the bolt and pull out the ignition coils

2 Set the engine to TDC on cylinder No 1 as described in Section 3. The inlet and exhaust cam lobes of No 1 cylinder will be pointing upwards (though not vertical), and the valve clearances can be checked.
3 Working on each valve, measure the clearance between the base of the cam lobe and the bucket tappet using feeler blades (see illustration). Record the thickness of the blade required to give a firm sliding fit on all the valves of No 1 cylinder. The desired clearances are given in the Specifications. Note that the clearances for inlet and exhaust valves are different. The inlet camshaft is at the front of the engine and the exhaust camshaft at the rear. Record all four clearances.

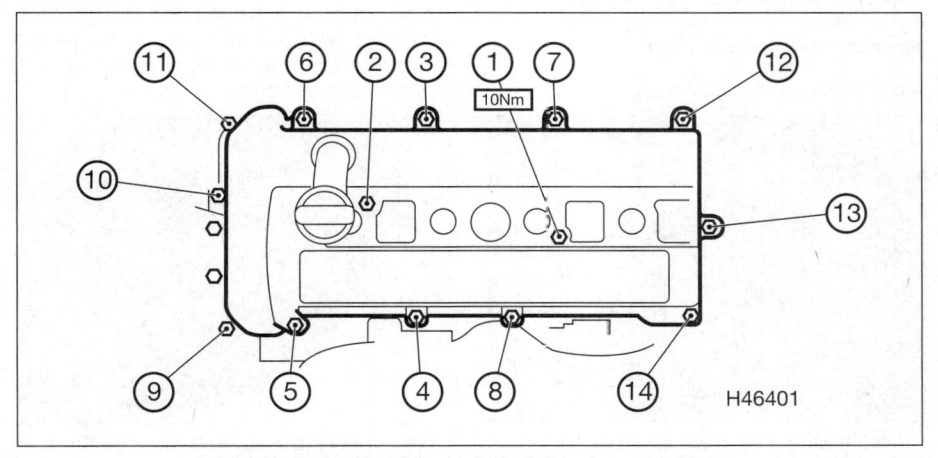

4.14 Cylinder head cover bolt tightening sequence

2B•6 1.8 & 2.0 litre engines (Duratec HE) in-car repair procedures

5.3 Measure the clearance between the base of the cam lobe and the tappet using feeler gauges

5.6 The tappet bucket has a number engraved on the underside

Removal

1 Remove the auxiliary drivebelts – either remove the drivebelts completely, or just secure them clear of the crankshaft pulley, depending on the work to be carried out (see Chapter 1).
2 Set the engine to TDC (see Section 3).
3 The crankshaft must now be locked to prevent its rotation while the pulley bolt is unscrewed. If the Ford special tools are not available proceed as follows:
  a) Remove the rubber plug from the transmission bellhousing, and use a large screwdriver or similar to lock the flywheel/driveplate ring gear teeth while an assistant slackens the pulley bolt; take care not to damage the teeth or the surrounding castings when using this method.
  b) If the engine/transmission has been removed and separated, lock the flywheel/driveplate using a locking tool (see illustration).
4 Unscrew the pulley bolt and remove the pulley.

4 Now turn the crankshaft clockwise through 180° so that the valves of cylinder No 3 are pointing upwards. Check and record the four valve clearances for cylinder No 3. The clearances for cylinders 4 and 2 can be checked after turning the crankshaft through 180° each time.

Adjustment

5 If adjustment is required, the bucket tappets must be changed by removing the camshafts as described in Section 9.
6 If the valve clearance was too small, a thinner bucket tappet must be fitted. If the clearance was too large, a thicker bucket tappet must be fitted. The bucket tappet has a number engraved on the inside (see illustration), if the marking is missing or illegible, a micrometer will be needed to establish bucket tappet thickness.
7 When the bucket tappet thickness and the valve clearance are known, the required thickness of the new bucket tappet can be calculated as follows:

New tappet thickness D
= Existing tappet thickness C
+ Measured clearance B
– Desired clearance A

Sample calculation

Desired clearance (A)	= 0.25
Measured clearance (B)	= 0.20
Existing tappet thickness (C)	= 2.55
Tappet thickness required (D)	= C+B−A = 2.5

All measurements in mm

8 With the correct thickness bucket tappets fitted in the cylinder head, refit the camshafts as described in Section 9.
9 Check the valve clearances are now correct, as described in paragraphs 2 to 4. If any clearances are still not within specification then carry out the adjustment procedure again.
10 It will be helpful for future adjustment if a record is kept of the thickness of bucket fitted at each position. The buckets required can be purchased in advance once the clearances and the existing bucket thicknesses are known.
11 When all the clearances are correct, refit the cylinder head cover as described in Section 4.

6 Crankshaft pulley – removal and refitting

Note: *Only turn the engine in the normal direction of rotation – clockwise from the right-hand side of the vehicle.*
Caution: *The pulley and crankshaft timing gear are not on a keyway, they are held in place by the crankshaft retaining bolt. Make sure the engine is set at TDC (see Section 3) before the pulley is removed.*
Note: *The crankshaft pulley retaining bolt is very tight and Ford use special tools (205-072 and 205-072-02) to lock the pulley to prevent it from turning. A new pulley retaining bolt will be required on refitting.*

Refitting

5 Refitting is the reverse of the removal procedure; making sure the engine has not moved from its setting at TDC (see Section 3).
6 Ensure that a new retaining bolt is used (see illustration), and tightened to the torque specified at the beginning of this Chapter.

7 Timing chain cover – removal and refitting

Note: *Only turn the engine in the normal direction of rotation – clockwise from the right-hand side of the vehicle.*

Removal

1 Remove the cylinder head cover as described in Section 4.
2 Apply the handbrake, then jack up the front of the vehicle and support it on axle stands (see Jacking and vehicle support). Remove the right-hand front roadwheel and remove the cover from under the right-hand front wheel arch.
3 Slacken the water pump pulley retaining bolts by approximately three turns.
4 Remove the auxiliary drivebelts (Chapter 1).
5 Undo the bolts securing the protective cover over the air conditioning compressor, and remove the cover. Disconnect the wiring plug, then undo the compressor mounting bolts, and the refrigerant pipe bracket bolt, and move the compressor to one side (see illustration). Suspend the compressor using wire or a strap from the vehicle bodywork/suspension. Note there is no need to disconnect any refrigerant pipes.
6 Remove the crankshaft pulley (Section 6).
7 Disconnect the crankshaft position (CKP) sensor wiring connector (see illustration).
8 Unscrew the retaining bolts and remove the water pump pulley.

6.3 Using a flywheel locking tool to prevent the flywheel from rotating

6.6 A new retaining bolt must be fitted

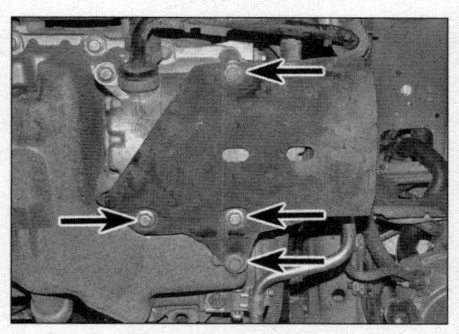

1.8 & 2.0 litre engines (Duratec HE) in-car repair procedures

7.5 Compressor protective cover retaining bolts (arrowed)

7.7 Disconnect the crankshaft position sensor wiring plug

7.11 Undo the right-hand mounting bolts/nuts (arrowed)

9 Detach the wiring harness from the studs on the lower edge of the timing chain cover.
10 Lift the coolant expansion tank from its mountings and move it to one side. If better access is required, drain sufficient coolant (see Chapter 1), then disconnect the lower coolant hose from the expansion tank.
11 Support the engine using a trolley jack and block of wood beneath the sump, then unscrew the nuts/bolts securing the engine/transmission right-hand mounting bracket and remove the mounting from the engine **(see illustration)**. Unclip the air conditioning pipe as the mounting is removed.
12 Remove the auxiliary drivebelt tensioner lower bolt.
13 Unscrew the timing chain cover retaining bolts (noting their positions for refitting) and withdraw the cover from the engine.

Refitting

14 Refitting is the reverse of the removal procedure (using the relevant Sections). Note the following points:
  a) Clean the sealant from the timing cover, cylinder block and cylinder head mating surfaces. When using a scraper and solvent to remove all traces of old gasket/sealant from the mating surfaces, be careful to ensure that you do not scratch or damage the material of either component – any solvents used must be suitable for this application. If the gasket was leaking, have the mating surfaces checked for warpage at an automotive engineering workshop.
  b) Renew the crankshaft oil seal fitted into the timing chain cover as described in Section 10.
  c) Ensure the drive shim is still fitted to the end of the crankshaft before the timing chain cover oil seal is fitted is refitted **(see illustration)**.
  d) Provided the relevant mating surfaces are clean and flat, apply a (3.0mm) bead of silicone sealant around the timing chain cover and the inner bolt holes **(see illustration)**. Note: The cover must be fitted within 10 minutes of applying the sealant.
  e) Tighten the timing chain cover bolts to the specified torque settings at the beginning of this Chapter, following the sequence shown **(see illustration)**.

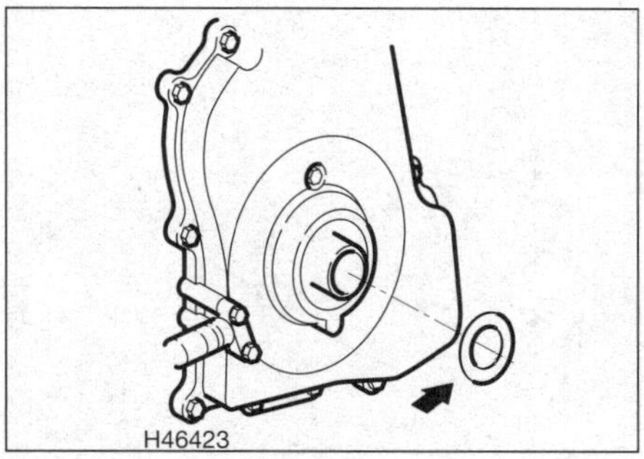

7.14a Ensure the crankshaft pulley drive shim (arrowed) is fitted before fitting the new oil seal

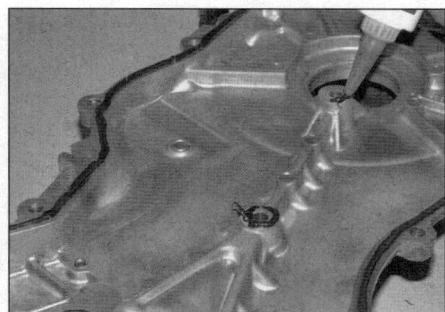

7.14b Apply a 3.0 mm bead of sealant around the timing chain cover, including the inner bolt holes

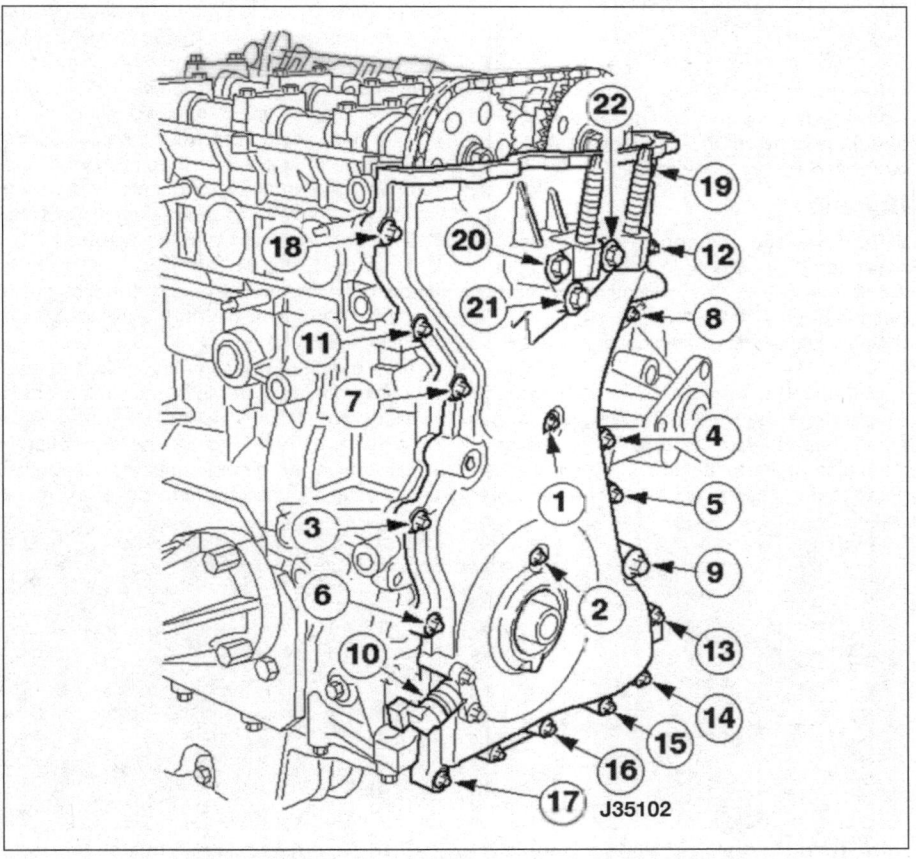

7.14c Timing chain cover bolt tightening sequence

2B•8   1.8 & 2.0 litre engines (Duratec HE) in-car repair procedures

8.4 Press against the timing chain guide and insert a locking pin (approximately 1.5 mm diameter)

8.6 Use a spanner to hold the camshafts whilst undoing the retaining bolts

8.7a Withdraw the tensioner guide from the pivot pin . . .

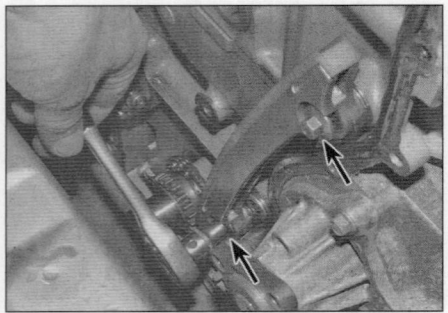

8.7b . . . then undo the retaining bolts (arrowed) and remove the fixed guide

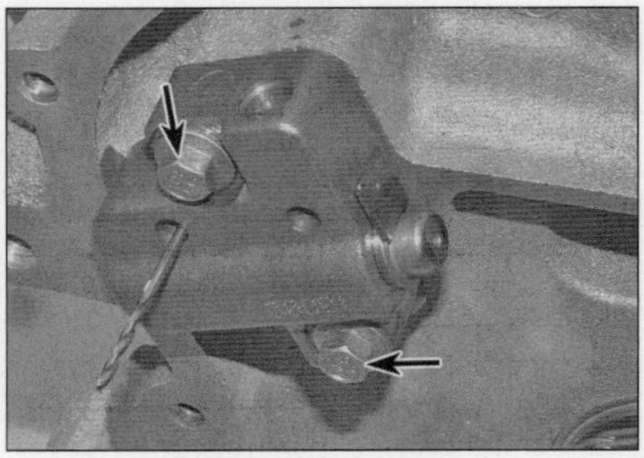

8.8 Timing chain tensioner bolts (arrowed)

8 Timing chain, tensioner and guides – removal, inspection and refitting

Note: *Only turn the engine in the normal direction of rotation – clockwise from the right-hand side of the vehicle.*

Removal

1 Remove the cylinder head cover as described in Section 4.
2 Set the engine to TDC as described in Section 3.
3 Remove the timing chain cover as described in Section 7.
4 Slacken the timing chain tensioner by inserting a small screwdriver into the access hole in the tensioner and releasing the pawl mechanism. Press against the timing chain guide to depress the piston into the tensioner housing. When fully depressed, insert a locking pin (approximately 1.5 mm) to lock the piston in its compressed position **(see illustration)**.
5 Hold the camshafts by the hexagon sections on the shafts to prevent them from turning, using an open-ended spanner.
6 With the camshafts held in position, undo the camshaft sprocket retaining bolts and remove the camshaft sprockets and timing chain. Do not rotate the crankshaft until the timing chain is refitted **(see illustration)**.
7 If required, unbolt the fixed timing chain guide and withdraw the tensioner timing chain guide from its pivot pin on the cylinder head **(see illustrations)**.
8 To remove the tensioner, undo the two retaining bolts and remove the timing chain tensioner from the cylinder block, taking care not to remove the locking pin **(see illustration)**.
9 To remove the timing chain sprocket from the crankshaft, the oil pump drive chain will need to be removed as described in Section 13. Note which way round it is fitted and mark the sprocket to ensure it is refitted the same way round.

Inspection

Note: *Keep all components identified for position to ensure correct refitting.*
10 Clean all components thoroughly and wipe dry.
11 Examine the chain tensioner and tensioner guide for excessive wear or other damage. Check the guides for deep grooves made by the timing chain. Renew them both if there is any doubt concerning their condition.
12 Examine the timing chain for excessive wear. Hold it horizontally and check how much movement exists in the chain links. If there is any doubt, compare it to a new chain. Renew as necessary.
13 Examine the teeth of the camshaft and crankshaft sprockets for excessive wear and damage.
14 Before refitting the timing chain tensioner, the piston must be compressed and locked until refitted (if not already done on removal). To do this, insert a small screwdriver into the access hole in the tensioner and release the pawl mechanism. Now lightly clamp the tensioner in a soft-jawed vice and slowly compress the piston. Do not apply excessive force and make sure that the piston remains aligned with its cylinder. When completely compressed, insert a locking pin/1.5 mm diameter wire rod into the special hole to lock the piston in its compressed position.

Refitting

15 If not already fitted, slide the crankshaft drive sprocket (and drive shim) onto the crankshaft. Ensure it is refitted the same way round as noted on removal (see Section 13 for further information on refitting the oil pump drive chain).
16 Refit the tensioner to the cylinder block and tighten the retaining bolts to the specified torque setting. Take care not to remove the locking pin **(see illustration)**.
17 Refit the fixed timing chain guide and tighten the two retaining bolts, then slide the tensioner timing chain guide back into place on the upper pivot pin **(see illustration)**.

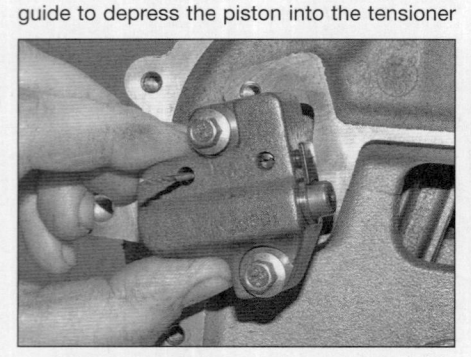

8.16 Refit the timing chain tensioner (still in the locked position)

8.17 Refit the tensioner guides to the engine

1.8 & 2.0 litre engines (Duratec HE) in-car repair procedures 2B•9

8.19 Refit the camshaft sprockets into position, complete with timing chain

8.20 Press against the tensioner guide and withdraw the locking pin (arrowed)

8.22 Use a spanner on the camshaft hexagon section to prevent them from rotating

18 Refit the inlet camshaft sprocket onto the camshaft, DO NOT tighten the retaining bolt at this stage.
19 With the timing chain around the exhaust camshaft sprocket refit the timing chain and sprocket, feeding the timing chain around the crankshaft drive sprocket and inlet camshaft sprocket **(see illustration)**.
20 With the timing chain in place, press against the tensioner guide and withdraw the tensioner locking pin. This will then tension the timing chain **(see illustration)**.
21 Check that the engine is still set to TDC (as described in Section 3).
22 Tighten the both camshaft sprocket retaining bolts to the torque setting specified in the Specifications at the beginning of this Chapter. **Note:** *Use an open-ended spanner on the hexagon on the camshafts to stop them from turning* **(see illustration)**.

23 Refit the timing chain cover as described in Section 7.
24 Remove the camshaft locking plate and crankshaft timing peg and turn the engine (in the direction of engine rotation) two full turns. Refit the camshaft locking plate and crankshaft timing peg to make sure the engine is still set at TDC (see Section 3 for further information).
25 Refit the cylinder head cover as described in Section 4.

9 Camshafts and tappets – removal, inspection and refitting

Note: *Only turn the engine in the normal direction of rotation – clockwise from the right-hand side of the vehicle.*

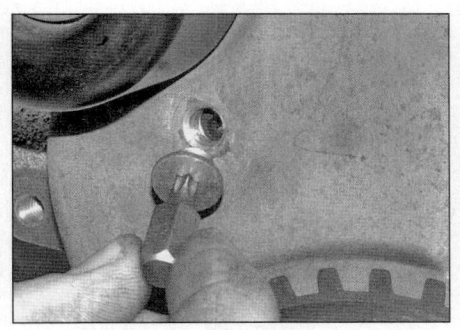

Removal

1 Remove the cylinder head cover as described in Section 4.
2 Set the engine to TDC on No 1 cylinder as described in Section 3.
3 Remove the timing chain cover lower and upper blanking plugs to gain access to the timing chain tensioner and guide **(see illustrations)**.
4 Slacken the timing chain tensioner by inserting a small screwdriver into the lower access hole in the timing chain cover and releasing the pawl mechanism in the tensioner **(see illustration)**.
5 Carefully turn the exhaust camshaft (by using an open-ended spanner on the hexagon on the shaft) in the normal direction of rotation (clockwise), to compress the timing chain tensioner **(see illustration)**.
6 Holding the exhaust camshaft in position, insert a bolt (M6 x 25 mm) into the upper access hole in the timing chain cover to lock the tensioner guide rail in position **(see illustration)**.
7 With the camshafts held in position (by using an open-ended spanner on the hexagon section on the shaft), slacken the camshaft sprocket retaining bolts.
8 Using a cable tie or similar, fasten the timing chain to the camshaft sprockets.
9 Remove the camshaft sprocket retaining bolts and remove the sprockets, complete with timing chain, away from the camshafts. Using a suitable piece of wire secure the sprockets and timing chain to prevent them dropping into the timing cover.

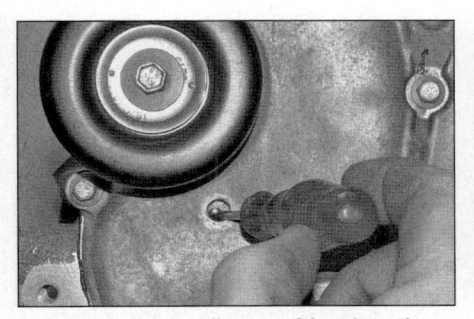

9.3a Remove the timing chain cover lower . . .

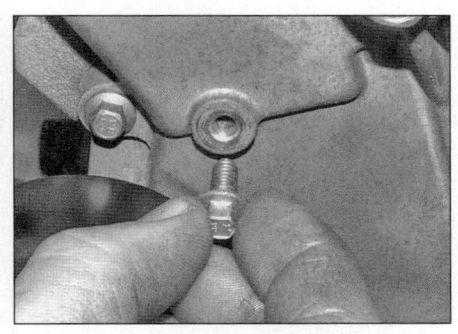

9.3b . . . and upper blanking plugs

9.4 Insert a small screwdriver into the lower access hole to release the timing chain tensioner

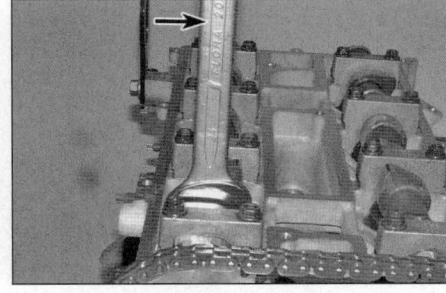

9.5 Carefully turn the exhaust camshaft in the direction of the arrow

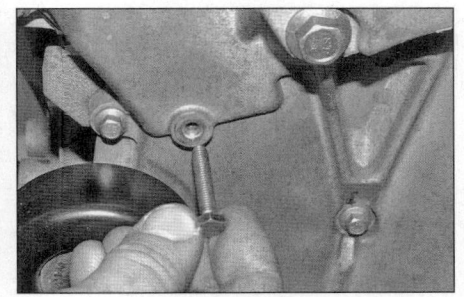

9.6 Whilst holding the exhaust camshaft in position, insert a bolt (M6 x 18 mm) to lock the tensioner guide rail

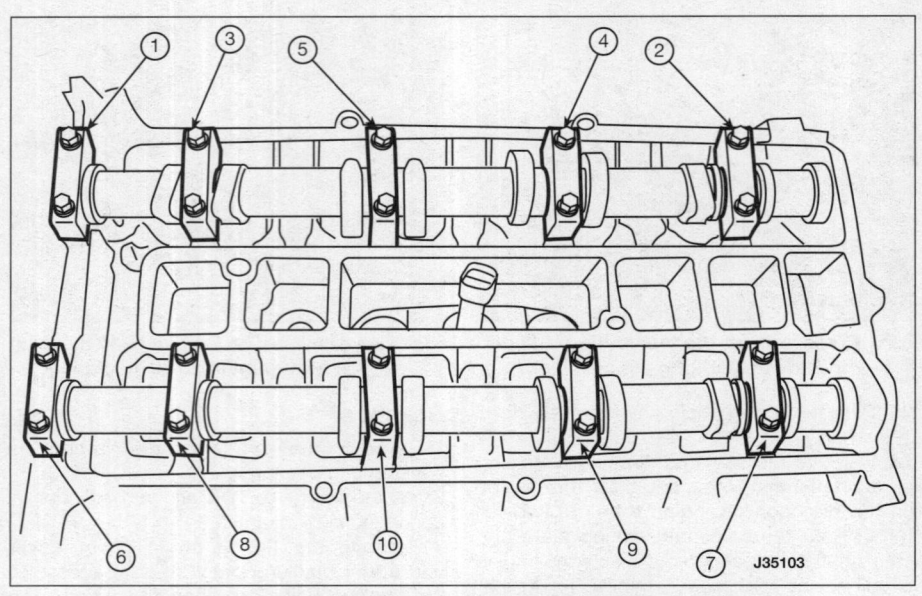

2B•10 1.8 & 2.0 litre engines (Duratec HE) in-car repair procedures

9.10 Sequence for slackening the camshaft bearing cap bolts

10 Working in sequence (see illustration), slacken the camshaft bearing cap bolts progressively by half a turn at a time. Work only as described to release gradually and evenly the pressure of the valve springs on the caps.

11 Withdraw the camshaft bearing caps, noting their markings, then remove the camshafts. The inlet camshaft can be identified by the reference lobe for the camshaft position sensor; therefore, there is no need to mark the camshafts (see illustrations).

12 Obtain sixteen small, clean containers, and number them 1 to 16. Using a rubber sucker, withdraw each bucket tappet in turn and place them in the containers. Do not interchange the bucket tappets as they are of different sizes; the shim is part of the bucket tappet (see illustrations). Different sizes of bucket tappets are available in the event of wear on the valves or repair on the cylinder head assembly.

Inspection

13 With the camshafts and tappets removed, check each for signs of obvious wear (scoring, pitting, etc) and for ovality, and renew if necessary.

14 Measure the outside diameter of each tappet (see illustration) – take measurements at the top and bottom of each tappet, then a second set at right-angles to the first; if any measurement is significantly different from the others, the tappet is tapered or oval (as applicable) and must be renewed. If the necessary equipment is available, measure the inside diameter of the corresponding cylinder head bore. If the tappets or the cylinder head bores are excessively worn, new tappets and/or a new cylinder head will be required.

15 Visually examine the camshaft lobes for score marks, pitting, galling (wear due to rubbing) and evidence of overheating (blue, discoloured areas). Look for flaking away of the hardened surface layer of each lobe (see illustration). If any such signs are evident, renew the component concerned.

16 Examine the camshaft bearing journals and the cylinder head bearing surfaces for signs of obvious wear or pitting. If any such signs are evident, renew the component concerned.

17 Using a micrometer, measure the diameter of each journal at several points (see illustration). If any measurement is significantly different from the others, renew the camshaft.

9.11a Note the identification markings (arrowed) on the camshaft bearing caps . . .

9.11b . . . and the reference lobe (arrowed) on the inlet camshaft for the position sensor

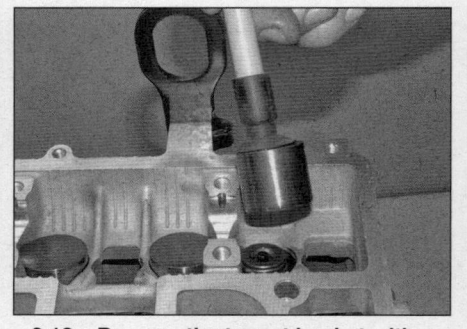

9.12a Remove the tappet bucket with a rubber sucker

9.12b Note the thickness number on the underside of the tappet bucket

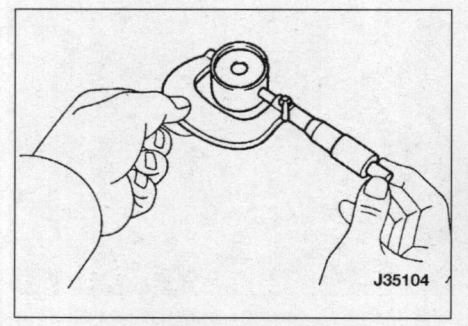

9.14 Use a micrometer to measure the diameter of the tappets

9.15 Check the cam lobes for pitting, wear and score marks – if necessary, renew the camshaft

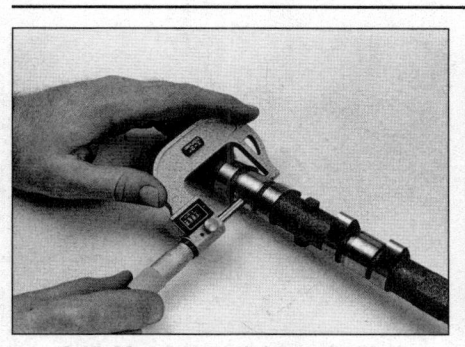

1.8 & 2.0 litre engines (Duratec HE) in-car repair procedures 2B•11

9.17 Measure each journal with a micrometer

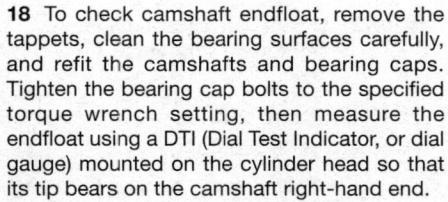

9.20 Liberally oil the tappets when refitting

9.22 Apply clean engine oil to the cam lobes and journals

18 To check camshaft endfloat, remove the tappets, clean the bearing surfaces carefully, and refit the camshafts and bearing caps. Tighten the bearing cap bolts to the specified torque wrench setting, then measure the endfloat using a DTI (Dial Test Indicator, or dial gauge) mounted on the cylinder head so that its tip bears on the camshaft right-hand end.

19 Tap the camshaft fully towards the gauge, zero the gauge, then tap the camshaft fully away from the gauge, and note the gauge reading. If the endfloat measured is found to be at or beyond the specified service limit, fit a new camshaft and repeat the check; if the clearance is still excessive, the cylinder head must be renewed.

Refitting

20 On reassembly, liberally oil the cylinder head tappet bores and the tappets **(see illustration)**. Carefully refit the tappets to the cylinder head, ensuring that each tappet is refitted to its original bore. Some care will be required to enter the tappets squarely into their bores.

21 Turn the engine back approximately 45° so that there are no pistons at the top of the cylinders.

22 Liberally oil the camshaft bearings and lobes **(see illustration)**. Ensuring that each camshaft is in its original location, refit the camshafts, locating each so that the slot in its left-hand end is approximately parallel to, and just above, the cylinder head mating surface.

23 All camshaft bearing caps have an identifying number and letter etched on them. The exhaust camshaft's bearing caps are numbered in sequence E1 to E5 and the inlet camshaft's bearing caps I1 to I5 **(see illustration 9.11a)**.

24 Ensuring that each cap is kept square to the cylinder head as it is tightened down, and working in sequence **(see illustration)**, tighten the camshaft bearing cap bolts slowly and by one turn at a time, until each cap touches the cylinder head. Next, go round again in the same sequence, tightening the bolts to the first stage torque wrench setting specified, then once more, tightening them to the second stage setting. Work only as described to impose gradually and evenly the pressure of the valve springs on the caps.

25 Fit the camshaft aligning tool; it should slip into place as described in Section 3 **(see illustration)**.

26 Refit the camshaft sprockets, complete with timing chain to the ends of the camshafts. DO NOT tighten the camshaft sprocket retaining bolts at this stage. Remove the cable ties from the timing chain and camshaft sprockets.

27 Remove the tensioner guide rail locking bolt from the upper access hole in the timing chain cover. It may be necessary to hold some pressure against the tensioner guide rail to remove the locking bolt.

28 Turn the engine (in the direction of rotation) approximately 45° to TDC. For further information on setting the engine to TDC, see Section 3.

29 With the camshafts held in position (by using an open-ended spanner on the hexagon on the shaft), tighten the camshaft sprocket retaining bolts to the specified torque.

30 Remove the camshaft locking plate and crankshaft timing peg and turn the engine (in the direction of engine rotation) two full turns. Refit the camshaft locking plate and crankshaft timing peg to make sure the engine is still set at TDC (see Section 3 for further information).

31 Refit the timing chain cover upper and lower blanking plugs, coat the blanking plug threads with a suitable sealant to prevent leaks.

32 Refit the cylinder head cover as described in Section 4.

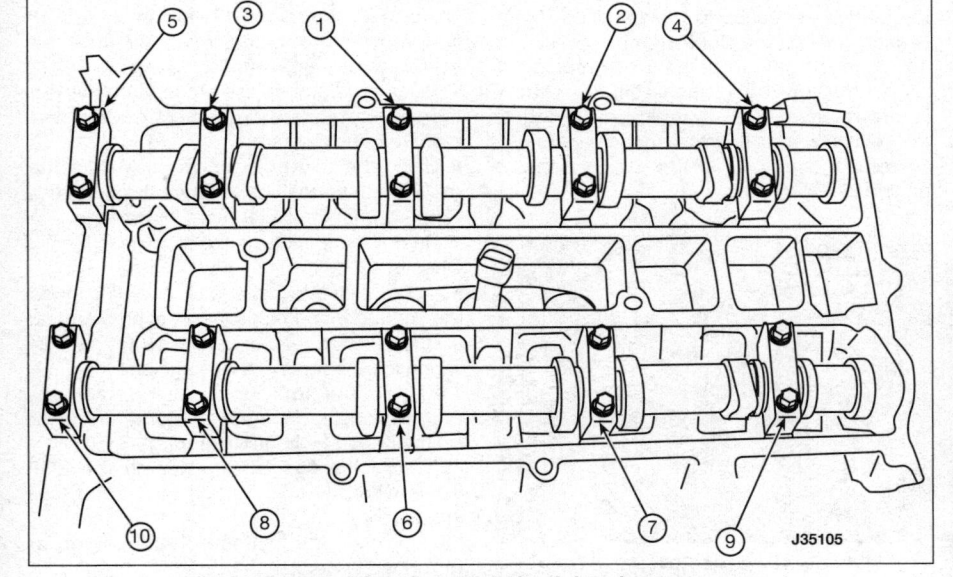

9.24 Camshaft bearing cap bolts tightening sequence

9.25 Fit the camshaft aligning tool to set TDC position

10.4a Ensure the oil seal remains square as it is being fitted

10.4b A socket of the correct size can be used for fitting the new seal

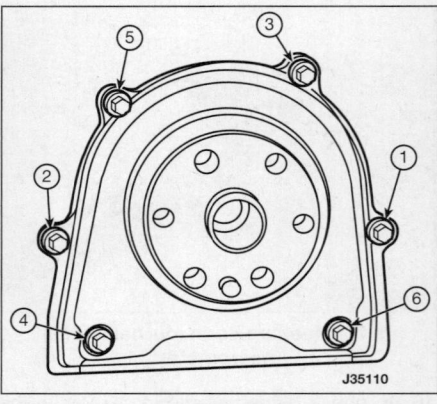

10.13 Oil seal carrier retaining bolts tightening sequence

10 Crankshaft oil seals – renewal

Timing chain end oil seal

1 Remove the crankshaft pulley as described in Section 6 of this Chapter.
2 Using a screwdriver, prise the old oil seal from the timing cover. Take care not to damage the surface of the timing cover and crankshaft. If the oil seal is tight, carefully drill two holes diagonally opposite each other in the oil seal, then insert self-tapping screws and use a pair of pliers to pull out the oil seal.
3 Wipe clean the seating in the timing cover and the nose of the crankshaft.
4 Smear clean engine oil on the outer periphery and sealing lips of the new oil seal, then start it into the timing cover by pressing it in squarely. Using a large socket or metal tubing, drive in the oil seal until flush with the outer surface of the timing cover. Make sure the oil seal remains square as it is being inserted. Wipe off any excess oil **(see illustrations)**.
5 Refit the crankshaft pulley as described in Section 6 of this Chapter.

Transmission end oil seal

Note: *The oil seal can only be renewed as a complete unit with the carrier.*

6 Remove the transmission (see the relevant Part of Chapter 7).
7 On manual models, remove the clutch assembly (see Chapter 6).
8 Unbolt the flywheel/driveplate (Section 15).
9 Remove the sump (see Section 12).
10 Undo the six retaining bolts and remove the oil seal carrier from the cylinder block. Where applicable, remove and discard its gasket.
11 Clean the seal housing and crankshaft, polishing off any burrs or raised edges which may have caused the seal to fail in the first place. Where applicable, clean also the mating surfaces of the cylinder block/crankcase, using a scraper to remove all traces of the old gasket/sealant – be careful not to scratch or damage the material of either – then use a suitable solvent to degrease them.
12 Use a special sleeve to slide the seal over the crankshaft, if this is not available, make up a guide from a thin sheet of plastic or similar, lubricate the lips of the new seal and the crankshaft shoulder with oil, then offer up the oil seal carrier, with the guide feeding the seal's lips over the crankshaft shoulder.
13 Being careful not to damage the oil seal, move the carrier into the correct position, aligning the guide pins, and tighten its bolts in the correct sequence to the specified torque wrench setting **(see illustration)**.
14 Wipe off any surplus oil or grease; the remainder of the reassembly procedure is the reverse of dismantling, referring to the relevant text for details where required. Check for signs of oil leakage when the engine is restarted.

11 Cylinder head – removal and refitting

Note: *Only turn the engine in the normal direction of rotation – clockwise from the right-hand side of the vehicle.*

Removal

1 Remove the battery as described in Chapter 5A.
2 Whenever you disconnect any vacuum lines, coolant and emissions hoses, wiring loom connectors, earth straps and fuel lines as part of the following procedure, always label them clearly so that they can be correctly reassembled.
3 Drain the cooling system as described in Chapter 1.
4 Remove the air cleaner assembly as described in Chapter 4A.
5 Remove the starter motor as described in Chapter 5A, then place it to one side.
6 Remove the exhaust manifold and heat shields as described in Chapter 4A.
7 Place rags around the pipes, then depress the locking tab and disconnect the fuel feed pipe from the fuel rail.
8 Undo the two bolts and remove the fuel rail. Plug the openings to prevent dirt ingress. Refer to Chapter 4A for more information.
9 Remove the inlet manifold as described in Chapter 4A.
10 Note their fitted locations, then disconnect the various wiring plugs from the components on the cylinder head, and release any relevant wiring loom from any retaining clips.
11 Undo the four bolts and detach the coolant housing from the left-hand end of the cylinder head **(see illustration)**.
12 Undo the two bolts securing the EGR valve (where fitted). Discard the gasket **(see illustration)**.
13 Remove the cylinder head cover as described in Section 5.
14 Remove the timing chain as described in Section 8.

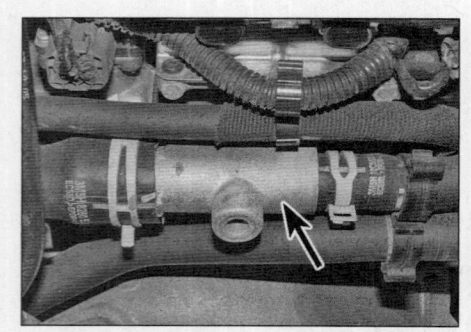

11.11 Remove the coolant outlet housing (arrowed) from the left-hand end of the cylinder head

11.12 Remove the EGR valve from the left-hand end of the cylinder head (arrowed)

1.8 & 2.0 litre engines (Duratec HE) in-car repair procedures

15 Remove the camshafts and tappets as described in Section 9.
16 Make a final check to ensure that all relevant coolant/vacuum hoses and wiring connectors have been disconnected.
17 Working in sequence **(see illustration)**, slacken the ten cylinder head bolts progressively and by one turn at a time. Remove each bolt in turn, and ensure that new ones are obtained for reassembly; these bolts are subjected to severe stresses and so must be renewed, regardless of their apparent condition, whenever they are disturbed.
18 Lift the cylinder head away; use assistance if possible, as it is a heavy assembly. Remove the gasket and discard it, note the position of the dowels.

Refitting

19 The mating faces of the cylinder head and cylinder block must be perfectly clean before refitting the head. Use a hard plastic or wood scraper to remove all traces of gasket and carbon; also clean the piston crowns. Take particular care, as the soft aluminium alloy is easily damaged. Also, make sure that the carbon is not allowed to enter the oil and water passages – this is particularly important for the lubrication system, as carbon could block the oil supply to any of the engine's components. Using adhesive tape and paper, seal the water, oil and bolt holes in the cylinder block. Clean all the pistons in the same way.
20 Check the mating surfaces of the cylinder block and the cylinder head for nicks, deep scratches and other damage. If excessive, machining may be the only alternative to renewal.
21 If warpage of the cylinder head gasket surface is suspected, use a straight-edge to check it for distortion. Refer to Part C of this Chapter, if necessary.
22 Wipe clean the mating surfaces of the cylinder head and cylinder block. Check that the locating dowels are in position in the cylinder block, and that all cylinder head bolt holes are free from oil.
23 Position a new gasket over the dowels on the cylinder block surface, making sure it is fitted the correct way around.
24 Rotate the crankshaft anti-clockwise so that No 1 cylinder's piston is lowered to approximately 20 mm before TDC, thus avoiding any risk of valve/piston contact and damage during reassembly.
25 Refit the cylinder head, locating it on the dowels. Lubricate the threads, then fit the new cylinder head bolts; carefully enter each into its hole and screw it in, by hand only, until finger-tight.
26 Working progressively and in sequence, use first a torque wrench, then an ordinary socket extension bar and an angle gauge to tighten the cylinder head bolts **(see illustrations)**. This is completed in stages given in the Specifications Section at the beginning of this Chapter. **Note:** *Once tightened correctly, following this procedure, the cylinder head bolts do not require check-tightening, and must not be retorqued.*
27 Refit the tappets, the camshafts, and the timing chain as described in Sections 8 and 9.
28 The remainder of reassembly is the reverse of the removal procedure, noting the following points:
a) See the refitting procedures in the relevant Sections and tighten all nuts and bolts to the torque wrench settings specified.
b) Refill the cooling system, and top-up the engine oil.
c) Check all disturbed joints for signs of oil or coolant leakage, once the engine has been restarted and warmed-up to normal operating temperature.

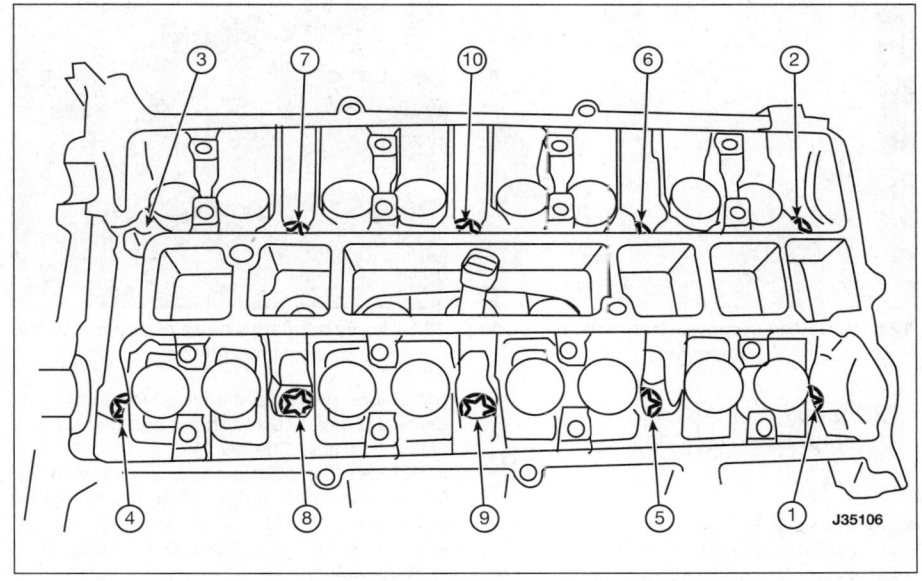

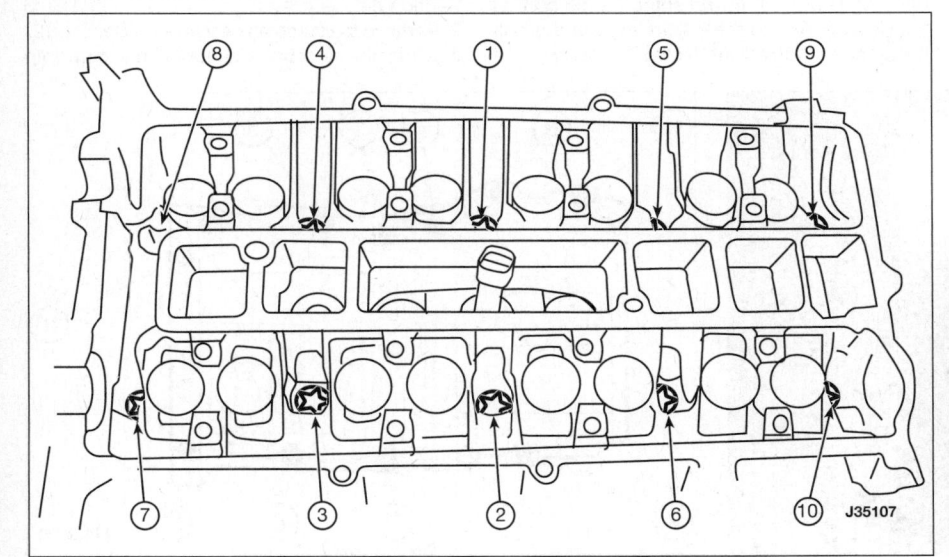

11.17 Cylinder head bolt slackening sequence

11.26a Cylinder head bolt tightening sequence

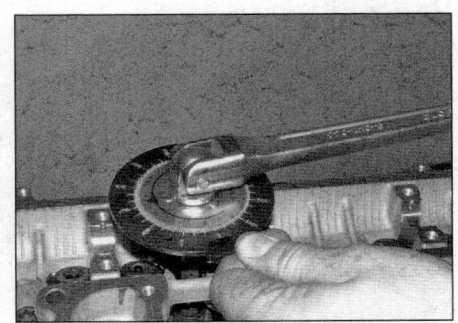

11.26b Use an angle-gauge for the final stages

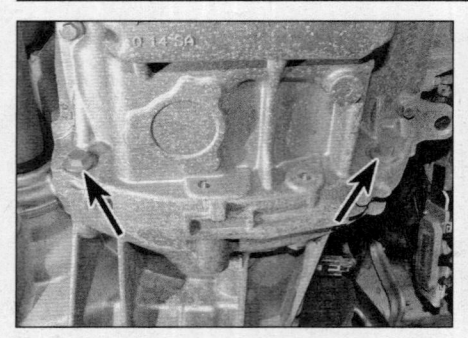

12.6 Undo the sump-to-transmission bolts (arrowed)

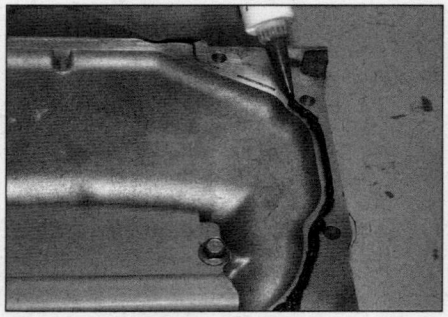

12.9 Apply a 3.0 mm bead of sealant to the sump flange

12 Sump – removal and refitting

Note: *To carry out this task with the engine/transmission installed in the vehicle it requires the assistance of at least one person, plus the equipment necessary to raise and support the front of the vehicle (high enough that the sump can be withdrawn from underneath). It will also need a support bar across the top of the engine bay to hold the complete engine/transmission unit in place while the vehicle is raised. Precise details of the procedure will depend on the equipment available – the following is typical.*

Removal

1 Apply the handbrake, then jack up the front of the vehicle and support it on axle stands (see *Jacking and vehicle support*). Undo the fasteners and remove the engine undershield.
2 Drain the engine oil, then clean and refit the engine oil drain plug, tightening it to the specified torque wrench setting. **Note:** *If the drain plug seal is damaged, a new drain plug will be required.* Although not strictly necessary as part of the dismantling procedure, owners are advised to remove and discard the oil filter, so that it can be renewed with the oil (see Chapter 1).
3 Remove the plastic cover from the top of the engine, then support the engine with a cross-beam or hoist.
4 Remove the timing chain cover as described in Section 7.
5 Undo the engine oil level dipstick guide tube retaining bolts, then pull the tube from the sump. Renew the seal at the base of the tube if necessary.
6 Unscrew and remove the sump-to-transmission bolts **(see illustration)**.
7 Progressively unscrew the sump retaining bolts. Use a scraper to break the sealant around the sump, taking care not to damage the mating surfaces of the sump and cylinder block. Lower the sump and withdraw it from the engine/transmission.

Refitting

8 On reassembly, thoroughly clean and degrease the mating surfaces of the cylinder block/crankcase and sump, then use a clean rag to wipe out the sump.
9 Apply a 3.0 mm bead of sealant (Ford No WSE-M4G323-A4) to the sump flange so that the bead is around the inside edge of the bolt holes **(see illustration)**. **Note:** *The sump must be refitted within 10 minutes of applying the sealant.*
10 Offer up the sump and insert the retaining bolts, do not tighten them at this stage.
11 Using a straight-edge, align the sump to the cylinder block on the timing chain end. With the sump held in position, progressively tighten the retaining bolts to the specified torque in sequence **(see illustrations)**.
12 Refit the sump-to-transmission bolts and tighten them to the specified torque.
13 Refit the timing chain cover as described in Section 7.
14 Refit the engine undershield, then lower the car to the ground and refill the engine with oil (and fit new oil filter) and the cooling system with coolant (see Chapter 1).
15 Check for signs of oil or coolant leaks once the engine has been restarted and warmed-up to normal operating temperature.

13 Oil pump – removal, inspection and refitting

Note: *While this task is theoretically possible when the engine is in place in the vehicle, in practise, it requires so much preliminary dismantling, and is so difficult to carry out due to the restricted access, that owners are advised to remove the engine from the vehicle first. All the illustrations used in this Section are with the engine out of the vehicle and the engine upside down on a work bench.*
Note: *In addition to the new pump gasket and other parts required, read through this Section, and ensure that the necessary tools and facilities are available.*

Removal

1 Remove the timing chain as described in Section 8.
2 Remove the sump as described in Section 12.
3 Undo the two bolts securing the oil pump

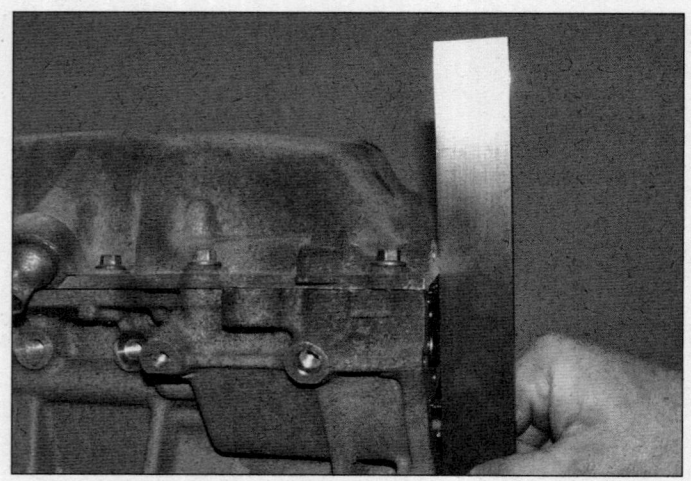

12.11a Use a straight-edge to align the sump to the cylinder block

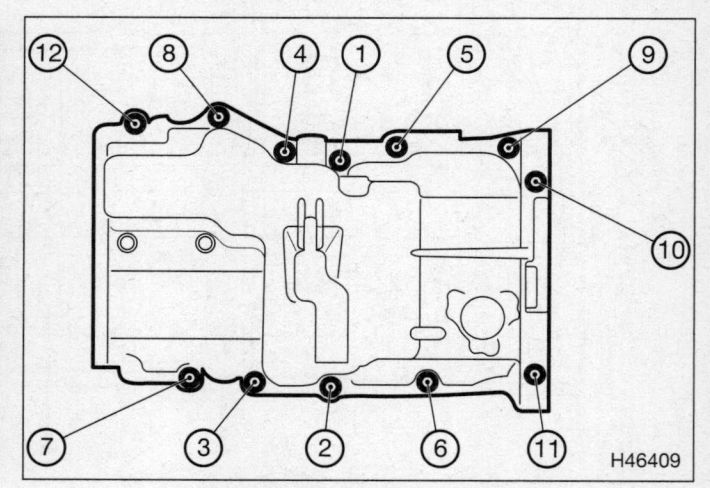

12.11b Sump bolt tightening sequence

1.8 & 2.0 litre engines (Duratec HE) in-car repair procedures 2B•15

13.3 Remove the oil pump pick-up pipe retaining bolts

13.4 Oil pump chain guide and tensioner retaining bolts (arrowed)

13.5 Hold the oil pump sprocket whilst undoing the sprocket bolt

13.7 Undo the 4 retaining bolts (arrowed) and remove the oil pump

13.11 Use one of the retaining bolts to locate the new gasket in place on the oil pump

13.12 Fit a new O-ring (arrowed) to the oil pump pick-up pipe

pick-up pipe to the pump (see illustration). Discard the O-ring/gasket.
4 Undo the two retaining bolts and remove the oil pump chain guide, then undo the retaining bolt and remove the oil pump chain tensioner (see illustration).
5 Hold the oil pump drive sprocket to prevent it from turning and slacken the sprocket retaining bolt (see illustration).
6 Undo the bolt and remove the oil pump sprocket complete with the oil pump drive chain.
7 Unbolt the pump from the cylinder block/crankcase (see illustration). Withdraw and discard the gasket.

Inspection
8 At the time of writing there were no parts for the pump, if there is any doubt in the operation of the oil pump, then the complete pump assembly should be renewed.

Refitting
9 Thoroughly clean and degrease all components, particularly the mating surfaces of the pump, the sump, and the cylinder block/crankcase. When using a scraper and solvent to remove all traces of old gasket/sealant from the mating surfaces, be careful to ensure that you do not scratch or damage the material of either component – any solvents used must be suitable for this application.
10 The oil pump must be primed on installation by pouring clean engine oil into it and rotating its inner rotor a few turns.
11 Fit the new gasket in place on the oil pump

using one of the retaining bolts to locate it, refit the pump to the cylinder block/crankcase and insert the retaining bolts, tightening them to the specified torque wrench setting (see illustration).
12 Fit the new O-ring/gasket in place and refit the pump pick-up pipe to the pump, tightening its retaining bolts securely (see illustration).
13 Refit the oil pump drive chain complete with oil pump sprocket (see illustration) and tighten the retaining bolt to the specified torque setting. Hold the oil pump drive sprocket (using the same method as removal) to prevent it from turning when tightening the sprocket retaining bolt.
14 Refit the oil pump chain tensioner to the cylinder block, making sure the spring is located correctly (see illustration). Tighten the retaining bolt to its specified torque setting.
15 Refit the oil pump chain guide to the

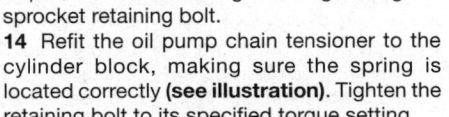

cylinder block, tightening the two retaining bolts to their specified torque setting.
16 Refit the timing chain as described in Section 8.
17 Refit the sump as described in Section 12.

14 Oil pressure warning light switch – removal and refitting

Removal
1 The switch is screwed into the oil filter housing on the front of the cylinder block (see illustration).
2 With the vehicle parked on firm level ground, open the bonnet and disconnect the battery negative (earth) lead (as described in Chapter 5A)

13.13 Align the flats (arrowed) on the oil pump driveshaft and oil pump sprocket when refitting

13.14 Ensure the spring on the tensioner is hooked behind the bolt (arrowed) to tension the chain

2B•16 1.8 & 2.0 litre engines (Duratec HE) in-car repair procedures

14.1 Oil pressure wiring light switch (arrowed)

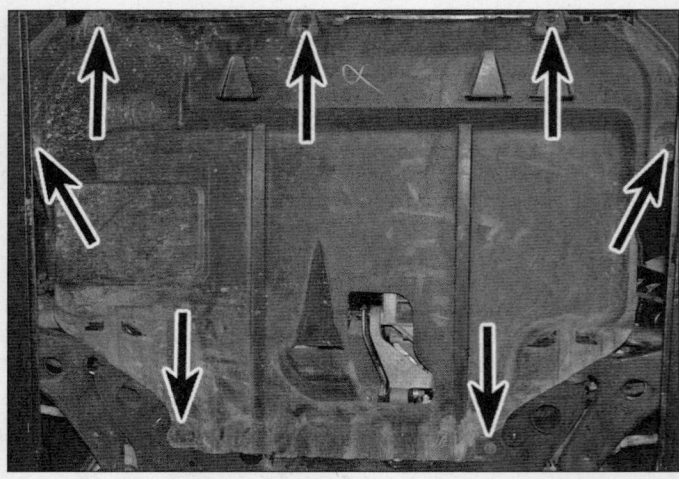

14.3 Undo the fasteners (arrowed) and remove the engine undershield – where fitted

3 If required, raise the front of the vehicle, and support it securely on axle stands, this will give better access to the switch. Where fitted, undo the bolts and remove the engine undershield **(see illustration)**.
4 Disconnect the wiring connector from the switch, and unscrew it; be prepared for some oil loss.

Refitting

5 Refitting is the reverse of the removal procedure; apply a thin smear of suitable sealant to the switch threads, and tighten it to the specified torque wrench setting. Check the engine oil level, and top-up as necessary (see *Weekly checks*). Check for signs of oil leaks once the engine has been restarted and warmed-up to normal operating temperature.

15 Flywheel/driveplate – removal, inspection and refitting

Removal

1 Remove the transmission (see the relevant Part of Chapter 7). Now is a good time to check components such as oil seals and renew them if necessary.

2 Where appropriate, remove the clutch (Chapter 6). Now is a good time to check or renew the clutch components.
3 Use a centre-punch or paint to make alignment marks on the flywheel/driveplate and crankshaft, to ensure correct alignment during refitting.
4 Prevent the flywheel/driveplate from turning by locking the ring gear teeth, or by bolting a strap between the flywheel/driveplate and the cylinder block/crankcase **(see illustration)**. Slacken the bolts evenly until all are free.
5 Remove each bolt in turn, and ensure that new ones are obtained for reassembly; these bolts are subjected to severe stresses, and so must be renewed, regardless of their apparent condition, whenever they are disturbed.
6 Withdraw the flywheel/driveplate from the end of the crankshaft. **Note:** *Take care when removing the flywheel/driveplate as it is a very heavy component.*

Inspection

7 Clean the flywheel/driveplate to remove grease and oil. Inspect the surface for cracks, rivet grooves, burned areas and score marks. Light scoring can be removed with emery cloth. Check for cracked and broken ring gear teeth. Lay the flywheel/driveplate on a flat surface, and use a straight-edge to check for warpage.

8 Clean and inspect the mating surfaces of the flywheel/driveplate and the crankshaft. If the crankshaft left-hand oil seal is leaking, renew it (see Section 10) before refitting the flywheel/driveplate.
9 While the flywheel/driveplate is removed, clean carefully its inboard (right-hand) face. Thoroughly clean the threaded bolt holes in the crankshaft – this is important, since if old sealer remains in the threads, the bolts will settle over a period and will not retain their correct torque wrench settings.

Refitting

10 On refitting, fit the flywheel/driveplate to the crankshaft so that all bolt holes align – it will fit only one way – check this using the marks made on removal. Apply suitable sealer to the threads of the new bolts then insert them **(see illustration)**.
11 Lock the flywheel/driveplate by the method used on dismantling. Working in a diagonal sequence to tighten them evenly, and increasing to the final amount in stages, tighten the new bolts to the specified torque wrench setting **(see illustration)**.
12 The remainder of reassembly is the reverse of the removal procedure, referring to the relevant text for details where required.

15.4 Lock the flywheel whilst the bolts (arrowed) are removed

15.10 Apply suitable locking fluid to the threads of the new bolts on fitting

15.11 Tighten the new bolts, using method used on dismantling for locking the flywheel

16 Engine/transmission mountings – inspection and renewal

General

1 The engine/transmission mountings seldom require attention, but broken or deteriorated mountings should be renewed immediately, or the added strain placed on the driveline components may cause damage or wear.

2 While separate mountings may be removed and refitted individually, if more than one is disturbed at a time – such as if the engine/transmission unit is removed from its mountings – they must be reassembled and their fasteners tightened in the position marked on removal.

3 On reassembly, the complete weight of the engine/transmission unit must not be taken by the mountings until all are correctly aligned with the marks made on removal. Tighten the engine/transmission mounting fasteners to their specified torque wrench settings.

Inspection

4 During the check, the engine/transmission unit must be raised slightly, to remove its weight from the mountings.

5 Raise the front of the vehicle, and support it securely on axle stands. Position a jack under the sump, with a large block of wood between the jack head and the sump, then carefully raise the engine/transmission just enough to take the weight off the mountings.

⚠️ **Warning: DO NOT place any part of your body under the engine when it is supported only by a jack.**

6 Check the mountings to see if the rubber is cracked, hardened or separated from the metal components. Sometimes the rubber will split right down the centre.

7 Check for relative movement between each mounting's brackets and the engine/transmission or body (use a large screwdriver or lever to attempt to move the mountings). If movement is noted, lower the engine and check-tighten the mounting fasteners.

16.15 Undo the centre bolt (arrowed) to release the mounting from the transmission

Renewal

Note: *The following paragraphs assume the engine is supported beneath the sump as described earlier.*

Right-hand mounting

8 Pull the plastic cover on the top of the engine upwards from its mountings.

9 Lift up the coolant expansion tank and position it to one side. Note there is no need to disconnect the coolant pipes.

10 Mark the position of the mounting on the vehicle, right-hand inner wing panel, then unclip the refrigerant pipe from the clip on the mounting.

11 With the engine/transmission supported, unscrew the two locking nuts from the engine casing, then undo the two retaining bolts to the vehicle inner wing panel and withdraw the mounting from the vehicle **(see illustration 7.11)**.

12 On refitting, tighten all fasteners to the torque wrench settings specified. Tighten the two locking nuts to the engine casing first, then release the hoist or jack to allow the mounting bracket to rest on the vehicle inner wing panel. Re-align the marks made on removal, then tighten the two mounting bracket-to-inner wing retaining bolts.

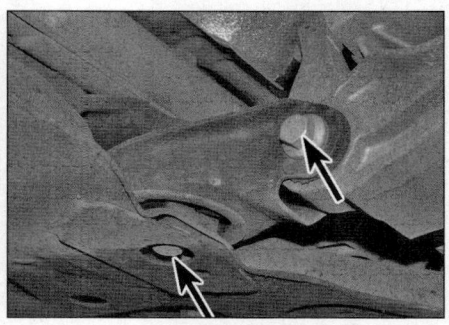

16.18 Undo the 2 bolts (arrowed) and remove the rear mounting

Left-hand mounting

13 Remove the air cleaner assembly as described in Chapter 4A.

14 Remove the battery as described in Chapter 5A, then undo the 3 bolts and remove the battery tray. Disconnect any wiring as the tray is withdrawn.

15 With the transmission supported, note the position of the mounting then unscrew the centre retaining bolt to release the mounting from the transmission **(see illustration)**.

16 Unscrew the 4 outer retaining nuts, and 2 bolts to dismantle the mounting from the mounting bracket.

17 On refitting, renew the self-locking nuts. Re-align the mounting in the position noted on removal, then tighten all fasteners to the specified torque wrench settings.

Rear mounting (roll restrictor)

18 Unbolt the mounting from the subframe and the transmission by unscrewing the mounting's centre bolts **(see illustration)**.

19 On refitting, ensure that the bolts are securely tightened to the specified torque wrench setting.

Notes

Chapter 2 Part C:
Engine removal and overhaul procedures

Contents

	Section number		Section number
Crankshaft	8	Engine overhaul – reassembly sequence	9
Cylinder head – dismantling, cleaning, inspection and reassembly	5	Engine/transmission removal – preparation and precautions	2
Engine and transmission – removal, separation and refitting	3	General information	1
Engine – initial start-up after overhaul and reassembly	10	Intermediate section/main bearing caps	6
Engine overhaul – preliminary information	4	Pistons and connecting rods	7

Degrees of difficulty

Easy, suitable for novice with little experience	Fairly easy, suitable for beginner with some experience	Fairly difficult, suitable for competent DIY mechanic	Difficult, suitable for experienced DIY mechanic	Very difficult, suitable for expert DIY or professional

Specifications

Cylinder head
Warp limit – maximum acceptable for use:
- 1.4 litre and 1.6 litre engines.............................. 0.03 mm
- 1.8 litre and 2.0 litre engines.............................. 0.10 mm

Inlet valves
Stem diameter:
- 1.4 litre and 1.6 litre engines.............................. Not available
- 1.8 litre and 2.0 litre engines.............................. 5.470 to 5.485 mm

Exhaust valves
Stem diameter:
- 1.4 litre and 1.6 litre engines.............................. Not available
- 1.8 litre and 2.0 litre engines.............................. 5.465 to 5.480 mm

Torque wrench settings
Refer to Chapter 2A or 2B Specifications for torque wrench settings.

2C•2 Engine removal and overhaul procedures

1 General information

Included in this part of Chapter 2 are details of removing the engine/transmission from the car and general overhaul procedures for the cylinder head, cylinder block and all other engine internal components.

Note: *On all engines covered by this manual, it is not possible to remove the intermediate/main bearing section or to remove the crankshaft or pistons. No separate parts appear to be available, and replacement/exchange units are supplied with crankshaft, pistons, connecting rods, etc, already fitted. Consult a Ford dealer or parts specialist.*

2 Engine/transmission removal – preparation and precautions

If you have decided that an engine must be removed for overhaul or major repair work, several preliminary steps should be taken.

Locating a suitable place to work is extremely important. Adequate work space, along with storage space for the car, will be needed. If a workshop or garage is not available, at the very least, a flat, level, clean work surface is required.

If possible, clear some shelving close to the work area, and use it to store the engine components and ancillaries as they are removed and dismantled. In this manner, the components stand a better chance of staying clean and undamaged during the overhaul. Laying out components in groups together with their fixing bolts, screws, etc, will save time and avoid confusion when the engine is refitted.

Clean the engine compartment and engine/transmission before beginning the removal procedure; this will help visibility and help to keep tools clean.

The help of an assistant should be available; there are certain instances when one person cannot safely perform all of the operations required to remove the engine from the vehicle.

Safety is of primary importance, considering the potential hazards involved in this kind of operation. A second person should always be in attendance to offer help in an emergency. If this is the first time you have removed an engine, advice and aid from someone more experienced would also be beneficial.

Plan the operation ahead of time. Before starting work, obtain (or arrange for the hire of) all of the tools and equipment you will need. Access to the following items will allow the task of removing and refitting the engine/transmission to be completed safely and with relative ease: an engine hoist – rated in excess of the combined weight of the engine/transmission, a heavy-duty trolley jack, complete sets of spanners and sockets as described at the rear this manual, wooden blocks, and plenty of rags and cleaning solvent for mopping-up spilled oil, coolant and fuel. A selection of different-sized plastic storage bins will also prove useful for keeping dismantled components grouped together. If any of the equipment must be hired, make sure that you arrange for it in advance, and perform all of the operations possible without it beforehand; this may save you time and money.

Plan on the vehicle being out of use for quite a while. Read through the whole of this Section and work out a strategy based on your own experience and the tools, time and workspace available to you. Some of the overhaul processes may have to be carried out by a Ford dealer or an engineering works – these establishments often have busy schedules, so it would be prudent to consult them before removing or dismantling the engine, to get an idea of the amount of time required to carry out the work.

When removing the engine from the vehicle, be methodical about the disconnection of external components. Labelling cables and hoses as they removed will greatly assist the refitting process.

Always be extremely careful when lifting the engine/transmission assembly from the engine bay. Serious injury can result from careless actions. If help is required, it is better to wait until it is available rather than risk personal injury and/or damage to components by continuing alone. By planning ahead and taking your time, a job of this nature, although major, can be accomplished successfully and without incident.

On all models covered by this manual the engine and transmission can be removed as a complete assembly downwards and out of the engine bay. The engine and transmission are then separated with the assembly on the bench. Alternatively, the transmission can be removed as described in Chapter 7A or 7B, and then the engine removed upwards.

3 Engine and transmission – removal, separation and refitting

Note: *This procedure describes removing the engine and transmission a complete assembly downwards out the of the engine compartment. When raising the vehicle bear in mind that the front underside of the vehicle must be at least 700 mm above the ground to provide sufficient clearance.*

Removal

1 Remove the fuel pump relay from the fusebox, then start the engine (if possible) and allow it to run until it stops (having relieved the fuel pressure).

2 Open the bonnet. If there is any possibility of the engine hoist being obstructed, remove the bonnet as described in Chapter 11.

3 Remove the battery and battery tray as described in Chapter 5A.

4 Drain the coolant as described in Chapter 1.

5 Pull the plastic cover on top of the engine (where fitted) straight up, then undo the bolts and remove the engine undershield (where fitted).

6 Remove the crash box from the front of the suspension subframe (where fitted).

7 Remove both front driveshafts.

8 Remove the exhaust manifold as described in Chapter 4A.

9 Remove the auxiliary drivebelt(s) as described in Chapter 1.

10 Remove the radiator as described in Chapter 3.

11 On models with air conditioning, disconnect the compressor wiring plug, undo the mounting bolts, and move the compressor to one side. Suspend the compressor from the vehicle bodywork using wire/cables ties, etc, to avoid placing any strain on the refrigerant pipes. On 1.8 and 2.0 litre models, undo the bolts and remove the cover under the compressor prior to disconnecting the wiring plug.

12 Disconnect the engine wiring loom from the engine compartment fusebox, the positive connection junction box, and the earth leads from the left-hand suspension turret, transmission mounting and left-hand chassis member **(see illustrations)**. Disconnect the engine management PCM wiring connectors – see Chapter 4A.

13 Pull the coolant tank upwards from its mountings and move it to one side.

3.12a Press back the clip . . .

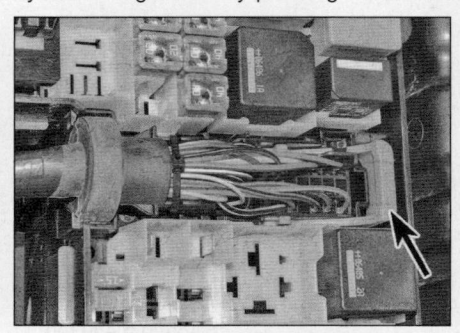

3.12b . . . then pull the locking catch (arrowed) to disconnect the engine loom from the fusebox

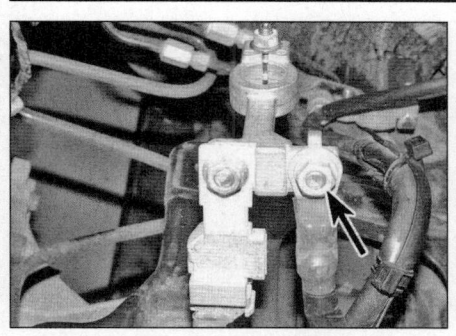

Engine removal and overhaul procedures 2C•3

3.12c Disconnect the lead from the positive connection junction box (arrowed)

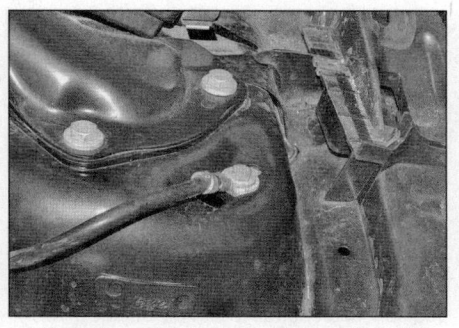

3.12d Disconnect the earth lead from the suspension turret . . .

3.12e . . . and the left-hand chassis member (arrowed)

3.14 Power steering fluid reservoir bolt (arrowed)

3.16a Prise out the catch . . .

3.16b . . . and depress the release button to disconnect the fuel hose

Models with conventional power steering

14 Undo the bolt securing the power steering reservoir and secure it to the front panel using cable ties **(see illustration)**.

15 Remove the power steering pump as described in Chapter 10.

All models

16 Disconnect the fuel hoses at the quick-release connections **(see illustrations)**.

17 Disconnect the coolant hoses from the heater connections at the engine compartment bulkhead, then disconnect the hoses from the coolant expansion tank to the engine **(see illustrations)**. Note their fitted positions and routing.

18 Disconnect the transmission gearchange/selector cable(s) from the transmission as described in Chapter 7A or 7B.

19 On manual transmission models, prise up the wire clip and disconnect the clutch slave cylinder hydraulic pipe from the top of the transmission housing **(see illustration)**.

20 On automatic transmission models, disconnect the fluid cooling hoses from the transmission as described in Chapter 7B.

21 Note their fitted positions and disconnect any vacuum hoses between the engine and brake servo/EGR/EVAP valves **(see illustration)**. On iB5 transmissions, disconnect the breather hose from the top of the transmission.

3.16c Depress the release button and disconnect the purge hose

3.17a Rotate the collar (arrowed) 30° anti-clockwise . . .

3.17b . . . and pull the hose from the connection

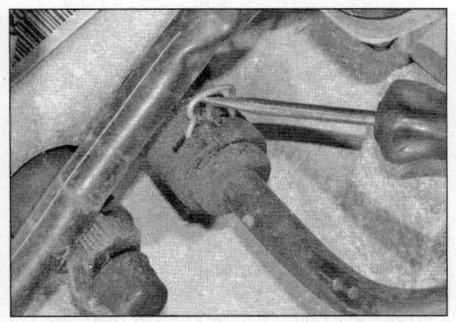

3.19 Prise out the clip and disconnect the clutch slave cylinder hose

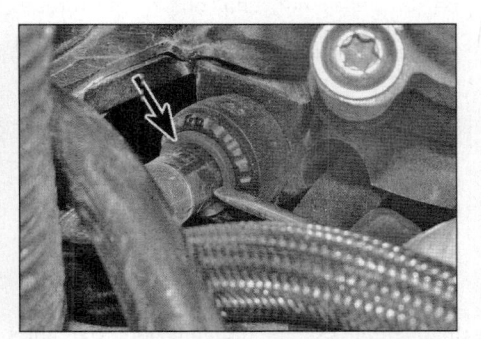

3.21 Push in the red collar (arrowed) and pull the servo vacuum hose from the manifold

2C•4 Engine removal and overhaul procedures

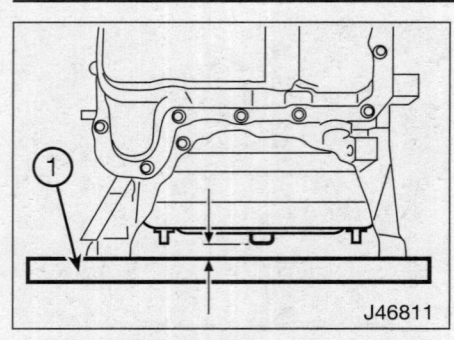

3.37 The distance between the straight edge (1) and the torque converter spigot must be 15 mm

22 Attach lifting chains/straps to the engine/transmission lifting eyes, and position an engine hoist to take the weight of the engine/transmission assembly.
23 Undo the nuts and bolts, then remove the right-hand engine mounting assembly.
24 Remove the central bolt from the left-hand transmission mounting. The engine and transmission should now be suspended from the hoist. Check to ensure nothing will obstruct the engine/transmission assembly as it is lowered.
25 Make a final check to ensure all wiring connectors, coolant hoses, and vacuum hoses that would prevent the engine from being removed have been disconnected.
26 Enlist the help of an assistant, and lower the engine/transmission downwards onto a trolley jack or similar. Once the assembly is fully lowered, disconnect the engine hoist and pull the assembly from under the vehicle.

Separation
27 Remove the starter motor.

Manual transmission models
28 Remove the bolts securing the transmission to the engine. Note the fitted positions of any brackets.
29 With the aid of an assistant, draw the transmission off the engine. Once it is clear of the dowels, do not allow it to hang on the input shaft.

Automatic transmission models
30 Rotate the crankshaft, using a socket on the pulley nut, until one of the torque converter-to-driveplate retaining bolts/nuts becomes accessible through the opening on the rear facing side of the engine. Working through the opening, undo the bolt. Rotate the crankshaft as necessary and remove the remaining bolts in the same way. Note that new bolts will be required for refitting.
31 Remove the bolts securing the transmission to the engine.
32 With the aid of an assistant, draw the transmission squarely off the engine dowels making sure that the torque converter remains in position on the transmission. Use the access hole in the transmission housing to hold the converter in place.

Refitting
Manual transmission models
33 Make sure that the clutch is correctly centred and that the clutch release components are fitted to the bellhousing. Do not apply any grease to the transmission input shaft, the guide sleeve, or the release bearing itself, as these components have a friction-reducing coating which does not require lubrication.
34 Manoeuvre the transmission squarely into position, and engage it with the engine dowels. Refit the bolts securing the transmission to the engine, and tighten them to the specified torque. Refit the starter motor.

Automatic transmission models
35 Before refitting the transmission, flush out the fluid cooler with fresh transmission fluid. To do this, attach a hose to the upper union, pour ATF through the hose and collect it in a container positioned beneath the return hose.
36 Clean the contact surfaces on the torque converter and driveplate, and the transmission and engine mating faces. Lightly lubricate the torque converter guide projection and the engine/transmission locating dowels with grease.
37 Place a straight-edge across the bellhousing, and measure the distance between the torque converter spigot and the straight-edge. Position the torque converter so the distance is 15 mm **(see illustration)**.
38 Manoeuvre the transmission squarely into position, and engage it with the engine dowels. Refit the bolts securing the transmission to the engine and tighten lightly first in a diagonal sequence, then again to the specified torque.
39 Attach the torque converter to the driveplate using new bolts. Rotate the crankshaft for access to the bolts as was done for removal, then rotate the torque converter by means of the access hole in the transmission housing. Fit and tighten all the bolts hand-tight first, then tighten again to the specified torque.

All models
40 The remainder of refitting is essentially a reversal of removal, noting the following points:
a) Tighten all fastenings to the specified torque and, where applicable, torque angle. Refer to the relevant Chapters of this manual for torque wrench settings not directly related to the engine.
b) Reconnect and if necessary, adjust the manual transmission selector cables as described in Chapter 7A.
c) On automatic transmission models, reconnect and adjust the selector cable as described in Chapter 7B.
d) Refit the air cleaner assembly as described in Chapter 4A.
e) Refit the auxiliary drivebelts, then refill the engine with coolant and oil as described in Chapter 1.
f) Refill the transmission with lubricant if necessary as described in Chapter 1, 7A or 7B as applicable.
g) Refer to Section 10 before starting the engine.

4 Engine overhaul – preliminary information

It is much easier to dismantle and work on the engine if it is mounted on a portable engine stand. These stands can often be hired from a tool hire shop. Before the engine is mounted on a stand, the flywheel/driveplate should be removed so that the stand bolts can be tightened into the end of the cylinder block/crankcase.

If a stand is not available, it is possible to dismantle the engine with it suitably-supported on a sturdy, workbench or on the floor. Be careful not to tip or drop the engine when working without a stand.

If you intend to obtain a reconditioned engine, all ancillaries must be removed first, to be transferred to the new engine (just as they will if you are doing a complete engine overhaul yourself). These components include the following:
a) Engine mountings and brackets (Chapter 2A or 2B).
b) Alternator including accessories mounting bracket (Chapter 5A).
c) Starter motor (Chapter 5A).
d) The ignition system and HT components including all sensors, ignition coils, spark plugs, as applicable (Chapters 1 and 5B).
e) Exhaust manifold (Chapter 4A).
f) Inlet manifold with fuel injection components (Chapter 4A).
g) All electrical switches, actuators and sensors, and the engine wiring harness (Chapters 4A and 5B).
h) Coolant pump, thermostat, hoses, and distribution pipe (Chapter 3).
i) Clutch components – manual transmission models (Chapter 6).
j) Flywheel/driveplate (Chapter 2A or 2B).
k) Oil filter (Chapter 1).
l) Dipstick, tube and bracket.

Note: *When removing the external components from the engine, pay close attention to details that may be helpful or important during refitting. Note the fitting positions of gaskets, seals, washers, bolts and other small items.*

If you are obtaining a 'short' engine (cylinder block/crankcase, crankshaft, pistons and connecting rods all assembled), then the cylinder head, timing belt/chain (together with tensioner, tensioner and idler pulleys and covers) and auxiliary drivebelt tensioner will have to be removed also.

If a complete overhaul is planned, the engine can be dismantled in the order given below:
a) Inlet and exhaust manifolds and turbocharger (where applicable).
b) Timing belt/chain, sprockets, tensioner, pulleys and covers.

Engine removal and overhaul procedures

c) Cylinder head.
d) Oil pump.
e) Flywheel/driveplate.
f) Sump.
g) Oil pick-up pipe.

Note: *On all engines covered by this manual, it is not possible to remove the intermediate/main bearing section or to remove the crankshaft or pistons. No separate parts appear to be available, and replacement/exchange units are supplied with crankshaft, pistons, connecting rods, etc, already fitted. Consult a Ford dealer or parts specialist.*

5 Cylinder head – dismantling, cleaning, inspection and reassembly

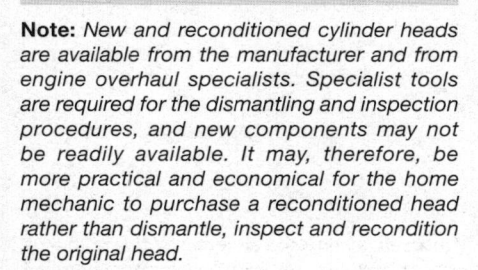

Note: *New and reconditioned cylinder heads are available from the manufacturer and from engine overhaul specialists. Specialist tools are required for the dismantling and inspection procedures, and new components may not be readily available. It may, therefore, be more practical and economical for the home mechanic to purchase a reconditioned head rather than dismantle, inspect and recondition the original head.*

Dismantling

1 Remove the cylinder head as described in Part A or B of this Chapter.
2 According to components still fitted, remove the thermostat housing (Chapter 3), the spark plugs (Chapter 1), and any other unions, pipes, sensors or brackets as necessary.
3 Tap each valve stem smartly, using a light hammer and drift, to free the spring and associated items.
4 Fit a deep-reach type valve spring compressor to each valve in turn, and compress each spring until the collets are exposed **(see illustration)**. Lift out the collets; a small screwdriver, a magnet or a pair of tweezers may be useful. Carefully release the spring compressor and remove it.
5 Remove the valve spring upper seat and the valve spring. Pull the valve out of its guide.
6 Pull off the valve stem oil seal with a pair of long-nosed pliers **(see illustration)**. It may be necessary to use a tool such as a pair of electrician's wire strippers, the 'legs' of which will engage under the seal, if the seal is tight.
7 Recover the valve spring lower seat. If there is much carbon build-up round the outside of the valve guide, this will have to be scraped off before the seat can be removed.
8 It is essential that each valve is stored together with its collets, spring and seats. The valves should also be kept in their correct sequence, unless they are so badly worn or burnt that they are to be renewed. If they are going to be kept and used again, place each valve assembly in a labelled polythene bag or similar container **(see illustration)**.
9 Continue removing all the remaining valves in the same way.

5.4 Compress the valve spring with a suitable valve spring compressor

Cleaning

10 Thoroughly clean all traces of old gasket material and sealing compound from the cylinder head upper and lower mating surfaces. Use a suitable liquid gasket dissolving agent together with a soft putty knife; do not use a metal scraper, or the faces will be damaged.
11 Remove the carbon from the combustion chambers and ports, then clean all traces of oil and other deposits from the cylinder head, paying particular attention to the bearing journals, tappet bores, valve guides and oilways.
12 Wash the head thoroughly with paraffin or a suitable solvent. Take plenty of time and do a thorough job. Be sure to clean all oil holes and galleries very thoroughly, dry the head completely and coat all machined surfaces with light oil.
13 Scrape off any heavy carbon deposits that may have formed on the valves, then use a power-operated wire brush to remove deposits from the valve heads and stems.

Inspection

Note: *Be sure to perform all the following inspection procedures before concluding that the services of an engineering works are required. Make a list of all items that require attention.*

Cylinder head

14 Inspect the head very carefully for cracks, evidence of coolant leakage, and other damage. If cracks are found, a new cylinder head should be obtained.

5.8 Keep groups of components together in labelled bags or boxes

5.6 Special pliers are available specifically designed to remove valve stem seals

15 Use a straight-edge and feeler blade to check that the cylinder head gasket surface is not distorted **(see illustration)**. If it is, it may be possible to resurface it; consult your dealer or engine overhaul specialist.
16 Examine the valve seats in each of the combustion chambers. If they are severely pitted, cracked or burned, then they will need to be renewed or recut by an engine overhaul specialist. If they are only slightly pitted, this can be removed by grinding-in the valve heads and seats with fine valve-grinding compound, as described below.
17 If the valve guides appear worn, indicated by a side-to-side motion of the valve, new guides must be fitted. Measure the diameter of the existing valve stems and the bore of the guides, renew the valves or guides as necessary. The renewal of valve guides should be carried out by an engine overhaul specialist.
18 If the valve seats are to be recut, this must be done *only after* the guides have been renewed.
19 The threaded holes in the cylinder head must be clean to ensure accurate torque readings when tightening fixings during reassembly. Carefully run the correct size tap (which can be determined from the size of the relevant bolt which fits in the hole) into each of the holes to remove rust, corrosion, thread sealant or other contamination, and to restore damaged threads. If possible, use compressed air to clear the holes of debris produced by this operation. Do not forget to clean the threads of all bolts and nuts as well.

5.15 Measure the distortion of the cylinder head surface using a straight-edge and feeler gauges

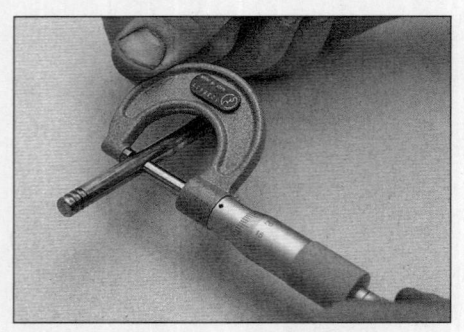

5.22 Measure the valve stem diameter with a micrometer

20 Any threads which cannot be restored in this way can often be reclaimed by the use of thread inserts. If any threaded holes are damaged, consult your dealer or engine overhaul specialist and have them install any thread inserts where necessary.

Valves

21 Examine the head of each valve for pitting, burning, cracks and general wear, and check the valve stem for scoring and wear ridges. Rotate the valve, and check for any obvious indication that it is bent. Look for pits and excessive wear on the tip of each valve stem. Renew any valve that shows any such signs of wear or damage.

22 If the valve appears satisfactory at this stage, measure the valve stem diameter at several points, using a micrometer **(see illustration)**. Any significant difference in the readings obtained indicates wear of the valve stem. Should any of these conditions be apparent, the valve(s) must be renewed.

23 If the valves are in satisfactory condition, they should be ground (lapped) into their respective seats, to ensure a smooth gas-tight seal. If the seat is only lightly pitted, or if it has been recut, fine grinding compound *only* should be used to produce the required finish. Coarse valve-grinding compound should *not* be used unless a seat is badly burned or deeply pitted; if this is the case, the cylinder head and valves should be inspected by an expert, to decide whether seat recutting, or even the renewal of the valve or seat insert, is required.

24 Valve grinding is carried out as follows.

5.33 Push the valve stem seal into place using a socket or tube

Place the cylinder head upside-down on a bench, with a block of wood at each end to give clearance for the valve stems.

25 Smear a trace of (the appropriate grade) valve-grinding compound on the seat face, and press a suction grinding tool onto the valve head. With a semi-rotary action, grind the valve head to its seat, lifting the valve occasionally to redistribute the grinding compound. A light spring placed under the valve head will greatly ease this operation.

26 If coarse grinding compound is being used, work only until a dull, matt even surface is produced on both the valve seat and the valve, then wipe off the used compound, and repeat the process with fine compound. When a smooth unbroken ring of light grey matt finish is produced on both the valve and seat, the grinding operation is complete. *Do not grind in the valves any further than absolutely necessary*, or the seat will be prematurely sunk into the cylinder head.

27 When all the valves have been ground-in, carefully wash off *all* traces of grinding compound, using paraffin or a suitable solvent, before reassembly of the cylinder head.

Valve components

28 Examine the valve springs for signs of damage and discoloration, and also measure their free length by comparing each of the existing springs with a new component.

29 Stand each spring on a flat surface, and check it for squareness. If any of the springs are damaged, distorted, or have lost their tension, obtain a complete set of new springs. It is normal to fit new springs as a matter of course if a major overhaul is being carried out.

30 Renew the valve stem oil seals regardless of their apparent condition.

Reassembly

31 Oil the stem of one valve and insert it into its guide then fit the spring lower seat.

32 The new valve stem oil seals may be supplied with a plastic fitting sleeve to protect the seal when it is fitted over the valve. If not, wrap a thin piece of polythene around the valve stem allowing it to extend about 10 mm above the end of the valve stem.

33 With the fitting sleeve, or polythene in place around the valve, fit the valve stem oil seal, pushing it onto the valve guide as far as it will go with a suitable socket or piece of tube **(see illustration)**. Once the seal is seated, remove the protective sleeve or polythene.

34 Fit the valve spring and upper seat. Compress the spring and fit the two collets in the recesses in the valve stem. Carefully release the compressor.

> **HAYNES HINT** *Use a little dab of grease to hold the collets in position on the valve stem while the spring compressor is released.*

35 Cover the valve stem with a cloth and tap it smartly with a light hammer to verify that the collets are properly seated.

36 Repeat these procedures on all the other valves.

37 Refit the remainder of the disturbed components then refit the cylinder head as described in Part A or B of this Chapter.

6 Intermediate section/main bearing caps

Note: *On all engines covered by this manual it is not possible to remove the intermediate/main bearing section or to remove the crankshaft or pistons. No separate parts appear to be available, and replacement/exchange units are supplied with crankshaft, pistons, connecting rods, etc, already fitted. Consult a Ford dealer or parts specialist.*

7 Pistons and connecting rods

Note: *On all engines covered by this manual it is not possible to remove the intermediate/main bearing section or to remove the crankshaft or pistons. No separate parts appear to be available, and replacement/exchange units are supplied with crankshaft, pistons, connecting rods, etc, already fitted. Consult a Ford dealer or parts specialist.*

8 Crankshaft

Note: *On all engines covered by this manual it is not possible to remove the intermediate/main bearing section or to remove the crankshaft or pistons. No separate parts appear to be available, and replacement/exchange units are supplied with crankshaft, pistons, connecting rods, etc, already fitted. Consult a Ford dealer or parts specialist.*

9 Engine overhaul – reassembly sequence

1 Before reassembly begins, ensure that all new parts have been obtained and that all necessary tools are available. Read through the entire procedure to familiarise yourself with the work involved, and to ensure that all items necessary for reassembly of the engine are at hand. In addition to all normal tools and materials, thread-locking compound will be needed in most areas during engine reassembly. A tube of Ford liquid gasket solution together with a short-haired application roller will also be needed to assemble the main engine sections.

2 In order to save time and avoid problems, engine reassembly can be carried out in the following order:
a) *Sump.*
b) *Oil pump.*
c) *Flywheel/driveplate.*
d) *Cylinder head.*
e) *Camshaft and tappets.*
f) *Timing belt/chain, tensioner, sprockets and idler pulleys.*
g) *Engine external components.*

3 At this stage, all engine components should be absolutely clean and dry, with all faults repaired. The components should be laid out (or in individual containers) on a completely clean work surface.

10 Engine – initial start-up after overhaul and reassembly

1 Refit the remainder of the engine components, then refit the engine and transmission to the vehicle as described in Section 3 of this Part. Double-check the engine oil and coolant levels and make a final check that everything has been reconnected. Make sure that there are no tools or rags left in the engine compartment.

2 Remove the spark plugs and disable the ignition system by disconnecting the ignition coil wiring at the connector. Remove the fuel pump relay from the fusebox.

3 Turn the engine over on the starter motor until the oil pressure warning light goes out. If the light fails to extinguish after several seconds of cranking, check the engine oil level and that the oil filter is fitted securely. Assuming these are correct, check the security of the oil pressure sensor wiring – do not progress any further until you are sure that oil is being pumped around the engine at sufficient pressure.

4 Refit the spark plugs and ignition wiring (ignition coils and wiring), and refit the fuel pump fuse.

5 Start the engine, noting that this also may take a little longer than usual, due to the fuel system components being empty.

6 While the engine is idling, check for fuel, coolant and oil leaks. Don't be alarmed if there are some odd smells and smoke from parts getting hot and burning off oil deposits.

7 Keep the engine idling until hot water is felt circulating through the top hose, check that it idles reasonably smoothly and at the usual speed, then switch it off.

8 After a few minutes, recheck the oil and coolant levels, and top-up as necessary (see *Weekly checks*).

9 If new components such as pistons, rings or crankshaft bearings have been fitted, the engine must be run-in for the first 500 miles. Do not operate the engine at full-throttle, or allow it to labour in any gear during this period. It is recommended that the oil and filter be changed at the end of this period.

Notes

Chapter 3
Cooling, heating and air conditioning systems

Contents

	Section number
Air conditioning system – general information and precautions	11
Air conditioning system components – removal and refitting	12
Auxiliary drivebelt check and renewal	See Chapter 1
Coolant level check	See Weekly checks
Coolant pump – checking, removal and refitting	8
Coolant renewal	See Chapter 1
Cooling system checks (coolant leaks, hose condition)	See Chapter 1
Cooling system electronic components – removal and refitting	6
Cooling system hoses – disconnection and renewal	3

	Section number
Cooling system servicing (draining, flushing and refilling)	See Chapter 1
Engine coolant (antifreeze) – general information	2
General information	1
Heater/air conditioning controls – removal and refitting	10
Heater/ventilation components – removal and refitting	9
Pollen filter renewal	See Chapter 1
Radiator and expansion tank – removal, inspection and refitting	7
Radiator electric cooling fan(s) – testing, removal and refitting	5
Thermostat – removal, testing and refitting	4

Degrees of difficulty

Easy, suitable for novice with little experience	Fairly easy, suitable for beginner with some experience	Fairly difficult, suitable for competent DIY mechanic	Difficult, suitable for experienced DIY mechanic	Very difficult, suitable for expert DIY or professional

Specifications

Coolant
Mixture type .... See *Lubricants and fluids* on page 0•17
Cooling system capacity .... See Chapter 1

System pressure
Pressure test .... 1.3 to 1.5 bars approximately – see cap for actual value

Expansion tank filler cap
Pressure rating .... 1.3 to 1.5 bars approximately – see cap for actual value

Thermostat
1.4 litre and 1.6 litre non-Ti-VCT:
   Starts to open .... 82°C
   Fully-open .... 112°C
1.6 litre Ti-VCT (electronically-controlled) .... 98°C
1.8 litre and 2.0 litre:
   Starts to open .... 92°C
   Fully-open .... 99°C

Air conditioning system
Refrigerant R134a
Refrigerant quantity .... 600 g
Refrigerant oil .... Ford WSH-M1C231-B
Refrigerant oil capacity:
   When refilling .... 200 ml
   When renewing the condenser .... 30 ml
   When renewing the evaporator .... 30 ml
   When renewing the accumulator/dehydrator .... 90 ml
   When renewing the compressor:
      If the oil drained from the faulty compressor is less than 150 ml .. 150 ml
      If the oil drained from the faulty compressor is more than 150 ml . 200 ml
   When renewing the refrigerant pipes .... 200 ml

3•2 Cooling, heating and air conditioning systems

Torque wrench settings

	Nm	lbf ft
Air conditioning accumulator/dehydrator-to-subframe bolts	7	5
Air conditioning compressor mounting bolts	24	18
Air conditioning condenser mounting bolts	24	18
Air conditioning high-pressure cut-off switch	10	7
Auxiliary drivebelt tensioner bolts	25	18
Compressor centre pulley bolt	13	10
Coolant outlet connector	20	15
Coolant pump bolts	9	7
Coolant pump pulley bolts	24	18
Coolant temperature sensor	12	9
Door check strap bolts	23	17
Door hinge bolts	15	11
Facia crossmember bolts:		
Inner	20	15
Outer	25	18
Side bolts	80	59
Radiator mounting bracket-to-subframe bolts	25	18
Refrigerant line connection	8	6
Refrigerant line to compressor	20	15
Refrigerant line to evaporator	20	15
Thermostat housing bolts	9	7

1 General information

Warning: DO NOT attempt to remove the expansion tank filler cap, or to disturb any part of the cooling system, while it or the engine is hot, as there is a very great risk of scalding. If the expansion tank filler cap must be removed before the engine and radiator have fully cooled down (even though this is not recommended) the pressure in the cooling system must first be released. Cover the cap with a thick layer of cloth, to avoid scalding, and slowly unscrew the filler cap until a hissing sound can be heard. When the hissing has stopped, showing that pressure is released, slowly unscrew the filler cap further until it can be removed; if more hissing sounds are heard, wait until they have stopped before unscrewing the cap completely. At all times, keep well away from the filler opening.

Warning: Do not allow coolant to come in contact with your skin, or with the painted surfaces of the vehicle. Rinse off spills immediately with plenty of water. Never leave coolant lying around in an open container, or in a puddle in the driveway or on the garage floor. Children and pets are attracted by its sweet smell, but coolant is fatal if ingested.

Warning: If the engine is hot, the electric cooling fan may start rotating even if the engine is not running, so be careful to keep hands, hair and loose clothing well clear when working in the engine compartment.

Engine cooling system

All vehicles covered by this manual employ a pressurised engine cooling system with thermostatically-controlled coolant circulation. The coolant is circulated by an impeller-type pump, bolted to the right-hand end of the cylinder block, inboard of the timing belt. On all models the pump is driven by the crankshaft pulley via the auxiliary drivebelt. The coolant flows through the cylinder block around each cylinder; in the cylinder head, cast-in coolant passages direct coolant around the inlet and exhaust ports, near the spark plug areas and close to the exhaust valve guides.

A wax type thermostat is located in a housing attached to the engine. During warm-up, the closed thermostat prevents coolant from circulating through the radiator. Instead, it returns through the coolant pipe running across the front of the engine to the radiator or expansion bottle. The supply to the heater is made from the rear of the thermostat housing. As the engine nears normal operating temperature, the thermostat opens and allows hot coolant to travel through the radiator, where it is cooled before returning to the engine. On some models, an electrically-heated thermostat is fitted, where the engine management ECM controls the position of the thermostat to improve engine efficiency and reduce harmful exhaust emissions.

The radiator is of aluminium construction, and has plastic end tanks. On models with automatic transmission, the fluid cooler is located across the front of the radiator.

The cooling system is sealed by a pressure-type filler cap in the expansion tank. The pressure in the system raises the boiling point of the coolant, and increases the cooling efficiency of the radiator. When the engine is at normal operating temperature, the coolant expands, and the surplus is displaced into the expansion tank. When the system cools, the surplus coolant is automatically drawn back from the tank into the radiator.

The temperature gauge and cooling fan(s) are controlled by the engine coolant temperature sensor that transmits a signal to the engine electronic control module (ECM) to operate them.

Heating/ventilation system

The heating system consists of a blower fan and heater matrix (radiator) located in the heater unit, with hoses connecting the heater matrix to the engine cooling system. Hot engine coolant is circulated through the heater matrix. When the heater temperature control on the facia is operated, a flap door opens to expose the heater box to the passenger compartment. When the blower control is operated, the blower fan forces air through the unit according to the setting selected. The heater controls are linked to the flap doors by cables.

Incoming fresh air for the ventilation system passes through a pollen filter mounted at the front of the heater housing (see Chapter 1) – this ensures that most particles will be removed before the air enters the cabin. However, it is vital that the pollen filter is changed regularly, since a blocked filter will significantly reduce airflow to the cabin, leading to ineffective de-misting.

The ventilation system air distribution is controlled by flap doors on the heater housing. All the vehicles have a recirculated air function, with the flap being controlled by a servo motor.

Air conditioning system

See Section 11.

Cooling, heating and air conditioning systems 3•3

2 Engine coolant (antifreeze) – general information

Warning: *Engine coolant (antifreeze) contains monoethylene glycol and other constituents, which are toxic if taken internally. They can also be absorbed into the skin after prolonged contact.*

Note: *Refer to Chapter 1 for further information on coolant renewal.*

The cooling system should be filled with a water/monoethylene glycol-based coolant solution, of a strength which will prevent freezing down to at least –25°C, or lower if the local climate requires it. Coolant also provides protection against corrosion, and increases the boiling point.

The cooling system should be maintained according to the schedule described in Chapter 1. If the engine coolant used is old or contaminated it is likely to cause damage, and encourage the formation of corrosion and scale in the system. Use coolant which is to Ford's specification and to the correct concentration.

Before adding the coolant, check all hoses and hose connections, because coolant tends to leak through very small openings. Engines don't normally consume coolant, so if the level goes down, find the cause and correct it.

The engine coolant concentration should be between 40% and 55%. If the concentration drops below 40% there will be insufficient protection, this must then be brought back to specification. Hydrometers are available at most automotive accessory shops to test the coolant concentration.

3 Cooling system hoses – disconnection and renewal

Note: *Refer to the warnings given in Section 1 of this Chapter before starting work.*

1 If the checks described in Chapter 1 reveal a faulty hose, it must be renewed as follows.

3.3 You can buy special tools specifically designed to release spring type hose clamps

2 First drain the cooling system (see Chapter 1); if the coolant is not due for renewal, the drained coolant may be re-used, if it is collected in a clean container.

3 To disconnect any hose, use a pair of pliers to release the spring clamps (or a screwdriver to slacken screw-type clamps), then move them along the hose clear of the union. Carefully work the hose off its stubs **(see illustration)**. The hoses can be removed with relative ease when new – on an older car, they may have stuck.

4 If a hose proves stubborn, try to release it by rotating it on its unions before attempting to work it off. Gently prise the end of the hose with a blunt instrument (such as a flat-bladed screwdriver), but do not apply too much force, and take care not to damage the pipe stubs or hoses. Note in particular that the radiator hose unions are fragile; do not use excessive force when attempting to remove the hoses. If all else fails, cut the hose with a sharp knife, then slit it so that it can be peeled off in two pieces. While expensive, this is preferable to buying a new radiator. Check first, however, that a new hose is readily available.

5 When refitting a hose, first slide the clamps onto the hose, then work the hose onto its unions. If the hose is stiff, use soap (or washing-up liquid) as a lubricant, or soften it by soaking it in boiling water, but take care to prevent scalding.

6 Work each hose end fully onto its union, then check that the hose is settled correctly and is properly routed. Slide each clip along the hose until it is behind the union flared end, before tightening it securely.

7 Refill the system with coolant (see Chapter 1).

8 Check carefully for leaks as soon as possible after disturbing any part of the cooling system.

4 Thermostat – removal, testing and refitting

Note: *Refer to the warnings given in Section 1 of this Chapter before starting work.*

Removal

1 Disconnect the battery negative (earth) lead (see Chapter 5A).

2 Drain the cooling system (see Chapter 1). If the coolant is relatively new or in good condition, drain it into a clean container and re-use it.

1.4 litre and 1.6 litre engines

3 Remove the alternator as described in Chapter 5A.

4 Disconnect the coolant hoses from the thermostat housing **(see illustration)**. On some 1.6 litre Ti-VCT engines, disconnect the wiring plug from the thermostat housing.

5 Unbolt the thermostat cover and withdraw the thermostat. Note the position of the air bleed valve (where fitted), and how the thermostat is installed (ie, which end is facing outwards) **(see illustration)**. **Note:** *On some 1.6 litre Ti-VCT engines, the electrically-heated thermostat is integral with the housing. If defective, the complete assembly must be renewed.*

1.8 litre and 2.0 litre engines

6 Remove the auxiliary drivebelt as described in Chapter 1.

7 Unclip the wiring harness, then undo the 3 bolts and remove the auxiliary drivebelt tensioner assembly.

8 Release the clips and disconnect the coolant hoses from the thermostat cover **(see illustration)**.

9 Slacken and remove the three bolts from the thermostat cover and withdraw from the thermostat housing. If improved

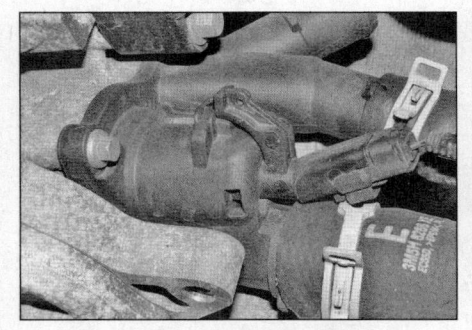

4.4 Release the clamps and disconnect the hoses from the thermostat housing – 1.6 litre Ti-VCT engine

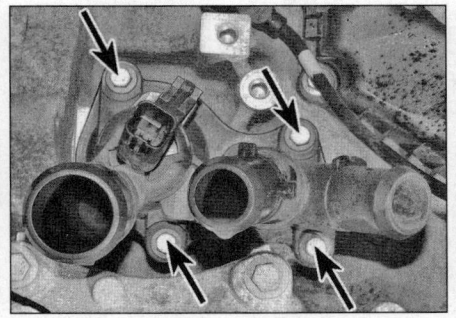

4.5 Undo the bolts (arrowed) and remove the thermostat housing

4.8 Disconnect the coolant hoses from the thermostat housing – 1.8 and 2.0 litre engines

3•4 Cooling, heating and air conditioning systems

access is required to the lower bolt, remove the alternator as described in Chapter 5A. Note that the thermostat is integral with the housing. If defective, the complete assembly must be renewed.

Testing

General

Note: *The following does not apply to 1.6 litre Ti-VCT engines, with electrically-heated thermostats. If a fault develops with the cooling system of this model, have the engine management ECM interrogated using a diagnostic fault code reader.*

10 Before assuming the thermostat is to blame for a cooling system problem, check the coolant level (see *Weekly checks*), the auxiliary drivebelt tension and condition (see Chapter 1) and the temperature gauge operation.

11 If the engine seems to be taking a long time to warm up (based on heater output or temperature gauge operation), the thermostat may be stuck open. Renew the thermostat.

12 Equally, a lengthy warm-up period might suggest that the thermostat is missing – it may have been removed or inadvertently omitted by a previous owner or mechanic. Don't drive the vehicle without a thermostat – the engine management system's ECM will stay in warm-up mode for longer than necessary, causing emissions and fuel economy to suffer.

13 If the engine runs hot, use your hand to check the temperature of the radiator top hose. If the hose isn't hot, but the engine is, the thermostat is probably stuck closed, preventing the coolant inside the engine from escaping to the radiator – renew the thermostat.

14 If the radiator top hose is hot, it means that the coolant is flowing and the thermostat is open. Consult the *Fault finding* Section at the end of this manual to assist in tracing possible cooling system faults.

Thermostat test

Note: *The following does not apply to 1.6 litre Ti-VCT engines, with electrically-heated thermostats. If a fault develops with the cooling system of this model, have the engine management ECM interrogated using a diagnostic fault code reader.*

15 If the thermostat remains in the open position at room temperature, it is faulty, and must be renewed as a matter of course.

16 To test it fully, suspend the (closed) thermostat on a length of string in a container of cold water, with a thermometer beside it; ensure that neither touches the side of the container.

17 Heat the water, and check the temperature at which the thermostat begins to open; compare this value with that specified. Checking the fully-open temperature may not be possible in an open container if it is higher than the boiling point of water at atmospheric pressure. Remove the thermostat and allow it to cool down; check that it closes fully.

18 If the thermostat does not open and close as described, if it sticks in either position, or if it does not open at the specified temperature, it must be renewed.

Refitting

19 Refitting is the reverse of the removal procedure, noting the following points:
a) Clean the mating surfaces carefully, and renew the thermostat's sealing ring/gasket.
b) Fit the thermostat in the same position as noted on removal.
c) Tighten the thermostat cover/housing bolts to the specified torque wrench setting.
d) Remake all the coolant hose connections, then refill the cooling system as described in the relevant part of Chapter 1.
e) Start the engine and allow it to reach normal operating temperature, then check for leaks and proper thermostat operation.

5 Radiator electric cooling fan(s) – testing, removal and refitting

Note: *Refer to the warnings given in Section 1 of this Chapter before starting work.*

Testing

1 The radiator cooling fan is controlled by the engine management system's ECM, acting on the information received from the cylinder head temperature sensor and engine coolant temperature sensor.

2 First, check the relevant fuses and relays (see Chapter 12).

3 To test the fan motor, unplug the electrical connector, and use fused jumper wires to connect the fan directly to the battery. If the fan still does not work, renew the motor.

4 If the motor proved sound, the fault lies in the engine coolant temperature sensor (see Section 6), in the wiring loom (see Chapter 12 for testing details) or in the engine management system (see Chapter 4A).

Removal

5 Disconnect the battery negative (earth) lead (see Chapter 5A).

6 Undo the fasteners and remove the engine undershield (where fitted), followed by the shield under the radiator **(see illustration)**.

7 Unplug the cooling fan electrical connector, and release the wiring loom from the fan shroud.

8 Undo the radiator support bracket front retaining bolts, and substitute them with M8 x 30 mm bolts, leaving at least 15 mm of thread exposed **(see illustration)**.

9 Remove the radiator support bracket rear retaining bolts **(see illustration)**.

10 Unclip the shroud from its upper and lower mountings, then lift the assembly to disengage it from its mountings **(see illustration)**.

5.6a Undo the fasteners (arrowed) and remove the engine undershield

5.6b Undo the bolts (left-hand side bolts arrowed) and remove the shield under the radiator

Cooling, heating and air conditioning systems 3•5

5.8 Radiator support bracket bolts (arrowed)

5.9 With the rear bolts removed, and the longer front bolts installed, allow the support bracket to drop

5.10 Depress the clip (arrowed) on each lower mounting and lift the cooling fan shroud upwards

11 Withdraw the fan and shroud as an assembly from underneath the vehicle.

Refitting

12 Refitting is the reverse of the removal procedure, noting the following points:
a) When refitting the fan to the motor, make sure it has located correctly before refitting the retaining clip.
b) Ensure that the shroud is settled correctly at all four mounting points before finally clipping into position.

6 Coolant system electronic components – removal and refitting

Coolant temperature sensor

Note: *Refer to the warnings given in Section 1 of this Chapter before starting work.*

1 On all models, the sensor is located at the coolant outlet housing at the left-hand end of the cylinder head.

Removal

⚠️ **Warning: Ensure the coolant is cold before attempting this procedure.**

2 Where applicable, remove the plastic cover from the top of the cylinder head.
3 Disconnect the wiring connector from the sensor.
4 Two different types of sensor may be fitted. The first type is screwed into the coolant outlet housing, and the second type is clipped into place. Unscrew the sensor from the housing, or pull out the clip as applicable **(see illustrations)**. Be prepared for coolant spillage and have rag or a rubber plug handy to force into the sensor aperture. This way only a little coolant will be lost.

Refitting

5 Refitting is the reverse of the removal procedure, noting the following points:
a) Screw the sensor into position and tighten it to the specified torque, or refit the sensor and insert the clip, as applicable.
b) Renew the sensor seal if necessary.
c) Refill the cooling system as described in Chapter 1.

Coolant degas shut-off valve

Note: *This valve is only fitted to some 1.6 litre Ti-VCT engines.*

6 This valve, located in the left-hand front corner of the engine compartment, controls the flow of coolant back to the expansion tank. In cold temperatures, whilst the engine is warming-up, the valve is closed, trapping the coolant in the cylinder head. This decreases warm-up time. When the coolant is warmed, the valve opens.
7 Use hose clamps on the coolant hoses to and from the shut-off valve, or be prepared for coolant spillage.
8 Disconnect the hoses and wiring connector from the valve.
9 Undo the bolts and remove the valve.
10 Refitting is a reversal of removal, remembering to refill the cooling system as described in Chapter 1.

7 Radiator and expansion tank – removal, inspection and refitting

Note: *Refer to the warnings given in Section 1 of this Chapter before starting work.*

Radiator removal

Note: *If leakage is the reason for removing the radiator, bear in mind that minor leaks can often be cured using a radiator sealant added to the coolant with the radiator in situ.*

1 Drain the coolant system as described in Chapter 1.
2 To provide greater clearance for the radiator to be lowered and removed, ensure that the handbrake is firmly applied, then raise and support the front of the car on axle stands (see *Jacking and vehicle support*). Remove the radiator lower cover **(see illustration 5.6b)**.
3 Remove the radiator fan and shroud assembly as described in Section 5.

Models with air conditioning

4 Undo the 4 scrivets and remove the air deflector panel behind the radiator grille **(see illustrations)**.
5 Release the 2 clips securing the bonnet lock cylinder to the front grille **(see illustration)**.
6 Undo the scrivet at each end and remove the radiator grille **(see illustration)**.
7 Remove the sponge padding at the base of the condenser.
8 Release the clips at the condenser lower

6.4a Unscrew the engine coolant temperature sensor (arrowed) . . .

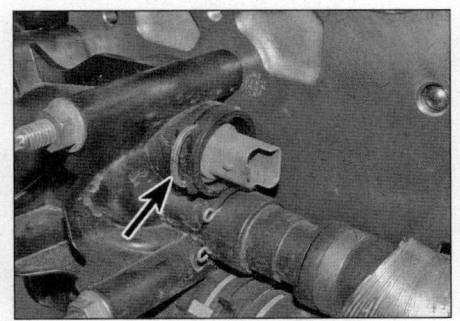

6.4b . . . or pull out the retaining clip (arrowed) followed by the sensor

7.4a Undo the 4 bolts (arrowed) . . .

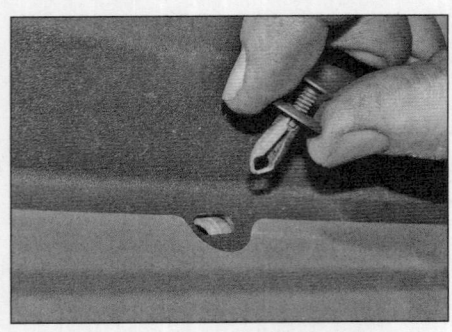

3•6 Cooling, heating and air conditioning systems

7.4b ... pull out the 'scrivets' ...

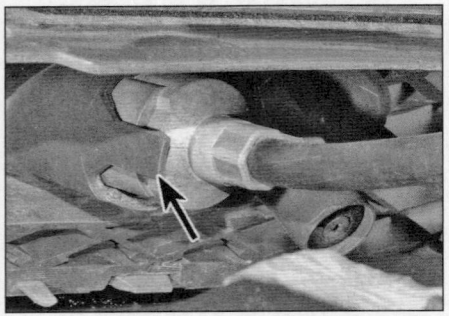

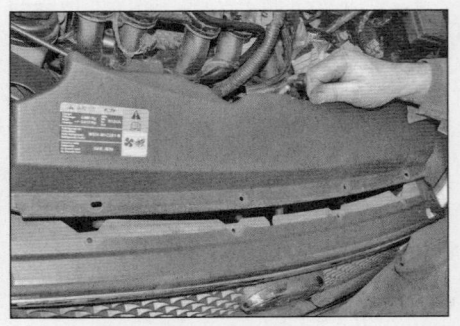

7.4c ... and remove the air deflector panel

7.5 Prise out the clip (arrowed) each side securing the lock cylinder

7.6 Remove the 'scrivet' (arrowed) at each end of the radiator grille

Radiator inspection

12 With the radiator removed, it can be inspected for leaks and damage. If it needs repair, have a radiator specialist or dealer service department perform the work, as special techniques are required.

13 Insects and dirt can be removed from the radiator with a garden hose or a soft brush. Take care not to damage the cooling fins as this is being done.

Radiator refitting

14 Refitting is the reverse of the removal procedure, noting the following points:
a) Be sure the mounting rubbers are seated properly at the base of the radiator.
b) After refitting, refill the cooling system with the recommended coolant (see Chapter 1).
c) Start the engine, and check for leaks. Allow the engine to reach normal operating temperature, indicated by the radiator top hose becoming hot. Once the engine has cooled (ideally, leave overnight), recheck the coolant level, and add more if required.

Expansion tank

Removal

15 With the engine completely cool, remove the expansion tank filler cap to release any pressure, then refit the cap.

16 Disconnect the hoses from the tank (see illustration), upper hose first. As each hose is disconnected, drain the tank's contents into a clean container. If the coolant is not due for

mountings, lift the condenser a little, then secure it to the front panel using cable ties or similar (see illustrations).

All models

9 Release the clamps, disconnect the radiator upper, lower and expansion tank hoses (see illustrations).

10 Undo the bolts and remove the radiator lower support bracket (see illustration 5.8).

11 Slide the radiator downwards from place.

7.8a Depress the clip (arrowed) on the lower condenser mountings

7.8b Secure the condenser to the front panel using cable ties

7.9a Release the spring clamps and disconnect the radiator upper hose ...

7.9b ... lower hose ...

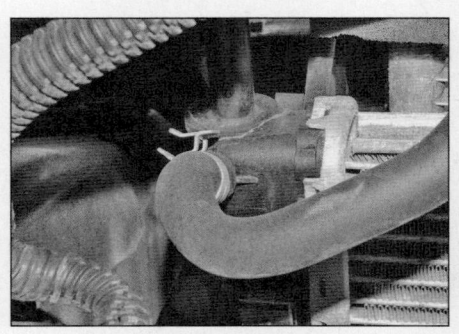

7.9c ... and expansion tank hose

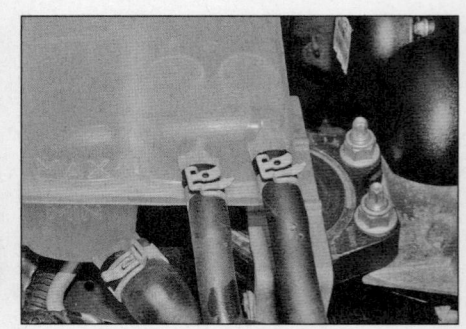

7.16 Release the clips and disconnect the hoses from the expansion tank

Cooling, heating and air conditioning systems 3•7

renewal, the drained coolant may be re-used, if it is kept clean.
17 Pull the expansion tank upwards to release it from the mounting lugs **(see illustration)**.
18 Wash out the tank, and inspect it for cracks and chafing – renew it if damaged.

Refitting
19 Refitting is the reverse of the removal procedure. Refill the cooling system with the recommended coolant (see Chapter 1), then start the engine and allow it to reach normal operating temperature, indicated by the radiator top hose becoming hot. Recheck the coolant level and add more if required, then check for leaks.

8 Coolant pump – checking, removal and refitting

Note: *Refer to the warnings given in Section 1 of this Chapter before starting work.*

Checking
1 A failure in the coolant pump can cause serious engine damage due to overheating.
2 There are three ways to check the operation of the coolant pump while it's installed on the engine. If the pump is defective, fit a new or rebuilt unit.
3 With the engine running at normal operating temperature, squeeze the radiator top hose. If the coolant pump is working properly, a pressure surge should be felt as the hose is released.

⚠ **Warning: Keep your hands away from the radiator electric cooling fan blades.**

4 Coolant pumps are equipped with weep or vent holes. If a failure occurs in the pump seal, coolant will leak from the hole. In most cases you'll need an electric torch to find the hole on the coolant pump from underneath to check for leaks.
5 If the coolant pump shaft bearings fail, there may be a howling sound at the drivebelt end of the engine while it's running. Shaft wear can be felt if the coolant pump pulley is rocked up and down.
6 Don't mistake drivebelt slippage, which causes a squealing sound, for coolant pump bearing failure.

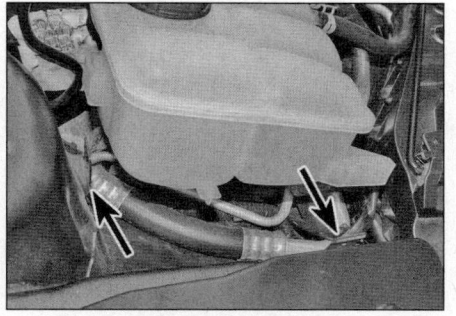

7.17 Pull the expansion tank upwards from the mounting lugs (arrowed)

Removal
7 Drain the cooling system (see Chapter 1).

1.4 and 1.6 litre models up to April 2005
8 Remove the upper timing belt cover as described in Chapter 2A.

1.4 and 1.6 litre models from April 2005
9 Remove the timing belt and tensioner as described in Chapter 2A.

All 1.4 and 1.6 litre models
10 Undo the bolts and remove the coolant pump **(see illustration)**. On models pre-April 2005, protect the timing belt from coolant with rags, etc.

1.8 & 2.0 litre engines
11 Remove the plastic cover on the top of the engine.
12 Slacken the coolant pump pulley bolts, then remove the auxiliary drivebelt as described in Chapter 1.

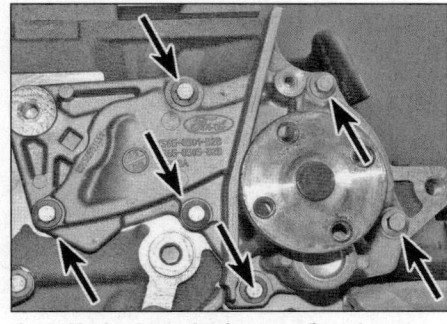

8.10 Undo the bolts (arrowed) and remove the coolant pump

13 Unscrew the bolts and remove the coolant pump pulley.
14 Undo the 3 bolts and remove the coolant pump **(see illustrations)**. Remove the O-ring seal and discard it.

Refitting
15 Clean the pump mating surfaces carefully; the gasket/O-ring must be renewed whenever it is disturbed **(see illustration)**. Refit the pump and tighten the bolts to the specified torque wrench setting.
16 The remainder of the refitting procedure is the reverse of dismantling, noting the following points:
 a) *Tighten all fixings to the specified torque wrench settings (where given).*
 b) *Where applicable, check the timing belt for contamination and renew if required, as described in Chapter 2A.*
 c) *On completion, refill the cooling system as described in Chapter 1.*

9 Heater/ventilation components – removal and refitting

Heater blower motor
Note: *This is a difficult procedure requiring patience and dexterity to release the blower motor retaining clip. It's much easier if the facia is removed as described in Chapter 11.*

1 Disconnect the battery negative lead as described in Chapter 5A.
2 Squeeze together the side of the fasteners

8.14a Unscrew the mounting bolts (arrowed) . . .

8.14b . . . remove the coolant pump . . .

8.14c . . . and remove the O-ring seal

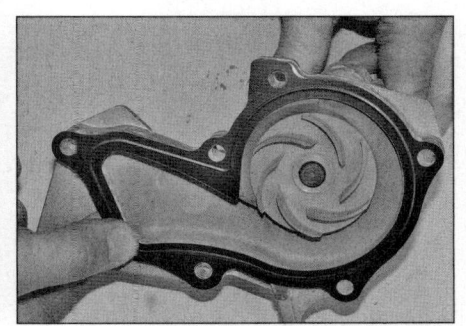

8.15 Renew the coolant pump gasket – 1.6 litre Ti-VCT engine

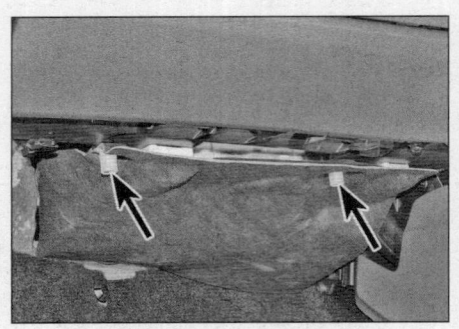

3•8 Cooling, heating and air conditioning systems

9.2 Squeeze together the side of the fasteners (arrowed) and pull them downwards

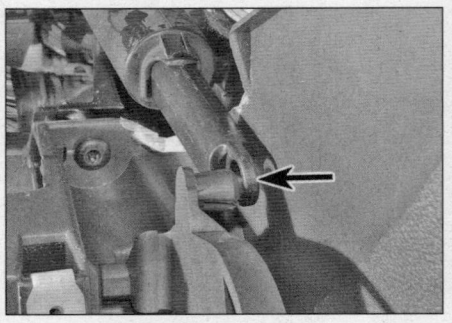

9.4 Push the support strut (arrowed) from the lug on the glovebox lid

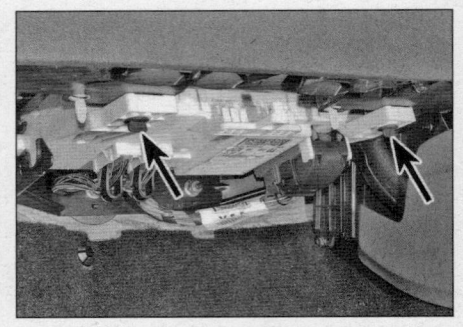

9.5a Rotate the fasteners (arrowed) anti-clockwise . . .

9.5b . . . and lower the junction box/fusebox

9.6 Undo the 2 nuts (arrowed) and remove the bracket

9.7 Recirculation flap housing bolts (arrowed)

and remove the lower passenger side footwell trim (see illustration), then withdraw the panel from the vehicle.
3 Remove the passenger glovebox as described in Chapter 11.

9.9a The motor retaining clip is at the front edge of the housing (arrowed)

9.9b Depress the clip, rotate the housing (see text) . . .

9.9c . . . and gently pull the motor from the other side of the housing

9.12 Heater blower motor resistor

4 Disconnect the support strut, then pull the glovebox lid from the facia (see illustration).
5 Undo the 2 fasteners and pivot the central junction box/fusebox downwards, then lift it from place. Disconnect the engine wiring harness from the junction/fusebox, and move it to one side (see illustrations).
6 Undo the 2 nuts securing the junction/fusebox bracket (see illustration).
7 Disconnect the flap wiring plug, then undo the 3 bolts and remove the air recirculation flap housing (see illustration).
8 On RHD models with manual transmission and air conditioning, remove the clutch pedal assembly as described in Chapter 6.
9 Disconnect the blower motor wiring plug, then depress the release clip, and rotate the blower motor clockwise (RHD) or anti-clockwise (LHD) and pull the motor from the housing (see illustrations). Take great care not to damage the motor fan – it's extremely delicate. Do not pull on the fan, or allow the motor to rest on the fan.
10 Refitting is the reverse of the removal procedure.

Blower motor resistor

11 Proceed as described in Paragraphs 1 to 5 in this Section.
12 Disconnect the wiring plug, undo the 2 bolts, and pull the resistor from the housing (see illustration).
13 Refitting is a reversal of removal.

Heater matrix removal

14 Disconnect the battery negative (earth) lead (see Chapter 5A).

Models with a plastic panel in front of the brake master cylinder

15 Remove the battery as described in

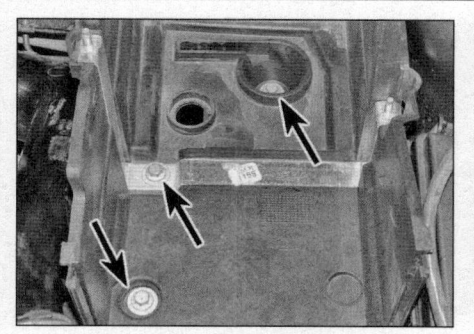

Cooling, heating and air conditioning systems 3•9

9.15 Battery tray bolts (arrowed)

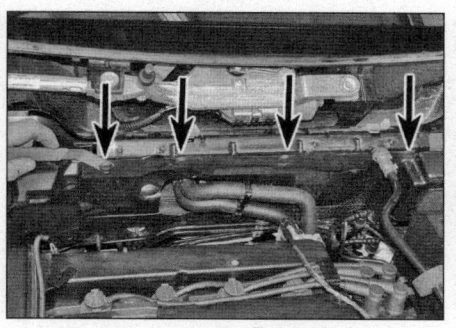

9.16a Prise out the 4 clips (arrowed)

9.16b Undo the 2 inner bolts, slacken the outer bolt, remove the nuts and pivot the cross-stay each side away

9.16c Remove the plastic panel

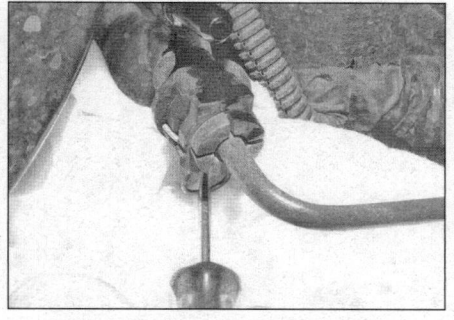

9.19a Prise down the clip and pull the pressure pipe from the clutch master cylinder

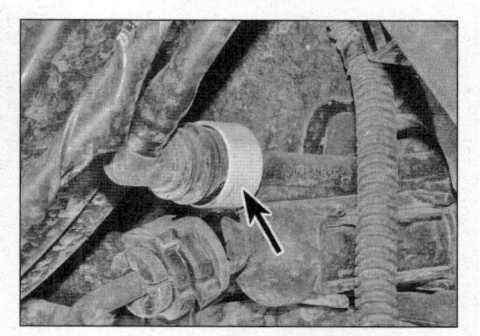

9.19b Pull back the collar (arrowed) and disconnect the fluid supply pipe

Chapter 5A, then undo the 3 bolts and slide the battery tray forward a little **(see illustration)**.

16 Prise out the 4 plastic clips securing the plastic panel to the engine compartment bulkhead, then undo the inner 2 retaining bolts on the suspension turret, slacken the outer bolt, remove the nuts and pivot the cross-stay each side away from the bulkhead. Lift the plastic panel from place **(see illustrations)**. Refit the bolts to secure the tops of the suspension struts to the vehicle body.

All models

17 Jack up the front of the vehicle and support it securely on axle stands. Undo the fasteners and remove the engine undershield.
18 Drain the cooling system as described in Chapter 1.
19 Pull back the collar/prise out the clip and disconnect the pressure pipe from the clutch master cylinder connection at the engine compartment bulkhead, then disconnect the fluid supply hose from the master cylinder **(see illustrations)**. Be prepared for fluid spillage – wipe up any spills immediately – the fluid could damage paintwork, etc.
20 Remove the plastic cover from the top of the engine, where fitted.
21 Rotate the collars anti-clockwise 30° and detach the heater hoses from the connections at the engine compartment bulkhead **(see illustrations)**.
22 Working inside the passenger compartment, remove the facia as described in Chapter 11.

23 On models with manual transmission, remove the clutch pedal assembly as described in Chapter 6.
24 Unclip the wiring harness, then undo the

9.21a Rotate the collar (arrowed) 30° anti-clockwise . . .

9.21b . . . and pull the hose from the connection

9.24 Note the earth connection (arrowed) at the top of the bracket

nuts and remove the support bracket from the right-hand side of the heater housing **(see illustration)**.

25 Remove the rear vent tube, then undo the

9.25a Remove the rear vent tube

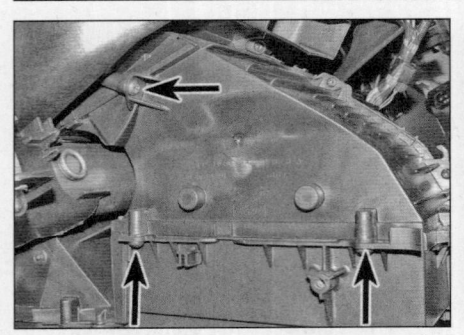

3•10 Cooling, heating and air conditioning systems

9.25b Undo the heater matrix upper cover bolts (left-hand side ones arrowed) . . .

9.25c . . . and remove the upper cover

9.26a Undo the 2 bolts (arrowed) and remove the cover . . .

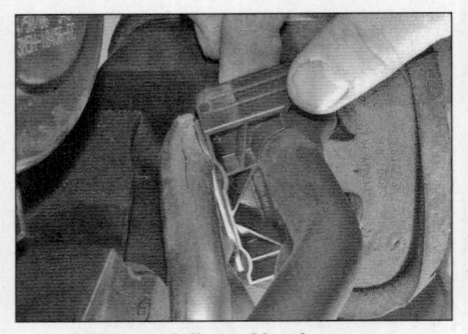

9.26b . . . followed by the spacer

9.27a Cut through the heater matrix pipes with a hacksaw (see text)

9.27b Lift the matrix from the housing

6 bolts and remove the heater matrix upper cover **(see illustrations)**.

26 Undo the 2 bolts and remove the bulkhead aperture cover and spacer around the heater matrix pipes **(see illustrations)**.

27 On models up to 10/2004, release the clamps securing the two halves of the matrix pipes, and remove the matrix from the housing. On models after this date, cut through the matrix pipes as shown, and remove the matrix. In production, these later models were fitted with one-piece pipes, whereas new matrices are supplied with two-piece pipes and suitable clamps **(see illustrations)**. Be prepared for fluid spillage.

Heater matrix refitting

28 Refitting is the reverse of the removal procedure. Note that new matrices are supplied with two-piece pipes and suitable clamps. Push the pipes into the aperture in the bulkhead, before installing the matrix in the housing, then use the clamps and seals supplied to join the pipes.

29 Refill the cooling system with the recommended coolant (see Chapter 1). Start the engine and allow it to reach normal operating temperature, indicated by the radiator top hose becoming hot. Recheck the coolant level and add more if required, then check for leaks. Check the operation of the heater.

Pollen filter

30 Refer to Chapter 1.

10 Heater/air conditioning controls – removal and refitting

Heater control panel

1 Disconnect the battery negative (earth) lead (see Chapter 5A).

2 Remove the facia-mounted audio unit as described in Chapter 12

Manual temperature control

3 On models up to 03/2007, undo the 2 bolts and unclip the heater control panel trim **(see illustrations)**.

4 Undo the 2 retaining bolts and manoeuvre the control panel away from the facia a little **(see illustration)**.

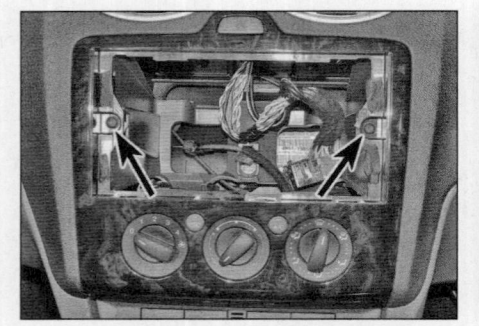

10.3a Undo the panel retaining bolts (arrowed)

10.3b Release the clips (arrowed)

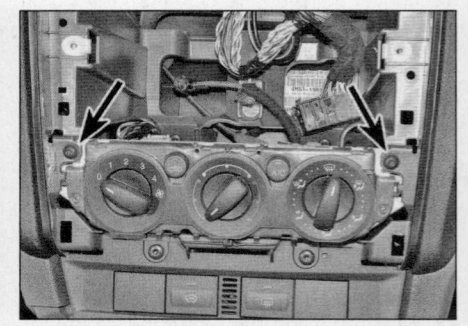

10.4 Heater control panel retaining bolts (arrowed)

Cooling, heating and air conditioning systems 3•11

5 Taking careful note of all their locations, disconnect the various wiring connectors from the rear of the panel and unclip the heater operating cables from the temperature and direction controls (see illustration).
6 Make sure that nothing remains attached to the panel, then withdraw it from the facia.

Automatic temperature control

7 On models up to 03/2007, undo the 2 bolts and unclip the heater control panel trim (see illustrations 10.3a and 10.3b).
8 Undo the 2 retaining bolts and manoeuvre the control panel away from the facia a little (see illustration 10.4).
9 Taking careful note of all their locations, disconnect the various wiring connectors from the rear of the panel.
10 Make sure that nothing remains attached to the panel, then withdraw it from the facia

DVD navigation system

11 The climate control function is built-into the DVD navigation touch screen. Removal of the screen assembly is described in Chapter 12.
12 Undo the bolt each side and remove the climate control module from the unit.

Blower motor switch – manual control only

13 Remove the heater control panel as described above.
14 Ensure the switch control knob is in position I during removal and refitting. Pull the control knob from the switch.
15 Cut through the retaining tabs and remove the switch cover from the rear of the panel (see illustration).
16 Pull the switch from place.
17 Refitting is the reverse of the removal procedure. Note that new switches are supplied with a cover that is retained by 2 bolts (also supplied). Check the operation of the controls on completion.

11 Air conditioning system – general information and precautions

General information

The air conditioning system consists of a condenser mounted in front of the radiator, an evaporator mounted adjacent to the heater matrix, a compressor driven by an auxiliary drivebelt, an accumulator/dehydrator, and the plumbing connecting all of the above components – this contains a choke (or 'venturi') mounted in the inlet to the evaporator, which creates the drop in pressure required to produce the cooling effect.
A blower fan forces the warmer air of the passenger compartment through the evaporator core (rather like a radiator in reverse), transferring the heat from the air to the refrigerant. The liquid refrigerant boils off into low-pressure vapour, taking the heat with it when it leaves the evaporator.

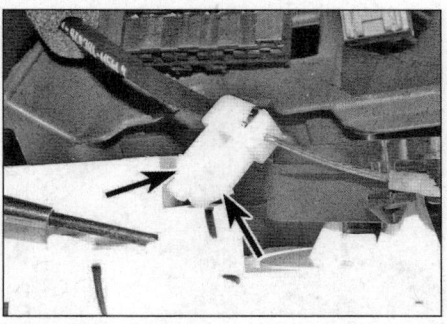

10.5 Squeeze together the sides of the clip (arrowed) and pull the outer cable fitting from the panel

The refrigerant circuit high- and low-pressure service ports are located on the right-hand side of the engine compartment (see illustration).

Precautions

⚠ **Warning: The air conditioning system is under high pressure. Do not loosen any fittings or remove any components until after the system has been discharged. Air conditioning refrigerant should be properly discharged at a dealer service department or an automotive air conditioning repair facility capable of handling R134a refrigerant. Always wear eye protection when disconnecting air conditioning system fittings.**

When an air conditioning system is fitted, it is necessary to observe the following special precautions whenever dealing with any part of the system, its associated components, and any items which necessitate disconnection of the system:
a) While the refrigerant used is less damaging to the environment than the previously-used R12, it is still a very dangerous substance. It must not be allowed into contact with the skin or eyes, or there is a risk of frostbite. It must also not be discharged in an enclosed space – while it is not toxic, there is a risk of suffocation. The refrigerant is heavier than air, and so must never be discharged over a pit.
b) The refrigerant must not be allowed to come in contact with a naked flame,

11.3 Air conditioning refrigerant circuit high- and low-pressure service ports (arrowed)

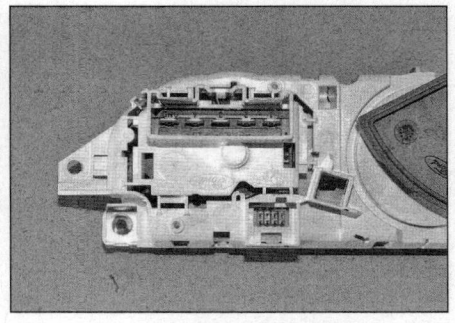

10.15 Cut through the retaining tabs and remove the switch

otherwise a poisonous gas will be created – under certain circumstances, this can form an explosive mixture with air. For similar reasons, smoking in the presence of refrigerant is highly dangerous, particularly if the vapour is inhaled through a lighted cigarette.
c) Never discharge the system to the atmosphere – R134a is not an ozone-depleting ChloroFluoroCarbon (CFC) like R12, but is instead a hydrofluorocarbon, which causes environmental damage by contributing to the 'greenhouse effect' if released into the atmosphere.
d) R134a refrigerant must not be mixed with R12; the system uses different seals (now green-coloured, previously black) and has different fittings requiring different tools, so that there is no chance of the two types of refrigerant becoming mixed accidentally.
e) If for any reason the system must be discharged, entrust this task to your Ford dealer or an air conditioning specialist.
f) It is essential that the system be professionally discharged prior to using any form of heat – welding, soldering, brazing, etc – in the vicinity of the system, before having the vehicle oven-dried at a temperature exceeding 70°C after repainting, and before disconnecting any part of the system.

12 Air conditioning system components – removal and refitting

⚠ **Warning: The air conditioning system is under high pressure. Do not loosen any fittings or remove any components until after the system has been discharged. Air conditioning refrigerant should be properly discharged into an approved type of container at a dealer service department or an automotive air conditioning repair facility capable of handling R134a refrigerant. Cap or plug the pipe lines as soon as they are disconnected to prevent the entry of moisture. Always wear eye protection when disconnecting air conditioning system fittings.**

3•12 Cooling, heating and air conditioning systems

12.9 Depress the clip each side (arrowed) and lift the condenser upwards

12.18 Unscrew the bolt securing each end of the facia crossmember to the door pillars

12.24 Undo the bolt (arrowed) and pull the refrigerant pipes from the bulkhead

Note: *This Section refers to the components of the air conditioning system itself – refer to Sections 9 and 10 for details of components common to the heating/ventilation system.*

Condenser

1 Have the refrigerant discharged at a dealer service department or an automotive air conditioning repair facility.
2 Disconnect the battery negative (earth) lead (see Chapter 5A).
3 Apply the handbrake, then raise the front of the vehicle and support on axle stands.
4 Undo the bolts and remove the radiator undershield **(see illustration 5.6b)**.
5 Disconnect the refrigerant lines from the condenser. Immediately cap the open fittings, to prevent the entry of dirt and moisture.
6 On automatic transmission models, remove the air deflectors from the front bumper cover.
7 Undo the nuts securing the power steering fluid cooler (where fitted) to the radiator crossmember.
8 Remove the two bolts from each side of the radiator support bracket (note that the condenser is also mounted on the brackets in front of the radiator), have a jack or pair of axle stands ready to support the weight.
9 Disengage the condenser upper mountings, then unclip it from the radiator and remove it from below **(see illustration)**. Store it upright, to prevent fluid loss. Take care not to damage the condenser fins.
10 Refitting is the reverse of removal. Renew the O-rings and lubricate with refrigerant oil.
11 Have the system evacuated, charged and leak-tested by the specialist who discharged it.

Evaporator

12 The evaporator is mounted inside the heater housing with the heater matrix. In order to remove the evaporator, the complete heater housing must be removed.
13 Have the refrigerant discharged at a dealer service department or an automotive air conditioning repair facility.
14 Disconnect the battery negative (earth) lead (see Chapter 5A).
15 Drain the cooling system as described in Chapter 1.
16 Remove the facia as described in Chapter 11.
17 Remove both front doors as described in Chapter 11.
18 Prise out the grommet then undo the bolt each end securing the facia crossmember to the door pillars **(see illustration)**.
19 Remove the front wiper motor and linkage as described in Chapter 12.
20 Remove the plastic cover from the top of the engine, where fitted.

Models with a plastic panel in front of the brake master cylinder

21 Remove the battery as described in Chapter 5A, then undo the 3 bolts and slide the battery tray forward a little.
22 Prise out the 4 plastic clips securing the plastic panel to the engine compartment bulkhead, then undo the inner 2 retaining bolts, slacken the outer bolt, remove the nuts and pivot the cross-stay each side away from the bulkhead. Lift the plastic panel from place **(see illustrations 9.16a, 9.16b and 9.16c)**. Refit the bolts to secure the tops of the suspension struts to the vehicle body.

All models

23 Rotate the collars anti-clockwise 30° approximately, and detach the heater hoses from the connections at the engine compartment bulkhead **(see illustration 9.21a and 9.21b)**.
24 Undo the bolt and detach the refrigerant pipes at the engine compartment bulkhead **(see illustration)**. Plug or cover the openings to prevent contamination. Renew the O-ring seals.
25 Working in the footwell, unscrew and remove the steering column universal joint pinch-bolt **(see illustration)**. Discard the bolt, a new one must be fitted.
26 Disconnect the wiring plugs, undo the 4 mounting bolts, and remove the steering column – refer to Chapter 10 if necessary.
27 Undo the bolt and remove the footwell air duct each side **(see illustration)**.
28 Undo the bolt each side securing the heater/evaporator housing to the support brackets, then undo the nuts and remove the support bracket each side. Note the routing, then release any wiring harnesses from their clips as the brackets are withdrawn **(see illustration 9.24)**.
29 Unclip and remove the rear footwell air duct **(see illustration 9.25a)**, then undo the 6 bolts and remove the heater matrix upper cover **(see illustration 9.25b and 9.25c)**.
30 Pull away the rubber weatherstrips from the door aperture adjacent to the A-pillar on each side, then remove both A-pillar trim panels as described in Chapter 11.
31 Pull up the door sill trim each side, then pull the footwell kick panel away from the A-pillar to release the retaining clips **(see illustrations)**.
32 Note their fitted positions, and the harness routing, then unplug all electrical connectors that would prevent the facia crossmember assembly being removed.
33 Undo the 2 bolts securing the crossmember to the heater housing in the centre **(see illustration)**.

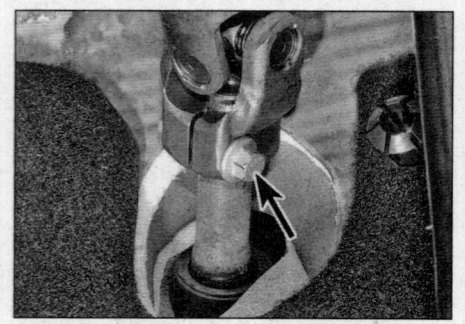

12.25 Undo the steering column UJ pinch-bolt (arrowed)

12.27 Undo the bolt (arrowed) and remove the footwell air duct each side

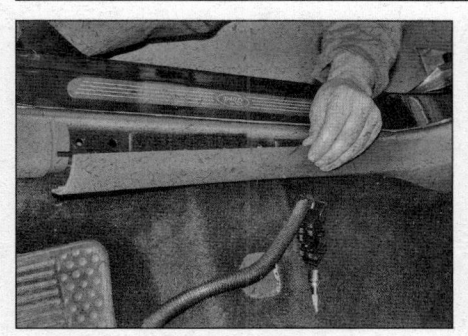

Cooling, heating and air conditioning systems 3•13

12.31a Pull the door sill trim upwards . . .

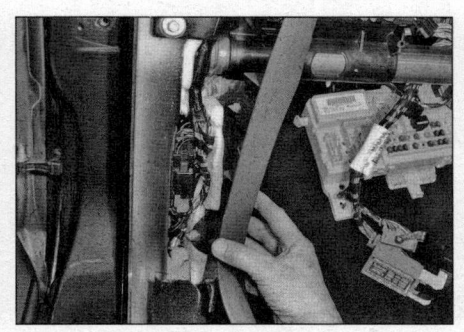

12.31b . . . then pull the footwell kick panel away from the pillar

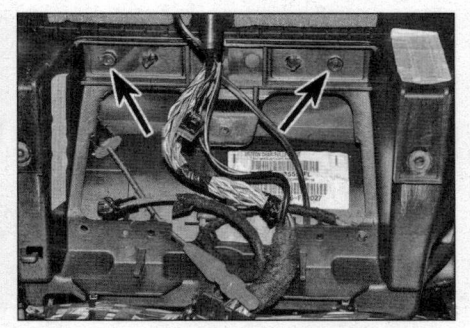

12.33 Undo the 2 bolts (arrowed) in the centre aperture

12.34a Undo the 2 bolts accessible from the engine compartment (arrowed) . . .

12.34b . . . and the 2 at each end of the facia crossmemeber (arrowed)

12.35 Disconnect the drain tube (arrowed) as the heater is withdrawn

34 Mark the position of the facia crossmember in relation to the door pillars, then undo the 2 inner bolts and the 4 outer bolts, pull the crossmember rearwards and lift it from place. The help of an assistant during this procedure is absolutely essential **(see illustrations)**.
35 Ensure all relevant electrical connectors are disconnected then lift the heater housing from position. Disconnect the evaporator drain tube as the housing is removed **(see illustration)**.
36 Undo the bolts securing the bulkhead aperture cover around the heater matrix and evaporator pipes **(see illustration 9.26a and 9.26b)**.
37 Undo the retaining bolts and remove the evaporator cover **(see illustration)**.
38 Withdraw the heater matrix and evaporator from the heater housing at the same time **(see illustration)**.

39 Refitting is the reverse of removal, noting the following points:
a) Align the crossmember with the previously-made marks, then refit and tighten the four bolts securing it to the A-pillar before inserting the bolt each end from the sides.
b) Tighten all fasteners to the specified torque where given.
c) Have the system evacuated, charged and leak-tested by the specialist who discharged it.

Compressor

40 Have the refrigerant discharged at a dealer service department or an automotive air conditioning repair facility.
41 Disconnect the battery negative (earth) lead (see Chapter 5A).
42 Apply the handbrake, then raise the front of the vehicle and support on axle stands. Remove the right-hand front roadwheel.
43 Remove the right-hand front wheel arch liner, and engine undershield.
44 Using a sharp knife cut the compressor drivebelt and discard it. Obviously, a new belt will be required.
45 Unscrew the clamping bolt to disconnect the refrigerant lines from the compressor **(see illustration)**. Plug the line connections to prevent entry of any dirt or moisture. Discard the O-ring seals, new ones must be fitted.
46 Unbolt the compressor from the cylinder block/crankcase, then unplug its electrical connector, then withdraw the compressor from the vehicle. **Note:** *Keep the compressor level during handling and storage. If the compressor has seized, or if you find metal particles in the refrigerant lines, the system*

12.37 Undo the evaporator cover bolts (arrowed)

12.38 Withdraw the heater matrix at the same time as the evaporator

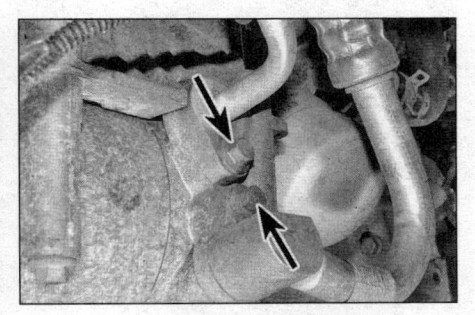

12.45 Undo the bolts and detach the refrigerant pipes from the compressor (arrowed)

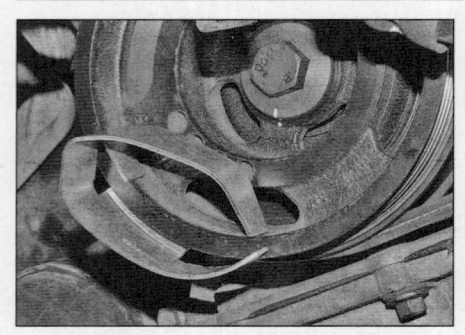

3•14 Cooling, heating and air conditioning systems

12.50 Fit the belt installation tool in the 7 o'clock position

12.51 Fit the belt around the installation tool

12.52 As the crankshaft is rotated clockwise, the belt is fed onto the pulley by the tool

must be flushed out by an air conditioning technician, and the accumulator/dehydrator must be renewed.

47 Prior to installation, turn the compressor clutch centre six times, to disperse any oil that has collected in the head.

48 Refit the compressor in the reverse order of removal; renew all seals disturbed.

49 If you are installing a new compressor, refer to the compressor manufacturer's instructions for adding refrigerant oil to the system.

1.4 and 1.6 litre models

50 Fit the belt installation tool (supplied with a new belt kit) to the crankshaft pulley in the 7 o'clock position **(see illustration)**.

51 Position the new belt around the compressor pulley, and under the crankshaft pulley, around the installation tool **(see illustration)**.

52 Rotate the installation tool clockwise until the tension on the belt increases, then rotate the crankshaft pulley clockwise, feeding the belt into place, until the tool is in the 3 o'clock position **(see illustration)**.

53 Remove the tool, rotate the crankshaft a further revolution and check the belt's ribs are correctly seated in the pulley grooves.

1.8 and 2.0 litre models

54 Fit the belt installation tool (supplied with a new belt kit) to the crankshaft pulley in the 9 o'clock position **(see illustration)**.

55 Position the new belt around the compressor pulley, and around the installation tool **(see illustration)**.

56 Fit the installation tool to the compressor belt. Note that the curved end of the tool fits around the belt and the flat end of the tool fits between the compressor and the sump **(see illustration)**.

57 Rotate the crankshaft pulley clockwise by hand, feeding the belt into place as the pulleys rotate. Stop when the upper tool is in the 6 o'clock position.

58 Remove the installation tool from the crankshaft pulley, then rotate the pulley one complete revolution and check the belt is correctly seated in the pulley grooves. If all is correct, remove the installation tool from the compressor pulley.

All models

59 Refit the wheel arch liner, undershield and roadwheel. Lower the vehicle to the ground.

60 Have the system evacuated, charged and leak-tested by the specialist that discharged it.

Accumulator/dehydrator

61 Have the refrigerant discharged at a dealer service department or an automotive air conditioning repair facility.

62 Apply the handbrake, then raise the front of the vehicle and support on axle stands.

63 Remove the right-hand front wheel. Unscrew the inner wheel arch liner and remove from the vehicle.

64 Remove the right-hand headlight as described in Chapter 12.

65 Undo the retaining nuts and detach the refrigerant pipes from the accumulator/dehydrator **(see illustration)**. Immediately cap the open fittings, to prevent the entry of dirt and moisture.

66 Undo the 3 mounting bolts/nuts (the rear one is accessible through the wheel arch) and withdraw the accumulator/dehydrator **(see illustration)**.

67 Refit the accumulator/dehydrator in the reverse order of removal; renew all seals disturbed.

68 If you are installing a new accumulator/dehydrator, top-up with new oil to the volume removed, plus 90 cc of extra refrigerant oil.

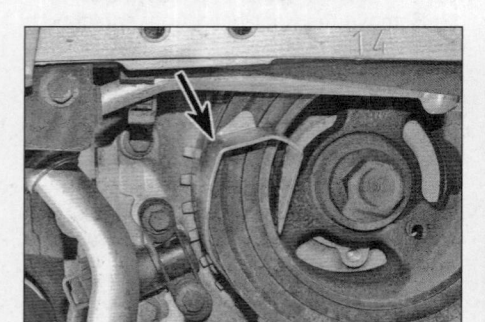

12.54 Fit the installation tool (arrowed) to the crankshaft pulley in the 9 o'clock position

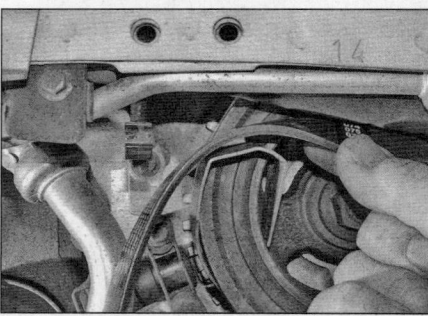

12.55 Fit the belt around the compressor pulley and the installation tool

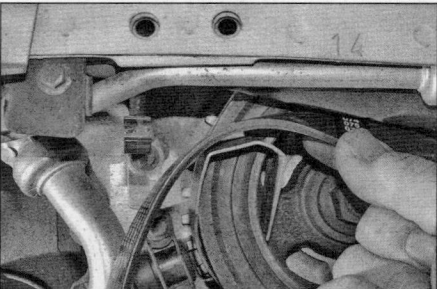

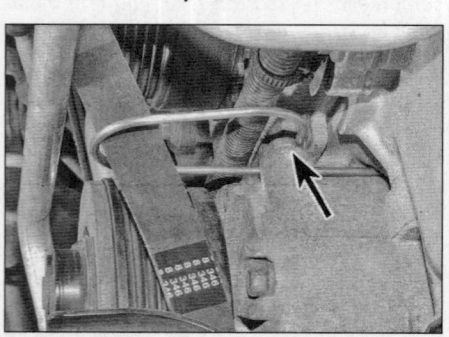

12.56 Insert the guide tool between the compressor and the sump. Note how the tool fits around the compressor bolt (arrowed)

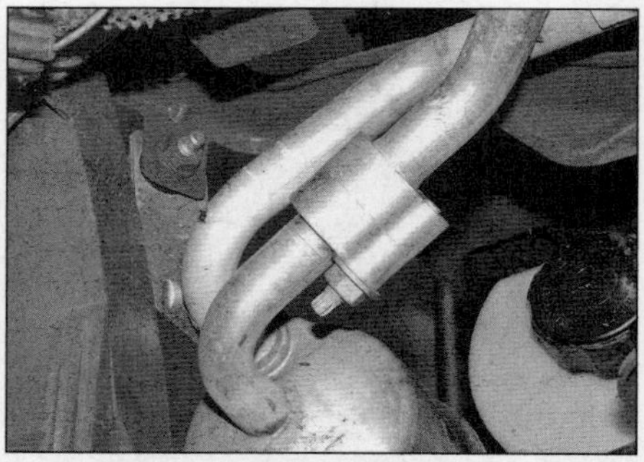

12.65 Disconnect the refrigerant pipes from the accumulator/dehydrator

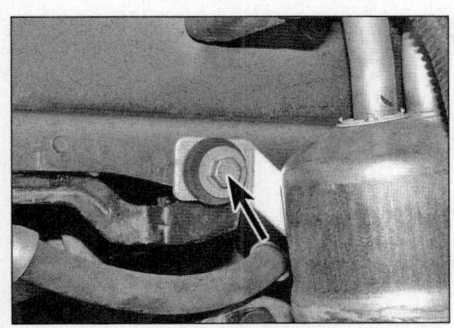

Cooling, heating and air conditioning systems 3•15

12.66 The rear mounting bolt (arrowed) is accessible through the wheel arch

12.73a Prise forwards the clips (arrowed) . . .

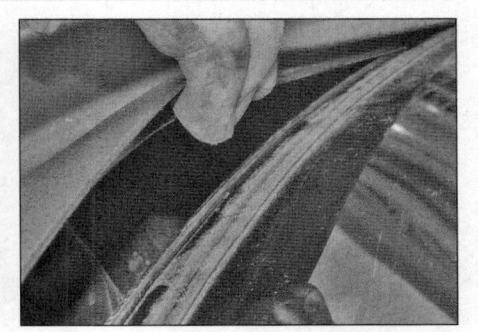

12.73b . . . then pull the scuttle cowling panel upwards from the base of the windscreen

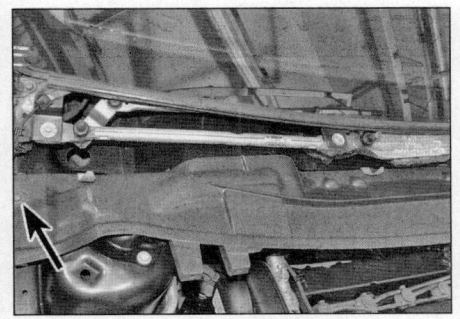

12.74 Undo the bolt at each end (right-hand one arrowed) and pull the bulkhead extension panel forwards

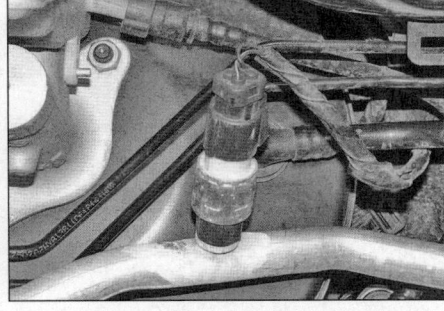

12.75a One pressure switch is located at the engine compartment bulkhead . . .

12.75b . . . whilst the other is behind the right-hand headlight (arrowed)

69 Refit the headlight and wheel arch liner.
70 Have the system evacuated, charged and leak-tested by the specialist that discharged it.

High- and low-pressure cut-off switches

71 Have the refrigerant discharged at a dealer service department or an automotive air conditioning repair facility.
72 Remove the wiper arms as described in Chapter 12.
73 Release the clips and remove the scuttle panel grille **(see illustrations)**.
74 Undo the bolts securing the brake fluid reservoir to the bulkhead extension (where fitted), then undo the bolts at each end and remove the extension **(see illustration)**.
75 Unplug the relevant switch electrical connector, and unscrew the switch **(see illustrations)**. Plug the openings to prevent contamination.
76 Refitting is the reverse of the removal procedure. Renew the O-rings and lubricate with refrigerant oil.
77 Have the system evacuated, charged and leak-tested by the specialist that discharged it. Check the operation of the air conditioning system.

Chapter 4 Part A:
Fuel and exhaust systems

Contents

	Section number		Section number
Accelerator pedal – removal and refitting	6	Fuel pump/fuel gauge sender unit – removal and refitting	8
Air cleaner assembly – removal and refitting	5	Fuel system – depressurisation	2
Air filter element renewal	See Chapter 1	Fuel tank – removal, inspection and refitting	7
Exhaust system – general information, removal and refitting	14	Fuel tank roll-over valve – removal and refitting	9
Fuel injection system – checking	11	General information and precautions	1
Fuel injection system components – removal and refitting	12	Hose and leak check	See Chapter 1
Fuel injection system shut-off (inertia) switch – removal and refitting	10	Manifolds – removal and refitting	13
Fuel lines and fittings – general information	4	Unleaded petrol – general information and usage	3

Degrees of difficulty

Easy, suitable for novice with little experience	Fairly easy, suitable for beginner with some experience	Fairly difficult, suitable for competent DIY mechanic	Difficult, suitable for experienced DIY mechanic	Very difficult, suitable for expert DIY or professional

Specifications

General
System type	Sequential multiport fuel indirect injection
Fuel octane requirement	95 RON unleaded
Regulated fuel pressure (nominal)	380 kpa (55 psi)

Torque wrench settings

	Nm	lbf ft
Accelerator pedal assembly nuts	8	6
Camshaft position sensor	8	6
Catalytic converter support bracket bolts	25	18
Crankshaft position sensor	8	6
Exhaust heat shield bolts	25	18
Exhaust manifold:		
Manifold nuts (to cylinder head)	48	35
Manifold to exhaust flexible section	48	35
Floor panel brace bolts	30	22
Fuel pulse damper (1.4 and 1.6 litre engines only)	10	7
Fuel rail mounting bolts:		
1.4 and 1.6 litre engines	15	11
1.8 and 2.0 litre engines	25	18
Fuel tank strap retaining bolts	25	18
Inlet manifold nuts/bolts:		
1.4 and 1.6 litre non-Ti-VCT engines	18	13
1.6 litre Ti-VCT engines	15	11
1.8 and 2.0 litre engines	Not available	
Oxygen sensors	48	35
Throttle body retaining bolts	10	7
Variable camshaft timing oil control solenoid (Ti-VCT engine only)	10	7

4A•2 Fuel and exhaust systems

1 General information and precautions

General information

The fuel system consists of a fuel tank (mounted under the floor, beneath the rear seats), fuel hoses, an electric fuel pump mounted in the fuel tank, and a sequential electronic fuel injection system controlled by an engine management electronic control unit (Powertrain Control Module).

The electric fuel pump supplies fuel under pressure to the fuel rail, which distributes fuel to the injectors. A pressure regulator integral with the pump controls the system pressure. From the fuel rail, fuel is injected into the inlet ports, just above the inlet valves, by four fuel injectors. The fuel rail is mounted to the cylinder head, just above the plastic inlet manifold.

The amount of fuel supplied by the injectors is precisely controlled by the Powertrain Control Module (PCM). The module uses the signals from the crankshaft position sensor and the camshaft position sensor to trigger each injector separately in cylinder firing order (sequential injection), with benefits in terms of better fuel economy and leaner exhaust emissions.

The Powertrain Control Module is the heart of the entire engine management system, controlling the fuel injection, ignition and emissions control systems. The module receives information from various sensors which is then computed and compared with preset values stored in its memory to determine the required period of injection.

Information on crankshaft position and engine speed is generated by a crankshaft position sensor. The inductive head of the sensor runs just above the engine flywheel and scans a series of protrusions on the flywheel periphery. As the crankshaft rotates, the sensor transmits a pulse to the system's ignition module every time a protrusion passes it. There is one missing protrusion in the flywheel periphery at a point corresponding to 90° BTDC. The ignition module recognises the absence of a pulse from the crankshaft position sensor at this point to establish a reference mark for crankshaft position. Similarly, the time interval between absent pulses is used to determine engine speed. This information is then fed to the Powertrain Control Module for further processing.

On all engines except the 1.6 litre Ti-VCT, the camshaft position sensor is located in the cylinder head so that it registers with a lobe on the camshaft. On 1.6 litre Ti-VCT engines, 2 camshaft position sensors are fitted, as each camshaft is fitted with variable timing units. The camshaft position sensor functions in the same way as the crankshaft position sensor, producing a series of pulses; this gives the Powertrain Control Module a reference point, to enable it to determine the firing order and operate the injectors in the appropriate sequence.

Engine temperature information is supplied by the coolant temperature sensor. The sensor is an NTC (Negative Temperature Coefficient) thermistor – that is, a semi-conductor whose electrical resistance decreases as its temperature increases. The sensor provides the Powertrain Control Module with a constantly-varying (analogue) voltage signal, corresponding to the temperature of the engine coolant. This is used to refine the calculations made by the module when determining the correct amount of fuel required to achieve the ideal air/fuel mixture ratio.

Inlet air temperature and density information for air/fuel mixture ratio calculations is provided by a temperature and manifold absolute pressure (TMAP) sensor. The TMAP sensor is located on the throttle housing, and consists of a pressure transducer and a temperature sensor which directly supersedes the mass airflow and inlet air temperature sensors. The TMAP sensor provides information to the Powertrain Control Module relating to inlet manifold vacuum and barometric pressure, and the temperature of the air in the inlet manifold. When the ignition is switched on with the engine stopped, the sensor calculates barometric pressure and, when the engine is running, the sensor calculates inlet manifold vacuum. Note that 1.6 litre Ti-VCT engines are fitted with a mass airflow sensor in the outlet duct from the air cleaner housing.

The throttle valve inside the throttle housing is controlled by the driver with the accelerator pedal. As the valve opens, the amount of air that can pass through the system increases. As the throttle valve opens further, the TMAP sensor signal alters, and the Powertrain Control Module opens each injector for a longer duration, to increase the amount of fuel delivered to the inlet ports.

All models features a throttle which is electronically-controlled – an accelerator cable is not fitted. Instead, a throttle position sensor fitted to the accelerator pedal provides the Powertrain Control Module with the throttle opening signal, and this is relayed to a motor-driven throttle valve. This system also enables the PCM to control the engine idle speed, varying the throttle opening as required by changes in engine temperature and load.

On all models, roadspeed is monitored by the ABS wheel sensors.

The clutch pedal position is monitored by a switch fitted to the pedal bracket. This sends a signal to the Powertrain Control Module.

A pressure-operated switch is screwed into the power steering system's high-pressure pipe. The switch sends a signal to the Powertrain Control Module to increase engine speed to maintain idle speed as pressure in the system rises – typically, when the steering is near full-lock.

Oxygen sensors in the exhaust system provides the module with constant feedback – 'closed-loop' control – which enables it to adjust the mixture to provide the best possible operating conditions for the catalytic converter. A further sensor is fitted, downstream of the converter, to monitor the converter's operation, and this provides an even finer degree of emission control.

The air inlet side of the system consists of an air cleaner housing, an inlet hose and duct, and a throttle housing.

Both the idle speed and mixture are under the control of the Powertrain Control Module, and cannot be adjusted.

Precautions

Before disconnecting any of the fuel injection system sensor wiring plugs, ensure at least that the ignition is switched off (ideally, disconnect the battery). If this is not done, it could result in a fault code being logged in the system memory, and may even cause damage to the component concerned.

Residual pressure will remain in the fuel lines long after the car was last used. When disconnecting any fuel line, first depressurise the fuel system as described in Section 2.

⚠️ **Warning: Many of the procedures in this Chapter require the removal of fuel lines and connections, which may result in some fuel spillage. Before carrying out any operation on the fuel system, refer to the precautions given in 'Safety first!' at the beginning of this manual, and follow them implicitly. Petrol is a highly-dangerous and volatile liquid, and the precautions necessary when handling it cannot be overstressed.**

2 Fuel system – depressurisation

⚠️ **Warning: The following procedure will merely relieve the pressure in the fuel system – remember that fuel will still be present in the system components, and take precautions accordingly before disconnecting any of them.**

Note: *Refer to the warning note in Section 1 before proceeding.*

1 The fuel system referred to in this Chapter is defined as the fuel tank and tank-mounted fuel pump/fuel gauge sender unit, the fuel filter, the fuel injector, and the metal pipes and flexible hoses of the fuel lines between these components. All these contain fuel, which will be under pressure while the engine is running and/or while the ignition is switched on.

2 The pressure will remain for some time after the ignition has been switched off, and must be relieved before any of these components is disturbed for servicing work.

3 The simplest depressurisation method is to disconnect the fuel pump electrical supply by removing the fuel pump fuse (refer to the wiring diagrams or the label on the engine

Fuel and exhaust systems 4A•3

compartment fusebox for exact location) and starting the engine; allow the engine to idle until it stops through lack of fuel. Turn the engine over once or twice on the starter to ensure that all pressure is released, then switch off the ignition; do not forget to refit the fuse when work is complete.

4 If an adapter is available to fit the Schrader-type valve on the fuel rail pressure test/release fitting (identifiable by its blue plastic cap, and located on the union of the fuel feed line and the fuel rail), this may be used to release the fuel pressure. The Ford adapter (tool number 23-033) operates like to a drain tap – turning the tap clockwise releases the pressure. If the adapter is not available, place cloth rags around the valve, then remove the cap and allow the fuel pressure to dissipate. Refit the cap on completion.

5 Note that, once the fuel system has been depressurised and drained (even partially), it will take significantly longer to restart the engine – perhaps several seconds of cranking – before the system is refilled and pressure restored.

3 Unleaded petrol – general information and usage

All petrol models are designed to run on fuel with a minimum octane rating of 95 (RON). All models have a catalytic converter, and so must be run on unleaded fuel **only**. Under no circumstances should leaded fuel (UK '4-star' or LRP) be used, as this will damage the converter.

Super unleaded petrol (98 octane) can also be used in all models if wished, though there is no advantage in doing so.

4 Fuel lines and fittings – general information

Note: *Refer to the warning note in Section 1 before proceeding.*

Quick-release couplings

1 Quick-release couplings are employed at many of the unions in the fuel feed and return lines.
2 Before disconnecting any fuel system component, relieve the residual pressure in the system (see Section 2), and equalise tank pressure by removing the fuel filler cap.

⚠ **Warning:** *This procedure will merely relieve the increased pressure necessary for the engine to run – remember that fuel will still be present in the system components, and take precautions accordingly before disconnecting any of them.*

3 Release the protruding locking lugs on each union by squeezing them together and carefully pulling the coupling apart (see illustration). Use rag to soak up any spilt fuel.

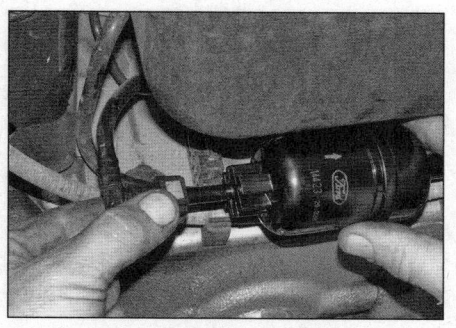

4.3 Squeeze the quick-release connectors to release them

Where the unions are colour-coded, the pipes cannot be confused. Where both unions are the same colour, note carefully which pipe is connected to which, and ensure that they are correctly reconnected on refitting.
4 To reconnect one of these couplings, press them firmly together. Switch the ignition on and off five times to pressurise the system, and check for any sign of fuel leakage around the disturbed coupling before attempting to start the engine.

Checking fuel lines

5 Checking procedures for the fuel lines are included in Chapter 1, Section 11.

Component renewal

6 If any damaged sections are to be renewed, use original-equipment hoses or pipes, constructed from exactly the same material as the section being renewed. Do not install substitutes constructed from inferior or inappropriate material; this could cause a fuel leak or a fire.
7 Before detaching or disconnecting any part of the fuel system, note the routing of all hoses and pipes, and the orientation of all clamps and clips. New sections must be installed in exactly the same manner.
8 Before disconnecting any part of the fuel system be sure to relieve the fuel system pressure (see Section 2), and equalise tank pressure by removing the fuel filler cap. Also disconnect the battery negative (earth) lead – see Chapter 5A. Cover the fitting being disconnected with a rag, to absorb any fuel that may spray out.

5 Air cleaner assembly – removal and refitting

1.4 and 1.6 litre non-Ti-VCT

1 Slacken the clamp at each end and remove the air cleaner outlet tube (see illustration).
2 Unhook the rubber retaining ring (see illustration).
3 Pull the collar away from the air cleaner assembly, and disconnect the crankcase ventilation hose from the air cleaner (see illustration).
4 On later models, undo the 4 scrivets and remove the air deflector panel above the radiator grille (see illustration).
5 Pull the air cleaner upwards to remove it. The pegs on the base of the cleaner fit into

5.1 Release the clamps (arrowed) and remove the outlet tube

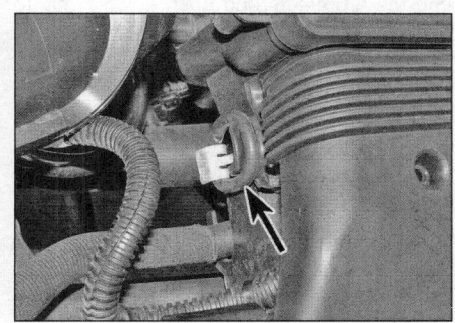

5.2 Unhook the rubber ring (arrowed)

5.3 Pull the collar and disconnect the ventilation hose

5.4 Undo the scrivets (arrowed) and remove the air deflector panel

4A•4 Fuel and exhaust systems

5.7 Prise up the red locking catch and disconnect the wiring plug

5.8 Slacken the outlet hose clamps (arrowed)

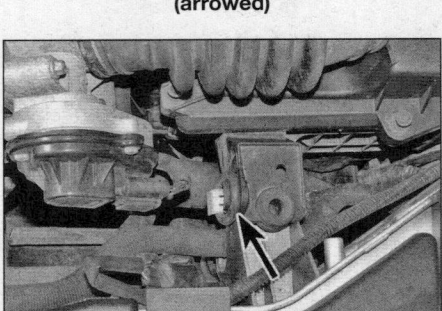

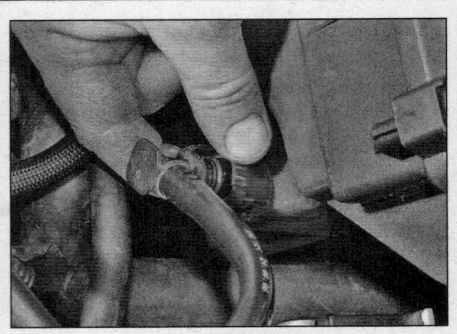

5.10 Squeeze together the sides of the collar and pull the ventilation hose from the air cleaner

5.15 Use a small screwdriver to prise apart the hose clips

5.16 Release the rubber strap (arrowed)

rubber grommets. These pegs may prove troublesome to release, and some effort may be needed – take care to avoid personal injury.

6 When refitting, locate the air cleaner pegs into the grommets and push down firmly to engage them in the grommets. Make sure the air cleaner duct clamps are securely refitted/tightened to prevent air leaks.

1.6 litre Ti-VCT

7 Disconnect the mass airflow sensor wiring plug, located in the outlet from the air cleaner cover **(see illustration)**.
8 Slacken the clamps and remove the air outlet hose from the between the air cleaner and the throttle body **(see illustration)**.
9 Disconnect the wiring plug from the coolant degas flow control valve (where fitted), then unclip the pipes, remove the 2 retaining bolts, and move the valve to one side.

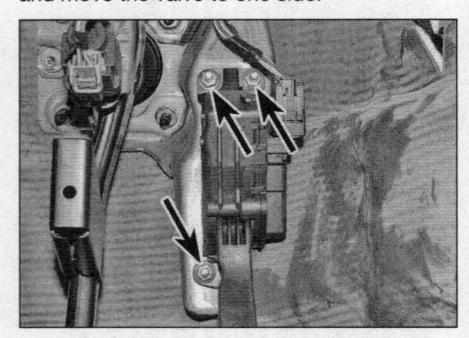

6.3 Accelerator pedal/sensor assembly mounting nuts (arrowed)

10 Squeeze together the sides of the collar and pull off the crankcase ventilation hose from the rear of the air cleaner **(see illustration)**.
11 Unhook the rubber retaining ring at the front right-hand corner of the air cleaner assembly **(see Illustration 5.2)**.
12 Pull the air cleaner upwards to remove it. The pegs on the base of the cleaner fit into rubber grommets. These pegs may prove troublesome to release, and some effort may be needed – take care to avoid personal injury.
13 When refitting, locate the air cleaner pegs into the grommets and push down firmly to engage them in the grommets. Make sure the air cleaner duct clamps are securely refitted/tightened to prevent air leaks.

1.8 and 2.0 litre

14 Remove the plastic cover from the top of the engine by pulling it upwards from its mountings.
15 Release the clips and remove the air cleaner outlet ducting **(see illustration)**.
16 Detach the rubber strap at the front of the housing **(see illustration)**.
17 Pull the air cleaner upwards from it rubber mountings. Squeeze together the sides of the collar and disconnect the crankcase ventilation hose from the air cleaner housing as it's withdrawn.
18 When refitting, locate the pegs on the base of the air cleaner housing into the mounting grommets and push the housing firmly downwards.

6 Accelerator pedal – removal and refitting

Removal

1 Remove the driver's side facia lower panel, as described in Chapter 11.
2 Disconnect the battery negative lead as described in Chapter 5A.
3 Disconnect the wiring plug from the throttle position sensor, then unscrew the 3 mounting nuts and remove the pedal/sensor assembly from the bulkhead studs **(see illustration)**. Note that the sensor is not available separately from the pedal assembly. **Note:** *Ford insist that the sensor wiring plug can only be disconnected 10 times before is becomes irreversibly damaged. Use a marker pen to record each disconnection on the side of the connector. Only disconnect the plug if it's absolutely necessary.*

Refitting

4 Refit in the reverse order of removal. On completion, check the action of the pedal to ensure that the throttle has full unrestricted movement, and fully returns when released.
5 Reconnect the battery as described in Chapter 5A.

7 Fuel tank – removal, inspection and refitting

Note: *Refer to the warning note in Section 1 before proceeding.*

Removal

1 Run the fuel level as low as possible prior to removing the tank. There is no drain plug fitted (and syphoning may prove difficult) but it may be possible to partially drain the tank.
2 Relieve the residual pressure in the fuel system (see Section 2), and equalise tank pressure by removing the fuel filler cap.
3 Disconnect the battery negative (earth) lead (see Chapter 5A).
4 Chock the front wheels, then jack up the rear of the car and support it on axle stands

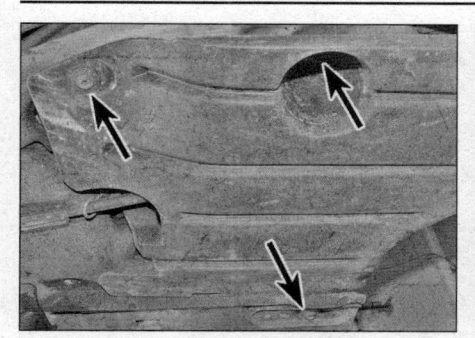

Fuel and exhaust systems 4A•5

7.7 Undo the 3 bolts (arrowed) and remove the left-hand side air deflector shield

7.8 Undo the nuts and remove the heat shields beneath the fuel tank

7.9 Take care not to damage the filler pipe stub (arrowed) when removing the pipe

7.10 Depress the release button (arrowed) and disconnect the vent pipe from the rear of the tank

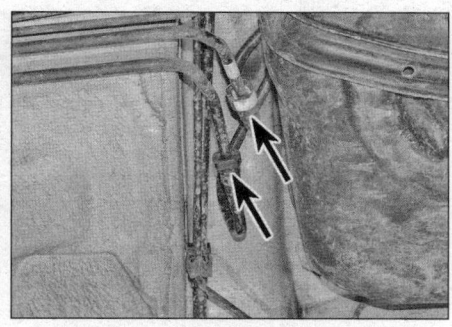

7.11a Disconnect the fuel supply and purge valve pipe at the front of the tank (arrowed)

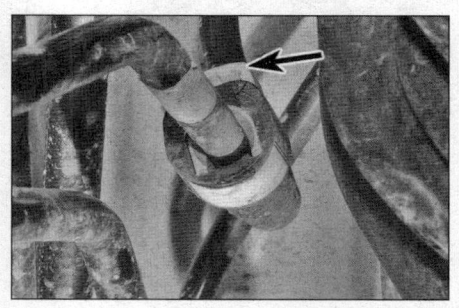

7.11b The top part of the catch (arrowed) must be prised out before the release button can be depressed on the fuel supply pipe

(see *Jacking and vehicle support*). Remove the rear roadwheels.

5 Unhook the exhaust system mounting rubbers from the centre and rear hangers, and allow the exhaust system to rest on the rear suspension crossmember.

6 Undo the nuts securing the flange of the exhaust system rear section, then manoeuvre the rear section to one side, and secure it in place using cable ties/wire/string.

7 Undo the 3 bolts and pull the left-hand side air deflector shield rearwards to release its retaining clip (see illustration).

8 Undo the nuts and remove the exhaust centre and rear section heat shields from the vehicle underside (see illustration).

9 Release the clips and disconnect the fuel tank filler pipes (see illustration). Do not use any sharp-edged tools to release the pipes from their stub, as the pipe is easily damaged.

10 Depress the release button and disconnect the fuel tank vent pipe from the rear of the tank to the evaporative emissions (see illustration).

11 Disconnect the fuel supply pipe and EVAP canister purge valve pipe from the front of the tank (see illustrations).

12 Support the tank using a trolley jack and a large sheet of wood to spread the load.

13 Note exactly how the fuel tank retaining straps are arranged to make refitting easier. In particular, note their fitted order under the retaining bolt heads, where applicable. The left-hand side strap is on top at the front fixing.

14 Unbolt and remove the fuel tank retaining straps (see illustrations), but do not lower the tank at this stage.

15 Partially lower the tank on the jack, taking care that no strain is placed on any fuel lines or wiring. As soon as the wiring

7.14a Undo the bolts at the rear (arrowed) . . .

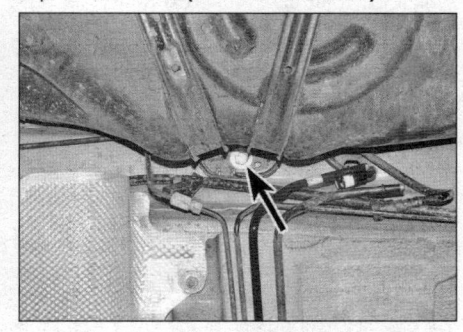

7.14b . . . and at the front (arrowed)

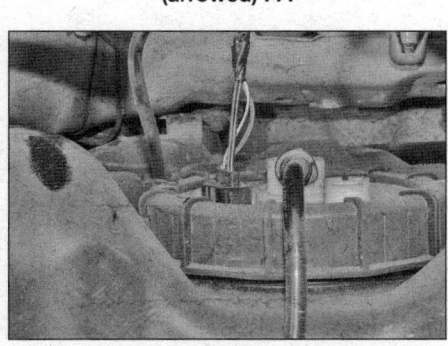

connector for the fuel pump/gauge sender on top of the tank is accessible, reach in and disconnect it, then release the clip and disconnect the breather hose from the top of the tank (see illustrations). Where

7.15a Disconnect the wiring plug . . .

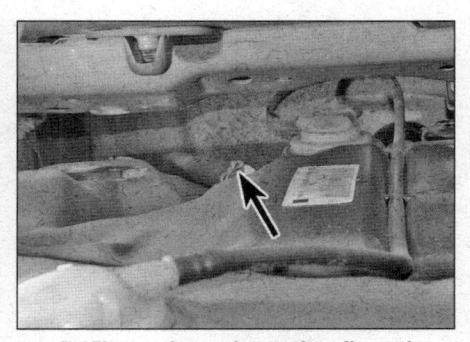

7.15b . . . then release the clip and disconnect the breather pipe (arrowed)

4A•6 Fuel and exhaust systems

8.3 Using a home-made tool to slacken the retaining ring

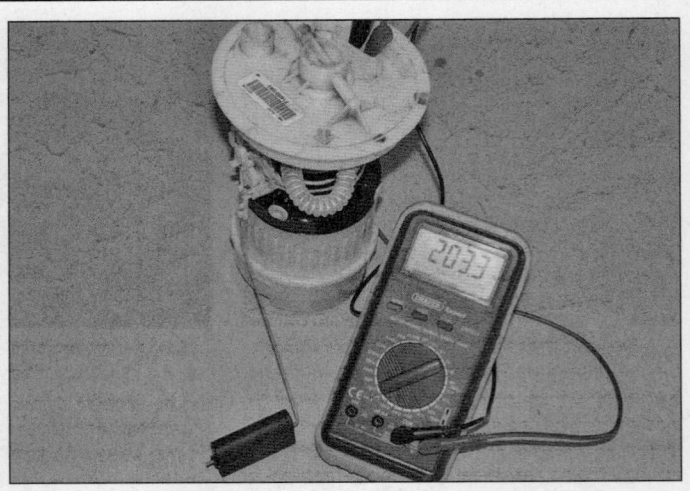

8.5 Measure the resistance of the sender unit at full and zero float arm deflection

applicable, unclip the EVAP canister hose from the top of the tank.
16 Lower the fuel tank to the ground, checking all the way down that no pipes or wiring are under any strain. Remove the tank from under the car.

Inspection

17 Whilst removed, the fuel tank can be inspected for damage or deterioration. Removal of the fuel pump/fuel gauge sender unit (see Section 8) will allow a partial inspection of the interior. If the tank is contaminated with sediment or water, swill it out with clean fuel. Do not under any circumstances undertake any repairs on a leaking or damaged fuel tank; this work must be carried out by a professional who has experience in this critical and potentially-dangerous work.
18 Whilst the fuel tank is removed from the car, it should be placed in a safe area where sparks or open flames cannot ignite the fumes coming out of the tank. Be especially careful inside garages where a natural-gas type appliance is located, because the pilot light could cause an explosion.
19 Check the condition of the lower filler pipe and renew it if necessary.

Refitting

20 Refitting is a reversal of the removal procedure, noting the following points:
a) Ensure that all pipe and wiring connections are securely fitted.
b) When refitting the quick-release couplings, press them together until the locking lugs snap into their groove.
c) Tighten the tank strap retaining bolts to the specified torque.
d) If evidence of contamination was found, do not return any previously-drained fuel to the tank unless it is carefully filtered first.

8 Fuel pump/fuel gauge sender unit – removal and refitting

Note: Refer to the warning note in Section 1 before proceeding. Ford specify the use of their service tool 310-069 (a large socket with projecting teeth to engage the fuel pump/sender unit retaining ring's raised edges) for this task. In practice, it was found that the ring could be loosened with conventional tools.

Removal

1 A combined fuel pump and fuel gauge sender unit is located in the top face of the fuel tank. The combined unit can only be detached and withdrawn from the tank after the tank is released and lowered from under the car. Refer to Section 7 and remove the fuel tank, then proceed as follows.
2 With the fuel tank removed, disconnect the fuel supply pipe (if still attached to the tank) from the stub by squeezing the quick-release lugs.
3 Unscrew and remove the special retaining ring, either by unscrewing it with the Ford tool, or by carefully tapping it round until it can be unscrewed by hand. If care is taken, the ring could also be loosened using an oil filter removal chain- or strap-wrench **(see illustration)**.
4 Take out the rubber seal, then carefully lift out the fuel pump/gauge sender unit from the tank. Take care that the sender unit float and arm are not damaged as the unit is removed.
5 The level sender unit can be tested by connecting an ohmmeter across the sender terminals, and measuring its resistance. At full deflection (full tank) we measured a resistance of 9 ohms, and at zero deflection (empty tank) we measured 203 ohms **(see illustration)**.

Refitting

6 Refitting is a reversal of removal, but fit a new rubber seal and tighten the retaining ring securely, aligning the arrow on the top of the module with the mark on the top of the tank **(see illustrations)**. Refit the fuel tank as described in Section 9.

9 Fuel tank roll-over valve – removal and refitting

1 The roll-over valve is built into the top of the fuel tank. It is not possible to access the valve. Its purpose is to prevent fuel loss if the car becomes inverted in a crash.

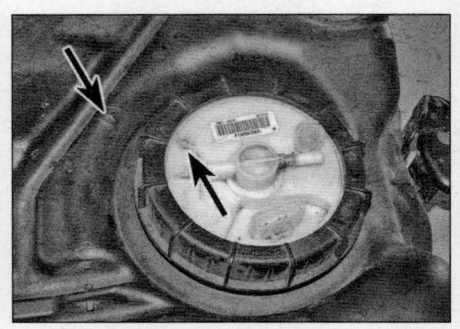

8.6a Renew the rubber seal

8.6b Align the arrow on the top of the module with the mark on the tank (arrowed)

10 Fuel injection system shut-off (inertia) switch – removal and refitting

1 The fuel injection system shut-off switch (also known as the inertia switch) is a safety feature, designed to reduce the loss of fuel following an accident. If a severe enough impact is detected by the switch, it will automatically shut off the car's high-pressure fuel pump, to reduce the chance of fuel escaping under pressure from the system.
2 It has been known for these switches to be triggered by non-life-threatening events, such as minor car parking bumps, or travelling over rough roads or potholes.
3 To reset the switch, depress the button on top of the switch. **Do not** reset the switch after an accident if fuel has escaped from the fuel system.

Removal
4 The fuel cut-off switch is located behind the driver's side footwell side trim panel. First disconnect the battery negative (earth) lead (see Chapter 5A).
5 Remove the footwell side panel trim as described in Chapter 11.
6 Unscrew and remove the switch retaining bolts, then disconnect the wiring plug and remove the switch **(see illustration)**.

Refitting
7 Refitting is a reversal of removal, but make sure that the switch is reset. Start the engine to prove this.

11 Fuel injection system – checking

Note: *Refer to the warning note in Section 1 before proceeding.*

1 If a fault appears in the fuel injection system, first ensure that all the system wiring connectors are securely connected and free of corrosion – also refer to paragraphs 6 to 9 below. Check that the inertia switch has not been triggered (Section 10). Then ensure that the fault is not due to poor maintenance; ie, check that the air cleaner filter element is clean, the spark plugs are in good condition and correctly gapped, the cylinder compression pressures are correct, the ignition system wiring is in good condition and securely connected, and the engine breather hoses are clear and undamaged, referring to Chapter 1, Chapter 2A or 2B and Chapter 5B.
2 If these checks fail to reveal the cause of the problem, the car should be taken to a suitably-equipped Ford dealer or specialist for testing. A diagnostic connector is fitted below the steering column, into which dedicated electronic test equipment can be plugged **(see illustration)**. The test equipment is capable of 'interrogating' the engine management system ECM (Powertrain Control Module)

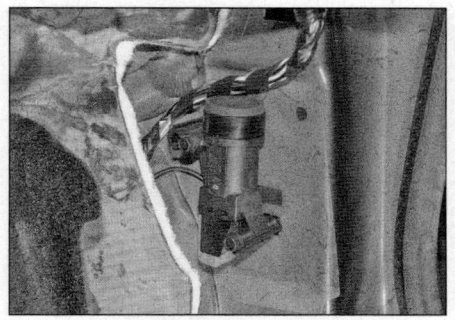

10.6 Fuel inertia shut-off switch

electronically and accessing its internal fault log (reading fault codes).
3 Fault codes can only be extracted from the ECM using a dedicated fault code reader. A Ford dealer will obviously have such a reader, but they are also available from other suppliers. It is unlikely to be cost-effective for the private owner to purchase a fault code reader, but a well-equipped local garage or auto-electrical specialist will have one.
4 Using this equipment, faults can be pinpointed quickly and simply, even if their occurrence is intermittent. Testing all the system components individually in an attempt to locate the fault by elimination is a time-consuming operation that is unlikely to be fruitful (particularly if the fault occurs dynamically), and carries a high risk of damage to the ECM's internal components.
5 Experienced home mechanics equipped with an accurate tachometer and a carefully-calibrated exhaust gas analyser may be able to check the exhaust gas CO content and the engine idle speed; if these are found to be out of specification, then the car must be taken to a suitably-equipped Ford dealer for assessment. Neither the air/fuel mixture (exhaust gas CO content) nor the engine idle speed are manually adjustable; incorrect test results indicate the need for maintenance (possibly, injector cleaning) or a fault within the fuel injection system.

Limited Operation Strategy
6 Certain faults, such as failure of one of the engine management system sensors, will cause the system will revert to a backup (or

12.1a Slacken the clamp and disconnect the outlet tube (arrowed) – 1.4/1.6 litre non-Ti-VCT engines . . .

11.2 Diagnostic connector (arrowed)

'limp-home') mode, referred to by Ford as 'Limited Operation Strategy' (LOS). This is intended to be a 'get-you-home' facility only – the engine management warning light will come on when this mode is in operation.
7 In this mode, the signal from the defective sensor is substituted with a fixed value (it would normally vary), which may lead to loss of power, poor idling, and generally-poor running, especially when the engine is cold.
8 However, the engine may in fact run quite well in this situation, and the only clue (other than the warning light) would be that the exhaust CO emissions (for example) will be higher than they should be.
9 Bear in mind that, even if the defective sensor is correctly identified and renewed, the engine will not return to normal running until the fault code is erased, taking the system out of LOS. This also applies even if the cause of the fault was a loose connection or damaged piece of wire – until the fault code is erased, the system will continue in LOS.

12 Fuel injection system components – removal and refitting

Note: *Refer to the precautions in Section 1 before proceeding.*

Throttle body

1.4 and 1.6 litre engines
1 Slacken the clamps and remove the air cleaner outlet tube **(see illustrations)**.
2 Slide up the red locking catch, and

12.1b . . . and 1.6 litre Ti-VCT engines (arrowed)

12.2 Slide up the red locking catch

12.4 Undo the 4 bolts and remove the throttle body

12.7 Pull the engine cover upwards

12.10a Disconnect the throttle body wiring plug . . .

12.10b . . . then undo the 4 bolts (arrowed)

disconnect the wiring plug from the throttle body **(see illustration)**.

3 On non-Ti-VCT engines, detach the engine breather pipe from the cylinder head cover.

4 On all engines, undo the 4 bolts and remove the throttle body **(see illustration)**.

5 Refitting is a reversal of removal. Use a new gasket/seal, and tighten the mounting bolts to the specified torque.

1.8 and 2.0 litre engines

6 Drain the cooling system as described in Chapter 1, or use hose clamps to prevent coolant loss when the hoses are disconnected from the throttle body.

7 Remove the plastic cover on the top of the engine **(see illustration)**.

8 Release the clamps and remove the ducting between the air cleaner and the throttle body **(see illustration 5.15)**.

9 Release the clamps and disconnect the coolant hoses from the throttle body. Use hose clamps if the system has not been drained (see Paragraph 6).

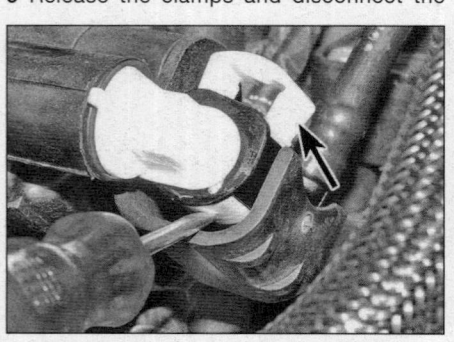

10 Disconnect the wiring plug, then undo the 4 bolts and remove the throttle body **(see illustrations)**.

11 Refitting is a reversal of removal. Use a new seal, and tighten the mounting bolts to the specified torque.

All engines

12 After refitting the throttle body, turn the ignition key to position II and wait for 1 minute for the throttle body to initialise, then turn the ignition off. Do not press the accelerator pedal during this procedure.

Fuel rail and injectors

13 Relieve the residual pressure in the fuel system (see Section 2), and equalise tank pressure by removing the fuel filler cap.

⚠ **Warning: This procedure will merely relieve the increased pressure necessary for the engine to run – remember that fuel will still be present in the system components, and take precautions accordingly before disconnecting any of them.**

14 Disconnect the battery negative (earth) lead (see Chapter 5A).

1.4 and 1.6 litre engines

15 Disconnect the engine breather hose from the cylinder head cover.

16 Unclip the fuel supply pipe from the support bracket, then prise out the locking catch, depress the release button and disconnect the pipe from the fuel rail **(see illustration)**.

17 Depress the wire locking clips and pull the wiring connectors assembly up from the injectors **(see illustrations)**. If necessary, disconnect the wiring plug from the oil pressure switch to allow the harness assembly to be moved to one side.

18 On 1.6 litre Ti-VCT engines, disconnect the wiring plugs from the throttle body, camshaft variable timing oil control solenoid at the right-hand end of the cylinder head, and the inlet camshaft position sensor at the left-hand end of the cylinder head.

19 On all engines, unscrew and remove the two fuel rail mounting bolts. Carefully pull the fuel rail upwards to release the injectors from place – there will be some resistance from the injector O-ring seals **(see illustrations)**.

20 Remove the retaining clips and carefully

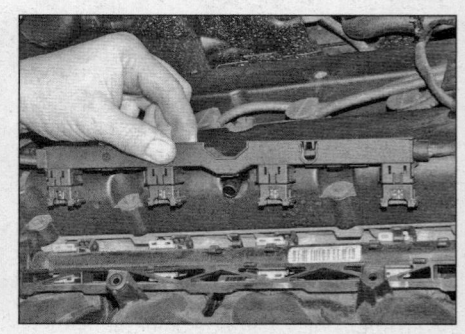

12.16 Prise out the locking catch (arrowed) then depress the release button

12.17a Push the locking clips (arrowed) forwards . . .

12.17b . . . and gently pull the connector assembly from the injectors

Fuel and exhaust systems 4A•9

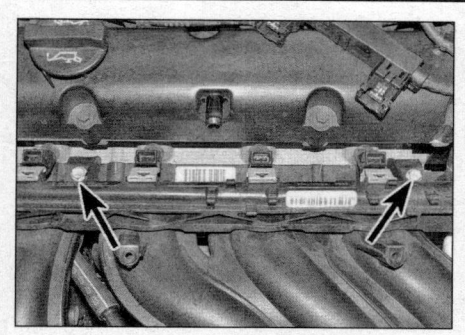

12.19a Undo the fuel rail mounting bolts (arrowed) . . .

12.19b . . . and pull the fuel upwards from place

12.20a Release the retaining clips from the rail . . .

12.20b . . . and pull the injector from the rail

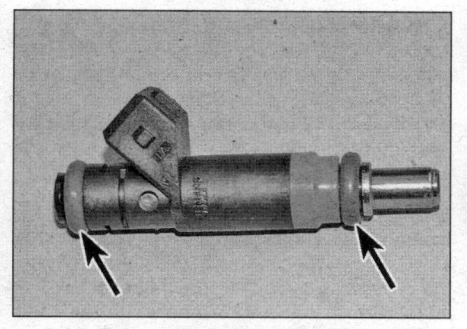

12.21 Renew the injector O-rings seals (arrowed)

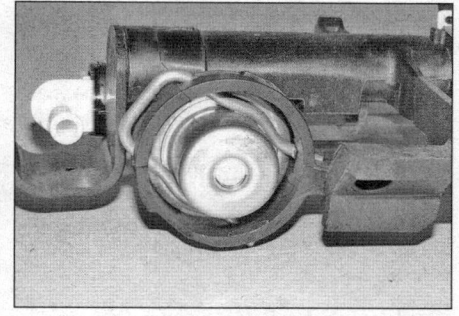

12.22 Prise out the clip and remove the fuel pulse damper

pull the injectors from the fuel rail **(see illustrations)**.

21 Using a screwdriver, prise the O-rings from the grooves at each end of the injectors **(see illustration)**. Discard the O-rings and obtain new ones.

22 If required, the fuel pulse damper can be removed after the retaining clip/bolts have been removed **(see illustration)**. When refitting the damper, lubricate the new O-ring seals with clean engine oil.

23 Refitting is the reverse of the removal procedure, noting the following points:
 a) Fit new injector O-rings, and lubricate them with clean engine oil to aid refitting.
 b) Tighten the fuel rail mounting bolts to the specified torque.
 c) Ensure that the hoses and wiring are routed correctly, and secured on reconnection by any clips or ties provided.
 d) On completion, switch the ignition on to activate the fuel pump and pressurise the system, without cranking the engine. Check for signs of fuel leaks around all disturbed unions and joints before attempting to start the engine.

1.8 and 2.0 litre engines

24 Remove the plastic cover from the top of the engine.

25 Disconnect the vacuum hose from the fuel pulse damper on the fuel rail (where fitted).

26 Depress the clips and disconnect the wiring plugs from the injectors, then unclip the wiring harness.

27 Disconnect the fuel supply pipe from the fuel rail by pushing the collar into the connector **(see illustration)**.

28 Unscrew the mounting nuts, then lift the fuel rail from the cylinder head – there will be some resistance from the injector O-ring seals **(see illustration)**.

29 To remove the injectors, first lift the retaining clips at the top, then slide them off sideways. Now pull the injectors out of the fuel rail.

30 Refitting is the reverse of the removal procedure, noting the following points:
 a) Fit new injector O-rings, and lubricate them with clean engine oil to aid refitting.
 b) Tighten the fuel rail mounting bolts to the specified torque.
 c) Ensure that the hoses and wiring are routed correctly, and secured on reconnection by any clips or ties provided.
 d) On completion, switch the ignition on to activate the fuel pump and pressurise the system, without cranking the engine. Check for signs of fuel leaks around all disturbed unions and joints before attempting to start the engine.

TMAP sensor

Non-Ti-VCT engines

31 The sensor is located beneath the throttle body. Remove the plastic cover from the top of the engine – where fitted.

32 With the ignition switched off, disconnect the sensor wiring plug, then remove the mounting bolt and withdraw it from the manifold. Check the condition of the sensor O-ring seal, and obtain a new one if necessary **(see illustrations)**.

33 Refitting is a reversal of removal. Use a new seal if necessary, and tighten the mounting bolt securely, to prevent air leaks.

12.27 Push in the collar (arrowed) and pull the connector from the fuel rail

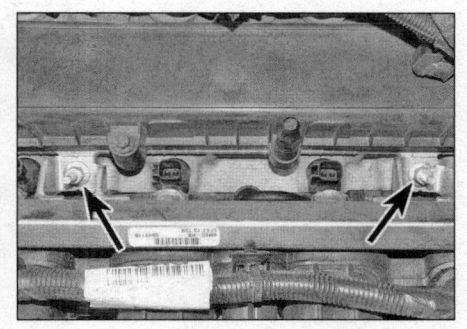

12.28 Undo the fuel rail mounting nuts (arrowed)

4A•10 Fuel and exhaust systems

12.32a TMAP sensor (arrowed) – shown with the throttle body removed for clarity – 1.4 and 1.6 litre non-Ti-VCT engines

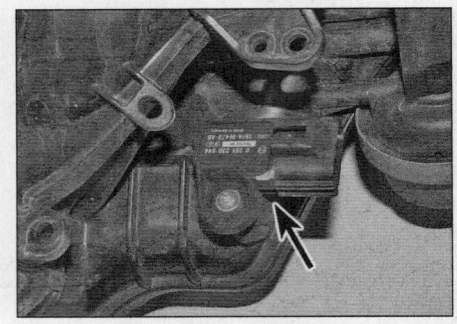

12.32b The TMAP sensor is located at the lower, left-hand edge of the manifold (arrowed)

Mass airflow sensor

1.6 litre Ti-VCT engines

34 Disconnect the wiring plug from the mass airflow sensor on the air cleaner cover **(see illustration 12.2)**.
35 Undo the 2 bolts and pull the sensor from the air cleaner cover.
36 Refitting is a reversal of removal. Note the arrow on the top of the sensor indicating airflow.

Powertrain Control Module

Note: *The module is fragile. Take care not to drop it, or subject it to any other kind of impact. Do not subject it to extremes of temperature, or allow it to get wet.*
Note: *If a new PCM is to be fitted, the configuration information stored within the module must be uploaded to Ford diagnostic equipment prior to the module being removed, and downloaded to the new PCM once installed. Entrust this task to a Ford dealer or suitably-equipped specialist.*
37 Disconnect the battery negative lead as described in Chapter 5A.

1.4 and 1.6 litre engines

38 Disconnect the wiring plug from the ignition coil assembly.
39 Depress the retaining clips and remove the cover over the PCM **(see illustration)**.
40 Undo the PCM retaining bolts. Take care not to damage the cylinder head cover. Note the upper rear bolt has a plastic spacer between the PCM and the battery tray.
41 Place the module squarely on the cylinder head cover, and drill out the shear-bolt securing the module wiring connector **(see illustration)**. A 6 mm drill bit will be required, and the hole must be drilled centrally, to avoid damaging the module – Ford dealers use a special guide tool (418-537) to ensure this, which is a short tube with a 6 mm hole down the centre. Alternatively, use suitable socket, and a centre-punch to mark the centre of the bolt, and drill a smaller pilot hole first.
42 Once the module connector starts to come free, indicating that the shear-bolt has been released, clean up all the swarf from the drilling operations before removing the connector completely.
43 Remove the module connector, and extract the remains of the shear-bolt with some grips. The module itself can now be removed from the car.
44 Refitting is a reversal of removal. A new shear-bolt should be obtained for refitting, and tightened until the head shears off. Note that the O-ring seal fits onto the bolt before it's inserted into the connector, then fit the retaining washer on the threads of the bolt before refitting the connector **(see illustrations)**.

1.8 and 2.0 litre engines up to 03/2007

45 Remove the plastic cover on the top of the engine, then depress the retaining clips and remove the cover over the PCM **(see illustration)**.
46 In order to remove the security shield, the retaining shear-bolts must be drilled out. Centre punch the holes, then drill out the bolts using a 6 mm drill **(see illustration)**. Remove the shield.
47 Lever over the locking catches and disconnect the wiring plugs from the PCM.
48 Undo the 3 retaining bolts, and slide the PCM from the bracket.

12.39 Release the clips (arrowed) and remove the cover over the PCM

12.41 Drill out the wiring connector shear-bolt

12.44a Fit the O-ring (arrowed) onto the new shear-bolt . . .

12.44b . . . then insert the bolt and fit the retaining washer

12.45 Unclip the PCM cover

12.46 Drill out the security shield shear-bolts (arrowed)

Fuel and exhaust systems 4A•11

49 Refitting is a reversal of removal. New shear-bolts should be obtained for refitting, and tightened until the heads shear off.

1.8 and 2.0 litre engines from 03/2007

50 Raise the front of the vehicle and support it securely on axle stands (see *Jacking and vehicle support*). Remove the left-hand front roadwheel.
51 Release the fasteners and remove the left-hand front wheel arch liner.
52 The PCM is fitted behind the front bumper. There may be a security shield fitted over the PCM. If this the case, remove the 4 retaining shear-bolts using an 8 mm drill. Where no shield is fitted, simply undo the 4 retaining bolts and remove the cover **(see illustrations)**.
53 Pull the PCM from place to release the retaining clips **(see illustration)**.
54 Lever over the locking catches and disconnect the wiring plugs from the PCM **(see illustration)**, then manoeuvre the PCM from position.
55 Refitting is a reversal of removal. New shear-bolts (where fitted) should be obtained for refitting, and tightened until the heads shear off.

Crankshaft position sensor

1.4 and 1.6 litre engines

56 The sensor is located on the front left-hand side of the engine, close to the transmission **(see illustration)**. For improved access, apply the handbrake, then jack up the front of the car and support it on axle stands (see *Jacking and vehicle support*). Remove the engine undershield (where fitted).
57 With the ignition switched off, disconnect the wiring plug, then unscrew the mounting bolt and withdraw the sensor.
58 Refitting is a reversal of removal. Ensure that the sensor is clean when refitting, and tighten the bolt to the specified torque.

1.8 and 2.0 litre engines

59 The sensor is located adjacent to the crankshaft pulley. Raise the front of the vehicle and support it securely on axle stands (see *Jacking and vehicle support*). Remove the engine undershield (where fitted) **(see illustration)**.
60 Disconnect the sensor wiring plug **(see illustration)**.
61 Undo the 2 retaining bolts and remove the sensor.
62 Refitting is a reversal of removal. Tighten the sensor retaining bolts securely.

Camshaft position sensor

1.4 and 1.6 litre engines

63 On the 1.4 and 1.6 litre non-Ti-VCT engines, one sensor is fitted, located on the right-hand rear of the cylinder head. On 1.6 litre Ti-VCT engines, there are 2 sensors fitted – one over each of the camshafts at the left-hand end of the cylinder head cover.
64 With the ignition switched off, disconnect the wiring from the camshaft position sensor(s) **(see illustration)**.

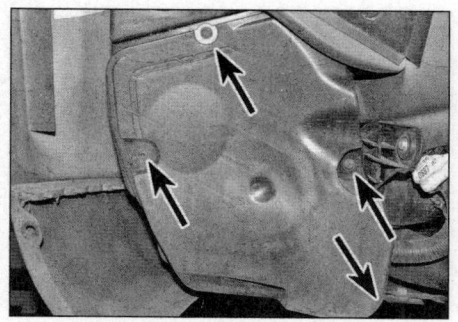

12.52a Undo the 4 bolts (arrowed) and remove the PCM cover

12.52b Drill out the shear-bolt (arrowed) and remove the security shield (where fitted)

12.53 Pull the PCM from the retaining clips

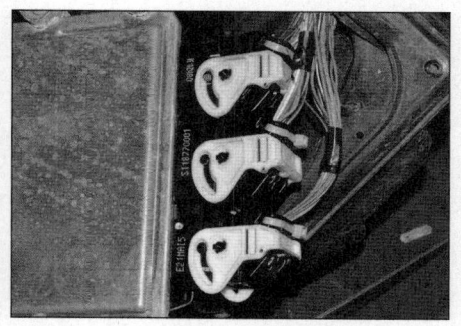

12.54 Lever over the locking catches to disconnect the PCM wiring plugs

65 Unscrew the mounting bolt(s) and withdraw the sensor(s) from the cylinder head or cylinder head cover (as applicable).
66 Refitting is a reversal of removal, but use a new seal. Smear a little engine oil on the seal before fitting the sensor, and tighten the bolt(s) to the specified torque.

1.8 and 2.0 litre engines

67 Remove the plastic cover on the top of the engine.

12.56 Crankshaft position sensor (arrowed)

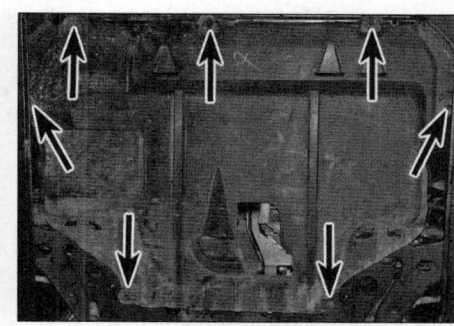

12.59 Undo the fasteners (arrowed) and remove the engine undershield

12.60 Crankshaft position sensor – 1.8 and 2.0 litre models

12.64 Disconnect the camshaft position sensor wiring plug – 1.4 and 1.6 litre engines

4A•12 Fuel and exhaust systems

12.68 Camshaft position sensor (arrowed) – 1.8 and 2.0 litre engines

12.71 Camshaft timing oil control solenoids (arrowed)

12.72 Undo the bolt and pull the solenoid from place

12.75 Clutch pedal position switch (arrowed)

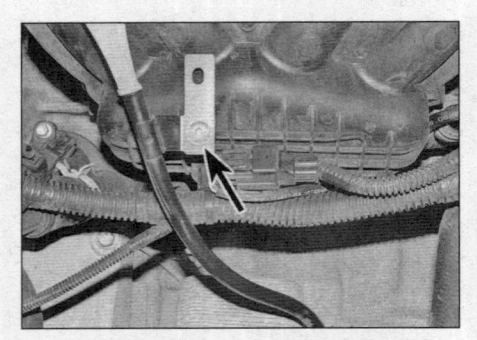

13.5 Undo the engine oil level dipstick guide tube bolt (arrowed)

13.6 Disconnect the breather hose (arrowed) – 1.6 litre Ti-VCT engine

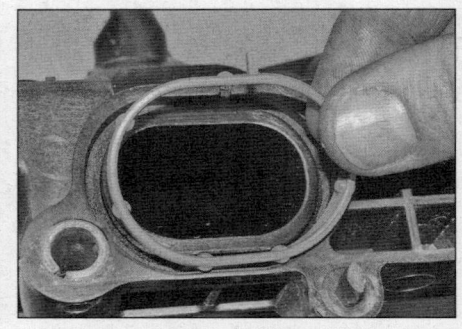

13.7 Renew the manifold-to-cylinder head seals

68 Disconnect the wiring plug, then undo the retaining bolt and remove the sensor (see illustration).
69 Refitting is a reversal of removal. Tighten the retaining bolt to the specified torque.

Coolant temperature sensor

70 See Chapter 3.

Variable camshaft timing oil control solenoids

71 The solenoids are located at the front, right-hand end of the cylinder head cover. Disconnect the solenoid wiring plug (see illustration).
72 Undo the retaining bolt and pull the solenoid from place (see illustration).
73 Refitting is a reversal of removal. Ensure the solenoid and aperture are scrupulously clean prior to refitting. Tighten the bolt to the specified torque.

Clutch pedal position switch

74 Remove the driver's side facia lower panel as described in Chapter 11.
75 With the ignition switched off, disconnect the wiring from the clutch switch (see illustration).
76 Rotate the switch anti-clockwise and remove it.
77 Refitting is a reversal of removal.

Power steering pressure switch

78 Refer to Chapter 10.

Oxygen sensor

79 Refer to Chapter 4B.

13 Manifolds – removal and refitting

Note: *Refer to the warning note in Section 1 before proceeding.*

Inlet manifold

1 Depressurise the fuel system as described in Section 2. On completion, disconnect the battery negative lead (refer to Chapter 5A).

1.4 and 1.6 litre engines

2 Remove the alternator as described in Chapter 5A.
3 Remove the fuel rail with injectors as described in Section 12.
4 Remove the throttle body as described in Section 12.
5 Undo the bolt securing the engine oil level dipstick guide tube to the manifold (see illustration).
6 Note their fitted locations and disconnect any vacuum hoses/pipes/wiring harnesses attached to the manifold (see illustration).
7 Undo the retaining bolts and remove the manifold. Renew the manifold-to-cylinder head seals/gasket (see illustration).
8 Refitting is a reversal of removal, noting the following points:
  a) Ensure that the mating faces are clean, and use a new manifold-to-cylinder head seals/gasket.
  b) Tighten all fixings to the specified torque.
  c) On completion, switch the ignition on to activate the fuel pump and pressurise the system, without cranking the engine. Check for signs of fuel leaks around all disturbed unions and joints before attempting to start the engine.

1.8 and 2.0 litre engines

9 Remove the plastic cover on the top of the engine.
10 Disconnect the battery as described in Chapter 5A.
11 Remove the throttle body as described in Section 12.
12 Remove the engine oil level dipstick guide tube upper and lower retaining bolts (see illustrations).
13 Remove the inlet manifold lower retaining bolt (see illustration).
14 Disconnect the wiring plugs from the left-hand knock sensor, MAP sensor (on the manifold), and unclip the harness from the manifold.

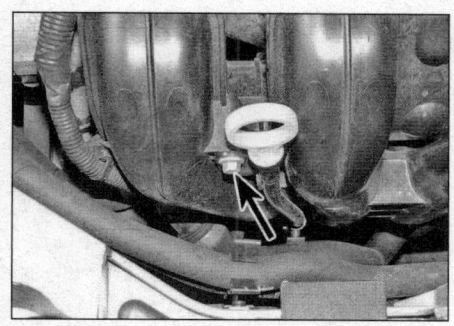

Fuel and exhaust systems 4A•13

13.12a Oil level dipstick guide tube upper bolt (arrowed) . . .

13.12b . . . and lower bolt (arrowed)

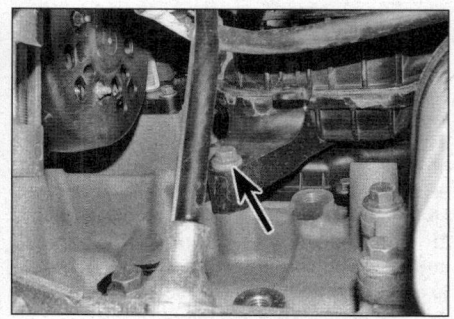

13.13 Manifold lower retaining bolt (arrowed)

15 For improved access, undo the bolts and move the bonnet catch to one side.
16 Disconnect the following around the manifold:
 a) Crankcase breather hose at the base of the manifold.
 b) Brake servo vacuum pipe from the manifold.
 c) Fuel pulse damper vacuum hose (where fitted).
17 Check carefully around the manifold, unclipping any remaining wiring or pipework which may still be attached to it.
18 Remove the retaining bolts, and withdraw the manifold from the front of the engine. Recover the gaskets (see illustration).
19 Refitting is a reversal of removal, noting the following points:
 a) Ensure that the mating faces are clean, and use new manifold gaskets if necessary.
 b) Tighten all fixings to the specified torque.

 c) On completion, switch the ignition on to activate the fuel pump and pressurise the system, without cranking the engine. Check for signs of fuel leaks around all disturbed unions and joints before attempting to start the engine.

Exhaust manifold

20 Disconnect the battery negative lead as described in Chapter 5A.

> **Warning: Do not attempt this procedure until the engine is completely cool – ideally, the car should be left overnight before starting work.**

21 The exhaust manifold is integral with the front catalytic converter. Remove the front subframe as described in Chapter 10.

1.8 and 2.0 litre models

22 Remove the plastic cover on the top of the engine, then remove the oil filler cap.

All models

23 Undo the bolts and detach the brake fluid reservoir (where fitted) from the scuttle cowl panel.
24 Remove the wiper arms as described in Chapter 12.
25 Remove the 5 clips and remove the scuttle cowl panel (see illustrations).
26 Undo the 2 bolts, release the clips and remove the bulkhead extension panel (see illustration).
27 Disconnect the oxygen sensors' wiring connectors behind the left-hand side of the engine (see illustration).
28 Remove the bolts securing the exhaust manifold heat shield (see illustration).
29 Working in a diagonal sequence, loosen and remove the exhaust manifold nuts. The manifold will remain in position for now, located on the cylinder head studs – do not try and slide it off the studs yet. **Note:** *If all of*

13.18 Renew the inlet manifold seals

13.25a Prise forwards the clips (arrowed) . . .

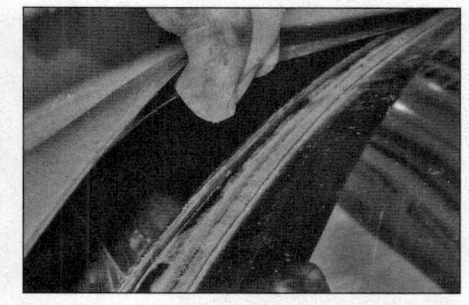

13.25b . . . then pull the scuttle cowling panel upwards from the base of the windscreen

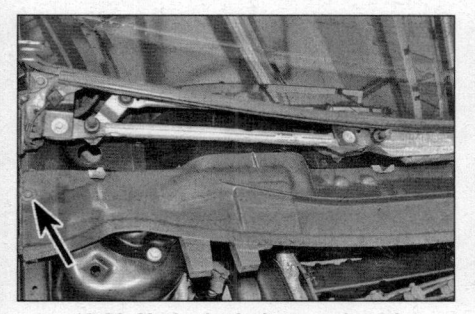

13.26 Undo the bolt at each end (right-hand one arrowed) and pull the bulkhead extension panel forwards

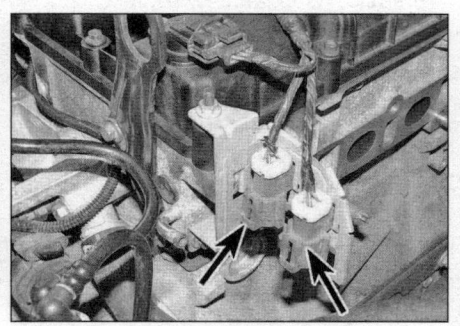

13.27 Disconnect the oxygen sensor wiring plugs (arrowed)

13.28 Remove the heat shield from over the exhaust manifold (arrowed)

the studs come out with the nuts, leave two of them in place to support the manifold.
30 Undo the bolts and remove the floor panel brace beneath the front of the exhaust system (see illustration).
31 Undo the 2 bolts securing the catalytic converter to the support bracket on its underside, and with the help of an assistant, slide the manifold off the cylinder head studs (or completely unscrew any remaining studs), and lower it down to remove it, taking care not to damage the sensors or their wiring. Recover and discard the gasket (see illustration).
32 Unscrew the oxygen sensors from the manifold and catalytic converter.
33 Refitting is a reversal of removal, noting the following points:
a) Ensure that the mating faces are clean, and use new manifold gaskets.
b) Use new manifold/catalytic converter nuts/bolt.
c) Do not fully tighten the manifold/catalytic converter mounting nuts/bolts until the front subframe has been refitted as described in Chapter 10.
d) Tighten the manifold nuts in a diagonal sequence, in the two stages specified.
e) Tighten all fixings to the specified torque.

14 Exhaust system – general information, removal and refitting

Caution: *Any work on the exhaust system should only be attempted once the system is completely cool – this may take several hours, especially in the case of the forward sections, such as the manifold and catalytic converter.*

General information

1 The exhaust system consists of the exhaust manifold with integral catalytic converter, the centre section, and a separate rear silencer. At the front, where the centre section joins the manifold, a flexible ('mesh') section is fitted, to allow for engine movement.
2 The system is suspended throughout its entire length by rubber mountings.

Removal

3 To remove a part of the system, first jack up the front or rear of the car, and support it on axle stands (see *Jacking and vehicle support*). Alternatively, position the car over an inspection pit, or on car ramps.

Manifold and catalytic converter

4 Refer to Section 13.

Centre section

5 To prevent damage to the exhaust flexible section, support it by attaching a pair of splints either side (two scrap strips of wood,

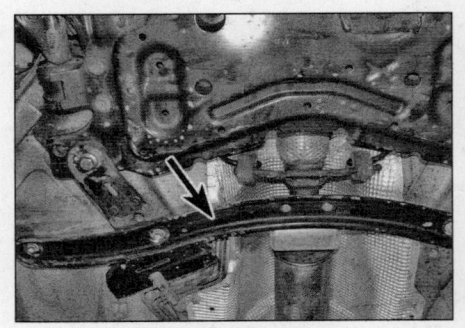

13.30 Remove the floor panel brace (arrowed)

13.31 Undo the bolts and remove support bracket under the catalytic converter

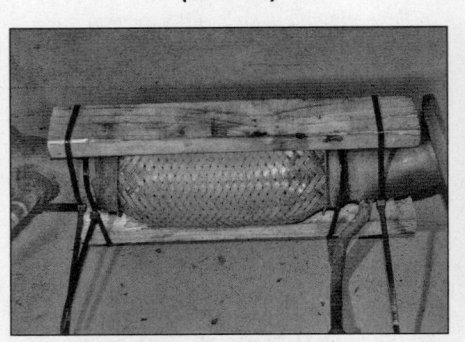

14.5 Make a 'splint' to support the flexible section of the exhaust

14.6 Undo the flange nuts (arrowed)

plant canes, etc) using some cable-ties (see illustration). If a new centre section is being fitted, this precaution only applies to the new section of exhaust.
6 Unscrew the nuts securing the centre section to the flexible joint, and separate the joint. Recover the gasket (see illustration).
7 Even if just the centre section is being removed, it still has to be separated from the rear silencer. Unbolt the clamp where the centre section joins the silencer, and separate the pipes (bear in mind that a corroded rear silencer may be damaged during removal – see paragraph 9).
8 Unhook the centre section's two rubber mountings, and remove it from under the car.

Rear silencer

9 When fitted in the factory, the exhaust system from the front section flange to the end of the tail pipe is one piece. However, if the rear silencer is to be renewed, new silencers should be available – check with your parts supplier. Using a hacksaw, cut through the exhaust pipe 150 mm behind the mounting, in front of the rear silencer.
10 Unhook the silencer rubber mountings, and remove it from under the car.

Heat shields

11 The heat shields are secured to the underside of the body by special nuts. Each shield can be removed separately, but note that they may overlap, making it necessary to loosen another section first. If a shield is being removed to gain access to a component located behind it, it may prove sufficient in some cases to remove the retaining nuts and/or bolts, and simply lower the shield, without disturbing the exhaust system. Otherwise, remove the exhaust section as described earlier.

Refitting

12 In all cases, refitting is a reversal of removal, but note the following points:
a) Always use new gaskets, nuts and clamps (as applicable), and coat all threads with copper grease. Make sure any new clamps are the same size as the original – overtightening a clamp which is too big will not seal the joint.
b) On a sleeved joint (such as that between the centre section and rear silencer), use a smear of exhaust jointing paste to achieve a gas-tight seal.
c) If any of the exhaust mounting rubbers are in poor condition, fit new ones.
d) Make sure that the exhaust is suspended properly on its mountings, and will not come into contact with the floor or any suspension parts. The rear silencer especially must be aligned correctly before tightening the clamp nuts.
e) Tighten all nuts/bolts to the specified torque, where given.

Chapter 4 Part B:
Emission control systems

Contents

	Section number
Catalytic converter – general information and precautions	2
Crankcase emission control system – checking and component renewal	3
Evaporative emission control system – checking and component renewal	4
Exhaust emission control systems – checking and component renewal	5
General information	1
Underbonnet check for fluid leaks and hose condition	See Chapter 1

Degrees of difficulty

Easy, suitable for novice with little experience	Fairly easy, suitable for beginner with some experience	Fairly difficult, suitable for competent DIY mechanic	Difficult, suitable for experienced DIY mechanic	Very difficult, suitable for expert DIY or professional

Specifications

Torque wrench setting	Nm	lbf ft
Oxygen sensor	42	31

1 General information

All models covered by this manual have various features built into the fuel and exhaust systems to help minimise harmful emissions. These features fall broadly into three categories; crankcase emission control, evaporative emission control, and exhaust emission control. The main features of these systems are as follows.

Crankcase emission control

To reduce the emissions of unburned hydrocarbons from the crankcase into the atmosphere, a Positive Crankcase Ventilation (PCV) system is used. The engine is sealed, and the blow-by gases and oil vapour are drawn from inside the crankcase, through an oil separator, into the inlet tract, to be burned by the engine during normal combustion.

Under conditions of high manifold depression (idling, deceleration) the gases will be sucked positively out of the crankcase. Under conditions of low manifold depression (acceleration, full-throttle running) the gases are forced out of the crankcase by the (relatively) higher crankcase pressure; if the engine is worn, the raised crankcase pressure (due to increased blow-by) will cause some of the flow to return under all manifold conditions.

Evaporative emission control

The evaporative emission control (EVAP) system is used to minimise the escape of unburned hydrocarbons into the atmosphere. To do this, the fuel tank filler cap is sealed, and a carbon canister is used to collect and store petrol vapours generated in the tank. When the engine is running, the vapours are cleared from the canister by an ECM-controlled electrically-operated EVAP purge valve into the inlet tract, to be burned by the engine during normal combustion.

To ensure that the engine runs correctly when idling, the valve only opens when the engine is running under load; the valve then opens to allow the stored vapour to pass into the inlet tract.

Exhaust emission control

Oxygen (lambda) sensors

To minimise the amount of pollutants which escape into the atmosphere, all models are fitted with a catalytic converter in the exhaust system. The system is of the closed-loop type, in which two heated oxygen sensors in the exhaust system provide the engine management ECM with constant feedback on the oxygen content of the exhaust gases. This enables the ECM to adjust the mixture by altering injector opening time, thus providing the best possible conditions for the converter to operate. The system functions in the following way.

The oxygen sensors (also known as a lambda sensors) have built-in heating elements, activated by the ECM to quickly bring the sensor's tip to an efficient operating temperature. The sensor's tip is sensitive to oxygen, and sends the control module a

4B•2 Emission control systems

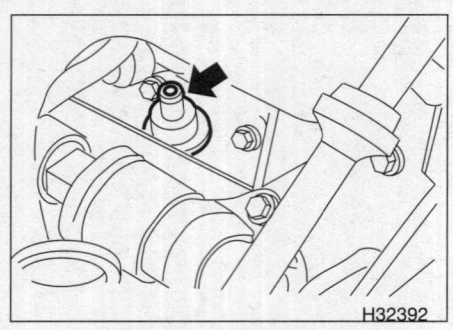

3.4 PCV valve location – 1.4 and 1.6 litre engines

varying voltage depending on the amount of oxygen in the exhaust gases; if the inlet air/fuel mixture is too rich, the exhaust gases are low in oxygen, so the sensor sends a voltage signal proportional to the oxygen detected, the voltage altering as the mixture weakens and the amount of oxygen in the exhaust gases rises. Peak conversion efficiency of all major pollutants occurs if the inlet air/fuel mixture is maintained at the chemically-correct ratio for complete combustion of petrol – 14.7 parts (by weight) of air to 1 part of fuel (the stoichiometric ratio). The sensor output voltage alters in a large step at this point, the ECM using the signal change as a reference point, and correcting the inlet air/fuel mixture accordingly, by altering the fuel injector opening time.

Exhaust gas recirculation (EGR)

This system is only fitted to some 1.8 and 2.0 litre models, and is designed to recirculate small quantities of exhaust gas into the inlet tract, and therefore into the combustion process. This reduces the level of oxides of nitrogen present in the final exhaust gas which is released into the atmosphere.

The volume of exhaust gas recirculated is controlled by an electrically-operated solenoid valve. The solenoid, and valve is mounted at the left-hand end of the cylinder head. The EGR system is controlled by the engine management ECM, which receives information on engine operating parameters from its various sensors.

Catalytic converters

Catalytic converters are fitted to all models.

3.5 Oil separator – 1.8 and 2.0 litre engines

The catalytic converter is integral with the exhaust manifold.

2 Catalytic converter – general information and precautions

On all models, a three-way catalytic converter is incorporated into the exhaust manifold. The catalytic converter is a reliable and simple device, which needs no maintenance in itself, but there are some facts of which an owner should be aware if the converter is to function properly for its full service life.

a) DO NOT use leaded petrol or LRP – the lead will coat the precious metals, reducing their converting efficiency, and will eventually destroy the converter.
b) Always keep the ignition and fuel systems well-maintained in accordance with the manufacturer's schedule (see Chapter 1).
c) If the engine develops a misfire, do not drive the vehicle at all (or at least as little as possible) until the fault is cured.
d) DO NOT push – or tow-start the vehicle – this will soak the catalytic converter in unburned fuel, causing it to overheat when the engine does start.
e) DO NOT switch off the ignition at high engine speeds, ie, do not blip the throttle immediately before switching off.
f) DO NOT use fuel or engine oil additives – these may contain substances harmful to the catalytic converter.
g) DO NOT continue to use the vehicle if the engine burns oil to the extent of leaving a visible trail of blue smoke.
h) Remember that the catalytic converter operates at very high temperatures. DO NOT, therefore, park the vehicle in dry undergrowth, over long grass or piles of dead leaves, after a long run.
i) Remember that the catalytic converter is FRAGILE. Do not strike it with tools during servicing work.
j) In some cases, a sulphurous smell (like that of rotten eggs) may be noticed from the exhaust. This is common to many catalytic converter-equipped vehicles. Once the vehicle has covered a few

4.5 The carbon canister (arrowed) is attached to the rear subframe

thousand miles, the problem should disappear – in the meantime, try changing the brand of petrol used.
k) The catalytic converter used on a well-maintained and well-driven vehicle should last for between 50 000 and 100 000 miles. If the converter is no longer effective, it must be renewed.

3 Crankcase emission control system – checking and component renewal

Checking

1 The components of this system require no attention other than to check that the hoses are clear and undamaged.

Oil separator renewal

2 Remove the inlet manifold as described in Chapter 4A.
3 The oil separator is located on the front facing side of the cylinder block, below the inlet manifold. Disconnect the breather hose from the top of the separator.
4 Pull the PCV valve from the top of the separator (see illustration). **Note:** On 1.8 and 2.0 litre models, depress the clip each side of the valve before pulling it from place.
5 Undo the bolts and remove the separator (see illustration). Recover the gasket.
6 On reassembly, fit a new gasket and tighten the bolts securely.

4 Evaporative emission control system – checking and component renewal

Checking

1 Poor idle, stalling and poor driveability can be caused by an inoperative canister vacuum valve, a damaged canister, split or cracked hoses, or hoses connected to the wrong fittings. Check the fuel filler cap for a damaged or deformed gasket.
2 Fuel loss or fuel odour can be caused by liquid fuel leaking from fuel lines, a cracked or damaged canister, an inoperative canister vacuum valve, and disconnected, misrouted, kinked or damaged vapour or control hoses.
3 Inspect each hose attached to the canister for kinks, leaks and cracks along its entire length. Repair or renew as necessary.
4 Inspect the canister. If it is cracked or damaged, renew it. Look for fuel leaking from the bottom of the canister. If fuel is leaking, renew the canister, and check the hoses and hose routing.

Component renewal

Carbon canister

5 The canister is located under the rear of the vehicle, attached to the rear subframe (see illustration).

Emission control systems 4B•3

4.6 Depress the release buttons (arrowed) and disconnect the hoses

4.10a Canister purge valve (arrowed) – 1.4 and 1.6 litre engines . . .

4.10b . . . and 1.8 and 2.0 litre engines (arrowed)

6 Note their fitted locations, then press in the release buttons, and disconnect the hoses from the canister **(see illustration)**.
7 Undo the two retaining screws and lower the canister from place.
8 Refitting is a reversal of removal.

Canister purge valve (EVAP)

9 The canister purge valve is mounted in the engine compartment, on the left-hand end of the cylinder head. Remove the battery and battery tray as described in Chapter 5A.
10 Note their fitted positions, then disconnect the vacuum pipes and wiring plug from the valve **(see illustrations)**.
11 Unclip the valve from the bracket.
12 Refitting is a reversal of removal.

5 Exhaust emission control systems – checking and component renewal

Checking

1 Checking of the system as a whole entails a close visual inspection of all hoses, pipes and connections for condition and security. Apart from this, any known or suspected faults should be attended to by a Ford dealer or suitably-equipped specialist.

Component renewal

Heated oxygen (lambda) sensors

Note: *The sensor is delicate, and will not work if it is dropped or knocked, if its power supply is disrupted, or if any cleaning materials are used on it.*

2 Disconnect the oxygen sensor wiring plugs at the rear of the engine **(see illustrations)**.
3 Unscrew the sensors from place **(see illustrations)**.
4 On refitting, clean the sealing washer (where fitted) and renew it if it is damaged or worn. Apply a smear of anti-seize compound to the sensor's threads, then refit the sensor, tightening it to the specified torque. Reconnect the wiring and secure with cable-ties where applicable.

Catalytic converter(s)

5 The catalytic converter(s) is part of the exhaust manifold. Refer to Part A of this Chapter for renewal procedures and additional information.

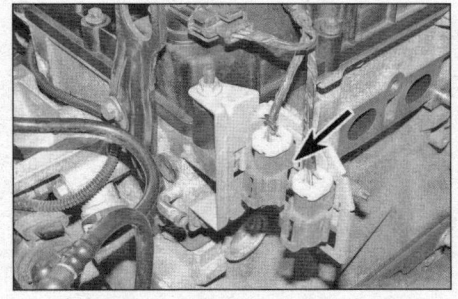

5.2a Oxygen sensor wiring plugs (arrowed) at the left-hand rear corner of the cylinder head – 1.4 and 1.6 litre engines . . .

5.3a An oxygen sensor is fitted to the exhaust manifold . . .

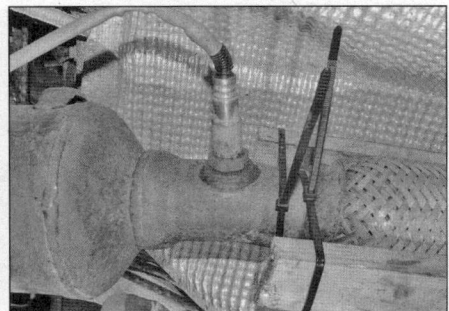

5.3b . . . and the front section of the exhaust pipe

EGR solenoid/valve

6 Remove the plastic cover on the top of the engine by pulling it straight up from its mountings.
7 Remove the air cleaner assembly as described in Chapter 4A.
8 Drain the coolant as described in Chapter 1. Alternatively, use hose clamps prior to disconnecting the coolant hoses from the EGR valve.
9 Slacken the clamps and remove the air cleaner outlet pipe.
10 Disconnect the EGR valve solenoid wiring plug **(see illustration)**.
11 Release the clamps and disconnect the coolant hoses from the EGR valve.
12 Undo the 2 bolts and remove the EGR valve/solenoid. Recover the gasket.
13 Refitting is a reversal of removal, renewing the gasket where applicable.

5.2b . . . and 1.8 and 2.0 litre engines (arrowed)

5.10 The EGR valve (arrowed) is located at the left-hand end of the cylinder head

Notes

Chapter 5 Part A:
Starting and charging systems

Contents

	Section number
Alternator – removal and refitting	5
Auxiliary drivebelt check and renewal	See Chapter 1
Battery – removal and refitting	3
Battery – testing and charging	2
Battery check	See *Weekly checks*
Charging system – testing	4
General information and precautions	1
Starter motor – removal and refitting	7
Starter motor – testing and overhaul	8
Starting system – testing	6

Degrees of difficulty

Easy, suitable for novice with little experience
Fairly easy, suitable for beginner with some experience
Fairly difficult, suitable for competent DIY mechanic
Difficult, suitable for experienced DIY mechanic
Very difficult, suitable for expert DIY or professional

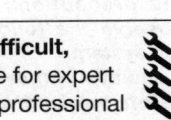

Specifications

System type	12 volt, negative earth

Battery

Type	Low-maintenance or maintenance-free sealed for life
Capacity	43, 50, 60 or 70 Ah (depending on model)
Charge condition:	
Poor	12.5 volts
Normal	12.6 volts
Good	12.7 volts

Torque wrench settings

	Nm	lbf ft
Alternator mounting bolts:		
1.4 and 1.6 litre engines	45	33
1.8 and 2.0 litre engines	25	18
Alternator pulley	80	59
Starter motor mounting bolts	35	26

1 General information and precautions

General information

The engine electrical system consists mainly of the charging and starting systems. Because of their engine-related functions, these components are covered separately from the body electrical devices such as the lights, instruments, etc (which are covered in Chapter 12). Information on the ignition system is covered in Part B of this Chapter.

The electrical system is of the 12 volt negative earth type.

The battery is of the low-maintenance or maintenance-free (sealed for life) type, and is charged by the alternator, which is belt-driven from the crankshaft pulley.

The starter motor is of the pre-engaged type, incorporating an integral solenoid. On starting, the solenoid moves the drive pinion into engagement with the flywheel ring gear before the starter motor is energised. Once the engine has started, a one-way clutch prevents the motor armature being driven by the engine until the pinion disengages from the flywheel.

Further details of the various systems are given in the relevant Sections of this Chapter. While some repair procedures are given, the usual course of action is to renew the component concerned.

Precautions

Warning: *It is necessary to take extra care when working on the electrical system to avoid damage to semi-conductor devices (diodes and transistors), and to avoid the risk of personal injury. In addition to the precautions given in Safety first!, observe the following when working on the system:*

• *Always remove rings, watches, etc, before working on the electrical system.* Even with the battery disconnected, capacitive discharge could occur if a component's live terminal is earthed through a metal object. This could cause a shock or nasty burn.

• *Do not reverse the battery connections.* Components such as the alternator, electronic control units, or any other components having semi-conductor circuitry could be irreparably damaged.

• Never disconnect the battery terminals, the alternator, any electrical wiring or any test instruments when the engine is running.

• Do not allow the engine to turn the alternator when the alternator is not connected.

• Never test for alternator output by 'flashing' the output lead to earth.

• Always ensure that the battery negative lead is disconnected when working on the electrical system.

• If the engine is being started using jump leads and a slave battery, connect the batteries *positive-to-positive* and *negative-to-negative* (see *Jump starting*). This also applies when connecting a battery charger.

• *Never* use an ohmmeter of the type incorporating a hand-cranked generator for circuit or continuity testing.

• Before using electric-arc welding equipment on the car, *disconnect the battery, alternator and components such as the electronic control units* (where applicable) to protect them from the risk of damage.

2 Battery – testing and charging

Testing

Standard and low-maintenance battery

1 If the vehicle covers a small annual mileage, it is worthwhile checking the specific gravity of the electrolyte every three months to determine the state of charge of the battery. Use a hydrometer to make the check, and compare the results with the following table. Note that the specific gravity readings assume an electrolyte temperature of 15°C; for every 10°C below 15°C subtract 0.007. For every 10°C above 15°C add 0.007.

	Ambient temperature	
	Above 25°C	Below 25°C
Fully-charged	1.210 to 1.230	1.270 to 1.290
70% charged	1.170 to 1.190	1.230 to 1.250
Discharged	1.050 to 1.070	1.110 to 1.130

2 If the battery condition is suspect, first check the specific gravity of electrolyte in each cell. A variation of 0.040 or more between any cells indicates loss of electrolyte or deterioration of the internal plates.

3 If the specific gravity variation is 0.040 or more, the battery should be renewed. If the cell variation is satisfactory but the battery is discharged, it should be charged as described later in this Section.

Maintenance-free battery

4 In cases where a sealed for life maintenance-free battery is fitted, topping-up and testing of the electrolyte in each cell may not be possible. The condition of the battery can therefore only be tested using a battery condition indicator or a voltmeter.

5 Certain models my be fitted with a maintenance-free battery, with a built-in charge condition indicator. The indicator is located in the top of the battery casing, and indicates the condition of the battery from its colour. The charge conditions denoted by the colour of the indicator should be printed on a label attached to the battery – if not, consult a Ford dealer or automotive electrician for advice.

All types

6 If testing the battery using a voltmeter, connect the voltmeter across the battery and note the voltage. The test is only accurate if the battery has not been subjected to any kind of charge for the previous six hours. If this is not the case, switch on the headlights for 30 seconds, then wait four to five minutes before testing the battery after switching off the headlights. All other electrical circuits must be switched off, so check that the doors and tailgate are fully shut when making the test.

7 If the voltage reading is less than 12.2 volts, then the battery is discharged, whilst a reading of 12.2 to 12.4 volts indicates a partially-discharged condition.

8 If the battery is to be charged, remove it from the vehicle and charge it as described later in this Section.

Charging

Note: *The following is intended as a guide only. Always refer to the manufacturer's recommendations (often printed on a label attached to the battery) before charging a battery.*

Standard and low-maintenance battery

9 Charge the battery at a rate equivalent to 10% of the battery capacity (eg, for a 45 Ah battery charge at 4.5 A) and continue to charge the battery at this rate until no further rise in specific gravity is noted over a four-hour period.

10 Alternatively, a trickle charger charging at the rate of 1.5 amps can safely be used overnight.

11 Specially rapid boost charges which are claimed to restore the power of the battery in 1 to 2 hours are not recommended, as they can cause serious damage to the battery plates through overheating. If the battery is completely flat, recharging should take at least 24 hours.

12 While charging the battery, note that the temperature of the electrolyte should never exceed 38°C.

Maintenance-free battery

13 This battery type takes considerably longer to fully recharge than the standard type, the time taken being dependent on the extent of discharge, but it can take anything up to three days.

14 A constant voltage type charger is required, to be set, when connected, to 13.9 to 14.9 volts with a charger current below 25 amps. Using this method, the battery should be useable within three hours, giving a voltage reading of 12.5 volts, but this is for a partially-discharged battery and, as mentioned, full charging can take far longer.

15 If the battery is to be charged from a fully-discharged state (condition reading less than 12.2 volts), have it recharged by your Ford dealer or local automotive electrician, as the charge rate is higher, and constant supervision during charging is necessary.

Starting and charging systems 5A•3

3.2 Release the clip and remove the battery cover

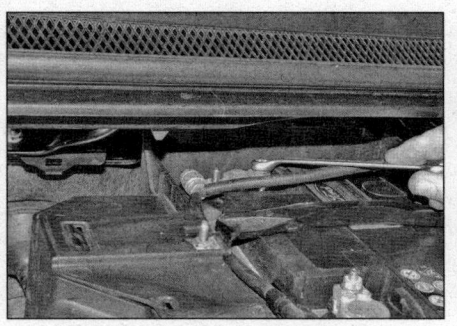

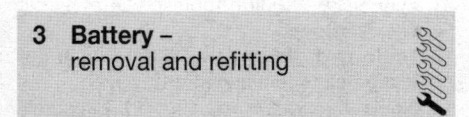

3.3 Slacken the nut and disconnect the battery negative terminal . . .

3.4 . . . followed by the positive terminal

3 Battery – removal and refitting

Caution: *Wait at least 5 minutes after turning off the ignition switch before disconnect the battery. This is to allow sufficient time for the various control modules to store information.*

Note: *Ensure you have the audio unit security code. This code will need to be inputted after reconnecting the battery – refer to the owner's handbook supplied with the vehicle.*

Removal

1 The battery is located on the left-hand side of the engine compartment. Begin by removing the air cleaner assembly as described in Chapter 4A.
2 Release the clip and remove the battery cover **(see illustration)**.
3 Slacken the clamp nut and disconnect the battery negative lead terminal **(see illustration)**.
4 Slacken the clamp nut and disconnect the battery positive lead terminal **(see illustration)**.
5 Using a screwdriver release the clips securing the cables to the battery box, then unclip and remove the front wall of the battery box.
6 Unscrew the nuts and remove the battery retaining clamp **(see illustration)**.
7 Lift the battery out of the engine compartment.
8 To remove the battery tray, begin by removing the air cleaner assembly as described in Chapter 4A.
9 On 1.4 and 1.6 litre models, and 1.8 and 2.0 litre models up to 03/2007, unclip the cover, then undo the 3 Torx bolts and move the engine management PCM from its location on the side of the battery tray and lay it over the engine – refer to Chapter 4A if necessary.
10 Undo the 3 bolts and remove the battery tray **(see illustration)**.

Refitting

11 Position the battery in the battery box.
12 Refit the retaining clamp and tighten the retaining nuts securely.
13 Reconnect the battery positive lead, followed by the negative lead. Smear a little petroleum jelly on the terminals. Ensure no-one is inside the vehicle whilst the battery is reconnected.
14 Refit the battery cover.
15 After reconnecting the battery, the engine may run erratically until it's been driven for a few minutes to allow the PCM to relearn. Also the electric windows may need to be re-initialised as follows:
 a) Press and hold the window control close button until the window is fully closed.
 b) Release the button, then press it again for 3 seconds.
 c) Briefly press the open button to the second detent, then release it. The window should open automatically.
 d) Briefly press the close button to the second detent, then release it. If the window does not close automatically, repeat the complete procedure.
 e) Repeat this procedure on each electric window.

4 Charging system – testing

Note: *Refer to the warnings given in Safety first! and in Section 1 of this Chapter before starting work.*

1 If the ignition/no-charge warning light fails to illuminate when the ignition is switched on, first check the alternator wiring connections for security. If all is satisfactory, the alternator maybe at fault and should be renewed or taken to an auto-electrician for testing and repair.
2 If the ignition warning light illuminates when the engine is running, stop the engine and check that the drivebelt is correctly tensioned (see Chapter 1) and that the alternator connections are secure. If all is so far satisfactory, have the alternator checked by an auto-electrician for testing and repair.
3 If the alternator output is suspect even though the warning light functions correctly, the regulated voltage may be checked as follows.
4 Connect a voltmeter across the battery terminals and start the engine.
5 Increase the engine speed until the voltmeter reading remains steady; the reading should be between 13.5 and 14.8 volts.
6 Switch on as many electrical accessories (eg, the headlights, heated rear window and heater blower) as possible, and check that the alternator maintains the regulated voltage between 13.5 and 14.8 volts.
7 If the regulated voltage is not as stated, the fault may be due to worn brushes, weak brush springs, a faulty voltage regulator, a faulty diode, a severed phase winding, or worn or damaged slip-rings. At the time of writing, it would appear that no parts were available for the alternator. If faulty the complete assembly must be renewed. In doubt, the alternator should be renewed or taken to an auto-electrician for testing.

3.6 Undo the battery clamp nuts (arrowed)

3.10 Battery tray bolts (arrowed)

5A•4 Starting and charging systems

5.2 Power steering fluid reservoir bolt (arrowed)

5.4 Alternator upper mounting nut (arrowed)

5.5 Alternator lower mounting bolt (arrowed)

5 Alternator – removal and refitting

Removal

1 Disconnect the battery negative lead (see Section 3).
2 Undo the bolt and move the power steering reservoir to one side (models with conventional power steering only) **(see illustration)**.
3 Remove the auxiliary drivebelt as described in Chapter 1.

1.4 and 1.6 litre engines

4 Undo and remove the alternator upper mounting nut **(see illustration)**.
5 Undo the alternator lower retaining bolt **(see illustration)**.
6 Undo the remaining upper mounting bolt and remove the splash shield **(see illustration)**.

7 Unclip the alternator wiring harness, then disconnect the power steering pressure switch, and the plug from the rear of the alternator.
8 Prise off the plastic cap, then undo the nut and disconnect the remaining cable from the rear of the alternator.
9 Unscrew the alternator upper mounting stud. This can be done using two nuts locked together on the stud's threads, or pull the alternator forwards a little and use a pair of self-grip pliers to unscrew the stud. Support the alternator as the stud is removed, then lift the alternator from place.

1.8 and 2.0 litre engines

10 Remove the plastic cover on the top of the engine by pulling it straight upwards from its mountings.
11 Remove the right-hand side headlight assembly as described in Chapter 12.
12 Undo the upper bolt securing the engine oil level dipstick guide tube to the manifold **(see illustration)**.
13 Undo and remove the alternator upper mounting bolt **(see illustration)**.
14 Raise the vehicle and support it securely on axle stands (see *Jacking and vehicle support*). Where fitted, undo the fasteners and remove the engine undershield.
15 Working underneath, unclip the refrigerant pipe (where applicable) and move it to one side. There's no need to disconnect the refrigerant pipe.
16 Undo the lower retaining bolt and pull the engine oil level dipstick tube from place **(see illustration)**.
17 Disconnect the wiring plug, then prise out the rubber cap and disconnect the lead from the rear of the alternator **(see illustration)**.
18 Undo the 2 lower mounting bolts and lower the alternator **(see illustration)**.

5.6 Alternator upper mounting bolt (arrowed)

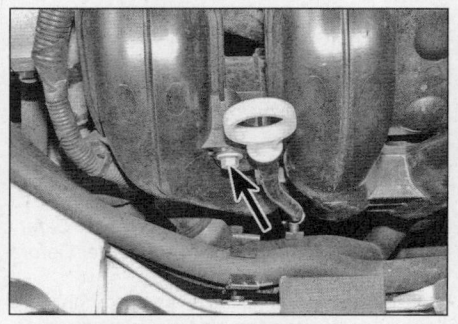

5.12 Undo the engine oil level dipstick guide tube bolt (arrowed)

5.13 Alternator upper mounting bolt (arrowed) – viewed through the headlight aperture

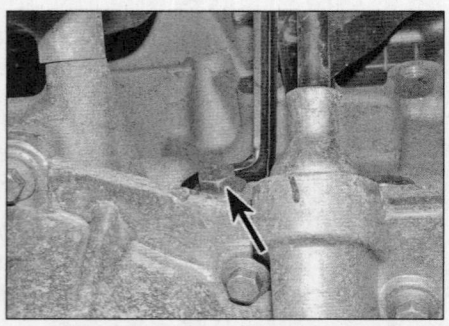

5.16 Engine oil level dipstick guide tube lower bolt (arrowed)

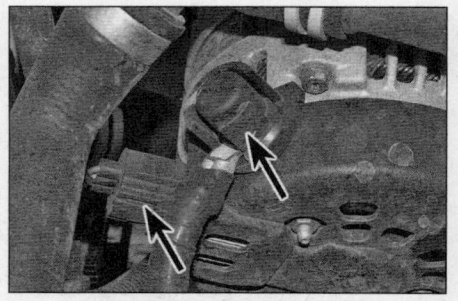

5.17 Disconnect the wiring plug, then pull away the rubber cap and disconnect the lead from the terminal stud (arrowed)

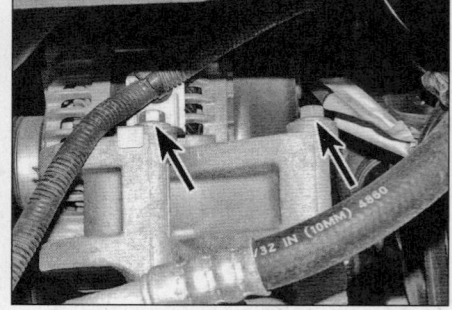

5.18 Alternator lower mounting bolts (arrowed)

Starting and charging systems 5A•5

Refitting

19 Refitting is a reversal of removal. Remembering to tighten the various fasteners to their specified torque where given.

6 Starting system – testing

Note: *Refer to the precautions given in Safety first! and in Section 1 of this Chapter before starting work.*

1 If the starter motor fails to operate when the ignition key is turned to the appropriate position, the following possible causes may be to blame:
a) The battery is faulty.
b) The electrical connections between the switch, solenoid, battery and starter motor are somewhere failing to pass the necessary current from the battery through the starter to earth.
c) The solenoid is faulty.
d) The starter motor is mechanically or electrically defective.

2 To check the battery, switch on the headlights. If they dim after a few seconds, this indicates that the battery is discharged – recharge (see Section 2) or renew the battery. If the headlights glow brightly, operate the ignition switch and observe the lights. If they dim, then this indicates that current is reaching the starter motor, therefore the fault must lie in the starter motor. If the lights continue to glow brightly (and no clicking sound can be heard from the starter motor solenoid), this indicates that there is a fault in the circuit or solenoid – see following paragraphs. If the starter motor turns slowly when operated, but the battery is in good condition, then this indicates that either the starter motor is faulty, or there is considerable resistance somewhere in the circuit.

3 If a fault in the circuit is suspected, disconnect the battery leads (including the earth connection to the body), the starter/solenoid wiring and the engine/transmission earth strap. Thoroughly clean the connections, and reconnect the leads and wiring, then use a voltmeter or test light to check that full battery voltage is available at the battery positive lead connection to the solenoid, and that the earth is sound. Smear petroleum jelly around the battery terminals to prevent corrosion – corroded connections are amongst the most frequent causes of electrical system faults.

4 If the battery and all connections are in good condition, check the circuit by disconnecting the wire from the solenoid blade terminal. Connect a voltmeter or test light between the wire end and a good earth (such as the battery negative terminal), and check that the wire is live when the ignition switch is turned to the start position. If it is, then the circuit is sound – if not, the circuit wiring can be checked as described in Chapter 12.

7.4 Undo the 2 nuts (arrowed) and disconnect the starter motor wiring

7.7 Undo the nut (arrowed) and slide the wiring terminal from the stud

5 The solenoid contacts can be checked by connecting a voltmeter or test light between the battery positive feed connection on the starter side of the solenoid, and earth. When the ignition switch is turned to the start position, there should be a reading or lighted bulb, as applicable. If there is no reading or lighted bulb, the solenoid is faulty and should be renewed.

6 If the circuit and solenoid are proved sound, the fault must lie in the starter motor. In this event, it may be possible to have the starter motor overhauled by a specialist, but check on the cost of spares before proceeding, as it may prove more economical to obtain a new or exchange motor.

7 Starter motor – removal and refitting

Removal

1 Disconnect the battery negative lead (see Section 3).

1.4 and 1.6 litre engines

2 Remove the air cleaner assembly as described in Chapter 4A.
3 On 1.6 litre Ti-VCT engines, remove the throttle body as described in Chapter 4A.
4 Disconnect the starter motor wiring connections **(see illustration)**.
5 Support the starter motor, then undo the

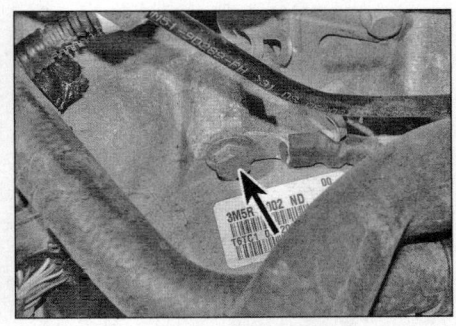

7.5 Note the earth connection on the rearmost starter mounting bolt (arrowed)

7.8 Remove the wiring harness bracket from the starter motor retaining studs/bolts

3 retaining bolts and manoeuvre it from place **(see illustration)**. Note the earth connection on the rearmost bolt and the bracket on the lower bolt.

1.8 and 2.0 litre engines

6 Raise the front of the vehicle and support it securely on axle stands (see *Jacking and vehicle support*). Where fitted, undo the fasteners and remove the engine undershield.
7 Disconnect the wiring from the starter solenoid **(see illustration)**.
8 Undo the retaining nuts and move the wiring bracket to one side **(see illustration)**.
9 Undo the mounting studs and remove the starter motor. Discard the gasket.

Refitting

10 Refitting is a reversal of removal. Tighten all fasteners to their specified torque where given.

8 Starter motor – testing and overhaul

If the starter motor is thought to be suspect, it should be removed from the vehicle and taken to an auto-electrician for testing. Most auto-electricians will be able to supply and fit brushes at a reasonable cost. However, check on the cost of repairs before proceeding, as it may prove more economical to obtain a new or exchange motor.

Notes

Chapter 5 Part B:
Ignition system

Contents

	Section number		Section number
Electronic ignition HT coil(s) – removal and refitting	3	Ignition timing – checking and adjustment	4
Ignition system – general information and precautions	1	Knock sensor – removal and refitting	5
Ignition system – testing	2	Spark plug renewal	See Chapter 1

Degrees of difficulty

| Easy, suitable for novice with little experience | Fairly easy, suitable for beginner with some experience | Fairly difficult, suitable for competent DIY mechanic | Difficult, suitable for experienced DIY mechanic | Very difficult, suitable for expert DIY or professional |

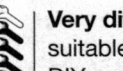

Specifications

General
System type .... Electronic distributorless ignition system controlled by engine management system (Powertrain Control Module)
Firing order 1-3-4-2
Location of No 1 cylinder .... Timing chain/belt end

Ignition system data
Ignition timing .... Controlled by the Powertrain Control Module (PCM)
Ignition coil resistances .... Not available

Torque wrench settings
	Nm	lbf ft
Ignition coil:		
1.4 and 1.6 litre engines	6	4
1.8 and 2.0 litre engines	10	7
Knock sensors	20	15

1 Ignition system – general information and precautions

General information

The ignition system is integrated with the fuel injection system to form a combined engine management system under the control of the Powertrain control module (PCM) (see Chapter 4A for further information). The main ignition system components include the ignition switch, the battery, the crankshaft speed/position sensor, the ignition coil, the camshaft position sensor(s), the knock sensor(s), and the spark plugs.

A Distributorless Ignition System (DIS) is fitted where the main functions of the conventional distributor are superseded by a computerised module within the Powertrain Control Module. On 1.4 and 1.6 litre engines, the remote ignition coil unit combines a double-ended pair of coils – each time a coil receives an ignition signal, two sparks are produced, one at each end of the secondary windings. One spark goes to a cylinder on its compression stroke and the other goes to the corresponding cylinder on its exhaust stroke. The first will give the correct power stroke, but the second spark will have no effect (a 'wasted spark'), occurring as it does during exhaust conditions. On 1.8 and 2.0 litre engines, one coil fitted for each spark plug. The coil fits above the spark plug, and has an integral power stage and HT cap.

The information contained in this Chapter concentrates on the ignition-related components of the engine management system. Information covering the fuel, exhaust and emission control components can be found in the applicable Parts of Chapter 4.

Precautions

The following precautions must be observed, to prevent damage to the ignition system components and to reduce risk of personal injury.

a) Do not keep the ignition on for more than 10 seconds if the engine will not start.
b) Ensure that the ignition is switched off before disconnecting any of the ignition wiring.
c) Ensure that the ignition is switched off before connecting or disconnecting any ignition test equipment, such as a timing light.
d) Do not earth the coil primary or secondary circuits.

Warning: Voltages produced by an electronic ignition system are considerably higher than those produced by conventional ignition systems. Extreme care must be taken when working on the system with the ignition switched on. Persons with surgically-implanted cardiac pacemaker devices should keep well clear of the ignition circuits, components and test equipment.

5B•2 Ignition system

3.2 Disconnect the ignition coil wiring plug (arrowed)

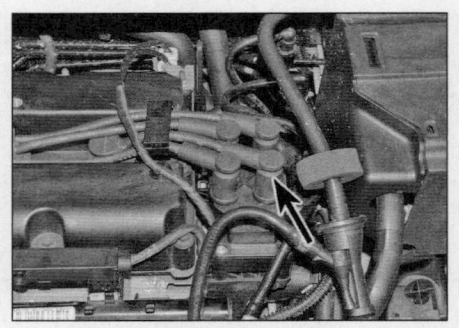

3.3 Pull the HT leads (arrowed) from the terminals on the coil

2 Ignition system – testing

Warning: *Voltages produced by an electronic ignition system are considerably higher than those produced by conventional ignition systems. Extreme care must be taken when working on the system if the ignition is switched on. Persons with surgically-implanted cardiac pacemaker devices should keep well clear of the ignition circuits, components and test equipment.*

General

1 The components of the ignition system are normally very reliable; most faults are far more likely to be due to loose or dirty connections, or to tracking of HT voltage due to dirt, dampness or damaged insulation, than to the failure of any of the system's components. **Always** check all wiring thoroughly before condemning an electrical component, and work methodically to eliminate all other possibilities before deciding that a particular component is faulty.

2 The old practice of checking for a spark by holding the live end of an HT cap a short distance away from the engine is **not** recommended; not only is there a high risk of a powerful electric shock, but the PCM or HT coil may be damaged. Similarly, **never** try to diagnose misfires by pulling off one HT coil at a time.

3 The following tests should be carried out when an obvious fault such as non-starting or a clearly detectable misfire exists. Some faults, however, are more obscure and are often disguised by the fact that the PCM will adopt an emergency program (limp-home) mode to maintain as much driveability as possible. Faults of this nature usually appear in the form of excessive fuel consumption, poor idling characteristics, lack of performance, knocking or pinking noises from the engine under certain conditions, or a combination of these conditions. Where problems such as this are experienced, the best course is to refer the car to a suitably-equipped garage for diagnostic testing using dedicated test equipment.

Engine will not start

Note: Remember that a fault with the anti-theft alarm or immobiliser will give rise to apparent starting problems. Make sure that the alarm or immobiliser has been deactivated, referring to the vehicle handbook for details.

4 If the engine either will not turn over at all, or only turns very slowly, check the battery and starter motor. Connect a voltmeter across the battery terminals (meter positive probe to battery positive terminal) then note the voltage reading obtained while turning the engine over on the starter for (no more than) ten seconds. If the reading obtained is less than approximately 9.5 volts, first check the battery, starter motor and charging system as described in Part A of this Chapter.

Engine misfires

5 An irregular misfire is probably due to a loose connection to one of the ignition coils or system sensors.

6 With the ignition switched off, check carefully through the system, ensuring that all connections are clean and securely fastened.

7 Regular misfiring indicates a problem with one of the ignition coils or spark plugs. As no resistance values are available, testing the coils is best left to a Ford dealer or suitably-equipped specialist.

8 Any further checking of the system components should be carried out after first checking the PCM for fault codes.

3 Electronic ignition HT coil(s) – removal and refitting

Removal

1.4 and 1.6 litre engines

1 The ignition coil is bolted to the coolant outlet elbow on the left-hand end of the cylinder head.

2 Make sure the ignition is switched off, then disconnect the main wiring plug from the coil **(see illustration)**.

3 Identify the HT leads for position (mark the leads and the coil terminals) then carefully pull them from the terminals on the coil **(see illustration)**.

4 Unscrew the four mounting bolts and remove the ignition coil from the engine compartment. Where applicable, recover the heat shield/mounting plate.

1.8 and 2.0 litre engines

5 Remove the plastic cover from the top of the engine, by pulling it upwards from the mountings.

6 Disconnect the ignition coil(s) wiring plug(s) **(see illustration)**. It is safest to work on one coil at a time. However, if the coils and the wiring plugs are marked for position, all 4 could be removed at once.

7 Each coil is secured by 1 bolt. Undo the bolt and pull the coil from the cylinder head **(see illustration)**.

Refitting

8 Refitting is a reversal of removal. Tighten the retaining bolts to the specified torque.

4 Ignition timing – checking and adjustment

Due to the nature of the ignition system, the ignition timing is constantly being monitored and adjusted by the engine management PCM, and nominal values cannot be given. Therefore, it is not possible for the home mechanic to check the ignition timing.

3.6 Press down the clip and disconnect the coil wiring plug

3.7 Undo the bolts and pull the coil from place

Ignition system 5B•3

The only way in which the ignition timing can be checked is using special electronic test equipment, connected to the engine management system diagnostic connector (refer to Chapter 4A). No adjustment of the ignition timing is possible. Should the ignition timing be incorrect, then a fault must be present in the engine management system.

5 Knock sensor – removal and refitting

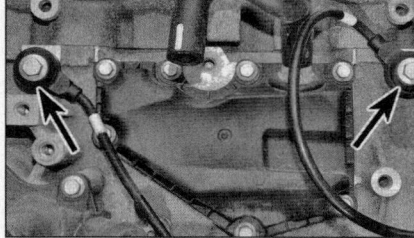

5.4 The knock sensors (arrowed) are located under the inlet manifold – 1.6 litre Ti-VCT engine

5.8 Knock sensor (arrowed) – 1.8 and 2.0 litre engines

Removal

1.4 and 1.6 litre models

1 Remove the alternator as described in Chapter 5A.
2 The knock sensor is located on the front facing side of the cylinder block under the inlet manifold.
3 Trace the wiring back from the sensor to the connector, then slide the retaining clip down and disconnect the wiring plug.
4 Note its fitted position, then undo the bolt and remove the sensor **(see illustration)**.

1.8 and 2.0 litre models

5 The knock sensors are located on the front facing side of the cylinder block under the inlet manifold.
6 Refer to Chapter 4A and remove the inlet manifold.
7 Disconnect the wiring connector from the knock sensor(s).
8 Note the fitted position of the sensor(s), it is essential that it is refitted to its original positions. Undo the retaining bolt and remove the sensor **(see illustration)**.

Refitting

9 Refitting is a reversal of removal, noting the following points:
a) *The sensor(s) must be refitted in their original positions, with the wiring harness angle exactly as before.*
b) *Tightening the retaining bolt to the specified torque is absolutely essential. Failure to do so could impair the performance of the sensor, causing engine damage.*

Notes

Chapter 6
Clutch

Contents

	Section number
Clutch assembly – removal, inspection and refitting	6
Clutch fluid level check	See Weekly checks
Clutch hydraulic system – bleeding	5
Clutch master cylinder – removal and refitting	3
Clutch pedal – removal and refitting	2

	Section number
Clutch pedal position switch – renewal	See Chapter 4A
Clutch release bearing – removal, inspection and refitting	7
Clutch slave cylinder – removal and refitting	4
General information	1
Hose and fluid leak check	See Chapter 1

Degrees of difficulty

Easy, suitable for novice with little experience	Fairly easy, suitable for beginner with some experience	Fairly difficult, suitable for competent DIY mechanic	Difficult, suitable for experienced DIY mechanic	Very difficult, suitable for expert DIY or professional

Specifications

General
Clutch type.. Single dry plate, diaphragm spring, hydraulic actuation

Driven plate
Warp limit... 0.2 mm

Torque wrench settings
	Nm	lbf ft
Pressure plate retaining bolts	29	21
Release bearing and slave cylinder mounting bolts	10	7

1 General information

A single dry plate diaphragm spring clutch is fitted to all manual transmission models. The clutch is hydraulically operated via a master and slave cylinder. All models have an internally-mounted slave cylinder and release bearing combined into one unit.

The main components of the clutch are the pressure plate, the driven plate (sometimes called the friction plate or disc) and the release bearing. The pressure plate is bolted to the flywheel, with the driven plate sandwiched between them. The centre of the driven plate carries female splines which mate with the splines on the transmission input shaft. The release bearing acts on the diaphragm spring fingers of the pressure plate.

When the engine is running and the clutch pedal is released, the diaphragm spring clamps the pressure plate, driven plate and flywheel firmly together. Drive is transmitted through the friction surfaces of the flywheel and pressure plate to the linings of the driven plate, and thus to the transmission input shaft.

The slave cylinder is incorporated into the release bearing – when the slave cylinder operates, the release bearing moves against the diaphragm spring fingers. As the spring pressure on the pressure plate is relieved, the flywheel and pressure plate spin without moving the driven plate. As the pedal is released, spring pressure is restored and the drive is gradually taken up.

The clutch hydraulic system consists of a master cylinder, a slave cylinder and the associated pipes and hoses. The fluid reservoir is shared with the brake master cylinder.

2 Clutch pedal – removal and refitting

Warning: *Hydraulic fluid is poisonous; wash off immediately and thoroughly in the case of skin contact, and seek immediate medical advice if any fluid is swallowed or gets into the eyes. Certain types of hydraulic fluid are inflammable, and may ignite when allowed into contact with hot components; when servicing any hydraulic system, it is safest to assume that the fluid IS inflammable, and to take precautions against the risk of fire as though it is petrol that is being handled. Hydraulic fluid is also an effective paint stripper, and will attack plastics; if any is spilt, it should be washed off immediately, using copious quantities of clean water. Finally, it is hygroscopic (it absorbs moisture from the air) – old fluid may be contaminated and unfit for further use. When topping-up or renewing the fluid, always use the recommended type, and ensure that it comes from a freshly-opened sealed container.*

Note: *Renewal of the clutch pedal return spring supposedly involves removal of the pedal assembly as described here. However, some owners report that it can be renewed in situ, although it is difficult to get at. The spring can be seen in illustration 2.8, top right.*

Removal

1 Remove the facia as described in Chapter 11, then remove the steering column as described in Chapter 10.

Models with a plastic panel in front of the brake master cylinder

2 Remove the battery as described in Chapter 5A, then undo the 3 bolts and slide the battery tray forward a little (see illustration).

3 Prise out the 4 plastic clips securing the plastic panel to the engine compartment

2.2 Battery tray retaining bolts (arrowed)

6•2 Clutch

2.3a Prise out the 4 clips (arrowed)

2.3b Undo the 2 inner bolts, slacken the outer bolt, undo the 2 nuts and pivot the cross-stay (arrowed) each side away from the engine compartment bulkhead . . .

2.3c . . . so the plastic panel in front of the master cylinder can be removed

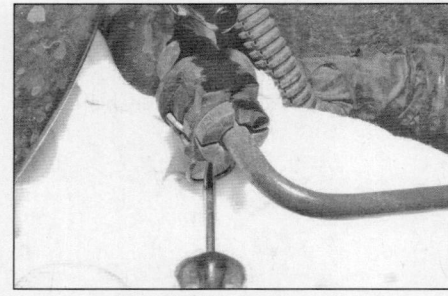

2.4a Prise down the clip and pull the pressure pipe from the clutch master cylinder

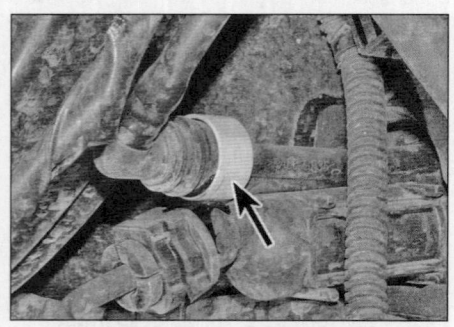

2.4b Pull back the collar (arrowed) and disconnect the fluid supply pipe

2.5 Disconnect the wiring plug (arrowed) from the clutch pedal position sensor

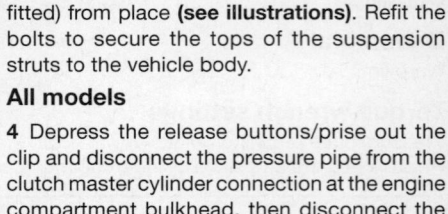

bulkhead, then undo the inner 2 retaining bolts, slacken the outer bolt, remove the nuts and pivot the cross-stay each side away from the bulkhead. Lift the plastic panel (where fitted) from place **(see illustrations)**. Refit the bolts to secure the tops of the suspension struts to the vehicle body.

All models

4 Depress the release buttons/prise out the clip and disconnect the pressure pipe from the clutch master cylinder connection at the engine compartment bulkhead, then disconnect the fluid supply hose from the master cylinder **(see illustrations)**. Be prepared for fluid spillage – wipe up any spills immediately – the fluid could damage paintwork, etc.

5 Disconnect the clutch pedal position sensor wiring plug **(see illustration)**.

6 Undo the retaining nuts and manoeuvre the clutch pedal complete with the bracket and master cylinder from place **(see illustration)**.

7 To separate the master cylinder from the pedal bracket, begin by squeezing the sides of the retaining clip and pull the pushrod from the pedal **(see illustration)**.

8 Rotate the master cylinder 60° clockwise and pull it from the bracket **(see illustration)**.

2.6 Undo the nuts (arrowed) and remove the pedal/master cylinder assembly

2.7 Squeeze the sides of the clip (arrowed) and pull the pushrod from the pedal

2.8 Rotate the master cylinder 60° clockwise and pull it from the bracket

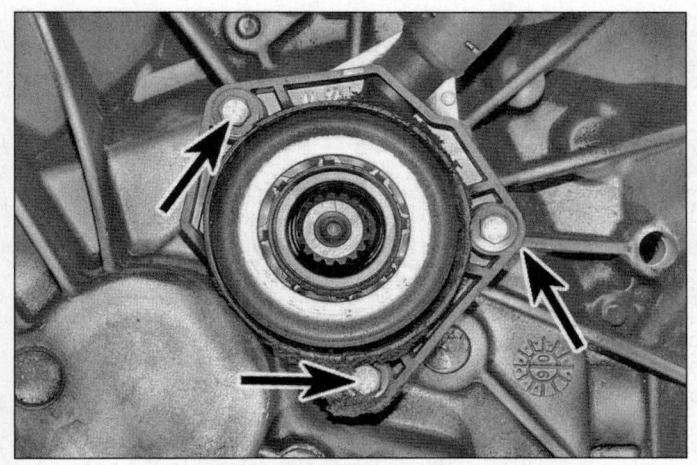

4.3 Slave cylinder mounting bolts (arrowed)

4.4 Apply a bead of sealant to the slave cylinder around the edge (arrowed)

Refitting

9 Refit by reversing the removal operations. Note the following points:
a) Tighten all fasteners securely.
b) Renew the seal between the master cylinder and the bulkhead if necessary.
c) Bleed the clutch hydraulic system as described in Section 5.
d) Check the operation of the clutch before refitting the lower facia panel.

3 Clutch master cylinder – removal and refitting

Note: *At the time of writing, it would appear that master cylinder internal components are not available separately, and therefore no repair or overhaul of the cylinder is possible. In the event of a hydraulic system fault, or any sign of visible fluid leakage on or around the master cylinder or clutch pedal, the unit should be renewed – consult a Ford dealer or specialist.*

1 Removal and refitting of the master cylinder is included in the pedal removal and refitting procedure described previously.

4 Clutch slave cylinder – removal and refitting

Note 1: *Slave cylinder internal components are not available separately, and no repair or overhaul of the cylinder is possible. In the event of a hydraulic system fault, or any sign of fluid leakage, the unit should be renewed.*
Note 2: *Refer to the warning at the beginning of Section 2 before proceeding.*

Removal

1 Remove the transmission as described in Chapter 7A. The internal slave cylinder cannot be removed with the transmission in place.
2 Release the rubber seal from the transmission.

3 Remove the mounting bolts securing the cylinder and release bearing assembly to the transmission, and remove the assembly, feeding the fluid pipe in through the transmission aperture **(see illustration)**.

Refitting

4 Ensure the release bearing/slave cylinder and transmission casing mating surfaces are clean. Apply a bead of sealant (Ford No ESK-M4G269-A) to the rear of the bearing/cylinder as shown **(see illustration)**.
5 Lubricate the inner lips of the seal with a little grease, then position the release bearing/slave cylinder on the input shaft, and tighten the bolts to the specified torque. Take care not to damage the seal lips with the input shaft splines – wrap adhesive tape around the splines prior to fitting the cylinder.
6 Refit the rubber seal around the pipes, ensuring it is correctly positioned.
7 The remainder of refitting is a reversal of removal, noting the following points:
a) Refit the transmission as described in Chapter 7A.
b) Remove the adhesive tape from the input shaft splines.
c) Bleed the clutch hydraulic system on completion (Section 5).

5 Clutch hydraulic system – bleeding

Note: *Refer to the warning at the beginning of Section 2 before proceeding.*

1 Top-up the hydraulic fluid reservoir on the brake master cylinder with fresh clean fluid of the specified type (see *Weekly checks*).
2 Remove the air cleaner assembly as described in Chapter 4A.
3 Remove the dust cover, and fit a length of clear hose over the bleed nipple on the slave cylinder **(see illustration)**. Place the other end of the hose in a jar containing a small amount of hydraulic fluid.

4 Slacken the bleed nipple half a turn, then have an assistant depress the clutch pedal. Tighten the bleed screw when the pedal is depressed. Have the assistant release the pedal, then slacken the bleed screw again.
5 Repeat the process until clean fluid, free of air bubbles, emerges from the bleed nipple. Tighten the nipple at the end of a pedal downstroke, and remove the hose and jar. Refit the dust cover.
6 Top-up the hydraulic fluid reservoir.
7 Pressure bleeding equipment may be used if preferred.

6 Clutch assembly – removal, inspection and refitting

⚠️ **Warning:** *Dust created by clutch wear and deposited on the clutch components may contain asbestos, which is a health hazard. DO NOT blow it out with compressed air or inhale any of it. DO NOT use petrol or petroleum-based solvents to clean off the dust. Brake system cleaner or methylated spirit should be used to flush the dust into a suitable receptacle. After the clutch components are wiped clean with rags, dispose of the contaminated rags and the used cleaner in a sealed, marked container.*

5.3 Connect the hose to the bleed nipple on the top of the transmission housing

6.3a Undo the pressure plate retaining bolts

6.3b Using a home-made tool to lock the flywheel

Removal

1 Access to the clutch may be gained in one of two ways. Either the engine/transmission assembly can be removed as described in Chapter 2C, and the transmission then separated from the engine, or the engine may be left in the car and the transmission removed independently as described in Chapter 7A. If the clutch is to be refitted, use paint or marker pen to mark the position of the pressure plate relative to the flywheel.

2 Having separated the transmission from the flywheel, check if there are any marks identifying the relation of the pressure plate to the flywheel. If not, make your own marks using a dab of paint or a scriber. These marks will be used if the original pressure plate is refitted, and will help to maintain the balance of the unit. A new pressure plate may be fitted in any position allowed by the locating dowels.

3 Unscrew and remove the 6 pressure plate retaining bolts, working in a diagonal sequence, and slackening the bolts only a turn at a time. If necessary, the flywheel may be held stationary using a home-made locking tool (see illustrations).

4 Ease the pressure plate off its locating dowels. Be prepared to catch the driven plate, which will drop out as the pressure plate is removed. Note which way round the driven plate is fitted.

Inspection

5 With the clutch assembly removed, clean off all traces of clutch dust using a dry cloth. This is best done outside or in a well-ventilated area.

6 Examine the linings of the driven plate for wear and loose rivets, and the rim for distortion, cracks, broken torsion springs and worn splines. The surface of the friction linings may be highly glazed, but, as long as the friction material pattern can be clearly seen, this is satisfactory.

7 If there is any sign of oil contamination, indicated by a continuous or patchy, shiny black discolouration, the plate must be renewed and the source of the contamination traced and rectified. This will be either a leaking crankshaft oil seal or transmission input shaft oil seal – or both.

8 The driven plate must also be renewed if the lining thickness has worn down to, or just above, the level of the rivet heads. Given the amount of dismantling work necessary to gain access to the driven plate, it may be wise to fit a new plate regardless of the old one's condition.

9 Check the machined faces of the flywheel and pressure plate. If either is grooved, or heavily scored, renewal is necessary. Providing the damage is not too serious, the flywheel can be removed as described in Chapter 2A or 2B, and taken to an engineering works, who may be able to clean up the surface by machining.

10 The pressure plate must be renewed if any cracks are apparent, if the diaphragm spring is damaged or its pressure suspect, or if there is excessive warpage of the pressure plate face.

11 With the transmission removed, check the condition of the release bearing, as described in Section 7.

Refitting

12 It is advisable to refit the clutch assembly with clean hands, and to wipe down the pressure plate and flywheel faces with a clean dry rag before assembly begins.

13 Fit an appropriate centring tool into the hole at the end of the crankshaft. The tool must be a sliding fit in the crankshaft hole and the driven plate centre. Ford centring tool No 308-204 may also be available, or a suitable equivalent may be fabricated.

14 Place the friction plate in position with the longer side of the centre boss towards the flywheel (1.4, 1.6 and 1.8 litre models), or with the spring hub assembly facing away from the flywheel (2.0 litre models), or as noted on removal. Note that the new driven plate will be marked to indicate which side faces the flywheel (see illustrations).

15 Place the pressure plate over the dowels. Refit the retaining bolts, and tighten them finger-tight so that the driven plate is gripped lightly, but can still be moved.

16 The driven plate must now be centralised so that, when the engine and transmission are mated, the splines of the gearbox input shaft will pass through the splines in the centre of the driven plate hub.

17 Centralisation can be carried out by inserting a round bar through the hole in the centre of the driven plate, so that the end of the bar rests in the hole in the rear end of the crankshaft. Move the bar sideways or up-and-down, to move the plate in whichever direction is necessary to achieve centralisation. Centralisation can then be checked by removing the bar and viewing the driven plate hub in relation to the diaphragm spring fingers, or by viewing through the side apertures of the pressure plate, and checking that the driven plate is central in relation to the outer edge of the pressure plate.

18 An alternative and more accurate method of centralisation is to use a commercially-available clutch-aligning tool, obtainable from most accessory shops (see illustration 6.14b).

19 Once the clutch is centralised, progressively tighten the pressure plate bolts in a diagonal sequence to the specified torque setting.

20 The engine and/or transmission can now be refitted by referring to the appropriate Chapters of this manual.

6.14a The clutch driven plate should be marked to indicate which side faces the transmission or flywheel

6.14b Position the driven plate using a clutch aligning tool

7 Clutch release bearing – removal, inspection and refitting

Removal

1 Access to the clutch release bearing may be gained in one of two ways. Either the engine/

transmission assembly can be removed as described in Chapter 2C, and the transmission then separated from the engine, or the engine may be left in the car and the transmission removed independently as described in Chapter 7A.

2 The release bearing and slave cylinder are combined into one unit, and cannot be separated. Refer to the slave cylinder removal procedure in Section 4.

Inspection

3 Check the bearing for smoothness of operation, and renew it if there is any roughness or harshness as the bearing is spun. It is a good idea to renew the bearing as a matter of course during clutch overhaul, regardless of its apparent condition, considering the amount of dismantling work necessary to gain access to it.

Refitting

4 Refer to Section 4.

Chapter 7 Part A:
Manual transmission

Contents

	Section number		Section number
Gearchange cables – adjustment	2	Transmission – removal and refitting	7
Gearchange cables and gear lever – removal and refitting	3	Transmission oil – draining and refilling	6
General information	1	Transmission oil level check	See Chapter 1
Oil seals – renewal	5	Transmission overhaul – general information	8
Reversing light switch – removal and refitting	4		

Degrees of difficulty

Easy, suitable for novice with little experience	Fairly easy, suitable for beginner with some experience	Fairly difficult, suitable for competent DIY mechanic	Difficult, suitable for experienced DIY mechanic	Very difficult, suitable for expert DIY or professional

Specifications

General
Transmission type.................................... Five forward speeds, one reverse. Synchromesh on all forward gears (and reverse gear on MTX 75 transmission). Gearchange linkage operated by twin cables

Transmission code:
- 1.4, 1.6 and 1.8 litre models................... iB5
- 2.0 litre models............................... MTX 75

Transmission oil type................................ See end of *Weekly checks* on page 0•17
Transmission oil capacity............................ See Chapter 1 Specifications

Gear ratios (typical)

iB5 transmission
- 1st.. 3.58:1
- 2nd... 2.04:1
- 3rd... 1.41:1
- 4th... 1.11:1
- 5th... 0.88:1
- Reverse... 3.62:1

MTX 75 transmission
- 1st.. 3.417:1
- 2nd... 2.136:1
- 3rd... 1.448:1
- 4th... 1.028:1
- 5th... 0.805:1
- Reverse... 3.737:1

Final drive ratios
- iB5 transmission.................................. 4.06:1
- MTX 75 transmission............................... 4.06:1

7A•2 Manual transmission

Torque wrench settings	Nm	lbf ft
Battery tray bolts	25	18
Crashbox-to-subframe bolts	40	30
Engine/transmission left-hand mounting lower section	80	59
Engine/transmission left-hand mounting upper section:		
Centre bolt*	148	109
Four outer nuts	48	35
Engine/transmission rear mounting through-bolts	80	59
Gearchange cable bracket bolts	20	15
Gearchange cable bushing	9	7
Gearchange mechanism to floor	9	7
Oil filler/level plug	35	26
Reversing light switch	18	13
Selector lever securing bolt	25	18
Slave cylinder pressure pipe bracket	28	21
Transmission to engine	48	35

* Do not re-use

1 General information

The transmission is contained in a cast-aluminium alloy casing bolted to the engine's left-hand end, and consists of the gearbox and final drive differential – often called a transaxle. The transmission unit type is stamped on a plate attached to the transmission. The 5-speed manual transmissions used in the Focus are the iB5 and MTX 75 types – refer to the Specifications for application details.

The iB5 unit is similar to that used in the previous Focus range, albeit with improved synchromesh components to improve the quality of gearchange. The MTX 75 transmission was also fitted to the previous Focus range. Both transmissions are equipped with cable operated gearchange linkage.

Drive is transmitted from the crankshaft via the clutch to the input shaft, which has a splined extension to accept the clutch driven plate. From the input shaft, drive is transmitted to the output shaft, from where the drive is transmitted to the differential crownwheel, which rotates with the differential and planetary gears, thus driving the sun gears and driveshafts. The rotation of the planetary gears on their shaft allows the inner roadwheel to rotate at a slower speed than the outer roadwheel when the car is cornering.

The input and output shafts are arranged side-by-side, parallel to the crankshaft and driveshafts, so that their gear pinion teeth are in constant mesh. In the neutral position, the output shaft gear pinions rotate freely, so that drive cannot be transmitted to the crownwheel.

Gear selection is via a floor-mounted lever and selector cable mechanism.

The transmission selector mechanism causes the appropriate selector fork to move its respective synchro-sleeve along the output shaft, to lock the gear pinion to the synchro-hub. Since the synchro-hubs are splined to the output shaft, this locks the pinion to the shaft, so that drive can be transmitted. To ensure that gearchanging can be made quickly and quietly, a synchromesh system is fitted to all forward gears, consisting of baulk rings and spring-loaded fingers, as well as the gear pinions and synchro-hubs. The synchromesh cones are formed on the mating faces of the baulk rings and gear pinions. The MTX 75 has synchromesh on reverse gear, and dual synchromesh on 1st, 2nd and 3rd gears, whilst the iB5 has no synchromesh on reverse, but dual synchromesh on 1st and 2nd gears.

Transmission overhaul

Because of the complexity of the assembly, possible unavailability of new parts and special tools necessary, internal repair procedures for the transmission are not recommended for the home mechanic. The bulk of the information in this Chapter is devoted to removal and refitting procedures.

2 Gearchange cables – adjustment

iB5 transmission

Note: *A 3 mm drill bit will be required for this adjustment.*

1 Inside the car, move the gear lever to neutral.

2 Carefully unclip the surround panel at the base of the gear lever gaiter, and move the panel aside for access to the base of the gear lever, disconnecting the switch wiring if necessary.

3 Move the gear lever to the 4th gear position, then insert a 3 mm drill bit into the gear lever base mechanism, making sure that it is fully inserted (see illustration).

4 Apply the handbrake, then jack up the front of the car, supporting it on axle stands (see *Jacking and vehicle support*). Where applicable, remove the engine undershield.

5 At the front face of the transmission housing, remove the selector mechanism cover by working around the edge, releasing a total of seven clips (see illustration).

6 Only the selector cable is to be adjusted during this procedure – this is the cable which comes to the lowest point on the front of the transmission, with its end fitting nearest the engine.

7 Unlock the selector cable by pressing the coloured insert towards the engine, and move the transmission selector lever (**not** the gear lever inside the car) to the 4th gear position by moving it up or down as necessary (see illustration).

8 Lock the selector cable in position by moving the coloured insert away from the engine.

9 Refit the selector mechanism cover, ensuring that the clips engage correctly, and lower the car to the ground.

2.3 Insert a 3 mm drill bit (arrowed) into the gear lever base mechanism

2.5 Unclip the cover from the front of the transmission

Manual transmission 7A•3

2.7 Prise out the locking insert

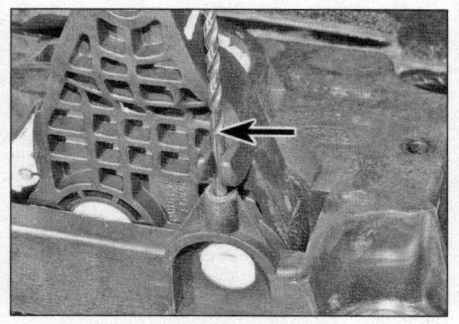

2.13 Insert a 3.0 mm drill bit (arrowed) through the lever assembly into the base to hole the lever in 4th

2.16 Prise the coloured insert (arrowed) upwards to unlock the selector cable

10 Inside the car, remove the drill bit from the gear lever base mechanism, and refit the surround panel.
11 Start the engine, keeping the clutch pedal depressed, and check for correct gear selection.

MTX 75 transmission

Note: *A 3 mm drill bit will be required for this adjustment.*

12 Carefully unclip the surround panel at the base of the gear lever gaiter, and move the panel aside for access to the base of the gear lever, disconnecting the switch wiring if necessary.
13 Move the gear lever to the 4th gear position, then insert a 3 mm drill bit into the gear lever base mechanism, making sure that it is fully inserted **(see illustration)**.
14 Apply the handbrake, then jack up the front of the car, supporting it on axle stands (see *Jacking and vehicle support*). Where applicable, remove the engine undershield.
15 Only the selector cable is to be adjusted during this procedure – this is the cable which comes to the lowest point on the front of the transmission, with its end fitting nearest the engine.
16 Unlock the selector cable by prising the coloured insert upwards, and move the transmission selector lever (**not** the gear lever inside the car) to the 4th gear position by moving it forwards or backwards as necessary **(see illustration)**.
17 Press the selector cable locking insert down to lock the cable.
18 Lower the car to the ground, remove the drill bit from the gear lever base mechanism, and refit the surround panel. Start the engine, keeping the clutch pedal depressed, and check for correct gear selection.

3 Gearchange cables and gear lever – removal and refitting

Removal

1 Remove the air cleaner assembly as described in Chapter 4A.
2 Apply the handbrake, then jack up the front of the car, supporting it on axle stands (see *Jacking and vehicle support*). Where applicable, remove the engine undershield.
3 At the transmission, unclip the cover (where fitted) from the selector mechanism. Remove the cables from the support brackets by twisting the spring-loaded knurled collars anti-clockwise. Depress the release button and detach the selector cable from the lever on the transmission, then prise the shift cable end fitting from the its lever on the transmission – note their fitted locations **(see illustration)**. Unclip the cables from the clips on the transmission casing.
4 Remove the washer-type fasteners, and slide the exhaust heat shield rearwards.
5 Unclip the cables from the vehicle body underside.
6 Remove the centre console as described in Chapter 11.

3.3 Twist the knurled collar anti-clockwise

3.8a Depress the release button (arrowed)

7 Undo the bolts and remove the bracket each side between the facia crossmember centre supports and the floor **(see illustration)**. Take care as the edges of the brackets are extremely sharp.
8 Press the release buttons and disconnect the shift (white) and selector (black) inner cables from the gear lever. Disconnect the cable outers from the floor brackets by twisting the collars and sliding them from the housing **(see illustrations)**.
9 Fold back the carpet and insulation material under the centre part of the facia for access to the selector cable floor grommet. Remove the two nuts and release the grommet from the floor **(see illustration)**.
10 Pass the cables up through the floor.
11 If required, the gear lever knob simply unscrews from place.
12 If required, the gear lever assembly can be

3.7 Remove the bracket each side of the crossmember supports

3.8b Twist the collars and slide the cables upwards

7A•4 Manual transmission

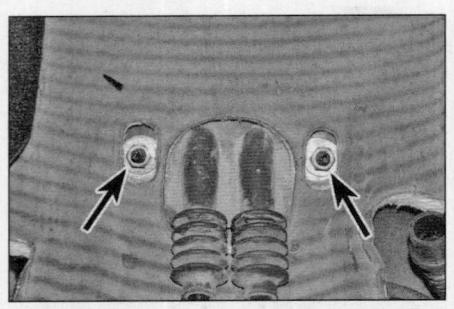

3.9 Undo the nuts (arrowed) to release the grommet – shown with the heater removed for clarity

removed by unscrewing the mounting bolts **(see illustration)**.

Refitting

13 Refitting is a reversal of removal. Use new clips when reconnecting the gearchange cables, and adjust the cables as described in Section 2.

4 Reversing light switch – removal and refitting

iB5 transmission

1 The switch is located on the front of the transmission, next to the selector cable front cover. To improve access, jack up the front left-hand side of the car (see *Jacking and vehicle support*). Where fitted, remove the engine undershield.

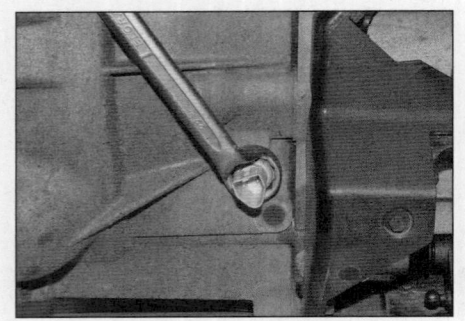

4.3 Unscrew the reversing light switch – iB5 transmission

5.4 Prise the driveshaft oil seal from place

3.12 Gear lever assembly mounting bolts (arrowed)

2 Disconnect the wiring plug from the switch.
3 Unscrew and remove the switch from the front of the transmission – anticipate a little oil spillage as this is done **(see illustration)**.
4 Refitting is a reversal of removal. Tighten the switch to the specified torque.

MTX 75 transmission

5 The switch is located on top of the transmission. Remove the air cleaner as described in Chapter 4A, and the battery and battery tray, as described in Chapter 5A.
6 Disconnect the wiring leading to the reversing light switch on the top of the transmission **(see illustration)**.
7 Unscrew the mounting bolts and remove the reversing light switch from the cover housing on the transmission.
8 Refitting is a reversal of the removal procedure.

4.6 Reversing light switch (arrowed) – MTX 75 transmission

5.7 Drive the oil seal into place using a tube or socket

5 Oil seals – renewal

1 Oil leaks frequently occur due to wear or deterioration of the driveshaft oil seals, or the selector shaft oil seal (iB5 transmission). Renewal of these seals is relatively easy, since the repairs can be performed without removing the transmission from the vehicle.

Driveshaft oil seals

2 The driveshaft oil seals are located at the sides of the transmission, where the driveshafts enter the transmission. If leakage at the seal is suspected, raise the vehicle and support it securely on axle stands. If the seal is leaking, oil will be found on the side of the transmission below the driveshaft.
3 Refer to Chapter 8 and remove the appropriate driveshaft.
4 Using a large screwdriver or lever, carefully prise the oil seal out of the transmission casing, taking care not to damage the transmission casing **(see illustration)**.

> **HAYNES HiNT** *If an oil seal is difficult to remove, it sometimes helps to drive the seal into the transmission a little way, applying force at one point only (at the top, for instance). This can have the effect of swivelling the opposite side of the seal out of the casing, and it can then be pulled out.*

5 Wipe clean the oil seal seating in the transmission casing.
6 Dip the new oil seal in clean oil, then press it a little way into the casing by hand, making sure that it is square to its seating.
7 Using suitable tubing or a large socket, carefully drive the oil seal fully into the casing until it contacts the seating **(see illustration)**.
8 When refitting the left-hand driveshaft on the iB5 transmission, use the protective sleeve which should be provided with Ford parts. The sleeve is fitted into the seal, and the driveshaft is then fitted through it – the sleeve is then withdrawn and cut free.
9 Refit the driveshaft (see Chapter 8).

Selector shaft oil seal (iB5 transmission)

10 Apply the handbrake, then jack up the front of the car, supporting it on axle stands (see *Jacking and vehicle support*). Where fitted, remove the engine undershield.
11 At the front face of the transmission housing, remove the selector mechanism cover by working around the edge, releasing a total of seven clips.
12 Prise off the retaining clips, then pull the shift and selector cables from the transmission levers, and detach them from the cable support brackets by turning the knurled collars clockwise.

Manual transmission 7A•5

13 Unscrew and remove the four bolts securing the selector mechanism rear cover to the transmission housing.
14 Remove the transmission shift lever by prising off the protective cap and extracting the retaining clip.
15 With the shift lever removed, unscrew the securing bolt and take off the selector lever and dust cover.
16 The selector shaft oil seal can now be prised out of its location. If using a screwdriver or similar sharp tool, take great care not to mark or gouge the selector shaft or the seal housing as this is done, or the new seal will also leak.
17 Before fitting the new oil seal, carefully clean the visible part of the selector shaft, and the oil seal housing. Wrap a little tape around the end of the shaft, to protect the seal lips as they pass over it.
18 Smear the new oil seal with a little oil, then carefully fit it over the end of the selector shaft, lips facing inwards (towards the transmission).
19 Making sure that the seal stays square to the shaft, press it fully along the shaft (if available, a 16 mm ring spanner is ideal for this).
20 Press the seal fully into its housing, again using the ring spanner or perhaps a deep socket. Remove the tape from the end of the shaft.
21 Further refitting is a reversal of removal. Tighten the selector lever securing bolt to the specified torque, and use new clips when reconnecting the gearchange cables.
22 On completion, check and if necessary adjust the cables as described in Section 2.

6 Transmission oil – draining and refilling

Note: *Although not included in the maintenance schedule by the manufacturers, it is a good idea to drain and renew the manual transmission oil on a regular basis. The frequency with which this needs to carried out can be left to the individual, but it is certainly advisable on a vehicle that has covered a high mileage.*

iB5 transmission

1 The iB5 transmission has no drain plug; the most effective way to drain the oil is to remove one or both driveshafts, as described in Chapter 8.
2 When refilling the transmission, remember that the vehicle must be level for the oil level to be correct. Refill the transmission using the information in Chapter 1 – refer to the table at the end of *Weekly checks* for the type of oil to be used.

MTX 75 transmission

3 The drain plug is located in the base of the differential housing – like the oil filler/level plug, a special hexagonal socket (or large Allen key) will be required for removal.

7.5 Undo the 3 bolts and remove the battery tray

4 The oil is best drained when the transmission is hot, but bear in mind the risk of burning yourself on hot exhaust components, etc. Apply the handbrake, then jack up the front of the car, and support it on axle stands (see *Jacking and vehicle support*).
5 Where applicable, remove the engine undershield. Position a suitable container under the transmission drain plug, then unscrew and remove it, and allow the oil to drain.
6 When the flow of oil stops, clean and refit the drain plug, and tighten it securely.
7 When refilling the transmission, remember that the vehicle must be level for the oil level to be correct. Refill the transmission using the information in Chapter 1 – refer to the table at the end of *Weekly checks* for the type of oil to be used.

7 Transmission – removal and refitting

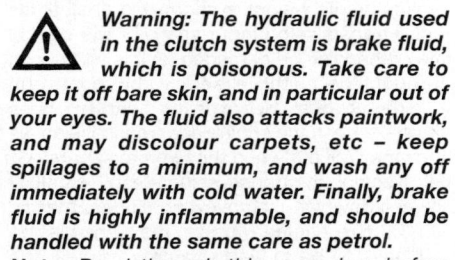

⚠ **Warning:** *The hydraulic fluid used in the clutch system is brake fluid, which is poisonous. Take care to keep it off bare skin, and in particular out of your eyes. The fluid also attacks paintwork, and may discolour carpets, etc – keep spillages to a minimum, and wash any off immediately with cold water. Finally, brake fluid is highly inflammable, and should be handled with the same care as petrol.*

Note: *Read through this procedure before starting work to see what is involved,*

7.11a Disconnect the reversing light wiring plug earth cable . . .

7.8 Undo the bolts and remove the radiator support bracket

particularly in terms of lifting equipment. Depending on the facilities available, the home mechanic may prefer to remove the engine and transmission together, then separate them on the bench, as described in Chapter 2C. The help of an assistant is highly recommended if the transmission is to be removed (and later refitted) on its own.

Removal

1 Remove the plastic cover from the top of the engine (where fitted).
2 Remove the air cleaner and inlet duct as described in Chapter 4A.
3 Remove the battery and starter motor as described in Chapter 5A.
4 Remove the engine management PCM as described in Chapter 4A.
5 Undo the 3 bolts and remove the battery tray **(see illustration)**.
6 Remove both front headlights as described in Chapter 12.
7 Secure the radiator to the bonnet slam panel with cable ties.
8 Remove the radiator undershield, then undo the bolts and remove the radiator support bracket **(see illustration)**.
9 On 1.8 and 2.0 litre models, undo the bolts and remove the crashbox from the front subframe (where fitted).
10 Undo the 2 upper transmission-to-engine retaining bolts.
11 Disconnect the reversing light wiring plug, and transmission earth cable(s), then unclip the wiring harness **(see illustrations)**.
12 Disconnect the gearchange cables from the transmission as described in Section 3.

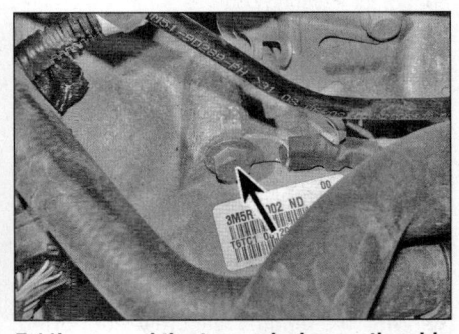

7.11b . . . and the transmission earth cable

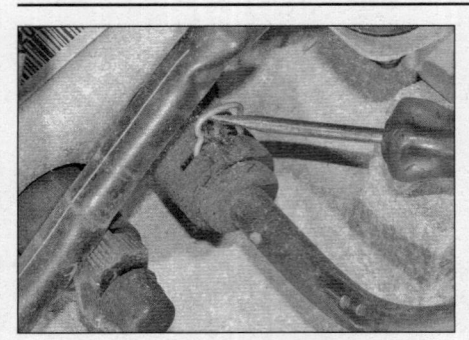

7.13 Pull out the securing clip

13 Make sure that the gear lever is in neutral. Taking adequate precautions against brake fluid spillage (refer to the *Warning* at the start of this Section), pull out the securing clip, then pull the pipe fitting out of the clutch slave cylinder at the top of the transmission. Plug or tape over the pipe end, to avoid losing fluid, and to prevent dirt entry.
14 Unclip the slave cylinder fluid pipe from the support bracket, and move it clear of the transmission.
15 Remove both driveshafts from the transmission as described in Chapter 8.
16 Unscrew and remove the two nuts/bolts, and separate the exhaust front pipe at the first flange joint under the car. Unhook the exhaust pipe from the rubber mountings.
17 Where fitted, undo the bolts and remove the floor brace from beneath the front section of the exhaust system.
18 Unscrew the two through-bolts and remove the engine/transmission rear mounting from the subframe.
19 The engine/transmission must now be supported, as the left-hand mounting must be dismantled and removed. Ford technicians use a support bar which locates in the tops of the inner wings – proprietary engine support bars are available from tool outlets.
20 If a support bar is not available, an engine hoist should be used. With an engine hoist, the engine/transmission can be manoeuvred more easily and safely. In the workshop, we found the best solution was to move the engine to the required position, and support it from below – using the hoist on the transmission then gave excellent manoeuvrability, and total control for lowering out.
21 Supporting both the engine and transmission from below should be considered a last resort, and should only be done if a heavy-duty hydraulic ('trolley') jack is used, with a large, flat piece of wood on the jack head to spread the load and avoid damage to the sump. A further jack will be needed to lower the transmission out. *Note: Always take care when using a hydraulic jack, as it is possible for this type to collapse under load – generally, a scissor-type jack avoids this problem, but is also less stable, and offers no manoeuvrability.*
22 With the engine securely supported, progressively unscrew and remove the left-hand mounting central bolt **(see illustration)**.

23 Remove three further nuts/bolts, and remove the lower section of the engine left-hand mounting.
24 Taking care that nothing which is still attached to the engine is placed under strain, lower the transmission as far as possible.
25 Remove the lower transmission-to-engine bolts, noting that, on some models, one of the bolts also retains the power steering pipe support bracket. The flange bolts are of different lengths, so note their positions carefully for refitting.
26 On 1.4 and 1.6 litre engines, swing the transmission forwards, and wedge it in position with a stout piece of wood, about 300 mm long, between the engine and the subframe.
27 Check that, apart from the remaining flange bolts, there is nothing preventing the transmission from being lowered and removed. Make sure that any wiring or hoses lying on top of the transmission are not going to get caught up and stretched as the transmission is lowered.

> **HAYNES HiNT** *Before removing the transmission from the engine, it is helpful for refitting to paint or scratch an alignment mark or two across the engine/transmission, so that the transmission can be offered up in approximately the right alignment to engage the dowels.*

28 Unscrew the remaining flange bolts. If the transmission does not separate on its own, it must be rocked from side-to-side, to free it from the locating dowels. As the transmission is withdrawn from the engine, make sure its weight is supported at all times – the transmission input shaft (or the clutch) may otherwise be damaged as it is withdrawn through the clutch assembly bolted to the engine flywheel. Recover the adapter plates fitted between the engine and transmission, as they may fall out when the two are separated.
29 Keeping the transmission steady, carefully lower it down and remove it from under the car. On 1.8 litre engine models, the transmission will have to be moved forwards to clear the subframe as it is lowered – if the transmission

7.22 Unscrew and remove the left-hand mounting central bolt

is being supported from below, take care that it is kept steady.
30 The clutch components can now be inspected with reference to Chapter 6, and renewed if necessary. Unless they are virtually new, it is worth renewing the clutch components as a matter of course, even if the transmission has been removed for some other reason.

Refitting

31 If removed, refit the clutch components (see Chapter 6). Also ensure that the engine-to-transmission adapter plates (where fitted) are in position on the engine.
32 Apply a very thin smear of high-temperature anti-seize grease to the splines of the transmission input shaft. Take care not to apply too much or the clutch plates may become contaminated.
33 Where a block of wood was used to wedge the engine forwards for transmission removal, make sure that it is in place for refitting.
34 With the transmission secured to the hoist/trolley jack as on removal, raise it into position, and then carefully slide it onto the engine, at the same time engaging the input shaft with the clutch driven plate splines. If marks were made between the transmission and engine on removal, these can be used as a guide to correct alignment.
35 Do not use excessive force to refit the transmission – if the input shaft does not slide into place easily, readjust the angle of the transmission so that it is level, and/or turn the input shaft so that the splines engage properly with the plate. If problems are still experienced, check that the clutch driven plate is correctly centred (Chapter 6).
36 Once the transmission is successfully mated to the engine, insert as many of the flange bolts as possible, and tighten them progressively to draw the transmission fully onto the locating dowels.
37 Refit the lower section of the engine left-hand mounting, and tighten the nuts to the specified torque. On the iB5 transmission, refit the mounting pipe support bracket, and tighten the mounting bolts.
38 Where applicable, remove the wedge fitted between the engine and subframe. Raise the transmission into position, then refit the upper section of the engine left-hand mounting. Tighten the nuts to the specified torque, noting that the centre nut is tightened considerably more than the four outer ones.
39 Refit the remaining transmission-to-engine bolts, and tighten all of them to the specified torque.
40 Refit the engine/transmission rear mounting to the subframe, and tighten the through-bolts to the specified torque.
41 Once the engine/transmission mountings have been refitted, the support bar, engine hoist or supporting jack can be removed.
42 Further refitting is a reversal of removal, noting the following points:
 a) *Refit the starter motor as described in Chapter 5A.*

b) *Refit the driveshafts as described in Chapter 8.*
c) *On completion, adjust the gearchange cables as described in Section 2.*

8 Transmission overhaul – general information

The overhaul of a manual transmission is a complex (and often expensive) engineering task for the DIY home mechanic to undertake, which requires access to specialist equipment. It involves dismantling and reassembly of many small components, measuring clearances precisely and if necessary, adjusting them by the selection shims and spacers. Internal transmission components are also often difficult to obtain and in many instances, extremely expensive. Because of this, if the transmission develops a fault or becomes noisy, the best course of action is to have the unit overhauled by a specialist repairer or to obtain an exchange reconditioned unit.

Nevertheless, it is not impossible for the more experienced mechanic to overhaul the transmission if the special tools are available and the job is carried out in a deliberate step-by-step manner, to ensure that nothing is overlooked.

The tools necessary for an overhaul include internal and external circlip pliers, bearing pullers, a slide hammer, a set of pin punches, a dial test indicator, and possibly a hydraulic press. In addition, a large, sturdy workbench and a vice will be required.

During dismantling of the transmission, make careful notes of how each component is fitted to make reassembly easier and accurate.

Before dismantling the transmission, it will help if you have some idea of where the problem lies. Certain problems can be closely related to specific areas in the transmission which can make component examination and renewal easier. Refer to *Fault finding* at the end of this manual for more information.

Notes

Chapter 7 Part B:
Automatic transmission

Contents

	Section number		Section number
Automatic transmission – removal and refitting	9	General information	1
Automatic transmission fluid level check	See Chapter 1	Oil seals – renewal	6
Automatic transmission overhaul – general information	10	Selector cable – removal, refitting and adjustment	3
Fault finding – general	2	Selector components – removal and refitting	4
Fluid cooler – removal and refitting	8	Transmission sensors – removal and refitting	5
Fluid pan – removal and refitting	7		

Degrees of difficulty

Easy, suitable for novice with little experience	Fairly easy, suitable for beginner with some experience	Fairly difficult, suitable for competent DIY mechanic	Difficult, suitable for experienced DIY mechanic	Very difficult, suitable for expert DIY or professional

Specifications

General
Transmission type... Electronically-controlled automatic, four forward speeds (one overdrive) and reverse. Torque converter lock-up in 3rd and 4th gears
Transmission code... 4F27E

Gear ratios
1st.. 2.816:1
2nd... 1.498:1
3rd.. 1.000:1
4th.. 0.726:1
Reverse.. 2.649:1

Torque wrench settings

	Nm	lbf ft
Engine/transmission left-hand mounting lower section	80	59
Engine/transmission left-hand mounting upper section:		
Centre bolt	148	109
Four outer nuts	48	35
Engine/transmission rear mounting bolts	48	35
Fluid cooler union nuts	25	18
Fluid pan bolts	7	5
Torque converter to driveplate (use new nuts)	37	27
Transmission lever bolt	10	7
Transmission range sensor bolts	10	7
Transmission to engine	48	35

1 General information

Available on 1.6 and 2.0 litre models, the 4F27E automatic transmission is controlled electronically by the engine management electronic control unit. This is a four-speed unit, featuring an overdrive top gear and a lock-up torque converter. This unit, which was developed by Mazda and is built in the USA, has been designed specifically for front-wheel-drive applications, and is particularly light and compact.

The transmission control module (TCM) is located on the engine bulkhead on the left-hand side of the engine compartment. The electronic control system has a fail-safe mode, which gives the transmission limited operation in order to drive the vehicle home or to a repair garage. A warning light on the instrument panel tells the driver when this occurs. The module uses all the information

7B•2 Automatic transmission

1.8 Press down to release the locking lever

available from the various transmission and engine management-related sensors (also see Chapters 4A and 5B) to determine the optimum gearshift points for smoothness, performance and economy. Depending on throttle position and vehicle speed, the module can 'lock-up' the torque converter in 3rd and 4th gear, eliminating torque converter 'slip' and improving fuel consumption.

The unit has been designed to have a low maintenance requirement, the fluid level being checked periodically (see Chapter 1). The fluid is intended to last the life of the transmission, and is cooled by a separate cooler located next to the radiator.

There is no kickdown switch, as kickdown is controlled by the throttle position sensor in the engine management system.

As is normally the case with automatic transmissions, a starter inhibitor relay is fitted, which prevents the engine from being started (by interrupting the supply to the starter solenoid) when the selector is in any position other than P or N. The intention is to prevent the car moving, which might otherwise happen if the engine were started in position D, for example. The inhibitor system is controlled by the module, based on signals received from the engine and transmission sensors. For more details on relay locations, see Chapter 12.

As a further safety measure, the ignition key can only be removed from the ignition switch when the selector is in P; it is also necessary for the ignition to be on, and for the brake pedal and selector lever locking button (on the side of the lever) to be depressed in order to move the selector from position P. If the vehicle battery is discharged, the selector lever release solenoid will not function. If it is required to move the vehicle in this state, prise up the flap, and insert a pen or a similar small instrument into the aperture on the right-hand side of the centre console **(see illustration)**. Push the locking lever downwards and move the selector lever to the required position.

2 Fault finding – general

In the event of a fault occurring on the transmission, first check that the fluid level is correct (see Chapter 1). If there has been a loss of fluid, check the oil seals as described in Section 6. Also check the hoses to the fluid cooler in the radiator for leaks. The only other tasks possible for the home mechanic are the renewal of the various transmission sensors (Section 5); however, it is not advisable to go ahead and renew any sensor until the fault has been positively identified by reading the transmission fault codes.

Any serious fault which occurs will result in the transmission entering the fail-safe mode, and a fault code (or several codes) will be logged in the control module. These codes can be read using an electronic fault code reader. A Ford dealer will obviously have such a reader, but they are also available from other suppliers. It is unlikely to be cost-effective for the private owner to purchase a fault code reader, but a well-equipped local garage or auto-electrical specialist will have one.

If the fault still persists, it is necessary to determine whether it is of an electrical, mechanical or hydraulic nature; to do this, special test equipment is required. It is therefore essential to have the work carried out by an automatic transmission specialist or Ford dealer if a transmission fault is suspected.

Do not remove the transmission from the vehicle for possible repair before professional fault diagnosis has been carried out, since most tests require the transmission to be in the vehicle.

3 Selector cable – removal, refitting and adjustment

Removal

1 Loosen the left-hand front wheel nuts. Apply the handbrake, jack up the front of the vehicle and support it on axle stands. Remove the left-hand front wheel. Where applicable, remove the engine undershield.
2 Remove the 'flat nut' fasteners, and slide the exhaust heat shield rearwards.
3 Locate the end of the selector cable, which is on the front of the transmission.
4 Disconnect the cable end fitting by prising it off the transmission selector lever **(see illustration)**.
5 Lift the locking tab, slide up the locking catch, then squeeze together the sides of the clip and slide the cable outer from the bracket on the transmission **(see illustrations)**.
6 Trace the cable back from the selector lever, releasing it from the various clips attaching it to the transmission and underside of the car.
7 Remove the centre console as described in Chapter 11.
8 Unscrew the bolts securing the left-hand side brackets fitted between the centre section of the facia panel and the floor, and remove the brackets. Release the wiring harness from any clips.
9 Move the selector lever to P. Working through the front of the selector housing, disconnect the cable inner from the lever by prising the end fitting sideways, then pull the

3.4 Prise the cable end fitting from the lever on the transmission

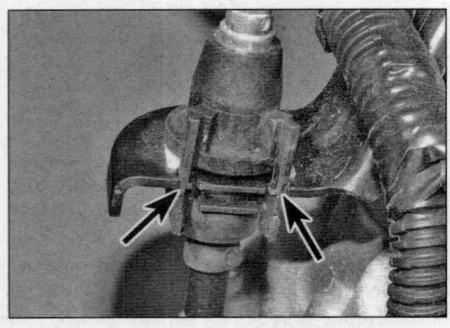

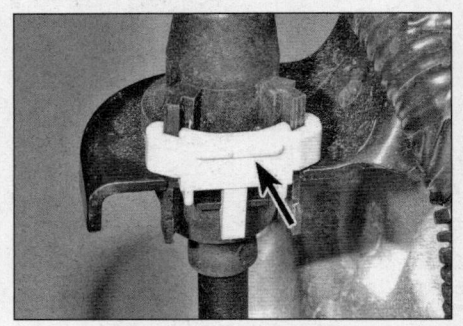

3.5a Prise out the locking catch (arrowed) . . .

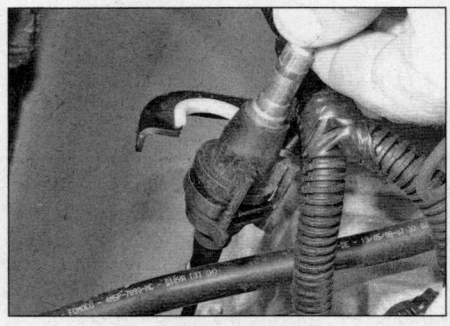

3.5b . . . squeeze together the clips (arrowed) . . .

3.5c . . . and slide the cable from the bracket

Automatic transmission 7B•3

3.9a Prise the end fitting (arrowed) from the lever

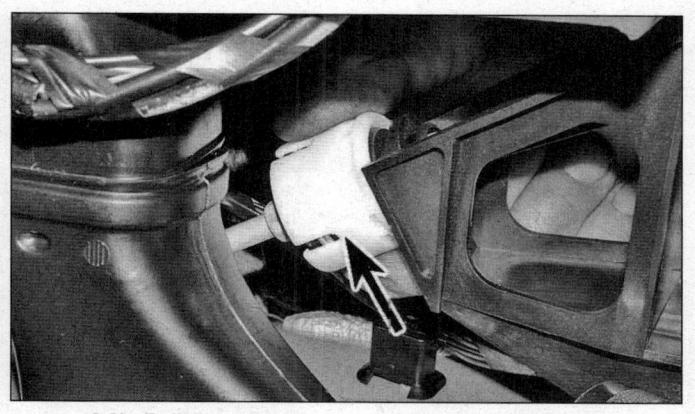

3.9b Pull the outer cable collar (arrowed) forwards

collar forwards, and lift the cable outer from the bracket **(see illustrations)**.
10 Fold back the carpet and insulation material under the centre part of the facia, for access to the selector cable floor grommet. Remove the two nuts and release the grommet from the floor.
11 Pass the cable down through the vehicle floor, and remove it from under the car.

Refitting

12 Refitting is a reversal of removal, noting the following points:
a) Once the cable has been reconnected to the selector lever, shift the lever to position D before reconnecting the cable end fitting at the transmission lever.
b) Before securing the cable to the transmission bracket or transmission lever, check the cable adjustment as described below.

Adjustment

13 Inside the vehicle, move the selector lever to position D.
14 With the inner cable disconnected from the lever on the transmission, check that the transmission lever is in the D position. To do this, it will be necessary to move the lever slightly up and down until it is positioned correctly. A further check can be made by observing that the D mark on the selector lever position sensor is correctly aligned

with the mark on the transmission lever **(see illustration)**.
15 Unclip the cable locking catch at the transmission end **(see illustration)**.
16 With both the selector levers inside the vehicle and on the side of the transmission in position D, refit the cable end fitting to the transmission lever, then press the catch on the cable into place to lock it.
17 Refit the left-hand front wheel, then lower the vehicle to the ground. Tighten the wheel nuts to the specified torque.
18 Road test the vehicle to check the operation of the transmission.

4 Selector components – removal and refitting

Selector assembly

Removal

1 Remove the centre console as described in Chapter 11.
2 Working through the front of the selector housing, disconnect the cable inner from the lever as described in Section 3.
3 Disconnect the multiplug wiring connectors at the rear of the assembly, noting their positions, and move the wiring harness clear.
4 Unscrew the four mounting nuts, and

withdraw the selector lever assembly **(see illustration)**.
5 If required, the assembly can be further dismantled (after removing the selector lever knob, as described below) by unclipping the top cover and removing the illumination bulb and inner cover.

Refitting

6 Refitting is a reversal of the removal procedure, but adjust the selector cable as described in Section 3.

Selector lever knob

Removal

7 Remove the centre console as described in Chapter 11.
8 Remove the grub screw at the side of the knob, then pull the knob upwards off the lever.

Refitting

9 Refitting is a reversal of removal.

5 Transmission sensors – removal and refitting

Transmission range sensor

1 The transmission range sensor is effectively a selector position sensor, the signal from which is used by the engine management module

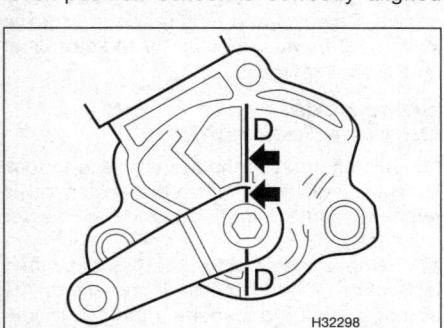

3.14 Selector lever position sensor/ transmission lever alignment markings

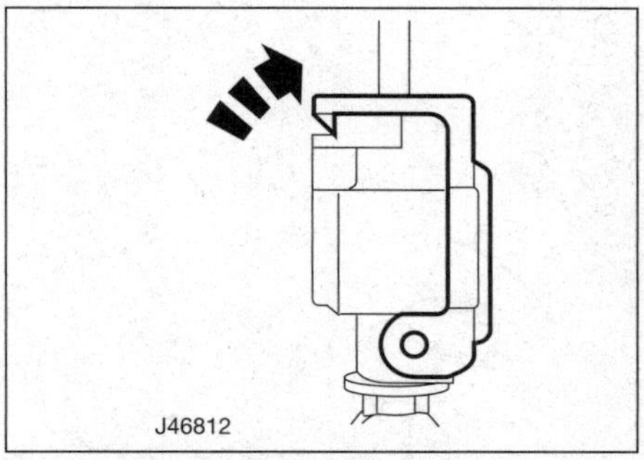

3.15 Prise up the cable locking catch

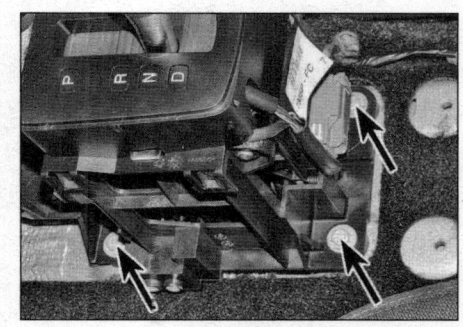

4.4 Undo the selector lever housing bolts (3 arrowed)

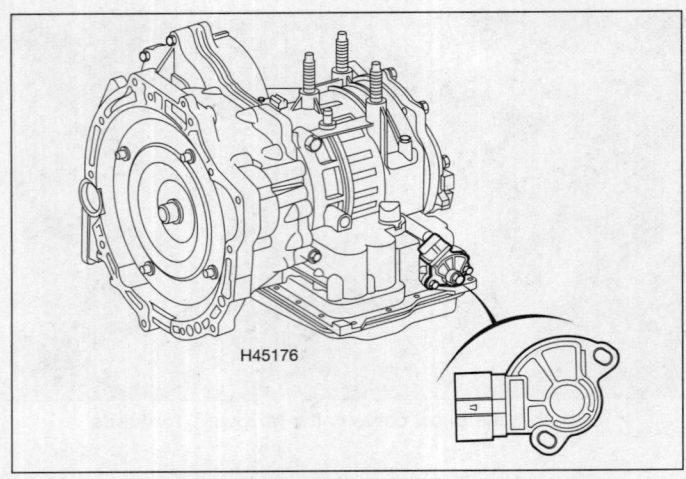

7B•4 Automatic transmission

5.2 Transmission range sensor location

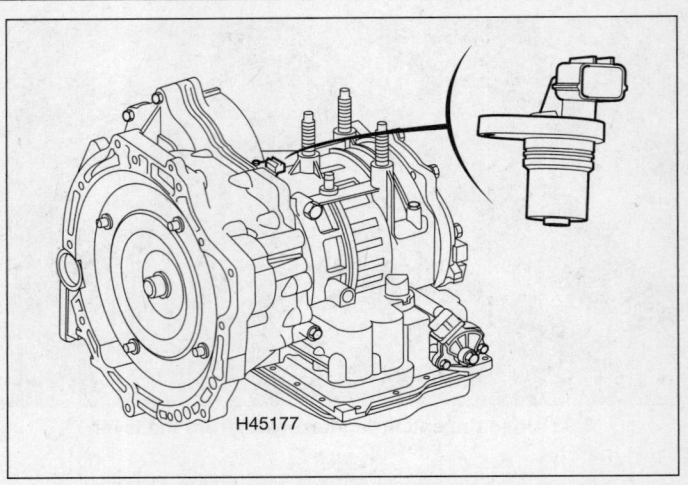

5.13 Turbine (output) shaft speed sensor location

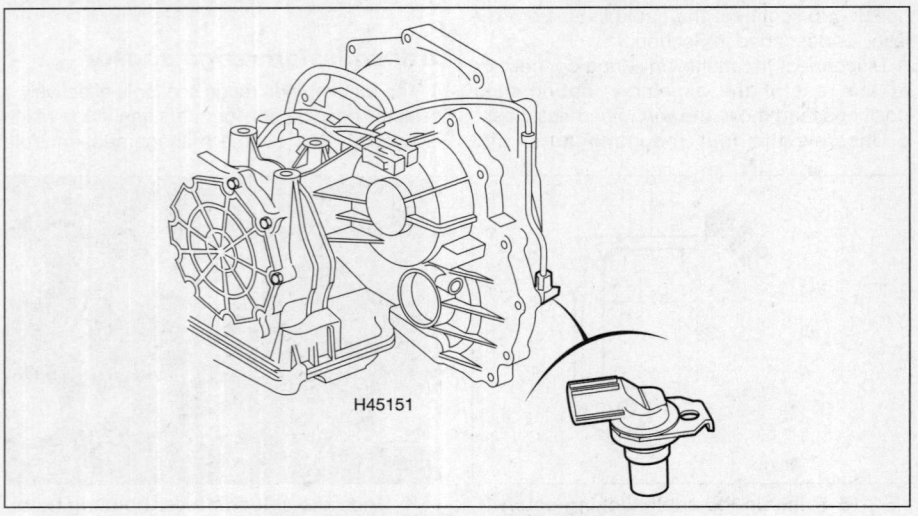

5.22 Output shaft speed sensor location

to modify the operation of the transmission, dependent on which 'gear' is selected. For example, besides controlling gearshift points, depending on the signal received, the module may actuate the starter inhibitor relay, the reversing lights, or the ignition key lock. **Note:** *To set the range sensor in its working position, Ford special tool 307-415 is required. If this tool is not available, the sensor position must be carefully marked before removal.*

2 Access to the range sensor is easiest from below – the sensor is at the front of the transmission, near the transmission selector lever **(see illustration)**. Apply the handbrake, then jack up the front of the car and support it on axle stands (see *Jacking and vehicle support*). Remove the engine undershield (where fitted).

3 Prise the selector cable end fitting off the transmission lever, and disconnect the wiring plug from the sensor.

4 Hold the transmission lever against rotation, then unscrew the lever retaining bolt, and remove the lever from the sensor.

Caution: *If the lever is not held as its bolt is undone, the force required to loosen the bolt will be transmitted to the sensor itself, which may well lead to the sensor being damaged. The same applies when retightening the bolt on completion.*

5 Before removing the sensor, make a couple of alignment marks between the sensor and the transmission, for use when refitting.

6 Take precautions against the possible spillage of transmission fluid. Unscrew the two sensor retaining bolts, and withdraw the sensor from the transmission.

7 Clean the sensor location in the transmission, and the sensor itself. If a new sensor is being fitted, transfer the alignment marks from the old unit to the new one – this will provide an approximate setting, which should allow the car to be driven.

8 Refit the sensor, and secure it loosely in position with the two bolts, tightened by hand only at this stage.

9 Ford special tool 307-415 must now be used to set the sensor in its working position.

If the tool is not available, realign the marks made prior to removal. When correctly aligned, tighten the two sensor retaining bolts to the specified torque.

10 Refit the transmission lever. Tighten the lever retaining bolt to the specified torque, holding the lever against rotation as the bolt is tightened (refer to the *Caution* earlier in this Section).

11 Reconnect the selector cable to the transmission lever, and check the cable adjustment as described in Section 3.

12 On completion, lower the car to the ground.

Turbine (input) shaft speed sensor

13 The turbine shaft speed sensor is located on top of the transmission, and is an inductive pick-up sensor which senses the speed of rotation of the input shaft **(see illustration)**. This information is used by the ECM to control gearchanging and the torque converter lock-up clutch. Removal and refitting details are similar to the output shaft speed sensor described earlier in this Section.

Brake pedal position switch

14 The signal from the switch is used by the ECM to disengage the torque converter lock-up, and to allow the selector lever to be moved from the P position when starting the engine. Removal and refitting details for the switch will be the same as for the stop-light switch in Chapter 9.

Brake pedal shift interlock actuator

16 This unit part of the system used to lock the selector lever in P when the ignition key is removed, and is incorporated in the selector lever itself.

17 Remove the selector knob as described in Section 4. With the knob removed, the actuator pushrod can be pulled out and removed.

18 Refitting is a reversal of removal. Check the operation of the system on completion.

Automatic transmission 7B•5

5.28 Battery tray retaining bolts (arrowed)

5.29a Prise out the 4 clips (arrowed)

5.29b Undo the 2 inner bolts, slacken the outer bolt, undo the 2 nuts and pivot the cross-stay (arrowed) each side away from the engine compartment bulkhead . . .

Selector lever shift interlock solenoid

19 The main solenoid controlling the shift interlock system (used to lock the selector lever in P when the ignition key is removed) is located at the base of the selector lever. For access to the solenoid, remove the centre console as described in Chapter 11. At the time of writing, no further removal details were available from Ford.

Transmission fluid temperature sensor

20 The fluid temperature sensor signal is used by the ECM to determine whether to allow the operation the torque converter lock-up clutch, and the selection of the overdrive 4th gear. The sensor is located among the transmission solenoid valves inside the fluid pan – no renewal procedure is suggested by Ford, so any suspected problems should be referred to a Ford dealer.

Output shaft speed sensor

21 Access to the speed sensor is easiest from below. Apply the handbrake, then loosen the left-hand front wheel nuts. Jack up the front of the car and support it on axle stands (see *Jacking and vehicle support*). Remove the engine undershield (where fitted).

22 Remove the left-hand front wheel and the wheel arch liner – the sensor is located at the rear of the transmission, behind the driveshafts **(see illustration)**.

23 Disconnect the wiring plug from the sensor, then position a suitable container below the sensor to catch any transmission fluid which may be spilt as the sensor is removed.

24 Unscrew the sensor securing bolt, and slowly withdraw the sensor from its location.

25 Check the condition of the O-ring seal fitted to the sensor body – fit a new seal if the old one is in poor condition.

26 Refitting is a reversal of the removal procedure, but clean the sensor location and lightly oil the O-ring before inserting the assembly in the transmission casing. Check the transmission fluid level as described in Chapter 1 on completion.

Transmission control module

27 Disconnect the battery negative lead as described in Chapter 5A.

Models with a plastic panel in front of the brake master cylinder

28 Remove the battery as described in Chapter 5A, then undo the 3 bolts and slide the battery tray forward a little **(see illustration)**.

29 Prise out the 4 plastic clips securing the plastic panel to the engine compartment bulkhead, then undo the inner 2 retaining bolts, slacken the outer bolt, remove the nuts and pivot the cross-stay each side away from the bulkhead. Lift the plastic panel from place **(see illustrations)**. Refit the bolts to secure the tops of the suspension struts to the vehicle body.

All models

30 Release the retaining clips and pull the TCM from the bulkhead bracket **(see illustration)**

31 Pivot down the locking catch, and disconnect the wiring plug and remove the TCM **(see illustration)**.

32 Refitting is a reversal of removal. Note that if a new TCM is fitted, it must be initialised using Ford diagnostic equipment (WDS). Entrust this task to a Ford dealer or suitably-equipped specialist.

6 Oil seals – renewal

Driveshaft oil seals

The procedure is the same as that for the manual transmission (refer to Chapter 7A).

Output shaft speed sensor oil seal

The procedure is covered in Section 5.

7 Fluid pan – removal and refitting

Note: *This procedure is provided principally to cure any leak developing from the fluid pan joint. It is not advisable for the DIY mechanic to remove the fluid pan for any other reason, since it gives access to internal transmission components, servicing of which is considered beyond the scope of this Manual.*

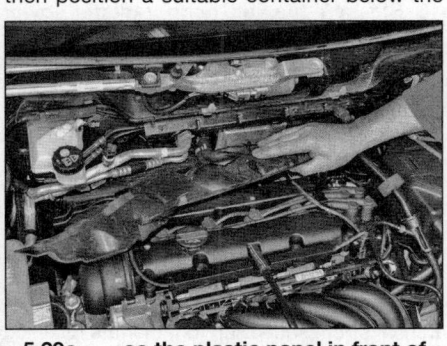

5.29c . . . so the plastic panel in front of the TCM can be removed

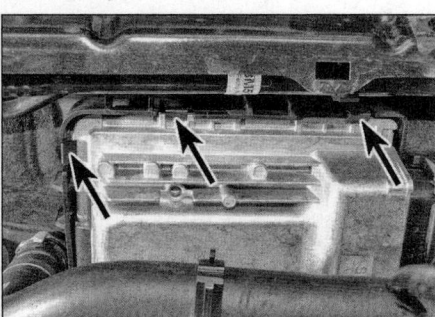

5.30 Release the clips (arrowed)

5.31 Pivot down the locking catch and disconnect the wiring plug

7B•6 Automatic transmission

Removal

1 Apply the handbrake, then jack up the front of the car and support it on axle stands (see *Jacking and vehicle support*). Remove the engine undershield (where fitted)
2 Place a suitable container below the pan, as most of the contents of the transmission will drain when the pan is removed.
3 Progressively unscrew and remove the fluid pan bolts.
4 The fluid pan is 'stuck' to the base of the transmission by a bead of sealant, so it is unlikely that the pan will fall off once the bolts are removed. Care must now be taken to break the sealant without damaging the mating surfaces. Do not prise the pan down, as this may bend it, or damage the sealing surfaces. The most successful method found is to run a sharp knife around the joint – this should cut through sufficiently to make removal possible without excess effort.

Refitting

5 With the fluid pan removed, clean off all traces of sealant from the pan and the mating face on the transmission. Again, take care not to mark either mating surface.
6 Apply a 1.5 mm thick bead of suitable sealant (Ford recommend Loctite 5699, or equivalent) to the fluid pan mating face, running the bead on the inside of the bolt holes. Do not apply excess sealant, or a bead much thicker than suggested, since the excess could end up inside the pan, and contaminate the internal components.
7 Offer the pan up into position, and insert a few of the bolts to locate it. Refit all the remaining bolts, and tighten them progressively to the specified torque.
8 Give the sealant time to cure, then trim off any excess with a knife. Refill the transmission via the dipstick tube, with reference to Chapter 1.
9 On completion, take the car for a run of several miles to get the fluid up to operating temperature, then recheck the fluid level, and check for signs of leakage.

8 Fluid cooler – removal and refitting

Removal

1 This procedure should only be attempted when the engine and transmission are completely cool, otherwise there is a great risk of scalding. The fluid cooler is mounted in front of the radiator **(see illustration)**.
2 Apply the handbrake, then jack up the front of the car and support it on axle stands (see *Jacking and vehicle support*).
3 Remove the three screws securing the radiator lower splash shield, and remove the shield from under the car.
4 Undo the fasteners and remove the air

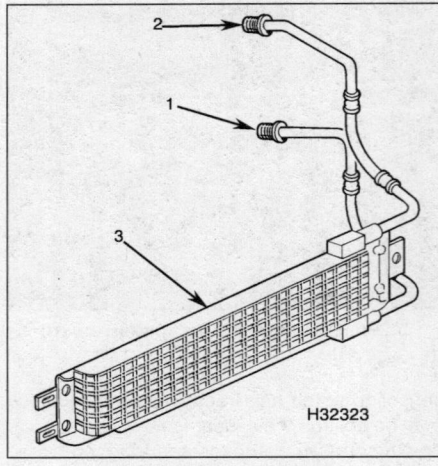

8.1 Fluid cooler details
1 Return hose
2 Supply hose
3 Fluid cooler

deflector panels under the right- and left-hand sides of the radiator.
5 Place a container below the fluid cooler connections to catch the escaping fluid; also note that, if the engine is still warm, the fluid may be extremely hot. Note the positions of the hose connections for refitting, then push the quick-release connector towards the cooler, press together the retaining tabs and pull the hose from the cooler. Tie the hoses up out of the way, and plug the hose ends to prevent the ingress of dirt.
6 Pull the retaining clip forwards, and lift each side of the cooler upwards from the brackets. Manoeuvre the cooler from place.

Refitting

7 Clean the fluid cooler fins of any debris as necessary, using a small brush – do not use any other tools, as the fins can easily be damaged.
8 Refitting is a reversal of removal, noting the following points:
a) Top-up the transmission fluid level using the information in Chapter 1.
b) Start the engine and check for signs of fluid leakage from the disturbed connections.

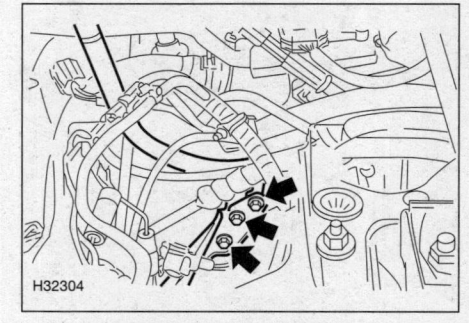

9.10 Selector cable/fluid filler tube support bracket bolts (arrowed)

9 Automatic transmission – removal and refitting

Removal

1 Remove the plastic cover from the top of the engine (where fitted).
2 Remove the air cleaner and intake duct as described in Chapter 4A.
3 Remove the battery and starter motor as described in Chapter 5A. Note that one of the mounting bolts also secures the transmission earth strap.
4 Remove the engine management PCM as described in Chapter 4A.
5 Undo the 3 bolts and remove the battery tray **(see illustration 5.28)**.
6 Remove both front headlights as descrbead in Chapter 12.
7 Before jacking up the front of the car, loosen the front wheel nuts, and if possible, the driveshaft retaining bolts.
8 Apply the handbrake, and chock the rear wheels. Jack up the front of the car, and support it on axle stands (see *Jacking and vehicle support*). There must be sufficient clearance below the car for the transmission to be lowered and withdrawn. Remove the front wheels and the engine undershield.
9 Undo the fasteners and remove the splash shield beneath the radiator.
10 Remove the three bolts securing the selector cable/fluid filler tube support bracket to the front of the transmission **(see illustration)**. Move the bracket to one side, clear of the transmission.
11 Disconnect the selector cable end fitting from the transmission lever as described in Section 3.
12 Disconnect the wiring plugs from the vehicle/output shaft speed sensor, turbine shaft speed sensor and transmission range sensor, as described in Section 5.
13 Remove the front section of the exhaust pipe, referring to Chapter 4A as necessary. Note particularly that the flexible section of the exhaust must not be bent too far during removal.
14 Remove both driveshafts from the transmission as described in Chapter 8.
15 Slacken the left-hand radiator lower support bracket front bolt 3 turns, then remove the rear bolt.
16 Wipe clean around the fluid supply and return pipes on the front of the transmission. It is essential that no dirt is introduced into the transmission. Undo the bolts and remove the crashbox (where fitted) from the front subframe.
17 Noting their respective positions, disconnect the fluid pipes from the transmission. The connectors are released by pushing the connector towards the transmission, squeezing together the retaining tags, and pulling the connector away **(see illustrations)**. Be prepared for loss of fluid,

Automatic transmission 7B•7

9.17a Fluid pipe at the left-hand end . . .

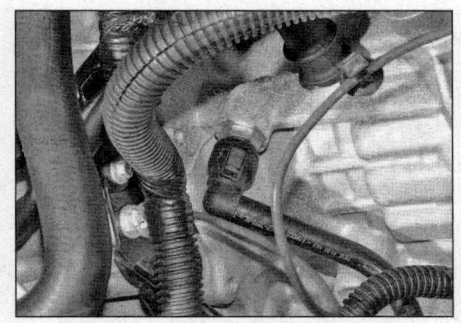

9.17b . . . and right-hand front face of the transmission

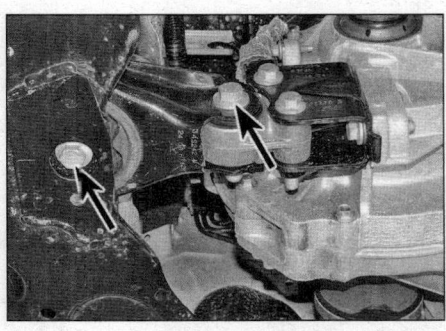

9.18 Remove the through-bolts (arrowed)

and cover the pipe ends and transmission pipe fittings to prevent further loss or dirt entry.

> **HAYNES HiNT**: *Fingers cut from old rubber gloves, secured with elastic bands, are a useful means of sealing off open pipes.*

18 Working from below, unscrew the through-bolts and remove the engine/transmission rear mounting (see illustration).
19 The engine/transmission must now be supported, as the left-hand mounting must be dismantled and removed. Ford technicians use a support bar which locates in the tops of the inner wings – proprietary engine support bars are available from tool outlets.
20 If a support bar is not available, an engine hoist should be used. Supporting the engine from below should be considered a last resort, and should only be done if a heavy-duty hydraulic ('trolley') jack is used, with a large, flat piece of wood on the jack head to spread the load and avoid damage to the sump. Note that a further jack will be needed to lower the transmission out.
21 With the engine securely supported, progressively unscrew the centre bolt, and remove the nuts securing the top section of the engine/transmission left-hand mounting, and lift it off.
22 Remove three further nuts/bolts, and remove the lower section of the engine left-hand mounting.
23 Locate the transmission fluid filler tube, and remove the screw at its base where it enters the transmission. Pull the tube out of its location, and remove it.
24 Remove the cover (where fitted) from the base of the transmission bellhousing, for access to the four large torque converter nuts. It will be necessary to turn the engine (using a spanner or socket on the crankshaft pulley bolt) in order to bring each of the nuts into view. It may also prove necessary to jam the driveplate ring gear with a suitable tool to prevent the engine turning as the nuts are unscrewed. Before removing the last nut, paint an alignment mark between the converter and driveplate to use when refitting. New nuts must be obtained for refitting.

25 Swing the transmission forwards, and wedge it in position with a stout piece of wood, about 300 mm long, between the engine and the subframe.
26 Support the transmission from below, ideally using a trolley jack (if one is not available, a sturdy jack with a large, flat piece of wood on top of the jack head will suffice).
27 Have an assistant ready to help steady the transmission as the flange bolts are removed – attempting to remove the transmission single-handed is not recommended, as it is a heavy assembly which can be awkward to handle.
28 Check that, apart from the remaining flange bolts, there is nothing preventing the transmission from being lowered and removed. Make sure that any wiring or hoses lying on top of the transmission are not going to get caught up and stretched as the transmission is lowered.

> **HAYNES HiNT**: *Before removing the transmission from the engine, it is helpful for refitting to paint or scratch an alignment mark or two across the engine/transmission, so that the transmission can be offered up in approximately the right alignment to engage the dowels.*

29 Unscrew and remove the flange bolts – there are three inserted from the transmission side, and six from the engine side (see illustration). Note the bolt locations carefully, as they are of different lengths.
30 If the transmission does not separate on its own, it must be rocked from side-to-side, to free it from the locating dowels. As the transmission is withdrawn from the engine, make sure its weight is supported at all times – care must be taken that the torque converter (which is a large, heavy, circular component) does not fall out.
31 Keeping the transmission steady on the jack head, and maintaining a supporting hand on the torque converter, carefully lower it and remove it from under the car.
32 Once the transmission has been fully lowered and steadied, bolt a strip of wood or metal across the bellhousing face, with suitable packing, to secure the torque converter firmly in position. The converter centre spigot should be 25 mm below the bellhousing face – this can be determined by placing a straight-edge across the bellhousing, and measuring between it and the centre of the converter (see illustration).

Refitting

33 Prior to refitting, clean the contact surfaces of the driveplate and torque converter.

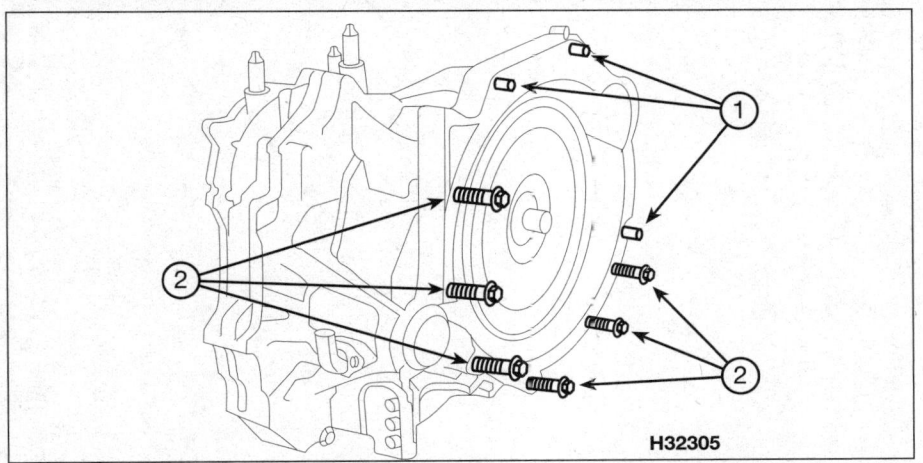

9.29 Engine-to-transmission bolts

1 Three bolts inserted from the transmission side
2 Six bolts inserted from the engine side

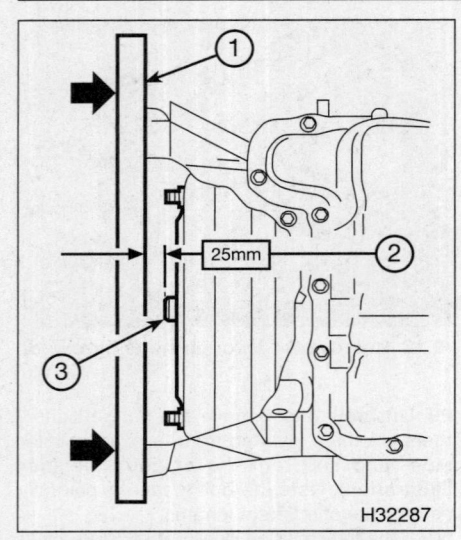

9.32 Check the torque converter is fully entered into the transmission

1 Straight-edge
2 Depth = 25 mm
3 Torque converter centre spigot

34 Check that the torque converter is fully entered in the transmission, as described in paragraph 32. *Caution: This procedure is important, to ensure that the torque converter is engaged with the fluid pump. If it is not fully engaged, serious damage will occur.*

35 As for removal, use a block of wood to wedge the engine forwards for refitting.

36 With the help of an assistant, raise the transmission, and locate it on the rear of the driveplate. The torque converter must remain in full engagement during the fitting procedure. Use the markings made prior to removal to help align the transmission.

37 Refit the transmission-to-engine flange bolts to the locations noted on removal, and tighten them progressively to draw the transmission fully onto the locating dowels.

38 Align the mark made on removal between the torque converter and driveplate. Refit and tighten the torque converter-to-driveplate nuts to the specified torque – new nuts must be used. Turn the engine as necessary to bring each nut into view, and lock the ring gear to prevent it turning as the nuts are tightened.

39 Refit the lower section of the engine left-hand mounting, and tighten the nuts to the specified torque.

40 Remove the wedge fitted between the engine and subframe. Raise the transmission into position, then refit the upper section of the engine left-hand mounting. Tighten the nuts to the specified torque, noting that the centre nut is tightened considerably more than the four outer ones.

41 Working from below, refit the through-bolts to the engine/transmission rear mounting, and tighten them to the specified torque.

42 Once the engine/transmission mountings have been refitted, the support bar, engine hoist or supporting jack can be removed.

43 Further refitting is a reversal of removal, noting the following points:

a) Refit the starter motor as described in Chapter 5A.
b) Refit the driveshafts as described in Chapter 8.
c) Tighten all fasteners to the specified torque (where given).
d) On completion, adjust the selector cable as described in Section 3, and top-up the fluid level as described in Chapter 1.
e) Recheck the transmission fluid level once the car has been driven.
f) Note that, since the battery has been disconnected, the ECM will take time to 'relearn' various settings which will have an adverse effect on how the transmission performs. After the car has completed a few miles of varied driving, however, the ECM's adaptive values should have been re-established.

10 Automatic transmission overhaul – general information

Overhaul of the automatic transmission should be left to an automatic transmission specialist or a Ford dealer. Refer to the information given in Section 2 before removing the unit.

Note that, if the vehicle is still within the warranty period, in the event of a fault it is important to take it to a Ford dealer who will carry out a comprehensive diagnosis procedure using specialist equipment. Failure to do this will invalidate the warranty.

Chapter 8
Driveshafts

Contents

	Section number
Driveshaft gaiter check	See Chapter 1
Driveshaft overhaul – general information	6
Driveshafts – removal and refitting	2
General information	1
Inner constant velocity joint gaiter – renewal	4
Outer constant velocity joint gaiter – renewal	3
Right-hand driveshaft support bearing – removal and refitting	5

Degrees of difficulty

Easy, suitable for novice with little experience	**Fairly easy,** suitable for beginner with some experience	**Fairly difficult,** suitable for competent DIY mechanic	**Difficult,** suitable for experienced DIY mechanic	**Very difficult,** suitable for expert DIY or professional

Specifications

General

Driveshaft type .... Equal-length solid-steel shafts, splined to inner and outer constant velocity joints. Intermediate shaft incorporated in right-hand driveshaft assembly
Outer constant velocity joint type .... Ball-and-cage
Inner constant velocity joint type .... Tripod

Lubrication

Lubricant type .... Special grease supplied in repair kit, or suitable molybdenum disulphide grease – consult a Ford dealer or parts specialist

CV joint grease capacity (approximate):	Outboard joint	Inboard joint
1.4 and 1.6 litre models	100 g	100 g
1.8 and 2.0 litre models	100 g	170 g

Torque wrench settings

	Nm	lbf ft
Crashbox bolts	40	30
Driveshaft bolt:*		
Stage 1	45	33
Stage 2	Angle-tighten a further 90°	
Headlight levelling sensor bracket to lower arm	8	6
Lower arm balljoint to hub carrier*	70	52
Right-hand driveshaft support bearing cap nuts*	25	18
Roadwheel nuts:		
Gold nuts for steel wheels	90	60
Silver nuts for steel wheels	130	96
One-piece alloy nuts for alloy wheels and 5-spoke steel wheels	130	96
Two-piece alloy nuts with conical washer	110	81

Do not re-use

1 General information

Drive is transmitted from the differential to the front wheels by means of two solid-steel, equal-length driveshafts equipped with constant velocity (CV) joints at their inner and outer ends. Due to the position of the transmission, an intermediate shaft and support bearing are incorporated into the right-hand driveshaft assembly.

A ball-and-cage type CV joint is fitted to the outer end of each driveshaft. The joint has an outer member, which is splined at its outer end to accept the wheel hub, and is threaded so that it can be fastened to the hub by a large bolt. The joint contains six balls within a cage, which engage with the inner member. The complete assembly is protected by a flexible gaiter secured to the driveshaft and joint outer member.

At the inner end, the driveshaft is splined to engage a tripod type CV joint, containing needle roller bearings and cups. On the left-hand side, the driveshaft inner CV joint engages directly with the differential sun wheel. On the right-hand side, the inner joint is integral with the intermediate shaft, the inner end of which engages with the differential sun wheel. As on the outer joints, a flexible gaiter secured to the driveshaft and CV joint outer member protects the complete assembly.

8•2 Driveshafts

2.3a Slacken the driveshaft retaining bolt (arrowed)

2.3b On some models, prise out the centre cap and slacken the bolt

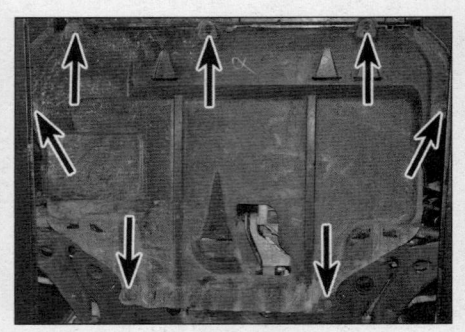

2.4 Undo the bolts (arrowed) and remove the engine undershield

2 Driveshafts – removal and refitting

Removal

1 Firmly apply the handbrake and chock the rear wheels. When the driveshaft bolt is to be loosened (or tightened), it is preferable to do so with the car resting on its wheels. If the car is jacked up, this places a high load on the jack, and the car could slip off.
2 If the car has steel wheels, remove the wheel trim on the side being worked on – the driveshaft bolt can then be loosened with the wheel on the ground. On models with alloy wheels, the safest option is to remove the wheel on the side being worked on, and to fit the temporary spare (see *Wheel changing* at the front of this Manual) – this wheel allows access to the driveshaft bolt.
3 With an assistant firmly depressing the brake pedal, slacken the driveshaft retaining bolt using a socket and a long extension bar **(see illustrations)**. Note that this bolt is extremely tight – ensure that the tools used to loosen it are of good quality, and a good fit.
4 Loosen the front wheel nuts, then jack up the front of the car and support it on axle stands (see *Jacking and vehicle support*). Remove the appropriate front roadwheel, then undo the 7 Torx bolts and remove the engine undershield (where fitted) **(see illustration)**.
5 Remove the previously-slackened driveshaft retaining bolt. Discard the bolt – a new one must be fitted.
6 Tap the end of the driveshaft approximately 15 to 20 mm into the wheel hub.
7 Undo the bolt/nut and detach the headlight levelling sensor bracket from the lower arm (where applicable).
8 Undo the bolts and remove the crash box from the subframe (where fitted).
9 Slacken the lower control arm balljoint nut until the end of the balljoint shank is level with the top of the nut.
10 Detach the lower control arm balljoint from the hub carrier using a balljoint separator tool **(see illustration)**.
11 Push down on the suspension arm using a stout bar to release the balljoint shank from the hub carrier. Take care not to damage the balljoint dust cover during and after disconnection.
12 Swivel the suspension strut and hub carrier assembly outwards, and withdraw the driveshaft CV joint from the hub flange **(see illustration)**.
13 If removing the left-hand driveshaft, free the inner CV joint from the transmission by levering between the edge of the joint and the transmission casing with a large screwdriver or similar tool. Take care not to damage the transmission oil seal or the inner CV joint gaiter. Withdraw the driveshaft from under the wheel arch.
14 If removing the right-hand driveshaft, undo the two nuts and remove the cap from the intermediate shaft support bearing **(see illustration)**. Pull the intermediate shaft out of the transmission, and remove the driveshaft assembly from under the wheel arch. **Note:** *Do not pull the outer shaft from the intermediate shaft – the coupling will separate.*

Refitting

15 Refitting is a reversal of removal, but observe the following points.
 a) Prior to refitting, remove all traces, rust, oil and dirt from the splines of the outer CV joint, and lubricate the splines of the inner joint with wheel bearing grease.
 b) Apply a little grease to the driveshaft seal lips in the transmission casing.
 c) If working on the left-hand driveshaft, ensure that the inner CV joint is pushed fully into the transmission, so that the retaining circlip locks into place in the differential gear.
 d) Always use a new driveshaft-to-hub retaining bolt **(see illustration)**.
 e) Fit the same wheel as was used for

2.10 Use a balljoint separator tool to detach the balljoint from the hub carrier

2.12 Push the lower control arm downwards, pull the hub carrier outwards, and withdraw the driveshaft

2.14 Undo the 2 nuts (arrowed) and remove the intermediate bearing cap

2.15 Always renew the driveshaft retaining bolt

Driveshafts 8•3

3.3 Cut the gaiter retaining clips

3.7 Pack the outer CV joint with about half the grease supplied

3.10a Locate the outer clip on the gaiter . . .

3.10b . . . then using a special pair of pliers . . .

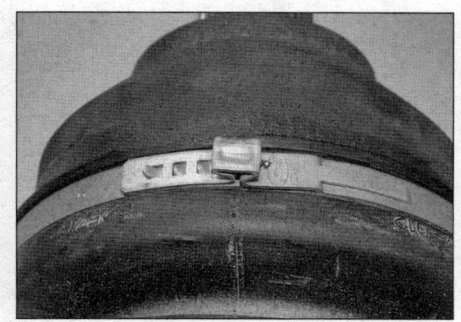

3.10c . . . remove any slack in the clip

3.11 Lift the inner edge of the gaiter to equalise the air pressure

loosening the driveshaft bolt, and lower the car to the ground.
f) Tighten all nuts and bolts to the specified torque (see Chapters 9 and 10 for brake and suspension component torque settings). When tightening the driveshaft bolt, tighten first using a torque wrench, then further, through the specified angle, using an angle-tightening gauge.
g) Ford insist that when refitting the right-hand driveshaft the intermediate shaft bearing cap nuts must be renewed.
h) Where applicable, refit the alloy wheel on completion. Tighten the roadwheel nuts to the specified torque.

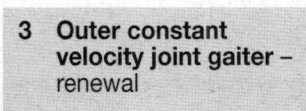

3 Outer constant velocity joint gaiter – renewal

1 Dismantle the inner constant velocity joint as described in Section 4.

Automatic models with a vibration damper fitted

2 On these vehicles, after removing the inner CV joint, measure and note the distance from the end of the shaft to the edge of the damper. The damper must then be pressed from the shaft, the outer joint boot renewed, then the damper pressed back into its original position using the dimensions previously-noted. If access to a hydraulic press in not available, most engineering workshops (automotive or otherwise) would be prepared to carry out this task for a modest fee.

All models

3 Cut off the gaiter retaining clips, then slide the gaiter down the shaft to expose the outer constant velocity joint (see illustration).
Caution: Do not disassemble the outer CV joint.
4 Scoop out as much grease as possible from the joint.
5 Inspect the ball tracks on the inner and outer members. If the tracks have widened, the balls will no longer be a tight fit. At the same time, check the ball cage windows for wear or cracking between the windows. If the joints appear worn, complete renewal may be the only option – check with a Ford dealer or specialist.
6 If the joint is in satisfactory condition, obtain a repair kit from your Ford dealer, consisting of a new gaiter, retaining clips, driveshaft bolt, circlip and grease.
7 Pack the joint with the half of the grease supplied, working it well into the ball tracks, and into the driveshaft opening in the inner member (see illustration).
8 Slide the rubber gaiter onto the shaft.
9 Apply the remaining grease to the joint and the inside of the gaiter.
10 Locate the outer lip of the gaiter in the groove on the joint outer member, then fit the retaining clip. Remove any slack in the clips by carefully compressing the raised section using a special pair of pincers (see illustrations).
Note: Ensure no grease is on the surfaces between the gaiter and the joint housing.
11 Use a small screwdriver to lift the inner lip of the gaiter, allowing the air pressure inside the gaiter to equalise, then fit the inner clip to the gaiter (see illustration).
12 Where applicable, press the damper into its original position.
13 Reassembly the inner constant velocity joint as described in Section 4.

4 Inner constant velocity joint gaiter – renewal

1 Remove the driveshaft(s) as described in Section 2.
2 Cut through the metal clips, and slide the gaiter from the inner CV joint.
3 Clean out some of the grease from the joint, then make alignment marks between the housing and the shaft, to aid reassembly (see illustration).
4 Carefully pull the housing from the tripod,

4.3 Make alignment marks between the shaft and housing

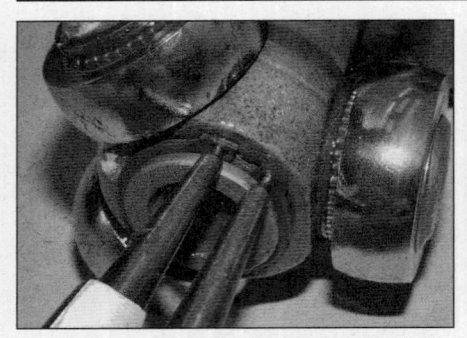

8•4 Driveshafts

4.6a Remove the circlip from the end of the shaft . . .

4.6b . . . then carefully drive the tripod from the shaft

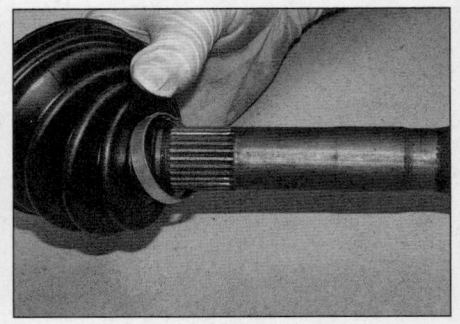

4.7 Slide the new gaiter and smaller diameter clip onto the shaft

4.8a Fit the tripod with the bevelled edge (arrowed) towards the shaft . . .

4.8b . . . then fit the new circlip

twisting the housing so the tripod rollers come out one at a time. If necessary, use a soft-faced hammer or mallet to tap the housing off.

5 Clean the grease from the tripod and housing.

6 Remove the circlip, and carefully drive the tripod from the end of the shaft **(see illustrations)**. Discard the circlip, a new one (supplied in the repair kit) must be fitted. Remove the gaiter if still on the shaft.

7 Slide the new gaiter onto the shaft along with the smaller clip **(see illustration)**.

8 Refit the tripod with the bevelled edge towards the driveshaft, and drive it fully into place, until the new circlip can be installed **(see illustrations)**.

9 Lubricate the tripod rollers with some of the grease supplied in the gaiter kit, then fill the housing and gaiter with the remainder.

10 Refit the housing to the tripod, tapping it gently into place using a soft-hammer or mallet if necessary.

11 Slide the new gaiter into place ensuring the smaller diameter of the gaiter locates over the grooves in the shaft **(see illustration)**.

12 Fit the new retaining clips **(see illustration)**.

13 Fit the new circlip to the end of the shaft **(see illustration)**.

5 Right-hand driveshaft support bearing – removal and refitting

Note: *At the time of writing, it would appear the support bearing was not available as a separate part. If the bearing is worn of damaged, the complete driveshaft must be renewed. Exchange driveshafts may be available – check with a Ford dealer or specialist.*

6 Driveshaft overhaul – general information

Road test the car, and listen for a metallic clicking from the front as the car is driven slowly in a circle with the steering on full-lock. Repeat the check on full-left and full-right lock. This noise may also be apparent when pulling away from a standstill with lock applied. If a clicking noise is heard, this indicates wear in the outer constant velocity joints.

If vibration, consistent with road speed, is felt through the car when accelerating, there is a possibility of wear in the inner constant velocity joints.

If the joints are worn or damaged, it would appear at the time of writing that no parts are available, other then boot renewal kits, and the complete driveshaft must be renewed. *Exchange driveshafts may be available – check with a Ford dealer or specialist.*

4.11 The smaller diameter of the gaiter must locate over the groove in the shaft (arrowed)

4.12 Equalise the air pressure before tightening the gaiter clip

4.13 The circlip on the end of the shaft must be renewed

Chapter 9
Braking system

Contents

	Section number
ABS hydraulic unit – removal and refitting	17
ABS wheel sensor – testing, removal and refitting	18
Brake check	See Chapter 1
Brake fluid renewal	See Chapter 1
Brake pedal – removal and refitting	12
Brake switches – removal, refitting and adjustment	21
Electronic stability control components – removal and refitting	19
Front brake caliper – removal, overhaul and refitting	3
Front brake disc – inspection, removal and refitting	4
Front brake pads – renewal	2
General information	1
Handbrake cables – removal and refitting	23
Handbrake lever – removal and refitting	22
Hydraulic pipes and hoses – inspection, removal and refitting	13
Hydraulic system – bleeding	14
Master cylinder – removal and refitting	11
Rear brake caliper – removal, overhaul and refitting	9
Rear brake disc – inspection, removal and refitting	10
Rear brake drum – removal, inspection and refitting	5
Rear brake pads – renewal	8
Rear brake shoes – renewal	6
Rear wheel cylinder – removal, overhaul and refitting	7
Traction control system – general information	20
Vacuum servo unit – testing, removal and refitting	15
Vacuum servo unit vacuum hose and non-return valve – removal, testing and refitting	16

Degrees of difficulty

Easy, suitable for novice with little experience | **Fairly easy,** suitable for beginner with some experience | **Fairly difficult,** suitable for competent DIY mechanic | **Difficult,** suitable for experienced DIY mechanic | **Very difficult,** suitable for expert DIY or professional

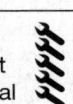

Specifications

Front brakes
Type	Ventilated disc, with single sliding piston caliper
Disc diameter:	
1.4, 1.6 and 1.8 litre models	278 mm
2.0 litre models	300 mm
Disc thickness:	
New	25.0 mm
Minimum	23.0 mm
Maximum disc thickness variation	0.020 mm
Maximum disc/hub run-out (installed)	0.050 mm
Caliper piston diameter	54.0 mm
Brake pad friction material minimum thickness	1.5 mm

Rear drum brakes
Type	Leading and trailing shoes, with automatic adjusters
Drum diameter:	
New	228.3 mm
Maximum	230.2 mm
Shoe width	38.0 mm
Brake shoe friction material minimum thickness	1.0 mm

Rear disc brakes
Type	Solid disc, with single-piston floating caliper
Disc diameter:	
1.6 and 1.8 litre models	265 mm
2.0 litre models	280 mm
Disc thickness:	
New	11.0 mm
Minimum	9.0 mm
Maximum disc thickness variation	0.020 mm
Maximum disc/hub runout (installed)	0.050 mm
Brake pad friction material minimum thickness	1.5 mm

9•2 Braking system

Torque wrench settings	Nm	lbf ft
ABS wheel sensor securing bolts	5	4
Brake pipe to master cylinder	17	13
Brake pipe to hydraulic control unit	11	8
Brake pipe unions	15	11
Front caliper guide bolts	28	21
Front caliper mounting bracket bolts	120	89
Handbrake lever mountings	35	26
Master cylinder to servo mountings	25	18
Pedal bracket to servo mountings	23	17
Rear caliper bracket	70	52
Rear caliper guide bolts	35	26
Rear wheel cylinder bolts	10	7
Roadwheel nuts:		
Gold nuts for steel wheels	90	60
Silver nuts for steel wheels	130	96
One-piece alloy nuts for alloy wheels and 5-spoke steel wheels	130	96
Two-piece alloy nuts with conical washer	110	81
Yaw rate sensor bracket to body	5	4

1 General information

The braking system is of diagonally-split, dual-circuit design, with ventilated discs at the front, and drum or disc brakes (according to model) at the rear. The front calipers are of single sliding piston design, and (where fitted) the rear calipers are of a single-piston floating design, using asbestos-free pads. The rear drum brakes are of the leading and trailing shoe type, and are self-adjusting during footbrake operation. The rear brake shoe linings are of different thicknesses, in order to allow for the different proportional rates of wear.

The vacuum servo unit uses inlet manifold depression (generated only when a petrol engine is running) to boost the effort applied by the driver at the brake pedal and transmits this increased effort to the master cylinder pistons.

The handbrake is cable-operated, and acts on the rear brakes. On rear drum brake models, the cables operate on the rear trailing brake shoe operating levers; on rear disc brake models, they operate on levers on the rear calipers. The handbrake lever incorporates an automatic adjuster, which will adjust the cable when the handbrake is operated several times.

The anti-lock braking system (ABS) uses the basic conventional brake system, together with an ABS hydraulic unit fitted between the master cylinder and the four brake units at each wheel. The hydraulic unit consists of a hydraulic actuator, an ABS brake pressure pump, and an ABS module. Braking at each of the four wheels is controlled by separate solenoid valves in the hydraulic actuator. If wheel lock-up is detected by one of the wheel sensors, when the vehicle speed is above 3 mph, the valve opens; releasing pressure to the relevant brake until the wheel regains a rotational speed corresponding to the speed of the vehicle. The cycle can be repeated many times a second. In the event of a fault in the ABS system, the conventional braking system is not affected. Diagnosis of a fault in the ABS system requires the use of special equipment, and this work should therefore be left to a Ford dealer or suitably-equipped specialist. The wheel speed sensor signal rings are built-into the oil seals of the wheel bearings.

Where fitted, the traction control systems are integrated with the ABS, and use the same wheel sensors. The hydraulic control unit has additional solenoid valves incorporated to enable control of the wheel brake pressure. The system is only active at speeds up to 53 mph – when the system is active the warning light on the instrument panel illuminates to warn the driver. This uses controlled braking of the spinning driving wheel when the grip at the driven wheels are different. The spinning wheel is braked by the ABS system, transferring a greater proportion of the engine torque through the differential to the other wheel, which increases the use of the available traction control.

On several models in the range, there is an Electronic Stability Program (ESP) available. This system supports the vehicle's stability and steering through a combination of ABS and traction control operations. There is a switch on the centre console, so that if required the system can be switched off. This will then illuminate the warning light on the instrument panel, to inform the driver that the ESP is not in operation. The stability of the vehicle is measured by Yaw rate and Accelerometer sensors, which sense the movement of the vehicle about its vertical axis, and also lateral acceleration.

Note: *When servicing any part of the system, work carefully and methodically; also observe scrupulous cleanliness when overhauling any part of the hydraulic system. Always renew components (in axle sets, where applicable) if in doubt about their condition, and use only genuine Ford parts, or at least those of known good quality. Note the warnings given in 'Safety first!' and at relevant points in this Chapter concerning the dangers of asbestos dust and hydraulic fluid.*

2 Front brake pads – renewal

Warning: *Renew both sets of front brake pads at the same time – never renew the pads on only one wheel, as uneven braking may result. Note that the dust created by wear of the pads may contain asbestos, which is a health hazard. Never blow it out with compressed air, and don't inhale any of it. An approved filtering mask should be worn when working on the brakes. DO NOT use petrol or petroleum-based solvents to clean brake parts; use brake cleaner or methylated spirit only.*

1 Apply the handbrake, then slacken the front roadwheel nuts. Jack up the front of the vehicle and support it on axle stands. Remove both front roadwheels.

2 Follow the accompanying photos (**illustrations 2.2a to 2.2p**) for the actual pad renewal procedure. Be sure to stay in order and read the caption under each illustration, and note the following points:

a) *New pads may have an adhesive foil on the backplates. Remove this foil prior to installation.*
b) *Thoroughly clean the caliper guide surfaces, and apply a little brake assembly (polycarbamide) grease.*
c) *When pushing the caliper piston back to accommodate new pads, keep a close eye on the fluid level in the reservoir.*

Caution: *Pushing back the piston causes a reverse-flow of brake fluid, which has been known to 'flip' the master cylinder rubber seals, resulting in a total loss of braking. To avoid this, clamp the caliper flexible hose and open the bleed screw – as the piston is pushed back, the fluid can be directed into a suitable container using a hose attached to the bleed screw. Close the screw just before the piston is pushed fully back, to ensure no air enters the system.*

Braking system 9•3

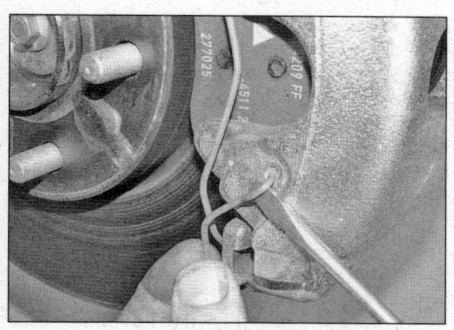

2.2a Use a flat-bladed screwdriver to carefully prise off the caliper retaining spring

2.2b Prise out the rubber caps . . .

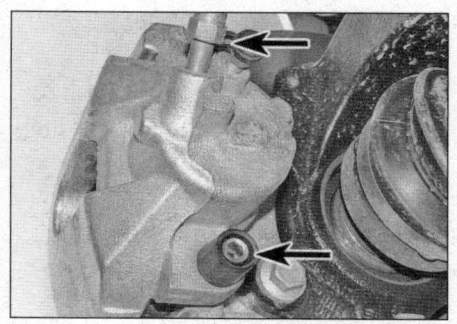

2.2c . . . and use an Allen key to undo the caliper guide bolts (arrowed)

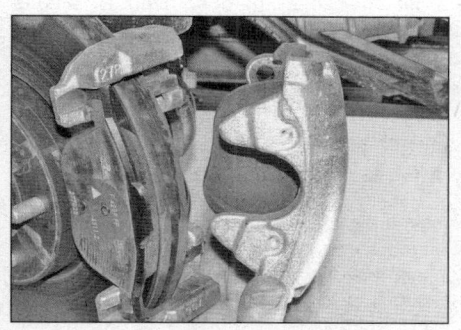

2.2d Slide the caliper and inner pad from the disc

2.2e Pull the inner brake pad from the caliper piston . . .

2.2f . . . and lift the outer pad from the caliper bracket

2.2g If you're fitting new pads, push the piston back into the caliper using a piston retraction tool or G-clamp

2.2h Clean the pad mounting surfaces with a wire brush

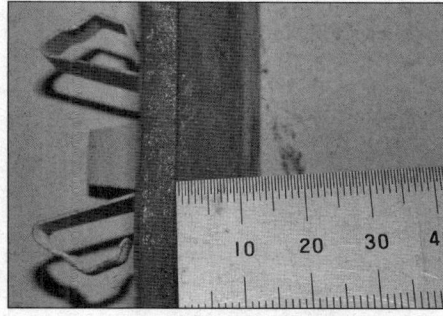

2.2i Measure the thickness of the pad's friction material. If it's 1.5 mm or less, renew all the front pads

2.2j Fit the outer pad to the caliper mounting bracket . . .

2.2k . . . then fit the inner pad to the caliper piston

2.2l Slide the caliper with the inner panel fitted over the disc and outer pad

9•4 Braking system

2.2m Refit the caliper guide bolts and tighten them to the specified torque

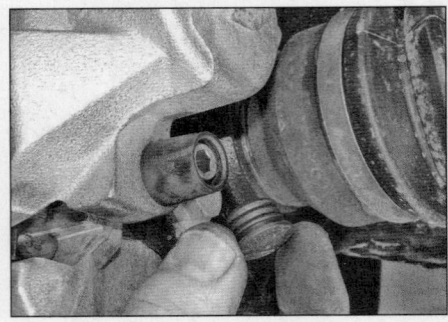

2.2n Press the rubber caps into position

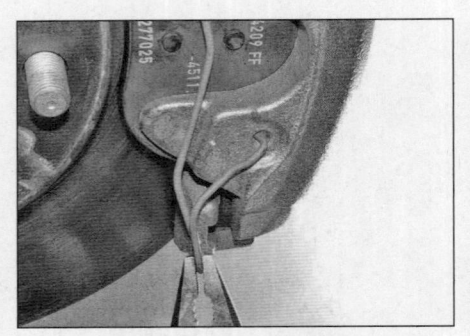

2.2o Use a pair of pliers . . .

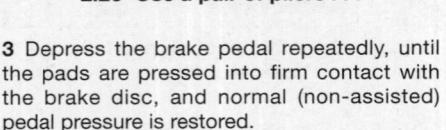

2.2p . . . to refit the caliper retaining spring

3 Depress the brake pedal repeatedly, until the pads are pressed into firm contact with the brake disc, and normal (non-assisted) pedal pressure is restored.
4 Repeat the above procedure on the remaining front brake caliper.

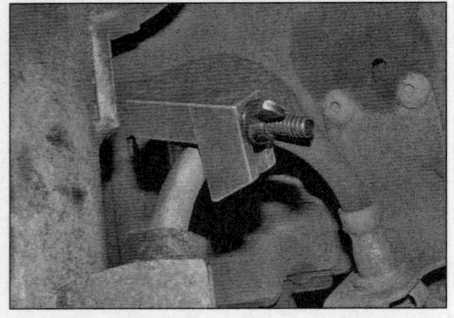

3.2 Use a hose clamp on the flexible hoses

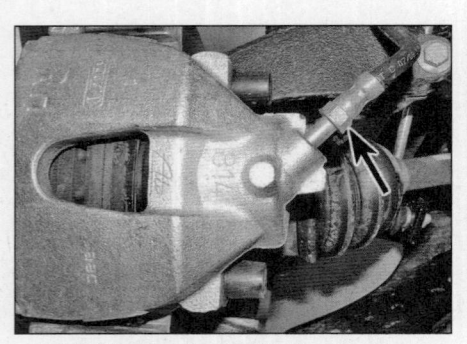

3.3 Slacken the flexible hose union (arrowed)

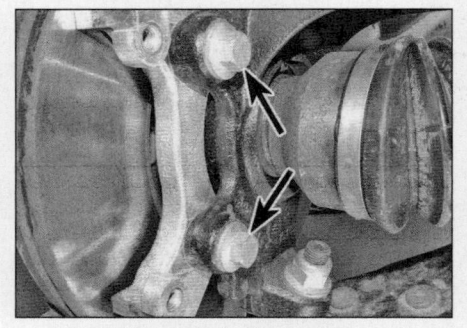

3.6 Caliper bracket bolts (arrowed)

5 Refit the roadwheels, then lower the vehicle to the ground and tighten the roadwheel nuts to the specified torque.
6 Check the hydraulic fluid level as described in *Weekly checks*.
Caution: New pads will not give full braking efficiency until they have bedded-in. Be prepared for this, and avoid hard braking as far as possible for the first hundred miles or so after pad renewal.

3 Front brake caliper – removal, overhaul and refitting

Note: *Refer to the warning at the beginning of the previous Section before proceeding.*

Removal

1 Apply the handbrake. Loosen the front wheel nuts, then jack up the front of the vehicle and support it on axle stands. Remove the appropriate front wheel.
2 Fit a brake hose clamp to the flexible hose leading to the caliper **(see illustration)**. This will minimise brake fluid loss during subsequent operations.
3 Loosen the union on the caliper end of the flexible brake hose **(see illustration)**. Once loosened, do not try to unscrew the hose at this stage.
4 Remove the brake pads as described in Section 2.
5 Support the caliper in one hand, and prevent the hydraulic hose from turning with the other hand. Unscrew the caliper from the hose, making sure that the hose is not twisted unduly or strained. Once the caliper is detached, plug the open hydraulic unions in the caliper and hose, to keep out dust and dirt.
6 If required, the caliper bracket can be unbolted from the hub carrier **(see illustration)**.

Overhaul

Note: *Before starting work, check on the availability of parts (caliper overhaul kit/seals).*
7 With the caliper on the bench, brush away all traces of dust and dirt, but take care not to inhale any dust, as it may be harmful to your health.
8 Pull the dust cover rubber seal from the end of the piston.
9 Apply low air pressure to the fluid inlet union, to eject the piston. Only low air pressure is required for this, such as is produced by a foot-operated tyre pump.
Caution: The piston may be ejected with some force. Position a thin piece of wood between the piston and the caliper body to prevent damage to the end face of the piston in the event of it being ejected suddenly.
10 Using a suitable blunt instrument, prise the piston seal from the groove in the cylinder bore. Take care not to scratch the surface of the bore.
11 Clean the piston and caliper body with methylated spirit, and allow to dry. Examine the surfaces of the piston and cylinder bore for wear, damage and corrosion. If the piston alone is unserviceable, a new piston must be obtained, along with seals. If the cylinder bore is unserviceable, the complete caliper must be renewed. The seals must be renewed, regardless of the condition of the other components.
12 Coat the piston and seals with clean brake fluid, then manipulate the piston seal into the groove in the cylinder bore.
13 Push the piston squarely into its bore, taking care not to damage the seal.
14 Fit the dust cover rubber seal onto the piston and caliper, then depress the piston fully.

Refitting

15 If removed, refit the caliper bracket and tighten the bolts to the specified torque.

Braking system 9•5

4.2 Suspend the caliper from the spring using wire or string

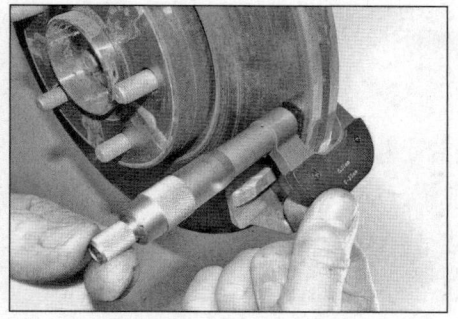

4.4 Measure the thickness of the disc using a micrometer

4.10 Lift the brake disc from the studs

16 Refit the brake pads as described in Section 2, but screw the caliper onto the flexible hose before refitting it to the caliper bracket.
17 Tighten the flexible hose union ensuring the hose is not kinked/twisted.
18 Bleed the brake circuit according to the procedure given in Section 14, remembering to remove the brake hose clamp from the flexible hose. Make sure there are no leaks from the hose connections. Test the brakes carefully before returning the vehicle to normal service.

4 Front brake disc – inspection, removal and refitting

Note: *To prevent uneven braking, BOTH front brake discs should be renewed or reground at the same time.*

Inspection

1 Apply the handbrake. Loosen the relevant wheel nuts, jack up the front of the vehicle and support it on axle stands. Remove the appropriate front wheel.
2 Remove the front brake caliper from the disc with reference to Section 3, and undo the two caliper bracket securing bolts. Do not disconnect the flexible hose. Support the caliper on an axle stand, or suspend it out of the way with a piece of wire, taking care to avoid straining the flexible hose **(see illustration)**.
3 Temporarily refit two of the wheel nuts to diagonally-opposite studs, with the flat sides of the nuts against the disc. Tighten the nuts progressively, to hold the disc firmly.
4 Scrape any corrosion from the disc. Rotate the disc, and examine it for deep scoring, grooving or cracks. Using a micrometer, measure the thickness of the disc in several places **(see illustration)**. The minimum thickness is stamped on the disc hub. Light wear and scoring is normal, but if excessive, the disc should be removed, and either reground by a specialist, or renewed. If regrinding is undertaken, the minimum thickness must be maintained. Obviously, if the disc is cracked, it must be renewed.
5 Using a dial gauge or a flat metal block and feeler gauges, check that the disc run-out 10 mm from the outer edge does not exceed the limit given in the Specifications. To do this, fix the measuring equipment, and rotate the disc, noting the variation in measurement as the disc is rotated. The difference between the minimum and maximum measurements recorded is the disc run-out.
6 If the run-out is greater than the specified amount, check for variations of the disc thickness as follows. Mark the disc at eight positions 45° apart then, using a micrometer, measure the disc thickness at the eight positions, 15 mm in from the outer edge. If the variation between the minimum and maximum readings is greater than the specified amount, the disc should be renewed.
7 The hub face run-out can also be checked in a similar way. First remove the disc as described later in this Section, fix the measuring equipment, then slowly rotate the hub, and check that the run-out does not exceed the amount given in the Specifications. If the hub face run-out is excessive, this should be corrected (by renewing the hub bearings – see Chapter 10) before rechecking the disc run-out.

Removal

8 With the wheel, caliper and bracket removed, remove the wheel nuts which were temporarily refitted in paragraph 3.
9 Mark the disc in relation to the hub, if it is to be refitted.
10 Remove the washer/retaining clip(s) (where fitted), and withdraw the disc over the wheel studs **(see illustration)**.

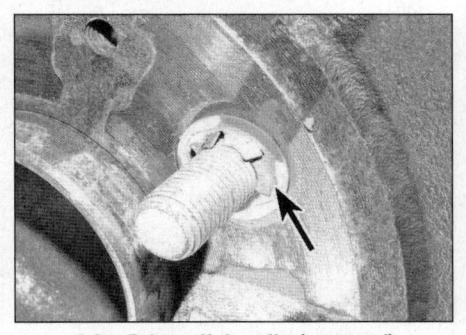

Refitting

11 Make sure that the disc and hub mating surfaces are clean, then locate the disc on the wheel studs. Align the previously-made marks if the original disc is being refitted.
12 Refit the washer/retaining clip(s), where fitted.
13 Refit the brake caliper and bracket with reference to Section 2.
14 Refit the wheel, and lower the vehicle to the ground. Tighten wheel nuts to their specified torque.
15 Test the brakes carefully before returning the vehicle to normal service.

5 Rear brake drum – removal, inspection and refitting

Note: *Refer to the warning at the beginning of Section 6 before proceeding.*
Note: *To prevent uneven braking, BOTH rear brake drums should be renewed at the same time.*

Removal

1 Chock the front wheels, release the handbrake and engage 1st gear (or P). Loosen the relevant wheel nuts, jack up the rear of the vehicle and support it on axle stands. Remove the appropriate rear wheel.
2 Prise off the spring clip (where fitted), and pull the drum from place. If the drum is reluctant to move, use two 8.0 mm bolts screwed into the threaded holes provided, and draw the drum from place **(see illustrations)**.

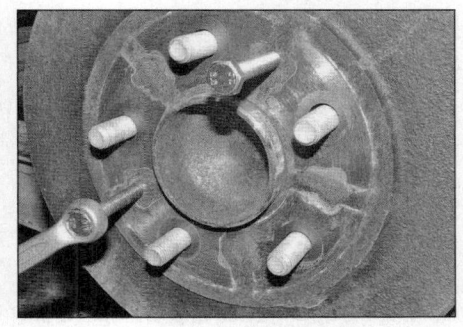

5.2a Prise off the clip (arrowed)

5.2b Use 2 x 8 mm bolts to force the drum from place

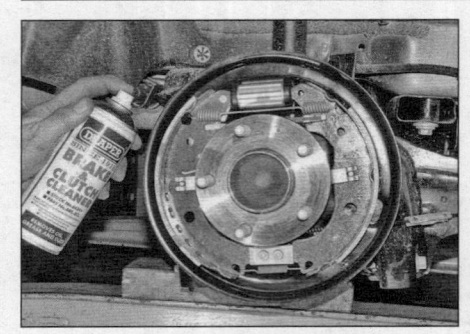

9•6 Braking system

6.3 Clean the components with brake cleaner

6.4 Depress the hold-down spring, and slide it from under the head of the pin

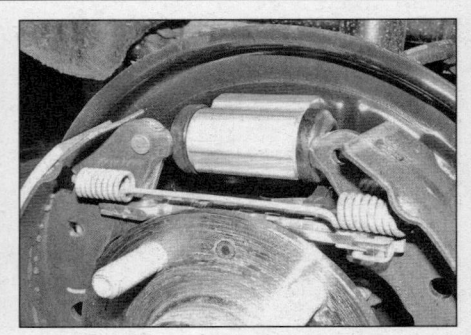

6.5 Pull the top end of the shoe assembly outwards from the wheel cylinder

6.7a Pull the bottom end of the shoes from the anchor . . .

6.7b . . . then pivot the whole brake shoe assembly outwards

3 With the brake drum removed, clean the dust from the drum, brake shoes, wheel cylinder and backplate, using brake cleaner or methylated spirit. Take care not to inhale the dust, as it may contain asbestos.

Inspection

4 Clean the inside surfaces of the brake drum, then examine the internal friction surface for signs of scoring or cracks. If it is cracked, deeply scored, or has worn to a diameter greater than the maximum given in the Specifications, then it should be renewed, together with the drum on the other side.
5 Regrinding of the brake drum is not recommended.

Refitting

6 Refitting is a reversal of removal, tightening relevant bolts to their specified torque. Where necessary, adjust the handbrake as described in Section 22.

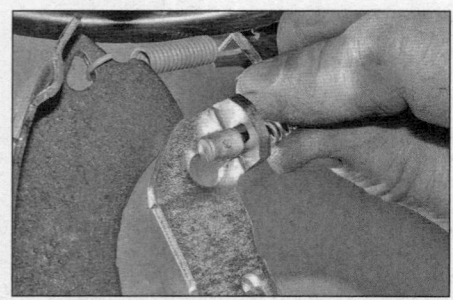

6.8 Pull the spring back and disengage the handbrake lever cable end fitting from the lever on the shoe

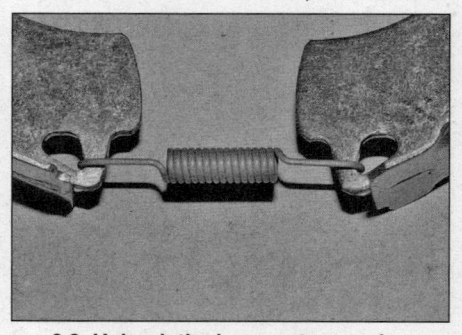

7 Test the brakes carefully before returning the vehicle to normal service.

6 Rear brake shoes – renewal

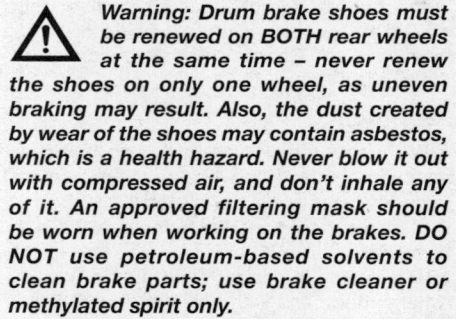

⚠️ **Warning:** *Drum brake shoes must be renewed on BOTH rear wheels at the same time – never renew the shoes on only one wheel, as uneven braking may result. Also, the dust created by wear of the shoes may contain asbestos, which is a health hazard. Never blow it out with compressed air, and don't inhale any of it. An approved filtering mask should be worn when working on the brakes. DO NOT use petroleum-based solvents to clean brake parts; use brake cleaner or methylated spirit only.*

1 Chock the front wheels, release the

6.9 Unhook the lower return spring

handbrake and engage 1st gear (or P). Loosen the relevant wheel nuts, jack up the rear of the vehicle and support it on axle stands. Remove the rear wheels. Work on one brake assembly at a time, using the assembled brake for reference if necessary.
2 Remove the rear brake drum as described in Section 5.
3 Note the fitted position of the springs and the brake shoes, then clean the components with brake cleaner, and allow to dry (see illustration); position a tray beneath the backplate, to catch the cleaner and residue.
4 Remove the two shoe hold-down springs, use a pair of pliers to depress the ends so that they can be withdrawn off the pins. If required, remove the hold-down pins from the backplate (see illustration). Note that on some models, it's not possible to remove the rearmost hold-down pin with the backplate in place.
5 Disconnect the top ends of the shoes from the wheel cylinder, taking care not to damage the rubber boots (see illustration).
6 To prevent the wheel cylinder pistons from being accidentally ejected, fit a suitable elastic band or wire lengthways over the cylinder/pistons. DO NOT press the brake pedal while the shoes are removed.
7 Pull the bottom end of the brake shoes from the bottom anchor (see illustrations). Use pliers or an adjustable spanner over the edge of the shoe to lever it away, if required.
8 Pull the handbrake cable spring back from the operating lever on the rear of the trailing shoe. Unhook the cable end from the cut-out in the lever, and remove the brake shoes (see illustration).
9 Working on a clean bench, move the bottom ends of the brake shoes together, and unhook the lower return spring from the shoes, noting the location holes (see illustration).
10 Pull the leading shoe from the strut and brake shoe adjuster (see illustration).
11 Pull the adjustment strut to release it from the trailing brake shoe, then unhook the upper return spring from the shoes, noting the location holes (see illustrations). Ford insist that the upper return spring is renewed.
12 If the wheel cylinder shows signs of fluid

Braking system 9•7

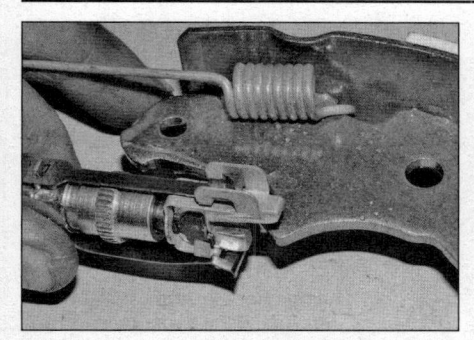

6.10 Pull the shoe from the strut and brake shoe adjuster

6.11a Pull the adjustment strut from the trailing shoe . . .

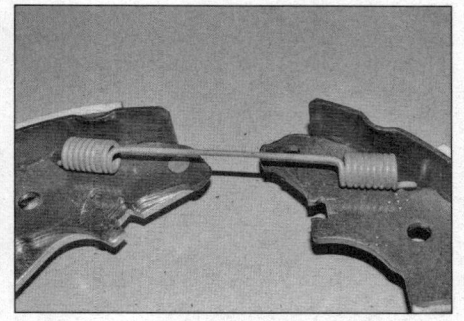

6.11b . . . then unhook the upper return spring

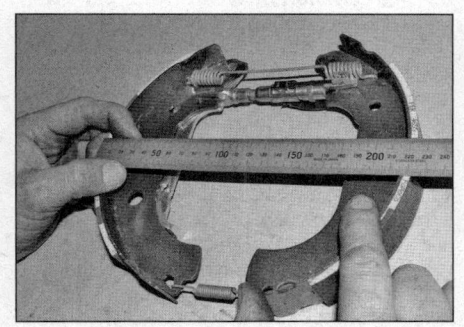

6.15a Set the adjustment strut so the diameter of the shoe assembly is 228 mm

6.15b When reassembled, the top of the assembly should look like this . . .

6.15c . . . and the lower end should look like this

leakage, or if there is any reason to suspect it of being defective, inspect it now, as described in the next Section.

13 Clean the backplate, and apply small amounts of high melting-point brake grease to the brake shoe contact points. Be careful not to get grease on any friction surfaces.

14 Lubricate the sliding components of the brake shoe adjuster with a little high melting-point brake grease.

15 Fit the new brake shoes using a reversal of the removal procedure, but set the adjustment strut so the diameter of the shoe assembly is 228 mm **(see illustrations)**.

16 Before refitting the brake drum, it should be inspected as described in Section 5.

17 With the drum in position and all the securing bolts and nuts tightened to their specified torque, refit the wheel, then carry out the renewal procedure on the remaining rear brake.

18 Lower the vehicle to the ground, and tighten the wheel nuts to the specified torque.

19 Depress the brake pedal several times, in order to operate the self-adjusting mechanism and set the shoes at their normal operating position.

20 Make several forward and reverse stops, and operate the handbrake fully two or three times (adjust the handbrake as required). Give the vehicle a road test, to make sure that the brakes are functioning correctly, and to bed-in the new shoes to the contours of the drum. Remember that the new shoes will not give full braking efficiency until they have bedded-in.

7 Rear wheel cylinder – removal, overhaul and refitting

Note: *Before starting work, check on the availability of parts (wheel cylinder, or overhaul kit/seals). Also bear in mind that if the brake shoes have been contaminated by fluid leaking from the wheel cylinder, they must be renewed. The shoes on BOTH sides of the vehicle must be renewed, even if they are only contaminated on one side.*

Removal

1 Remove the brake drum as described in Section 5.

2 Minimise fluid loss either by removing the master cylinder reservoir cap, and then tightening it down onto a piece of polythene to obtain an airtight seal, or by using a brake hose clamp, a G-clamp, or similar tool, to clamp the flexible hose at the nearest convenient point to the wheel cylinder.

3 Pull the brake shoes apart at their top ends, so that they are just clear of the wheel cylinder. The automatic adjuster will hold the shoes in this position, so that the cylinder can be withdrawn.

4 Wipe away all traces of dirt around the hydraulic union at the rear of the wheel cylinder, then undo the union nut.

5 Unscrew the two bolts securing the wheel cylinder to the backplate **(see illustration)**.

6 Withdraw the wheel cylinder from the backplate so that it is clear of the brake shoes.

Plug the open hydraulic unions, to prevent the entry of dirt, and to minimise further fluid loss whilst the cylinder is detached.

Overhaul

7 No overhaul procedures or parts were available at the time of writing, check availability of spares before dismantling. Renewing a wheel cylinder as a unit is recommended.

Refitting

8 Wipe clean the backplate and remove the plug from the end of the hydraulic pipe. Fit the cylinder onto the backplate and screw in the hydraulic union nut by hand, being careful not to cross-thread it.

9 Tighten the mounting bolts, then fully tighten the hydraulic union nut.

10 Retract the automatic brake adjuster mechanism, so that the brake shoes engage

7.5 Undo the 2 bolts (arrowed) and remove the wheel cylinder

9•8 Braking system

with the pistons of the wheel cylinder. To do this, prise the shoes apart slightly, turn the automatic adjuster to its minimum position, and release the shoes.
11 Remove the clamp from the flexible brake hose, or the polythene from the master cylinder (as applicable).
12 Refit the brake drum with reference to Section 5.
13 Bleed the hydraulic system as described in Section 14. Providing suitable precautions were taken to minimise loss of fluid, it should only be necessary to bleed the relevant rear brake.
14 Test the brakes carefully before returning the vehicle to normal service.

8 Rear brake pads – renewal

Warning: *Renew both sets of rear brake pads at the same time – never renew the pads on only one wheel, as uneven braking may result. Note that the dust created by wear of the pads may contain asbestos, which is a health hazard. Never blow it out with compressed air, and don't inhale any of it. An approved filtering mask should be worn when working on the brakes. DO NOT use petrol or petroleum-based solvents to clean brake parts; use brake cleaner or methylated spirit only.*

1 Chock the front wheels, slacken the rear road-wheel nuts, then jack up the rear of the vehicle and support it on axle stands (see *Jacking and vehicle support*). Remove the rear wheels.
2 With the handbrake lever fully released, follow the accompanying photos **(see illustrations 8.2a to 8.2u)** for the actual pad renewal procedure. Be sure to stay in order and read the caption under each illustration, and note the following points:
  a) If re-installing the original pads, ensure they are fitted to their original position.
  b) Thoroughly clean the caliper guide surfaces and guide bolts.
  c) If new pads are to be fitted, use a piston retraction tool to push the piston back and twist it clockwise at the same time – keep an eye on the fluid level in the reservoir whilst retracting the piston.

Caution: *Pushing back the piston causes a reverse-flow of brake fluid, which has been known to 'flip' the master cylinder rubber seals, resulting in a total loss of braking. To avoid this, clamp the caliper flexible hose and open the bleed screw – as the piston is pushed back, the fluid can be directed into a suitable container using a hose attached to the bleed screw. Close the screw just before the piston is pushed fully back, to ensure no air enters the system.*

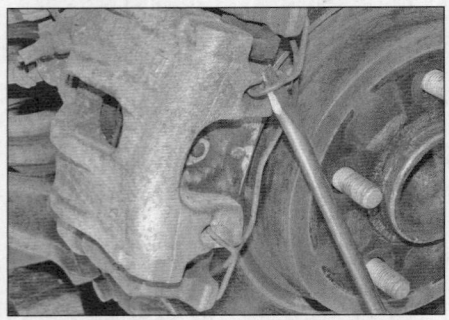

8.2a Prise away the retaining spring

8.2b Pull out the rubber caps . . .

8.2c . . . and use a 7 mm Allen key or bit to unscrew the guide bolts

8.2d Unclip the brake hose from the bracket

8.2e Lift away the caliper . . .

8.2f . . . and suspend it from the suspension using cable ties/string

8.2g Remove the outer brake pad . . .

8.2h . . . and the inner pad

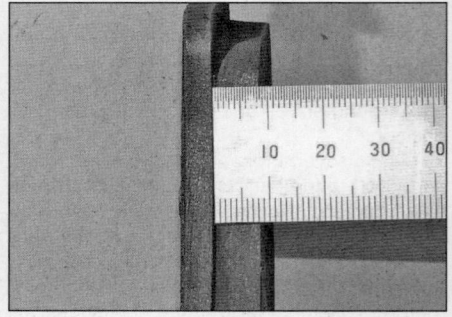

8.2i Measure the thickness of the pad friction material

Braking system 9•9

8.2j Use a wire brush to clean the pad mounting bracket

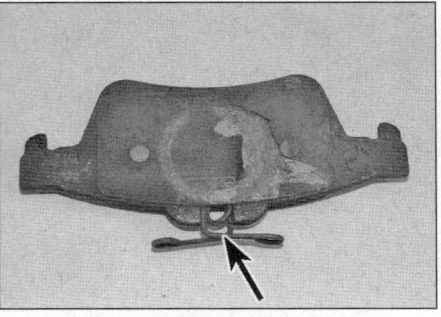

8.2k Note that the inner pad has an anti-rattle spring (arrowed)

8.2l Apply a little high-temperature anti-seize grease (Copperslip) to the rear of the pad . . .

8.2m . . . and the areas where the pad backing plate contacts the mounting bracket

8.2n Fit the inner pad – friction material side against the disc . . .

8.2o . . . followed by the outer pad

8.2p If new pads have been fitted, use a retraction tool to rotate the caliper piston clockwise, at the same time as pushing it into the caliper

8.2q Refit the caliper over the pads . . .

8.2r . . . then refit and tighten the guide bolts to the specified torque

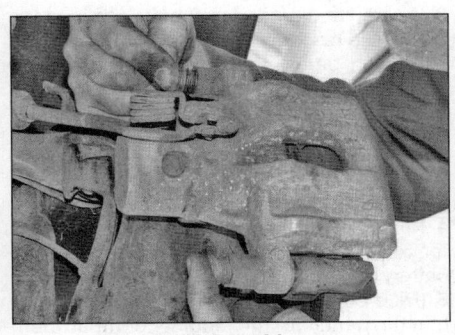

8.2s Refit the rubber caps

8.2t Clip the brake hose back into the bracket

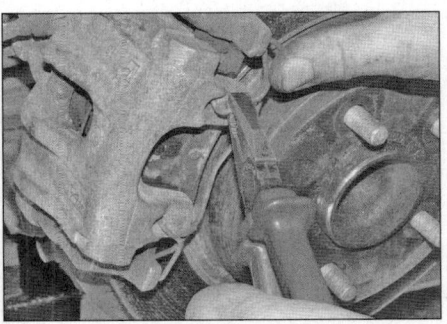

8.2u Use pliers to refit the caliper retaining spring

9•10 Braking system

9.4 Unclip the cable end fitting (arrowed) from the caliper lever

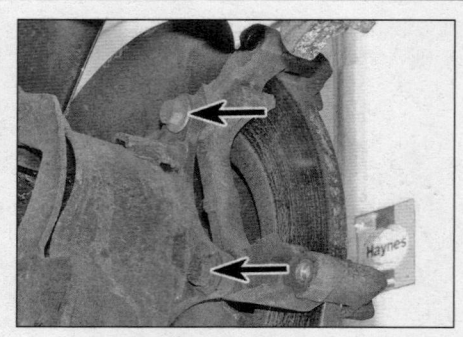

9.6 Undo the caliper mounting bracket bolts (arrowed)

3 Depress the brake pedal repeatedly, until the pads are pressed into firm contact with the brake disc, and normal (non-assisted) pedal pressure is restored.
4 Repeat the above procedure on the remaining brake caliper.
5 If necessary, adjust the handbrake as described in Section 22.
6 Refit the roadwheels, then lower the vehicle to the ground and tighten the roadwheel nuts to the specified torque.
7 Check the hydraulic fluid level as described in *Weekly checks*.
Caution: *New pads will not give full braking efficiency until they have bedded-in. Be prepared for this, and avoid hard braking as far as possible for the first hundred miles or so after pad renewal.*

9 Rear brake caliper – removal, overhaul and refitting

Removal

1 Chock the front wheels, and engage 1st gear (or P). Loosen the rear wheel nuts, jack up the rear of the vehicle and support it on axle stands. Remove the appropriate rear wheel.
2 Fit a brake hose clamp to the flexible hose leading to the caliper **(see illustration 3.2)**. This will minimise brake fluid loss during subsequent operations.
3 Slacken (but do not completely unscrew) the union on the caliper end of the flexible hose.
4 Unclip the handbrake inner cable fitting from the lever on the caliper, then detach the outer cable from the bracket **(see illustration)**.
5 Unscrew the caliper from the hydraulic brake hose, making sure that the hose is not twisted or strained unduly. Plug the open hydraulic unions to keep dust and dirt out.
6 If necessary, unbolt the caliper bracket from the hub carrier **(see illustration)**.

Overhaul

7 No overhaul procedures, or parts, were available at the time of writing. Check the availability of spares before dismantling the caliper. Do not attempt to dismantle the handbrake mechanism inside the caliper; if the mechanism is faulty, the complete caliper assembly must be renewed.

Refitting

8 Refit the caliper, and where applicable the bracket, by reversing the removal operations. Refer to the points made in Section 22 when reconnecting the handbrake cable. Tighten the mounting bolts and wheel nuts to the specified torque, and do not forget to remove the brake hose clamp from the flexible brake hose.
9 Bleed the brake circuit according to the procedure given in Section 14. Make sure there are no leaks from the hose connections. Test the brakes carefully before returning the vehicle to normal service.

10 Rear brake disc – inspection, removal and refitting

Removal

1 Remove the rear caliper and pads as described in Section 8.
2 Unbolt the caliper carrier bracket from the hub **(see illustration 9.6)**, then mark the disc in relation to the hub, if it is to be refitted.
3 Remove the retaining clip from the wheel stud (where fitted), and withdraw the disc over the wheel studs **(see illustration)**.
4 Procedures for inspection of the rear brake discs are the same as the front brake discs as described in Section 4.

Refitting

5 Refitting is a reversal of removal, as described in the relevant Sections. Apply a little thread locking compound to the caliper bracket-to-hub carrier bolts.

11 Master cylinder – removal and refitting

> **Warning:** *Brake fluid is poisonous. Take care to keep it off bare skin, and in particular not to get splashes in your eyes. The fluid also attacks paintwork and plastics – wash off spillages immediately with cold water. Finally, brake fluid is highly inflammable, and should be handled with the same care as petrol.*

Removal

1 Exhaust the vacuum in the servo by pressing the brake pedal a few times, with the engine switched off.
2 Disconnect the battery negative lead. **Note:** *Before disconnecting the battery, refer to Chapter 5A for precautions.*

> **Warning:** *Do not syphon the fluid by mouth; it is poisonous. Any brake fluid spilt on paintwork should be washed off with clean water, without delay – brake fluid is also a highly-effective paint-stripper.*

3 Where fitted, undo the 2 bolts securing the brake fluid reservoir extension to the bulkhead extension panel, then depress the release button and detach the reservoir extension hose from the reservoir above the master cylinder.

Models with a plastic panel in front of the brake master cylinder

4 Remove the battery as described in Chapter 5A, then undo the 3 bolts and slide the battery tray forward a little **(see illustration)**.
5 Prise out the 4 plastic clips securing the plastic panel to the engine compartment bulkhead, then undo the inner 2 retaining bolts, slacken the outer bolt, remove the nuts

10.3 Pull the rear brake disc over the wheel studs

11.4 Battery tray retaining bolts (arrowed)

Braking system 9•11

11.5a Prise out the 4 clips (arrowed)

11.5b Undo the 2 inner bolts, slacken the outer bolt, undo the 2 nuts and pivot the cross-stay (arrowed) each side away from the engine compartment bulkhead . . .

11.5c . . . so the plastic panel in front of the master cylinder can be removed

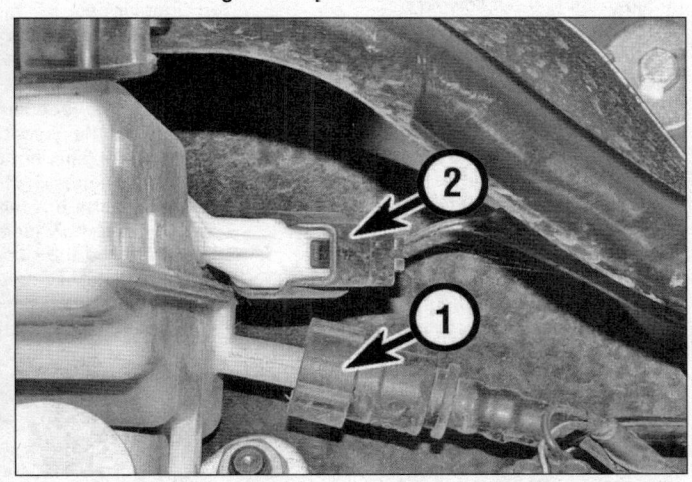

11.7 Depress the release button (on the reverse of the connector – 1), and disconnect the clutch fluid supply hose, then disconnect the level warning sensor wiring plug (2)

and pivot the cross-stay each side away from the bulkhead. Lift the plastic panel (where fitted) from place **(see illustrations)**. Refit the bolts to secure the tops of the suspension struts to the vehicle body.

All models

6 Raise the vehicle and remove the wheels. Slacken the front bleed nipples, attach a rubber hose to the nipple, and place the other end of the hose in a suitable container. Operate the brake pedal until the fluid level is down to the base of the reservoir.

7 Depress the release button and detach the clutch master cylinder fluid supply hose from the side of the brake fluid reservoir **(see illustration)**. Plug the openings to prevent contamination.

8 Disconnect the wiring plug from the fluid level sensor on the side of the reservoir **(see illustration 11.7)**.

9 Identify the locations of each brake pipe on the master cylinder, then place rags beneath

the master cylinder to catch spilt hydraulic fluid.

10 Clean around the hydraulic union nuts. Unscrew the nuts, and disconnect the hydraulic lines from the master cylinder. If the nuts are tight, a split ring spanner should be used in preference to an open-ended spanner **(see illustration)**.

Cap the end of the pipes and the master cylinder to prevent any dirt contamination.

11 Undo the master cylinder securing nuts, and withdraw the master cylinder from the studs on the servo unit **(see illustration)**.

12 Recover the gasket/seal from the master cylinder.

11.10 Undo the brake pipe unions (arrowed)

11.11 Master cylinder retaining nuts (arrowed)

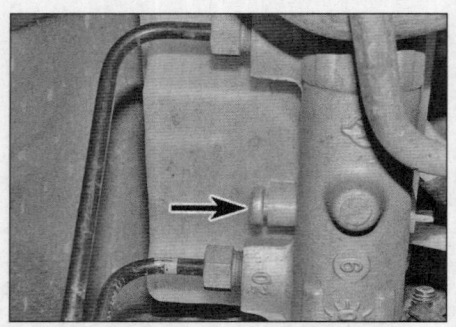

9•12 Braking system

11.17 Pull out the reservoir retaining pin (arrowed – viewed from underneath)

13 If the master cylinder is faulty, it must be renewed. At the time of writing, no overhaul kits were available.

Refitting

14 Refitting is a reversal of the removal procedure, noting the following points:
 a) Clean the contact surfaces of the master cylinder and servo, and locate a new gasket on the master cylinder.
 b) Refit and tighten the nuts to the specified torque.
 c) Carefully insert the brake pipes in the apertures in the master cylinder, then tighten the union nuts. Make sure that the nuts enter their threads correctly.
 d) Fill the reservoir with fresh brake fluid.
 e) Bleed the brake hydraulic system as described in Section 14.
 f) Test the brakes carefully before returning the vehicle to normal service.

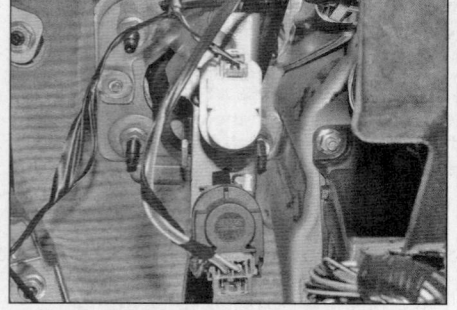

12.4 Disconnect the wiring plugs from the brake pedal switches

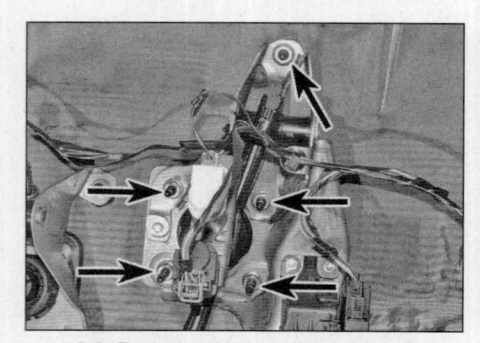

12.6 Brake pedal bracket assembly retaining nuts (arrowed)

Brake fluid reservoir

15 Carry out the procedure described in Paragraph 3 to 7 of this Section.
16 Disconnect the wiring plug from the fluid level sensor on the side of the reservoir.
17 Remove the retaining pin and detach the reservoir from the master cylinder (see illustration).

12 Brake pedal – removal and refitting

Removal

1 Working inside the vehicle, move the driver's seat fully to the rear, to allow maximum working area.
2 Remove the driver's side lower facia panel as described in Chapter 11.
3 Remove the accelerator pedal as described in Chapter 4A.
4 Disconnect the electrical connectors to the brake pedal switches. Remove the switches by turning them, then pulling them out of the pedal bracket (see illustration).
5 Prise out the pin securing the servo pushrod to the pedal (see illustration). Discard the pin – a new one must be fitted.
6 Slacken the 5 retaining nuts on the pedal bracket assembly (see illustration).
7 Manoeuvre the pedal assembly rearwards, and down from under the facia. No further dismantling of the assembly is recommended – it would appear that only the complete assembly is available.

12.5 Prise out and discard the servo pushrod pin

13.7 Use a brake pipe spanner to slacken the union nuts

Refitting

8 Refitting is a reversal of the removal procedure.
9 Refit the brake pedal switches as described in Section 21.

13 Hydraulic pipes and hoses – inspection, removal and refitting

Note: *Refer to the warning at the start of Section 14 concerning the dangers of brake fluid.*

Inspection

1 Jack up the front and rear of the vehicle, and support on axle stands (see *Jacking and vehicle support*). Making sure the vehicle is safely supported on a level surface.
2 Check for signs of leakage at the pipe unions, then examine the flexible hoses for signs of cracking, chafing and fraying.
3 The brake pipes should be examined carefully for signs of dents, corrosion or other damage. Corrosion should be scraped off, and if the depth of pitting is significant, the pipes renewed. This is particularly likely in those areas underneath the vehicle body where the pipes are exposed and unprotected.
4 Renew any defective brake pipes and/or hoses.

Removal

5 If a section of pipe or hose is to be removed, loss of brake fluid can be reduced by unscrewing the filler cap, and completely sealing the top of the reservoir with cling film or adhesive tape. Alternatively, the reservoir can be emptied (see Section 11).
6 To remove a section of pipe, hold the adjoining hose union nut with a spanner to prevent it from turning, then unscrew the union nut at the end of the pipe, and release it. Repeat the procedure at the other end of the pipe, then release the pipe by pulling out the clips attaching it to the body.
7 Where the union nuts are exposed to the full force of the weather, they can sometimes be quite tight. If an open-ended spanner is used, burring of the flats on the nuts is not uncommon, and for this reason, it is preferable to use a split ring (brake) spanner (see illustration), which will engage all the flats. If such a spanner is not available, self-locking grips may be used as a last resort; these may well damage the nuts, but if the pipe is to be renewed, this does not matter.
8 To further minimise the loss of fluid when disconnecting a flexible brake line from a rigid pipe, clamp the hose as near as possible to the pipe to be detached, using a brake hose clamp or a pair of self-locking grips with protected jaws.
9 To remove a flexible hose, first clean the ends of the hose and the surrounding area, then unscrew the union nuts from the hose ends. Remove the spring clip, and withdraw

the hose from the serrated mounting in the support bracket. Where applicable, unscrew the hose from the caliper.

10 Brake pipes supplied with flared ends and union nuts can be obtained individually or in sets from Ford dealers or accessory shops. The pipe is then bent to shape, using the old pipe as a guide, and is ready for fitting. Be careful not to kink or crimp the pipe when bending it; ideally, a proper pipe-bending tool should be used.

Refitting

11 Refitting of the pipes and hoses is a reversal of removal. Make sure that all brake pipes are securely supported in their clips, and ensure that the hoses are not kinked. Check also that the hoses are clear of all suspension components and underbody fittings, and will remain clear during movement of the suspension and steering.
12 On completion, bleed the hydraulic system as described in Section 14.

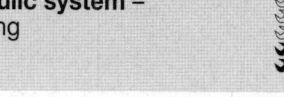

14 Hydraulic system – bleeding

Warning: Brake fluid contains polyglycol ethers and polyglycols which are poisonous. Take care to keep it off bare skin, and in particular not to get splashes in your eyes. Wash hands thoroughly after handling and if fluid contacts the eyes, flush out with cold running water. If irritation persists get medical attention immediately. The fluid also attacks paintwork and plastics – wash off spillages immediately with cold water. Finally, brake fluid is highly inflammable, and should be handled with the same care as petrol.

1 If the master cylinder has been disconnected and reconnected, then the complete system (all circuits) must be bled of air. If a component of one circuit has been disturbed, then only that particular circuit need be bled.
2 Bleeding should commence on the furthest bleed nipple from the master cylinder, followed by the next one until the bleed nipple remaining nearest to the master cylinder is bled last.
3 There are a variety of do-it-yourself 'one-man' brake bleeding kits available from motor accessory shops, and it is recommended that one of these kits be used wherever possible, as they greatly simplify the brake bleeding operation. Follow the kit manufacturer's instructions in conjunction with the following procedure. If a pressure-bleeding kit is obtained, then it will not be necessary to depress the brake pedal in the following procedure.
4 During the bleeding operation, do not allow the brake fluid level in the reservoir to drop below the minimum mark. If the level is allowed to fall so far that air is drawn in, the whole procedure will have to be started

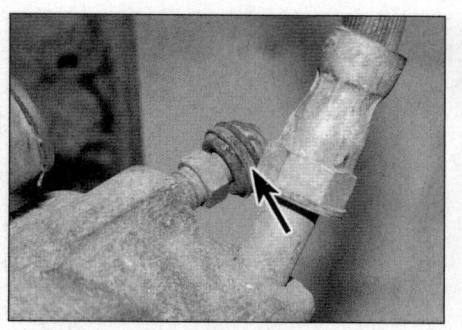

14.7a Prise off the dust cap from the bleed screw (arrowed)

again from scratch. Only use new fluid for topping-up, preferably from a freshly-opened container. Never re-use fluid bled from the system.
5 Before starting, check that all rigid pipes and flexible hoses are in good condition, and that all hydraulic unions are tight. Take great care not to allow hydraulic fluid to come into contact with the vehicle paintwork, otherwise the finish will be seriously damaged. Wash off any spilt fluid immediately with cold water.
6 If a brake bleeding kit is not being used, gather together a clean jar, a length of plastic or rubber tubing which is a tight fit over the bleed screw, and a new container of the specified brake fluid (see *Lubricants and fluids*). The help of an assistant will also be required.
7 Clean the area around the bleed screw on the rear brake unit to be bled (it is important that no dirt be allowed to enter the hydraulic system), and remove the dust cap. Connect one end of the tubing to the bleed screw, and immerse the other end in the jar **(see illustrations)**. The jar should be filled with sufficient brake fluid to keep the end of the tube submerged.
8 Open the bleed screw by half a turn, and have the assistant depress the brake pedal to the floor. Tighten the bleed screw at the end of the down stroke, then have the assistant release the pedal. Continue this procedure until clean brake fluid, free from air bubbles, can be seen flowing into the jar. Finally tighten the bleed screw with the pedal in the fully-depressed position.
9 Remove the tube, and refit the dust cap. Top-up the master cylinder reservoir if necessary, then repeat the procedure on the opposite rear brake.
10 Repeat the procedure on the front brake furthest from the master cylinder, followed by the brake nearest to the master cylinder.
11 Check the feel of the brake pedal – it should be firm. If it is spongy, there is still some air in the system, and the bleeding procedure should be repeated.
12 When bleeding is complete, top-up the master cylinder reservoir and refit the cap.
13 On models with manual transmission, check the clutch operation on completion; it may be necessary to bleed the clutch hydraulic system as described in Chapter 6.

14.7b Connect the kit and open the bleed screw

15 Vacuum servo unit – testing, removal and refitting

Testing

1 To test the operation of the servo unit, depress the footbrake four or five times to dissipate the vacuum, then start the engine while keeping the footbrake depressed. As the engine starts, there should be a noticeable give in the brake pedal as vacuum builds-up. Allow the engine to run for at least two minutes, and then switch it off. If the brake pedal is now depressed again, it should be possible to hear a hiss from the servo when the pedal is depressed. After four or five applications, no further hissing should be heard, and the pedal should feel harder.
2 Before assuming that a problem exists in the servo unit itself, inspect the non-return valve as described in the next Section.

Removal

RHD models

3 On models with air conditioning, have the refrigerant circuit evacuated as described in Chapter 3. When disconnecting the air conditioning pipes, cap the ends to prevent any contamination.
4 Refer to Section 11 and remove the master cylinder.
5 Remove the right-hand headlight assembly as described in Chapter 12.
6 Detach the coolant expansion tank from the right-hand side inner wing and move it to one side.
7 Disconnect the wiring plugs from the high- and low-pressure cut-off switches in the refrigerant pipes, then undo the bolt securing the pipes to the connection at the engine compartment bulkhead **(see illustrations)**. Discard the O-ring seals – new ones must be fitted.
8 Undo the bolts securing the refrigerant pipes to the connections at the condenser and accumulator/dehydrator, and unclip the pipes from the inner wing. Discard the O-ring seals – new ones must be fitted. Plug the openings to prevent contamination.

9•14 Braking system

15.7a Undo the bolt securing the refrigerant pipes (arrowed)

9 Carefully prise the vacuum non-return valve from the servo **(see illustration 16.5)**.
10 Remove the driver's side lower facia panel as described in Chapter 11.
11 Disconnect their wiring plugs, then remove the brake pedal position switch (coloured blue/white) and brake light switch (coloured black) from the bracket. Rotate the position switch anti-clockwise, and the light switch clockwise. Do not move the brake pedal during this procedure.
12 Carefully prise the pin from the servo actuator rod **(see illustration 12.5)**. Discard the pin – a new one must be fitted
13 Undo the 4 nuts securing the servo to the bulkhead/pedal bracket and manoeuvre it from the engine compartment.
14 Note that the servo unit cannot be dismantled for repair or overhaul and, if faulty, must be renewed.

LHD models
15 Remove the brake master cylinder as described in Section 11.
16 Undo the brake pipes to the hydraulic control unit. Cap the end of the pipes and the hydraulic unit to prevent any dirt contamination.
17 Disconnect the vacuum pipe from the servo.
18 Remove the driver's side lower facia panel as described in Chapter 11.
19 Disconnect their wiring plugs, then remove the brake pedal position switch (coloured blue/white) and brake light switch (coloured black) from the bracket. Rotate the position switch anti-clockwise, and the light switch clockwise.

16.5 The vacuum non-return valve is located in the pipe between the inlet manifold and the servo (arrowed)

15.7b Renew the refrigerant pipe O-ring seals (arrowed)

Do not move the brake pedal during this procedure.
20 Carefully prise the pin from the servo actuator rod **(see illustration 12.5)**. Discard the pin – a new one must be fitted
21 Undo the 4 nuts securing the servo to the bulkhead/pedal bracket and manoeuvre it from the engine compartment.
22 Note that the servo unit cannot be dismantled for repair or overhaul and, if faulty, must be renewed.

Refitting
23 Refitting is a reversal of the removal procedure, noting the following points:
 a) Refer to the relevant Sections/Chapters for details of refitting the other components removed.
 b) Compress the actuator rod into the brake servo, before refitting.
 c) Make sure the gasket is correctly positioned on the servo.
 d) Test the brakes carefully before returning the vehicle to normal service.

16 Vacuum servo unit vacuum hose and non-return valve – removal, testing and refitting

Removal
1 With the engine switched off, depress the brake pedal four or five times, to dissipate any remaining vacuum from the servo unit.
2 Disconnect the vacuum hose adapter at the servo unit, by pulling it free from the rubber

17.3 Release the clips (arrowed) and disconnect the ABS unit wiring plug

grommet. If it is reluctant to move, prise it free, using a screwdriver with its blade inserted under the flange.
3 Detach the vacuum hose from the inlet manifold connection, pressing in the collar to disengage the tabs, then withdrawing the collar slowly.
4 If the hose or the fixings are damaged or in poor condition, they must be renewed.

Testing
5 Examine the non-return valve **(see illustration)** for damage and signs of deterioration, and renew it if necessary. The valve may be tested by blowing through its connecting hoses in both directions. It should only be possible to blow from the servo end towards the inlet manifold.

Refitting
6 Refitting is a reversal of the removal procedure. If fitting a new non-return valve, ensure that it is fitted the correct way round.

17 ABS hydraulic unit – removal and refitting

Note: At the time of writing, no parts for the ABS hydraulic unit were available, and it must therefore be renewed as an assembly. Refer to the warning at the start of Section 14 concerning the dangers of brake fluid.

Removal
1 Remove the battery (see Chapter 5A) and the PCM (Chapter 4A), then undo the bolts and remove the battery tray **(see illustration 11.4)**.
2 Raise the vehicle and remove the wheels. Slacken the front bleed nipples, attach a rubber hose to the nipple, and place the other end of the hose in a suitable container. Operate the brake pedal until the fluid level is down to the base of the reservoir.

⚠ **Warning: Do not syphon the fluid by mouth; it is poisonous. Any brake fluid spilt on paintwork should be washed off with clean water, without delay – brake fluid is also a highly-effective paint-stripper.**

3 Depress the retaining clips, release the retainer and disconnect the wring plug from the ABS control unit **(see illustration)**. Cover the disconnected plug and socket to prevent contamination.
4 Undo the six brake pipes to the hydraulic control unit. Cap the end of the pipes and the hydraulic unit to prevent any dirt contamination. Unclip the brake lines from the retaining clips.
5 Undo the securing bolts from the brake hydraulic unit, and withdraw from the bulkhead. Remove it from the engine compartment, taking care not to damage any other components.

Refitting
6 Refitting is reversal of removal. Ensure

that the multiplug is securely connected, and that the brake pipe unions are tightened to the specified torque. On completion, bleed the hydraulic system as described in Section 14.

18 ABS wheel sensor – testing, removal and refitting

Testing
1 Checking of the sensors is done either by substitution for a known good unit, or interrogating the ABS ECU for stored fault codes, using dedicated test equipment found at Ford dealers or suitably-equipped specialists.

Removal

Front wheel sensor
2 Apply the handbrake and loosen the relevant front wheel nuts. Jack up the front of the vehicle and support it on axle stands. Remove the wheel.
3 Disconnect the sensor wiring plug.
4 Unscrew the sensor mounting bolt from the hub carrier and withdraw the sensor (see illustration). Withdraw the O-ring seal.

Rear wheel sensor
5 Chock the front wheels, and engage 1st gear (or P). Jack up the rear of the vehicle and support it on axle stands. Remove the relevant wheel.
6 Disconnect the sensor wiring plug.
7 Unscrew the sensor mounting bolt, and withdraw the sensor (see illustration). Withdraw the O-ring seal.

Refitting
8 Refitting is a reversal of the removal procedure. Fit a new O-ring seal to the hub carrier – not the sensor.

19 Electronic stability control components – removal and refitting

Note: *This system uses the same components as the ABS and Traction control system. The only additional components are the 'yaw rate' sensor and 'accelerometer sensor', which are mounted on the same bracket on the floor crossmember, and the steering wheel rotation sensor.*

Yaw rate and accelerometer sensor

Removal
1 Remove the driver's side front seat as describe in Chapter 11.
2 Open the relevant door, then pull the trim upwards from along the sill.
3 Remove the driver's side B-pillar trim panel as described in Chapter 11.

18.4 Front ABS sensor mounting bolt (arrowed)

4 Pull the carpet back to gain access to the sensors.
5 Disconnect the sensor wiring plug.
6 Undo the two retaining bolts and remove the sensor and bracket.

Refitting
7 Refitting is a reversal of the removal procedure. Ensure the sensor and bracket is correctly positioned.

Steering wheel rotation sensor
8 The steering wheel rotation sensor is integral with the driver's airbag contact unit, beneath the steering wheel. Removal of the unit is described in Chapter 12.

20 Traction control system – general information

1 The Traction control system is an expanded version of the ABS system. It is integrated with the ABS, and uses the same wheel sensors. It also uses the hydraulic control unit, which incorporates additional internal solenoid valves.
2 To remove the hydraulic unit or wheel sensors, carry out the procedures as described in Sections 17 and 18.

21 Brake switches – removal, refitting and adjustment

Removal

Brake pedal position switch
1 Disconnect the battery negative (earth) lead (see Chapter 5A).
2 Remove the driver's side lower facia panel as described in Chapter 11.
3 Disconnect the wiring connector from the brake pedal position switch. This is the upper of the two switches, and is coloured blue and white (see illustration 12.4).
4 Rotate the switch anti-clockwise by a quarter-turn, and withdraw it from the pedal bracket. Do not depress the brake pedal during the removal or refitting procedure – the pedal must be 'at rest'.

18.7 Rear ABS sensor retaining bolt (arrowed) – disc brake model

Brake light switch
5 Proceed as described in Paragraphs 1 and 2 in this Section.
6 Disconnect the wiring connector from the brake light switch. This is the lower of the two switches, and is coloured black (see illustration 12.4).
7 Rotate the switch *clockwise* by a quarter-turn, and withdraw it from the pedal bracket (see illustration). Do not depress the brake pedal during the removal or refitting procedure – the pedal must be 'at rest'.

Refitting and adjustment
8 Refitting is a reversal of the removal procedure. **Note:** *If both switches have been removed, the brake pedal position switch must be installed before the light switch.*
9 Both switches are automatically adjusted/calibrated by the vehicle system.

22 Handbrake lever – removal and refitting

Removal
1 Chock the front wheels, and engage 1st gear (or P).
2 Remove the centre console as described in Chapter 11.
3 Disconnect the electrical connector from the handbrake warning switch (see illustration).
4 Slacken the locknut, then undo the handbrake adjusting nut (see illustration).

21.7 Rotate the brake light switch *clockwise* to remove it

9•16 Braking system

22.3 Disconnect the handbrake warning light switch (arrowed)

22.4 Handbrake adjusting nut (arrowed)

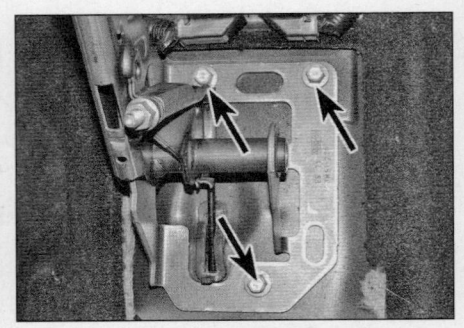

22.5 Handbrake lever bracket bolts (arrowed)

22.11 Insert a 0.7 mm feeler gauge between the caliper lever and the abutment (stop)

22.15 Insert a 2.0 mm feeler gauge between the lever end stop and the side of the shoe

5 Unscrew the mounting bolts securing the handbrake lever to the floor (see illustration).
6 Withdraw the handbrake from inside the vehicle.

Refitting

7 Refitting is a reversal of removal, ensuring the cable retaining tab is positioned away from the cable.
8 When refitting the lever, it will be necessary to adjust the mechanism, as follows. **Note:** *The handbrake should only be adjusted when the brakes are cool.*
9 Tighten the cable adjustment nut finger-tight, then raise the handbrake lever 12 notches.
10 Fully release the handbrake, then slacken the adjustment nut to the end of the threads.

Disc brake models

11 Insert a 0.7 mm feeler gauge between the handbrake lever and the caliper abutment on both sides (see illustration).
12 With the help of an assistant, tighten the adjustment nut until movement is observed on one of the caliper handbrake levers.
13 Remove the feeler gauges from both sides, then check the wheels rotate freely with no excess friction or drag caused by the brake. Tighten the adjustment locknut.

Drum brake models

14 Remove the brake drums as described in Section 5.
15 Ensure the handbrake lever is fully released, then insert a 2.0 mm feeler gauge between the handbrake lever end stop and the rear brake shoe on each side (see illustration).
16 With the help of an assistant, tighten the cable adjustment nut until movement is observed on one of the handbrake levers.
17 Remove the feeler gauges, and refit the drum brakes as described in Section 5.
18 Check the wheels rotate freely with no excess friction or drag caused by the brake. Tighten the cable locknut.

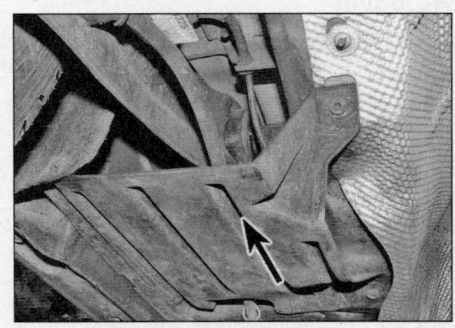

23.4 Remove the air deflector panel each side (arrowed)

23 Handbrake cables – removal and refitting

Removal

1 Starting at the rear, prise up and remove the gaiter/trim around the handbrake lever.
2 Slacken the handbrake adjustment nut to the end of the threads.
3 Chock the front wheels and engage 1st gear (or P). Loosen the wheel nuts on the relevant rear wheel, then jack up the rear of the vehicle and support it on axle stands. Fully release the handbrake lever.
4 Release the fasteners and remove the air deflector panel on each side (see illustration).
5 Remove the exhaust system as described in Chapter 4A.
6 Undo the fasteners and remove the exhaust front and centre heat shields.
7 Remove the relevant rear wheel and unclip the handbrake outer cable from its retaining clips (see illustration).

Disc brake models

8 Unbolt the cable guide from the arm on both sides (see illustration).
9 Use a pair of pliers to detach the handbrake

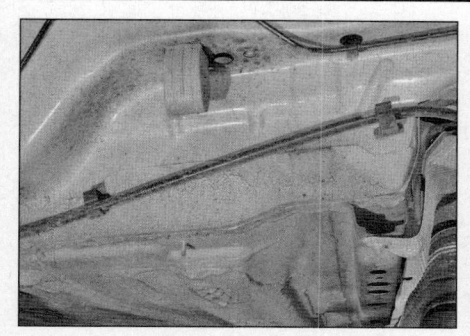

Braking system 9•17

23.7 Release the handbrake cable from the retaining clips

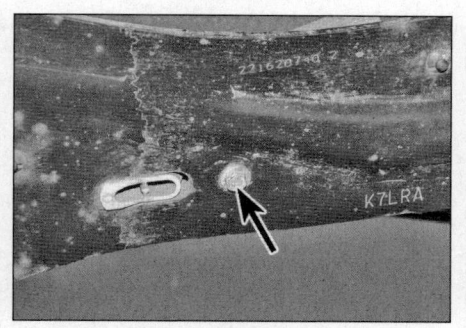

23.8 Undo the bolt (arrowed) securing the cable guide to the tie-bar

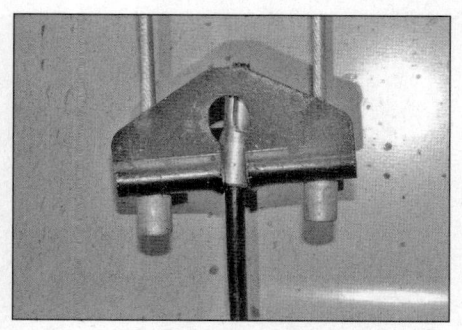

23.10a Disconnect the cables from the equaliser bracket

cable inner fitting from the lever on each caliper **(see illustration 9.4)**.

10 Detach each outer cable from the bracket on the vehicle underbody, then disengage them from the equaliser bracket **(see illustrations)**. Note that the left-hand cable has a black sleeve, and the right-hand cable has a white sleeve.

Drum brake models

11 Unbolt the outer cable guide from the tie-bar on both sides **(see illustration)**.
12 Unclip the handbrake cable from the arm both sides. Pull the cable through the tie-bar on both sides.
13 Unclip the cable from the support hangers. Note that there are marks on the cable outer sleeve to indicate the clip positions.
14 Rotate each cable through 90° and detach them from the equaliser, then depress the clips and pull the outer cables from the bracket **(see illustrations 23.10a and 23.10b)**. Withdraw

23.10b Note that the cables cross over when fitted correctly

the cables from beneath the vehicle. Note that the left-hand cable has a black sleeve, whilst the right-hand cable has a white sleeve.

Refitting

15 Refitting is a reversal of the removal procedure, noting the following points:

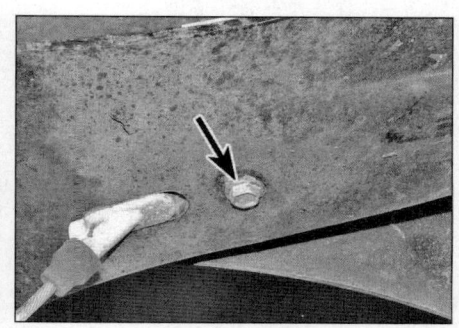

23.11 Undo the bolt (arrowed) securing the handbrake cable to the tie-bar

a) *Adjust the cable as described in Section 22.*
b) *Make sure that the cable end fittings are correctly located*
c) *Check the operation of the handbrake. Make sure that both wheels are locked, then free to turn, as the handbrake is operated.*

Chapter 10
Suspension and steering

Contents

	Section number
Front anti-roll bar – removal and refitting	6
Front hub carrier and bearing – removal and refitting	2
Front subframe – removal and refitting	21
Front suspension control arm and balljoint – removal, overhaul and refitting	5
Front suspension strut – dismantling, inspection and reassembly	4
Front suspension strut – removal and refitting	3
General information	1
Power steering fluid level check	See *Weekly checks*
Power steering pump – removal and refitting	18
Rear anti-roll bar – removal and refitting	12
Rear coil spring – removal and refitting	10
Rear hub bearings – renewal	7
Rear shock absorber – removal and refitting	9
Rear hub carrier/lateral link – removal and refitting	8
Rear suspension link arms – removal and refitting	11
Steering and suspension check	See Chapter 1
Steering column – removal and refitting	14
Steering rack – removal and refitting	15
Steering rack gaiters – renewal	16
Steering system – bleeding	17
Steering wheel – removal and refitting	13
Track rod end – removal and refitting	19
Tyre condition and pressure checks	See *Weekly checks*
Wheel alignment and steering angles – general information	20

Degrees of difficulty

Easy, suitable for novice with little experience	Fairly easy, suitable for beginner with some experience	Fairly difficult, suitable for competent DIY mechanic	Difficult, suitable for experienced DIY mechanic	Very difficult, suitable for expert DIY or professional

Specifications

Front suspension
Type .... Independent, with MacPherson struts incorporating coil springs and telescopic shock absorbers. Anti-roll bar fitted to all models

Rear suspension
Type .... Fully-independent, multi-link with separate coil springs and hydraulic telescopic shock absorbers. Anti-roll bar fitted to all models

Steering
Type .... Power-assisted rack-and-pinion. Electro-hydraulic on some models
Steering fluid type .... See end of *Weekly checks* on page 0•17

Wheel alignment and steering angles
Front wheel:
  Hatchback and Saloon models:
    Camber angle:
      Standard chassis .... 0.36° to -1°58'
      Sports chassis .... 0.25° to -2°0.7'
    Castor angle:
      Standard chassis .... 4°13' to 2°09'
      Sports chassis .... 4°14' to 2°13'
    Toe setting .... 0°06' ± 0°15' toe-in
  Estate models:
    Camber angle .... 0°35' to -1°58'
    Caster angle .... 4°16' to 2°14'
    Toe setting .... 0°06' ± 0°15' toe-in
Rear wheel:
  Camber angle:
    Standard chassis .... 0° to -2°35'
    Sports chassis .... -0°08' to -2°38'
  Toe setting .... 0°38' to 0°08' toe-in

Tyres
Tyre pressures .... See sticker on the driver's side door pillar

Torque wrench settings

	Nm	lbf ft
Front suspension		
ABS sensor	10	7
Anti-roll bar clamp bolts*	50	37
Anti-roll bar connecting link nuts*	50	37
Balljoint-to-control arm bolts	70	52
Balljoint nut to hub carrier*	70	52
Brake caliper mounting bracket bolts*	120	89
Control arm to subframe:*		
Rear bolt	115	85
Front bolt	175	129
Driveshaft bolt	See Chapter 8	
Lower balljoint to control arm	70	52
Lower torque rod bolts:		
M10	60	44
M12	80	59
Subframe front and rear mounting bolts:*		
Front	120	89
Rear	280	207
Subframe rear mounting brackets	70	52
Suspension strut piston nut*	50	37
Suspension strut to hub carrier*	90	66
Suspension strut upper mounting/brace to body	32	24
Suspension upper mount brace-to-bulkhead nuts	20	15
Rear suspension		
Anti-roll bar link to lower control arms (link with balljoints)	50	37
Anti-roll bar link to lower arm (solid link)	25	18
Anti-roll bar link to anti-roll bar (link with balljoints)	70	52
Anti-roll bar-to-subframe bolts	50	37
Lateral link/hub carrier to body	115	85
Lower control arm to hub carrier	115	85
Lower control arm to subframe	90	66
Rear hub bearing assembly	55	41
Shock absorber lower mounting bolt	115	85
Shock absorber upper mounting nut*:		
Normal suspension	25	18
Self-levelling suspension (Nivomat)	60	44
Shock absorber upper mounting bolts		
Hatchback and Saloon models	25	18
Estate models	115	85
Tie-rod bolts	115	85
Upper control arm to hub carrier/lateral link and subframe	115	85
Steering		
Belt-driven steering pump bolts	23	17
EHPS pump bolts	23	17
Steering column mounting bolts*	25	18
Steering rack mounting bolts	90	66
Steering wheel bolt	48	35
Steering shaft universal joint pinch-bolt*	28	21
Track rod end balljoint nuts*	50	37
Track rod locknuts	62	46
Roadwheels		
Roadwheel nuts:		
Gold nuts for steel wheels	90	60
Silver nuts for steel wheels	130	96
One-piece alloy nuts for alloy wheels and 5-spoke steel wheels	130	96
Two-piece alloy nuts with conical washer	110	81

* Do not re-use

1 General information

The independent front suspension is of the MacPherson strut type, incorporating coil springs and integral telescopic shock absorbers. The struts are located by transverse control arms, which are attached to the front subframe via rubber bushes at their inner ends, and incorporate a balljoint at their outer ends. The hub carriers, which carry the hub bearings, brake calipers and the hub/disc assemblies, are bolted to the MacPherson struts, and connected to the control arms through the balljoints. A front anti-roll bar is fitted to all models, and is attached to the subframe and to the MacPherson struts via link arms (see illustration).

The rear suspension is of the fully independent, multilink type, consisting of an upper and lower control arm mounted via rubber bushes, to the lateral link/hub carrier and rear subframe. The lateral link is attached to the vehicle body at the front end and incorporate the hub carrier at the rear. The

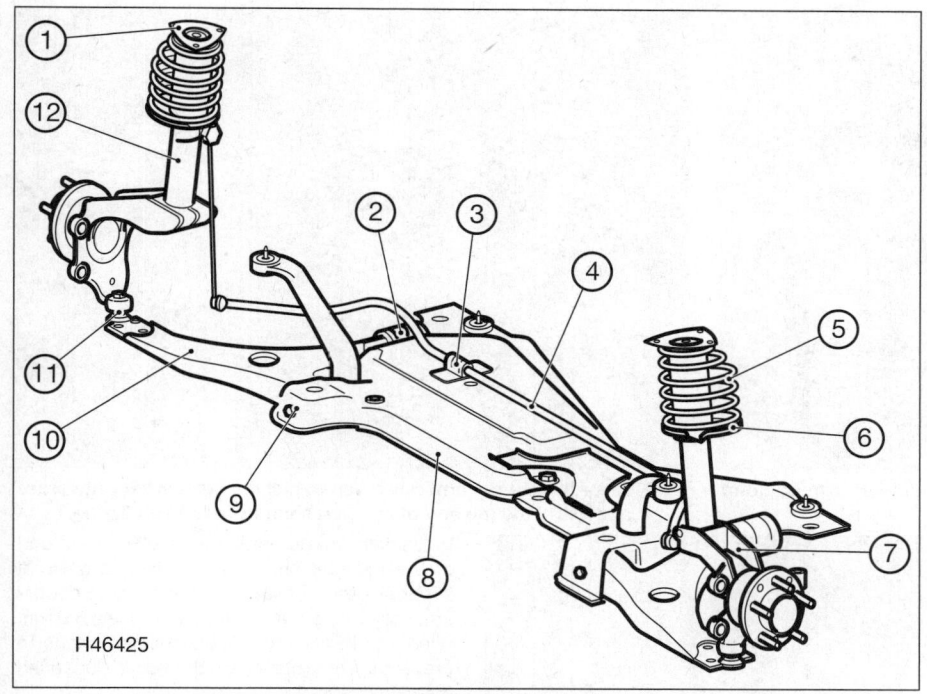

Suspension and steering 10•3

assembly is located by a tie rod each side. Coil springs are fitted between the lower control arm and the subframe. Separate hydraulic telescopic shock absorbers are fitted between the hub carrier between the lower control arm and the vehicle body **(see illustration)**.

Power-assisted rack and pinion steering is fitted as standard equipment. On some models, power assistance is derived from a hydraulic pump, driven by an electric motor, controlled by the Electro-Hydraulic Power Steering module (EHPS). On other models, the hydraulic pump is driven the auxiliary drivebelt.

2 Front hub carrier and bearing – removal and refitting

Note: *The hub bearing is a sealed, pre-adjusted and pre-lubricated, double-row ball type, and is intended to last the car's entire service life without maintenance or attention. The hub flange and bearing are serviced as a complete assembly, and these components cannot be dismantled or renewed individually.*

Removal

1 Loosen the appropriate front wheel nuts, then jack up the front of the car and support it on axle stands (see *Jacking and vehicle support*). Remove the appropriate front roadwheel.

2 Undo the bolt securing the headlight levelling sensor bracket to the right-hand front lower arm (where applicable).

3 Slacken and remove the bolt securing the driveshaft to the hub **(see illustration)**. Have an assistant depress the brake pedal to prevent the hub from rotating. Discard the bolt, a new one must be used.

4 Remove the front brake disc as described in Chapter 9.

5 Disconnect the wiring plug, undo the bolt and remove the ABS wheel sensor from the hub carrier – refer to Chapter 9 if necessary.

6 Undo the retaining nut, then disconnect the steering track rod end balljoint from the hub carrier. If necessary, use a balljoint separator tool **(see illustrations 19.3a and 19.3b)**.

7 Undo the bolt and remove the lower arm balljoint heat shield.

1.1 Front suspension

1. Upper bearing, mounting and spring seat
2. Rear bush
3. Clamp
4. Anti-roll bar
5. Spring
6. Lower spring seat
7. Hub carrier
8. Front subframe
9. Front bush
10. Control arm
11. Balljoint
12. MacPherson strut

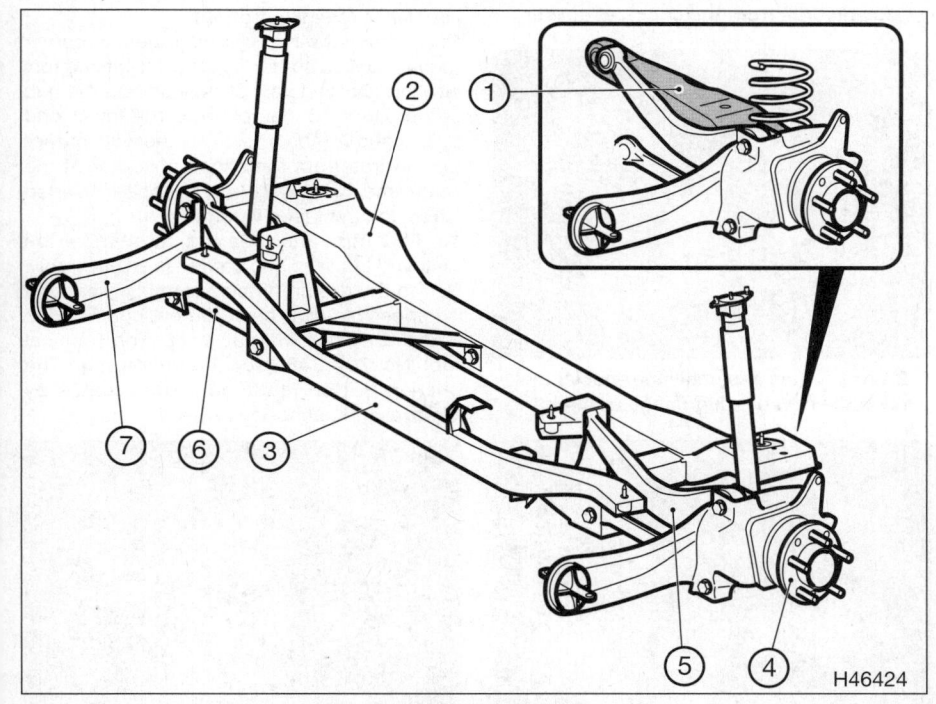

1.2 Rear suspension

1. Lower control arm
2. Subframe
3. Anti-roll bar
4. Wheel speed sensor
5. Upper control arm
6. Tie rod
7. Lateral link/hub carrier

2.3 Slacken the driveshaft bolt (arrowed)

10•4 Suspension and steering

2.8 Use a balljoint separator tool to detach the lower arm balljoint from the hub carrier

2.10 Lever the control arm downwards, pull the hub carrier outwards, and withdraw the end of the driveshaft from the hub flange

2.11a With the bolt removed, spread the hub carrier slightly using a large screwdriver . . .

2.11b . . . then gently tap the hub carrier downwards from the shock absorber

2.12a Using the Ford special tool to support the hub carrier, press the hub flange and bearing out . . .

2.12b . . . then assembly the special tool around the new bearing/flange assembly . . .

2.12c . . . position the hub carrier over the new bearing, and the special tool in place on the hub carrier . . .

2.12d . . . then press the hub carrier . . .

2.12e . . . fully onto the bearing

8 Slacken the nut until it is level with the end of the balljoint shank, then using a balljoint separator tool, detach the suspension control arm balljoint from the hub carrier. Use a 6.0 mm Allen key in the end of the balljoint shank to prevent it from rotating as the nut is slackened (see illustration).

9 Use a stout bar to lever the control arm downwards and move the hub carrier over the end of the balljoint shank. Take care not to damage the balljoint dust cover during and after disconnection.

10 Swivel the hub carrier assembly outwards, and withdraw the driveshaft CV joint from the hub flange (see illustration).

11 Remove the bolt securing the hub carrier to the shock absorber. Insert a flat-bladed tool into the gap and very slightly spread the hub carrier where it clamps onto the lower end of the shock absorber. Tap the hub carrier downwards from the shock absorber at the same time. Note which way the bolt is inserted – from the front (see illustrations).

12 The hub and bearing must now be removed from the hub carrier as an assembly. Due to the design of the assembly, we found it impossible to press the new hub/bearing into the carrier without using Ford special tool No 204-348 (see illustrations). The bearing will be rendered unserviceable by removal and cannot be re-used.

Suspension and steering 10•5

3.5a Prise forward the clips (arrowed) . . .

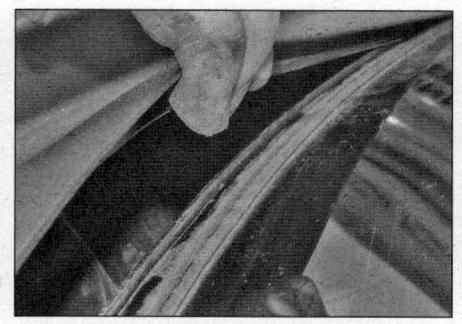

3.5b . . . and pull the scuttle cowl panel upwards from the base of the windscreen

3.6 Undo the 2 bolts (arrowed) and pull the panel forwards to release it from the clips (arrowed)

Refitting

13 Prior to refitting, remove all traces of metal adhesive, rust, oil and dirt from the splines and threads of the driveshaft outer CV joint and the bearing housing mating surface on the hub carrier.

14 The remainder of refitting is a reversal of removal, but observe the following points:
 a) Ensure that the hub and brake disc mating faces are spotlessly clean, and refit the disc with the orientation marks aligned.
 b) A new driveshaft retaining bolt should be used.
 c) Ensure that the ABS sensor, and the sensor location in the hub carrier, are perfectly clean before refitting.
 d) Tighten all nuts and bolts to the specified torque (see Chapter 9 for brake component torque settings).

3 Front suspension strut – removal and refitting

Removal

1 Loosen the appropriate front wheel nuts, then jack up the front of the car and support it on axle stands (see *Jacking and vehicle support*). Remove the appropriate front roadwheel.
2 Remove the plastic cover from the top of the engine (where fitted).
3 Undo the 2 bolts securing the brake fluid remote reservoir (where fitted) to the cowl panel.
4 Remove the wiper arms as described in Chapter 12.
5 Release the 5 clips and remove the scuttle cowl panel **(see illustrations)**.
6 Undo the 2 bolts at each end and pull the bulkhead extension panel forwards to release it from the clips release the clips and remove the bulkhead extension panel **(see illustration)**.
7 Undo the nut securing the anti-roll bar link balljoint to the suspension strut. Use an Allen key to counterhold the balljoint shank **(see illustration)**. A new nut will be required.
8 Unclip the brake hose from the bracket on the suspension strut.

3.7 Use an Allen key to counterhold the anti-roll bar link balljoint nut

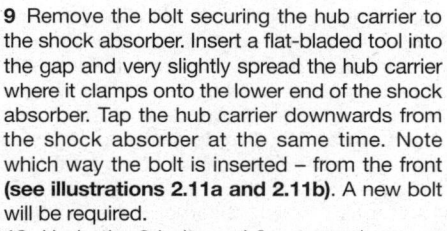

9 Remove the bolt securing the hub carrier to the shock absorber. Insert a flat-bladed tool into the gap and very slightly spread the hub carrier where it clamps onto the lower end of the shock absorber. Tap the hub carrier downwards from the shock absorber at the same time. Note which way the bolt is inserted – from the front **(see illustrations 2.11a and 2.11b)**. A new bolt will be required.
10 Undo the 3 bolts and 2 nuts, and remove the brace between the suspension top mountings and the bulkhead **(see illustration)**. Have an assistant support the strut assembly.
11 Manoeuvre the strut out from underneath the wheel arch.

Refitting

12 Refitting is a reversal of removal, but tighten all nuts and bolts to the specified torque, using new nuts/bolts where necessary.

4.2 Hold the strut piston rod with an Allen key, and slacken the retaining nut

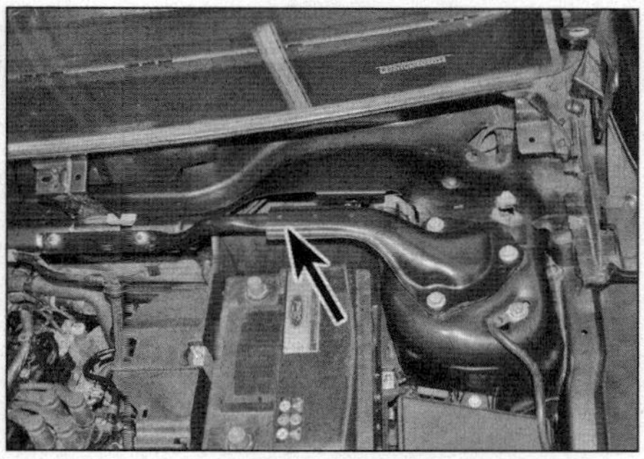

3.10 Undo the 3 bolts and 2 nuts, then remove the brace (arrowed)

4 Front suspension strut – dismantling, inspection and reassembly

> **Warning:** Before attempting to dismantle the suspension strut, a suitable tool to hold the coil spring in compression must be obtained. Adjustable coil spring compressors which can be positively secured to the spring coils are readily available, and are recommended for this operation. Any attempt to dismantle the strut without such a tool is likely to result in damage or personal injury.

Dismantling

1 Remove the strut from the car as described in Section 3.
2 Slacken the strut mounting nut 1/2 a turn, while holding the protruding portion of the piston rod with an Allen key **(see illustration)**. Do not remove the nut at this stage.
3 Fit the spring compressors to the coil springs, and tighten the compressors until the load is taken off the spring seats **(see illustration)**.
4 Remove the piston nut, then make alignment marks where the ends of the spring contact the upper and lower seats **(see illustration)**. Discard the nut – a new one must be fitted.
5 Remove the upper mounting/spring seat, bump stop and gaiter followed by the spring **(see illustration)**. Do not attempt to separate the spring seat from the mounting or the bearing balls will fall out.

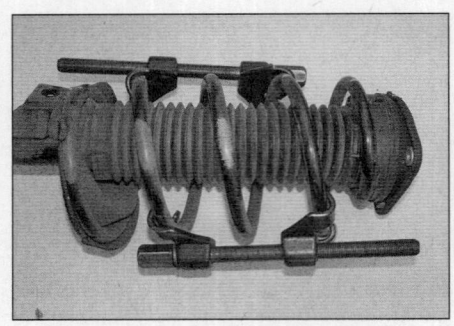

10•6 Suspension and steering

4.3 Fit the compressors to the springs

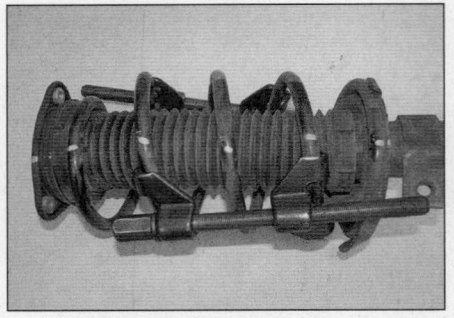

4.4 Make alignment marks between the spring and seats

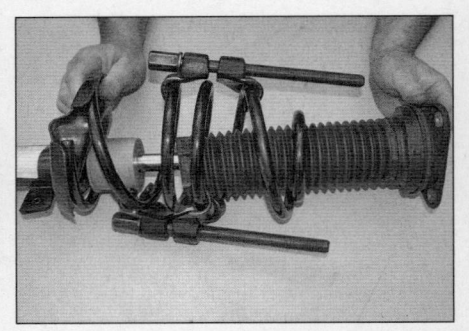

4.5 With the springs fully compressed, remove the mounting/seat/bump stop and gaiter, followed by the spring

5 Front suspension control arm and balljoint – removal, overhaul and refitting

4.11a Ensure the spring ends are correctly located in their seats

4.11b Tighten the new piston rod nut to the specified torque

Inspection

6 With the strut assembly now completely dismantled, examine all the components for wear, damage or deformation. Renew any of the components as necessary.

7 Examine the shock absorber for signs of fluid leakage, and check the strut piston for signs of pitting along its entire length. Test the operation of the shock absorber, while holding it in an upright position, by moving the piston through a full stroke and then through short strokes of 50 to 100 mm. In both cases, the resistance felt should be smooth and continuous. If the resistance is jerky, or uneven, or if there is any visible sign of wear or damage, renewal is necessary.

8 If any doubt exists about the condition of the coil spring, gradually release the spring compressor, and check the spring for distortion and signs of cracking. Since no minimum free length is specified by Ford, the only way to check the tension of the spring is to compare it to a new component. Renew the spring if it is damaged or distorted, or if there is any doubt as to its condition.

9 Inspect all other components for signs of damage or deterioration, and renew any that are suspect.

10 If a new shock absorber is being fitted, hold it vertically and pump the piston a few times to prime it.

Reassembly

11 Reassembly is a reversal of dismantling, but ensure that the spring is fully compressed before fitting. Make sure that the spring ends are correctly located in the upper and lower seats, aligning the marks made on removal, then tighten the new shock absorber piston retaining nut and strut mounting bolts to specified torque **(see illustrations)**.

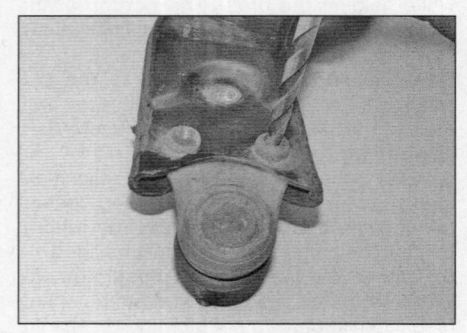

Balljoint

Removal

1 Loosen the appropriate front wheel nuts. Chock the rear wheels and apply the handbrake, then jack up the front of the vehicle and support it on axle stands (see *Jacking and vehicle support*). Remove the appropriate front roadwheel, then release the fasteners and remove the engine undershield (where fitted).

2 Undo the bolt securing the headlight levelling sensor bracket to the control arm (where fitted).

3 Slacken the nut until it is level with the end of the balljoint shank, then using a balljoint separator tool, detach the suspension control arm balljoint from the hub carrier. Use an Allen key in the end of the balljoint shank to prevent it from rotating as the nut is slackened **(see illustration 2.8)**. Discard the nut – a new one must be fitted.

4 Use a stout bar to lever the control arm downwards and over the end of the balljoint shank. Take care not to damage the balljoint dust cover during and after disconnection.

5 If the original balljoint is being removed, use a drill to remove the 3 balljoint-to-control arm retaining rivets **(see illustrations)**. Pull the balljoint from the control arm.

6 If the balljoint being removed is not the original, undo the 3 bolts and pull the balljoint from the control arm.

Refitting

7 New balljoints may be supplied with suitable retaining bolts. If not, obtain 3 bolts, M10 x 30 mm, and 3 suitable self-locking nuts. Position the new balljoint in the end of the control arm, insert the bolts from underneath, and tighten the nuts to the specified torque. Note that 2 different balljoints may be available. The balljoints are identical apart from the diameter of the taper of the balljoint shank. The shank with the larger diameter taper is identified by a blue band on the gaiter, and the smaller diameter taper by a yellow

5.5a Drill out the 3 rivets . . .

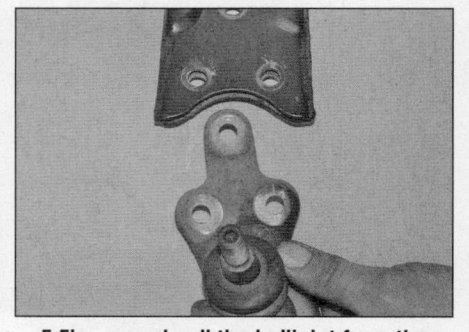

5.5b . . . and pull the balljoint from the control arm

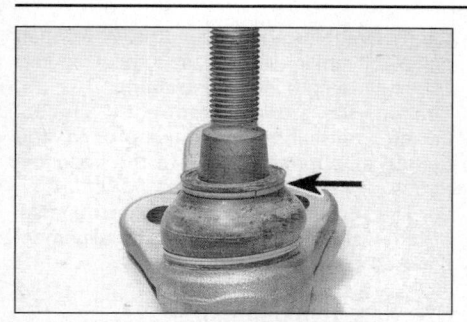

Suspension and steering 10•7

5.7a The colour of the rubber band (arrowed) determines the diameter of the balljoint shank

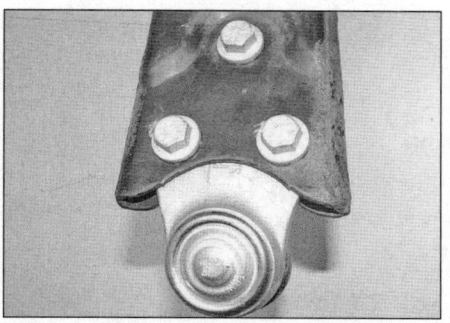

5.7b Insert the bolts from the underside of the control arm . . .

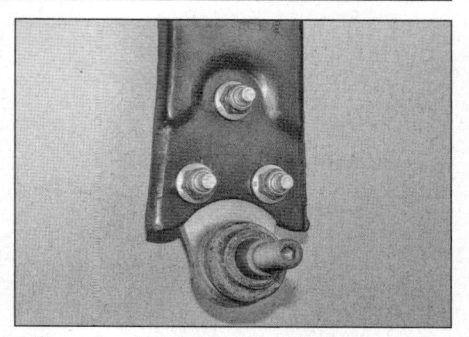

5.7c . . . and fit the self-locking nuts on the upper side

band **(see illustrations)**. Select the balljoint that matches the one to be renewed.

8 The remainder of refitting is a reversal of removal. Tighten all fasteners to their specified torque, where given.

Control arm

Removal

9 Proceed as described in Paragraphs 1 to 4.
10 Undo the two bolts securing the control arm rear mounting and the single bolt securing the front mounting and manoeuvre the control arm from under the vehicle **(see illustrations)**. Discard the bolts, new one must be fitted.

Overhaul

11 Thoroughly clean the control arm and the area around the control arm mountings. Inspect the arm for any signs of cracks, damage or distortion, and carefully check the inner pivot bushes for signs of swelling, cracks or deterioration of the rubber.
12 If either bush requires renewal, the work should be entrusted to a Ford dealer or specialist. A hydraulic press and suitable spacers are required to remove and refit the bushes and a setting gauge is needed for accurate positioning of the bushes in the arm.

Refitting

13 Locate the arm in its mountings, and starting at the rear, fit the new mounting bolts finger-tight only. Once all the bolts are in place, tighten the bolts to their specified torque. Do not allow the control arm to move during the tightening procedure.
14 Engage the balljoint shank in the control arm, then tighten the new nut to the specified torque.
15 The remainder of refitting is a reversal of removal. Have the front wheel alignment checked at the earliest opportunity.

6 Front anti-roll bar – removal and refitting

Removal

1 Loosen the appropriate front wheel nuts. Chock the rear wheels and apply the handbrake, then jack up the front of the vehicle and support it on axle stands (see *Jacking*

5.10a Control arm rear mounting bolts (arrowed) . . .

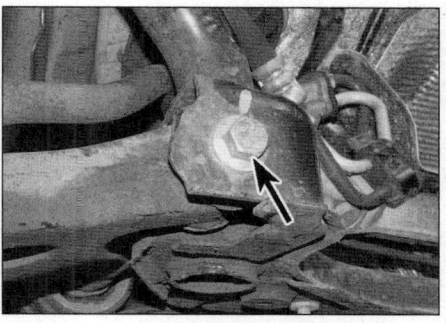

and vehicle support). Remove the appropriate front roadwheel, then release the fasteners and remove the engine undershield (where fitted) **(see illustration)**
2 Slacken the nut until it is level with the end of the balljoint shank, then using a balljoint separator tool, detach the suspension control arm balljoint from the hub carrier. Use an Allen key in the end of the balljoint shank to prevent it from rotating as the nut is slackened **(see illustration 2.8)**.
3 Use a stout bar to lever the control arm downwards and over the end of the balljoint shank. Take care not to damage the balljoint dust cover during and after disconnection.
4 Ensure the wheels are in the straight-ahead position, then working under the facia, undo and remove the steering column lower universal joint pinch-bolt **(see illustration 14.8)**. Discard the bolt – a new one must be fitted.
5 Undo the nut each side securing the lower

6.1 Undo the fasteners (arrowed) and remove the engine undershield

5.10b . . . and front mounting bolt (arrowed)

end of the anti-roll bar links to the bar. Use a Torx bit to counterhold the nut.
6 Undo the nut and detach the track rod end balljoint from the hub carrier each side, using a balljoint separator tool as described in Section 19.
7 Undo the bolt at the lower rear of the engine securing the lower torque rod to the bracket on the transmission/engine.
8 Attach splints each side of the exhaust flexible section (two wooden strips secured by cable tie will suffice) to prevent excessive bending, then undo the bolts/nuts securing the centre exhaust section to the front section.
9 Unhook the exhaust mounting rubbers at the front.
10 Position a sturdy trolley jack beneath, and in contact with, the rear of the subframe.
11 Undo the bolt each side securing the front of the subframe to the body approximately 6 turns **(see illustration)**. Note that new

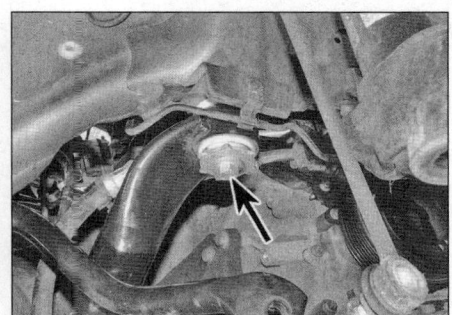

6.11 Slacken the subframe front mounting bolt each side (arrowed) about 6 turns

10•8 Suspension and steering

6.12 Undo the subframe rear mounting bolts (arrowed)

6.14 Anti-roll bar clamp bolts (arrowed)

6.15 The anti-roll bar bushes are split to facilitate renewal, and are shaped to fit the bar profile

6.18 Align the front subframe by inserting aligning tools (arrowed) through the holes in the subframe into the corresponding holes in the vehicle body

subframe front mounting bolts will be required for refitting.

12 Undo the bolts each side securing the rear mounting brackets to the subframe and vehicle body, and recover the washers **(see illustration)**. Note that new subframe mounting bolts will be required for refitting.

13 Carefully lower the jack and allow the subframe to drop slightly at the rear, so that the anti-roll bar clamp bolts are accessible. Take care not to damage the power steering hoses.

14 Undo the bolts securing the anti-roll bar clamps on each side of the subframe, and manipulate the anti-roll bar out from under the car **(see illustration)**. Discard the bolts, new ones must be fitted.

15 Examine the anti-roll bar for signs of damage or distortion, and the connecting links and mounting bushes for signs of deterioration of the rubber. The bushes are split along their length and must be fitted in their original positions **(see illustration)**.

Refitting

16 Manipulate the anti-roll bar into position on the subframe. Fit the new clamp bolts and tighten to the specified torque.

17 Raise the subframe at the rear, fit the rear mounting brackets to the body, and tighten the bolts (new where applicable) hand-tight only at this stage.

18 The alignment of the subframe must be checked by inserting round tools can be inserted through the holes in the sidemembers. Ford tools (part No 205-316) may be available.

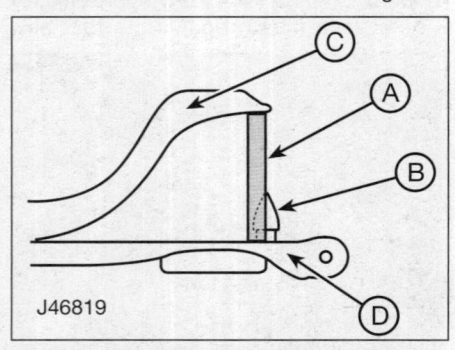

8.7 Remove the bump stop (B), and insert the spacer (A) between the lower control arm (D) and the spring upper seat (C)

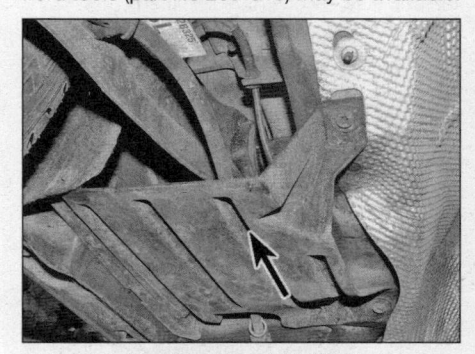

8.8 Remove the air baffle plate (arrowed)

Alternatively, using two lengths of wooden dowel, 20 mm in diameter, and approximately 150 mm in length **(see illustration)**.

19 With the subframe correctly aligned, fit new front subframe mounting bolts, and tighten all subframe bolts to the specified torque.

20 The remainder of refitting is a reversal of removal. Have the front wheel alignment checked at the earliest opportunity.

7 Rear hub bearings – renewal

1 The rear hub bearings cannot be renewed separately, and are supplied with the rear hub as a complete assembly.
2 Remove the brake disc or drum (as applicable) as described in Chapter 9.
3 Undo the bolt and remove the ABS wheel speed sensor from the hub carrier.
4 Undo the four Torx bolts and withdrawn the bearing assembly from the hub carrier.
5 Fit the new assembly to the hub carrier then insert and tighten the bolts to the specified torque.
6 Refit the ABS wheel speed sensor and brake disc or drum as described in Chapter 9.

8 Rear hub carrier/lateral link – removal and refitting

Removal

1 Remove the rear hub as described in the previous Section. On models with disc brakes, unbolt and remove the disc shield.
2 Undo the bolt securing the handbrake cable retaining clip to the lateral link, then unhook the cable from the connecting sleeve. Pull the cable through the lateral link/hub carrier.
3 Unclip the brake hose from the hub carrier.
4 Unclip the handbrake cable from the hub carrier.
5 Release the ABS wheel speed sensor wiring harness from the clips on the lateral link.
6 Remove the relevant rear coil spring as described in Section 10.
7 Fabricate a spacer, 20 mm in diameter, and 113 mm (Hatchback and Saloon) or 184 mm (Estate) long. Unscrew the suspension bump stop, insert the spacer between the lower control arm and the coil spring upper seat, then raise the lower control arm with a trolley jack until the spacer is lightly trapped **(see illustration)**. Ensure the spacer is vertical.
8 Undo the fasteners and remove the air baffle plate from the relevant side **(see illustration)**.
9 Undo the retaining bolt and withdraw the ABS wheel sensor from hub carrier/lateral link. Do not disconnect the wheel sensor wiring plug.
10 Undo the bolts securing the upper control

Suspension and steering 10•9

arm and tie rod to the lateral link/hub carrier (see illustrations 11.4 and 11.10b).
11 Undo the bolt and detach the lower control arm from the lateral link/hub carrier (see illustration 11.14a).
12 Undo the 2 bolts securing the front mounting to the vehicle body, and withdrawn the lateral link from under the vehicle (see illustration).
13 Renewal of the bush at the front of the lateral link requires the use of Ford special tools and a hydraulic press. Therefore it is recommended that this task should be entrusted to a Ford dealer or suitably-equipped specialist.

Refitting

14 Manoeuvre the lateral link into position and tighten the 2 front mounting bolts to the specified torque.
15 Refit the ABS wheel speed sensor wiring harness clips to the link.
16 Position the handbrake cable and refit the cable retaining clip.
17 Refit the upper control arm, lower control arm and tie rod, but don't tighten the bolts yet.
18 Ensure the fabricated spacer (paragraph 7) is still in place between the lower control arm and the spring seat (see illustration 8.7).
19 Tighten the upper control arm, lower control arm and tie rod bolts to their specified torque. Remove the spacer, and refit the bump stop.
20 The remainder of refitting is a reversal of removal. Have the rear wheel alignment checked at the earliest opportunity.

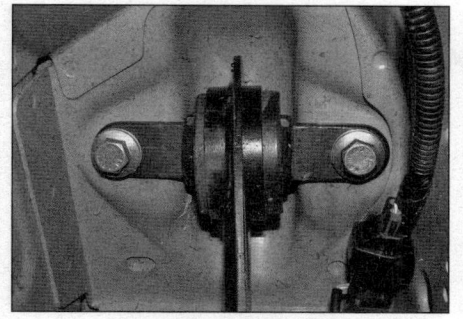

8.12 Lateral link/hub carrier front mounting bolts

9 Rear shock absorber – removal and refitting

Removal

1 Slacken the rear roadwheel nuts, then chock the front wheels then jack up the rear of the vehicle and support it on axle stands (see *Jacking and vehicle support*). Remove the rear wheels.
2 Place a trolley jack under the hub carrier and raise the suspension a little to take the load off the shock absorber.

Hatchback and Saloon models

3 Undo the 2 bolts securing the upper end of the shock absorber to the vehicle body (see illustration).
4 Undo the lower mounting bolt, and pull the shock absorber from the hub carrier (see illustration).
5 If required, undo the nut and pull the upper mounting from the shock absorber (see illustration).
6 Check the condition of the shock absorber and renew as necessary.

Estate models

7 If removing the left-hand shock absorber, unhook the rear silencer from the rubber mountings, undo the fasteners, and remove the exhaust heat shield (see illustration).
8 Undo the shock absorber upper mounting bolt (see illustration).
9 Undo and remove the shock absorber lower mounting bolt (see illustration). Manoeuvre the shock absorber from under the vehicle.

Refitting

10 Refitting is a reversal of removal, tightening all nuts and bolts to the specified torques.

10 Rear coil spring – removal and refitting

Removal

1 Slacken the road wheel nuts, then chock the front wheels and raise the rear of the vehicle. Support it securely on axle stands (see *Jacking and vehicle support*). Remove the roadwheels.
2 Undo the nut securing the anti-roll bar link to the lower control arm (see illustration 12.2).

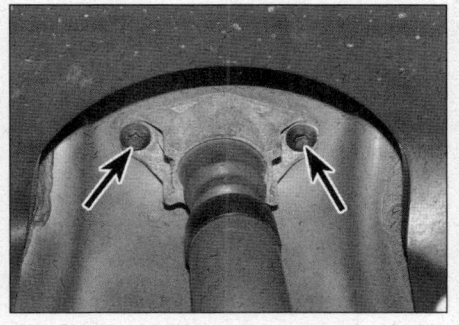

9.3 Shock absorber upper mounting bolts (arrowed)

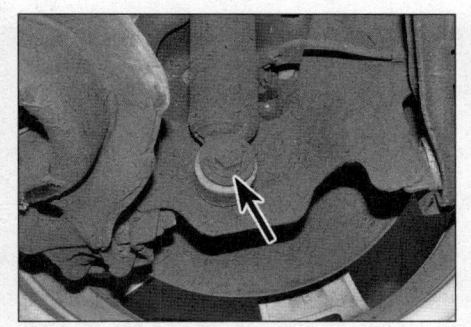

9.4 Shock absorber lower mounting bolt (arrowed)

9.5 Undo the shock absorber upper mounting nut (arrowed)

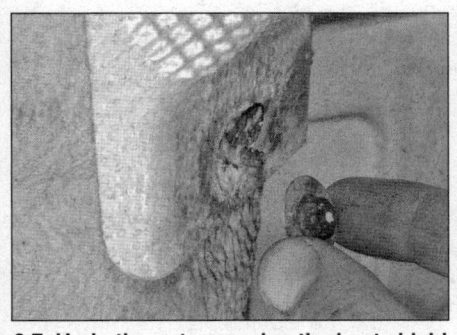

9.7 Undo the nuts securing the heat shield

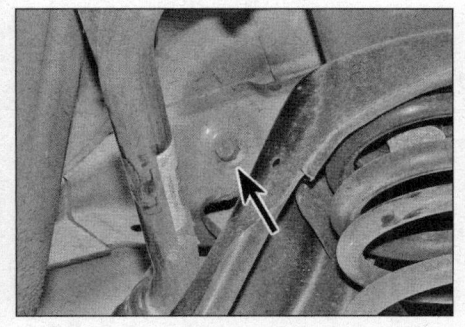

9.8 Rear shock absorber upper mounting bolt (arrowed)

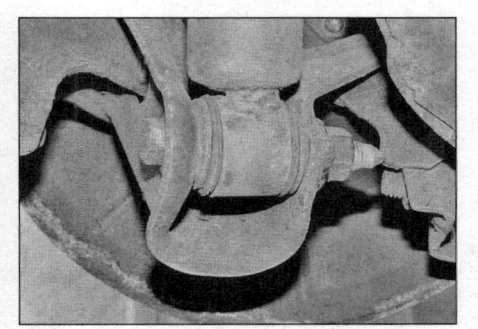

9.9 Rear shock absorber lower mounting bolt

10•10 Suspension and steering

10.5 Remove the rear springs using spring compressors

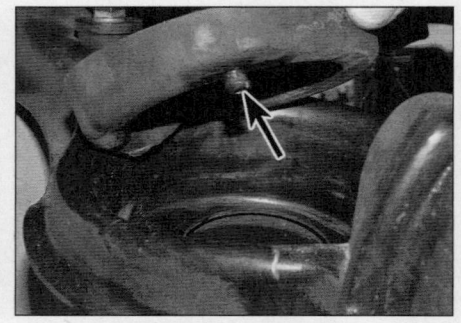

10.8a The lug (arrowed) on the underside of the seat must locate in the hole in the arm

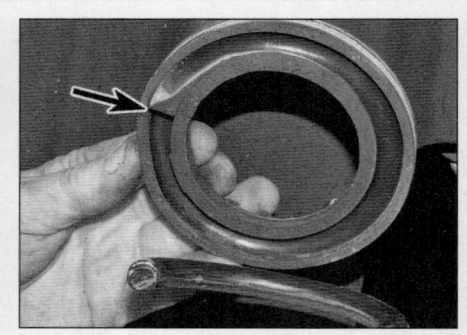

10.8b The end of the spring must fit against the stop in the rubber seat (arrowed)

3 Position a trolley jack under the hub carrier, and take the weight.
4 Remove the shock absorber lower mounting bolt.
5 Attach spring compressors to the spring and compress the spring. Ford specify tools No 204-215 and 204-167. Alternative spring compressors may be available **(see illustration)**.
6 Remove the trolley jack, and remove the spring.
7 Examine all the components for wear or damage, and renew as necessary.

Refitting

8 Refit the rubbers seats to the control arm and spring, ensuring the ends of the spring locate correctly **(see illustrations)**.
9 Refit the compressed spring onto the seat in the lower control arm. Rotate the spring until the spring engages correctly in the control arm grooves.
10 Raise the control arm by means of the jack, and engage the upper end of the spring in its recess in the body.
11 Refit the shock absorber lower mounting bolt, securing it in place before removing the jack. Tighten all nuts and bolts to the specified torque.
12 Release and remove the spring compressor.
13 Remainder of refitting is a reversal of removal.

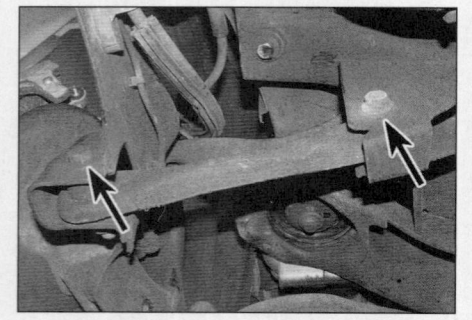

11 Rear suspension link arms – removal and refitting

Removal

1 Loosen the rear wheel bolts. Chock the front wheels, then jack up the rear of the vehicle and support it on axle stands (see *Jacking and vehicle support*). Remove the appropriate rear roadwheel(s).

Tie-rod – Hatchback and Saloon models

2 Remove the rear spring as described in Section 10.
3 Fabricate a spacer, 20 mm in diameter, and 113 mm long. Unscrew the suspension bump stop, insert the spacer between the lower control arm and the coil spring upper seat, then raise the lower control arm with a trolley jack until the spacer is lightly trapped (see illustration 8.7). Ensure the spacer is vertical.
4 Undo the outer and inner bolts, then remove the tie-rod **(see illustration)**. Note that the tie-rod is marked FRONT on one side.

Tie-rod – Estate models

5 Remove the rear spring as described in Section 10.
6 Fabricate a spacer, 20 mm in diameter, and 184 mm long. Insert the spacer between the lower control arm and the coil spring upper seat, then raise the lower control arm with a trolley jack until the spacer is lightly trapped (see illustration 8.7). Ensure the spacer is vertical.
7 Undo the outer and inner bolts, then remove the tie-rod (see illustration 11.4). Note that the tie-rod is marked FRONT on one side.

Upper control arm – Hatchback and saloon models

8 Remove the rear spring as described in Section 10.
9 Fabricate a spacer, 20 mm in diameter, and 113 mm long. Unscrew the suspension bump stop, insert the spacer between the lower control arm and the coil spring upper seat, then raise the lower control arm with a trolley jack until the spacer is lightly trapped (see illustration 8.7). Ensure the spacer is vertical.
10 Undo the outer and inner bolts, then remove the control arm **(see illustrations)**.

Upper control arm – Estate models

11 Fabricate a spacer, 20 mm in diameter, and 184 mm long. Insert the spacer between the lower control arm and the coil spring upper seat, then raise the lower control arm with a trolley jack until the spacer is lightly trapped (see illustration 8.7). Ensure the spacer is vertical.
12 Undo the outer and inner bolts, then remove the control arm **(see illustrations 11.10a and 11.10b)**.

Lower control arm

13 Remove the coil spring as described in Section 10.
14 Mark the position of the inner bolt eccentric washer in relation to the arm, then undo the inner and outer control arm bolts,

11.4 Tie-rod mounting bolts (arrowed)

11.10a Upper control arm inner bolt (arrowed) . . .

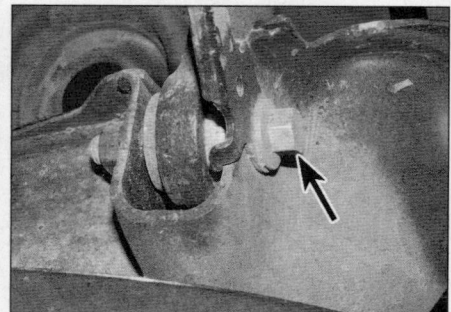

11.10b . . . and outer bolt (arrowed)

Suspension and steering 10•11

rotate the anti-roll bar approximately 30° and remove the control arm (see illustrations).

15 Examine the condition of the metal-elastic bushes in the control arm. If renewal is necessary, the bushes must be pressed from the arm and new ones pressed into place. This necessitates the use of an hydraulic press. Entrust this task to a Ford dealer or suitably-equipped garage.

Refitting

16 Refitting any of the control arms/tie rods is essentially a reversal of removal, noting the following points:
a) Tighten all fasteners to their specified torque where given, using a little thread-locking compound.
b) Before tightening any control arm/tie rod mounting bolts, ensure the suspension is in the 'normal' position using the fabricated spacers as described in the removal procedures.

12 Rear anti-roll bar – removal and refitting

Removal

1 Chock the front wheels, then jack up the rear of the vehicle and support it on axle stands (see *Jacking and vehicle support*).
2 Undo the nuts securing the outer ends of the anti-roll bar to the links (see illustration). Take care not to damage the rubber boots.
3 Undo the bolts securing the anti-roll bar clamps to the subframe, manoeuvre the anti-roll bar from under the vehicle (see illustration).
4 Examine the anti-roll bar for signs of damage or distortion, and the connecting links and mounting bushes for signs of deterioration of the rubber. The bushes are split along their length and must be fitted in their original positions.

Refitting

5 Position the anti-roll bar, then fit and tighten the bolts securing the anti-roll bar clamps to the subframe.
6 Refit the anti-roll bar links and tighten the

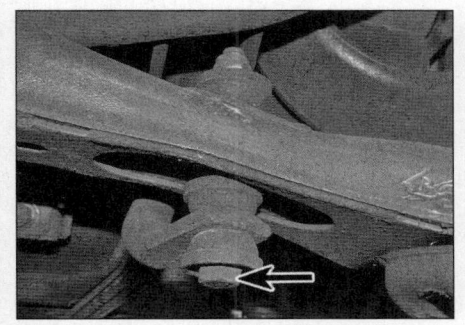

12.2 Rear anti-roll bar-to-control arm bolt (arrowed)

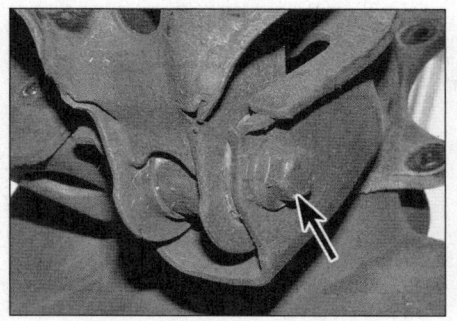

11.14a Undo the lower control arm outer bolt (arrowed) . . .

nuts to the specified torque, using a Torx bit to counterhold the nuts.
7 The remainder of refitting is a reversal of removal.

13 Steering wheel – removal and refitting

> **Warning:** Handle the airbag unit with extreme care as a precaution against personal injury, and always hold it with the cover facing away from the body. If in doubt concerning any proposed work involving the airbag unit or its control circuitry, consult a Ford dealer.

Removal

1 Drive the car forwards, and park it with the front wheels in the straight-ahead position.
2 Remove the driver's airbag as described in Chapter 12. Secure the rotary contact unit in place using tape to prevent any rotation.
3 Disconnect the wiring plug at the top of the steering wheel aperture.
4 Undo the steering wheel centre retaining bolt (see illustration).
5 On vehicles built up to 01/2005, if a new steering wheel is being fitted, but the original driver's airbag is to be used, undo the bolt and remove the earth spring from the wheel. This must be fitted to the new wheel.
6 Make alignment marks between the steering wheel centre and the column shaft, then lift the steering wheel off the column shaft, and

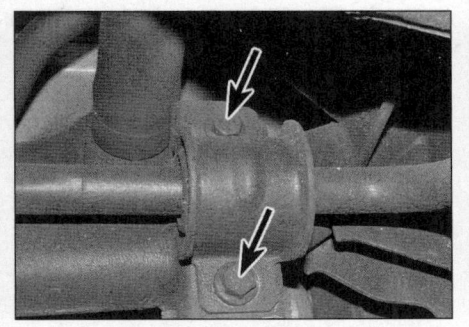

12.3 Undo the bolts (arrowed) securing the anti-roll bar clamps

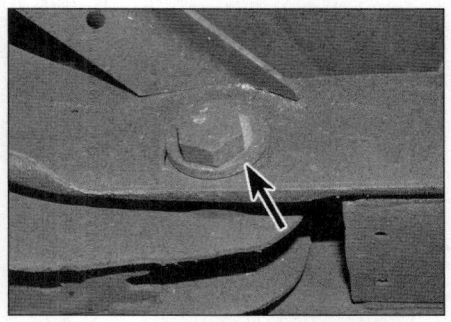

11.14b . . . then mark the position of the eccentric washer (arrowed) and remove the bolt

feed the wiring and plastic strip through the hole in the wheel.

Refitting

7 Ensure that the front wheels are still in the straight-ahead position.
8 On vehicles built up to 01/2005, if a new steering wheel is being fitted, but the original driver's airbag is to be used, undo the bolt and remove the earth cable from the new wheel, then attach the old earth spring.
9 Check the airbag rotary contact unit is still aligned. Refer to Chapter 12 if necessary. Remove the securing tape.
10 Feed the wiring through the hole in the steering wheel, then engage the wheel with the steering column shaft. Ensure that the marks made on removal are aligned, and that the pegs on the contact reel engage with the recesses on the steering wheel hub.
11 Refit the steering wheel retaining bolt, and tighten it to the specified torque.
12 Refit the airbag unit to the steering wheel as described in Chapter 12.

14 Steering column – removal and refitting

Removal

1 Disconnect the battery negative lead – see Chapter 5A.
2 Fully extend the steering column, then on models with an audio control switch fitted to the column shroud, release the locking tang,

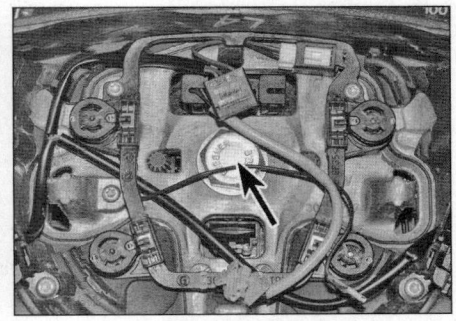

13.4 Steering wheel retaining bolt (arrowed)

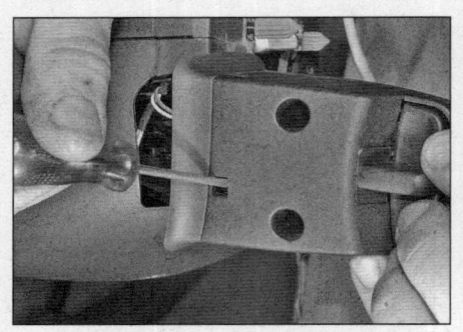

10•12 Suspension and steering

14.2 Release the clip and pull the audio control switch from the column shroud

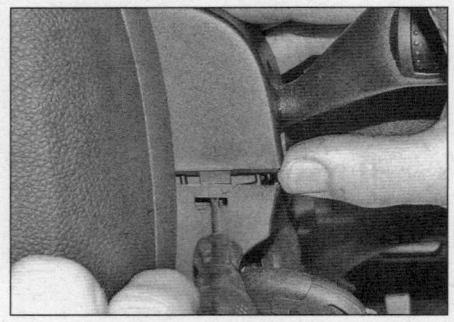

14.4 Release the clip each side securing the column upper shroud to the lower

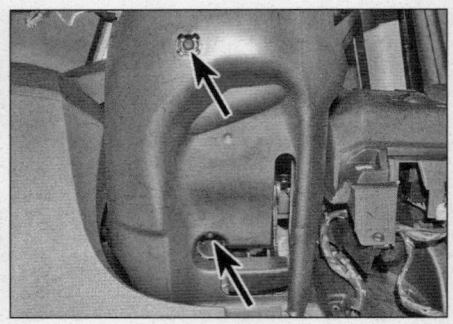

14.5 Undo the bolts (arrowed) securing the column lower shroud

pull the switch from place and disconnect the wiring plug **(see illustration)**.
3 Undo the fasteners and remove the lower facia panel on the driver's side – see Chapter 11.
4 Turn the steering wheel for access, then release the retaining clips and remove the steering column upper shroud **(see illustration)**. Turn the steering wheel back to the straight-ahead position.
5 Undo the 2 retaining bolts, and remove the steering column lower shroud **(see illustration)**. Release the steering column locking lever to remove the shroud completely.
6 Remove the steering wheel as described in Section 13.
7 Note their fitted positions and routing, then disconnect the various column wiring plugs and release the loom retaining clips.
8 Undo the steering column lower pinch-bolt and pull the joint upwards from the pinion **(see illustration)**. Ensure the column adjustment lever is released before detaching the joint from the pinion. Discard the pinch-bolt, a new one must be fitted.
9 Undo the 4 retaining bolts and manoeuvre the column from the vehicle **(see illustration)**. Discard the bolts, new ones must be fitted.
10 If required, drill out the security bolts, and remove the steering lock from the column **(see illustration)**. No further dismantling of the assembly is recommended.

Refitting

11 Refitting is a reversal of removal, bearing in mind the following points:

a) Lubricate universal joint splines with grease before engaging the steering column.
b) When fitting the new column retaining bolts, the shortest bolts are nearest the bulkhead.
c) Use a new universal joint pinch-bolt.
d) If refitting the steering lock, tighten the new security bolts until their heads snap off.
e) If the steering column has been rotated, or the front wheels turned from straight-ahead, reset the airbag contact reel as described in Chapter 12.

15 Steering rack – removal and refitting

Removal

1 Drive the car forwards and park it with the steering wheels in the straight-ahead position. Remove the ignition key to lock the steering in this position.
2 Remove the lower facia panel (where fitted) on the driver's side as described in Chapter 11.
3 Remove the steering column lower gaiter (where fitted), then undo the pinch-bolt and pull the joint upwards from the pinion **(see illustration 14.8)**. Ensure the column adjustment lever is released before detaching the joint from the pinion. Discard the pinch-bolt, a new one must be fitted.
4 Loosen the front wheel nuts. Chock the rear wheels then jack up the front of the vehicle

and support it on axle stands (see *Jacking and vehicle support*). Remove both front roadwheels.
5 Undo the fasteners and remove the engine undershield (where fitted) **(see illustration 6.1)**.
6 Undo the bolt securing the headlight levelling sensor bracket to the lower control arm (where applicable).
7 On some models, disconnect the steering angle sensor wiring plug (located at the steering column pinion in the engine compartment).
8 Attach splints each side of the exhaust flexible section (two wooden strips secured by cable tie will suffice) to prevent excessive bending, then undo the bolts/nuts securing the centre exhaust section to the front section.
9 Unhook the exhaust mounting rubbers at the front.
10 Slacken the nut until it is level with the end of the balljoint shank, then using a balljoint separator tool, detach the suspension control arm balljoint from the hub carrier. Use an Allen key in the end of the balljoint shank to prevent it from rotating as the nut is slackened **(see illustration 2.8)**.
11 Use a stout bar to lever the control arm downwards and over the end of the balljoint shank. Take care not to damage the balljoint dust cover during and after disconnection.
12 Undo the nut each side securing the lower end of the anti-roll bar links to the bar. Use a Torx bit to counterhold the nut.
13 Undo the nut and detach the track rod end balljoint from the hub carrier each side, using a balljoint separator tool as described in Section 19.

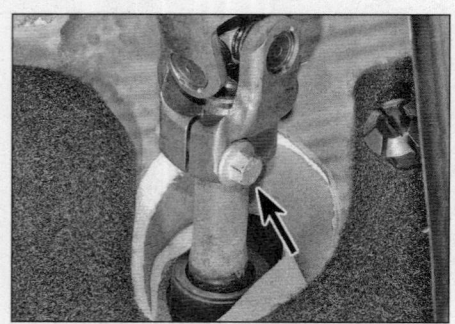

14.8 Steering column lower pinch-bolt (arrowed)

14.9 Steering column upper mounting bolts (arrowed)

14.10 Drill out the security bolt (arrowed) each side

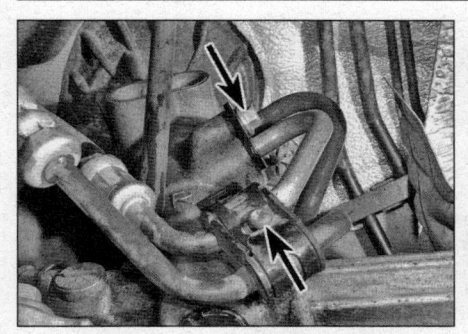

Suspension and steering 10•13

15.15 Steering rack pipes clamp bolts (arrowed)

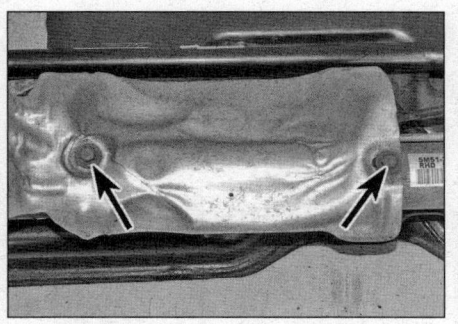

15.21 Steering rack heat shield bolts (arrowed)

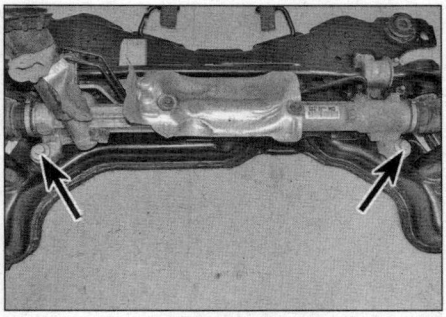

15.22 Steering rack retaining bolts (arrowed)

14 Undo the bolt at the lower rear of the engine securing the lower torque rod to the bracket on the transmission/engine.
15 Remove the bolt, unclip the power steering pipes from the steering rack, then undo the bolt, rotate the clamp plate and disconnect the pipes from the steering rack pinion **(see illustration)**.
16 Position a sturdy trolley jack beneath, and in contact with, the rear of the subframe.
17 Undo the bolt each side securing the front of the subframe **(see illustration 6.11)**. Note that new subframe front mounting bolts will be required for refitting.
18 Undo the bolts each side securing the rear mounting brackets to the subframe and vehicle body, and recover the washers **(see illustration 6.12)**. Note that new subframe mounting bolts will be required for refitting.
19 Carefully lower the jack and subframe. Take care not to damage the power steering hoses.
20 Undo the bolts and remove the anti-roll bar **(see illustration 6.14)**. Discard the bolts – new ones must be fitted.
21 Undo the bolts and remove the steering rack heat shield **(see illustration)**.
22 Undo the retaining bolts, and lift the steering rack from the subframe **(see illustration)**.

Refitting

23 Manipulate the steering rack into position and tighten the bolts to the specified torque.
24 Refit the steering rack heat shield and tighten the bolts securely.
25 Refit the anti-roll bar to the subframe and tighten the new bolts to the specified torque.
26 Ensure the steering rack pinion bulkhead seal is in place, then raise the subframe into position.
27 Fit the subframe rear mounting brackets to the body, then insert the new front and rear subframe mounting bolts. Only hand tighten them at this stage.
28 The alignment of the subframe must be checked by inserting round tools though the holes in the side members. Ford tools (part No 205-316) may be available. Alternatively, using two lengths of wooden dowel, 20 mm in diameter, and approximately 150 mm in length **(see illustration 6.18)**.

29 With the subframe correctly aligned, tighten all subframe bolts to the specified torque.
30 Engage the steering shaft universal joint with the pinion shaft, and push it fully home.
31 Fit the new universal joint pinch-bolt and tighten it to the specified torque.
32 Refit the fluid pipes to the steering rack using new O-ring seals, and tighten the retaining bolt securely.
33 The remainder of refitting is a reversal of removal, noting the following points:
a) Tighten all fasteners to their specified torque where given.
b) Bleed the power steering system as described in Section 17.
c) Have the front wheel alignment checked at the earliest opportunity.

16 Steering rack gaiters – renewal

1 Remove the track rod end on the side concerned as described in Section 19. Unscrew the locknut from the track rod.
2 Release the two clips and peel off the gaiter. Disconnect the breather hose as the gaiter is withdrawn **(see illustration)**
3 Clean out any dirt and grit from the inner end of the track rod and (when accessible) the rack.
4 Wrap insulating tape around the track rod threads to protect the new gaiter whilst installing.
5 Refit the track rod end locknut.
6 Refit the track rod end as described in Section 19.

17 Steering system – bleeding

Belt-driven pump

1 Wipe clean the area around the reservoir filler neck, and unscrew the filler cap/dipstick from the reservoir.
2 If topping-up is necessary, use clean fluid of the specified type (see *Weekly checks*). Check for leaks if frequent topping-up is required.

Do not run the engine without fluid in the reservoir.
3 After component renewal, or if the fluid level has been allowed to fall so low that air has entered the hydraulic system, bleeding must be carried out as follows:
4 Fill the reservoir to the MAX mark as described in *Weekly checks*. Note that the power steering fluid should be cold, and poured slowly to minimise aeration.
5 Raise the front of the vehicle until the tyres are just clear of the ground, then support the vehicle securely on axle stands (see *Jacking and vehicle support*).
6 Without starting the engine, slowly turn the steering wheel from lock to lock, and add power steering fluid until the fluid level ceases to drop.
7 Start the engine and turn the steering wheel repeatedly from full lock one way, to full lock the other way, then top-up the fluid level as necessary.
8 Turn the steering wheel slowly to the full right lock position, and hold it there for 2 seconds.
9 Now turn the steering wheel slowly to the full left lock position, and hold it there for 2 seconds.
10 Top-up the fluid level again if necessary.
11 Repeat paragraphs 8 and 9 until the steering operation is satisfactory.
12 If the steering is still noisy (indicating air in the system), leave the vehicle overnight, and then try again. If this still fails to remove the air, the vehicle must be taken to a Ford dealer or suitably-equipped specialist, who will be

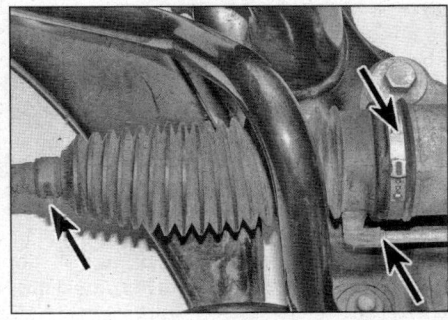

16.2 Steering rack gaiter clips and breather hose (arrowed) – shown with the rack removed for clarity

10•14 Suspension and steering

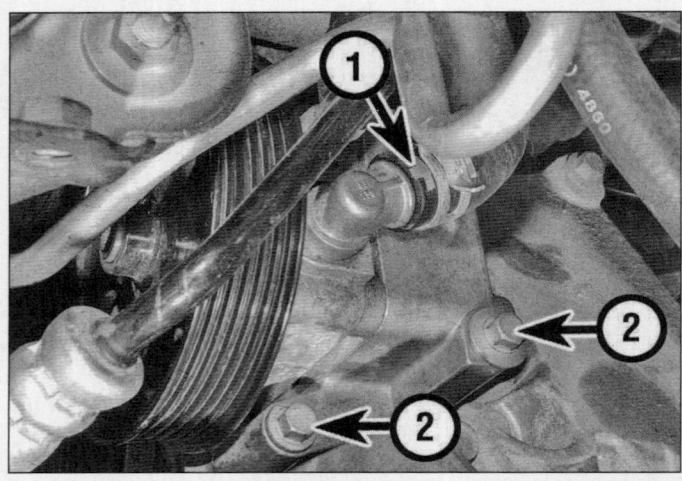

18.6 Power steering pump fluid supply hose (1) and lower mounting bolts (2)

18.14 Disconnect the wiring plugs from the EHPS module

able to apply a vacuum to the reservoir using special tools.

13 On completion, stop the engine, lower the vehicle to the ground, and recheck the fluid level.

Electro-Hydraulic power steering

14 Remove the right-hand headlight as described in Chapter 12.

15 Wipe clean the area around the reservoir filler neck, and unscrew the filler cap/dipstick from the reservoir.

16 If topping-up is necessary, use clean fluid of the specified type (see *Weekly checks*). Check for leaks if frequent topping-up is required. Do not run the engine without fluid in the reservoir.

17 After component renewal, or if the fluid level has been allowed to fall so low that air has entered the hydraulic system, bleeding must be carried out as follows.

18 Fill the reservoir to the MAX mark as described in *Weekly checks*. Note that the power steering fluid should be cold, and poured slowly into the reservoir to minimise aeration.

19 Raise the front of the vehicle until the tyres are just clear of the ground, then support the vehicle securely on axle stands (see *Jacking and vehicle support*).

20 Start the engine, slowly turn the steering wheel from lock to lock, and add power steering fluid until the fluid level ceases to drop.

21 Switch off the engine and check the fluid level. Top-up if necessary.

22 Start the engine and turn the steering from lock to lock. If excessive noise is still apparent (indicating air in the system), leave the vehicle overnight, then try again.

23 If the steering is still noisy, it may be that the pump is faulty. Consult a Ford dealer or specialist.

24 On completion, stop the engine, lower the vehicle to the ground, and recheck the fluid level.

18 Power steering pump – removal and refitting

Removal – belt-driven pump

1 Remove the auxiliary drivebelt as described in Chapter 1.

2 Jack up the front of the vehicle and support it securely on axle stands (see *Jacking and vehicle support*).

3 Undo the fasteners and remove the splash shield under the radiator.

4 Undo the bolts and remove the right-hand wheel arch liner.

Models with a fluid cooler

5 Release the clamp and disconnect the hose from the power steering cooler to the pump. Be prepared for fluid spillage. Plug the openings to prevent contamination.

Models without a fluid cooler

6 Release the clamp and disconnect the hose from the power steering reservoir to the pump (see illustration). Be prepared for fluid spillage. Plug the openings to prevent contamination.

All models

7 Disconnect the fluid supply hose from the

18.19 Disconnect the fluid return and pressure pipes

pump. Be prepared for fluid spillage. Plug the openings to prevent contamination.

8 Undo the 2 lower mounting bolts from the pump **(see illustration 18.6)**.

9 Remove the alternator as described in Chapter 5A.

10 Disconnect the power steering pump pressure switch wiring plug.

11 Slacken the power steering pump pressure pipe union nut.

12 Undo the upper mounting bolts and remove the pump. Disconnect the pressure pipe as the pump is withdrawn.

Removal – Electro-Hydraulic power steering

Note: *If a new EHPS pump/module is to be fitted, the relevant program code needs to be extracted and reloaded to the module. Entrust this task to a Ford dealer or suitably-equipped specialist.*

13 Remove the right-hand side headlight as described in Chapter 12.

14 Disconnect the pump wiring plugs **(see illustration)**.

15 Jack up the front of the vehicle and support it securely on axle stands (see *Jacking and vehicle support*).

16 Undo the fasteners and remove splash shield under the radiator and the engine undershield.

17 Undo the Torx bolts and remove the right-hand wheel arch liner.

18 Use a syringe to extract as much fluid as possible from the pump reservoir.

19 Undo the union nut and disconnect the pump pressure pipe **(see illustration)**. Be prepared for fluid spillage. Plug the openings to prevent contamination.

20 Release the clamp and disconnect the fluid return hose from the pump **(see illustration 18.19)**. Be prepared for fluid spillage. Plug the openings to prevent contamination.

21 Undo the 3 bolts and remove the assembly **(see illustration)**.

Suspension and steering 10•15

22 No individual parts are available. If faulty, exchange units are available from Ford.

Refitting

23 Refitting is a reversal of removal, bearing in mind the following points:
a) Use a new O-ring on pressure pipe union.
b) Tighten the mounting bolts to the specified torque.
c) If a new EHPS has been fitted, suitable software will need to be downloaded from Ford. Consult your local dealer or specialist.
d) Refill/top-up the fluid reservoir, and bleed the system as described in Section 17.

19 Track rod end – removal and refitting

Removal

1 Loosen the appropriate front wheel nuts. Chock the rear wheels, then jack up the front of the vehicle and support it on axle stands (see *Jacking and vehicle support*). Remove the appropriate front roadwheel.

2 Counterhold the track rod, and slacken the track rod end locknut by half a turn **(see illustration)**. If the locknut is now left in this position, it will act as a further guide for refitting.

3 Unscrew the track rod end balljoint nut, using and Allen key to counterhold the balljoint shank. Separate the balljoint from the steering arm with a proprietary balljoint separator, then remove the nut and disengage the balljoint from the arm **(see illustrations)**.

4 Unscrew the track rod end from the track rod, counting the number of turns needed to remove it. Make a note of the number of turns, so that the tracking can be reset (or at least approximated) on refitting.

Refitting

5 Screw the track rod end onto the track rod by the same number of turns noted during removal.

6 Engage the balljoint in the steering arm. Fit a new nut and tighten it to the specified torque.

7 Counterhold the track rod and tighten the locknut.

8 Refit the front wheel, lower the car and tighten the wheel bolts in a diagonal sequence to the specified torque.

9 Have the front wheel toe-in (tracking) checked and adjusted by a Ford dealer or suitably-equipped repairer.

20 Wheel alignment and steering angles – general information

1 A car's steering and suspension geometry is defined in four basic settings – all angles are expressed in degrees (toe settings are also expressed as a measurement); the relevant settings are camber, castor, steering axis inclination, and toe setting **(see illustration)**. On the models covered by this manual, only the front and rear wheel toe settings are adjustable.

2 Camber is the angle at which the front wheels are set from the vertical when viewed from the front or rear of the car. Negative camber is the amount (in degrees) that the wheels are tilted inward at the top from the vertical.

3 The front camber angle is adjusted by slackening the steering knuckle-to-suspension strut mounting bolts and repositioning the hub carrier assemblies as necessary.

4 Castor is the angle between the steering axis and a vertical line when viewed from each side of the car. Positive castor is when the steering axis is inclined rearward at the top.

18.21 EHPS module retaining bolts (arrowed)

19.2 Slacken the track rod end locknut (arrowed)

19.3a Use an Allen key to counterhold the track rod end balljoint shank

19.3b Use a separator tool to detach the track rod end from the hub carrier

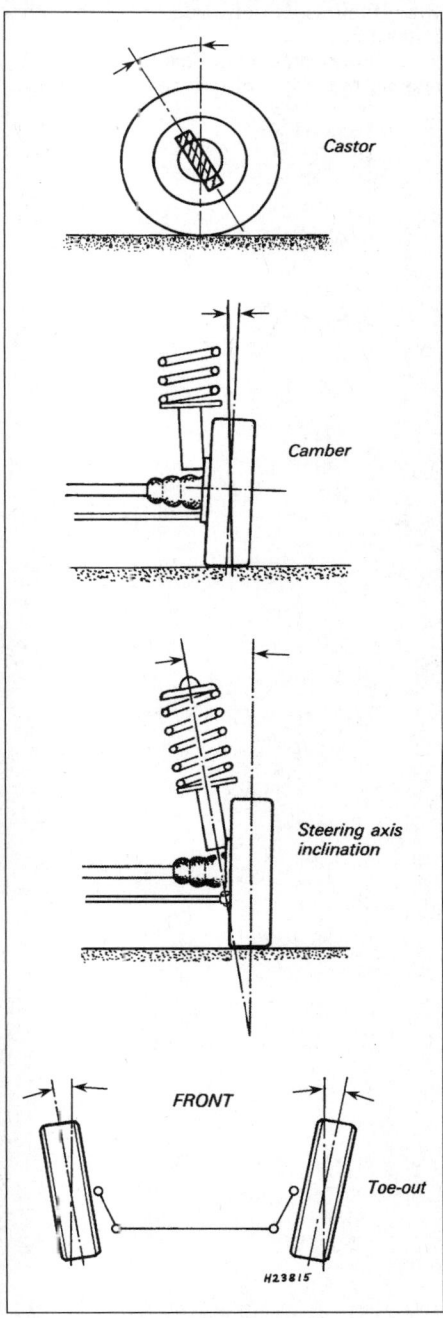

20.1 Front wheel geometry

5 Steering axis inclination is the angle (when viewed from the front of the vehicle) between the vertical and an imaginary line drawn through the front suspension strut upper mounting and the control arm balljoint.
6 Toe setting is the amount by which the distance between the front inside edges of the roadwheels (measured at hub height) differs from the diametrically opposite distance measured between the rear inside edges of the roadwheels. Toe-in is when the roadwheels point inwards, towards each other at the front, while toe-out is when they splay outwards from each other at the front.
7 The front wheel toe setting is adjusted by altering the length of the steering track rods on both sides. This adjustment is normally referred to as the tracking.
8 The rear wheel toe setting is adjusted by rotating the lateral link front mounting bolt in the chassis. The bolt incorporates an eccentric washer, and the pivot point for the link varies as the bolt is rotated.
9 All other suspension and steering angles are set during manufacture, and no adjustment is possible. It can be assumed, therefore, that unless the vehicle has suffered accident damage, all the preset angles will be correct.
10 Special optical measuring equipment is necessary to accurately check and adjust the front and rear toe settings and front camber angles, and this work should be carried out by a Ford dealer or similar expert. Most tyre-fitting centres have the expertise and equipment to carry out at least a front wheel toe setting (tracking) check for a nominal charge.

21 Front subframe – removal and refitting

1 The front subframe removal and refitting is described within the steering rack removal and refitting procedure, as described in Section 15. If the subframe is to be removed as part of another procedure (eg, catalytic converter renewal), the steering rack and anti-roll bar can be left in place on the subframe.

Chapter 11
Bodywork and fittings

Contents

	Section number
Body side-trim mouldings and adhesive emblems – removal and refitting	24
Bonnet – removal, refitting and adjustment	8
Bonnet lock – removal, refitting and adjustment	9
Boot lid – removal and refitting	17
Boot lid lock components – removal and refitting	18
Bumpers – removal and refitting	6
Central locking system – testing, reprogramming, removal and refitting	22
Centre console – removal and refitting	29
Door – removal and refitting	14
Door handle and lock components – removal and refitting	13
Door inner trim panel – removal and refitting	10
Door window glass – removal and refitting	11
Door window regulator – removal and refitting	12
Exterior mirror and glass – removal and refitting	15
Facia – removal and refitting	32
General information	1
Glovebox – removal and refitting	31
Interior mirror – removal and refitting	16
Interior trim panels – removal and refitting	28
Maintenance – bodywork and underframe	2
Maintenance – upholstery and carpets	3
Major body damage – repair	5
Minor body damage – repair	4
Overhead console – removal and refitting	30
Radiator grille – removal and refitting	7
Seat belts – removal and refitting	27
Seats – removal and refitting	26
Sunroof – general information and adjustment	25
Support struts – removal and refitting	20
Tailgate – removal and refitting	19
Tailgate lock components – removal and refitting	21
Wheel arch liner – removal and refitting	33
Windscreen and fixed windows – removal and refitting	23

Degrees of difficulty

Easy, suitable for novice with little experience | **Fairly easy,** suitable for beginner with some experience | **Fairly difficult,** suitable for competent DIY mechanic | **Difficult,** suitable for experienced DIY mechanic | **Very difficult,** suitable for expert DIY or professional

Specifications

Torque wrench settings	Nm	lbf ft
Bumper bar mounting:		
Front bolts	25	18
Rear bolts	20	15
Front seat mounting bolts	35	26
Passenger's airbag module lower support bracket:		
Bolts	9	6
Nuts	7	5
Rear seat backrest catch retaining bolts	23	17
Rear seat hinge	35	26
Seat belt mounting nuts and bolts:		
Front inertia reel bolt	38	28
Front lower anchorage	38	28
Front seat belt buckle stake	47	35
Front seat bolts shoulder height adjuster	35	26
Front upper anchorage	38	28
Rear centre belt buckle stalk	55	41
Rear centre inertia reel	35	26
Rear centre lower anchorage	55	41
Rear outer inertia reel	40	30
Rear outer lower anchorage	38	28

1 General information

The bodyshell and underframe on all models feature variable thickness steel. Achieved by laser-welded technology, used to join steel panels of different gauges. This gives a stiffer structure, with mounting points being more rigid, which gives an improved crash performance.

An additional safety crossmember is incorporated between the A-pillars in the upper area of the bulkhead, and the facia and steering column are secured to it. The lower bulkhead area is reinforced by additional systems of members connected to the front of the vehicle. The body side rocker panels (sills) have been divided along the length of the vehicle by internal reinforcement, this functions like a double tube which increases its strength. All doors are reinforced and incorporate side impact protection, which is secured in the door structure. There are additional impact absorbers to the front and rear of the vehicle, behind the bumper assemblies.

All sheet metal surfaces which are prone to corrosion are galvanised. The painting process includes a base colour which closely matches the final topcoat, so that any stone damage is not as noticeable. The front wings are of a bolt-on type to ease their renewal if required.

Automatic seat belts are fitted to all models, and the front seat safety belts are equipped with a pyrotechnic pretension seat belt buckle, which is attached to the seat frame of each front seat. In the event of a serious front impact, the system is triggered and pulls the stalk buckle downwards to tension the seat belt. It is not possible to reset the tensioner once fired, and it must therefore be renewed. The tensioners are fired by an explosive charge similar to that used in the airbag, and are triggered via the airbag control module. The safety belt retractor, which is fitted in the base of the B-pillar, has a device to control the seat belt, if the deceleration force is enough to activate the airbags.

In the UK, central locking is standard on all models. In other countries, it is available on certain models only. Where double-locking is fitted, the lock mechanism is disconnected (when the system is in use) from the interior door handles, making it impossible to open any of the doors or the tailgate/boot lid from inside the vehicle. This means that, even if a thief should break a side window, he will not be able to open the door using the interior handle. In the event of a serious accident, a crash sensor unlocks all doors if they were previously locked.

Many of the procedures in this Chapter require the battery to be disconnected; refer to Chapter 5A.

2 Maintenance – bodywork and underframe

The general condition of a vehicle's bodywork is the one thing that significantly affects its value. Maintenance is easy, but needs to be regular. Neglect, particularly after minor damage, can lead quickly to further deterioration and costly repair bills. It is important also to keep watch on those parts of the vehicle not immediately visible, for instance the underside, inside all the wheel arches, and the lower part of the engine compartment.

The basic maintenance routine for the bodywork is washing – preferably with a lot of water, from a hose. This will remove all the loose solids which may have stuck to the vehicle. It is important to flush these off in such a way as to prevent grit from scratching the finish. The wheel arches and underframe need washing in the same way, to remove any accumulated mud, which will retain moisture and tend to encourage rust. Paradoxically enough, the best time to clean the underframe and wheel arches is in wet weather, when the mud is thoroughly wet and soft. In very wet weather, the underframe is usually cleaned of large accumulations automatically, and this is a good time for inspection.

Periodically, except on vehicles with a wax-based underbody protective coating, it is a good idea to have the whole of the underframe of the vehicle steam-cleaned, engine compartment included, so that a thorough inspection can be carried out to see what minor repairs and renovations are necessary. Steam-cleaning is available at many garages, and is necessary for the removal of the accumulation of oily grime, which sometimes is allowed to become thick in certain areas. If steam-cleaning facilities are not available, there are some excellent grease solvents available which can be brush-applied; the dirt can then be simply hosed off. Note that these methods should not be used on vehicles with wax-based underbody protective coating, or the coating will be removed. Such vehicles should be inspected annually, preferably just prior to Winter, when the underbody should be washed down, and any damage to the wax coating repaired. Ideally, a completely fresh coat should be applied. It would also be worth considering the use of such wax-based protection for injection into door panels, sills, box sections, etc, as an additional safeguard against rust damage, where such protection is not provided by the vehicle manufacturer.

After washing paintwork, wipe off with a chamois leather to give an unspotted clear finish. A coat of clear protective wax polish will give added protection against chemical pollutants in the air. If the paintwork sheen has dulled or oxidised, use a cleaner/polisher combination to restore the brilliance of the shine. This requires a little effort, but such dulling is usually caused because regular washing has been neglected. Care needs to be taken with metallic paintwork, as special non-abrasive cleaner/polisher is required to avoid damage to the finish. Always check that the door and ventilator opening drain holes and pipes are completely clear, so that water can be drained out. Brightwork should be treated in the same way as paintwork. Windscreens and windows can be kept clear of the smeary film which often appears, by the use of proprietary glass cleaner. Never use any form of wax or other body or chromium polish on glass.

3 Maintenance – upholstery and carpets

Mats and carpets should be brushed or vacuum-cleaned regularly, to keep them free of grit. If they are badly stained, remove them from the vehicle for scrubbing or sponging, and make quite sure they are dry before refitting. Seats and interior trim panels can be kept clean by wiping with a damp cloth. If they do become stained (which can be more apparent on light-coloured upholstery), use a little liquid detergent and a soft nail brush to scour the grime out of the grain of the material. Do not forget to keep the headlining clean in the same way as the upholstery. When using liquid cleaners inside the vehicle, do not over-wet the surfaces being cleaned. Excessive damp could get into the seams and padded interior, causing stains, offensive odours or even rot.

Caution: If the inside of the vehicle gets wet accidentally, it is worthwhile taking some trouble to dry it out properly, particularly where carpets are involved. Do not leave oil or electric heaters inside the vehicle for this purpose.

4 Minor body damage – repair

Minor scratches in bodywork

If the scratch is very superficial, and does not penetrate to the metal of the bodywork, repair is very simple. Lightly rub the area of the scratch with a paintwork renovator, or a very fine cutting paste, to remove loose paint from the scratch, and to clear the surrounding bodywork of wax polish. Rinse the area with clean water.

Apply touch-up paint to the scratch using a fine paint brush; continue to apply fine layers of paint until the surface of the paint in the scratch is level with the surrounding paintwork. Allow the new paint at least two weeks to harden, then blend it into the surrounding paintwork by rubbing the scratch area with a paintwork renovator or a very fine cutting paste. Finally, apply wax polish.

Where the scratch has penetrated right through to the metal of the bodywork, causing the metal to rust, a different repair technique is required. Remove any loose rust from the bottom of the scratch with a penknife, then apply rust-inhibiting paint to prevent the formation of rust in the future. Using a rubber or nylon applicator, fill the scratch with bodystopper paste. If required, this paste can be mixed with cellulose thinners to provide a very thin paste which is ideal for filling narrow scratches. Before the stopper-paste in the scratch hardens, wrap a piece of smooth cotton rag around the top of a finger. Dip the finger in cellulose thinners, and quickly sweep it across the surface of the stopper-paste in the scratch; this will ensure that the surface of the stopper-paste is slightly hollowed. The scratch can now be painted over as described earlier in this Section.

Dents in bodywork

When deep denting of the vehicle's bodywork has taken place, the first task is to pull the dent out, until the affected bodywork almost attains its original shape. There is little point in trying to restore the original shape completely, as the metal in the damaged area will have stretched on impact, and cannot be reshaped fully to its original contour. It is better to bring the level of the dent up to a point which is about 3 mm below the level of the surrounding bodywork. In cases where the dent is very shallow anyway, it is not worth trying to pull it out at all. If the underside of the dent is accessible, it can be hammered out gently from behind, using a mallet with a wooden or plastic head. Whilst doing this, hold a suitable block of wood firmly against the outside of the panel, to absorb the impact from the hammer blows and thus prevent a large area of the bodywork from being 'belled-out'.

Should the dent be in a section of the bodywork which has a double skin, or some other factor making it inaccessible from behind, a different technique is called for. Drill several small holes through the metal inside the area – particularly in the deeper section. Then screw long self-tapping screws into the holes, just sufficiently for them to gain a good purchase in the metal. Now the dent can be pulled out by pulling on the protruding heads of the screws with a pair of pliers.

The next stage of the repair is the removal of the paint from the damaged area, and from an inch or so of the surrounding 'sound' bodywork. This is accomplished most easily by using a wire brush or abrasive pad on a power drill, although it can be done just as effectively by hand, using sheets of abrasive paper. To complete the preparation for filling, score the surface of the bare metal with a screwdriver or the tang of a file, or alternatively, drill small holes in the affected area. This will provide a really good 'key' for the filler paste.

To complete the repair, see the Section on filling and respraying.

Rust holes or gashes in bodywork

Remove all paint from the affected area, and from an inch or so of the surrounding 'sound' bodywork, using an abrasive pad or a wire brush on a power drill. If these are not available, a few sheets of abrasive paper will do the job most effectively. With the paint removed, you will be able to judge the severity of the corrosion, and therefore decide whether to renew the whole panel (if this is possible) or to repair the affected area. New body panels are not as expensive as most people think, and it is often quicker and more satisfactory to fit a new panel than to attempt to repair large areas of corrosion.

Remove all fittings from the affected area, except those which will act as a guide to the original shape of the damaged bodywork (e.g. headlight shells etc). Then, using tin snips or a hacksaw blade, remove all loose metal and any other metal badly affected by corrosion. Hammer the edges of the hole inwards, in order to create a slight depression for the filler paste.

Wire-brush the affected area to remove the powdery rust from the surface of the remaining metal. Paint the affected area with rust-inhibiting paint, if the back of the rusted area is accessible, treat this also.

Before filling can take place, it will be necessary to block the hole in some way. This can be achieved by the use of aluminium or plastic mesh, or aluminium tape.

Aluminium or plastic mesh, or glass-fibre matting, is probably the best material to use for a large hole. Cut a piece to the approximate size and shape of the hole to be filled, then position it in the hole so that its edges are below the level of the surrounding bodywork. It can be retained in position by several blobs of filler paste around its periphery.

Aluminium tape should be used for small or very narrow holes. Pull a piece off the roll, trim it to the approximate size and shape required, then pull off the backing paper (if used) and stick the tape over the hole; it can be overlapped if the thickness of one piece is insufficient. Burnish down the edges of the tape with the handle of a screwdriver or similar, to ensure that the tape is securely attached to the metal underneath.

Filling and respraying

Before using this Section, see the Sections on dent, deep scratch, rust holes and gash repairs.

Many types of bodyfiller are available, but generally speaking, those proprietary kits which contain a tin of filler paste and a tube of resin hardener are best for this type of repair. A wide, flexible plastic or nylon applicator will be found invaluable for imparting a smooth and well-contoured finish to the surface of the filler.

Mix up a little filler on a clean piece of card or board – measure the hardener carefully (follow the maker's instructions on the pack), otherwise the filler will set too rapidly or too slowly. Using the applicator, apply the filler paste to the prepared area; draw the applicator across the surface of the filler to achieve the correct contour and to level the surface. As soon as a contour that approximates to the correct one is achieved, stop working the paste – if you carry on too long, the paste will become sticky and begin to 'pick-up' on the applicator. Continue to add thin layers of filler paste at 20-minute intervals, until the level of the filler is just proud of the surrounding bodywork.

Once the filler has hardened, the excess can be removed using a metal plane or file. From then on, progressively-finer grades of abrasive paper should be used, starting with a 40-grade production paper, and finishing with a 400-grade wet-and-dry paper. Always wrap the abrasive paper around a flat rubber, cork, or wooden block – otherwise the surface of the filler will not be completely flat. During the smoothing of the filler surface, the wet-and-dry paper should be periodically rinsed in water. This will ensure that a very smooth finish is imparted to the filler at the final stage.

At this stage, the 'dent' should be surrounded by a ring of bare metal, which in turn should be encircled by the finely 'feathered' edge of the good paintwork. Rinse the repair area with clean water, until all of the dust produced by the rubbing-down operation has gone.

Spray the whole area with a light coat of primer – this will show up any imperfections in the surface of the filler. Repair these imperfections with fresh filler paste or bodystopper, and once more smooth the surface with abrasive paper. Repeat this spray-and-repair procedure until you are satisfied that the surface of the filler, and the feathered edge of the paintwork, are perfect. Clean the repair area with clean water, and allow to dry fully.

The repair area is now ready for final spraying. Paint spraying must be carried out in a warm, dry, windless and dust-free atmosphere. This condition can be created artificially if you have access to a large indoor working area, but if you are forced to work in the open, you will have to pick your day very carefully. If you are working indoors, dousing the floor in the work area with water will help to settle the dust which would otherwise be in the atmosphere. If the repair area is confined to one body panel, mask off the surrounding panels; this will help to minimise the effects of a slight mis-match in paint colours. Bodywork fittings (e.g. chrome strips, door handles etc) will also need to be masked off. Use genuine masking tape, and several thicknesses of newspaper, for the masking operations.

Before commencing to spray, agitate the aerosol can thoroughly, then spray a test area (an old tin, or similar) until the technique is mastered. Cover the repair area with a thick coat of primer; the thickness should be built up

6.4 Undo the bolt and prise out the scrivet each side of the radiator grille aperture

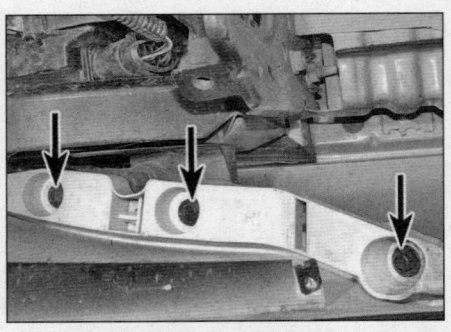

6.7 Undo the 3 bolts securing the bumper to the wing (arrowed) – viewed from under the wheel arch

6.9a The bumper is retained by 3 clips in the centre (arrowed) . . .

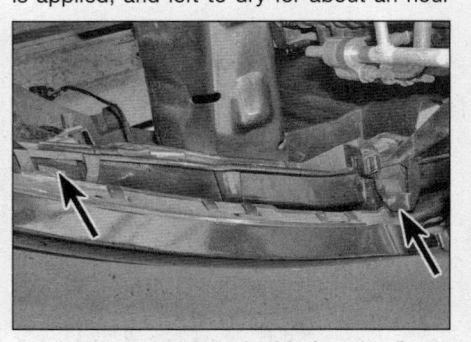

6.9b . . . and 2 each side (arrowed)

using several thin layers of paint, rather than one thick one. Using 400-grade wet-and-dry paper, rub down the surface of the primer until it is really smooth. While doing this, the work area should be thoroughly doused with water, and the wet-and-dry paper periodically rinsed in water. Allow to dry before spraying on more paint.

Spray on the top coat, again building up the thickness by using several thin layers of paint. Start spraying at one edge of the repair area, and then, using a side-to-side motion, work until the whole repair area and about 2 inches of the surrounding original paintwork is covered. Remove all masking material 10 to 15 minutes after spraying on the final coat of paint.

Allow the new paint at least two weeks to harden, then, using a paintwork renovator, or a very fine cutting paste, blend the edges of the paint into the existing paintwork. Finally, apply wax polish.

Plastic components

With the use of more and more plastic body components by the vehicle manufacturers (e.g. bumpers. spoilers, and in some cases major body panels), rectification of more serious damage to such items has become a matter of either entrusting repair work to a specialist in this field, or renewing complete components. Repair of such damage by the DIY owner is not really feasible, owing to the cost of the equipment and materials required for effecting such repairs. The basic technique involves making a groove along the line of the crack in the plastic, using a rotary burr in a power drill. The damaged part is then welded back together, using a hot-air gun to heat up and fuse a plastic filler rod into the groove. Any excess plastic is then removed, and the area rubbed down to a smooth finish. It is important that a filler rod of the correct plastic is used, as body components can be made of a variety of different types (e.g. polycarbonate, ABS, polypropylene).

Damage of a less serious nature (abrasions, minor cracks etc) can be repaired by the DIY owner using a two-part epoxy filler repair material. Once mixed in equal proportions, this is used in similar fashion to the bodywork filler used on metal panels. The filler is usually cured in twenty to thirty minutes, ready for sanding and painting.

If the owner is renewing a complete component himself, or if he has repaired it with epoxy filler, he will be left with the problem of finding a suitable paint for finishing which is compatible with the type of plastic used. At one time, the use of a universal paint was not possible, owing to the complex range of plastics encountered in body component applications. Standard paints, generally speaking, will not bond to plastic or rubber satisfactorily. However, it is now possible to obtain a plastic body parts finishing kit which consists of a pre-primer treatment, a primer and coloured top coat. Full instructions are normally supplied with a kit, but basically, the method of use is to first apply the pre-primer to the component concerned, and allow it to dry for up to 30 minutes. Then the primer is applied, and left to dry for about an hour before finally applying the special-coloured top coat. The result is a correctly-coloured component, where the paint will flex with the plastic or rubber, a property that standard paint does not normally posses.

5 Major body damage – repair

Where serious damage has occurred, or large areas need renewal due to neglect, it means that complete new panels will need welding-in; this is best left to professionals. If the damage is due to impact, it will also be necessary to check completely the alignment of the bodyshell; this can only be carried out accurately by a Ford dealer, using special jigs. If the body is left misaligned, it is primarily dangerous, as the car will not handle properly, and secondly, uneven stresses will be imposed on the steering, suspension and possibly transmission, causing abnormal wear or complete failure, particularly to items such as the tyres.

6 Bumpers – removal and refitting

Front bumper removal

1 Apply the handbrake, jack up the front of the vehicle and support it on axle stands. Undo the fasteners and remove the engine undershield.

Models up to 12/2007

2 Undo the fasteners and remove the splash shield under the radiator.
3 Remove the radiator grille as described in Section 7.
4 Remove the scrivet each side of the radiator grille aperture **(see illustration)**.
5 Remove both front headlights as described in Chapter 12.
6 Undo the 2 bolts each side securing the wheel arch liner to the bumper.
7 Undo the 3 bolts each side securing the bumper to the underside of the wing **(see illustration)**.
8 Pull the headlight washer jets forwards (where fitted), then release the clips and detach the jet assembly from the pipe.
9 Release the 7 clips at the upper edge, then with the help of an assistant to support one end of the bumper, pull the sides away from the body and withdraw it forwards from the vehicle **(see illustrations)**. Disconnect the foglamp connectors as the bumper is withdrawn.

Models from 12/2007

10 Undo the fasteners and remove the splash shield under the radiator.
11 Remove the front headlights as described in Chapter 12.

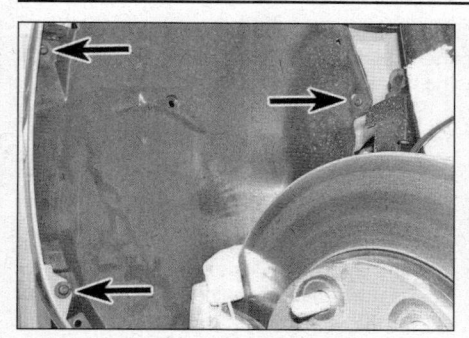

Bodywork and fittings 11•5

6.12a Undo the bolts at the front of the wheel arch liner (arrowed) . . .

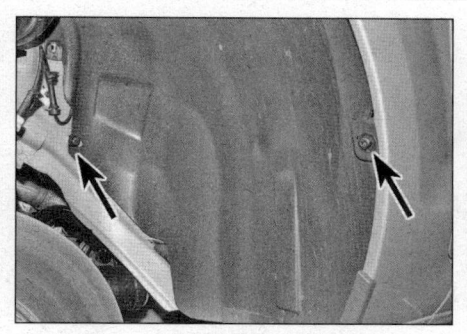

6.12b . . . and at the rear (arrowed)

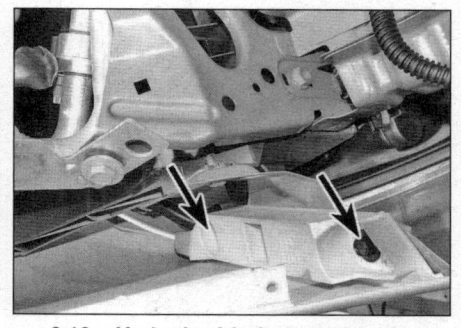

6.13a Undo the 2 bolts securing the bumper to the wing (arrowed)

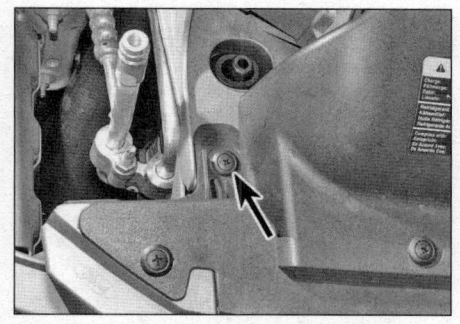

6.13b Undo the scrivet each side of the radiator grille (arrowed)

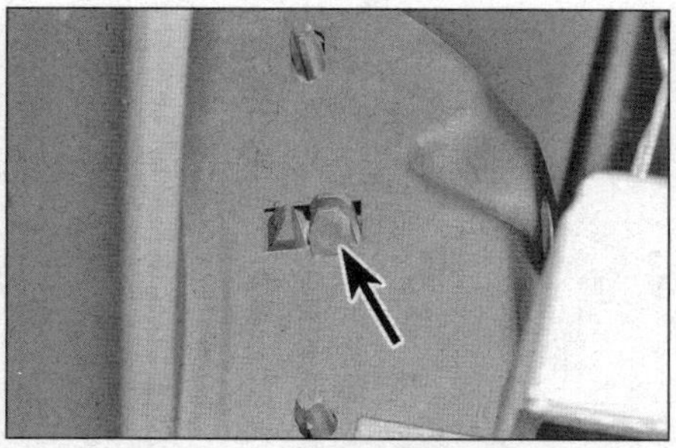

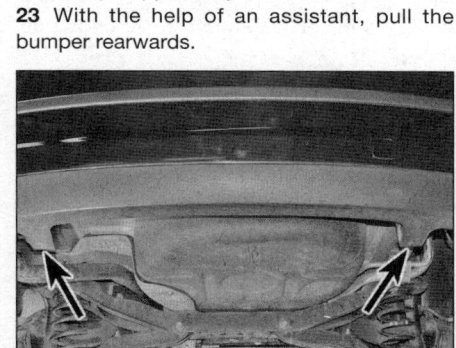

6.16a Squeeze together the sides of the clip securing the wing to the bumper each side (arrowed)

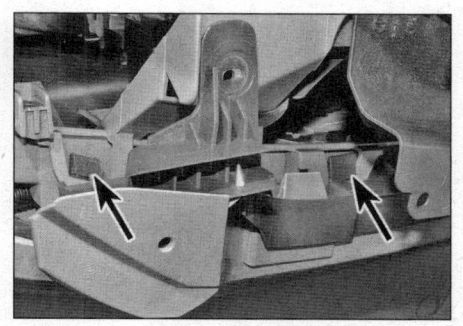

6.16b Release the clips (arrowed) at the top edge of the bumper

12 Undo the bolts securing the wheel arch liners to the front bumper **(see illustrations)**.
13 Undo the 2 bolts each side securing the bumper to the front wing, and the scrivet each side of the radiator grille **(see illustrations)**.
14 Remove the radiator grille as described in Section 7.
15 Pull the headlight washer jets forwards (where fitted), then release the clips and detach the jet assembly from the pipe.
16 Release the clips at the upper and outer edges, then with the help of an assistant to support one end of the bumper, withdraw it forwards from the vehicle **(see illustrations)**. Disconnect the foglamp connectors as the bumper is withdrawn.

Rear bumper removal

Hatchback models up to 12/2007

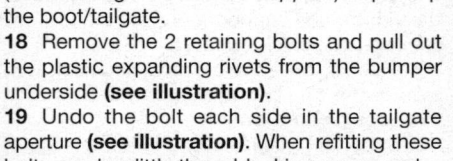

17 Chock the front wheels, jack up the rear of the vehicle and support it on axle stands (see *Jacking and vehicle support*). Open up the boot/tailgate.
18 Remove the 2 retaining bolts and pull out the plastic expanding rivets from the bumper underside **(see illustration)**.
19 Undo the bolt each side in the tailgate aperture **(see illustration)**. When refitting these bolts, apply a little thread-locking compound.
20 Undo the 2 bolts each side securing the bumper to the wheel arch liner **(see illustration)**.
21 Undo the nut each side in the wheel arch securing the bumper to the wing, and pull the front edges of the bumper outwards to release the guide pin each side **(see illustration)**.

22 Disconnect the wiring plug for the rear foglamp/reversing light/parking assistance sensors (as applicable).
23 With the help of an assistant, pull the bumper rearwards.

Hatchback models from 12/2007

24 Chock the front wheels, jack up the rear of the vehicle and support it on axle stands (see *Jacking and vehicle support*). Open up the tailgate.

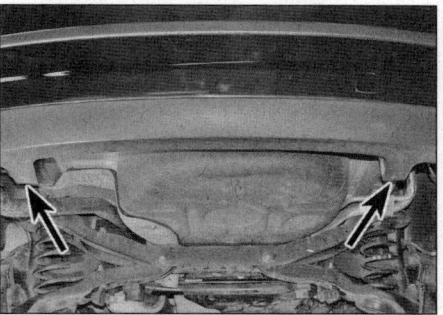

6.18 Undo the bolts and prise out the plastic rivets (arrowed)

6.19 Undo the bolt each side in the tailgate aperture

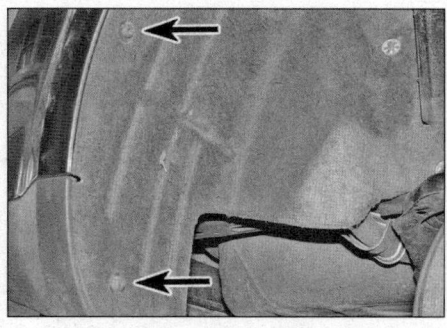

6.20 Wheel arch liner-to-bumper bolts (arrowed)

6.21 Undo the nut each side securing the bumper to the wing

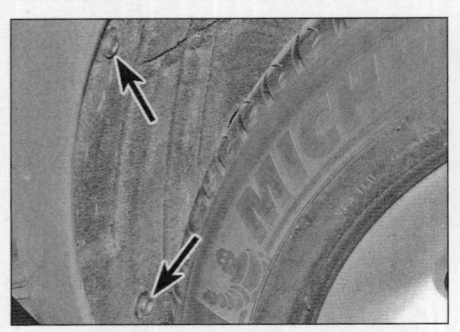

6.25 2 bolts (arrowed) secure the wheel arch liner to the bumper each side

6.27a Undo the bolt in the tailgate aperture . . .

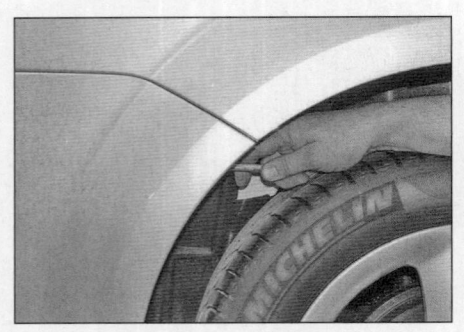

6.27b . . . and the nut securing the bumper to the wing

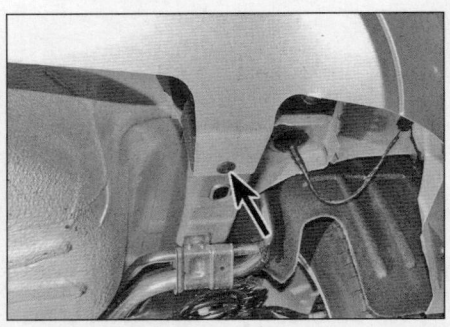

6.28 Undo the bolt each side (arrowed) on the underside of the bumper

6.32 Undo the bolt (arrowed) in the tailgate aperture

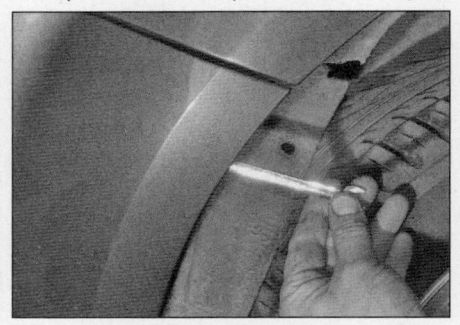

6.33 Undo the nut each side behind the wheel arch liner

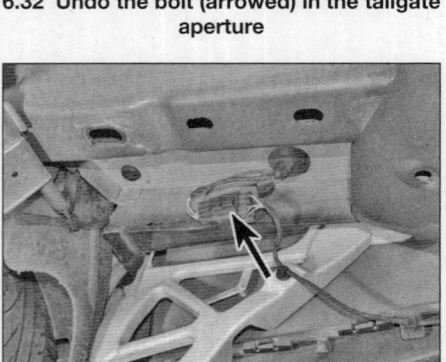

6.34 Disconnect the wiring plug under the right-hand side of the bumper (arrowed)

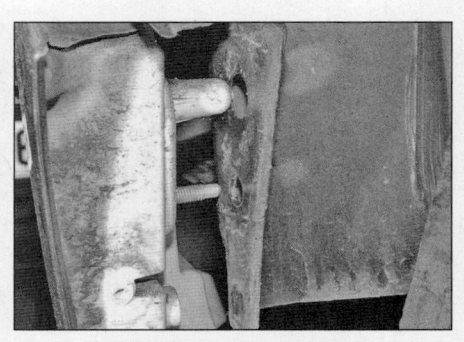

6.35 Pull the front edges of the bumper outwards to disengage the locating lugs

25 Undo the 2 bolts each side securing the mudflap/wheel arch liner to the bumper **(see illustration)**.
26 Disconnect the wiring plug for the rear foglamp/reversing light/parking assistance sensors (as applicable).
27 The bumper is retained by 1 bolt each side in the tailgate aperture, and a nut each side at its front, inner edge **(see illustrations)**. Remove the bolts and nuts.
28 Undo the bolts on the bumper underside, and prise out the plastic inserts **(see illustration)**. With the help of an assistant, pull the sides away from the body, and withdraw the bumper rearwards.

Estate models up to 12/2007

29 Chock the front wheels, jack up the rear of the vehicle and support it on axle stands (see *Jacking and vehicle support*).
30 Undo the 2 bolts each side securing the mudflap/wheel arch liner to the bumper.
31 Remove the 2 retaining bolts and pull out the plastic expanding rivets from the bumper underside **(see illustration 6.28)**.
32 Undo the bolt each side in the tailgate aperture **(see illustration)**.
33 Pull forwards the wheel arch liner, then undo the nut each side securing the bumper **(see illustration)**.
34 Disconnect the wiring plug for the rear foglamp/reversing light/parking assistance sensors (as applicable) **(see illustration)**.
35 With the help of an assistant, pull out the front edges, and manoeuvre the bumper rearwards **(see illustration)**.

Estate models from 12/2007

36 Chock the front wheels, jack up the rear of the vehicle and support it on axle stands (see *Jacking and vehicle support*).
37 Disconnect the wiring plug for the rear foglamp/reversing light/parking assistance sensors (as applicable).
38 Undo the 2 bolts each side securing the mudflap/wheel arch liner to the bumper.
39 Remove the 2 retaining bolts and pull out the plastic expanding rivets from the bumper underside **(see illustration 6.28)**.
40 Undo the bolt each side in the tailgate aperture **(see illustration 6.32)**.
41 Undo the nut each side, and release the clip securing the bumper to the rear wings **(see illustration 6.33)**.
42 Disconnect the wiring plug for the rear foglamp/reversing light/parking assistance sensors (as applicable).
43 Release the 3 clips at the top edge of the bumper and, with the help of an assistant, pull the sides away from the body and manoeuvre the bumper rearwards.

Saloon models up to 12/2007

44 Chock the front wheels, jack up the rear of the vehicle and support it on axle stands (see *Jacking and vehicle support*).
45 Carefully prise out the moulding strip each side of the bumper, and undo the bolt each side **(see illustrations)**.
46 Undo the 2 scrivets on the lower edge of the bumper **(see illustration 6.28)**.
47 Disconnect the wiring plug for the rear foglamp/reversing light/parking assistance sensors (as applicable).
48 Undo the 2 bolts each side securing the mudflap/wheel arch liner to the bumper.
49 Undo the bolt each side in the boot lid aperture **(see illustration)**.

Bodywork and fittings 11•7

50 Undo the nut each side, and release the clip securing the bumper to the rear wings **(see illustration)**.
51 Release the 3 clips at the top edge of the bumper and, with the help of an assistant, pull the sides away from the body and manoeuvre the bumper rearwards.

Saloon models from 12/2007

52 Chock the front wheels, jack up the rear of the vehicle and support it on axle stands (see *Jacking and vehicle support*). Open up the boot.
53 Undo the 2 bolts each side securing the mudflap/wheel arch liner to the bumper.
54 Disconnect the wiring plug for the rear foglamp/reversing light/parking assistance sensors (as applicable).
55 The bumper is retained by 2 bolts each side in the boot lid aperture. Remove the bolts, then with the help of an assistant, pull the sides away from the body, and withdraw the bumper rearwards.

All models

56 If required, the parking distance sensors can be removed from the bumper cover, by depressing the retaining tangs and withdrawing the sensor.

Refitting

57 Refitting is a reversal of the removal procedure. Make sure that, where applicable, the bumper guides are located correctly. Check all electrical components that have been disconnected.

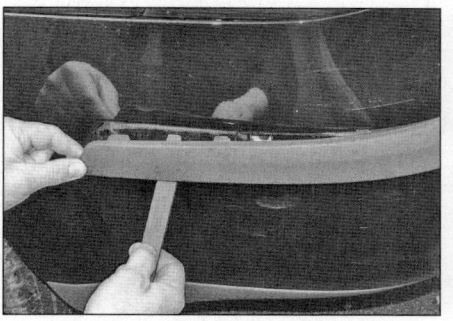

7 Radiator grille – removal and refitting

Removal

1 Support the bonnet in the open position. Undo the 4 scrivets and remove the plastic panel above the radiator grille **(see illustrations)**.
2 Release the 2 clips securing the bonnet lock linkage to the radiator grille **(see illustration)**.

6.45a Prise away the moulding . . .

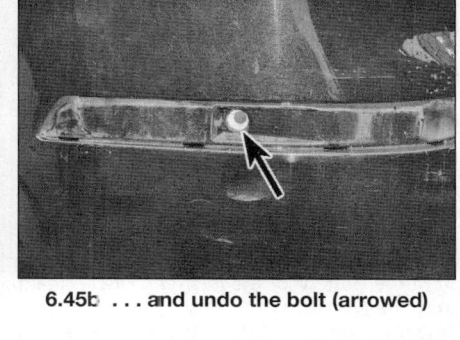

6.45b . . . and undo the bolt (arrowed)

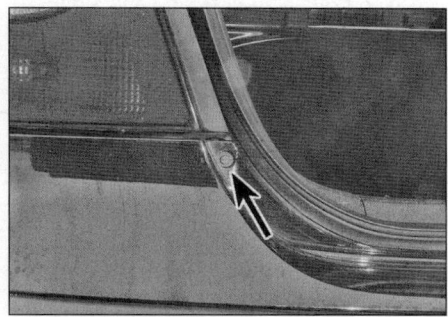

6.49 Undo the bolt (arrowed) in the boot lid aperture

6.50 Undo the nut each side behind the wheel arch liner

3 Unscrew the 2 radiator grille upper mounting scrivets **(see illustration)**.
4 Pivot the grille forwards, the undo the 2 lower clips and remove the grille **(see illustration)**.

Refitting

5 Refitting is a reversal of the removal procedure.

7.1a Undo the bolt and prise out the scrivets . . .

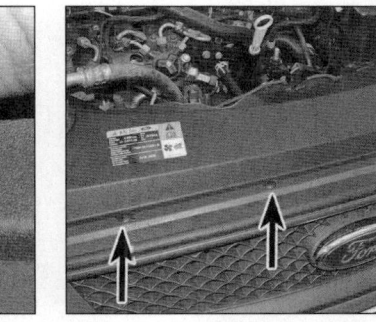

7.1b . . . along the front edge (arrowed) of the air deflector panel

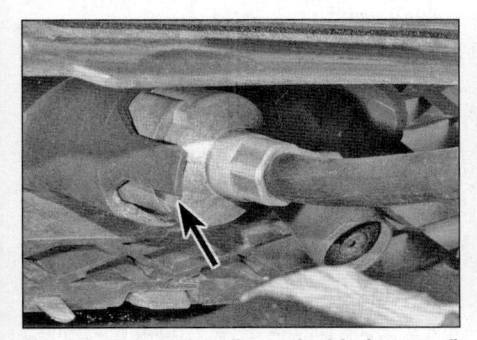

7.2 Prise apart the clip each side (arrowed) to release the bonnet lock linkage

7.3 Remove the scrivet each side of the radiator grille (arrowed)

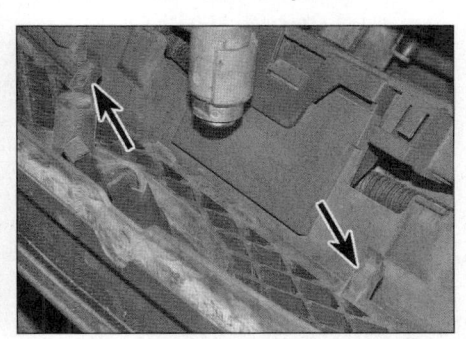

7.4 Radiator grille lower clips (arrowed)

8 Bonnet –
removal, refitting and adjustment

Removal

1 Open the bonnet, and support it in the open position using the stay. Where fitted, release the clips and remove the bonnet insulation panel.
2 Disconnect the windscreen washer hoses from the bottom of the jets, and unclip them from the bonnet.
3 Disconnect the windscreen washer wiring connector from the bottom of the jets, and unclip from the bonnet.
4 To assist in correctly realigning the bonnet when refitting it, mark the outline of the hinges with a soft pencil. Loosen the

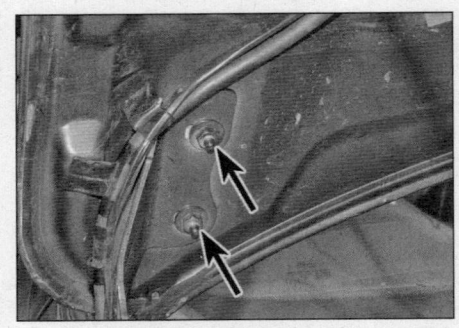

8.4 Bonnet hinge retaining nuts (arrowed)

two hinge retaining nuts on each side (see illustration).
5 With the help of an assistant, unscrew the four nuts, release the stay, and lift the bonnet from the vehicle.

Refitting and adjustment

6 Refitting is a reversal of the removal procedure, noting the following points:
a) Position the bonnet hinges within the outline marks made during removal, but if necessary, alter its position to provide a uniform gap all round.
b) Adjust the front height by repositioning the lock (see Section 9) and turning the rubber buffers on the engine compartment front cross panel up or down to support the bonnet.

9 Bonnet lock –
removal, refitting and adjustment

Removal

1 Undo the 4 bolts, release the 2 clips and remove the air deflector panel over the bonnet lock (see illustrations 7.1a and 7.1b).
2 Make alignment marks between the lock and panel, then undo the 2 bolts securing the lock assembly to the bonnet slam panel (see illustration).
3 Note its fitted position, then detach the bonnet lock key cylinder link rod from the lock assembly (see illustration).
4 Disconnect the wiring connector from the lock assembly, as it is being removed.
5 Push the lock cylinder from the housing, using a screwdriver to unclip it.

Refitting and adjustment

6 Refitting is a reversal of the removal procedure, starting by positioning the lock as noted before removal.
7 If the front of the bonnet is not level with the front wings, the lock may be moved up or down within the mounting holes. After making an adjustment, raise or lower the rubber buffers to support the bonnet correctly.

9.2 Undo the bonnet lock bolts

9.3 Release the clip (arrowed) each side of the link rod

10 Door inner trim panel –
removal and refitting

Removal

1 Disconnect the battery negative (earth) lead (Chapter 5A).

Front door

2 Operate the inner door release handle, and carefully pull the bezel from place (see illustrations). Disconnect the keyless entry/door lock/electric window (as applicable) switch wiring plug as the bezel is withdrawn (where fitted).
3 Insert a blunt, flat-bladed tool under the door grab handle, then twist it to unclip the cover trim. Undo the two bolts from behind the cover inside the door pull handle (see illustrations).
4 If working on the driver's door, disconnect the wiring connector from the window operating switch.

10.2a Starting at the front edge, carefully pull the interior handle bezel from place

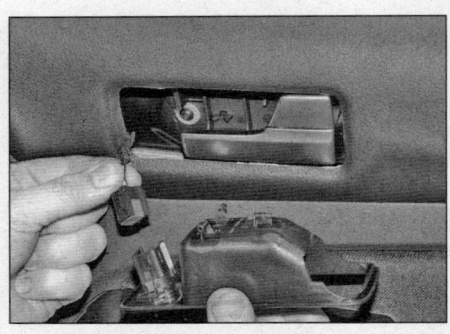

10.2b Disconnect the switch wiring plug

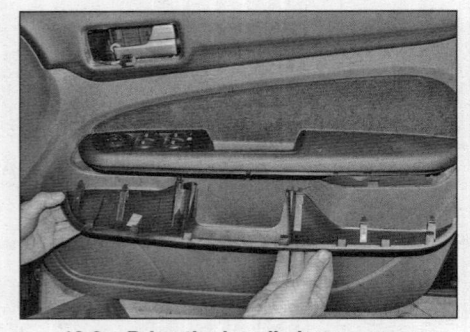

10.3a Prise the handle lower cover downwards . . .

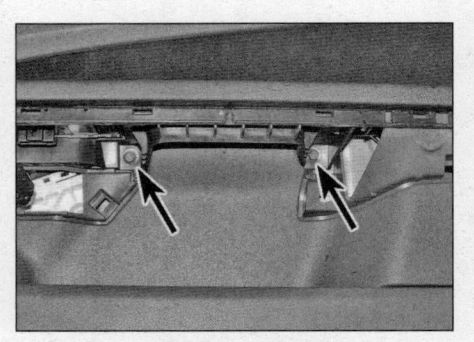

10.3b . . . and undo the 2 bolts in the recess (arrowed)

Bodywork and fittings 11•9

10.5a Use a forked tool to lever between the door panel retaining clips and their collars (arrowed) – shown with the panel removed for clarity

10.5b With the clips released, remove the panel

5 Working around the outer edge, use a forked trim release tool to release the retaining clips securing the trim panel **(see illustrations)**.

Rear door

6 Operate the inner door release handle, and carefully pull the bezel from place **(see illustration)**. Disconnect the window switch wiring plug as the bezel is withdrawn.

7 On models fitted with manual (ie, non-electric) rear windows, fully shut the window, and note the position of the regulator handle. Release the spring clip by inserting a clean cloth between the handle and the door trim. Using a 'sawing' action, pull the cloth against the open ends of the clip to release it, at the same time pulling the handle from the regulator shaft splines. Withdraw the handle and the spacer **(see illustrations)**.

8 Carefully prise the cover from the door grab handle. Undo the two bolts from behind the cover inside the door pull handle **(see illustrations)**.

9 Working around the outer edge, use a forked trim release tool to release the retaining clips **(see illustration 10.5a)** securing the trim panel **(see illustration)**. Disconnect the tweeter speaker wiring plug (where fitted) as the panel is withdrawn.

10.6 Carefully pull the handle bezel from place

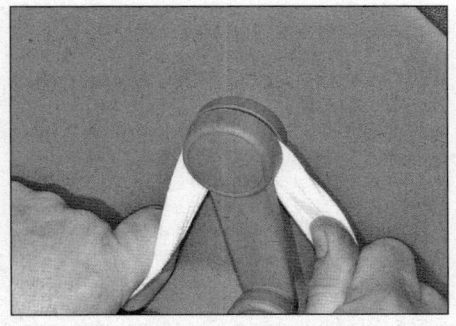

10.7a Use a clean cloth and a sawing motion to release the regulator handle retaining clip

10.7b The edges of the clip (arrowed) must be pushed towards the handle

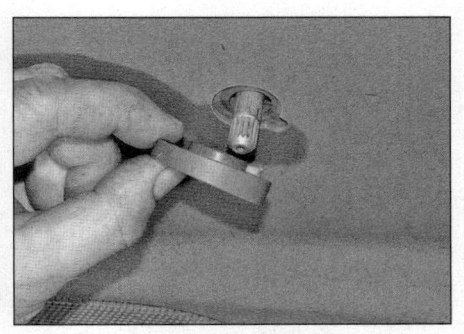

10.7c Recover the handle spacer

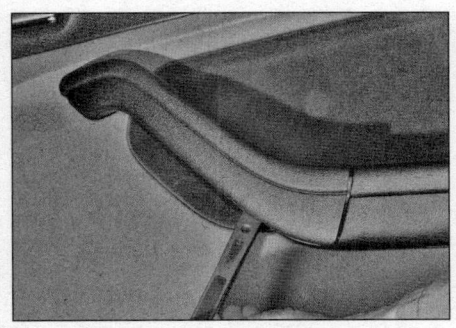

10.8a Prise the cover from the door grab handle . . .

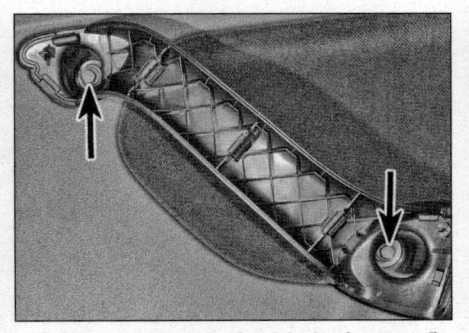

10.8b . . . and undo the 2 bolts (arrowed)

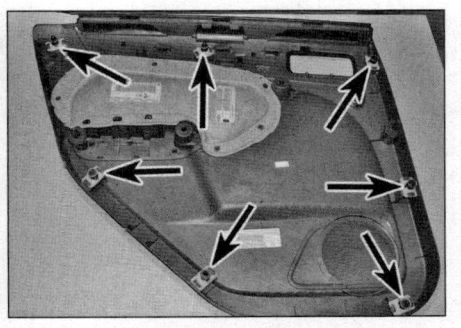

10.9 Rear inner door panel retaining clips (arrowed)

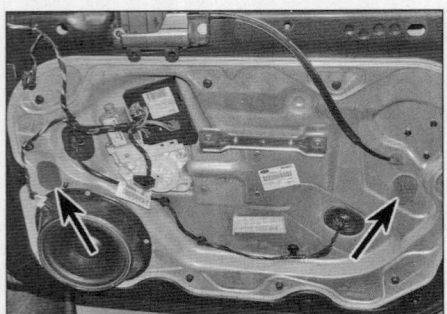

11•10 Bodywork and fittings

11.2 Prise the rubber grommets (arrowed) from the panel

11.3 Pull the inner weather strip up from the door

11.5 Align the window clamp bolts with the apertures in the panel

Refitting

10 Refitting is a reversal of the removal procedure. On the rear manual windows, ensure the retaining clip is fitted to the winder handle before refitting the handle to the regulator shaft.

11 Door window glass – removal and refitting

Removal

Front door

1 Remove the door inner trim panel as described in Section 10.
2 Prise the rubber grommet from the front and rear of the door panel to access the window clamps **(see illustration)**.

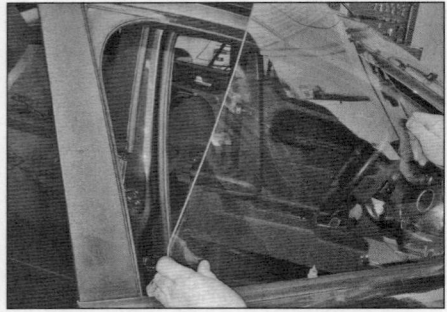

11.7 Lift the rear of the window and withdraw it from the outside of the door

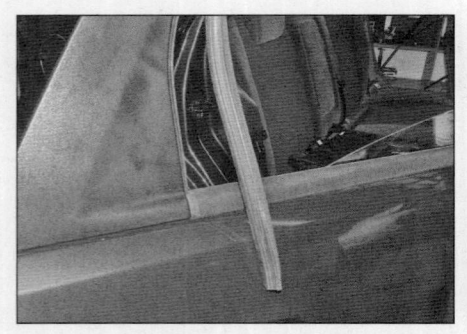

11.9b ... and rear window guide rubbers

3 Carefully prise the rubber inner weather strip from the door **(see illustration)**.
4 Reconnect the door window switch, and reconnect the battery negative lead.
5 Operate the window switch and align the window clamps bolts with the apertures exposed by removing the grommets **(see illustration)**.
6 Slacken each of the window clamp bolts by 2 turns.
7 Lift the window glass from the door while tilting it up at the rear, and withdraw it from the outside of the door frame **(see illustration)**.

Rear door

8 Remove the door window regulator panel as described in Section 12. Note that there is no need to drill out the rivets securing the regulator to the panel.
9 Lower the window, then prise out the lower sections of the window guide rubber at

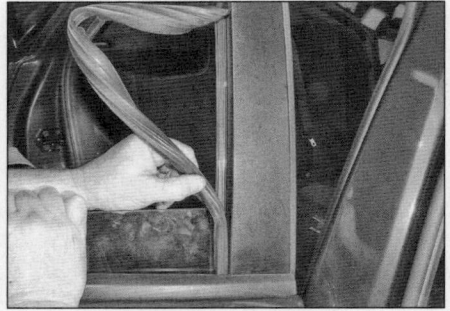

11.9a Prise out the front ...

11.10 Prise up the door inner weather strip

the front and rear of the window frame **(see illustrations)**.
10 Carefully prise the rubber inner weather strip from the door **(see illustration)**.
11 Lift the window glass from the door while tilting it up at the rear, and withdraw it from the outside of the door frame **(see illustration)**.

Refitting

12 Refitting is a reversal of the removal procedure, making sure that the glass is correctly located in the clamps.

12 Door window regulator – removal and refitting

Removal

Front door

1 Remove the front door window as described in Section 11.
2 Disconnect the wiring plugs, then undo the 3 bolts and remove the electric window motor **(see illustration)**.
3 Disconnect the cable from the door inner release handle **(see illustration)**.
4 Remove the exterior handle as described in Section 13.
5 Prise off the tweeter speaker cover **(see illustration)**.
6 Undo the retaining bolt, pull the exterior mirror trim panel from the door, and lift it from place **(see illustration)**. Disconnect the wiring plug(s) as the panel is withdrawn.

11.11 Tilt it up at the rear, and remove the glass from the door

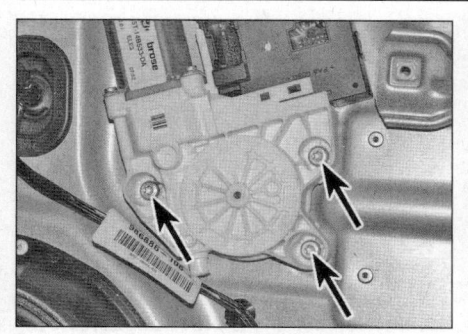

Bodywork and fittings 11•11

12.2 Window motor retaining bolts (arrowed)

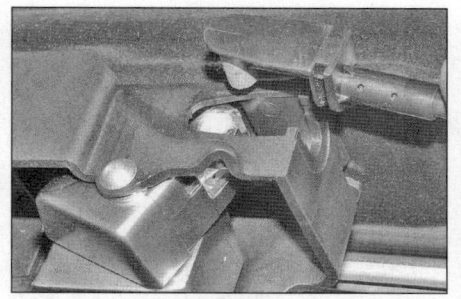

12.3 Push the lock button into the door, then lift the release cable end fitting from the handle

12.5 Prise the 'tweeter' cover from place

7 Undo the 10 bolts securing the inner panel to the door frame (see illustration).
8 Undo the 5 bolts securing the door lock to the door (see illustrations).
9 Manoeuvre the panel from the door (see illustration).
10 Using a suitable sized drill bit, remove the 6 (3-door models) or 4 (4/5-door models) rivets securing the window regulator to the door panel (see illustrations).

Rear door

11 Remove the rear door inner trim panel as described in Section 10.
12 Prise the foam/rubber grommet from the front and rear of the door panel to access the window clamps (see illustration).
13 On models with manual windows, refit the window winder handle, and fully lower the window.

12.6 Undo the bolt (arrowed) and pull the mirror trim panel from the door

14 On models with electric windows, reconnect the window switch and the battery negative lead, then fully lower the window.

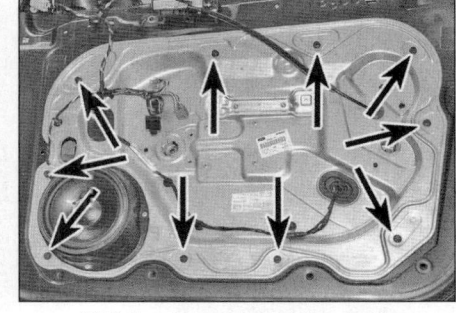

12.7 Inner panel retaining bolts (arrowed)

15 Operate the window switch/handle and align the window clamp bolts with the apertures exposed by removing the grommets (see illustration).

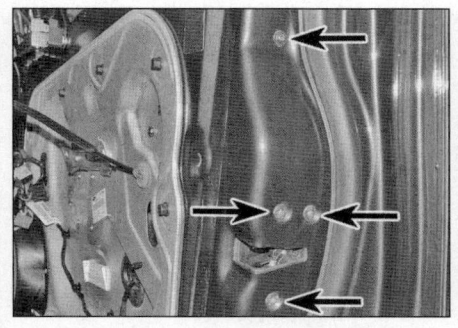

12.8a Undo the 4 bolts (arrowed) at the end of the door ...

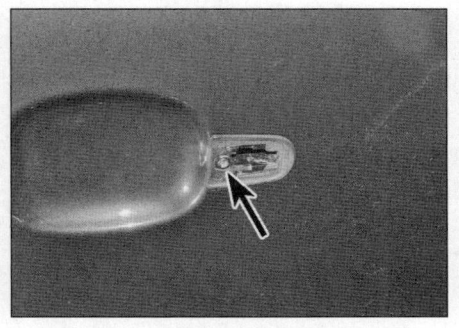

12.8b ... and the one (arrowed) on the outside of the door

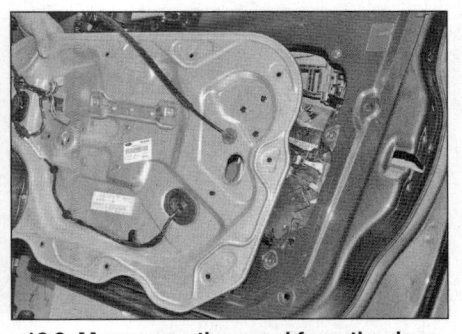

12.9 Manoeuvre the panel from the door

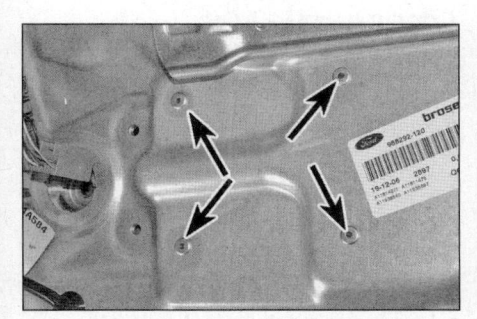

12.10a Drill out the rivets (arrowed) securing the regulator to the panel – 4/5-door model

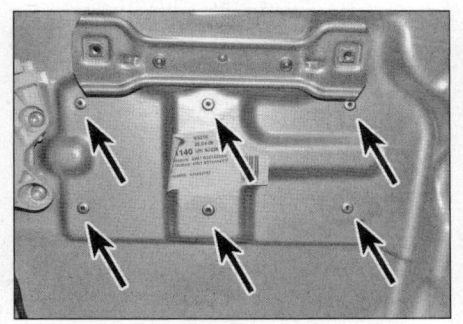

12.10b 3-door model regulator rivets (arrowed)

12.12 Prise out the grommets (arrowed) to access the window clamps

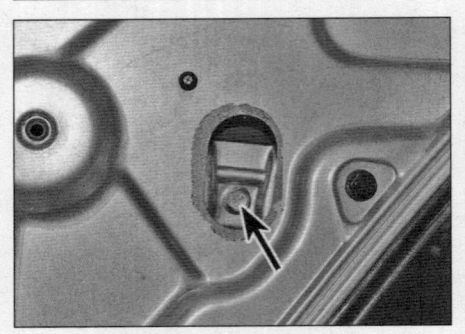

11•12 Bodywork and fittings

12.15 Raise the window until the clamp bolt is visible (arrowed)

12.17 Undo the bolts and pull the window motor from the panel

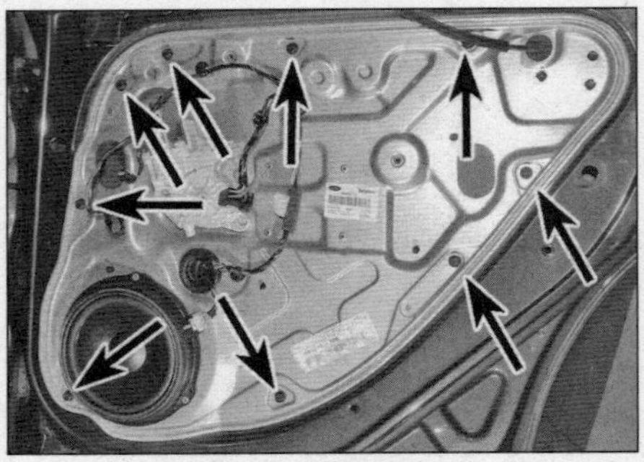

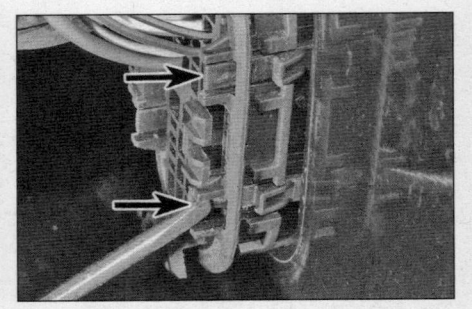

12.19a Release the 2 clips each side of the connector (arrowed) and pull it from the pillar

12.19b Disconnect the door wiring plug

12.21 Rear door panel bolts (arrowed)

16 Slacken the clamp bolts two turns, then lift the window to the top of the door and secure it in place using tape.
17 On models with electric windows, undo the 3 bolts and remove the window regulator motor (see illustration). Disconnect the wiring plug as the motor is withdrawn.
18 Set the handle in the 'Lock' position, then lift the interior door release handle operating cable end fitting upwards, and disconnect it (see illustration 12.3).
19 Close the door, prise away the rubber gaiter, release the 4 clips and pull the connector from the door pillar, then disconnect the door wiring plug (see illustrations). Push the wiring harness into the door.
20 Open the door, and remove the exterior handle as described in Section 13.
21 Undo the 9 bolts securing the inner panel to the door frame (see illustration).
22 Undo the 4 bolts securing the door lock at the rear edge of the door, and the single bolt securing the exterior handle frame to the door (see illustrations). Manoeuvre the panel/regulator from the door.
23 Using a suitable-sized drill bit, remove the 5 rivets (manual windows) or 4 rivets (electric windows) securing the window regulator to the door panel (see illustration).

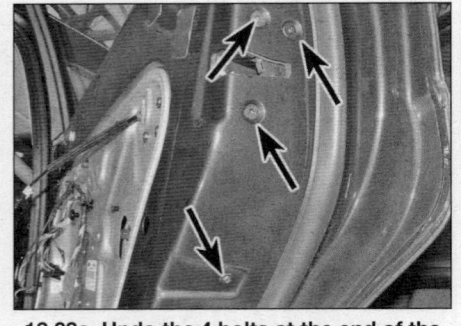

Refitting

24 Refitting is a reversal of the removal procedure.

13 Door handle and lock components – removal and refitting

12.22a Undo the 4 bolts at the end of the door (arrowed) . . .

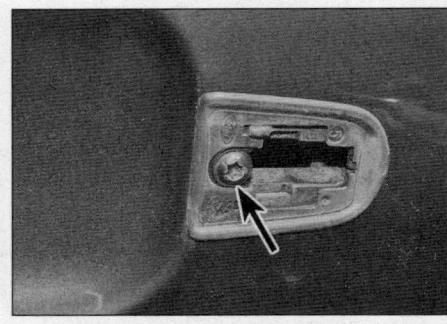

12.22b . . . and one on the outside of the door (arrowed)

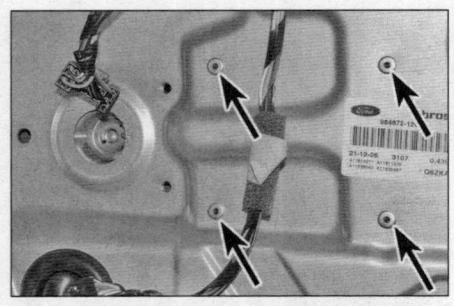

⚠ *Warning: before working on any electrical components, disconnect the battery negative (earth) lead (Chapter 5A).*

Removal

Exterior handle – front

1 Prise out the rubber grommet from the end of the door adjacent to the exterior handle (see illustration).
2 Working through the aperture, slacken the handle retaining bolt approximately 22 turns (see illustration).
3 Carefully pull the trim and lock cylinder from the door (see illustration). On models with the Keyless Entry system, remove the trim at the rear of the handle (where the lock cylinder would be on conventional systems).
4 Pull the exterior handle rearwards, and manoeuvre it from the door. Recover the seals between the handle and the door skin.

12.23 Drill out the rivets (arrowed) securing the regulator to the panel – electric window model

13.1 Prise out the grommet at the end of the door

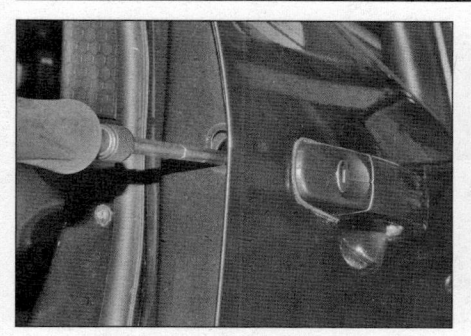

Bodywork and fittings 11•13

13.2 Slacken the handle retaining bolt approximately 22 turns . . .

13.3 . . . until the lock cylinder and trim can be pulled from the door

13.6 Prise out the grommet . . .

5 On models with the Keyless Entry system, gently pull the handle antenna wiring harness until an audible click is heard, and the harness connector is in the horizontal position. Disconnect the wiring plug.

Exterior handle – rear

6 Prise out the rubber grommet from the end of the door adjacent to the exterior handle **(see illustration)**.
7 Working through the aperture, slacken the handle retaining bolt approximately 7 turns **(see illustration)**.
8 Pull the trim at the rear of the handle outwards **(see illustration)**.
9 Pull the exterior handle rearwards, and manoeuvre it from the door. Recover the seals between the handle and the door skin.

Interior handle

10 Remove the door inner trim panel Section 10.
11 Detach the door release handle from the door by undoing the bolt, unclipping the front end, then slide the handle out in a forwards direction **(see illustrations)**.
12 Set the handle in the 'Lock' position, then lift the operating cable end fitting upwards, and disconnect it **(see illustration 12.3)**.

Lock motor/module – front

13 Proceed as described in paragraphs 1 to 10 of Section 12.
14 Press in the centre pins, prise out the plastic rivets securing the lock and latch retaining bracket to the door panel **(see illustration)**. Disconnect the lock wiring plugs as it's withdrawn.

13.7 . . . undo the bolt approximately 7 turns . . .

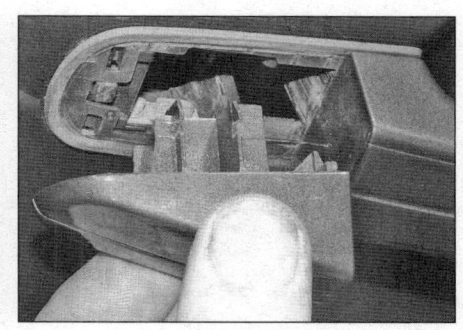

13.8 . . . until the trim can be removed

15 Depress the retaining clips each side of the lock remote control cable outer fitting, and pull it from the support bracket, then rotate the cable end fitting 90° and detach it from the lever on the lock **(see illustration)**.

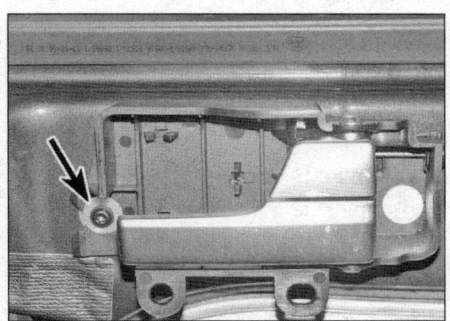

13.11a Undo the bolt (arrowed) . . .

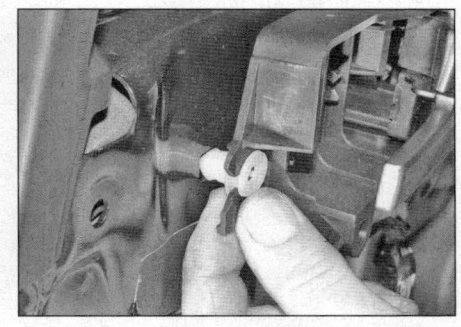

Repeat this procedure on the exterior handle cable.
16 Using a suitable-sized drill bit, remove the rivet securing the lock to the bracket **(see illustration)**.

13.11b . . . and pull the front end of the handle assembly from the door

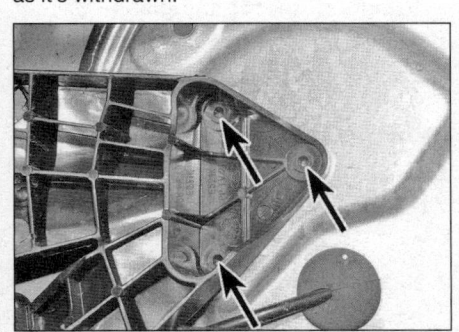

13.14 Push in the centre pins of the 3 rivets (arrowed)

13.15 Depress the clips (arrowed) and pull the fitting from the bracket

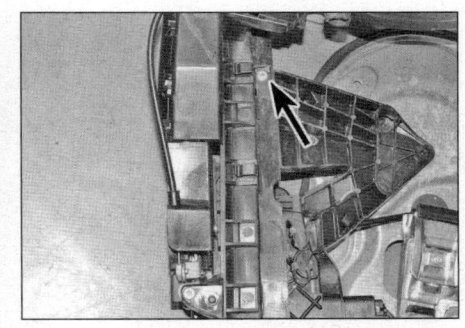

13.16 Drill out the rivet (arrowed) securing the lock to the bracket

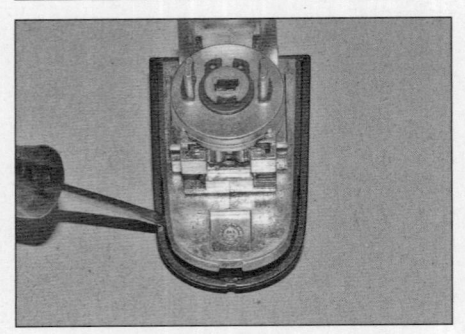

11•14 Bodywork and fittings

13.19a Release the clip each side . . .

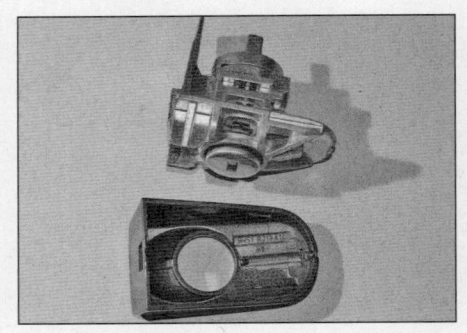

13.19b . . . and detach the cover from the lock cylinder

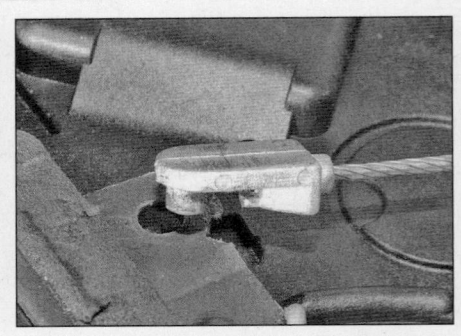

13.21 Rotate the end fitting and detach it from the lever

13.22 Press the centres from the 3 rivets . . .

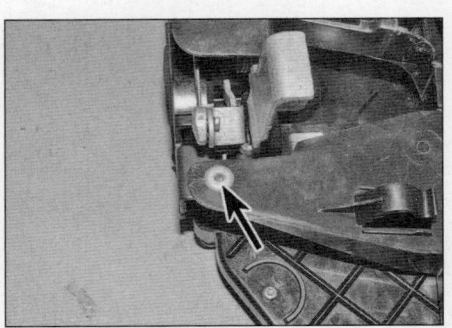

13.23 . . . and drill out the rivet securing the lock to the bracket (arrowed)

Lock cylinder

17 Prise out the rubber grommet from the end of the door adjacent to the exterior handle **(see illustration 13.1)**.
18 Working through the aperture, slacken the handle retaining bolt approximately 22 turns **(see illustration 13.2)**.
19 Pull the trim and lock cylinder from the door **(see illustration 13.3)**. If required, release the clip each side with a small screwdriver, and separate the lock cylinder from the trim **(see illustrations)**

Lock motor/module – rear

20 Proceed as described in paragraphs 12 to 22 of Section 12.
21 Depress the retaining clips each side of the lock remote control cable outer fitting, and pull it from the support bracket **(see illustration 13.15)**, then rotate the cable end fitting and detach it from the lever on the lock

(see illustration). Repeat this procedure on the exterior handle cable.
22 Using a suitably-sized rod, drive out the centres of the 3 plastic rivets securing the lock and latch retaining bracket to the door panel **(see illustration)**. Disconnect the lock wiring plugs as it's withdrawn.
23 Using a suitable-sized drill bit, remove the rivet securing the lock to the bracket **(see illustration)**.

Refitting

Handles (exterior and interior)

24 Refitting is a reversal of the removal procedure. When refitting the exterior handle on models with the Keyless Entry system, reconnect the antenna wiring connector and push it into the holder.

Lock cylinder

25 Refitting is a reversal of removal.

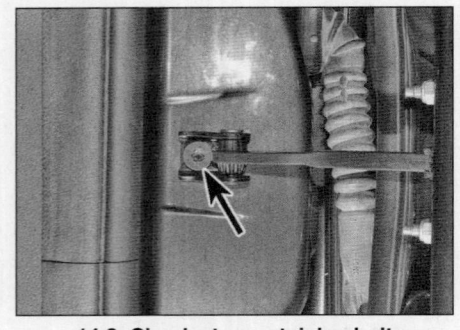

14.2 Check strap retaining bolt (arrowed)

14.3 Undo the upper and lower hinge bolts

Lock motor/modules

26 Refitting is a reversal of the removal procedure, but check that the door lock passes over the striker centrally. If necessary, reposition the striker before fully tightening the mounting bolts.

14 Door – removal and refitting

Removal

1 Disconnect the battery negative (earth) lead (Chapter 5A).
2 Using a Torx key, unscrew and remove the check strap mounting bolt from the door pillar **(see illustration)**.
3 Have an assistant support the door, then undo the retaining bolts in the top and bottom hinges **(see illustration)**.
4 Carefully lift the door from the hinges, and support it on a trolley jack or similar.
5 Prise out the rubber gaiter, and disconnect the wiring block connector **(see illustrations 12.19a and 12.19b)**.

Refitting

6 Refitting is a reversal of the removal procedure, but check that the door lock passes over the striker centrally. If necessary, reposition the striker.

15 Exterior mirror and glass – removal and refitting

Removal

Mirror

1 Unclip the trim panel from the front of the window opening over the tweeter speaker and remove it **(see illustration 12.6)**.
2 Undo the retaining bolt, then starting at the top, pull the exterior mirror trim panel from the door, and lift it from place **(see illustration 12.7)**. Disconnect the wiring plug as the panel is withdrawn

Bodywork and fittings 11•15

3 Unscrew the mirror mounting bolts, then release the clip and withdraw the mirror from the outside of the door. Recover the mirror seal as the wiring/cable is being drawn through the rubber grommet **(see illustrations)**.

Mirror glass
4 Pull the outer edge of the glass rearwards, insert a flat-bladed screwdriver and gently prise the glass from place **(see illustrations)**.
5 Withdraw the mirror glass and disconnect the wiring connectors for the heated mirrors.

Refitting
6 Refitting is a reversal of the removal procedure. Take care not to drop the rubber grommet inside the door panel when removing the mirror, as the interior door trim will have to be removed to retrieve it.

16 Interior mirror –
removal and refitting

Basic mirror
1 Press the retaining clip away from the windscreen, then slide the mirror up from the base **(see illustrations)**.
2 Refitting is a reversal of removal.

Auto-dimming mirror
3 Squeeze together the sides, and slide up the mirror base upper cover **(see illustration)**.
4 Pull apart the top edges and slide down the mirror base lower cover **(see illustration)**.
5 Disconnect the mirror wiring plug (where applicable).
6 Rotate the mirror base 60° anti-clockwise and detach it from the mounting **(see illustration)**.
7 Refitting is the reversal of the removal procedure.

17 Boot lid –
removal and refitting

Removal
1 Disconnect the battery negative (earth) lead (Chapter 5A), and open the boot lid.

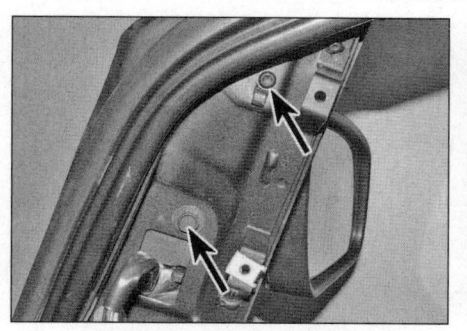

15.3a Mirror mounting bolts (arrowed)

15.3b Recover the mirror housing seal

15.4a Insert a screwdriver and gently prise the mirror from place

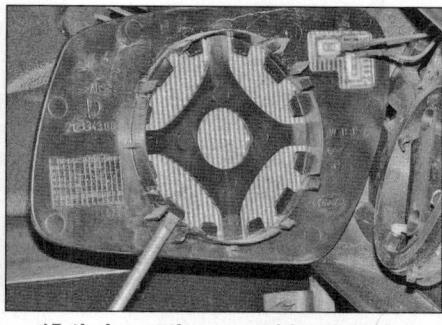

15.4b Insert the screwdriver into the mirror retaining clip as shown

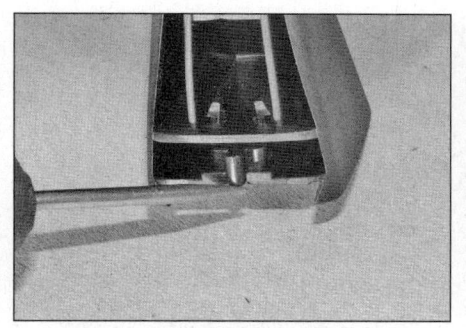

2 Undo the bolts, and prise out the scrivets securing the trim panel to the boot lid **(see illustration)**.

3 Pull down the edge of the boot lid trim panel, and carefully prise the interior grab handle from the lid **(see illustration)**.

16.1a Push the clip at the base of the mirror rearwards, and slide it up from the windscreen mounting

16.1b Mirror retaining clip – viewed from the front face of the mirror base

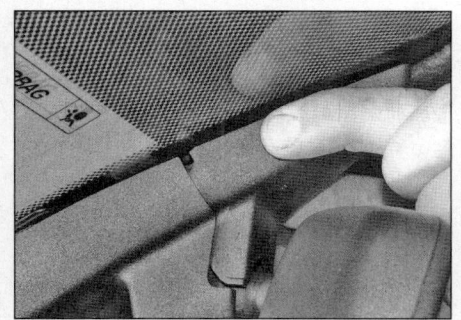

16.3 Squeeze together the sides and slide up the upper cover

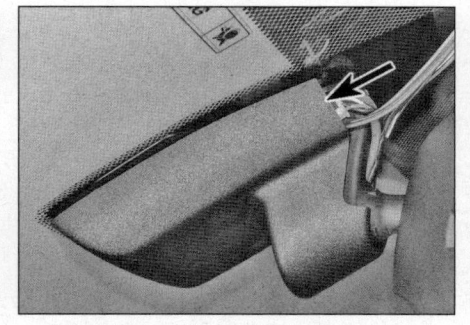

16.4 Pull apart the top edges (arrowed) and slide down the lower cover

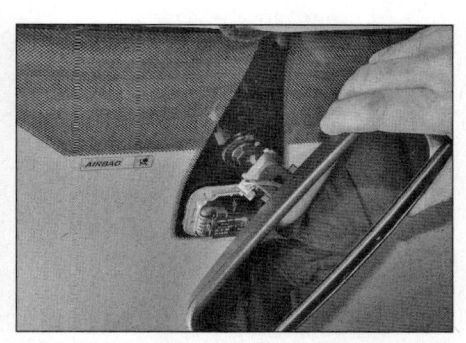

16.6 Rotate the mirror 60° anti-clockwise to release it

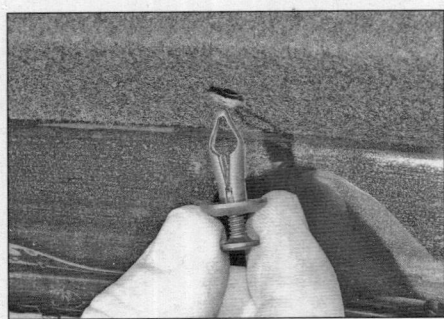

11•16 Bodywork and fittings

17.2 Undo the bolt and prise out the scrivets

17.3 Pull down the edge of the boot lid trim, and prise the grab handle from the lid

17.5 Pull the rubber grommet from the boot lid

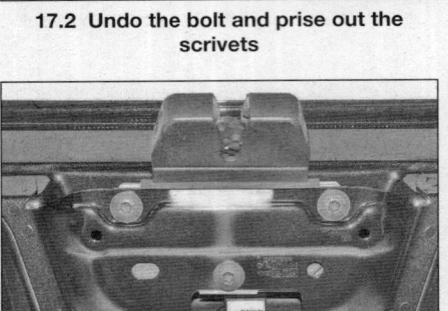

18.3 Boot lid lock wiring plug (arrowed)

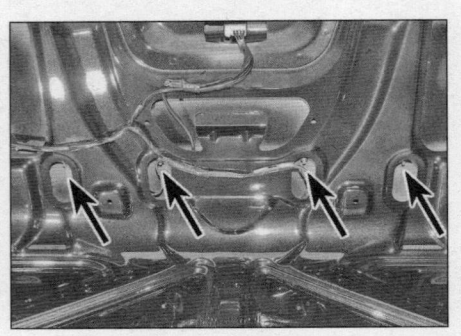

18.5 Undo the 4 nuts (arrowed) and remove the release button assembly

4 Note their fitted positions, then disconnect the various wiring connectors on the inside of the boot lid.
5 Prise the rubber grommet from the left-hand corner of the boot lid, and pull the wiring loom through (see illustration).
6 Mark the position of the hinge arms with a pencil. Place rags beneath each corner of the boot lid, to prevent damage to the paintwork.
7 With the help of an assistant, unscrew the mounting bolts and lift the boot lid from the car.

Refitting

8 Refitting is a reversal of the removal procedure, noting the following points:
 a) Check that the boot lid is correctly aligned with the surrounding bodywork, with an equal clearance around its edge.
 b) Adjustment can be made by loosening the hinge bolts, and moving the boot lid within the elongated mounting holes.
 c) Check that the lock enters the striker centrally when the boot lid is closed.

18 Boot lid lock components – removal and refitting

Removal

1 Undo the bolts, and prise out the scrivets securing the trim panel to the boot lid (see illustration 17.2).
2 Pull down the edge of the boot lid trim panel, and carefully prise the interior grab handle from the lid (see illustration 17.3).
3 Disconnect the wiring plug from the lock assembly (see illustration).
4 Using a Torx key, unscrew the lock mounting bolts, and withdraw the lock.
5 If required, undo the nuts and remove the boot lid lock release button assembly (see illustration).

Refitting

6 Refitting is a reversal of the removal procedure.

19 Tailgate – removal and refitting

Removal

1 Disconnect the battery negative (earth) lead (Chapter 5A).
2 The tailgate may be unbolted from the hinges and the hinges left in position.
3 On models without a rear spoiler, remove the two bolts from the high-level brake light cover, and disconnect the bulbholder wiring and washer pipe (see illustrations). On models with a rear spoiler, undo the bolts, remove the high-level brake light and disconnect the wiring plug, then starting at the front edge, prise out the washer jet and disconnect the hose.
4 Undo the retaining bolts in the handle recesses, then pull trim panel away from the tailgate to release the retaining clips.
5 Carefully unclip the upper central tailgate trim (where fitted), then pull the rear window side trims inwards to release the clips (see illustrations).

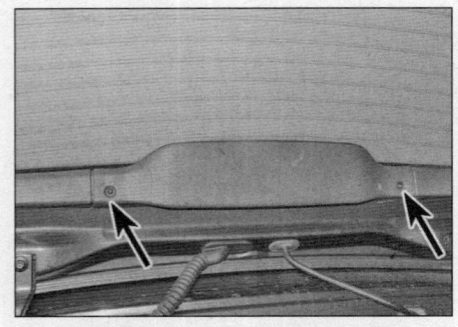

19.3a Undo the 2 bolts (arrowed) and remove the high-level brake light cover

19.3b Disconnect the washer jet pipe

19.3c On models with a rear spoiler, prise out the washer jet and disconnect the pipe

Bodywork and fittings 11•17

6 Disconnect the wiring loom connectors through the tailgate inner skin aperture including the earth wiring. Attach a strong fine cord to the end of the wiring loom, to act as an aid to guiding the wiring through the tailgate when it is refitted.
7 Prise the rubber grommet from the tailgate aperture, and pull out the wiring loom. Untie the cord, leaving it in position in the tailgate for guiding the wire through on refitting.
8 Have an assistant support the tailgate in its open position.
9 Using a small screwdriver, prise off the clip securing the struts to the tailgate. Pull the sockets from the ball-studs, and move the struts downwards (see illustration 20.2).
10 Unscrew and remove the hinge bolts (two each side) from the tailgate (see illustration). Withdraw the tailgate from the body aperture, taking care not to damage the paintwork.
11 If the hinges are to be removed from the roof panel, remove the D-pillar trim panels as described in Section 28.
12 Carefully pull down the rear edge of the headlining for access to the nuts and bolts. Take care not to damage the headlining.
13 Unscrew the mounting nuts and bolts for the hinges from the rear roof panel.

Refitting
14 Refitting is a reversal of the removal procedure, but check that the tailgate is located centrally in the body aperture, and that the striker enters the lock centrally. If necessary, loosen the mounting nuts and reposition the tailgate as required.

20 Support struts – removal and refitting

Removal
1 Have an assistant support the tailgate, boot or bonnet in its open position.
2 Prise off the upper spring clip securing the strut to the tailgate, boot or bonnet, then pull the socket from the ball-stud (see illustration).
3 Similarly prise off the bottom clip, and pull the socket from the ball-stud. Withdraw the strut.

Refitting
4 Refitting is a reversal of the removal procedure, making sure that the strut is fitted the same way up as when it was removed.

21 Tailgate lock components – removal and refitting

Removal
Estate
1 With the tailgate open, undo the 2 bolts in

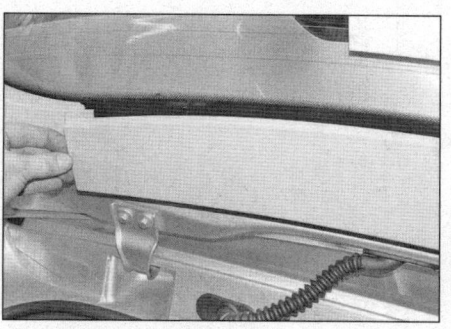

19.5a Pull away the upper, central tailgate trim (models with a rear spoiler)

19.10 Tailgate hinge bolts

the handle recesses and unclip the trim panel from the tailgate (see illustration).
2 Disconnect the electrical connector from the tailgate lock assembly (see illustration).
3 Undo the 3 lock securing bolts and remove the lock assembly.

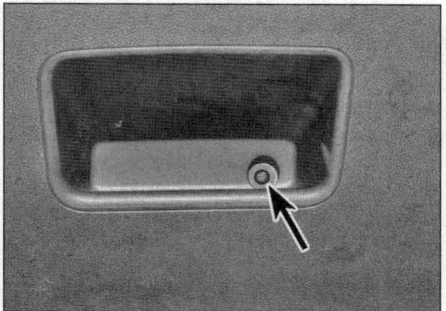

21.1 Undo the bolt in the tailgate handle recess (arrowed)

21.4 Undo the bolt (arrowed) each side in the handle recess

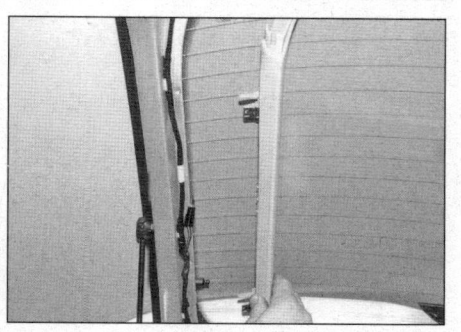

19.5b Pull the window side trims inwards

20.2 Prise the retaining clip from the ends of the strut

Hatchback
4 Undo the 2 bolts at the lower edge, and pull the interior trim panel from the tailgate (see illustration).
5 Disconnect the wiring plug from the lock assembly (see illustration).

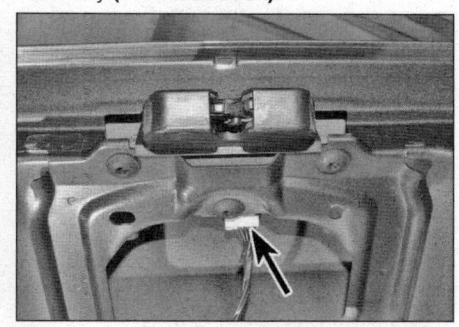

21.2 Tailgate lock wiring plug (arrowed)

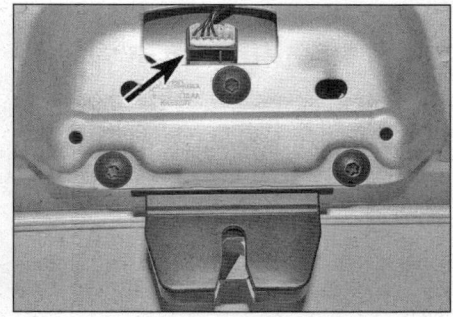

21.5 Tailgate lock wiring plug (arrowed)

11•18 Bodywork and fittings

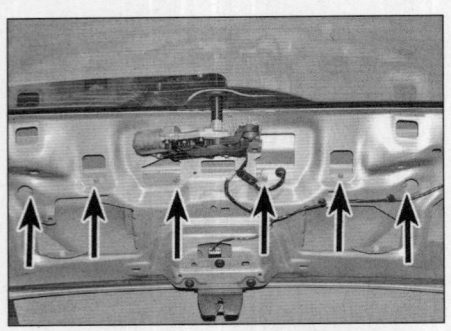

21.7 Undo the 6 nuts (arrowed) and remove the release button assembly

6 Using a Torx key, unscrew the lock mounting bolts, and withdraw the lock.
7 To remove the release button assembly, undo the 6 nuts and remove the panel from the tailgate **(see illustration)**. Unclip the button from the panel.

Refitting

8 Refitting is a reversal of the removal procedure.

22 Central locking system – testing, reprogramming, removal and refitting

Testing/reprogramming

1 Testing of the central locking/alarm system can only be carried out using Ford's WDS diagnostic tester.
2 Prior to reprogramming a remote locking transmitter, ensure the vehicle battery is fully-charged, and the alarm is not armed or triggered. Fasten all seat belts, and close all doors.
3 Turn the ignition switch from position I to position II four times within 6 seconds, then turn it to position 0 (off).
4 A chime will be heard to indicate that the 'learning mode' has begun.
5 Within 10 seconds of the previous step, press any button on the remote transmitter until a further chime is heard. This indicates the process has been successful. Turn the ignition switch to position II to exit the learning mode.

Removal

Generic electronic module (GEM)

Note: *If the GEM is to be renewed, the unit settings must be saved prior to removal, then initialised using the FORD WDS diagnostic tester.*

6 Removal and refitting of the GEM is described in Chapter 12.

Keyless entry system module

Note: *If the module is to be renewed, the unit settings must be saved prior to removal, then initialised using the FORD WDS diagnostic tester.*

7 Disconnect the battery negative lead as described in Chapter 5A.

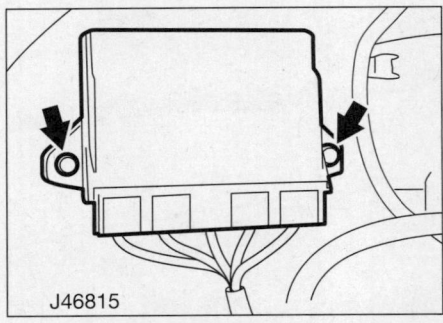

22.9 Keyless entry module retaining bolts (arrowed)

8 Remove the left-hand luggage compartment side panel, C-pillar panel and parcel shelf support as described in Section 28.
9 Undo the 2 retaining bolts, and remove the module **(see illustration)**. Disconnect the wiring plugs as the module is withdrawn.

Door motors

10 The door lock motors are integral with the locks. Refer to Section 13.

Boot lid/tailgate motor

11 The boot lid/tailgate motors are integral with the locks. Refer to Section 18 or 21 as applicable.

Refitting

12 In all cases, refitting is a reversal of the removal procedure.

23 Windscreen and fixed windows – removal and refitting

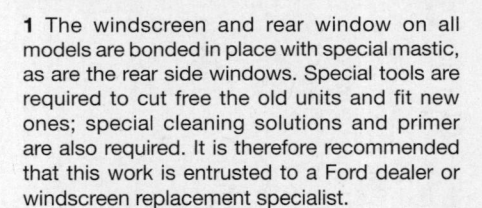

1 The windscreen and rear window on all models are bonded in place with special mastic, as are the rear side windows. Special tools are required to cut free the old units and fit new ones; special cleaning solutions and primer are also required. It is therefore recommended that this work is entrusted to a Ford dealer or windscreen replacement specialist.

24 Body side-trim mouldings and adhesive emblems – removal and refitting

Removal

1 Body side trims and mouldings are attached either by retaining clips or adhesive bonding. On bonded mouldings, insert a length of strong cord (fishing line is ideal) behind the moulding or emblem concerned. With a sawing action, break the adhesive bond between the moulding or emblem and the panel.
2 Thoroughly clean all traces of adhesive from the panel using methylated spirit, and allow the location to dry.
3 On mouldings with retaining clips, unclip the mouldings from the panel, taking care not to damage the paintwork.

Refitting

4 Peel back the protective paper from the rear face of the new moulding or emblem. Carefully fit it into position on the panel concerned, but take care not to touch the adhesive. When in position, apply hand pressure to the moulding/emblem for a short period, to ensure maximum adhesion to the panel.
5 Renew any broken retaining clips before refitting trims or mouldings.

25 Sunroof – general information and adjustment

Glass panel

1 Slide back the sun blind, and set the glass panel in the closed position.
2 Pull the panel guide arm covers inwards and remove them **(see illustration)**.
3 Undo the 2 retaining bolts each side, then lift the sunroof glass panel out from the vehicle.
4 When refitting, adjust the position of the rear edge of the panel so that it is flush with the roof, then tighten the bolts.
5 The remainder of refitting is a reversal of removal.

Sun blind

6 Remove the glass panel as described in paragraphs 1 to 3.
7 Close the sun blind, then undo the bolts each side securing the blind.
8 Manoeuvre the blind from the vehicle.
9 Refitting is a reversal of removal.

Sunroof mechanism and motor

10 Removal of the sunroof mechanism and/or motor involves removal of the headlining. This is a complex task, which requires patience and dexterity, and is considered to be beyond the scope of a DIYer. Consequently, we recommend this task be entrusted to a Ford dealer or upholstery specialist.

Adjustment

11 The sunroof should operate freely, without sticking or binding, as it is opened and closed. When in the closed position, check that the panel is flush with the surrounding roof panel.
12 If adjustment is required, slide back the sun blind, but leave the glass panel in the closed position.
13 Loosen the rear securing bolts (one each side). Adjust the glass panel up or down, so that it is flush at its back edge with the roof panel.
14 Loosen the front securing bolts (one each side). Adjust the glass panel up or down, so that it is flush at its front edge with the roof panel.
15 Retighten the four securing bolts.
16 Check the roof seal for wind noise and water leaks.

Bodywork and fittings 11•19

Drain tubes

17 There are four drain tubes, one located in each corner of the sunroof aperture.
18 To remove any obstruction insert a length of suitable nylon wire down through the tubes. If the obstruction cannot be cleared, access the drain tubes as follows:
19 The front drain tubes go down the front A-pillars; remove the lower trim panel to gain access to the drain tube.
20 The rear drain tubes go down the C-pillars (Hatchback and Saloon), or D-pillars (Estate); remove the rear side trims to gain access.

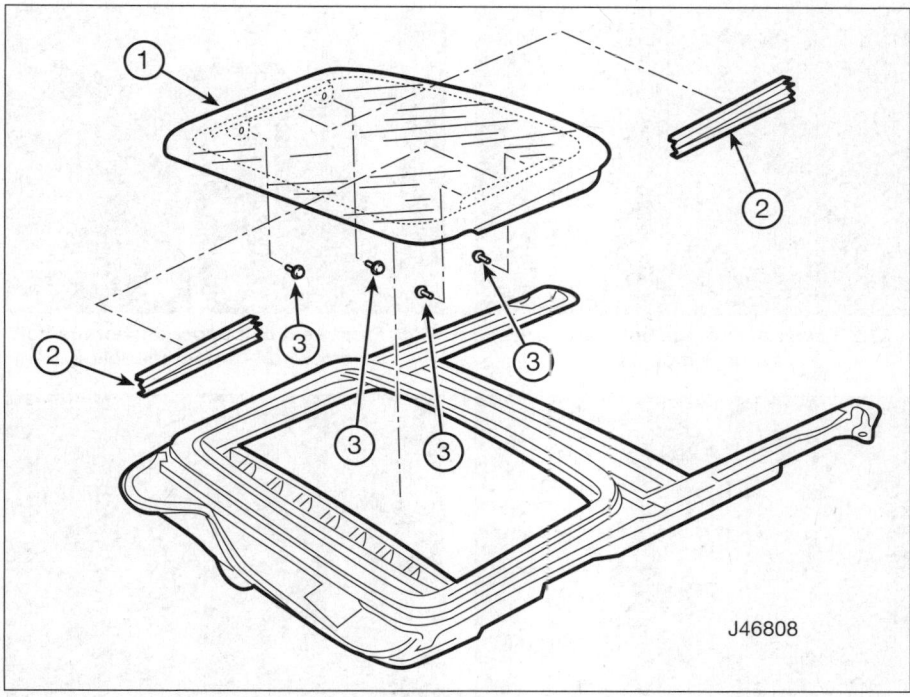

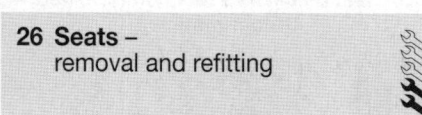

26 Seats – removal and refitting

Removal

Front seat

1 Disconnect the battery negative lead, and position the lead away from the battery (see Chapter 5A).

> **Warning:** Before proceeding, wait a minimum of 5 minutes, as a precaution against accidental firing of the airbag unit or seat belt pretensioner. This period ensures that any residual electrical energy is dissipated.

2 Undo the security bolt and disconnect the wiring plug under the front of the seat **(see illustration)**.
3 Undo the 4 seat retaining bolts and with the help of an assistant, manoeuvre the seat from the vehicle **(see illustration)**. Note that the seat is extremely heavy.

Rear seat cushion

4 On some models, unclip the plastic trim from the hinges at the front of each seat cushion.
5 Unscrew and remove the Torx mounting bolts from the hinges **(see illustration)**, then withdraw the seat cushion from inside the vehicle.

Rear seat backrest

6 Fold the rear seat cushion forwards (if not already removed), and fold the backrest forward.

7 Use a screwdriver to force rearwards the locking catch, and lift the outer end of the backrest from the hinge **(see illustration)**.
8 Pull the backrest from the centre pivot to disengage the mounting pin **(see illustration)**. If necessary, undo the seat belt stalk mounting bolt and manoeuvre the backrest from the vehicle.

25.2 Sunroof glass panel details

1 Glass panel   2 Guide arm covers   3 Retaining bolts

26.2 Undo the bolt (arrowed) and disconnect the seat wiring plug

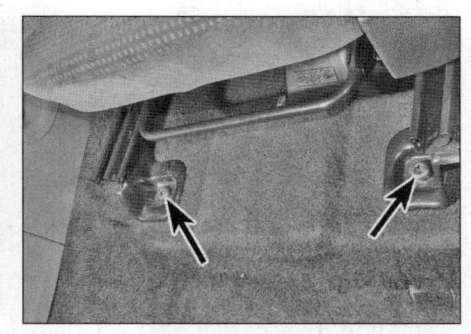

26.3 Seat front retaining bolts (arrowed)

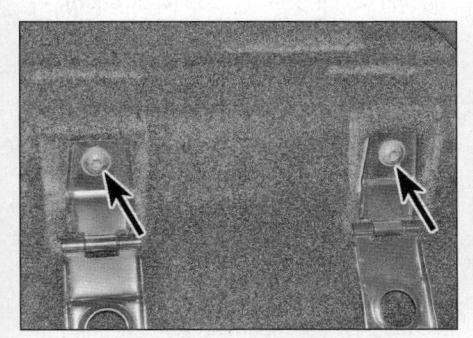

26.5 Undo the bolts securing the rear seat hinges (arrowed)

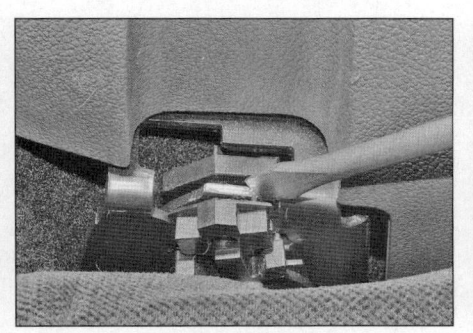

26.7 Release the catch and lift the outer end of the backrest

26.8 Pull the backrest from the pivot to disengage the mounting pin

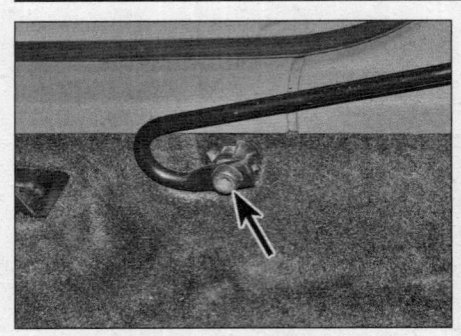

11•20 Bodywork and fittings

27.2 Lower anchorage bolt (arrowed) – 3-door models

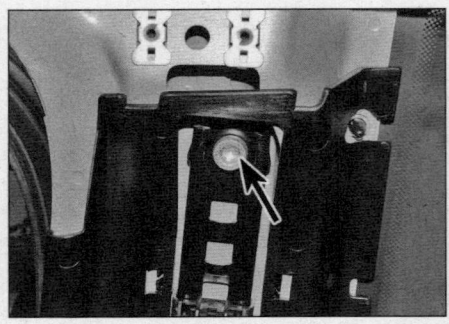

27.5 Front seat belt upper anchorage bolt (arrowed) – 3-door models

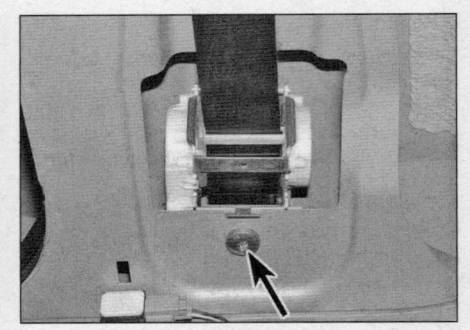

27.6 Seat belt inertia reel bolt (arrowed) – 3-door models

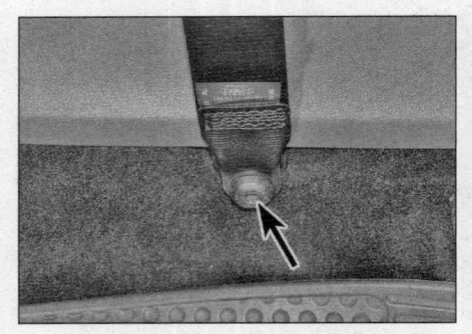

27.7 Front belt lower anchorage bolt (arrowed)

27.9 Front belt upper anchorage bolt (arrowed)

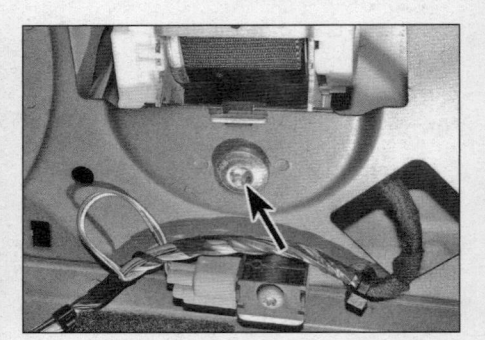

27.10 Inertia seat belt reel mounting bolt (arrowed)

Refitting

9 Refitting is a reversal of the removal procedure, tighten the mounting bolts to the specified torque.

27 Seat belts – removal and refitting

⚠ *Warning: Be careful when handling the seat belt tensioning device, it contains a small explosive charge (pyrotechnic device) similar to the one used to deploy the airbag(s). Clearly, injury could be caused if these are released in an uncontrolled fashion. Once fired, the tensioner cannot be reset, and must be renewed. Note also that seat belts and associated components which have been subject to impact loads must be renewed.*

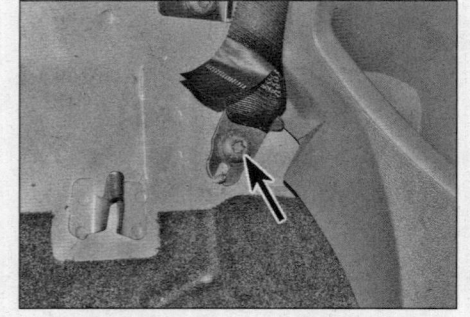

27.11 Rear belt lower anchorage bolt (arrowed)

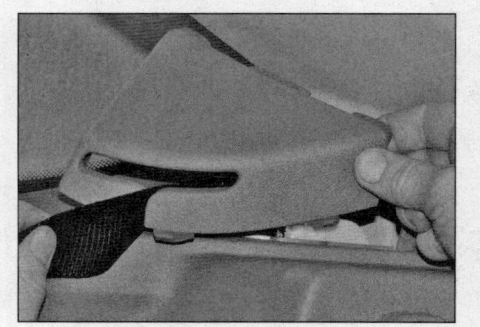

27.12 Unclip the cover over the seat belt reel

Removal – front seat belt

1 Disconnect the battery negative lead, and position the lead away from the battery (see Chapter 5A).

⚠ *Warning: Before proceeding, wait a minimum of 5 minutes, as a precaution against accidental firing of the seat belt tensioner. This period ensures that any residual electrical energy is dissipated.*

⚠ *Warning: There is a potential risk of the seat belt tensioning device firing during removal, so it should be handled carefully. Once removed, treat it with care – do not allow use chemicals on or near it, and do not expose it to high temperatures, or it may detonate.*

3-door models

2 Undo the anchorage rail bolt and slide the belt off **(see illustration)**. Note that the spacer and washer are integral with the bolt.

3 Remove the B-pillar trim panel and rear side panel as described in Section 28.

4 Rotate the seat belt guide loop anti-clockwise and remove it from the B-pillar.

5 Undo the seat belt upper anchorage bolt **(see illustration)**. Note that the spacer and washer are integral with the bolt.

6 Unscrew the mounting bolt, and lift the seat belt reel unit to remove from the base of the pillar **(see illustration)**.

4-door & 5-door models

7 Undo and remove the bolt for the lower seat belt anchorage **(see illustration)**. Note that the spacer and washer are integral with the bolt.

8 Remove the B-pillar trim panel as described in Section 28.

9 Undo the seat belt upper anchorage bolt from the height adjuster **(see illustration)**.

10 Unscrew the mounting bolt, and lift seat belt reel unit to remove from the base of the pillar **(see illustration)**.

Removal – rear side seat belt

3-door & 5-door models

11 Fold the rear seat cushions forward, and unscrew the seat belt lower anchorage bolt **(see illustration)**.

12 Prise up the front edge, and unclip the cover trim from over the seat belt reel **(see illustration)**.

13 Unscrew the mounting bolt securing the seat belt reel unit, and withdraw from the vehicle.

Bodywork and fittings 11•21

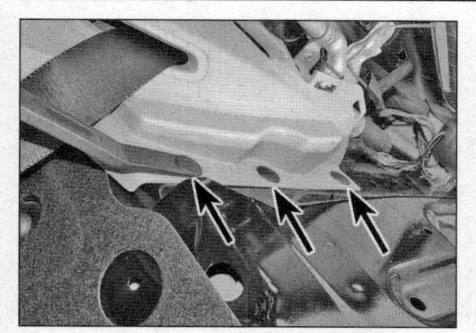

27.16a Prise out the 3 clips (arrowed)...

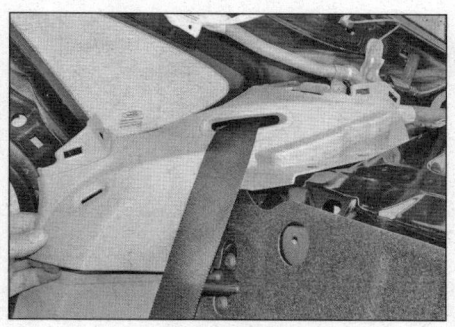

27.16b ...and remove the panel over the inertia reel

27.17 Undo the inertia reel bolt (arrowed)

Saloon

14 Fold the rear seat cushions forward, and unscrew the seat belt lower anchorage bolt.
15 Remove the C- and D-pillar trim panels as described in Section 28.
16 Fold the rear seat backrest forward, then remove the 3 clips securing the cover trim from over the seat belt reel (see illustrations). Feed the seat belt through the cover as it's withdrawn.
17 Unscrew the mounting bolt securing the seat belt reel unit, and withdraw from the vehicle (see illustration).

Removal – rear centre seat belt

18 The centre rear seat belt reel is attached to the rear seat backrest. Remove the backrest as described in Section 26.
19 Use a screwdriver to prise up the backrest release button surround trim, releasing the clips (see illustration). When refitting the trim, align the notch with the slot (see illustration).

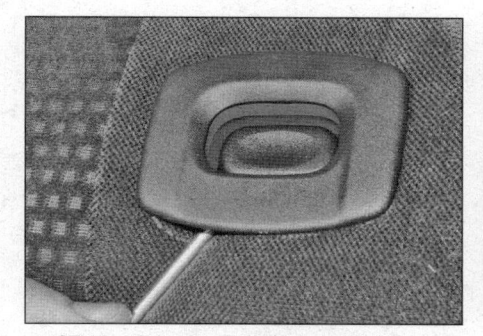

27.19a Prise up the backrest release button surround

20 Push down the backrest padding and use a screwdriver to depress the clip on the side of the headrest guide tubes (see illustrations). Pull the guide tubes from the backrest.
21 Depress the clips and remove the seat belt guide trim from the top of the backrest

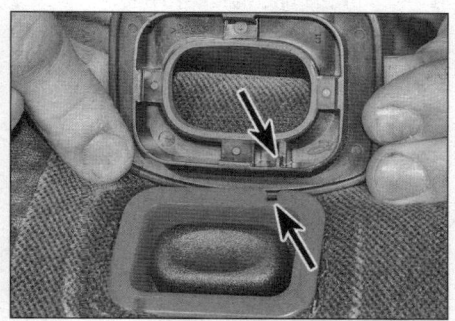

27.19b Align the notch with the slot (arrowed)

(see illustration). Feed the seat belt through the slot in the trim.
22 Gently prise out the beading securing the top half of the backrest seat fabric (see illustration).
23 Carefully pull the seat foam padding from the top part of the backrest (see illustrations).

27.20a Push-in the clip and pull the headrest guide tube from the backrest

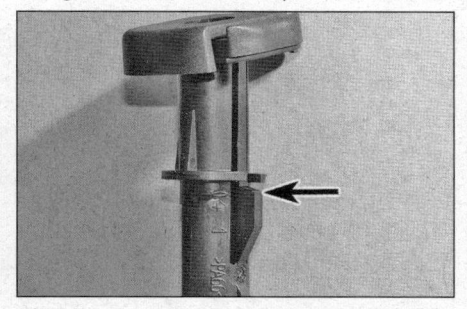

27.20b Depress the headrest guide tube clip (arrowed) – shown with the tube removed

27.21 Depress the clips and remove the belt guide trim

27.22 Prise out the beading securing the top part of the backrest fabric

27.23a Pull the foam padding from the top part of the backrest...

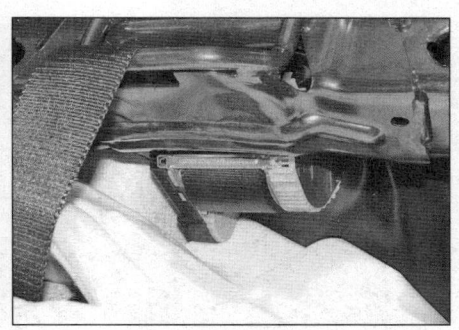

27.23b ...to access the inertia seat belt reel

11•22 Bodywork and fittings

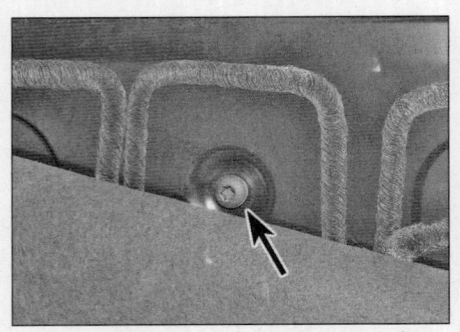

27.24 Peel away the top part of the seat backrest fabric to expose the inertia reel retaining bolt (arrowed)

24 Peel away the top part of the backrest fabric covering, which is glued in place (see illustration).
25 Undo the Torx bolt and manoeuvre the seat belt reel from the seat backrest. Feed the seat belt through the seat backrest bracket as the reel is withdrawn.

Removal – front seat belt stalks

26 The front seat belt stalks are bolted to the seat frame (see illustration) and can be removed after removing the front seat as described in Section 26.
27 Note its routing, then unclip the pretensioner wiring harness from the underside of the seat.
28 Unclip the pretensioner wiring plug from the seat frame.
29 Undo the Torx bolt and remove the pretensioner/stalk.

27.26 Seat belt pretensioner retaining bolt (arrowed)

Refitting

30 Refitting is a reversal of the removal procedure, noting the following points:
a) Tighten the mounting nuts and bolts to the specified torque.
b) Make sure the seat belt reel locating dowel is correctly positioned.
c) Refit spacers in their correct position.
d) On 3-door models, make sure the anchor rail is located correctly.

28 Interior trim panels – removal and refitting

Note: *This section covers the removal and installation of the interior trim panels. It may be necessary to remove an overlapping trim before you can remove the one required. For more information on trim removal, look at relevant Chapters and Sections, where the trims may need to be removed to carry out any other procedures (eg, to remove the steering column you will need to remove the shrouds).*

Sunvisor removal

1 Unscrew the mounting bolts and remove the visor (see illustration).
2 Disconnect the wiring for the vanity mirror light, where fitted.
3 Prise up the cover, unscrew the inner bracket mounting bolts, and remove the bracket (see illustration).

Passenger grab handle removal

4 Prise up the covers, then unscrew the mounting bolts and remove the grab handle (see illustration).

A-pillar trim removal

5 Pull the rubber weatherstrip away from the area adjacent to the pillar.
6 Starting at the top, carefully pull the A-pillar trim inwards to release the retaining clips (see illustration). Note that it is quite likely that some of the clips will be damaged during the removal procedure.

B-pillar trim removal

4 and 5-door models

7 Pull the rubber weatherstrip from the rear door aperture adjacent to the B-pillar trim.
8 Prise up the front edge of the rear door sill trim to access the B-pillar trim (see illustration).

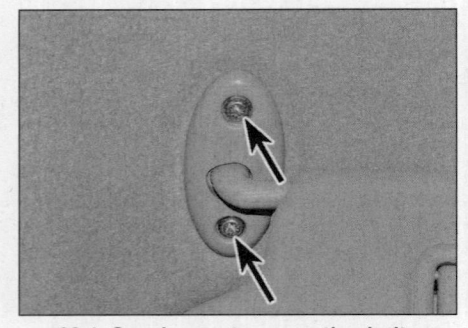

28.1 Sunvisor outer mounting bolts (arrowed)

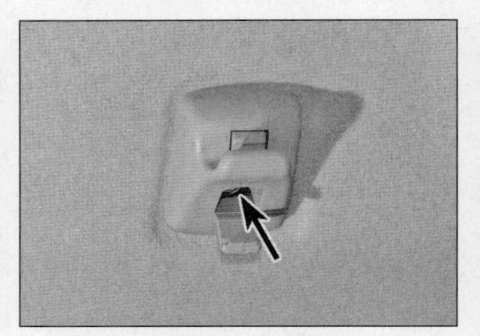

28.3 Prise up the cover to expose the sunvisor inner mounting bolt (arrowed)

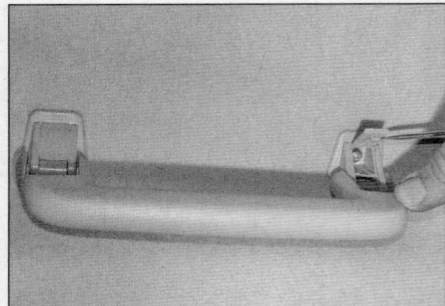

28.4 Prise up the covers to expose the grab handle bolts

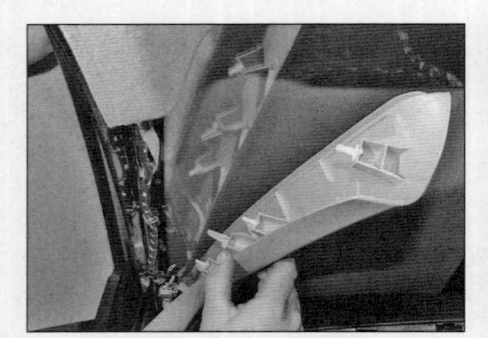

28.6 Pull the A-pillar trim inwards to release the clips

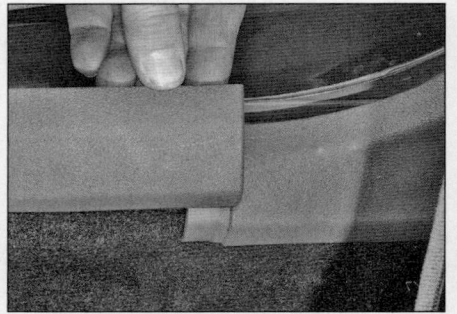

28.8 Prise up the front edge of the rear door sill trim . . .

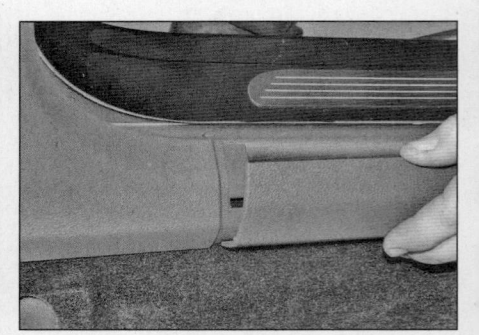

28.9 . . . and the rear edge of the front door sill trim

Bodywork and fittings 11•23

28.10a Prise out the cover . . .

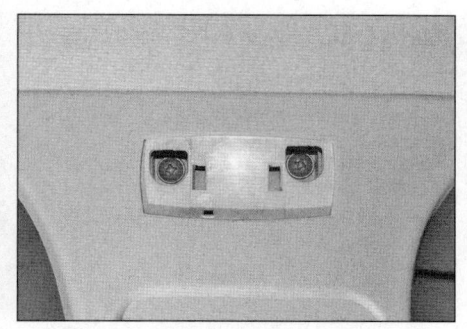

28.10b . . . and undo the 2 retaining bolts

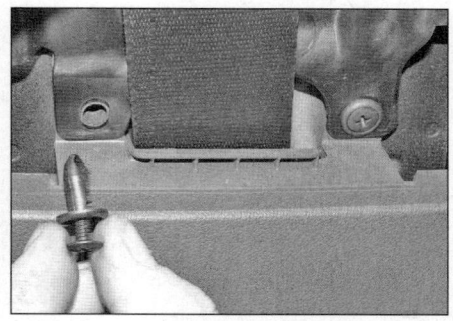

28.13a Undo the bolt, and prise out the scrivets . . .

28.13b . . . then pull the panel from the pillar

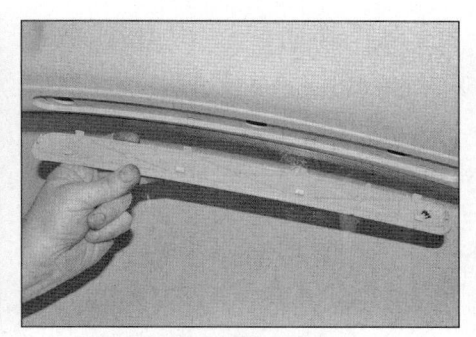

28.16a Prise down the cover . . .

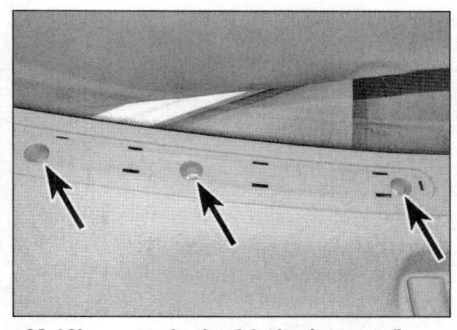

28.16b . . . undo the 3 bolts (arrowed) . . .

9 Pull up the rear edge of the front door sill scuff plate panel (see illustration).
10 Prise out the cover and undo the 2 bolts at the top of the B-pillar trim (see illustrations).
11 If required, unscrew the seat belt mounting bolt from its lower anchorage point.
12 Carefully pull the upper B-pillar trim from the pillar.
13 Slacken the two bolts and prise out the scrivets from the top of the lower trim panel, then unclip it from the B-pillar (see illustrations).

3-door models

14 Undo the bolt securing the lower seat belt anchorage rail (see illustration 27.2).
15 Pull the rubber weatherstrip from the area adjacent to the B-pillar.
16 Carefully prise the cover from the upper window trim, undo the 2 bolts and lower the front end of the trim adjacent to the window (see illustrations).
17 Prise the cover from the top of the B-pillar trim, and undo the 2 bolts (see illustrations).
18 Pull the B-pillar trim inwards to release the retaining clips. Feed the seat belt through the trim as it's withdrawn.

C-pillar trim removal

3-door models

19 Remove the rear parcel shelf
20 Fold the rear seat backrest cushion forwards.
21 Pull the rubber weatherstrip from the tailgate aperture adjacent to the C-pillar.
22 Undo the 2 bolts, and pull the parcel shelf support inwards to release the clips (see illustration 28.48). Disconnect any wiring plugs as the support is withdrawn.
23 Pull the C-pillar trim downwards/inwards to release the retaining clips (see illustration).

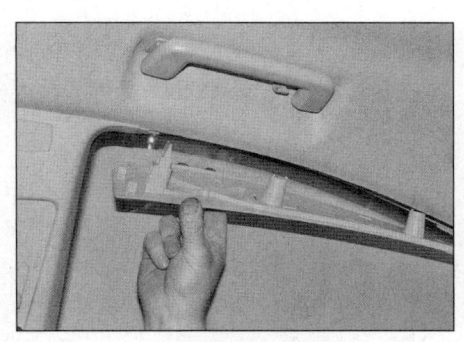

28.16c . . . and pull down the front edge of the window trim

28.17b . . . and undo the 2 bolts

4-door Saloon and 5-door Hatchback models

24 Pull the rubber weatherstrip from the door aperture adjacent to the C-pillar.
25 Starting at the lower edge, prise out the

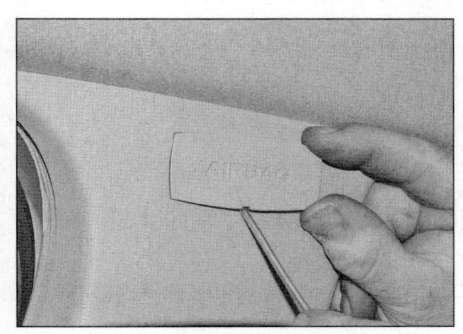

28.17a Prise away the cover . . .

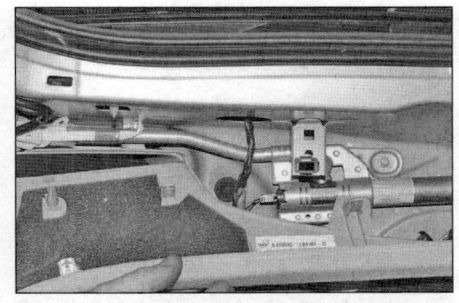

28.23 Pull the C-pillar trim panel forwards and inwards to release the clips – 3-door models

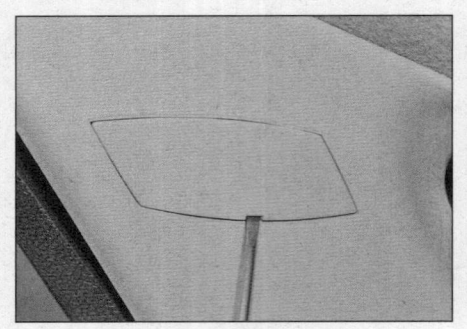

11•24 Bodywork and fittings

28.25a Prise out the cover ...

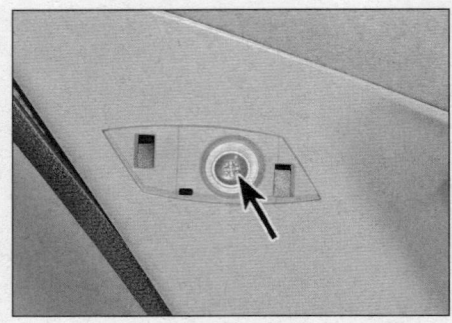

28.25b ... undo the bolt (arrowed) ...

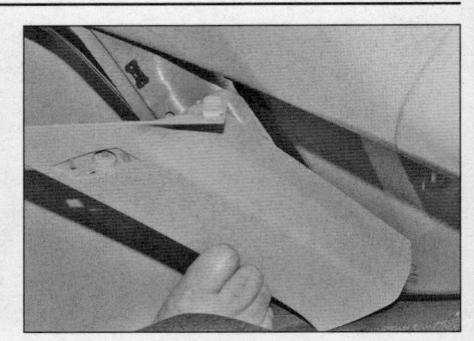

28.26 ... and pull the C-pillar trim panel from position

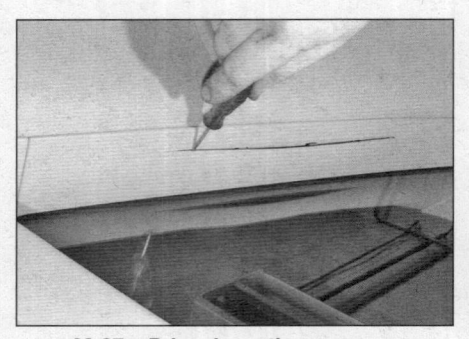

28.27a Prise down the cover ...

28.27b ... undo the 3 bolts ...

28.27c ... and pull down the panel

plastic cover at the top of the trim and undo the bolt **(see illustrations)**.

26 Pull the C-pillar trim inwards to release the retaining clips **(see illustration)**.

Estate models

27 Prise down the cover, undo the 3 bolts, then pull down the trim panel at the top of the rear side window aperture to release the clips **(see illustrations)**.

28 Pull the rubber weatherstrip from the door aperture adjacent to the C-pillar.

29 Starting at the front edge, prise out the plastic cover at the top of the trim and undo the bolt **(see illustrations)**.

30 Pull the C-pillar trim inwards to release the retaining clips **(see illustrations)**.

D-pillar trim removal

4-door Saloon models

31 Remove the parcel shelf and C-pillar trim panel as described in this Section.

32 Prise out the 2 clips at the base of the trim, then pull the rear window glass trim panel inwards to release the retaining clips **(see illustration)**.

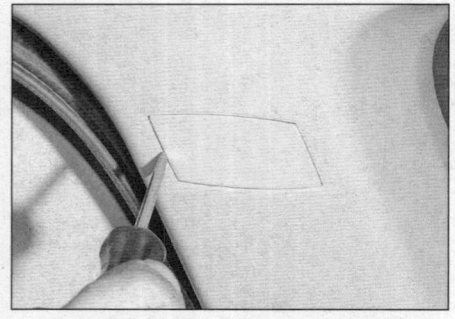

28.29a Prise out the cover ...

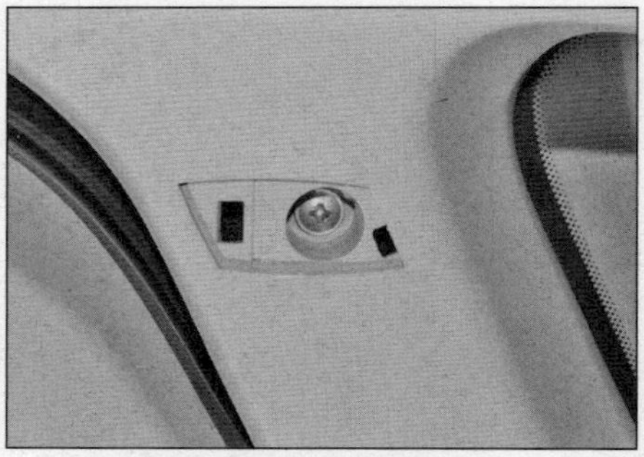

29.29b ... and undo the bolt

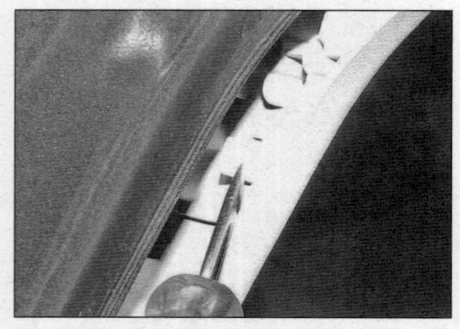

28.30a Release the clip at the front edge ...

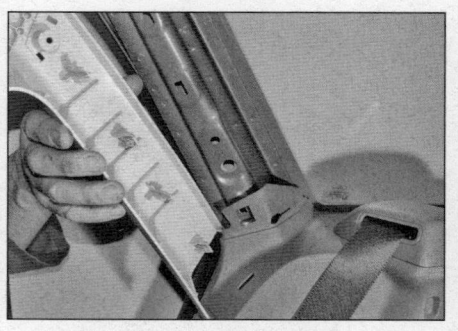

28.30b ... and pull the C-pillar trim inwards

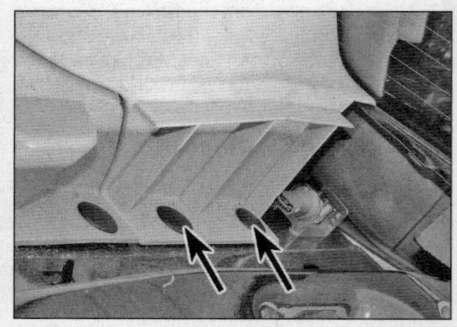

28.32 Prise out the clips (arrowed) at the base of the window trim panel

Bodywork and fittings 11•25

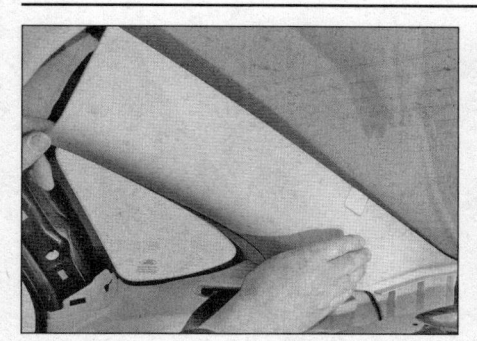

28.33 Starting at the top, pull the D-pillar trim forwards

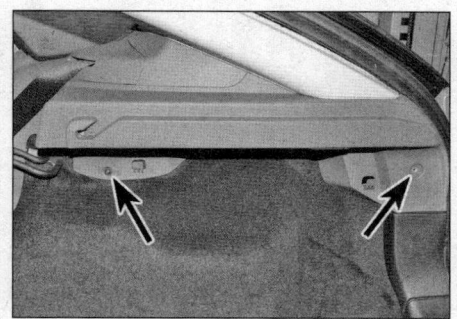

28.36 Parcel shelf support panel bolts (arrowed)

28.37 Prise out the cover to expose the bolts

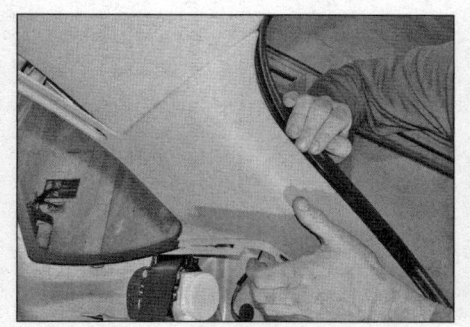

28.38 Pull the D-pillar trim panel forwards and downwards

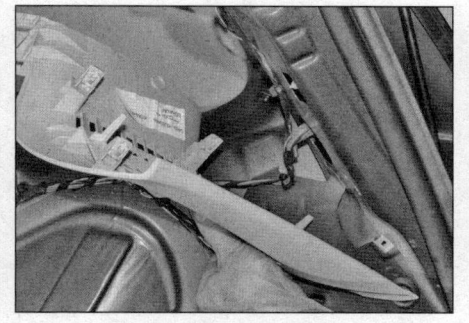

28.41 Pull the D-pillar trim inwards to release the clips

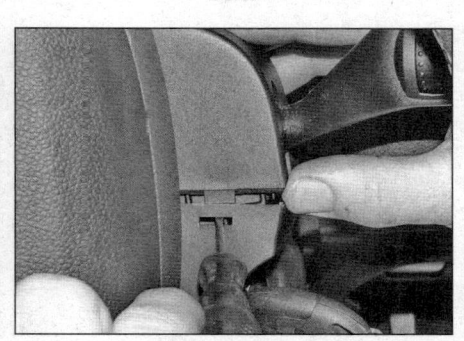

28.42 Rotate the steering wheel 90° and release the upper shroud clips

33 Pull the remaining D-pillar trim forwards to release it (see illustration).

5-door Hatchback models

34 Tilt the rear seat backrest forwards, then remove the C-pillar trim as described previously in this Section.
35 Pull the rubber weatherstrip from the tailgate aperture adjacent to the D-pillar
36 Undo the 2 bolts, and pull the parcel shelf support panel inwards to release the retaining clips (see illustration).
37 Carefully prise off the cover at the front, upper edge of the D-pillar, and undo the 2 bolts exposed (see illustration).
38 Pull the D-pillar trim forwards and downwards to release it (see illustration).

Estate models

39 Remove the luggage compartment side panel as described in this Section.
40 Pull the rubber weatherstrip from the tailgate aperture adjacent to the D-pillar.
41 Pull the D-pillar trim inwards to release the retaining clips (see illustration).

Steering column shrouds removal

42 To release the upper shroud from the lower shroud, turn the steering wheel 90°, insert a thin screwdriver into a hole at each side of the column (see illustration). Lift the upper shroud from the column and unclip from the bottom of the instrument panel.
43 Using a thin screwdriver unclip the radio control switch from the lower shroud (see illustration).

44 Release the steering column height lever. Undo the 2 securing bolts from the lower shroud, and remove from the column (see illustration).

Luggage area side panel removal

3-door models

45 Remove the parcel shelf and the luggage compartment floor covering.
46 Tilt the rear seat backrest and cushion forwards.
47 Pull the rubber weatherstrip from the tailgate aperture.
48 Undo the 2 bolts and pull the parcel shelf support inwards to release the retaining clips (see illustration). Disconnect any wiring plugs as the support is withdrawn.
49 Remove the 4 retaining clips and pull

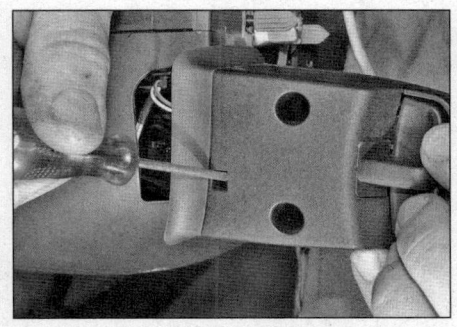

28.43 Depress the clip to release the audio switch from the shroud

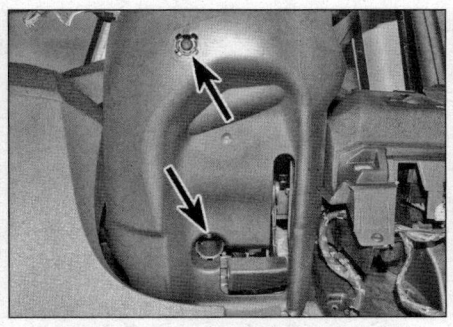

28.44 Lower shroud retaining bolts (arrowed)

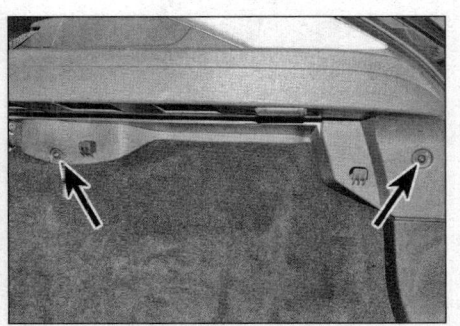

28.48 Undo the 2 parcel shelf support bolts (arrowed)

11•26 Bodywork and fittings

28.49 Prise out the tailgate sill trim clips

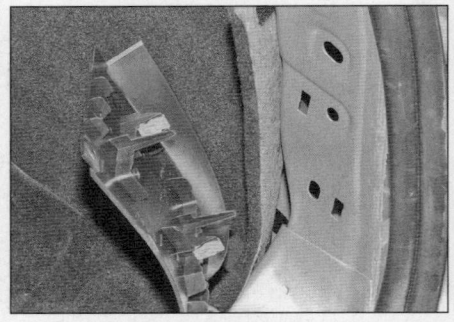

28.50 Pull the tailgate aperture corner trim panel inwards to release the clips

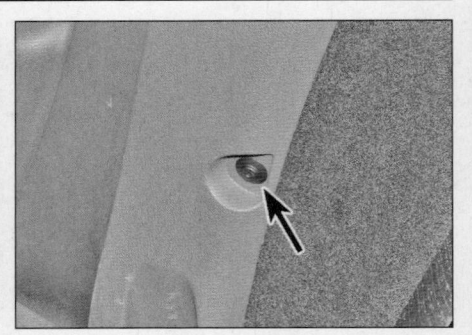

28.51 Prise out the clip (arrowed) at the front edge of the side panel

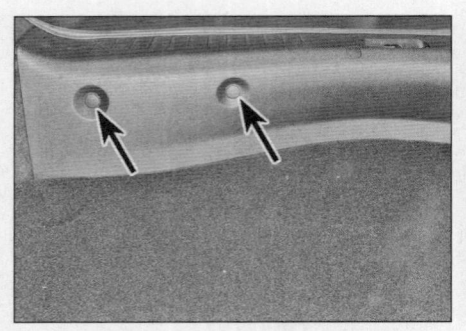

28.57a Prise out the 2 clips (arrowed) each side of the tailgate sill trim front face . . .

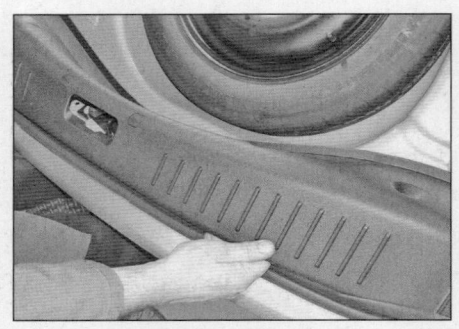

28.57b . . . the pull the trim upwards from place

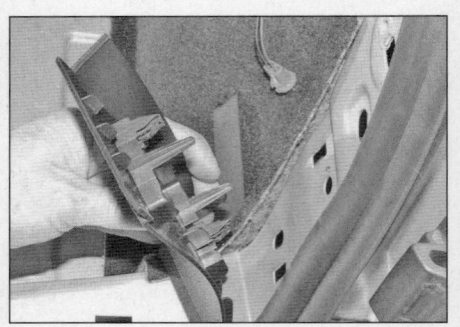

28.58 Pull away the trim panel in the lower corner of the tailgate aperture

the tailgate sill panel upwards to release the retaining clips **(see illustration)**.
50 Pull the trim panel in the lower corner of the tailgate aperture inwards to release the retaining clips **(see illustration)**.
51 Remove the retaining clip at the front edge of the luggage compartment side panel, then pull the panel inwards to remove it **(see illustration)**.

5-door Hatchback models
52 Remove the parcel shelf and the luggage compartment floor covering.

53 Tilt the rear seat backrest and cushion forwards.
54 Remove the C-pillar trim as described previously in this Section.
55 Pull the rubber weatherstrip from the tailgate aperture.
56 Undo the 2 bolts and pull the parcel shelf support inwards to release the retaining clips **(see illustration 28.36)**.
57 Remove the 4 retaining clips and pull the tailgate sill panel upwards to release the retaining clips **(see illustrations)**.
58 Pull the trim panel in the lower corner of the tailgate aperture inwards to release the retaining clips **(see illustration)**.
59 Remove the retaining clip at the front edge of the luggage compartment side panel, then pull the panel inwards to remove it **(see illustration)**.

Estate models
60 Remove the luggage compartment floor covering.
61 Tilt the rear seat backrest and cushion forwards.
62 Pull the rubber weatherstrip from the tailgate aperture.
63 Prise up and remove the cover over the rear seat belt reel, then undo the 3 bolts and pull the luggage compartment upper side panel inwards to release the clips **(see illustrations)**.
64 Pull the tailgate sill panel upwards to release the retaining clips.
65 Pull the trim panel in the lower corner of the tailgate aperture inwards to release the retaining clips **(see illustration)**.

28.59 Prise out the clip at the front edge of the panel

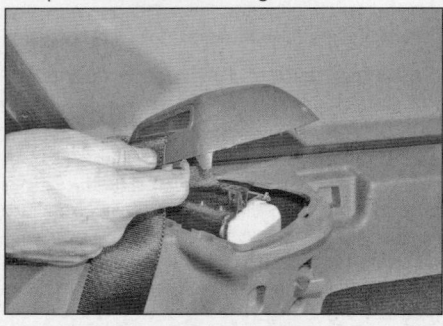

28.63a Prise up the cover over the inertia reel . . .

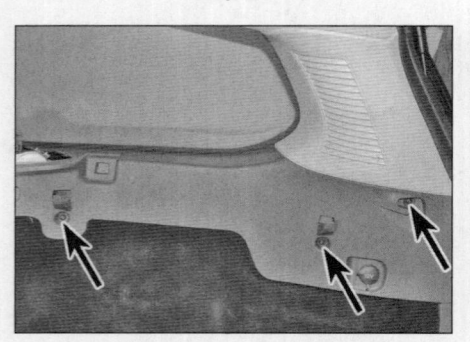

28.63b . . . then undo the 3 bolts (arrowed) at the top of the panel

28.65 Pull the trim panel (arrowed) inwards to release the clips

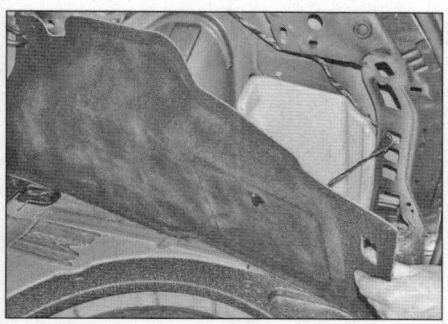

Bodywork and fittings 11•27

28.66 Pull the luggage compartment side panel inwards

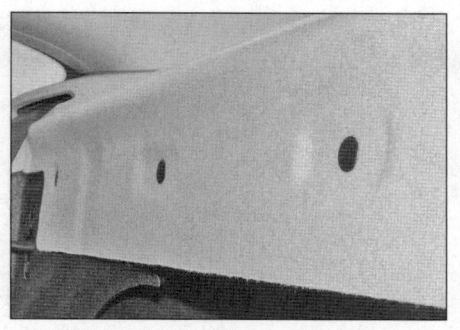

28.68 Prise out the clips at the front edge of the parcel shelf

28.69 Undo the lower facia panel bolt (arrowed)

28.70 Unclip the diagnostic socket as the facia panel is removed

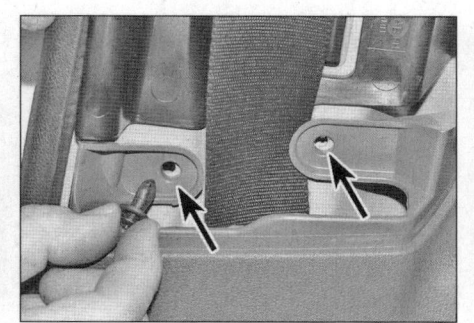

28.72 Undo the bolts and prise out the scrivets (arrowed)

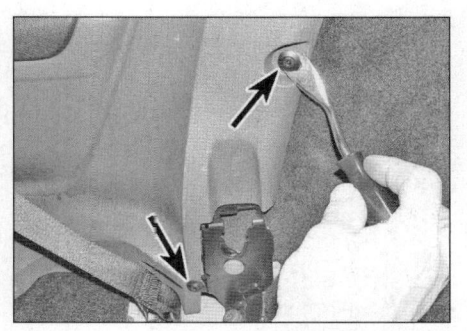

28.74 Prise out the clips (arrowed) at the rear of the side panel

66 Remove the retaining clip securing the side panel/storage compartment lid, then pull the side panel inwards and remove it **(see illustration)**.

Parcel shelf removal

Saloon only

67 Tilt the rear seat backrest forwards.
68 Remove the 4 retaining clips at the front edge, then pull the parcel shelf forwards **(see illustration)**.

Driver's lower facia panel removal

69 Undo the single bolt in the coin recess **(see illustration)**.
70 Pull the panel rearwards to release the clips, then unclip the diagnostic plug as the panel is withdrawn **(see illustration)**.

Rear side panel removal

3-door models

71 Remove the B-pillar trim panel as described previously in this Section.
72 Undo the 2 scrivets at the front upper edge of the panel **(see illustration)**.
73 Fold forwards the rear seat cushion and remove the rear seat backrest as described in Section 26.
74 Prise out the clips at the rear edge of the panel **(see illustration)**.
75 Pull up the rear edge of the door sill trim.
76 Starting at the front pull the rear side panel inwards to release the various push-in clips, and manoeuvre the panel from the vehicle.

Refitting

77 Refitting is a reversal of the removal procedure. Where seat belt fastenings have been disturbed, make sure that they are tightened to the specified torque. Renew any broken clips as required.

29 Centre console – removal and refitting

Manual transmission models

Models up to 03/2007 with an armrest

1 Prise out the covers, and remove the bolts at the front of the console side panels (2 on the left-hand side, and one on the right) **(see illustration)**.
2 Starting at the front edges, pull the console side panels from place **(see illustration)**.
3 Starting at the rear, unclip the gear lever gaiter trim from the surround trim, then unclip the surround trim from the centre console, leaving the gaiter on the gear lever **(see illustrations)**.

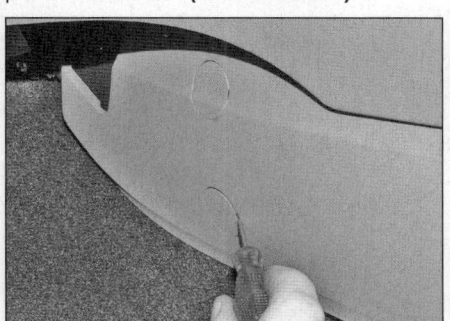

29.1 Prise out the covers, undo the bolts ...

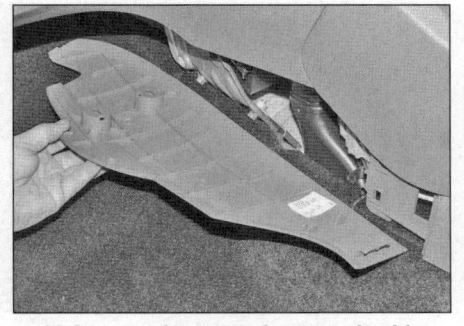

29.2 ... and remove the console side panels

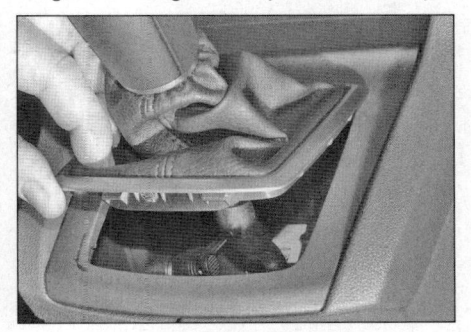

29.3a Unclip the gaiter trim ...

29.3b ... and the surround trim

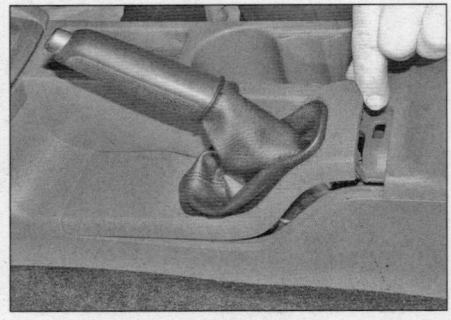

29.4a Unclip the handbrake lever trim ...

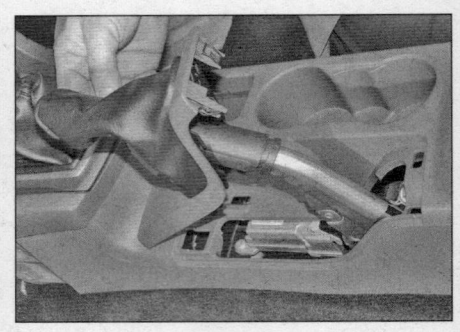

29.4b ... and pull it over the lever

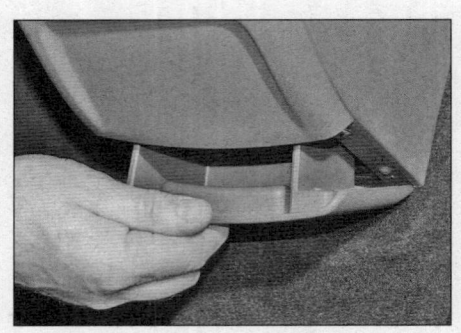

29.5 Lift the storage compartment to release the retaining clips

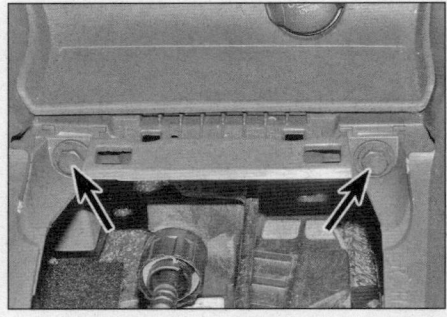

29.6a Undo the 2 bolts at the front of the gear lever aperture (arrowed) ...

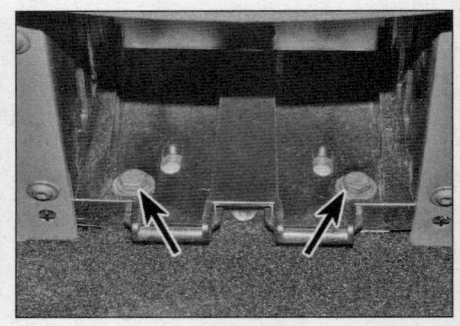

29.6b ... and the 2 (arrowed) in the rear storage compartment aperture

4 Starting at the rear, unclip the handbrake lever surround trim from the centre console and remove it from the handbrake lever (see illustrations).
5 Open the rear storage compartment, then lift it slightly to release the lower retaining clips, and remove it from the console (see illustration).
6 Undo the bolt each side of the gear lever aperture, and the bolts in the rear storage compartment aperture (see illustrations).
7 Manoeuvre the centre console from place, disconnecting any wiring plugs as it's withdrawn (see illustration).
8 Refitting is a reversal of the removal procedure.

Models from 03/2007 with an armrest

9 Prise up the gear lever surround trim (see illustration 29.3a and 29.3b).
10 Prise out the covers and undo the bolts each side (2 on the left, one on the right-hand side), then remove the console side panels (see illustrations 29.1 and 29.2).
11 Lift the armrest lid, and undo the 2 bolts exposed, then remove the trim panel at the front of the armrest pedestal/handbrake lever trim (see illustrations). Carefully work the gaiter over the handbrake lever as the panel is withdrawn.
12 Lift out the rubber mat from the cup holders, and undo the bolt beneath (see illustration)
13 Pull the top half of the console upwards to release the retaining clips (see illustration).

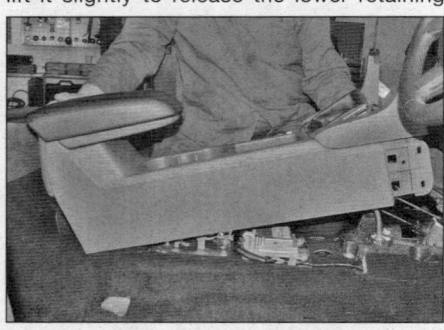

29.7 Manoeuvre the centre console over the gear lever and handbrake lever

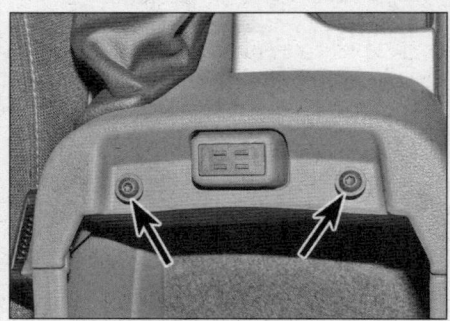

29.11a Undo the 2 bolts (arrowed) ...

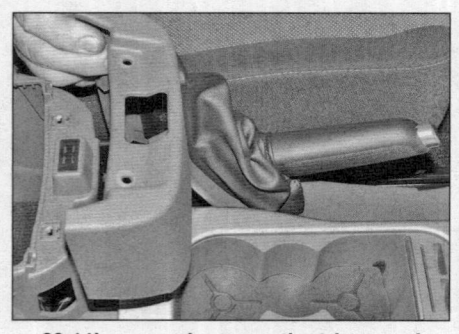

29.11b ... and remove the trim panel

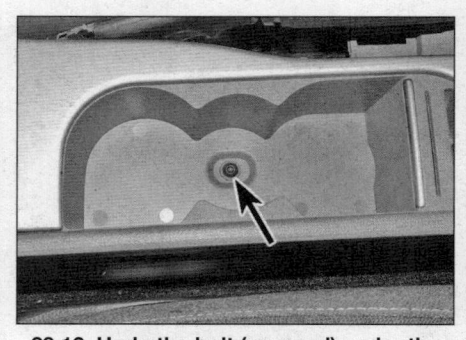

29.12 Undo the bolt (arrowed) under the cupholder mat

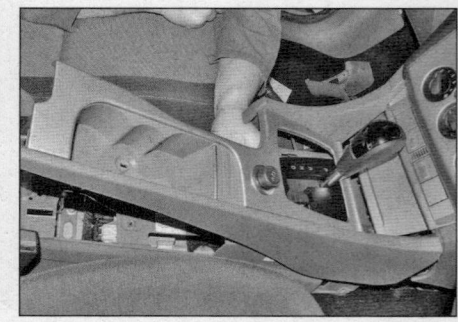

29.13 Pull the top half of the console upwards

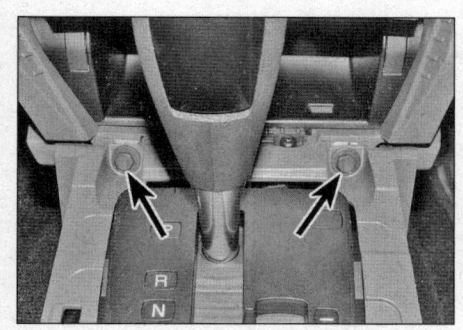

Bodywork and fittings 11•29

29.14a Undo the 2 bolts (arrowed) at the front of the console . . .

29.14b . . . and the bolt each side at the rear

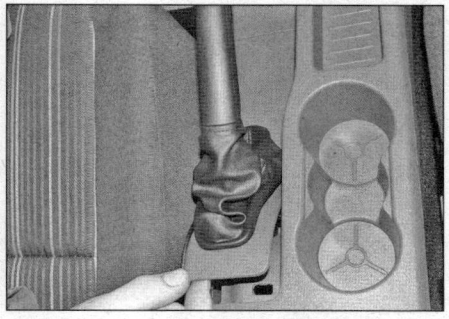

29.17 Prise up the handbrake lever surround trim

Disconnect the power outlet wiring plug as it becomes accessible.

14 Undo the 2 bolts at the front of the console, and the 2 at the rear each side **(see illustrations)**. Lift the console from place, and disconnect any wiring plugs as it's removed.

15 Refitting is a reversal of the removal procedure.

Models without an armrest

16 Prise up and remove the gear lever surround trim.

17 Starting at the rear, prise up and remove the handbrake lever surround trim **(see illustration)**.

18 Prise out the covers and undo the bolts each side (2 on the left, one on the right-hand side), then remove the console side panels **(see illustrations 29.1 and 29.2)**.

19 Prise up the plastic cover in the rear storage box and undo the 2 bolts exposed **(see illustrations)**.

20 Undo the 2 bolts at the front of the gearlever aperture and manoeuvre the console from place **(see illustration 29.14a)**.

21 Refitting is a reversal of the removal procedure.

Automatic transmission models

22 This procedure is the same as given above for manual transmission models, except for the following.

23 Move the selector lever to the rearmost position, then carefully prise up the selector lever trim panel and surround from the centre console. **Note:** *If necessary, the lever can be moved without turning on the ignition by prising up the cover on the selector lever surround trim, and depressing the release button with a screwdriver or similar* **(see illustrations)**.

24 Detach and disconnect the wiring plugs inside the centre console. Cut any cable-ties as necessary.

25 Refitting is a reversal of the removal procedure.

30 Overhead console – removal and refitting

Removal

1 Starting at the front edge, carefully prise the interior light unit from the console **(see illustration)**. Disconnect the wiring plug as the light is removed.

2 On models with an electrically-operated sunroof, remove the sunroof switch (Chapter 12, Section 4).

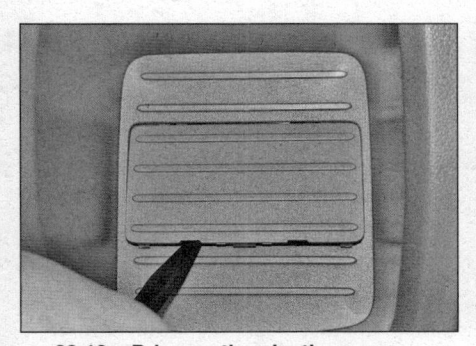

29.19a Prise up the plastic cover . . .

29.19b . . . and undo the 2 bolts

29.23a Prise up the selector lever panel trim . . .

29.23b . . . and the surround trim

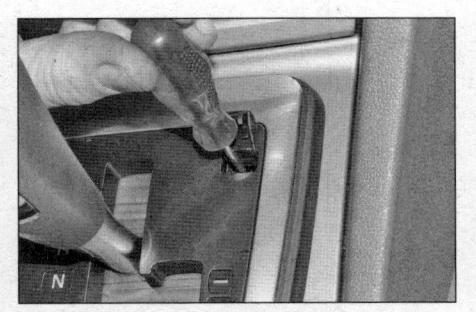

29.20c Prise up the cover and depress the release button to allow the selector lever to be moved

30.1 Insert a screwdriver, depress the clip, and pull the interior light from the console

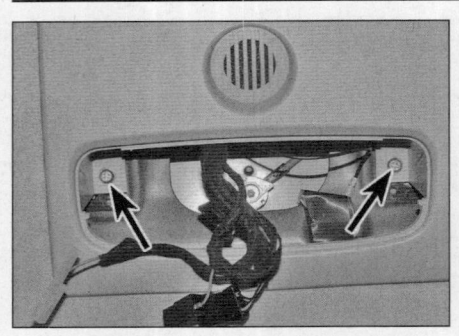

11•30 Bodywork and fittings

30.3 Console retaining bolts (arrowed)

3 Undo the 2 bolts in the light aperture, then starting at the front edge, prise down the console panel (see illustration). Disconnect any wiring plugs as the console is removed.

Refitting

4 Refitting is a reversal of the removal procedure.

31 Glovebox – removal and refitting

1 On models with an air conditioned glovebox, undo the fasteners and lower the GEM/fusebox from below the passenger's side of the facia, then reach up to the right-hand side of the glovebox and pull the cool air pipe from the fitting on the side of the box.
2 Open the glovebox lid, undo the 7 retaining bolts and pull the glovebox from place (see

31.2 Glovebox retaining bolts (arrowed)

illustration). Prise down the covers to access the lower 3 bolts. Take care not to lose the lock striker from the top of the glovebox as it's withdrawn.
3 Disconnect the wiring plugs as the glovebox is withdrawn. If required, the glovebox lid simply pulls from place.
4 Refitting is a reversal of the removal procedure, making sure that the glovebox is located correctly before tightening the bolts.

32 Facia – removal and refitting

Removal

1 Disconnect the battery negative (earth) lead (Chapter 5A).
2 Remove the centre console as described in Section 29.

Models up to 04/2006
3 Remove the passenger's airbag module as described in Chapter 12.

Models from 04/2006
4 Squeeze together the sides and remove the fasteners, then remove the cover under the central junction box under the facia (see illustration).
5 Rotate the fasteners anti-clockwise and detach the central junction box from the facia crossmember (see illustration).
6 On models with air conditioning, reach up and disconnect the cooling hose from the glovebox.
7 Remove the glovebox as described in Section 31.
8 Undo the passenger's airbag module lower support bracket bolts/nuts and remove the bracket (see illustration).
9 Use thin, flat-bladed screwdrivers (or similar) to release the passenger's side, inner air vent upper retaining clips, then manoeuvre the vent from the facia (see illustrations).
10 Disconnect the passenger's airbag module wiring plug, then undo the module outer retaining bolts (see illustrations).

All models
11 Remove the heater/climate control panel as described in Chapter 3.
12 Remove the instrument panel as described in Chapter 12.
13 Remove the driver's side lower facia panel as described in Section 28.
14 Remove the headlight switch, hazard

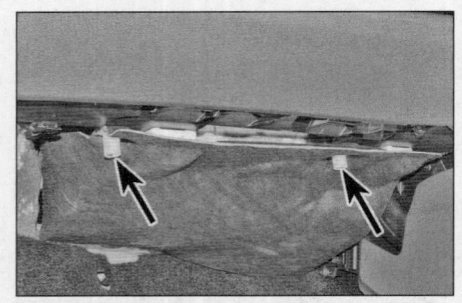

32.4 Release the fasteners (arrowed) securing the cover under the central junction box

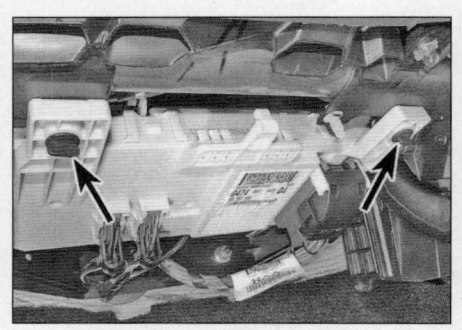

32.5 Undo the fasteners (arrowed) and lower the central junction box

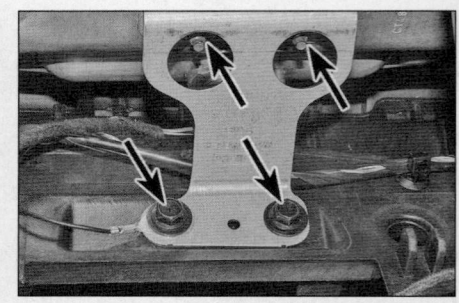

32.8 Remove the airbag lower support bracket nuts and bolts (arrowed). Note the earth lead attached to the lower bolt

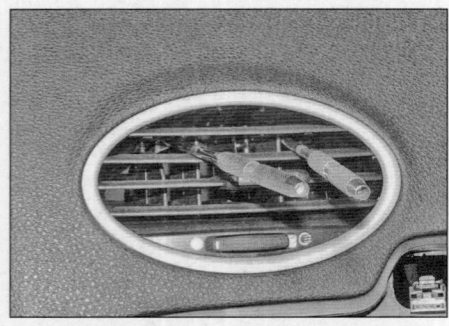

32.9a Insert screwdrivers into the passenger's side inner air vent . . .

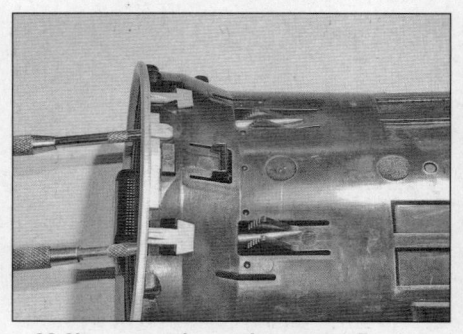

32.9b . . . to release the upper clips . . .

32.9c . . . and pull the vent from the facia

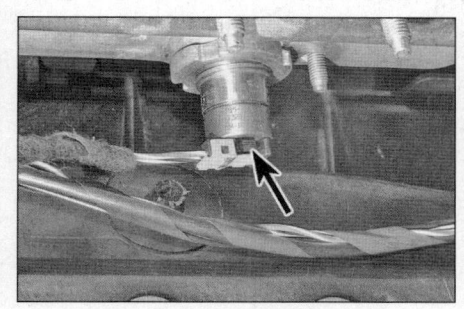

Bodywork and fittings 11•31

32.10a Squeeze together the clips (arrowed) and disconnect the airbag connector

32.10b Undo the airbag bracket inner bolt (arrowed) . . .

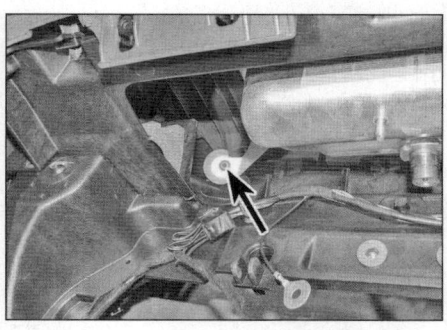

32.10c . . . and outer bolt (arrowed)

switch and facia centre console switch panel as described in Chapter 12.

15 Disconnect the passenger cabin temperature sensor wiring plug (where fitted).
16 Release the clips and remove the glovebox light switch **(see illustration)**.
17 Pull the passenger's side facia outer trim rearwards to release the retaining clips **(see illustration)**.
18 Use a thin, flat-bladed screwdriver to release the air vents' retaining clips, then manoeuvre the vents from the facia **(see illustration 32.9a, 32.9b and 32.9c)**.
19 Disconnect the wiring plug from the rear of the cigar lighter/power outlet and keyless entry module (where fitted).
20 Detach the glovebox damper from the lid **(see illustration)**.
21 Remove the left-hand steering column switch as described in Chapter 12.
22 Undo the 9 bolts and with the help of an assistant, manoeuvre the facia from the vehicle **(see illustrations)**.
23 With the help of an assistant, pull the facia rearwards to release the extension panel retaining clips, and manoeuvre it from the cabin.

Refitting

24 Refitting is a reversal of the removal procedure. On completion, check the operation of all electrical components.

33 Wheel arch liner – removal and refitting

Removal

Front

1 Apply the handbrake. If the wheel is to

32.16 Squeeze together the clips (arrowed) and push the glovebox light switch from place

be removed (to improve access), loosen the wheel nuts. Jack up the front of the vehicle and support it on axle stands (see *Jacking and vehicle support*). Remove the front wheel.

32.17 Pull the passenger's side outer trim rearwards

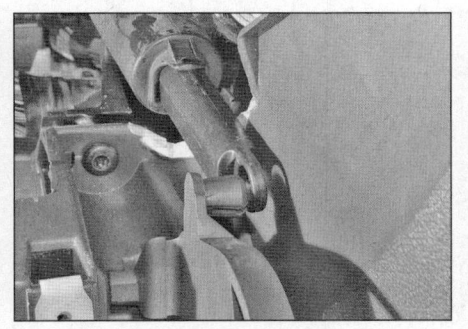

32.20 Slide the damper from the glovebox lid

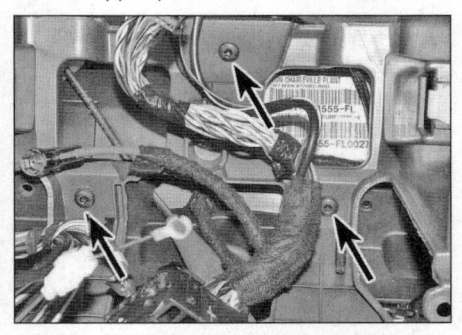

32.22a Undo the 3 bolts (arrowed) in the facia central aperture . . .

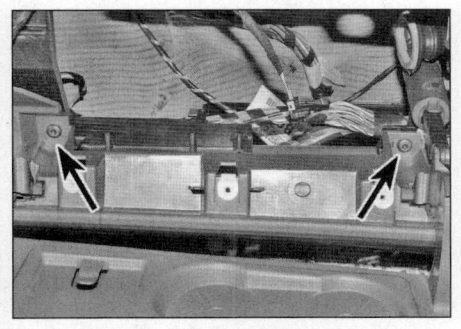

32.22b . . . 2 bolts (arrowed) in the glovebox aperture . . .

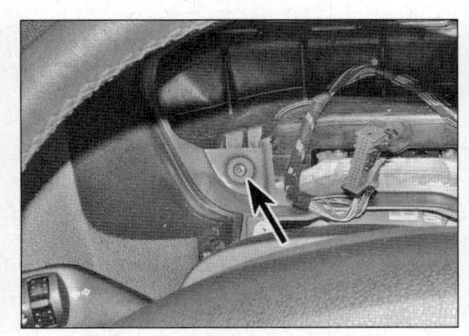

32.22c . . . 1 bolt (arrowed) in the instrument panel aperture . . .

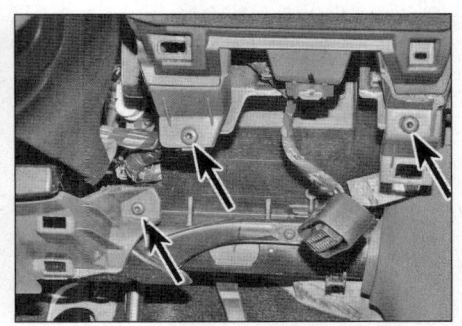

32.22d . . . and 3 bolts (arrowed) under the driver's side of the facia

11•32 Bodywork and fittings

2 Unscrew the bolts securing the liner to the inner wheel arch panel.
3 Remove the bolts and clips securing the liner to the outer edge of the wheel arch and bumper. Withdraw the liner from under the vehicle.

Rear

4 Chock the front wheels, and engage 1st gear (or P). If the wheel is to be removed (to improve access), loosen the wheel nuts. Jack up the rear of the vehicle and support it on axle stands (see *Jacking and vehicle support*). Remove the rear wheel.
5 Undo the bolts securing the liner to the outer edge of the wheel arch and bumper.
6 Remove the clips securing the liner to the inner wheel arch, and withdraw the liner from under the vehicle.

Refitting

7 Refitting is a reversal of the removal procedure. If the wheels were removed, tighten the wheel nuts to the specified torque.

Chapter 12
Body electrical system

Contents

	Section number
Aerial – removal and refitting	19
Airbag system – general information and precautions	21
Airbag system components – removal and refitting	22
Anti-theft alarm system – general information	23
Audio/DVD units – removal and refitting	18
Central locking system – general information	16
Electrical fault finding – general information	2
Electronic control modules – removal and refitting	24
Exterior light bulbs – renewal	6
Exterior light units – removal, refitting and beam adjustment	8
Fuel filler flap motor – removal and refitting	25
Fuses and relays – general information	3
General information and precautions	1
Horns – removal and refitting	14
Ignition switch – removal and refitting	4
Instrument panel – removal and refitting	10
Interior light bulbs – renewal	7
Parking aid components – general, removal and refitting	17
Speakers – removal and refitting	20
Sunroof motor – removal and refitting	15
Switches – removal and refitting	5
Tailgate wiper motor – removal and refitting	13
Washer system – general	12
Windscreen wiper components – removal and refitting	11
Xenon gas discharge headlight system – component removal, refitting and adjustment	9

Degrees of difficulty

Easy, suitable for novice with little experience

Fairly easy, suitable for beginner with some experience

Fairly difficult, suitable for competent DIY mechanic

Difficult, suitable for experienced DIY mechanic

Very difficult, suitable for expert DIY or professional

Specifications

System type	12 volt, negative earth

Bulbs
	Power rating (watts)
Direction indicators	21
Direction indicator side repeaters	5 capless
Foglamp:	
Front	35 H8
Rear	21
Headlight:	
Halogen:	
Dipped	55 H7
Main	55 H1
Gas discharge (Xenon):	
Dipped	35 DS2
Main	55 H1
Glovebox light	3 capless
High-level brake light	5
Interior light	10
Number plate light	5
Luggage compartment light	5 capless
Reading light	5
Reversing light	21
Sidelights	5
Stop/tail light	21/5
Stop-light	21
Vanity mirror	5

Torque wrench settings
	Nm	lbf ft
Airbag control unit nuts	7	5
Crash sensor bolts	6	4

12•2 Body electrical system

1 General information and precautions

Warning: *Before carrying out any work on the electrical system, read through the precautions given in 'Safety first!' at the beginning of this manual, and in Chapter 5A.*

1 The electrical system is of 12 volt negative earth type. Power for the lights and all electrical accessories is supplied by a lead-acid type battery which is charged by the alternator.

2 This Chapter covers repair and service procedures for the various electrical components not associated with the engine. Information on the battery, alternator and starter motor can be found in Chapter 5A.

3 It should be noted that prior to working on any component in the electrical system, the battery negative terminal should first be disconnected to prevent the possibility of electrical short-circuits and/or fires. **Note:** *If the vehicle has a security-coded radio, check that you have a copy of the code number before disconnecting the battery. Refer to your Ford dealer if in doubt.*

2 Electrical fault finding – general information

Note: *Refer to the precautions given in 'Safety first!' and in Chapter 5A before starting work. The following tests relate to testing of the main electrical circuits, and should not be used to test delicate electronic circuits (such as anti-lock braking systems), particularly where an electronic control unit is used.*

Caution: *The Ford Focus electrical system is extremely complex. Many of the ECMs are connected via a 'Databus' system, where they are able to share information from the various sensors, and communicate with each other. For instance, as the automatic gearbox approaches a gear ratio shift point, it signals the engine management ECM via the Databus. As the gearchange is made by the transmission ECM, the engine management ECM retards the ignition timing, momentarily reducing engine output, to ensure a smoother transition from one gear ratio to the next. Due to the design of the Databus system, it is not advisable to backprobe the ECMs with a multimeter in the traditional manner. Instead, the electrical systems are equipped with a sophisticated self-diagnosis system, which can interrogate the various ECMs to reveal stored fault codes, and help pinpoint faults. In order to access the self-diagnosis system, specialist test equipment (fault code reader/scanner) is required.*

General

1 Typically, electrical circuit consists of an electrical component, any switches, relays, motors, fuses, fusible links or circuit breakers related to that component, and the wiring and connectors which link the component to both the battery and the chassis. To help to pinpoint a problem in an electrical circuit, wiring diagrams are included at the end of this Chapter.

2 Have a good look at the appropriate wiring diagram before attempting to diagnose an electrical fault, to obtain a complete understanding of the components included in the particular circuit concerned. The possible sources of a fault can be narrowed down by noting if other components related to the circuit are operating properly. If several components or circuits fail at one time, the problem is likely to be related to a shared fuse or earth connection.

3 An electrical problem will usually stem from simple cause, such as loose or corroded connections, a faulty earth connection, a blown fuse, a melted fusible link, or a faulty relay (refer to Section 3 for details of testing relays). Visually inspect the condition of all fuses, wires and connections in a problem circuit before testing the components. Use the wiring diagrams to determine which terminal connections will need to be checked in order to pinpoint the trouble-spot.

4 The basic tools required for electrical fault finding include a circuit tester or voltmeter (a 12 volt bulb with a set of test leads can also be used for certain tests); a self-powered test light (sometimes known as a continuity tester); an ohmmeter (to measure resistance); a battery and set of test leads; and a jumper wire, preferably with a circuit breaker or fuse incorporated, which can be used to bypass suspect wires or electrical components. Before attempting to locate a problem with test instruments, use the wiring diagram to determine where to make the connections.

5 Sometimes, an intermittent wiring fault (usually caused to a poor or dirty connection, or damaged wiring insulation) can be pinpointed by performing a wiggle test on the wiring. This involves wiggling the wiring by hand to see if the fault occurs as the wiring is moved. It should be possible to narrow down the source of the fault to a particular section of wiring. This method of testing can be used in conjunction with any of the tests described in the following sub-Sections.

6 Apart from problems due to poor connections, two basic types of fault can occur in an electrical circuit: open-circuit, or short-circuit.

7 Largely, open-circuit faults are caused by a break somewhere in the circuit, which prevents current from flowing. An open-circuit fault will prevent a component from working, but will not cause the relevant circuit fuse to blow.

8 Low resistance or short-circuit faults are caused by a 'short'; a failure point which allows the current flowing in the circuit to 'escape' along an alternative route, somewhere in the circuit. This typically occurs when a positive supply wire touches either an earth wire, or an earthed component such as the bodyshell. Such faults are normally caused by a breakdown in wiring insulation, A short circuit fault will normally cause the relevant circuit fuse to blow.

9 Fuses are designed to protect a circuit from being overloaded. A blown fuse indicates that there may be problem in that particular circuit and it is important to identify and rectify the problem before renewing the fuse. Always renew a blown fuse with one of the correct current rating; fitting a fuse of a different rating may cause an overloaded circuit to overheat and even catch fire.

Finding an open-circuit

10 One of the most straightforward ways of finding an open-circuit fault is by using a circuit test meter or voltmeter. Connect one lead of the meter to either the negative battery terminal or a known good earth. Connect the other lead to a connector in the circuit being tested, preferably nearest to the battery or fuse. Switch on the circuit, bearing in mind that some circuits are live only when the ignition switch is moved to a particular position. If voltage is present (indicated either by the tester bulb lighting or a voltmeter reading, as applicable), this means that the section of the circuit between the relevant connector and the battery is problem-free. Continue to check the remainder of the circuit in the same fashion. When a point is reached at which no voltage is present, the problem must lie between that point and the previous test point with voltage. Most problems can be traced to a broken, corroded or loose connection.

Warning: *Under no circumstances may live measuring instruments such as ohmmeters, voltmeters or a bulb and test lead be used to test any of the airbag circuitry. Any testing of these components must be left to a Ford dealer or specialist, as there is a danger of activating the system if the correct procedures are not followed.*

Finding a short-circuit

11 Loading the circuit during testing will produce false results and may damage your test equipment, so all electrical loads must be disconnected from the circuit before it can be checked for short circuits. Loads are the components which draw current from a circuit, such as bulbs, motors, heating elements, etc.

12 Keep both the ignition and the circuit under test switched off, then remove the relevant fuse from the circuit, and connect a circuit test meter or voltmeter to the fuse connections.

13 Switch on the circuit, bearing in mind that some circuits are live only when the ignition switch is moved to a particular position. If voltage is present (indicated either by the tester bulb lighting or a voltmeter reading, as applicable), this means that there is a short-

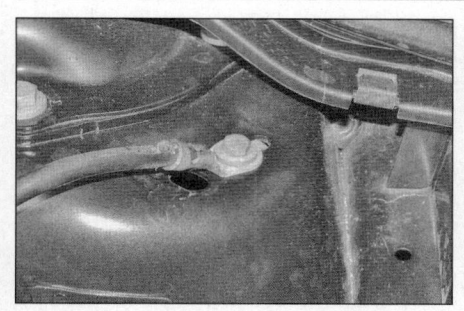

Body electrical system 12•3

2.14a Earth connection on the left-hand side suspension turret in the engine compartment ...

2.14b ... left-hand chassis member in the engine compartment (under the air filter) ...

2.14c ... left-hand transmission mounting (under the battery tray) ...

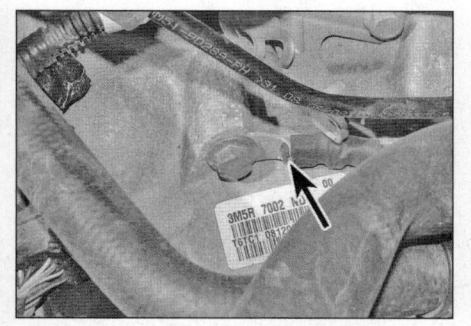

2.14d ... transmission bellhousing (arrowed) ...

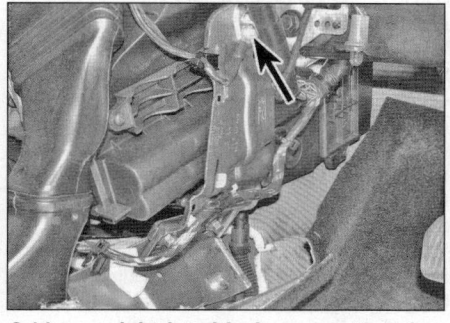

2.14e ... right-hand facia support bracket (arrowed) ...

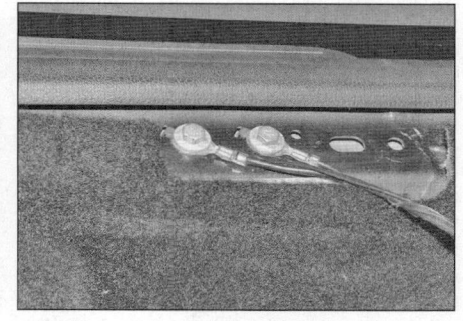

2.14f ... left- and right-hand front door sills (under the sill trims)

circuit. If no voltage is present, but the fuse still blows with the load(s) connected, this indicates an internal fault in the load(s).

Finding an earth fault

14 The battery negative terminal is connected to 'earth': the metal of the engine/transmission and the car body – and most systems are wired so that they only receive a positive feed, the current returning through the metal of the car body. This means that the component mounting and the body form part of that circuit. Loose or corroded mountings can therefore cause a range of electrical faults, ranging from total failure of a circuit, to a puzzling partial fault. In particular, lights may shine dimly (especially when another circuit sharing the same earth point is in operation), motors (eg, wiper motors or the radiator auxiliary cooling fan motor) may run slowly, and the operation of one circuit may have an apparently unrelated effect on another. Note that on many vehicles, earth straps are used between certain components, such as the engine/transmission and the body, usually where there is no metal-to-metal contact between components due to flexible rubber mountings, etc (see illustrations).

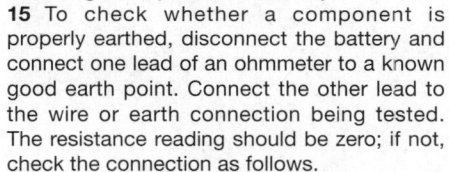

15 To check whether a component is properly earthed, disconnect the battery and connect one lead of an ohmmeter to a known good earth point. Connect the other lead to the wire or earth connection being tested. The resistance reading should be zero; if not, check the connection as follows.

16 If an earth connection is thought to be faulty, dismantle the connection and clean back to bare metal both the bodyshell and the wire terminal or the component earth connection mating surface. Be careful to remove all traces of dirt and corrosion, then use a knife to trim away any paint, so that a clean metal-to-metal joint is made. On reassembly, tighten the joint fasteners securely; if a wire terminal is being refitted, use serrated washers between the terminal and the bodyshell to ensure a clean and secure connection. When the connection is remade, prevent the onset of corrosion in the future by applying a coat of petroleum jelly or silicone-based grease or by spraying on (at regular intervals) a proprietary ignition sealer or a water dispersant lubricant.

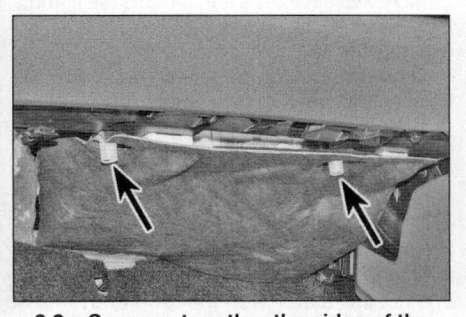

3 Fuses and relays – general information

Main fuses

1 The fuses are located on a single panel under the passenger's side of the facia (also known as the central junction box), and in a fusebox on the left-hand side of the engine compartment (also known as the engine junction box).

2 Access to the passenger cabin fuses is gained by removing the trim panel concealing the fusebox. The panel is secured by 2 fasteners. Undo the fasteners and allow the panel to drop down. Rotate the fusebox fasteners anti-clockwise, lower the fusebox from place, and pull it towards you. Hook the fusebox into the rear part of the bracket (see illustrations).

3 To access the engine compartment fusebox, open the bonnet, pull up on the lever and open the fusebox cover (see illustration).

4 Each fuse is numbered; the fuses' ratings

3.2a Squeeze together the sides of the fasteners to release them (arrowed) and lower the panel

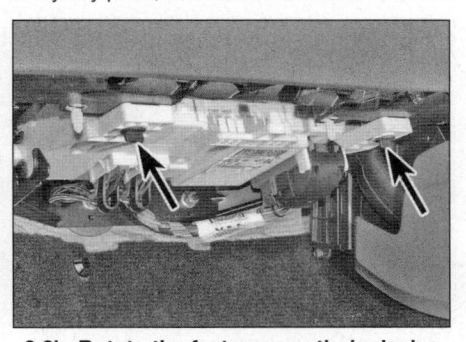

3.2b Rotate the fasteners anti-clockwise (arrowed) ...

12•4 Body electrical system

3.2c ... then pull the fusebox rearwards

3.3 Release the clip at the rear then lift off the engine compartment fusebox cover

and circuits they protect are listed on the rear face of the cover panel. A list of fuses is given with the wiring diagrams.

5 To remove a fuse, first switch off the circuit concerned (or the ignition), then pull the fuse out of its terminals – a pair of tweezers provided specifically for this purpose are fitted on the underside of the engine compartment fusebox cover. The wire within the fuse should be visible; if the fuse is blown the wire will have a break in it, which will be visible through the plastic casing.

6 Always renew a fuse with one of an identical rating; never use a fuse with a different rating from the original or substitute anything else. Never renew a fuse more than once without tracing the source of the trouble. The fuse rating is stamped on top of the fuse; note that the fuses are also colour-coded for easy recognition.

7 If a new fuse blows immediately, find the cause before renewing it again; a short to earth as a result of faulty insulation is most likely. Where a fuse protects more than one circuit, try to isolate the defect by switching on each circuit in turn (if possible) until the fuse blows again. Always carry a supply of spare fuses of each relevant rating on the vehicle, a spare of each rating should be clipped into the base of the fusebox.

8 Note that some circuits are protected by 'maxi' fuses fitted in the engine compartment fusebox. These fuses are physically much bigger than the normal fuses, and have correspondingly higher ratings. Should one of these fuses fail, have the circuit examined a Ford dealer or specialist prior to renewing the fuse.

9 Two fusible links are fitted to the battery positive lead. These are designed to protect the starter motor and alternator wiring harnesses from damage resulting from a major fault. If either of these two links should fail, do not renew them until the circuit concerned has been examined.

Relays

10 The main relays are located in the and engine compartment fusebox. The location and function of the relays is given on the underside of the fusebox lid.

11 The relays are of sealed construction, and cannot be repaired if faulty. The relays are of the plug-in type, and may be removed by pulling directly from their terminals. In some cases, it will be necessary to prise the two plastic clips outwards before removing the relay.

12 If a circuit or system controlled by a relay develops a fault and the relay is suspect, operate the system; if the relay is functioning, it should be possible to hear it click as it is energised. If this is the case, the fault lies with the components or wiring of the system. If the relay is not being energised, then either the relay is not receiving a main supply or a switching voltage, or the relay itself is faulty. Testing is by the substitution of a known good unit, but be careful; while some relays are identical in appearance and in operation, others look similar but perform different functions.

13 To renew a relay, first ensure that the ignition switch is off. The relay can then simply be pulled out from the socket and the new relay pressed in.

4 Ignition switch – removal and refitting

Removal

1 Ensure the battery negative lead has been disconnected as described in Chapter 5A, then turn the ignition switch to position I.

2 Using a thin screwdriver, release the locking clip at the front edge, the remove the audio control switch from the steering column (where fitted) **(see illustration)**. Disconnect the wiring plug as the switch is withdrawn.

3 Rotate the steering wheel as necessary to access the column upper shroud retaining clips. Release the clips and remove the shroud **(see illustration)**.

4 Undo the bolts and remove the steering column lower shroud **(see illustration)**. Release the steering column adjustment lever to remove the shroud.

5 Disconnect the wiring plug, then depress the clips and remove the ignition switch **(see illustration)**. Do not turn the lock cylinder (key) from position I whilst the ignition switch is removed.

6 With the key still in position I, insert a thin rod into the hole in the lower part of the cylinder housing and depress spring-loaded locking lug, and pull the cylinder from the housing **(see illustrations)**.

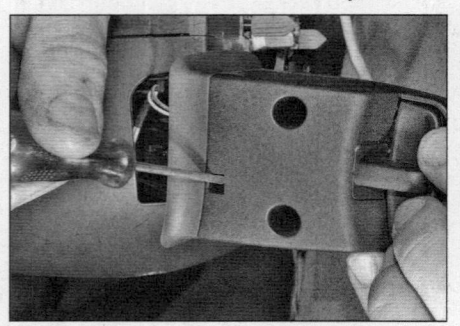

4.2 Depress the clip and remove the audio control switch from the column shroud

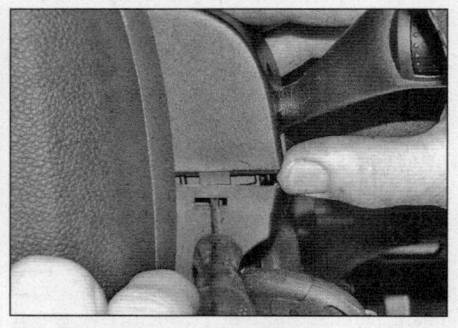

4.3 Rotate the steering wheel and release the upper shroud retaining clip each side

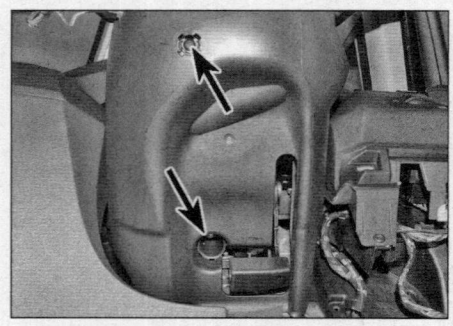

4.4 Lower steering column shroud bolts (arrowed)

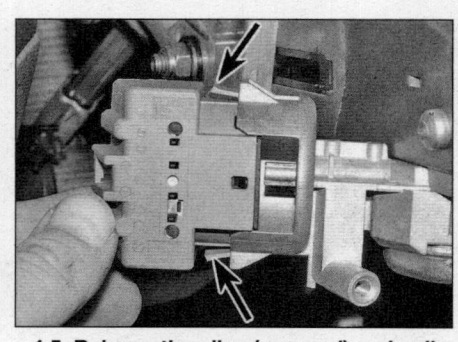

4.5 Release the clips (arrowed) and pull the switch from the lock

Body electrical system 12•5

Refitting

7 Refitting is a reversal of removal. Note that the lock cylinder (key) must be in position I prior to refitting the ignition switch.

5 Switches – removal and refitting

Steering column switches

1 Using a thin screwdriver, release the locking clip at the front edge, the remove the audio control switch from the steering column (where fitted) **(see illustration 4.2)**. Disconnect the wiring plug as the switch is withdrawn.
2 Rotate the steering wheel as necessary to access the column upper shroud retaining clips. Release the clips and remove the shroud **(see illustration 4.3)**.
3 Undo the 2 bolts and remove the steering column lower shroud **(see illustration 4.4)**. Release the steering column adjustment lever to remove the shroud.
4 Undo the bolts and slide the relevant switch from the assembly **(see illustration)**.
5 If the multifunction switch/rotary contact carrier is to be removed, begin by removing the steering wheel as described in Chapter 10.
6 Disconnect the wiring plugs, undo the 4 bolts and slide the assembly from the steering column **(see illustrations)**.
7 Refitting is a reversal of removal.

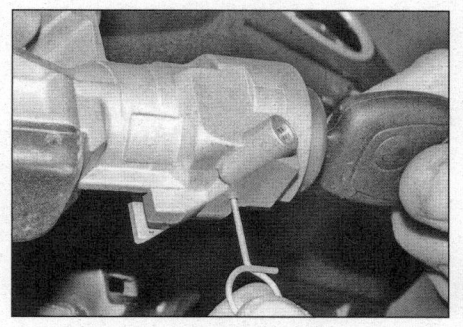

4.6a Insert a thin rod into the hole on the underside of the lock to release the locking lug . . .

Light switch

8 Remove the driver's side lower facia panel as described in Chapter 11.
9 Reach up, squeeze together the switch upper and lower retaining clips, and pull the switch from the facia **(see illustration)**. Disconnect the wiring plug as the switch is withdrawn.
10 Refitting is a reversal of removal.

Glovebox light switch

11 Remove the glovebox as described in Chapter 11.
12 Disconnect the switch wiring plug.
13 Release the clips and remove the switch **(see illustration)**.
14 Refitting is a reversal of removal.

4.6b . . . and pull the lock cylinder from the housing

Door mirror adjuster

15 The door mirror adjusters are integral with the window switch assemblies fitted to the door panels.
16 To remove the switch assemblies, using a flat-bladed, blunt tool, carefully prise away the grab handle recess trim **(see illustration)**.
17 Detach the wiring connector, then undo the retaining bolts and pull the switch from the surround **(see illustration)**.
18 Refit in the reverse order of removal.

Facia centre panel switches

19 Remove the facia-mounted audio unit as described in Section 18, then on models up to 03/2007, undo the 2 bolts and pull the surround trim from place **(see illustration)**.

5.4 Undo the bolts (arrowed) and slide the relevant switch from place

5.6a Undo the bolts (arrowed) on the top . . .

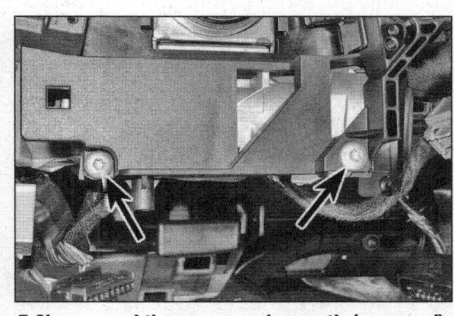

5.6b . . . and the ones underneath (arrowed), then slide the multifunction switch/contact carrier assembly from the column

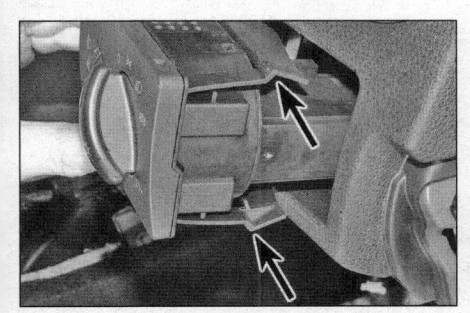

5.9 Reach up behind the facia and squeeze together the light switch clips (arrowed)

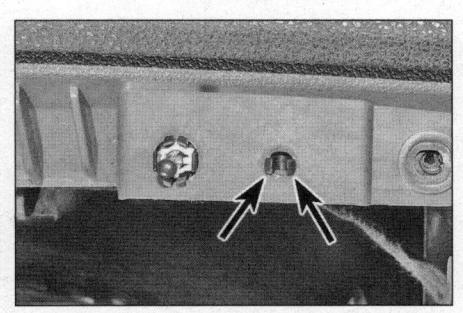

5.13 Squeeze together the clips (arrowed) and pull the glovebox light switch from place

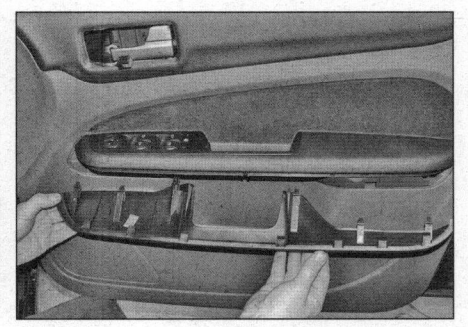

5.16 Carefully prise the grab handle recess trim downwards

12•6 Body electrical system

5.17 Undo the bolts (arrowed) securing the switch assembly

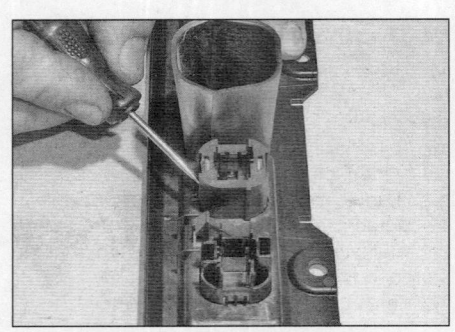

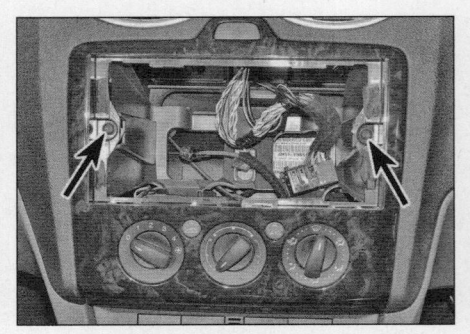

5.19 Audio unit surround trim bolts (arrowed)

5.20 Switch panel retaining bolts (arrowed)

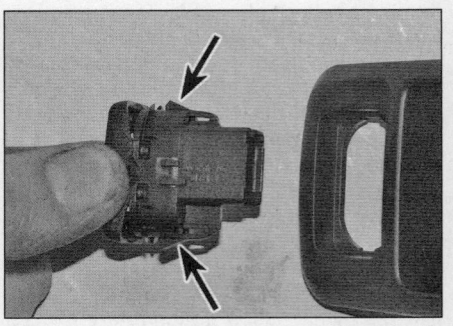

5.21 Release the clips and pull the switch from the panel

5.26 Prise out the front edge, and remove the handle surround

5.27 Depress the clips (arrowed) and pull the switch from the surround

20 Undo the 2 retaining bolts and pull the switch panel from the facia (see illustration). Disconnect the wiring plugs as the panel is withdrawn.
21 If required, release the clips and pull the relevant switch from the panel (see illustration).
22 Refitting is a reversal of removal.

Sunroof control switch
23 Remove the overhead console as described in Chapter 11.
24 Press-out the retaining clips and pull the switch from the console.
25 Refit in the reverse order of removal.

Central locking switches
26 Prise out the front edge and remove the interior release handle surround (see illustration). Disconnect the switch wiring plug as the surround is removed.

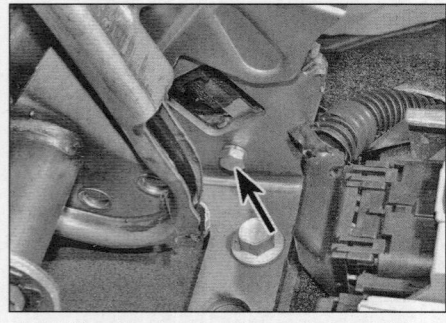

5.34 Handbrake warning switch retaining bolt (arrowed)

27 Disconnect the wiring plug from the switch, then depress the retaining clips and press the switch from the panel (see illustration).
28 Refitting is a reversal of removal.

Window switches
29 To remove the switch assemblies, using a flat-bladed, blunt tool, carefully prise the grab handle recess trim downwards (see illustration 5.16).
30 Detach the wiring connector, then undo the retaining bolts and pull the switch from the surround (see illustration 5.17).
31 Refit in the reverse order of removal.

Courtesy light switches
32 The courtesy lights are controlled by microswitches incorporated into the door locks. The switches are not available separately. If defective, the door lock assembly must be renewed (see Chapter 11).

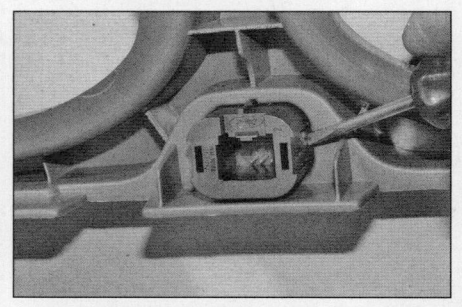

5.41 Depress the clips each side of the hazard warning switch – shown with the facia removed for clarity

Handbrake warning switch
33 Remove the centre console as described in Chapter 11.
34 Undo the single bolt and detach the switch (see illustration).
35 Detach the wiring connector from the switch.
36 Refit in the reverse order of removal.

Brake light switch
37 Refer to Chapter 9.

Headlight control/foglamp/instrument illumination
38 These switches are integral with the light switch module. Removal is described earlier in this Section.

Hazard warning switch
39 Remove the facia-mounted audio unit as described in Section 18. then on models up to 03/2007, undo the 2 bolts and pull the surround trim from place (see illustration 5.19).
40 Disconnect the wiring plug from the switch.
41 Depress the clips and push the switch from position (see illustration).
42 Refitting is a reversal of removal.

Steering wheel switches
43 Remove the driver's airbag as described in Section 22.
44 Undo the bolts and remove the relevant switch pad (see illustration). Disconnect the wiring plug as the switch pad is withdrawn.
45 Refitting is a reversal of removal.

Body electrical system 12•7

Seat heating switches

46 Remove the facia centre switch panel as described in Paragraph 19 and 20.
47 Release the clips and slide the switch from the panel (see illustration 5.21).

6 Exterior light bulbs – renewal

Note: *This section does not cover bulb renewal on models fitted with gas discharge headlights; refer to Section 9 for renewal details.*

1 Whenever a bulb is renewed, note the following points:
 a) Remember that if the light has just been in use, the bulb may be extremely hot.
 b) **Do not** touch the bulb glass with the fingers, as the small deposits can cause the bulb to cloud over.
 c) Always check the bulb contacts and holder, ensuring that there is clean metal-to-metal contact. Clean off any corrosion or dirt before fitting a new bulb.
 d) Wherever bayonet-type bulbs are fitted, ensure that the live contacts bear firmly against the bulb contact.
 e) Always ensure that the new bulb is of the correct rating and that it is completely clean before fitting it.

Halogen main beam

2 Remove the headlight unit as described in Section 8.

Models up to 12/2007

3 Push the retaining clips outwards and remove the plastic cover from the rear of the headlight **(see illustrations)**.
4 Pull the wiring plug from the bulb, then release the retaining clip and remove the bulb **(see illustrations)**. If the bulb is to be refitted, do not touch the glass with the fingers. If the glass is accidentally touched, clean it with methylated spirit.
5 Fit the new bulb using a reversal of the removal procedure.

Models from 12/2007

6 Peel away the plastic cap from the rear of the unit.

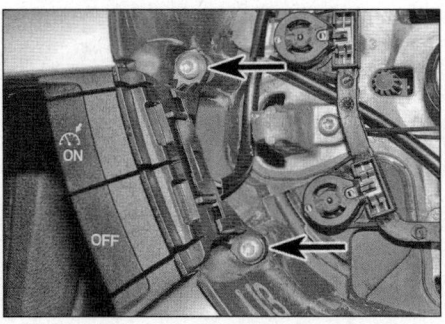

5.44 Steering wheel switch retaining bolts (arrowed)

7 Depress the clip and pull the wiring plug from the bulb **(see illustration)**.
8 Remove the bulb from the reflector **(see illustration)**. If the bulb is to be refitted, do not touch the glass with the fingers. If the glass is accidentally touched, clean it with methylated spirit.
9 Fit the new bulb using a reversal of the removal procedure.

Halogen dipped beam

10 Remove the headlight as described in Section 8.

Models up to 12/2007

11 Push the retaining clips outwards and remove the plastic cover from the rear of the headlight **(see illustration 6.3a and 6.3b)**.
12 Disconnect the wiring plug from the rear of the bulb, then release the retaining clip and remove the bulb from the headlight, noting which way around it's fitted **(see illustrations)**. If the bulb is to be refitted, do not touch the glass with the fingers. If the glass is accidentally touched, clean it with methylated spirit.

6.3a Release the clips around its edge . . .

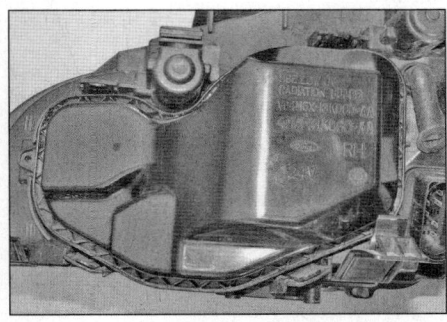

6.3b . . . and remove the plastic cover from the rear of the headlight

6.4a Disconnect the wiring plug and unhook the clip (arrowed) . . .

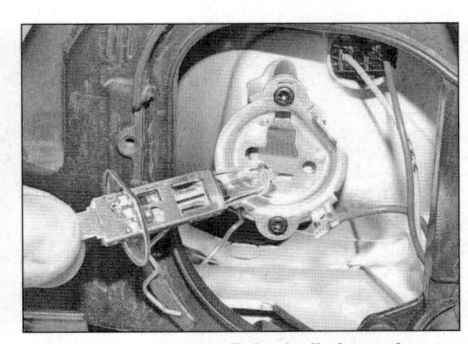

6.4b . . . then pull the bulb from the reflector

6.7 Depress the clip (arrowed) and pull the wiring plug from the bulb

6.8 Pull the bulb from the reflector

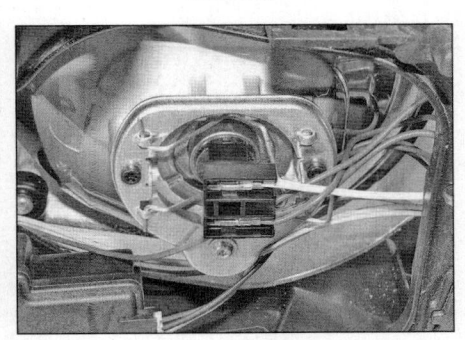

6.12a Pull the wiring plug from the bulb . . .

12•8 Body electrical system

6.12b ...then unhook the bulb retaining clip

6.15 Depress the clip (arrowed) and pull the wiring plug from the bulb

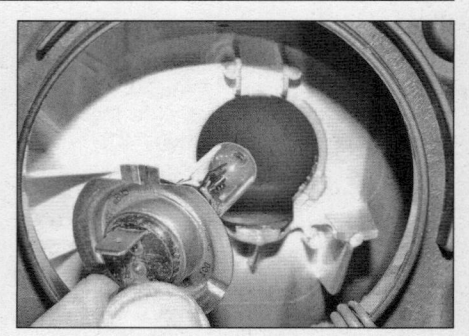

6.16 Pull the bulb from the reflector

13 Fit the new bulb using a reversal of the removal procedure.

Models from 12/2007

14 Peel away the plastic cap from the rear of the unit.
15 Depress the clip and pull the wiring plug from the bulb (see illustration).
16 Remove the bulb from the reflector (see illustration). If the bulb is to be refitted, do not touch the glass with the fingers. If the glass is accidentally touched, clean it with methylated spirit.
17 Fit the new bulb using a reversal of the removal procedure.

Sidelight

Models up to 12/2007

18 Remove the headlight unit as described in Section 8, then remove the cover from the rear of the headlight (see illustration 6.3a and 6.3b).
19 Squeeze together the clips and pull the bulbholder from the headlight unit (see illustration). Pull only on the bulbholder – not the cable.
20 Pull the wedge-type bulb directly from the bulbholder.
21 Fit the new bulb using a reversal of the removal procedure.

Models from 12/2007

22 Remove the headlight as described in Section 8, then pull the rubber cover from the rear of the sidelight location (see illustration).
23 Rotate the bulbholder clockwise and pull it from the reflector (see illustration).
24 Pull the wedge-type bulb from the holder (see illustration).
25 Fit the new bulb using a reversal of the removal procedure.

Front foglamp

26 Remove the foglamp as described in Section 8.
27 Disconnect the wiring from the bulbholder.
28 Rotate the bulbholder anti-clockwise and pull it from the foglamp (see illustration). Note that the bulb is integral with the bulbholder.
29 Fit the new bulb using a reversal of the removal procedure.

Front direction indicator

30 Remove the headlight as described in Section 8.
31 Rotate the bulbholder anti-clockwise and pull it from the headlight (see illustration).
32 Depress and twist the bulb to remove it from the bulbholder (see illustration).
33 Fit the new bulb using a reversal of the removal procedure.

6.19 Squeeze together the clips (arrowed)

6.22 Pull the rubber cover away to access the sidelight bulb

6.23 Rotate the bulbholder clockwise and withdraw it from the headlight

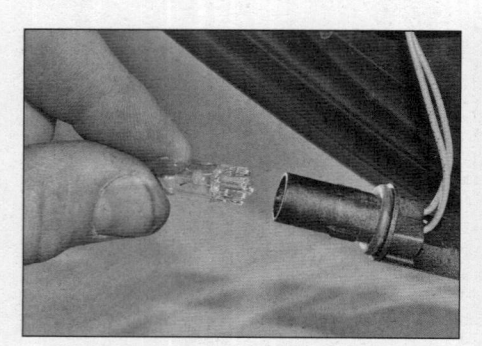

6.24 Pull the wedge-type bulb from the holder

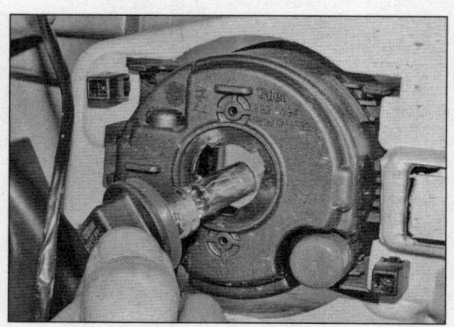

6.28 Rotate the foglamp bulbholder anti-clockwise

6.31 Rotate the bulbholder anti-clockwise

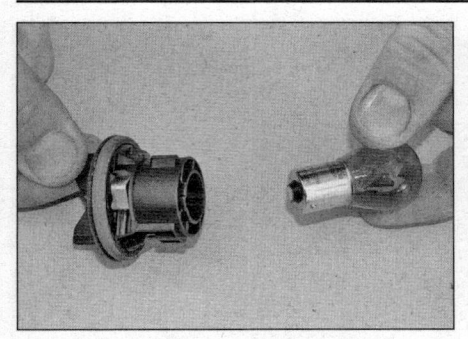

6.32 Depress and twist the bulb

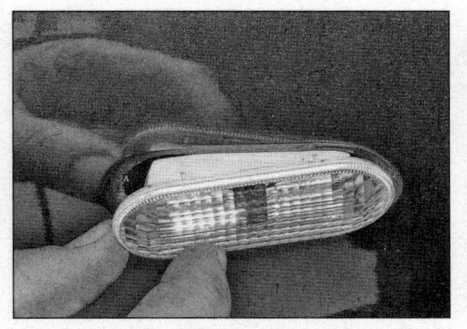

6.34 Push the repeater rearwards and pull the front edge outwards

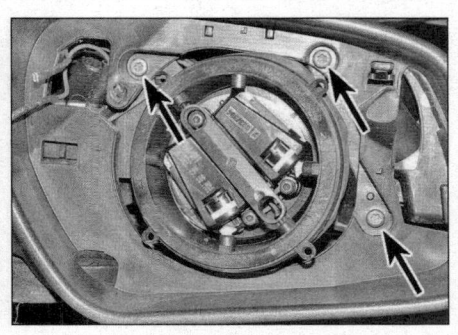

6.39a Undo the 3 bolts (arrowed) . . .

Direction indicator side repeater

In wing

34 Slide the side repeater lens rearwards, the pull the front edge from the wing (see illustration).
35 Holding the bulbholder, twist the lens anti-clockwise and it from the place.
36 Pull the wedge type bulb from the holder.
37 Refitting is a reversal of removal.

In mirror

38 Remove the mirror glass as described in Chapter 11.
39 Undo the 3 bolts, release the 2 clips and remove the plastic trim around the mirror motor (see illustrations)
40 Slide forward the cover over the mirror housing.
41 Release the clip and remove the repeater (see illustration).
42 Fold back the rubber sleeve, and pull the bulbholder from the repeater. Pull the wedge type bulb from the holder.
43 Refitting is a reversal of removal.

Approach light

44 Remove the door mirror glass as described in Chapter 11.
45 Release the clip and manoeuvre the lens from the mirror housing.
46 Pull the wedge-type bulb from the bulbholder.
47 Fit the new bulb using a reversal of the removal procedure.

Rear combination light

Hatchback models

48 Remove the rear light unit as described in Section 8.
49 Rotate the relevant bulbholder anti-clockwise and pull it from the light (see illustration 8.15).
50 Push and twist the bulb anti-clockwise, and pull it from the bulbholder.
51 Refitting is a reversal of removal.

Saloon models

52 Working in the luggage compartment, rotate the fasteners 90° and remove the appropriate access panel on the relevant side (see illustration).
53 Squeeze the plastic tabs and withdraw the bulbholder from the rear light unit (see illustration).
54 Press and twist the relevant bulb anti-clockwise, and withdraw it from the bulbholder.
55 Fit the new bulb using a reversal of the removal procedure.

Estate models

56 Remove the rear light unit as described in Section 8.
57 Undo the bolts, and remove the bulbholder (see illustrations).

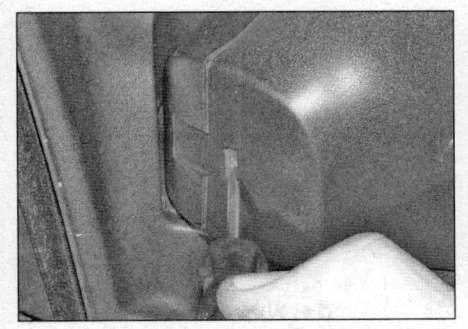

6.39b . . . release the clip at the inner edge . . .

6.39c . . . and the one at the lower, outer edge

6.41 Release the retaining clip

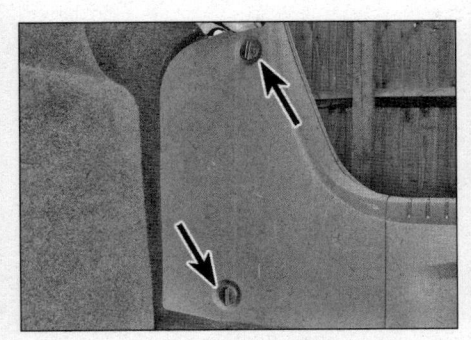

6.52 Rotate the fasteners (arrowed) and remove the panel

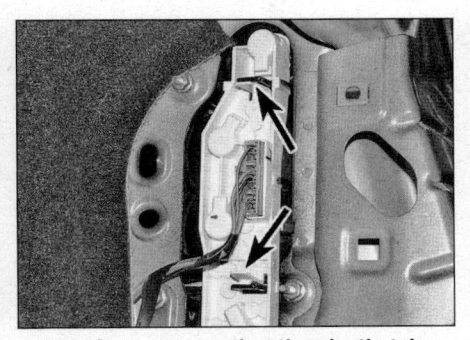

6.53 Squeeze together the plastic tabs (arrowed)

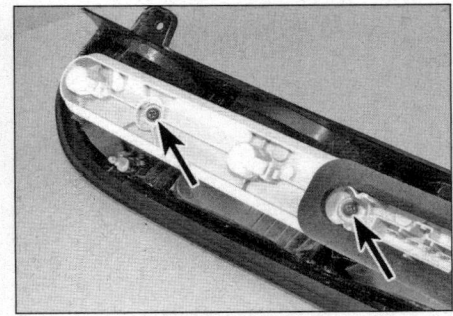

6.57a Undo the 2 bolts (arrowed) . . .

12•10 Body electrical system

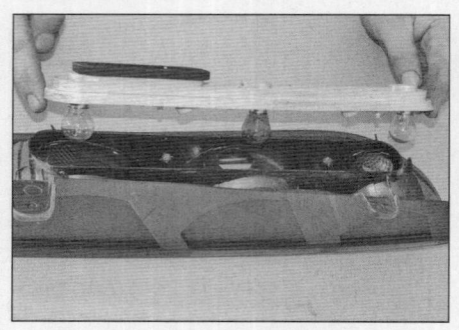

6.57b ... and withdraw the bulbholder

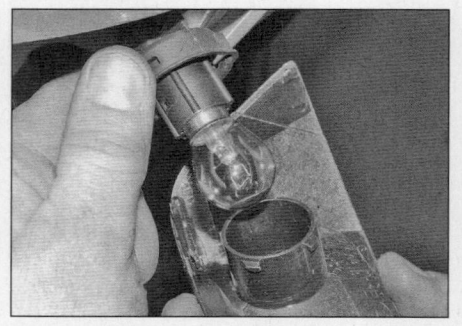

6.61 Rotate the bulbholder anti-clockwise

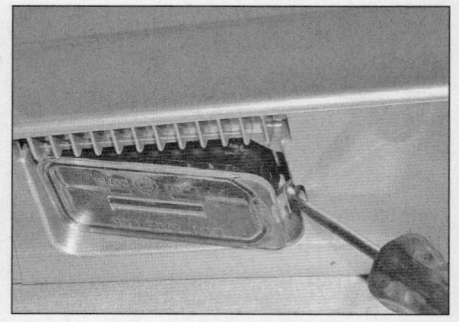

6.64 Release the clip and withdrawn the number plate light

58 Press and twist the relevant bulb anti-clockwise, and withdraw it from the bulbholder.
59 Fit the new bulb using a reversal of the removal procedure.

Rear foglamp/reversing light

60 Remove the relevant light unit as described in Section 8.
61 Rotate the relevant bulbholder anti-clockwise and pull it from the light **(see illustration)**.
62 Push and twist the bulb anti-clockwise, and pull it from the bulbholder.
63 Refitting is a reversal of removal.

Number plate light

64 On some models, undo the retaining bolts, and pull the lens from the tailgate/boot lid. On other models, using a small, flat-bladed screwdriver, release the clips and carefully prise the lens from the tailgate **(see illustration)**.
65 Pull the festoon-type or wedge type bulb from the contacts.
66 Fit the new bulb using a reversal of the removal procedure.

High-level brake light

Hatchback and Estate models

67 Undo the bolts and remove the light unit **(see illustration)**. Note that on models with a spoiler the bolts are accessed from the outside of the tailgate, whilst on models without a spoiler, they are accessed from inside.
68 Unclip the bulbholder, and pull the wedge-type bulb from place **(see illustration)**.
69 Fit a new bulb using a reversal of the removal procedure.

Saloon models

70 Starting at the rear edge, unclip the cover over the light unit **(see illustration)**.
71 Release the 2 clips and lower the light unit **(see illustration)**.
72 Disconnect the wiring plug, then unclip the bulbholder **(see illustration)**.
73 Pull the wedge-type bulb from place
74 Refitting is a reversal of removal.

7 Interior light bulbs – renewal

1 Whenever a bulb is renewed, note the following points:
   a) Remember that if the light has just been in use, the bulb may be extremely hot.
   b) Always check the bulb contacts and holder, ensuring that there is clean metal-to-metal contact between the bulb and its live and earth. Clean off any corrosion or dirt before fitting a new bulb.
   c) Wherever bayonet-type bulbs are fitted, ensure that the live contact(s) bear firmly against the bulb contact.
   d) Always ensure that the new bulb is of the correct rating and that it is completely clean before fitting it.

Reading lights

2 Inset a small flat-bladed screwdriver into the slot in the front face, depress the clip; and carefully prise the light unit from place **(see illustration)**.

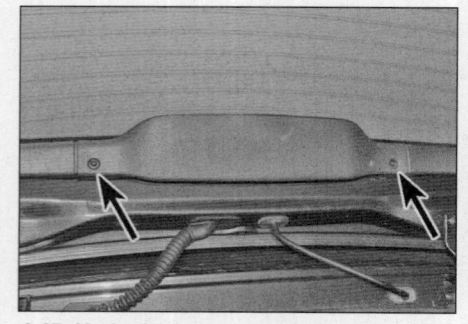

6.67 Undo the bolts (arrowed) and remove the high-level brake light unit

6.68 Release the clips (arrowed) and withdraw the bulbholder

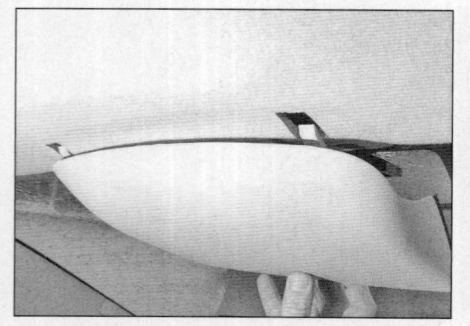

6.70 Pull down the rear edge of the brake light cover

6.71 Release the clips (arrowed) and remove the light unit

6.72 Bulbholder retaining clips (arrowed)

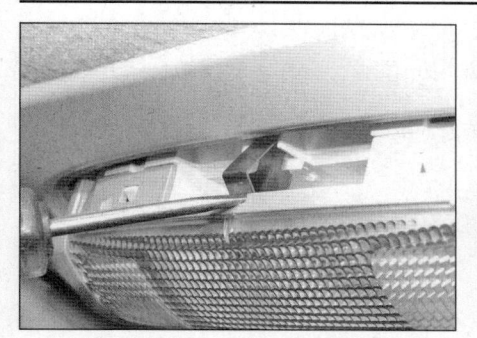

Body electrical system 12•11

7.2 Depress the clip at the front of the interior light

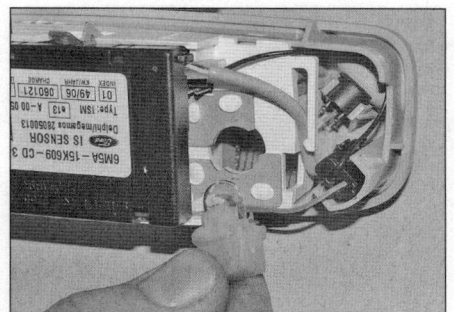

7.3 Twist the reading light bulbholder anti-clockwise and remove it

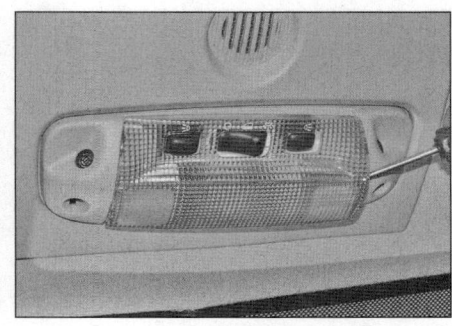

7.5a Prise the lens from place . . .

3 Twist the reading light bulbholder anti-clockwise and remove it **(see illustration)**. Pull the wedge type bulb from the holder.
4 Fit a new bulb using a reversal of the removal procedure.

Interior lights

5 Unclip the lens, and pull the interior light festoon type bulb from the contacts **(see illustrations)**.
6 Fit a new bulb using a reversal of the removal procedure.

Glovebox/luggage area light

7 Carefully prise the light unit from place **(see illustration)**.
8 Pull the wedge-type bulb from its holder.
9 Fit the new bulb using a reversal of the removal procedure. Note that the lens will only fit one-way round.

Footwell lights

10 Reach under the facia, and pull the wedge-type capless bulb from the holder **(see illustration)**.
11 Fit the new bulb using a reversal of the removal procedure.

Sunvisor/vanity mirror light

12 Carefully prise the light unit from place **(see illustration)**.
13 Pull the wedge-type bulb from the bulbholder **(see illustration)**.
14 Fit the new bulb using a reversal of the removal procedure.

Instrument panel bulbs

15 On all models covered by this Manual, it is not possible to renew the instrument panel bulbs individually as they are of LED design and soldered to a printed circuit board. It is not possible to renew a single LED. Where an LED is not functioning, the complete instrument panel must be renewed.

Switch illumination

16 The switches are illuminated by LEDs, and cannot be renewed separately. Refer to Section 5 and remove the switch.

Heater/air conditioning control panel illumination

17 The control panel is illuminated by non-renewable LEDs. If defective, the control panel may need to be renewed.

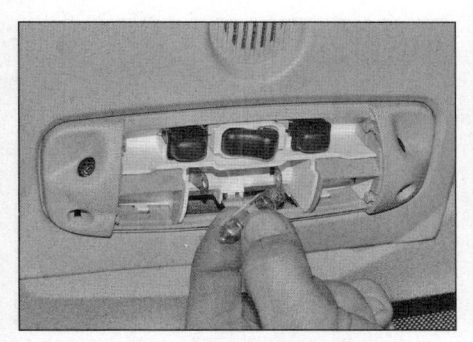

7.5b . . . then pull the interior light bulb from the contacts

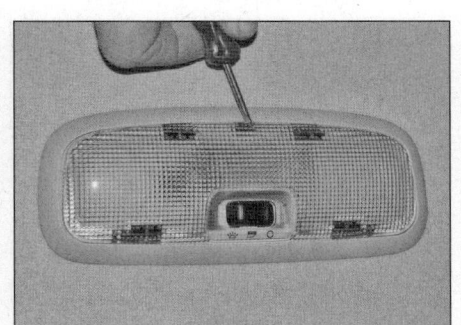

7.5c Prise the rear interior light lens from place

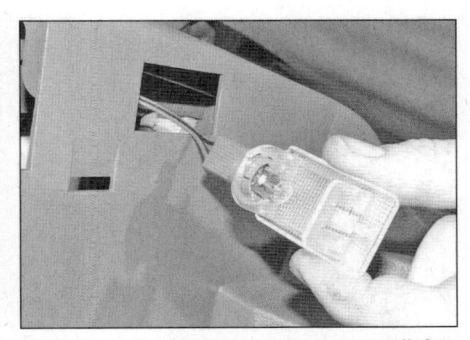

7.7 Prise the luggage compartment light from place

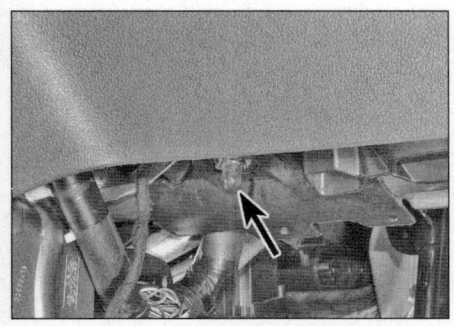

7.10 Pull the footwell light bulb (arrowed) from the holder

7.12 Carefully prise the vanity light lens from place

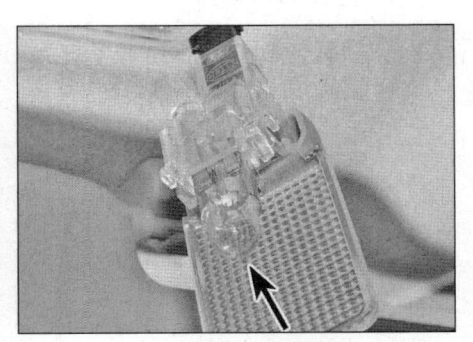

7.13 Pull the bulb (arrowed) from the holder

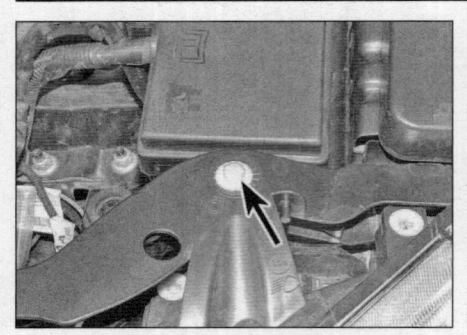

12•12 Body electrical system

8.1 Headlight retaining bolt (arrowed)

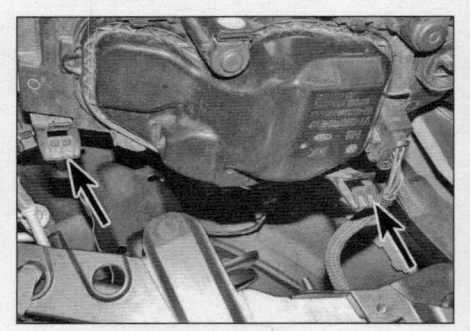

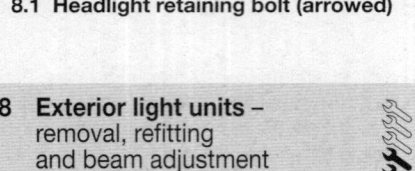

8.2 Depress the clips (arrowed) and pull the headlight forwards – shown with the headlight removed for clarity

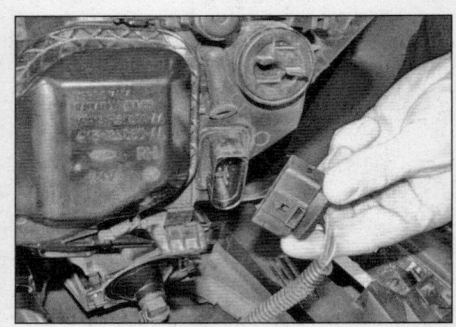

8.3 Disconnect the headlight wiring plug

8 Exterior light units – removal, refitting and beam adjustment

Headlight unit

Removal

Caution: On models equipped with gas discharge headlights, disconnect the battery negative lead, as described in Chapter 5A, prior to working on the headlights.

1 Open the bonnet, and undo the headlight upper retaining bolt **(see illustration)**.
2 Depress the retaining clips on the rear of the headlight, and pull the unit from place **(see illustration)**.
3 Disconnect the wiring plugs from the rear of the headlight as it's withdrawn **(see illustration)**.
4 If required, the headlight levelling motor can be renewed after the headlight has been removed, as follows: *Note: On models after 12/2007, it is not possible to renew the motor separately. If defective, it would appear that the complete headlight assembly must be renewed – check with your local dealer or parts specialist.*
5 Release the clips and remove the plastic cover from the rear of the headlight **(see illustration 6.3a and 6.3b)**.
6 Disconnect the motor wiring plug, then rotate the motor clockwise (left-hand headlight) or anti-clockwise (right-hand headlight), manoeuvre the motor ball-head from the guide on the reflector and pull it from the headlight **(see illustrations)**.

Refitting

7 Refitting is a reversal of the removal procedure. On completion check for satisfactory operation, and have the headlight beam adjustment checked as soon as possible (see below).

Front foglamp

Removal – models up to 12/2007

8 Carefully prise out the trim above the foglamp, and the foglamp surround trim **(see illustrations)**.
9 Undo the 2 mounting bolts, withdraw the foglamp from the front bumper, and disconnect the wiring **(see illustration)**.

Removal – models from 12/2007

10 Carefully prise out the foglamp surround trim **(see illustration)**.

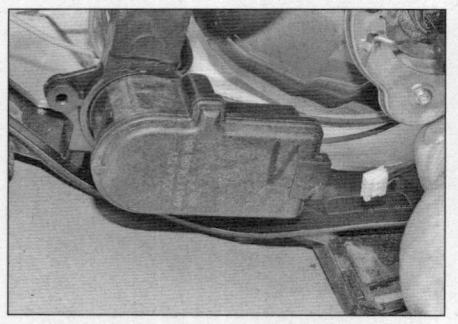

8.6a Disconnect the levelling motor wiring plug . . .

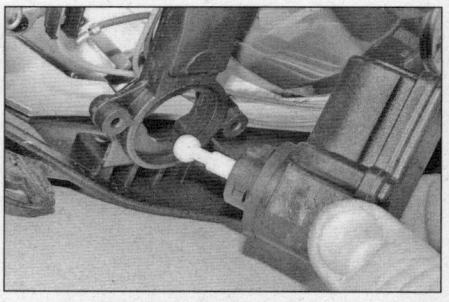

8.6b . . . then rotate the motor (see text) and disengage the ball-head from the guide on the reflector

8.8a Prise out the trim above the foglamp . . .

8.8b . . . and the trim around the foglamp

8.9 Foglamp mounting bolts (arrowed)

8.10 Prise away the foglamp surround trim

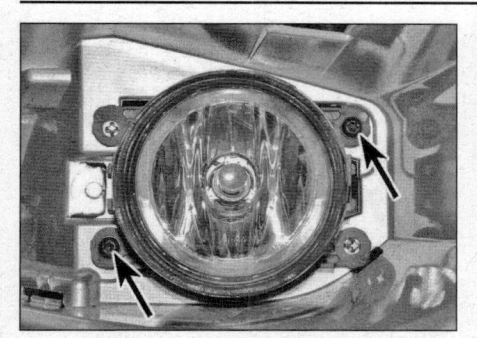

Body electrical system 12•13

8.11 Foglamp mounting bolts (arrowed)

8.12a Foglamp adjustment bolt (arrowed) – pre 12/2007 models . . .

8.12b . . . and post-12/2007 models

11 Undo the 2 mounting bolts, withdraw the foglamp from the front bumper, and disconnect the wiring **(see illustration)**.

Refitting

12 Refitting is a reversal of removal, but have the foglamp beam setting checked at the earliest opportunity. An approximate adjustment can be made by positioning the car 10 metres in front of a wall marked with the centre point of the foglamp lens. Turn the adjustment screw as required **(see illustrations)**. Note that only height adjustment is possible – there is no lateral adjustment.

Direction indicator side repeater

Removal and refitting

13 The procedure is as described for bulb renewal in Section 6.

Rear combination light

Hatchback and Estate models

14 Open the tailgate, and undo the 2 light unit retaining bolts **(see illustration)**.
15 Pull the light unit rearwards, and disconnect the wiring plug **(see illustration)**.
16 Refitting is a reversal of removal.

Saloon models

17 Remove the bulbholder as described in Section 6.
18 Undo the 3 retaining nuts, and remove the light unit **(see illustration)**.
19 Refitting is a reversal of removal. Ensure that the seal is correctly positioned.

Number plate light

20 The procedure is as described for bulb renewal in Section 6.

High-level brake light

Hatchback and Estate models

21 The procedure is as described for bulb renewal in Section 6.

Saloon models

22 Starting at the rear, unclip the plastic cover from the light unit **(see illustration 6.70)**.
23 Release the 2 clips and remove the light unit **(see illustration 6.71)**. Disconnect the wiring plug as the unit is withdrawn.
24 Refitting is a reversal of removal.

Rear foglamp/reversing lights

25 Reach up behind the light unit and release the retaining clips at its edge **(see illustration)**.

8.14 Rear light retaining bolts (arrowed)

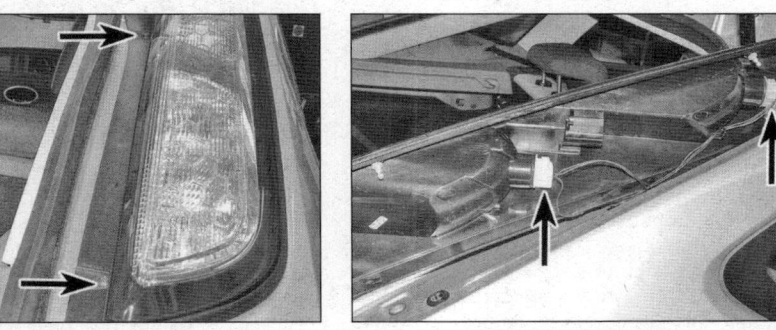

26 Pull the light unit rearwards, and disconnect the wiring plug.
27 Refitting is a reversal of removal.

Beam adjustment

Halogen headlights

28 Accurate adjustment of the headlight beam is only possible using optical beam setting equipment, and this work should therefore be carried out by a Ford dealer or suitably-equipped workshop.
29 For reference, the headlights can be adjusted using the adjuster screws, accessible via the top of each light unit **(see illustration)**.
30 Some models are equipped with an electrically-operated headlight beam adjustment system which is controlled through the switch in the facia. On these models, ensure that the switch is set to the basic 0 position before adjusting the headlight aim.

8.15 Rotate the bulbholders (arrowed) anti-clockwise

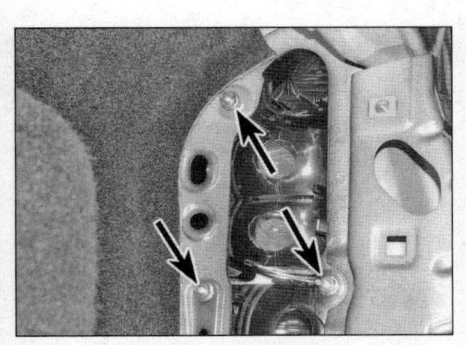

8.18 Rear light retaining nuts (arrowed) – Saloon models

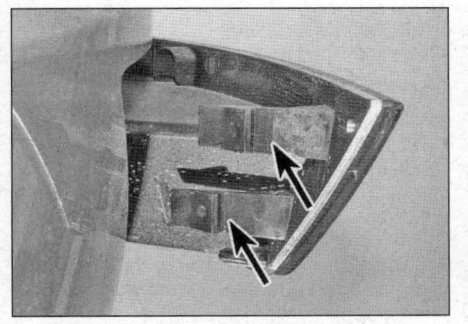

8.25 Release the clips (arrowed) at the edge of the rear foglamp/reversing light

8.29 Headlight beam adjustment bolts (arrowed)

12•14 Body electrical system

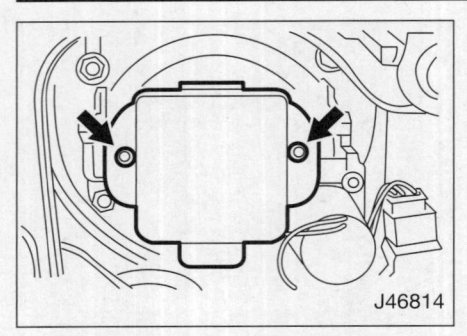

9.8 Undo the bolts (arrowed) and pull the bulb and module rearwards

31 On vehicles with adaptive front headlights (the headlight reflectors turn in the direction of the steering) It is possible to adjust the headlight beams for driving on the right-hand, or left-hand side of the road. Remove the headlight as described in this Section.
32 Release the clips and remove the cover from the rear of the headlight (see illustration 6.3a and 6.3b).
33 Press the lever on the side of the reflector upwards for driving on the right, and down for driving on the left.
34 For information on the lighting control module, see Section 9, paragraphs 19 to 21.

9 Xenon gas discharge headlight system – component removal, refitting and adjustment

General information

1 Xenon gas discharge headlights were available as an optional extra on all models covered in this manual. The headlights dipped beam bulbs produce light by means of an electric arc, rather than by heating a metal filament as in conventional halogen bulbs. An electronically-operated shutter is fitted in front of the bulb which angles the light for dipped beam, then re-angles the light for main beam. A conventional halogen bulb is also fitted to augment the main beam light output. The arc is generated by a control circuit which operates at voltages of above 28 000 volts. The intensity of the emitted light means that the headlight beam has to be controlled dynamically to avoid dazzling other road users. An electronic control unit monitors the vehicle's pitch and overall ride height by sensors mounted on the front and rear suspension and adjusts the beam range accordingly, using the range control motors built into the headlight units.

⚠ **Warning:** *The discharge bulb starter circuitry operates at extremely high voltages. To avoid the risk of electric shock, ensure that the battery negative cable is disconnected before working on the headlight units (see Chapter 5A), then additionally switch the dipped beam on and off to discharge any residual voltage.*

Headlight main beam

2 Remove the headlight as described in Section 8.
3 Push the retaining clips outwards, and remove the plastic cover from the rear of the headlight (see illustration 6.3a and 6.3b).
4 Disconnect the wiring plug from the rear of the bulb, then release the retaining clip and pull the bulb from the reflector (see illustration 6.4a and 6.4b). Note how the lugs on the bulb engage with the slots in the reflector. If the bulb is to be refitted, do not touch the glass with the fingers. If the glass is accidentally touched, clean it with methylated spirit.
5 Fit the new bulb using a reversal of the removal procedure.

Headlight dipped beam

Caution: *The dipped beam bulb is under gas pressure of at least 10 bars, therefore it is recommended that protective glasses are worn during this procedure.*
6 Remove the headlight as described in Section 8.

Models up to 12/2007

7 Release the retaining clips and detach the plastic cover from the rear of the light unit (see illustration 6.3a and 6.3b).
8 Disconnect the wiring plug, then undo the 2 retaining bolts and pull the bulb and module rearwards (see illustration). If the glass is accidentally touched, clean it with methylated spirit.
9 Fit the new bulb using a reversal of the removal procedure.

Models from 12/2007

10 Remove the plastic cap from the rear of the headlight, then disconnect the bulb module wiring plug.
11 Rotate the bulb locking collar anti-clockwise, and pull the bulb and module from the reflector (see illustration).
12 Slide the locking collar upwards and remove the bulb from the module (see illustration).
13 Fit the new bulb using a reversal of the removal procedure.

Sidelight

14 Remove the headlight unit as described in Section 8.
15 Pull the bulbholder from the headlight unit. Pull only on the bulbholder – not the cable.
16 Pull the wedge-type bulb directly from the bulbholder.
17 Fit the new bulb using a reversal of the removal procedure.

Lighting control module

Note: *If a new module is to be fitted, it must be configured using Ford dedicated diagnostic equipment (WDS). Entrust this task to a Ford dealer or suitably-equipped specialist.*
18 The lighting control module is fitted to vehicles with Xenon high-intensity gas discharge lights, or models with adaptive front lighting system (see Section 8, paragraph 31). The module is located behind the driver's side lower facia.
19 Undo the single bolt, and remove the facia panel beneath the main light control switch. Unclip the diagnostic plug connector as the panel is withdrawn.
20 Disconnect the wiring plug, then release the clip each side and remove the module.
21 Refitting is a reversal of removal.

Front ride height sensor

Removal

22 The sensor is mounted on the lower control arm of the right-hand wheel. Apply the handbrake, then jack up the front of the vehicle and support it on axle stands (see *Jacking and vehicle support*). Remove the wheel.
23 Undo the bolt securing the sensor arm bracket to the control arm.
24 Drill out the 2 rivets securing the sensor bracket to the vehicle body.
25 Disconnect the wiring plus as the sensor is withdrawn.

Refitting

26 Refitting is a reversal of removal. Note that if a new sensor has been fitted, then a calibration procedure must be carrier out. This requires access to Ford diagnostic equipment – entrust this task to a Ford dealer or suitably-equipped specialist.

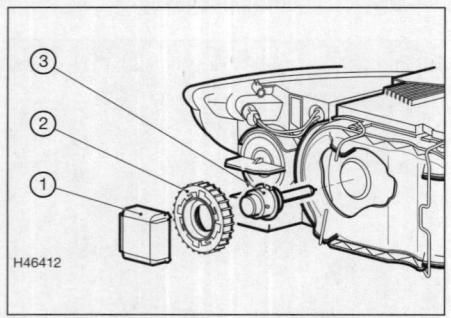

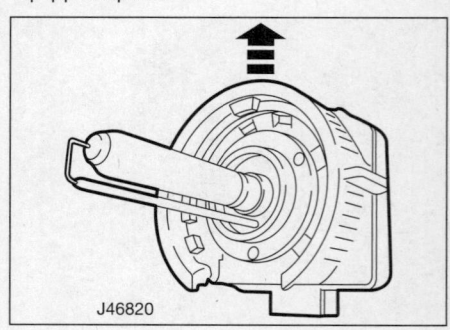

9.11 Xenon bulb details

1 Ignition module
2 Collar
3 Bulb

9.12 Slide the collar upwards

Rear ride height sensor

Removal

27 The sensor is secured to the left-hand lower control arm and the rear subframe. Chock the front wheels, then jack up the rear of the vehicle and support it on axle stands (see *Jacking and vehicle support*).
28 Disconnect the sensor wiring plug, then undo the bolts and remove the sensor, bracket and lever arm assembly.

Refitting

29 Refitting is a reversal of removal. Note that if a new sensor has been fitted, then a calibration procedure must be carried out. This requires access to Ford diagnostic equipment – entrust this task to a Ford dealer or suitably-equipped specialist.

Setting-up for left- or right-hand drive

Note: *This feature is also available on some halogen headlights (see Section 8, paragraphs 31 to 33).*

30 On models equipped with gas discharge headlights, the 'dipping' characteristics of the unit can be set-up for countries who drive on the left or right. Remove the headlight as described in Section 9.
31 Release the clips and remove the plastic cover from the rear of the headlight behind the dipped beam location.
32 Press the lever on the side of the reflector upwards for driving on the right, and down for driving on the left.

Beam adjustment

33 The basic alignment procedure of the headlights is the same as normal halogen headlights (see Section 8). However, before the procedure is attempted, the ride height sensors must be calibrated using dedicated Ford test equipment. Therefore this task should be entrusted to a Ford dealer or suitably-equipped specialist.

Range control positioning motor

34 Remove the headlight as described in Section 8.
35 Remove the cover from the rear of the headlight.

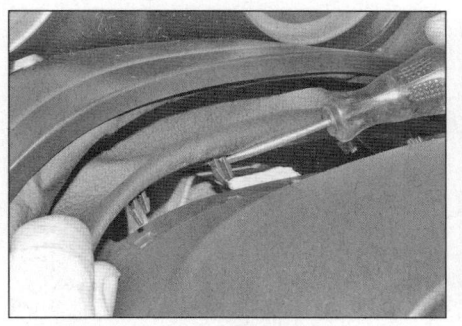

10.3 Unclip the gaiter from the column upper shroud

36 Disconnect the motor wiring plug, then undo the 2 retaining bolts.
37 Disengage the motor ball-head from the guide in the reflector and remove the motor.
38 Refitting is a reversal of removal.

10 Instrument panel – removal and refitting

Note: *The instrument panel and its function is included in the vehicle's self-diagnosis program. If the instrument panel has a fault, it would be prudent to have the vehicle's fault code memory interrogated by a Ford dealer or specialist, prior to removing the panel.*

Note: *If the instrument panel is being substituted with a new or exchange unit, the assistance of a Ford dealer or specialist is required to download necessary software, and initialise/adapt the various instrument panel functions.*

Removal

1 Disconnect the battery negative lead as described in Chapter 5A.
2 Fully extend the steering column, and move it to its lowest position.
3 Unclip the rubber gaiter from the steering column upper shroud, then pull the bezel attached to the lower part of the instrument panel rearwards and remove it **(see illustration)**.
4 Undo the 2 retaining bolts on the lower

10.4 Undo the bolts at the lower edge (arrowed) the pull the top of the instrument panel rearwards

edge of the instrument panel, then carefully pull the top edge of the panel rearwards and manoeuvre it from place **(see illustration)**.
5 Disconnect the wiring plug(s) as the panel is withdrawn.

Refitting

6 Refitting is a reversal of removal, but see the note at the beginning of this section.

11 Windscreen wiper components – removal and refitting

Wiper blades

1 Refer to *Weekly checks*.

Wiper arms

Removal

2 If the wipers are not in their parked position, switch on the ignition, and allow the motor to automatically park.
3 Before removing an arm, mark its parked position on the glass with a strip of adhesive tape. Prise off the cover and unscrew the spindle nut **(see illustrations)**. Ease the arm from the spindle by rocking it slowly from side-to-side.

Refitting

4 Refitting is a reversal of removal, but before tightening the spindle nuts, position the wiper blades as marked before removal.

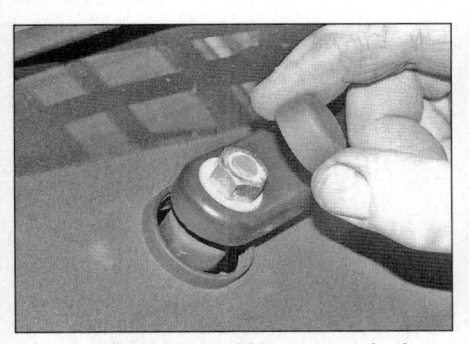

11.3a Pull of the rubber cap, undo the nut . . .

11.3b . . . and remove the wiper arm

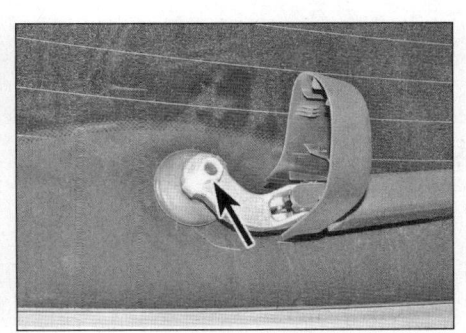

11.3c Lift the cover to expose the wiper spindle nut – rear wiper

12•16 Body electrical system

11.6a Prise forwards the clips (arrowed) . . .

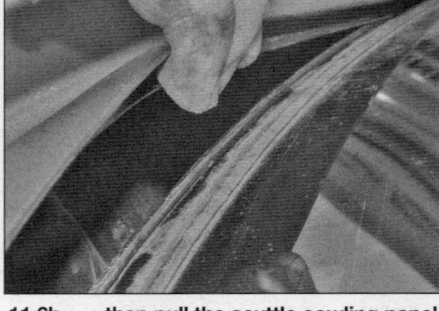

11.6b . . . then pull the scuttle cowling panel upwards from the base of the windscreen

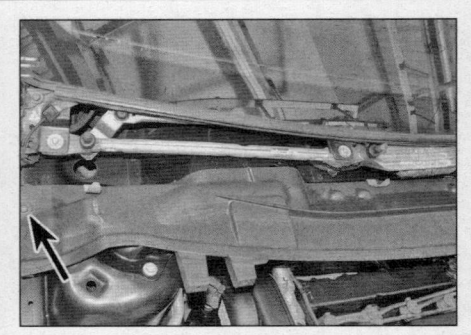

11.7 Undo the bolt at each end (right-hand one arrowed) and pull the bulkhead extension panel forwards

11.8 Undo the 3 bolts and slide the wiper linkage assembly 20 mm to the left . . .

11.9 . . . to release the rubber mounting lug from the bracket

clips and remove the bulkhead extension panel **(see illustration)**.
8 Undo the 3 bolts securing the motor linkage **(see illustration)**.
9 Move the assembly towards the left-hand side 20 mm to release the rubber mounting lug from the bracket on the bulkhead **(see illustration)**. Disconnect the wiper motor wiring plug as the assembly is withdrawn.
10 Using a screwdriver, carefully prise the linkage arm from the balljoint stud.
11 Undo the 3 bolts and remove the motor.

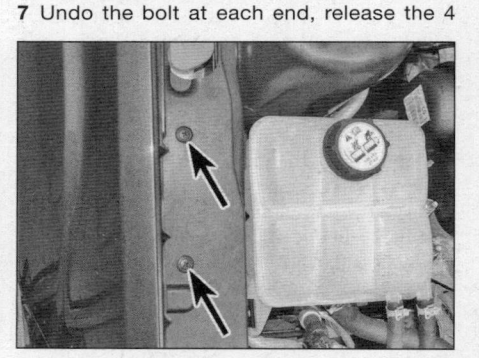

Refitting
12 When refitting, with the motor/linkage back in place, reconnect the wiring plug then operate the touch-wipe button to set the motor in the rest position. The remainder of refitting is a reversal of removal.

Wiper motor

Removal
5 Remove the wiper arms as described in the previous sub-Section.
6 Remove the clips at the front edge, then pull the scuttle cowling panel upwards to release it from the base of the windscreen **(see illustrations)**. Lift the panel from place.
7 Undo the bolt at each end, release the 4

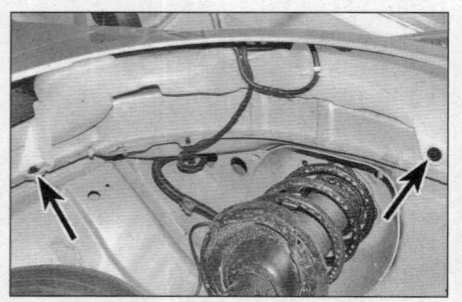

12 Washer system – general

1 All models are fitted with a windscreen washer system. Estate models also have a tailgate washer, and some models are fitted with headlight washers.
2 The fluid reservoir for the windscreen/headlight washer is located behind the right-hand side inner wing, behind the wheel arch liner. The windscreen washer fluid pump is attached to the side of the reservoir body **(see illustrations)** and where headlight washers are fitted, a lift cylinder/accumulator is located in the supply tube, behind the front

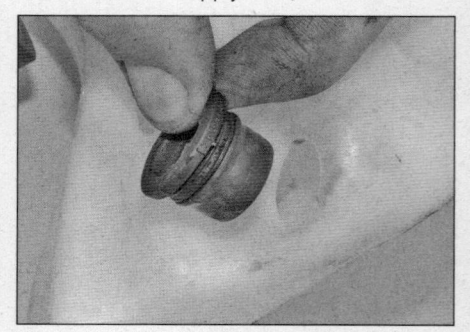

12.2a The washer fluid reservoir is retained by 2 bolts (arrowed) – viewed from under the wheel arch

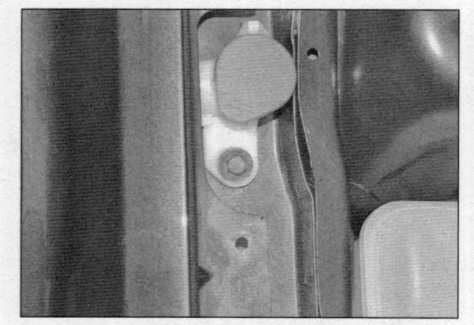

12.2b Remove the scrivets (arrowed) . . .

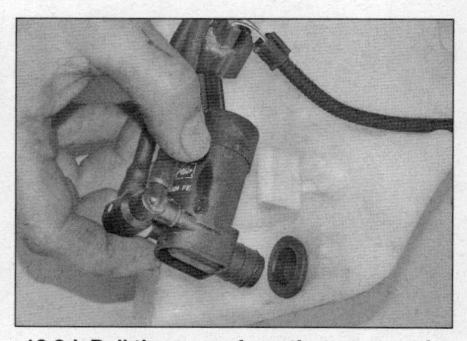

12.2c . . . to access the reservoir upper retaining bolt

12.2d Pull the pump from the grommet in the reservoir . . .

12.2e . . . then pull the grommet from the reservoir

Body electrical system 12•17

12.2f The grommet incorporates a coarse filter

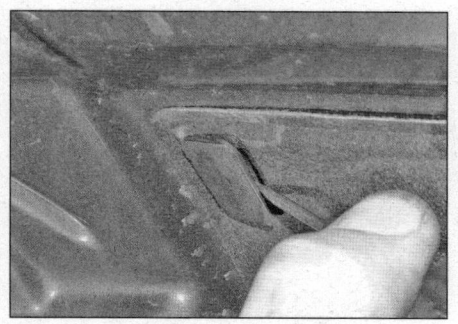

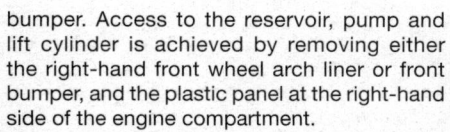

12.6a Prise out the bonnet insulation panel clips

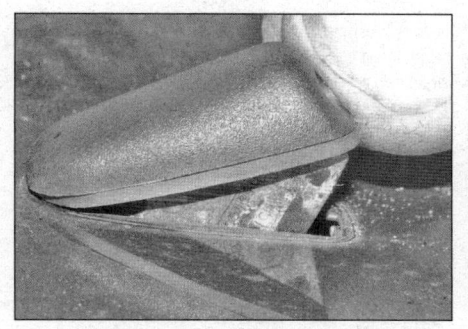

12.6b Disconnect the hose from the underside of the washer jet

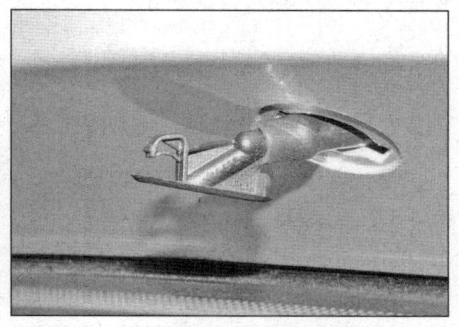

bumper. Access to the reservoir, pump and lift cylinder is achieved by removing either the right-hand front wheel arch liner or front bumper, and the plastic panel at the right-hand side of the engine compartment.

3 The tailgate washer is fed by the same reservoir, with a dual output pump.
4 The reservoir fluid level must be regularly topped-up with windscreen washer fluid containing an antifreeze agent, but not cooling system antifreeze – see *Weekly checks*.
5 The supply hoses are attached by rubber couplings to their various connections, and if required, can be detached by simply pulling them free from the appropriate connector.
6 The windscreen washer jets can be adjusted by inserting a pin into the jet and altering the aim as required. To remove a washer jet, open the bonnet, and disconnect the hose from the jet. Note that on some models, the bonnet insulation panel must be unclipped and removed **(see illustrations)**.
7 Where applicable, disconnect the wiring plug, then push the jet forwards, and lift the rear edge. Manoeuvre the jet from the bonnet **(see illustration)**.
8 The headlight washer jets are best adjusted using the Ford tool, and should therefore be entrusted to a Ford dealer or specialist to set.
9 On models with a rear spoiler, starting at the front edge, carefully prise the jet from place **(see illustration)**. Disconnect the hose as the jet is withdrawn.

13 Tailgate wiper motor – removal and refitting

Removal

1 Make sure the tailgate wiper is switched off and in its rest position, then remove the tailgate trim panel as described in Chapter 11.
2 Remove the wiper arm and blade as described in Section 11.
3 Detach the wiring connector from the wiper motor.
4 Undo the 3 wiper motor mounting bolts and remove the wiper motor from the tailgate **(see illustration)**. Check the condition of the spindle rubber grommet in the tailgate, and if necessary, renew it.

12.7 Press the jet forwards and lift the rear edge

Refitting

5 Refit in the reverse order of removal. Refit the wiper arm and blade so that the arm is parked correctly.

14 Horns – removal and refitting

Removal

1 The horns are located at the front end of the vehicle. Raise the front of the vehicle and support it securely on axle stands (see *Jacking and vehicle support*).
2 Release the fasteners and remove the splash shield under the radiator.
3 Disconnect the horn wiring plug, undo the mounting bolt and remove the horn from the vehicle **(see illustration)**.

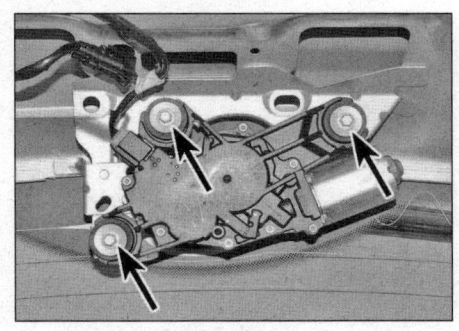

13.4 Tailgate wiper motor bolts (arrowed)

12.9 Carefully prise the front edge of the rear washer jet from place

Refitting

4 Refit in the reverse order of removal. Check for satisfactory operation on completion.

15 Sunroof motor – removal and refitting

Removal of the sunroof motor requires the headlining to be removed. This is an involved task, requiring patience and dexterity. Consequently we recommend you entrust this task to a Ford dealer or upholstery specialist.

16 Central locking system – general information

1 All models are equipped with a central door

14.3 Horn retaining bolt (arrowed) – viewed from above

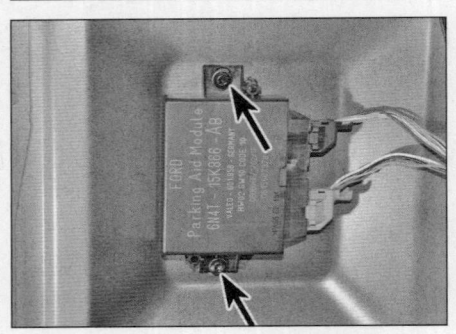

12•18 Body electrical system

17.4 Undo the parking aid module bolts (arrowed)

17.7 Press apart the clips (arrowed) and pull the sensor from place

locking system, which automatically locks all doors and the rear tailgate/boot lid in unison with the manual locking of the driver's front door. The system is operated electronically with motors/switches incorporated into the door lock assemblies. The system is controlled by the Generic Electronic Module (GEM) and the Keyless Vehicle Module (KVM) – where fitted. The GEM and the KVM communicate with the vehicle's other control modules via an information network known as a Databus. Control modules integral with electric window motors receive signals from the GEM via the databus, and directly control the operation of the door locks. The tailgate/boot lid has its own control module, integral with the lock assembly. If any module is renewed, new software for the unit must be downloaded from Ford. Entrust this task to a Ford dealer or suitably-equipped specialist.

2 The control unit is equipped with a self-diagnosis capability. Should the system develop a fault, have the control unit interrogated by a Ford dealer or suitably-equipped specialist. Once the fault has been established, refer to the relevant Section of Chapter 11 to renew a door module or tailgate/boot lid lock as applicable.

17 Parking aid components – general, removal and refitting

General information

1 The parking aid system is available on all models. Four ultrasound sensors located in the bumpers measure the distance to the closest object behind or in front the car, and inform the driver using acoustic signals from a buzzer located under the rear luggage compartment trim. The nearer the object, the more frequent the acoustic signals.

2 The system includes a control module and self-diagnosis program, and therefore, in the event of a fault, the vehicle should be taken to a Ford dealer or suitably-equipped specialist who will be able to interrogate the system.

Parking Aid Module (PAM)

Removal

3 The control unit is located behind the right-hand luggage compartment side trim panel. Remove the luggage compartment side panel trim as described in Chapter 11, and remove the foam padding behind the panel.
4 Undo the 2 retaining bolts, and remove the PAM **(see illustration)**. As the unit is removed, disconnect the wiring plugs.

Refitting

5 Refitting is a reversal of removal.

Range/distance sensor

Removal

6 Remove the relevant bumper as described in Chapter 11.
7 Disconnect the sensor wiring plug, then push the retaining clips apart, and pull the sensor from position **(see illustration)**.

Refitting

8 Refitting is a reversal of removal. Press the sensor firmly into position until the retaining clips engage.

Speaker

9 The parking aid warning speaker is located adjacent to the right-hand side rear seat belt inertia reel units. To access the speakers, remove the parcel shelf support brackets/luggage compartment side panels as described in Chapter 11.
10 Undo the 2 retaining bolts, and remove the speaker. Disconnect the wiring plug as the speaker is removed.

18 Audio/DVD units – removal and refitting

Note: *This Section applies only to standard-fit audio equipment.*
Note: *If a new audio unit is to be fitted, it must be configured using Ford diagnostic equipment (WDS). Entrust this task to a Ford dealer or suitably-equipped specialist.*

Removal

1 Disconnect the battery negative lead as described in Chapter 5A.

Audio unit – models up to 03/2007

2 Removal of the facia unit requires the use of Ford special tools No GV3301. Equivalent tools may be available from car audio specialist.
3 Insert the 4 tools into the slots in each corner of the audio control panel **(see illustrations)**. Note that the tools must be inserted with the straight-edges to the outside. Pull the audio unit from the facia.
4 Release the clocking catches and disconnect the wiring plug(s) as the unit is withdrawn.

Audio unit – models from 03/2007

5 Starting at the top edge, carefully prise the surround panel from the facia centre **(see illustration)**.
6 Undo the bolt in each corner of the audio unit **(see illustration)**. Pull the audio unit from place, and disconnect the wiring plugs.

Audio unit with DVD player – models up to 01/2008

7 Removal of the facia unit requires the use of

18.3a Insert the tools into the slots in the corners the unit

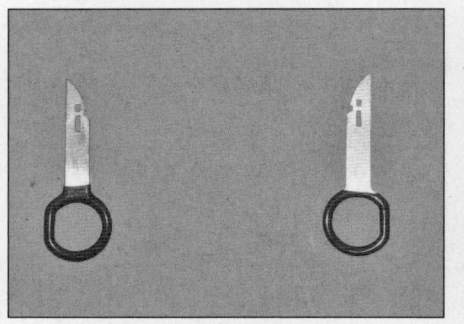

18.3b The tools must be inserted with the straight-edges to the outside

18.5 Carefully prise the top edge of the surround panel from the facia

Body electrical system 12•19

18.6 Undo the 4 bolts (arrowed) and pull the audio unit from place

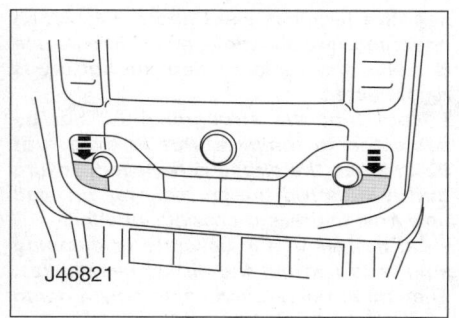

18.11 Prise out the blanking plugs (arrowed)

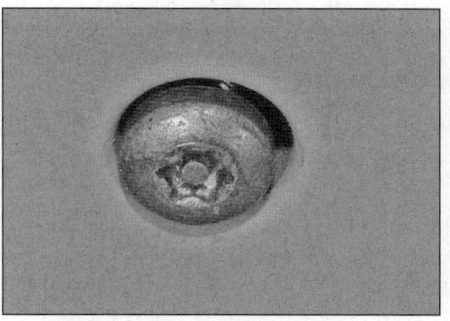

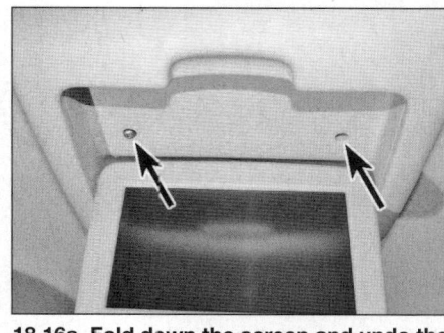

18.16a Fold down the screen and undo the security bolts (arrowed)

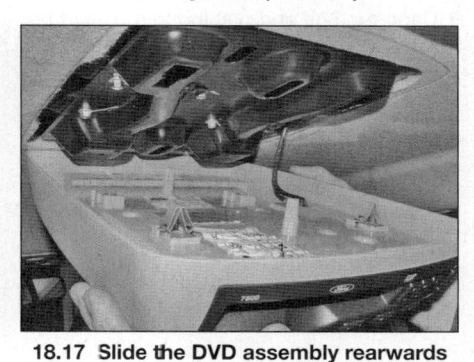

Ford special tools No GV3301. Equivalent tools may be available from car audio specialist.

8 Insert the 4 tools into the slots in each corner of the audio control panel **(see illustration 18.3a and 18.3b)**. Note that the tools are marked 'top left', etc. Pull the audio unit from the facia.

9 Release the clocking catches and disconnect the wiring plug(s) as the unit is withdrawn.

Audio unit with DVD player – models from 01/2008

10 Removal of the facia unit requires the use of Ford special tools No GV3301. Equivalent tools may be available from car audio specialist.

11 Carefully prise out the blanking plates in the lower corners of the control panel **(see illustration)**.

12 Insert the 4 tools into the slots in each corner of the audio control panel **(see illustration 18.3a and 18.3b)**. Note that the tools are marked 'top left', etc. Pull the audio unit from the facia.

13 Release the clocking catches and disconnect the wiring plug(s) as the unit is withdrawn

CD autochanger

Note: *If a new autochanger is to be fitted, the new unit must be configured using Ford diagnostic equipment (WDS). Entrust this task to a Ford dealer or suitably-equipped specialist.*

14 Remove the front seat as described in Chapter 11.

15 Undo the 5 retaining bolts and pull the autochanger from place. Disconnect the wiring plug as the unit is withdrawn.

Headlining-mounted DVD player

16 Fold down the DVD screen, and remove the 2 Torx security bolts **(see illustrations)**.

17 Slide the assembly rearwards and lower it from place **(see illustration)**. Disconnect the wiring plug as the assembly is withdrawn.

Note: *Handle the DVD assembly with care – it's very delicate.*

18 No further dismantling is recommended. When refitting the assembly, position it in line with the front mounting bolt holes, and push it upwards to engage the rear clips.

18.16b Note the pin in the centre of the security bolts

Refitting

19 Refitting is a reversal of removal, but if a new unit has been fitted, suitable software must be downloaded from Ford. Entrust this task to a Ford dealer or suitably-equipped specialist.

19 Aerial – removal and refitting

Removal and refitting of the aerial requires the headlining to be removed. This is an involved task, requiring patience and dexterity. Consequently, we recommend you entrust this task to a Ford dealer or upholstery specialist.

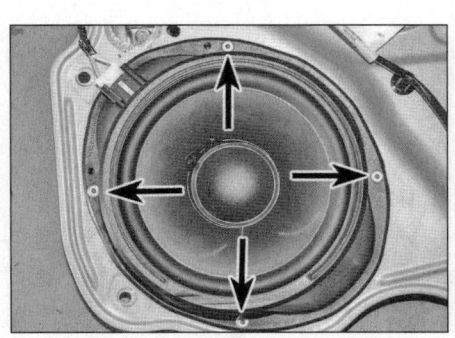

18.17 Slide the DVD assembly rearwards

20 Speakers – removal and refitting

Door speakers

1 To remove a door-mounted speaker, remove the appropriate door trim as described in Chapter 11.

2 Drill out the rivets securing the speaker to the door **(see illustration)**.

3 Disconnect the wiring plugs as the speaker is withdrawn.

4 Refit in the reverse order of removal.

Tweeter speaker

5 Pull the trim panel over the door mirror mounting from place **(see illustration)**.

20.2 Drill out the rivets (arrowed) and remove the speaker

20.5 Pull the mirror mounting trim panel from place

12•20 Body electrical system

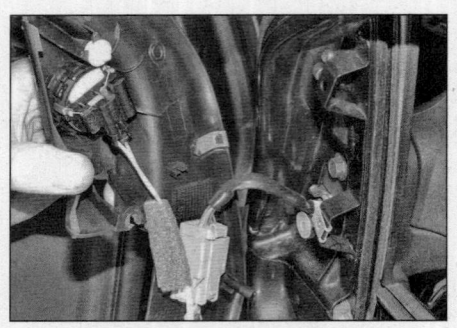

20.6 Undo the bolt and pull the trim panel from the door frame

6 Undo the bolt and pull the trim panel from the door frame **(see illustration)**.
7 Release the retaining clips and remove the speaker. Disconnect the speaker wiring plug as it's withdrawn.
8 Refitting is a reversal of removal.

Rear speakers – 3-door models

9 Remove the rear side panel as described in Chapter 11.
10 Disconnect the wiring plug, undo the 3 bolts and remove the speaker.
11 Refitting is a reversal of removal.

21 Airbag system – general information and precautions

Warning: Before carrying out any operations on the airbag system, disconnect the battery

22.4a Insert a flat-bladed screwdriver and push the handle down to release the airbag clip

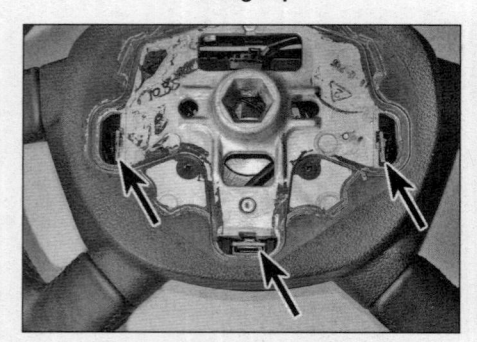

22.4c There are 3 airbag retaining clips (arrowed)

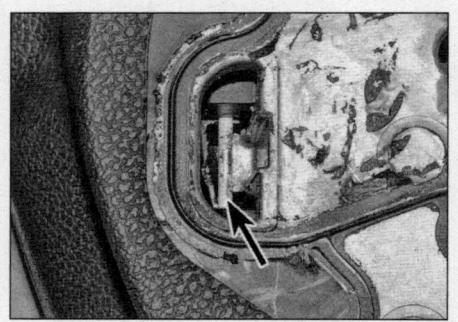

22.4b The airbag clips (arrowed) must be pushed outwards

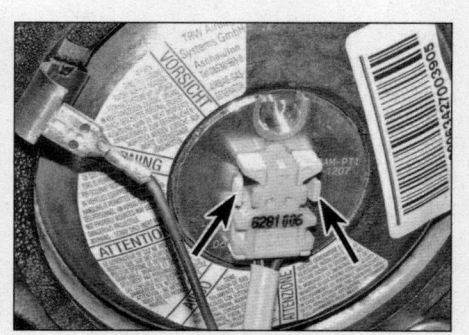

22.5 Squeeze together the clips (arrowed) and pull the connector from the airbag

negative terminal (see Chapter 5A). When operations are complete, make sure no one is inside the vehicle when the battery is reconnected.
• Note that the airbag(s) must not be subjected to temperatures in excess of 90°C. When the airbag is removed, ensure that it is stored the correct way up (pad upwards) to prevent possible inflation.
• Do not allow any solvents or cleaning agents to contact the airbag assemblies. They must be cleaned using only a damp cloth.
• The airbags and control unit are both sensitive to impact. If either is dropped or damaged they should be renewed.
• Disconnect the airbag control unit wiring plug prior to using arc-welding equipment on the vehicle.

A driver's and passenger's airbag, side airbags (seat mounted) and overhead curtain airbags were fitted as standard equipment to models in the Ford Focus range. The driver's airbag is fitted to the centre of the steering wheel. The passenger's airbag is fitted to the upper surface of the facia, above the glovebox. The airbag system comprises the airbag unit(s) (complete with gas generators), impact sensors, the control unit and a warning light in the instrument panel.

The airbag system is triggered in the event of a direct or offset frontal impact above a predetermined force. The airbag is inflated within milliseconds, and forms a safety cushion between the driver and the steering wheel or (where applicable) the passenger and the facia. This prevents contact between the upper body and the steering wheel, column and facia, and therefore greatly reduces the risk of injury. The airbag then deflates almost immediately through vents in the side of the airbag. The side airbags and overhead curtain airbags are triggered by side impacts, registered by the sensors fitted to the base of the B-pillars on each side.

Every time the ignition is switched on, the airbag control unit performs a self-test. The self-test takes approximately 7 seconds, and during this time the airbag warning light on the facia is illuminated. After the self-test has been completed, the warning light should go out. If the warning light fails to come on, remains illuminated after the initial 7 second period, or comes on at any time when the vehicle is being driven, there is a fault in the airbag system. The vehicle should then be taken to a Ford dealer or specialist for examination at the earliest possible opportunity.

22 Airbag system components – removal and refitting

Note: Refer to the warnings in Section 21 before carrying out the following operations.

1 Disconnect the battery negative terminal (see Chapter 5A). Wait at least 5 minutes for any residual electrical energy to dissipate before commencing work. **Note:** If removing the driver's airbag, turn the steering wheel 90° from straight-ahead before disconnecting the battery, otherwise the steering lock will engage.

Driver's airbag

2 Set the steering wheel and front wheels in the 'straight-ahead' position.
3 Rotate the steering wheel 90° in each direction to access the steering column upper shroud retaining clips. Release the clips and remove the shroud **(see illustrations 4.2, 4.3 and 4.4)**.
4 Locate the access hole in the reverse side of the steering wheel, and insert a flat-bladed screwdriver into the hole, then push the handle downwards to release the retaining clip **(see illustrations)**. Turn the steering wheel 180° and release the clip on the other side, followed by the clip at the base of the unit.
5 Temporarily touch the striker plate of the front door to discharge any electrostatic electricity. Return the steering wheel to the straight-ahead position, then carefully lift the airbag assembly away from the steering wheel and disconnect the wiring connectors from the rear of the unit **(see illustration)**. Note that the airbag must not be knocked or dropped, and should be stored the correct way up with its padded surface uppermost.
6 On refitting, reconnect the wiring connectors and locate the airbag unit in the steering wheel, making sure the wire does not become trapped, and push the airbag into place to

Body electrical system 12•21

22.8a Insert screwdrivers into the passengers side inner air vent ...

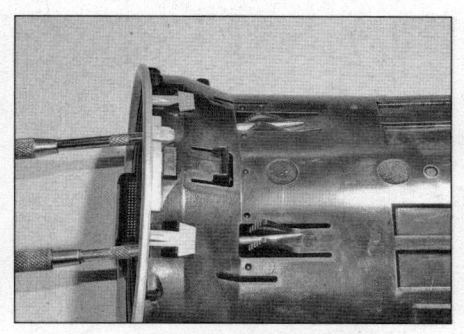

22.8b ... to release the upper clips ...

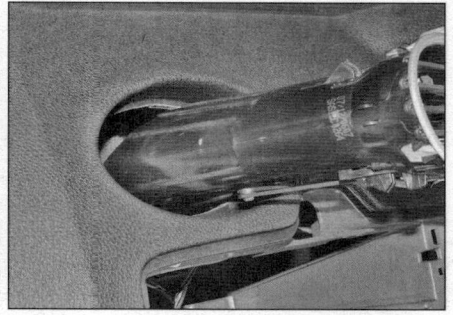

22.8c ... and pull the vent from the facia

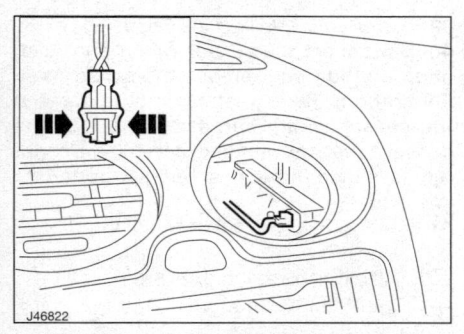

22.9 Squeeze together the sides and disconnect the airbag wiring plug

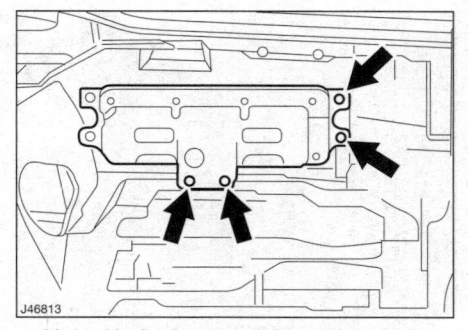

22.11 Undo the remaining airbag bolts (arrowed)

22.14 Passenger's airbag nuts (arrowed)

engage the retaining clips. Reconnect the battery negative lead (see Chapter 5A). Ensure no-one is in the vehicle when the battery is reconnected.

Passenger airbag

Models up to 04/2006

7 Remove the passenger's glovebox as described in Chapter 11.
8 Using a small screwdriver, release the upper retaining clips from the passenger's side central facia air vent, the pull the top edge forwards, release the lower clips and remove the vent **(see illustrations)**.
9 Disconnect the airbag wiring plug **(see illustration)**.
10 Undo the airbag module inner retaining bolts.
11 Working underneath the facia, undo the 4 remaining airbag mounting bolts **(see illustration)**. Manoeuvre the airbag from place.
12 Refitting is a reversal of removal. Ensure that the wiring connector is securely reconnected. Ensure that no-one is inside the vehicle. Reconnect the battery negative lead as described in Chapter 5A.

Models from 04/2006

13 Remove the facia as described in Chapter 11.
14 Undo the 6 nuts and remove the airbag from the facia **(see illustration)**.
15 Refitting is a reversal of removal. Ensure that the wiring connector is securely reconnected. Ensure that no-one is inside the vehicle. Reconnect the battery negative lead as described in Chapter 5A.

Airbag wiring contact unit

16 Remove the steering wheel as described in Chapter 10.
17 Fully extend the steering column, then on models with an audio control switch fitted to the column shroud, release the locking tang, pull the switch from place and disconnect the wiring plug **(see illustration 4.2)**.
18 Undo the fasteners and remove the lower facia panel on the driver's side – see Chapter 11.
19 Release the retaining clips and remove the steering column upper shroud **(see illustration 4.3)**.
20 Undo the retaining bolts, and remove the steering column lower shroud **(see illustration 4.4)**. Release the steering column locking lever to remove the shroud completely.
21 Disconnect the wiring plug from the contact unit and the steering angle sensor (where fitted).

22.22 Apply tape to secure the rotary contact unit

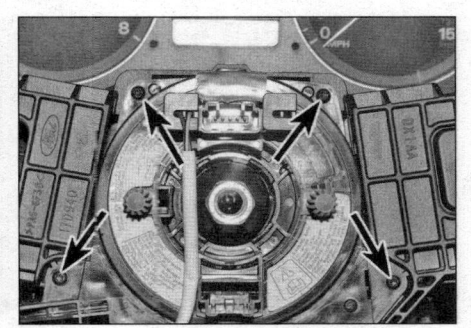

22.23 Contact unit retaining bolts (arrowed)

22 If the contact unit is to be refitted, apply tape to lock the unit in position **(see illustration)**. Do not attempt to rotate the unit.
23 Undo the 4 bolts and remove the contact unit **(see illustration)**.
24 If required, release the clips and detach the steering angle sensor from the contact unit.
25 Begin refitting by attaching the steering angle sensor to the contact unit. Ensure the retaining clips fully engage and the sensor locating tangs align with the ones on the contact unit. **Note:** *If a new sensor is being fitted, it must be configured and calibrated using Ford diagnostic equipment. Entrust this task to a Ford dealer or suitably-equipped specialist.*
26 Ensure the front wheels are still in the 'straight-ahead' position, and the directional indicator stalk is in the Off position, then fit the contact unit into position. Tighten the retaining bolts.

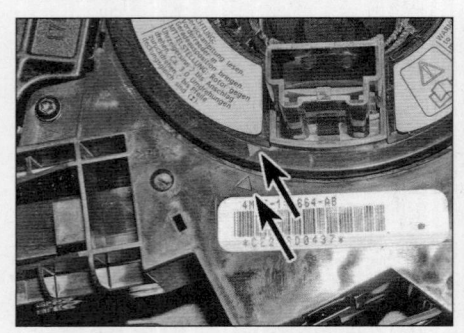

12•22 Body electrical system

22.27 Align the marks (arrowed) on the contact unit rotor and cover

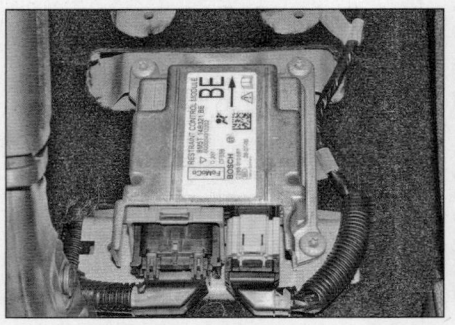

22.31 Note the arrow on the top of the RCM must point forwards

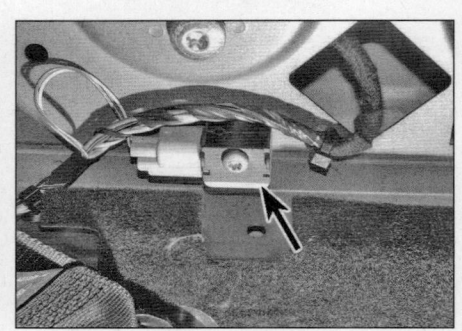

22.35a Undo the bolt and prise out the scrivets ...

22.35b ... along the front edge (arrowed) of the air deflector panel

22.40 Side crash sensor (arrowed)

27 If there is any doubt as to the position of the contact unit (eg, securing tape missing or disturbed), the unit must be centralised as follows:
a) Rotate the contact unit rotor anti-clockwise until a resistance is felt.
b) Rotate the rotor clockwise until the arrow marked on the rotor aligns with the raised V section on the outer cover, at approximately the 7 o'clock position (see illustration).
c) Rotate the rotor 3 turns in a clockwise direction.

28 The remainder of refitting is a reversal of removal.

Restraint Control Module (RCM)

29 Refer to Chapter 11 and remove the centre console.
30 Release the locking devices and disconnect the wiring plugs for the control unit.

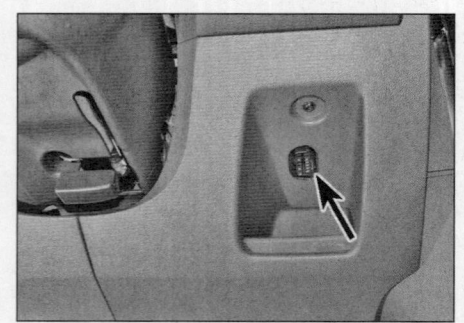

24.0 The diagnostic plug (arrowed) is located under the driver's side of the facia

31 Undo the retaining bolts and remove the control unit (see illustration).
32 Refitting is a reversal of removal, ensuring the module is refitted with the arrow mark on the top pointing forwards. Note that if a new module has been fitted, software for it will need to be downloaded from Ford. Entrust this task to a Ford dealer or suitably-equipped specialist.

Side airbags

33 The side airbags are incorporated into the side of the front and rear seats. Removal of the units requires the seat upholstery to be removed. This is a specialist task, which we recommend should be entrusted to a Ford dealer or specialist.

Head/overhead curtain airbags

34 Renewal of the head airbags/inflatable curtain requires removal of the headlining. This is a specialist task, and should be entrusted to a Ford dealer or specialist.

Crash/lateral acceleration sensors

Front sensor – vehicles up to 05/2005 only

35 Open the bonnet, undo the 4 scrivets and remove the air deflector panel (see illustrations).
36 Undo the retaining bolt and remove the sensor.
37 Refitting is a reversal of removal.

Side sensors

38 The side sensors are located in the vehicle's B-pillars each side.

39 Remove the B-pillar (see Chapter 11).
40 Disconnect the sensor wiring plug, then undo the bolt and remove the sensor (see illustration). Take great care not to damage the sensor wiring harness. Note that the sensor must be handled carefully. Do not refit a sensor that has been dropped or knocked.
41 Refitting is a reversal of removal.

23 Anti-theft alarm system – general information

An anti-theft alarm and immobiliser system is fitted as standard equipment. Should the system become faulty, the vehicle should be taken to a Ford dealer or specialist for examination. They will have access to a special diagnostic tester which will quickly trace any fault present in the system.

24 Electronic control modules – removal and refitting

Note: All of these modules are included in the vehicle's sophisticated self-diagnosis system. Should a fault occur, have the system interrogated using a fault code reader/Ford test equipment, via the diagnostic plug located under the driver's side of the facia, above the pedals (see illustration).

Removal

1 Disconnect the battery negative lead as described in Chapter 5A.

Generic Electronic Module (GEM)

2 The GEM is integral with the passenger compartment fusebox/central junction box. This module is responsible for the management of the following functions:
Current distribution.
Headlights.
Headlight range adjustment.
Foglamps.
Side lights.
Reversing lights.
High-level brake light.
Interior lights.

Body electrical system 12•23

25.2 Remove the wheel arch liner

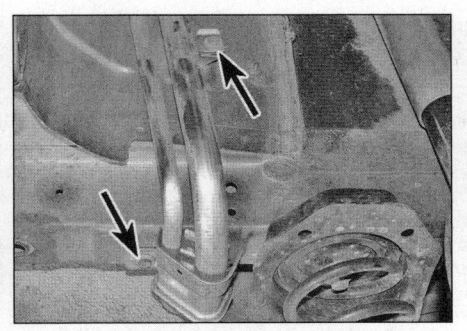

25.3 Undo the bolts (arrowed) securing the filler/breather pipe assembly

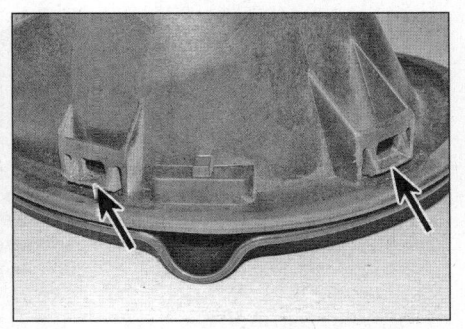

25.4a Reach up and depress the clips (arrowed)...

25.4b ...then manoeuvre the filler flap from the wing

25.5 Depress the clip each side (arrowed) then slide the cover and motor from the flap assembly

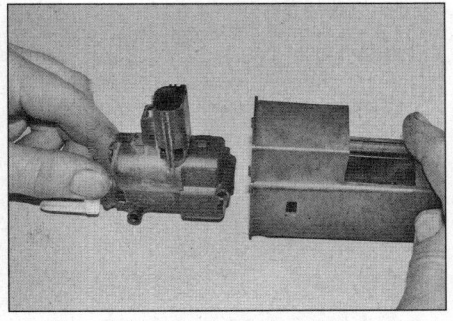

25.6 Slide the motor from the cover

Wipers.
Heated windscreen.
Cruise control.
Central locking.
Anti theft system.
Handbrake switch.
Brake fluid level monitoring.
Fuel pump.
Battery charging.
Databus communications.

3 Remove the trim panel above the passenger's side footwell **(see illustration 3.2a)**.
4 Undo the 2 fasteners and lift the GEM/junction/fusebox from the mounting bracket **(see illustration 3.2b and 3.2c)**.
5 Note their fitted positions, and disconnect the wiring plugs as the GEM is withdrawn.
6 If a new GEM is to be fitted, the unit must be configured and initialised using Ford diagnostic equipment (WDS). Entrust this task to a Ford dealer or suitably-equipped specialist.

Lighting control module (LCM)

7 This module is only fitted to vehicles equipped with adaptive front lights (AFS), or Xenon high-intensity gas discharge headlights (HID). On models with AFS it controls the movement of the reflectors as the steering is operated, and on models with HID, it controls the range control as the suspension compresses or extends.
8 Renewal of the module is described in Section 9.

Keyless vehicle module (KVM)

9 Renewal of the KVM is described in Chapter 11.

Climate control module (CCM)

10 Removal of the CCM is described in Chapter 3, Section 10.

Refitting

11 Refitting is a reversal of removal. If a new module has been fitted, software will need to be downloaded from Ford. Entrust this task to a Ford dealer or suitably-equipped specialist.

25 Fuel filler flap motor – removal and refitting

1 Slacken the right-hand rear roadwheel nuts, then raise the rear of the vehicle and support it securely on axle stands (see *Jacking and vehicle support*). Remove the roadwheel.
2 Undo the fasteners and remove the right-hand rear wheel arch liner **(see illustration)**.
3 Undo the bolts securing the filler pipe assembly to the inner wing and chassis member **(see illustration)**.
4 Reach up behind the wheel arch, depress the 2 retaining clips, and manoeuvre the filler flap assembly from place **(see illustrations)**. Disconnect the wiring plug and unclip with harness as the assembly is withdrawn.
5 Release the clip each side and slide the cover and motor from the filler funnel **(see illustration)**.
6 Slide the motor from the cover **(see illustration)**.
7 Refitting is a reversal of removal.

12•24 Wiring diagrams

Ford Focus wiring diagrams — Diagram 1

WARNING: This vehicle is fitted with a supplemental restraint system (SRS) consisting of a combination of driver (and passenger) airbag(s), side impact protection airbags and seatbelt pre-tensioners. The use of electrical test equipment on any SRS wiring systems may cause the seatbelt pre-tensioners to abruptly retract and airbags to explosively deploy, resulting in potentially severe personal injury. Extreme care should be taken to correctly identify any circuits to be tested to avoid choosing any of the SRS wiring in error.
For further information see airbag system precautions in body electrical systems chapter.
Note: The SRS wiring harness can normally be identified by yellow and/or orange harness or harness connectors.

Key to symbols

- Solenoid actuator
- Earth point and location (E7)
- Wire colour (blue with white tracer) — Bu/Wh
- Dashed outline denotes part of a larger item, containing in this case an electronic or solid state device (pins 1 and 3 of a single connector).
- Bulb
- Switch
- Fuse/Fusible link (F26)
- Resistor
- Variable resistor
- Variable resistor
- Wire splice, soldered joint, or unspecified connector
- Connecting wires
- Diode
- Light-emitting diode
- Item number (12)
- Motor/pump (M)
- Heating element

Engine fusebox 4

Fuse	Rating	Circuit
F1	50A	Engine cooling fan
F2	80A	Power steering
F3	60A	Passenger fusebox supply
F4	60A	Passenger fusebox supply
F5	80A	Auxiliary heater
F6	60A	Glow plug (Diesel only)
F7	30A	ABS, stability control pump
F8	20A	ABS, stability control valves
F9	20A	Engine management
F10	30A	Heater blower
F11	20A	Ignition switch
F12	40A	Ignition relay
F13	30A	Starter solenoid
F14	40A	Heated front screen RH
F15	30A	Engine cooling fan relay
F16	40A	Heated front screen LH
F17	30A	Convertible roof
F18	30A	Power inverter
F19	10A	ABS
F20	15A	Horn
F21	20A	Auxiliary heater
F22	10A	Power steering control unit
F23	30A	Headlight washer
F24	15A	Diesel auxiliary heater
F25	10A	Ignition relays
F26	15A	Automatic transmission
F27	10A	Air conditioning clutch
F28	10A	Diesel glow plug monitoring
F29	10A	Climate control
F30	3A	Engine management, auto. transmission
F31	10A	Battery smart charging
F32	10A	Automatic transmission
F33	10A	Heated oxygen sensor
F34	10A	Intercooler bypass valve
F34	10A	Engine management
F35	10A	Engine management
F36	10A	Engine management

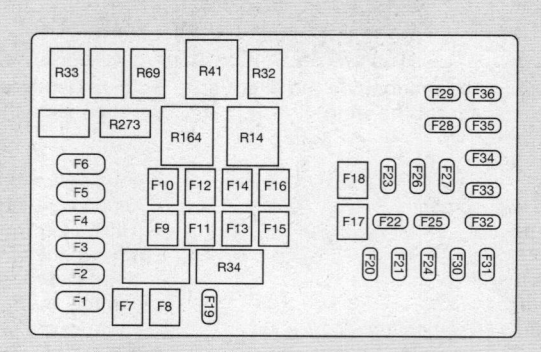

Passenger fusebox 18

Fuse	Rating	Circuit
F100	10A	Electronic control units ignition supply
F101	20A	Sunroof, driver's electric seat, convertible roof
F102	10A	Heater control, steering column, Diesel particulate filter, remote control receiver
F103	10A	Lighting
F104	10A	Battery saver, interior lights
F105	25A	Heated rear window
F106	20A	Keyless entry system
F107	10A	Instrument cluster, diagnostics
F108	7.5A	Instrument cluster (audio and navigation unit)
F109	20A	Cigar lighter, rear auxiliary power socket
F110	10A	Daytime running lights, lighting control switch
F111	15A	Fuel pump (petrol)
F112	15A	Audio supply
F113	10A	Daytime running lights (parking lights)
F114	10A	Instrument cluster, engine immobiliser
F115	7.5A	Lighting control
F116	20A	Foglights
F117	7.5A	Number plate lights
F118	20A	LH rear door control unit
F119	15A	Luggage compartment auxiliary power socket
F120	20A	RH rear door control unit
F121	20A	Heated front seats
F122	10A	Airbag
F123	7.5A	Heated mirrors
F124	7.5A	Parking lights, side & tail lights LHS
F125	7.5A	Parking lights, side & tail lights RHS
F126	20A	Keyless entry system
F127	25A	Electric windows
F128	-	Not used
F129	20A	Windscreen wiper
F130	-	Not used
F131	15A	Rear window wiper
F132	15A	Stop lights
F133	25A	Central locking, passenger door control unit
F134	20A	Central locking, driver's door control unit
F135	20A	Daytime running lights
F136	15A	Washer pump, heated washer jets
F137	10A	Battery backup sounder
F138	10A	Engine management, automatic transmission
F139	10A	RH main beam
F140	10A	LH main beam
F141	10A	Reversing light, electric mirrors
F142	15A	RH dip beam
F143	15A	LH dip beam

Earth locations

- E1 On engine
- E2 On engine
- E3 In engine bay, behind LH headlight
- E4 'A' pillar driver's side
- E5 In luggage compartment
- E6 LH side of luggage compartment
- E7 In engine bay, behind RH headlight
- E8 In passenger compartment, front of LH inner sill
- E9 In passenger compartment, front of LH inner sill
- E10 In engine bay, by LH strut tower
- E11 In passenger compartment, front of RH inner sill
- E12 In passenger compartment, front of RH inner sill
- E13 In passenger compartment, front of RH inner sill
- E14 Roof opening panel
- E15 Behind centre of dash
- E16 In passenger compartment, LH inner sill, below 'B' post

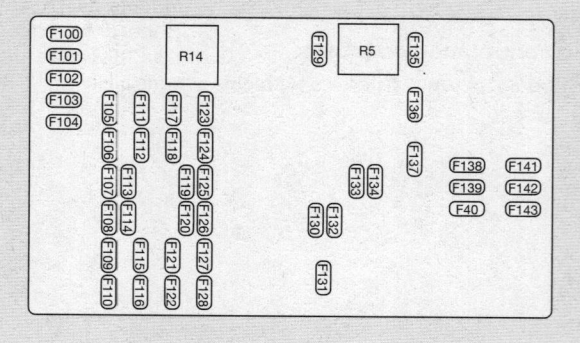

H33944

Wiring diagrams 12•25

Diagram 2

Colour codes

Wh	White	Og	Orange
Bu	Blue	Rd	Red
Gy	Grey	Pk	Pink
Ye	Yellow	Gn	Green
Bn	Brown	Vt	Violet
Bk	Black	Sr	Silver
Na	Natural	Lg	Light green

Key to items

1. Battery
2. Starter motor
3. Alternator
4. Engine fusebox
   - R13 = power hold relay
   - R22 = starter relay
   - R33 = horn relay
   - R212 = glow plug relay
5. Ignition switch
6. Engine cooling fan
7. Air conditioning pressure switch
8. Engine coolant temp. sensor
9. Horn (low tone)
10. Horn (high tone)
11. Steering wheel clock springs
12. Horn switch
13. Glow plug nc. 1
14. Glow plug nc. 2
15. Glow plug nc. 3
16. Glow plug nc. 4

H33945

Typical starting & charging

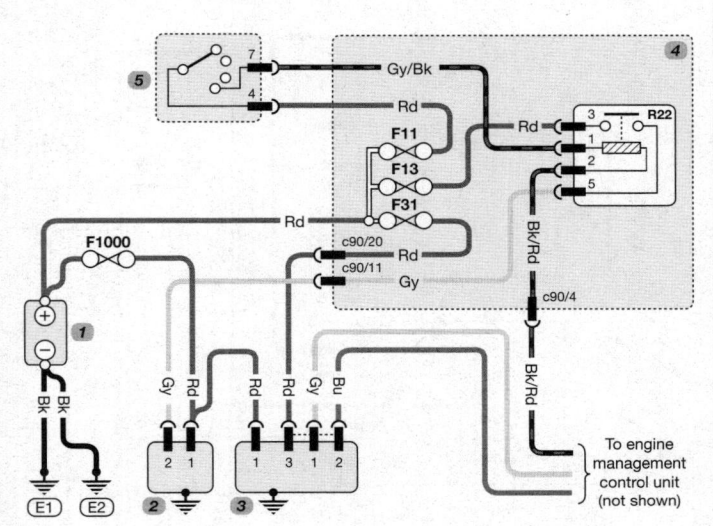

Typical engine cooling fan

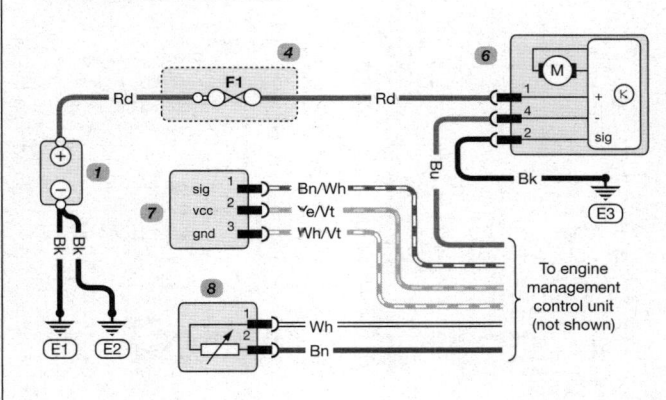

Typical horn

Typical pre-heating system

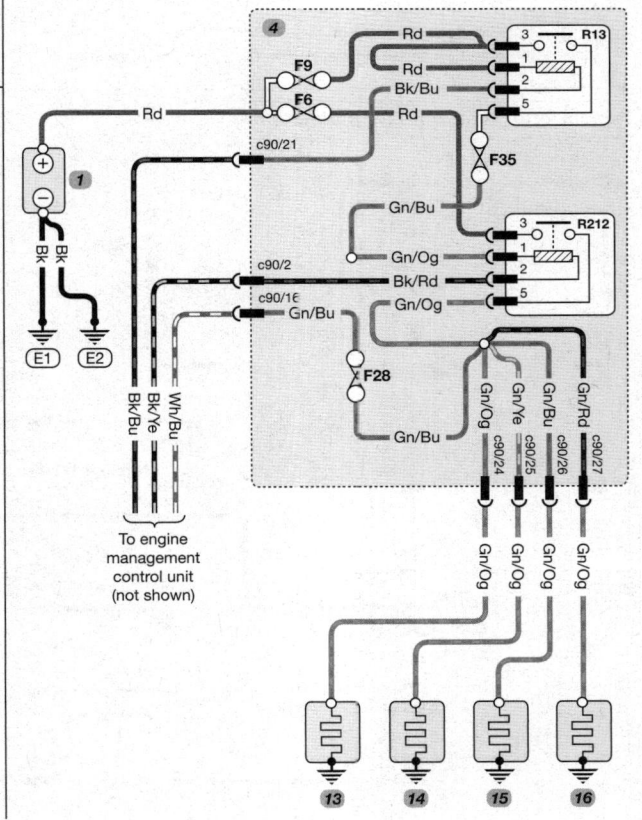

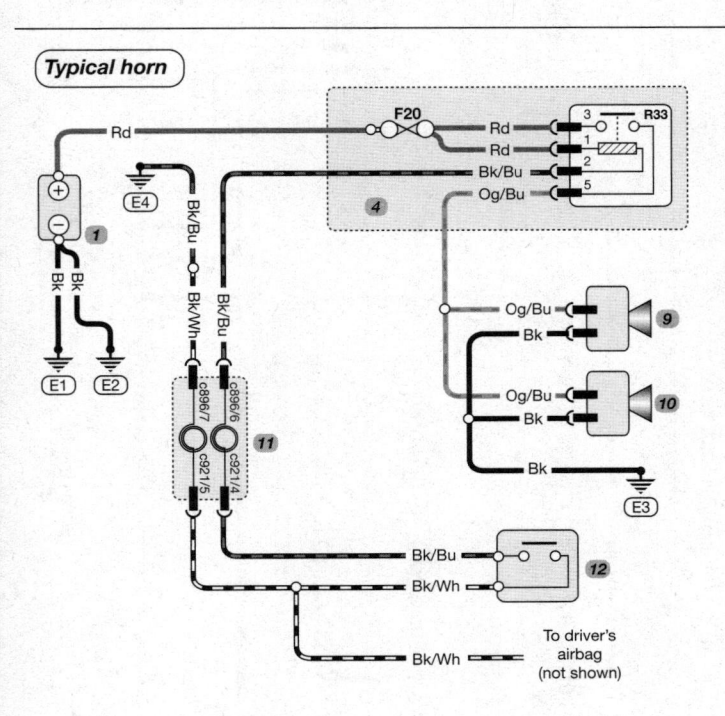

12•26 Wiring diagrams

Diagram 3

Colour codes
- **Wh** White
- **Bu** Blue
- **Gy** Grey
- **Ye** Yellow
- **Bn** Brown
- **Bk** Black
- **Na** Natural
- **Og** Orange
- **Rd** Red
- **Pk** Pink
- **Gn** Green
- **Vt** Violet
- **Sr** Silver
- **Lg** Light green

Key to items
1. Battery
4. Engine fusebox
   - R41 = ignition relay
5. Ignition switch
18. Passenger fusebox
   - a = GEM control unit
   - b = autolighting relay
   - c = dip beam relay
   - d = main beam relay
19. LH rear light
   - a = stop/tail light
20. RH rear light (as above)
21. Stop light switch
22. Reversing light switch
23. Reversing light
24. High level stop light
25. Number plate light
26. Light switch
   - a = park/off/side/head/auto
27. LH headlight
   - a = side light
   - b = dip beam
   - c = main beam
   - d = light shade
28. RH headlight (as above)
29. Autolighting/rain sensor
30. Multifunction switch
   - a = main beam/flasher

H33946

Typical stop & reversing lights

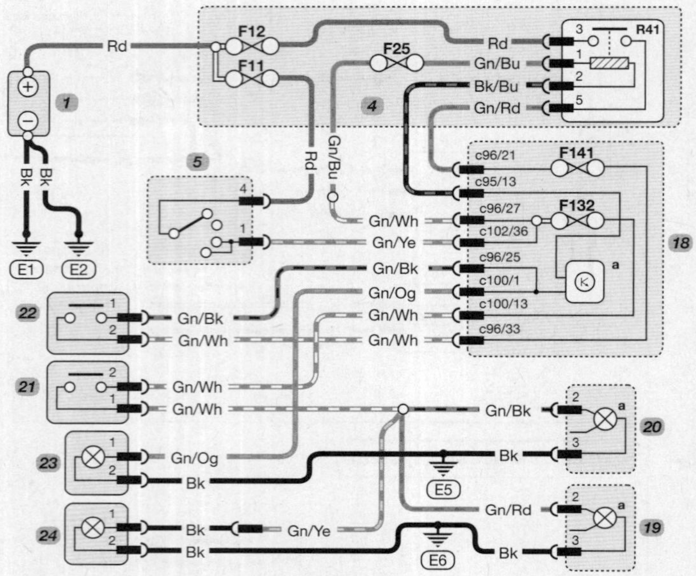

Typical side, tail & number plate lights

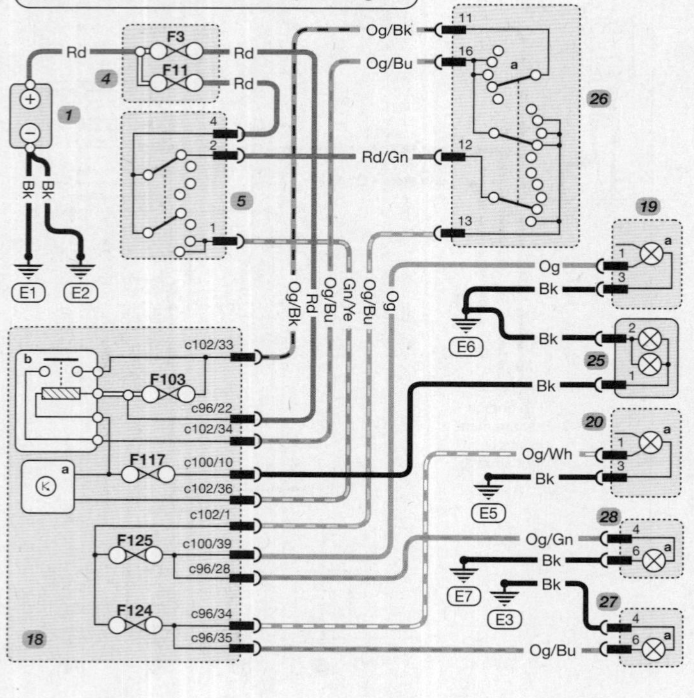

Typical headlights

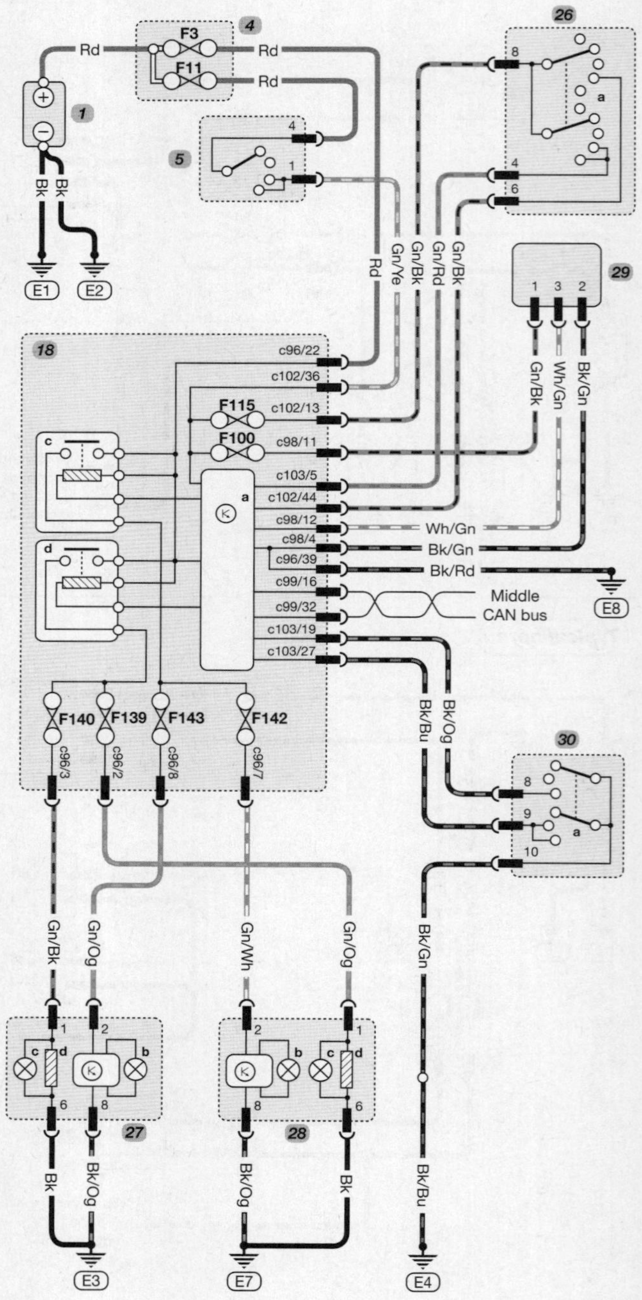

Wiring diagrams

Diagram 4

Colour codes
- Wh White
- Bu Blue
- Gy Grey
- Ye Yellow
- Bn Brown
- Bk Black
- Na Natural
- Og Orange
- Rd Red
- Pk Pink
- Gn Green
- Vt Violet
- Sr Silver
- Lg Light green

Key to items
1. Battery
4. Engine fusebox
   - R41 = ignition relay
5. Ignition switch
18. Passenger fusebox
    - a = GEM control unit
19. LH rear light
    - b = direction indicator
20. RH rear light
    - (as above)
26. Light switch
    - b = front/rear foglight
27. LH headlight
    - e = direction indicator
28. RH headlight
    - (as above)
30. Multifunction switch
    - b = direction indicator
33. LH front side repeater
34. RH front side repeater
35. Hazard warning switch
36. LH exterior mirror
    - a = indicator side repeater
37. RH exterior mirror
    - a = indicator side repeater
38. LH front foglight
39. RH front foglight
40. Rear foglight

H33947

Typical direction indicators & hazard warning lights

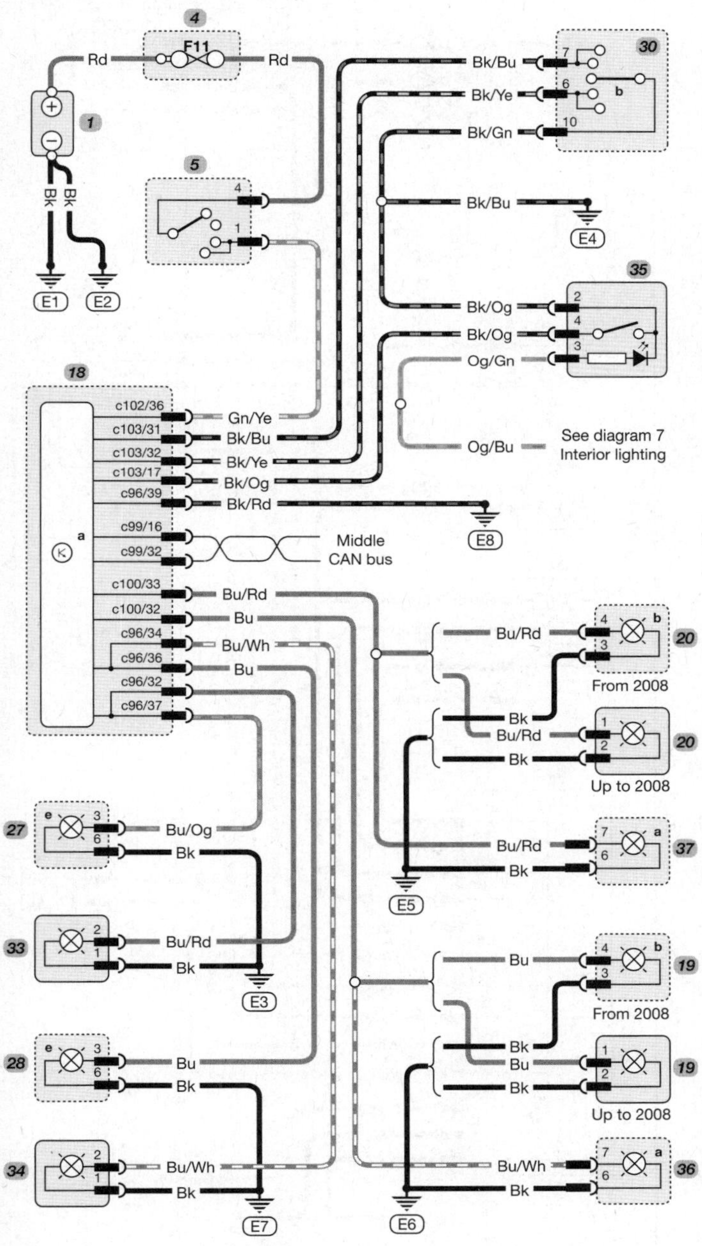

Typical foglights

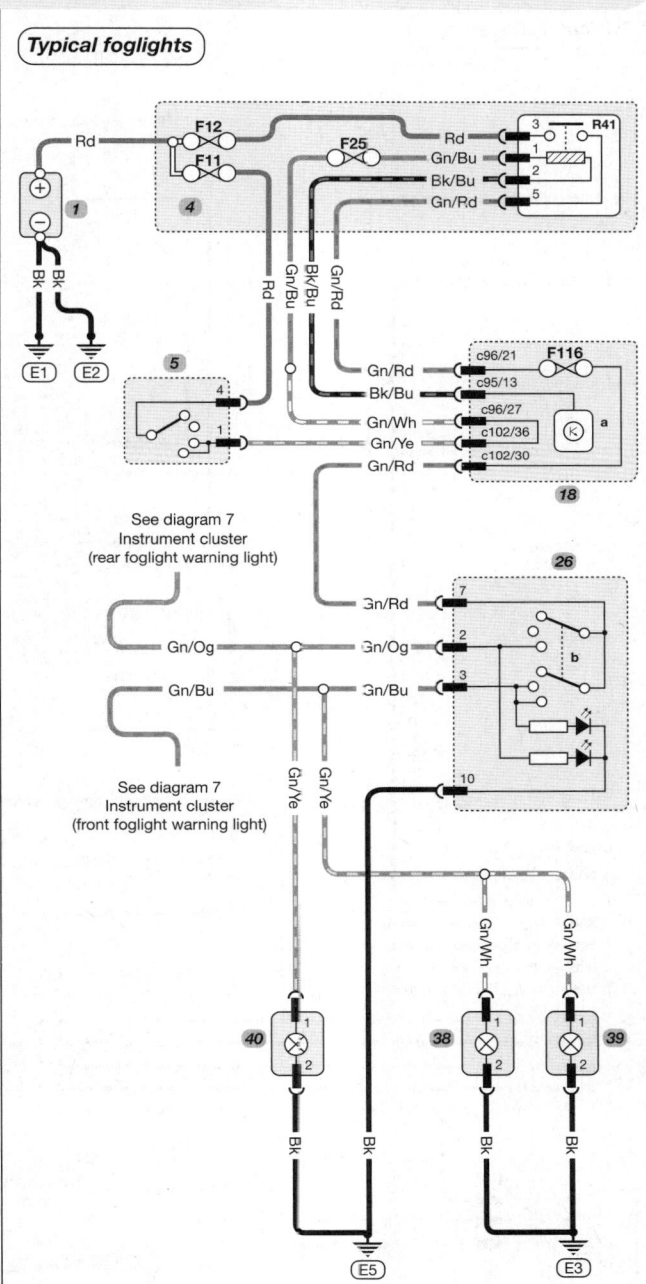

12•28 Wiring diagrams

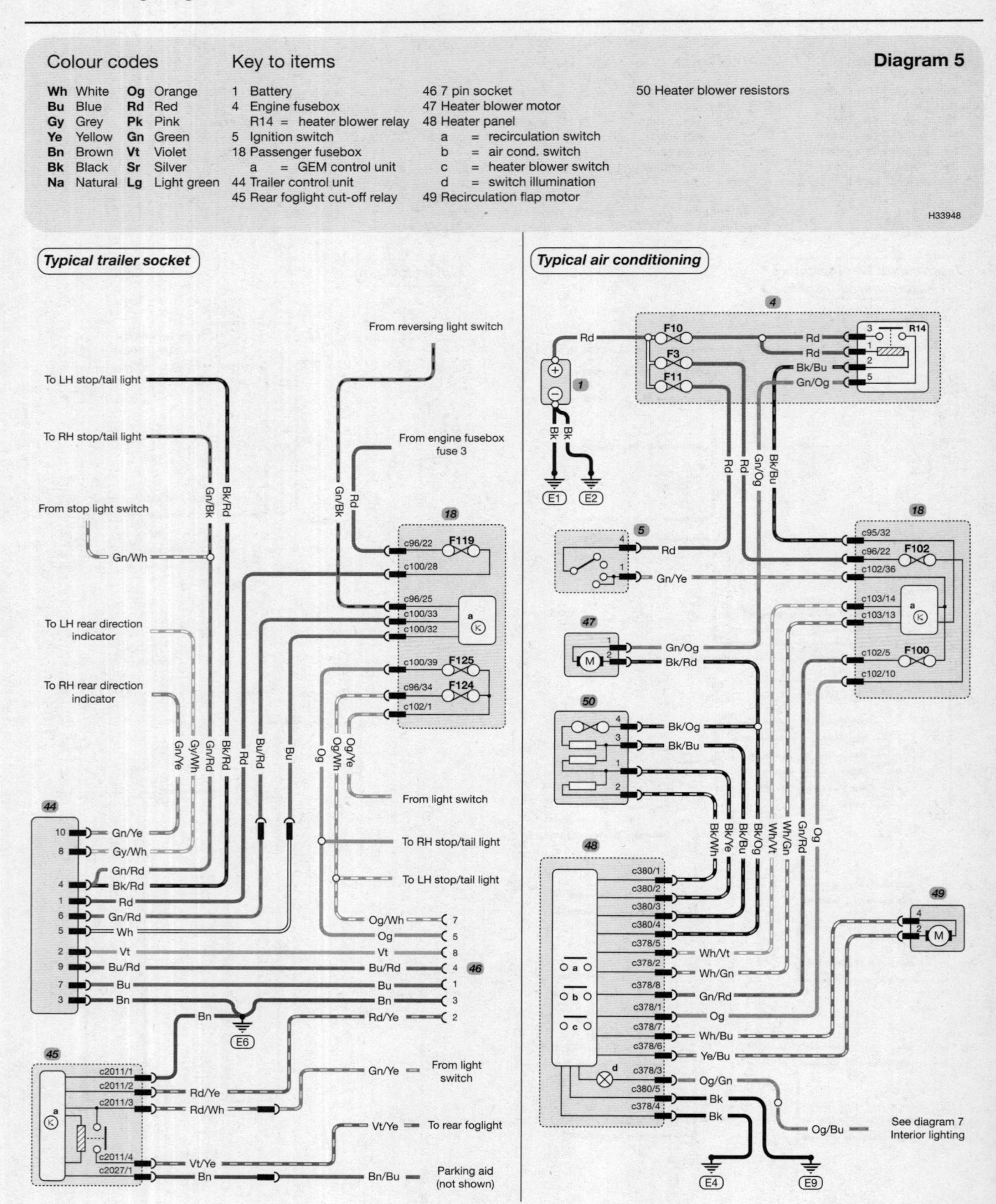

Diagram 5

Colour codes

Wh	White	Og	Orange
Bu	Blue	Rd	Red
Gy	Grey	Pk	Pink
Ye	Yellow	Gn	Green
Bn	Brown	Vt	Violet
Bk	Black	Sr	Silver
Na	Natural	Lg	Light green

Key to items

1 Battery
4 Engine fusebox
   R14 = heater blower relay
5 Ignition switch
18 Passenger fusebox
   a = GEM control unit
44 Trailer control unit
45 Rear foglight cut-off relay
46 7 pin socket
47 Heater blower motor
48 Heater panel
   a = recirculation switch
   b = air cond. switch
   c = heater blower switch
   d = switch illumination
49 Recirculation flap motor
50 Heater blower resistors

H33948

Typical trailer socket

Typical air conditioning

Wiring diagrams 12•29

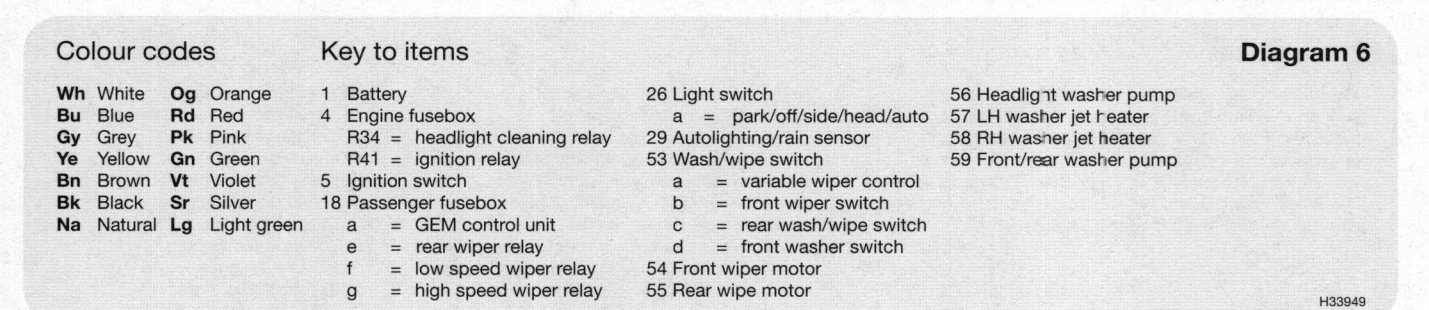

Colour codes
- Wh White
- Bu Blue
- Gy Grey
- Ye Yellow
- Bn Brown
- Bk Black
- Na Natural
- Og Orange
- Rd Red
- Pk Pink
- Gn Green
- Vt Violet
- Sr Silver
- Lg Light green

Key to items
1 Battery
4 Engine fusebox
   R34 = headlight cleaning relay
   R41 = ignition relay
5 Ignition switch
18 Passenger fusebox
   a = GEM control unit
   e = rear wiper relay
   f = low speed wiper relay
   g = high speed wiper relay
26 Light switch
   a = park/off/side/head/auto
29 Autolighting/rain sensor
53 Wash/wipe switch
   a = variable wiper control
   b = front wiper switch
   c = rear wash/wipe switch
   d = front washer switch
54 Front wiper motor
55 Rear wipe motor
56 Headlight washer pump
57 LH washer jet heater
58 RH washer jet heater
59 Front/rear washer pump

Diagram 6

H33949

Typical wash/wipe

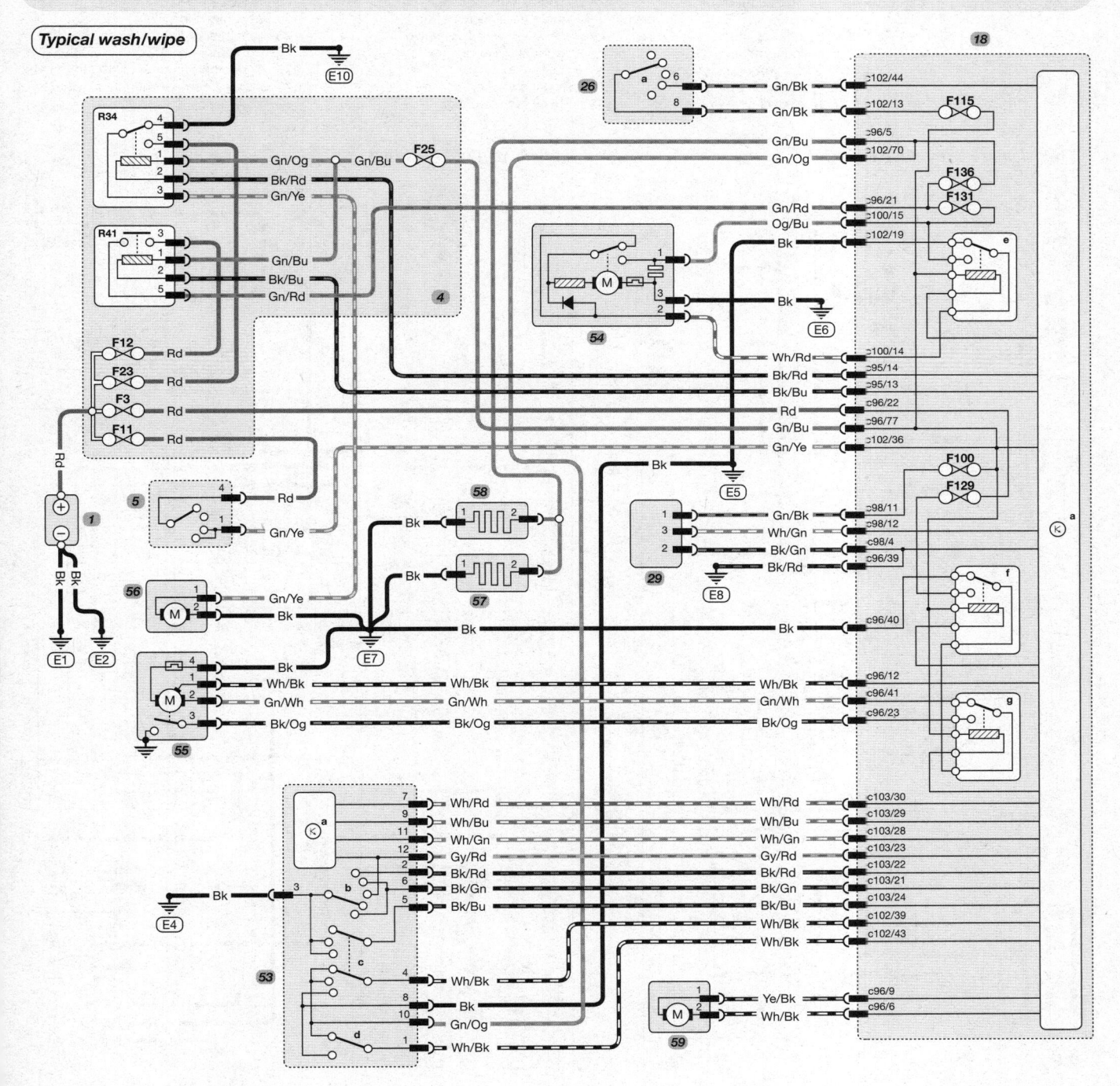

Wiring diagrams

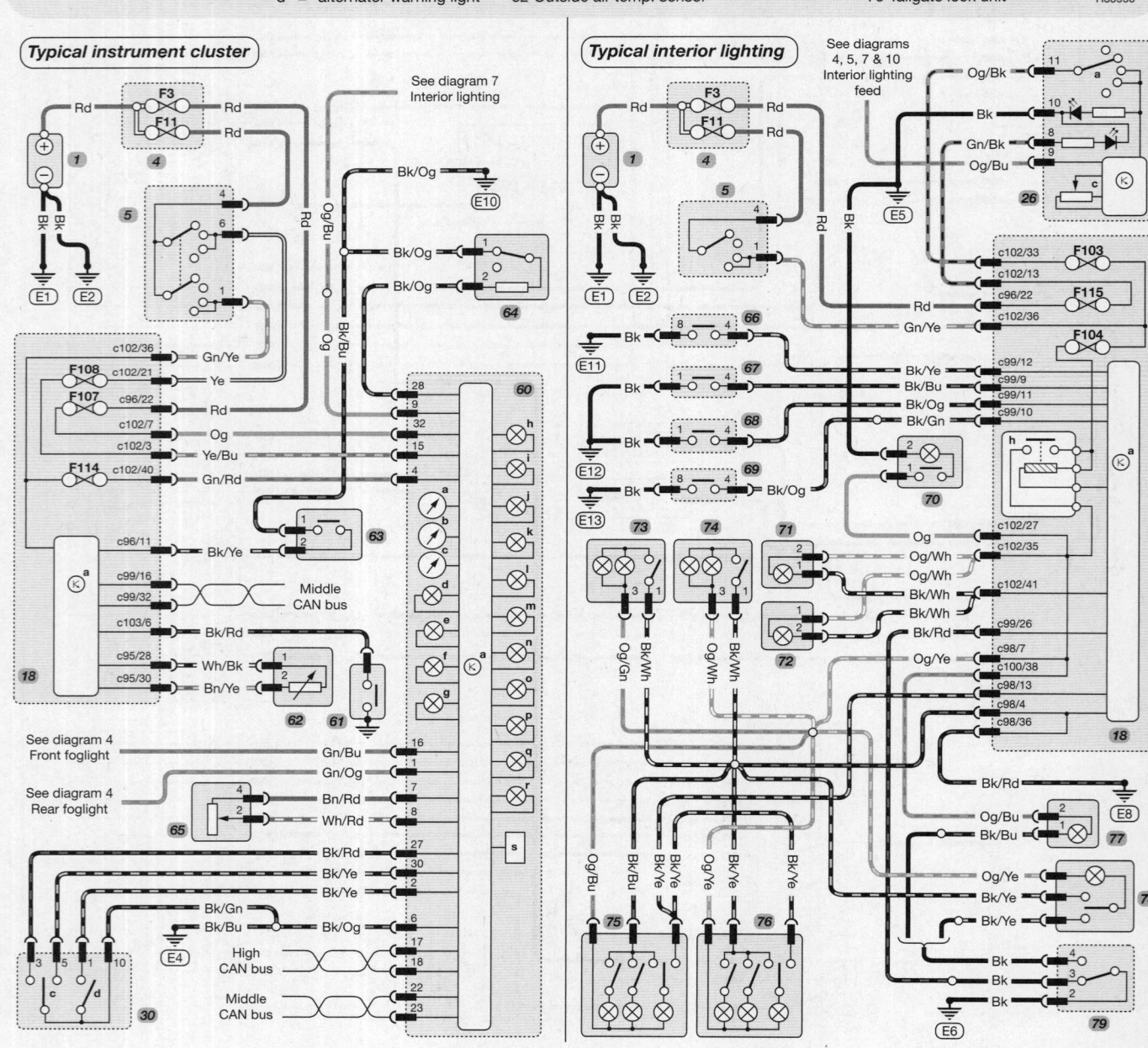

Colour codes

Wh	White	Og	Orange
Bu	Blue	Rd	Red
Gy	Grey	Pk	Pink
Ye	Yellow	Gn	Green
Bn	Brown	Vt	Violet
Bk	Black	Sr	Silver
Na	Natural	Lg	Light green

Key to items

1 Battery
4 Engine fusebox
5 Ignition switch
18 Passenger fusebox
  a = GEM control unit
  h = battery saver relay
26 Light switch
  a = park/off/side/head/auto
  c = interior lighting dimmer
30 Multifunction switch
  c = display mode
  d = set/reset
60 Instrument cluster
  a = tachometer
  b = coolant temp. gauge
  c = speedometer
  d = alternator warning light
  e = low oil pressure warning light
  f = shift up warning light
  g = MIL warning light
  h = speed control warning light
  i = check engine warning light
  j = preheater warning light
  k = ice warning light
  l = low brake fluid/handbrake warning light
  m = electric power stering warning light
  n = seatbelt warning light
  o = airbag warning light
  p = instrument illumination
  q = lights on warning light
  r = door ajar warning light
  s = LCD display
61 Handbrake switch
62 Outside air temp. sensor
63 Brake fluid level switch
64 Low washer fluid level switch
65 Fuel gauge sender unit
66 Driver's door lock assy
67 Passenger's door lock assy
68 LH rear door lock assy
69 RH rear door lock assy
70 Glovebox light/switch
71 LH footwell light
72 RH footwell light
73 LH vanity mirror light
74 RH vanity mirror light
75 Front interior light
76 Rear interior light
77 Luggae compartment light (not estate)
78 Luggage compartment light (estate)
79 Tailgate lock unit

Diagram 7

Typical instrument cluster

Typical interior lighting

Wiring diagrams 12•31

Diagram 8

Colour codes
- Wh White
- Bu Blue
- Gy Grey
- Ye Yellow
- Bn Brown
- Bk Black
- Na Natural
- Og Orange
- Rd Red
- Pk Pink
- Gn Green
- Vt Violet
- Sr Silver
- Lg Light green

Key to items
1. Battery
4. Engine fusebox
5. Ignition switch
18. Passenger fusebox
   - a = GEM control unit
   - h = door lock relay
   - i = double locking relay
   - j = driver's door lock relay
   - k = door unlock relay
64. Driver's door lock unit
65. Passenger's door lock unit
66. LH rear door lock unit
67. RH rear door lock unit
79. Tailgate lock unit
83. Remote control unit
88. Tailgate lock switch
89. Fuel filler lock motor

H33951

Typical central locking

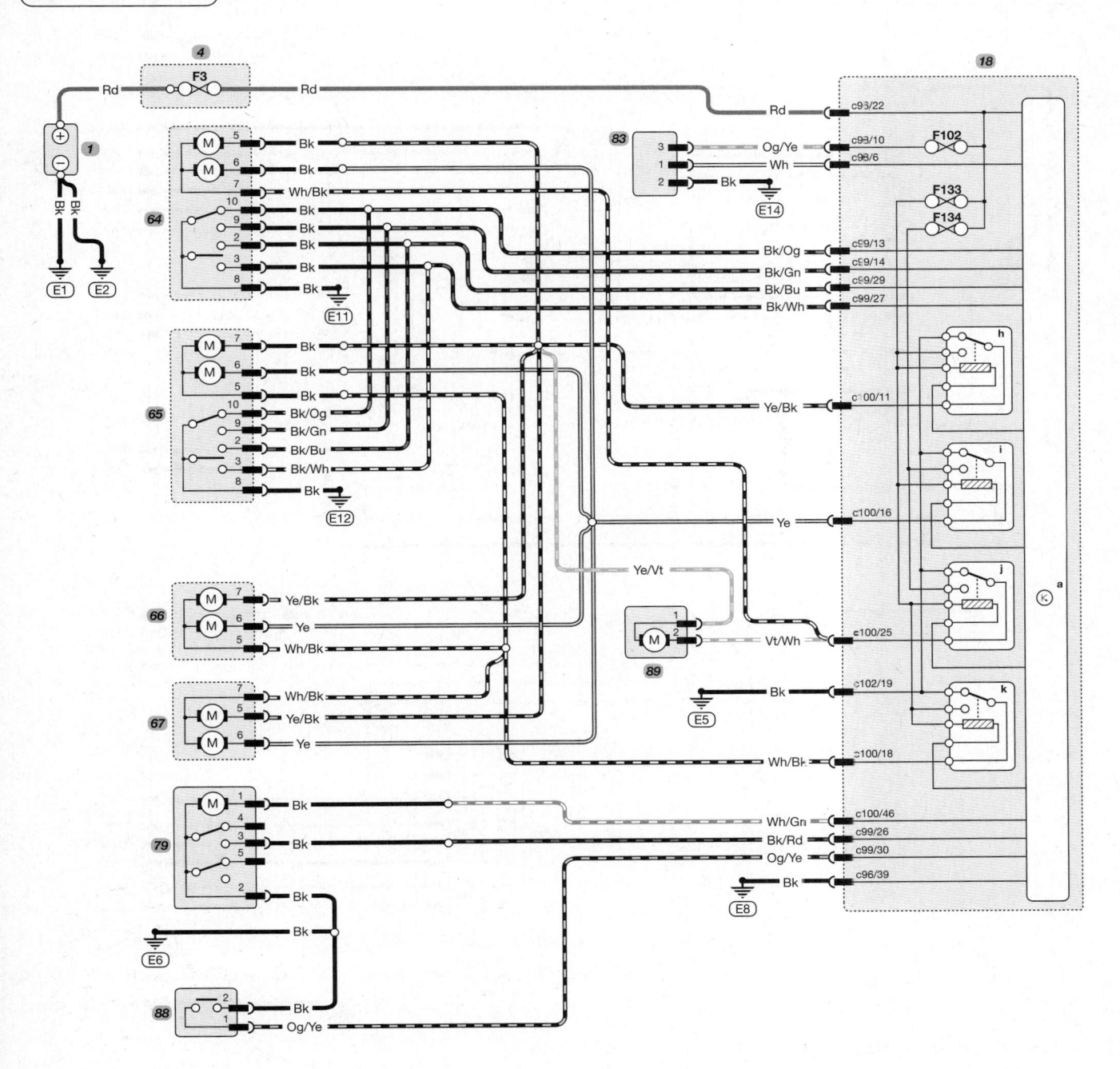

12•32 Wiring diagrams

Colour codes
- Wh — White
- Bu — Blue
- Gy — Grey
- Ye — Yellow
- Bn — Brown
- Bk — Black
- Na — Natural
- Og — Orange
- Rd — Red
- Pk — Pink
- Gn — Green
- Vt — Violet
- Sr — Silver
- Lg — Light green

Key to items
- 1 Battery
- 4 Engine fusebox
- 18 Passenger fusebox
- 36 LH exterior mirror
  - b = fold motor
  - c = up/down motor
  - d = left/right motor
  - e = heater element
  - f = puddle light
- 37 RH exterior mirror
  - b = fold motor
  - c = up/down motor
  - d = left/right motor
  - e = heater element
  - f = puddle light
- 92 Driver's window/mirror control switch
- 93 Electric mirror fold control unit
- 94 Electric mirror fold switch
- 95 Driver's door control unit
- 96 Passenger's door control unit

Diagram 9

H33952

Typical electric mirrors

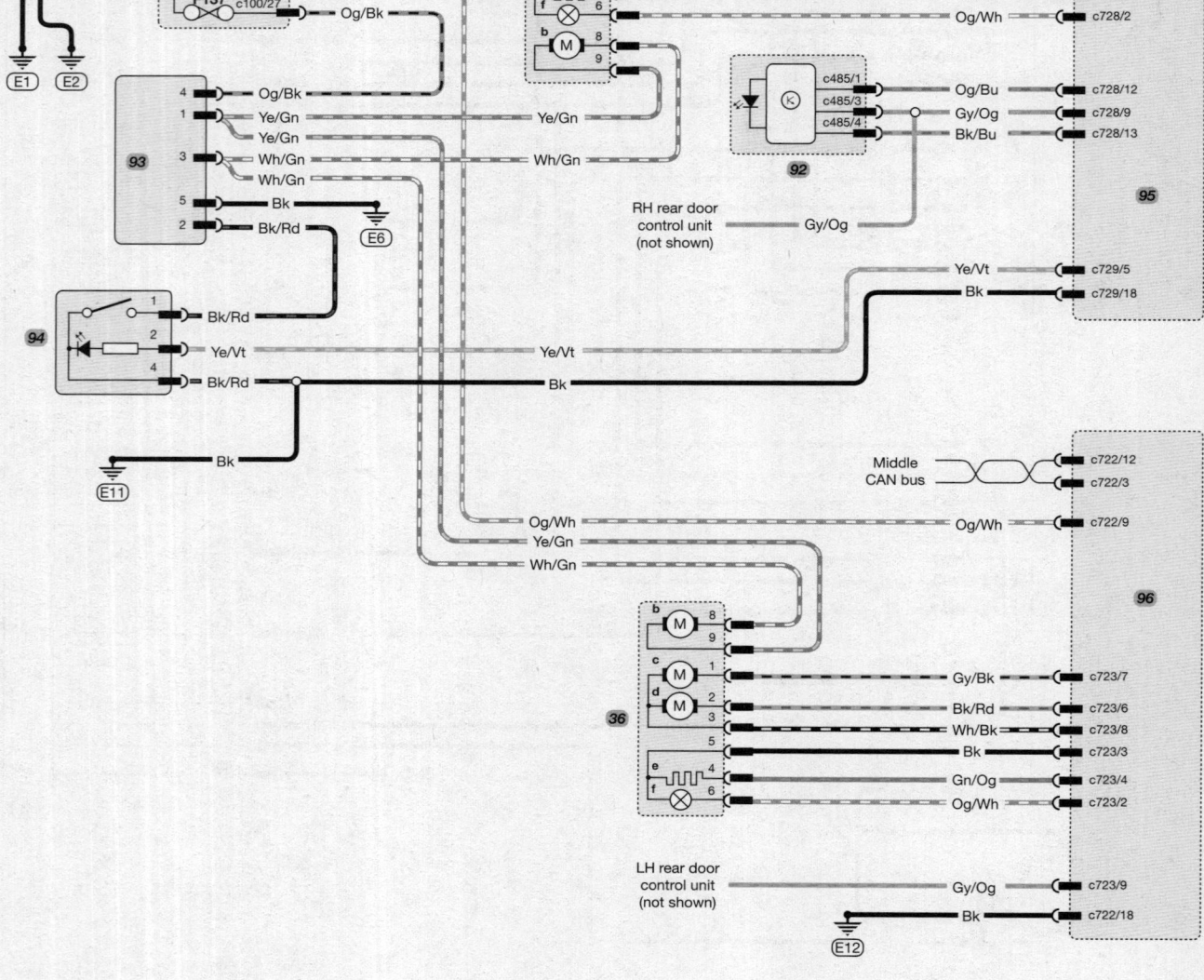

Wiring diagrams 12•33

Colour codes

Wh	White	**Og**	Orange
Bu	Blue	**Rd**	Red
Gy	Grey	**Pk**	Pink
Ye	Yellow	**Gn**	Green
Bn	Brown	**Vt**	Violet
Bk	Black	**Sr**	Silver
Na	Natural	**Lg**	Light green

Key to items

1 Battery
4 Engine fusebox
   R41 = ignition relay
5 Ignition switch
18 Passenger fusebox
   a = GEM control unit
92 Driver's window/mirror control switch
98 Passenger's window switch
99 Driver's window motor
100 Passenger's window motor
101 Audio unit
102 CD changer
103 Steering wheel remote control
104 LH front speaker 1
105 LH front speaker 2
106 RH front speaker 1
107 RH front speaker 2
108 LH rear door speaker 1
109 LH rear door speaker 2
110 RH rear door speaker 1
111 RH rear door speaker 2

Diagram 10

H33953

Typical electric windows

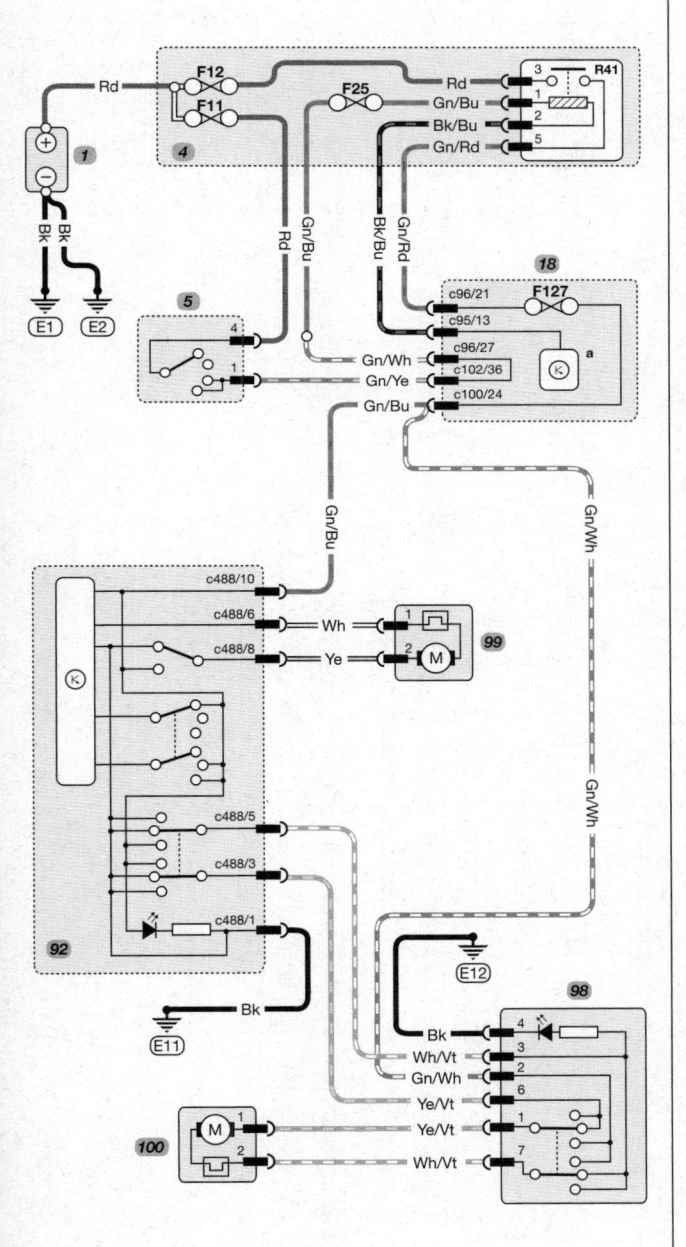

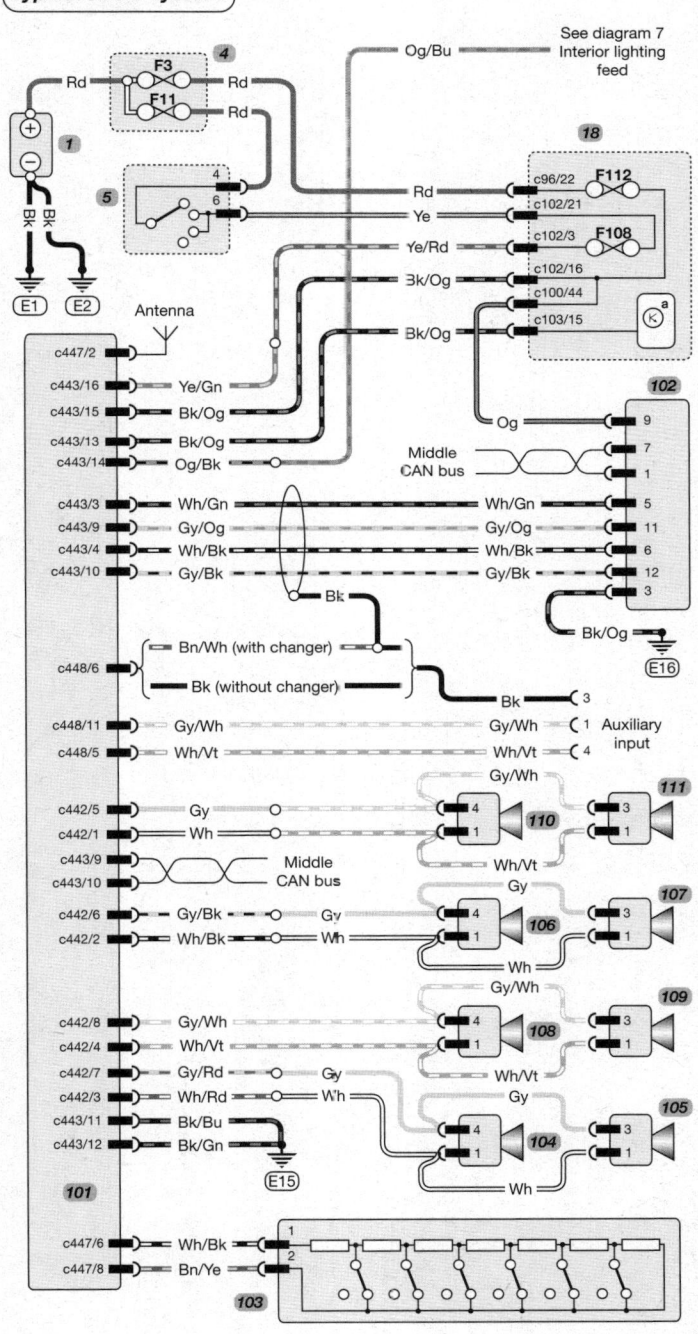

Typical audio system

Notes

Reference   REF•1

Dimensions and weights .... **REF•1**	Jacking and vehicle support .... **REF•9**
Fuel economy...................... **REF•2**	Tools and working facilities .... **REF•10**
Conversion factors.................. **REF•6**	MOT test checks .... **REF•12**
Buying spare parts.................. **REF•7**	Fault finding .... **REF•16**
Vehicle identification numbers .... **REF•7**	Glossary of technical terms .... **REF•23**
General repair procedures .... **REF•8**	Index........................... **REF•27**

Dimensions and weights

Note: *All figures are approximate, and may vary according to model. Refer to manufacturer's data for exact figures.*

Dimensions
Overall length:
    Hatchback models .... 4337 to 4351 mm
    Saloon models .... 4481 to 4488 mm
    Estate models.. 4472 to 4494 mm
Overall width (including mirrors)................................ 1991 to 2020 mm
Wheelbase .... 2640 mm
Height (without roof bars):
    Hatchback models .... 1454 to 1497 mm
    Saloon models .... 1454 to 1497 mm
    Estate models.. 1459 to 1503 mm

Weights
Gross vehicle weight .... See Vehicle identification plate
Maximum towing weight .... See Vehicle identification plate

REF•2 Fuel economy

Fuel economy

Although depreciation is still the biggest part of the cost of motoring for most car owners, the cost of fuel is more immediately noticeable. These pages give some tips on how to get the best fuel economy.

Working it out

Manufacturer's figures

Car manufacturers are required by law to provide fuel consumption information on all new vehicles sold. These 'official' figures are obtained by simulating various driving conditions on a rolling road or a test track. Real life conditions are different, so the fuel consumption actually achieved may not bear much resemblance to the quoted figures.

How to calculate it

Many cars now have trip computers which will display fuel consumption, both instantaneous and average. Refer to the owner's handbook for details of how to use these.

To calculate consumption yourself (and maybe to check that the trip computer is accurate), proceed as follows.

1. Fill up with fuel and note the mileage, or zero the trip recorder.
2. Drive as usual until you need to fill up again.
3. Note the amount of fuel required to refill the tank, and the mileage covered since the previous fill-up.
4. Divide the mileage by the amount of fuel used to obtain the consumption figure.

For example:

Mileage at first fill-up (a) = 27,903
Mileage at second fill-up (b) = 28,346
Mileage covered (b - a) = 443
Fuel required at second fill-up = 48.6 litres

The half-completed changeover to metric units in the UK means that we buy our fuel in litres, measure distances in miles and talk about fuel consumption in miles per gallon. There are two ways round this: the first is to convert the litres to gallons before doing the calculation (by dividing by 4.546, or see Table 1). So in the example:

48.6 litres ÷ 4.546 = 10.69 gallons
443 miles ÷ 10.69 gallons = 41.4 mpg

The second way is to calculate the consumption in miles per litre, then multiply that figure by 4.546 (or see Table 2).

So in the example, fuel consumption is:

443 miles ÷ 48.6 litres = 9.1 mpl
9.1 mpl x 4.546 = 41.4 mpg

The rest of Europe expresses fuel consumption in litres of fuel required to travel 100 km (l/100 km). For interest, the conversions are given in Table 3. In practice it doesn't matter what units you use, provided you know what your normal consumption is and can spot if it's getting better or worse.

Table 1: conversion of litres to Imperial gallons

litres	1	2	3	4	5	10	20	30	40	50	60	70
gallons	0.22	0.44	0.66	0.88	1.10	2.24	4.49	6.73	8.98	11.22	13.47	15.71

Table 2: conversion of miles per litre to miles per gallon

miles per litre	5	6	7	8	9	10	11	12	13	14
miles per gallon	23	27	32	36	41	46	50	55	59	64

Table 3: conversion of litres per 100 km to miles per gallon

litres per 100 km	4	4.5	5	5.5	6	6.5	7	8	9	10
miles per gallon	71	63	56	51	47	43	40	35	31	28

Fuel economy REF•3

Maintenance

A well-maintained car uses less fuel and creates less pollution. In particular:

Filters
Change air and fuel filters at the specified intervals.

Oil
Use a good quality oil of the lowest viscosity specified by the vehicle manufacturer (see *Lubricants and fluids*). Check the level often and be careful not to overfill.

Spark plugs
When applicable, renew at the specified intervals.

Tyres
Check tyre pressures regularly. Under-inflated tyres have an increased rolling resistance. It is generally safe to use the higher pressures specified for full load conditions even when not fully laden, but keep an eye on the centre band of tread for signs of wear due to over-inflation.

When buying new tyres, consider the 'fuel saving' models which most manufacturers include in their ranges.

Driving style

Acceleration
Acceleration uses more fuel than driving at a steady speed. The best technique with modern cars is to accelerate reasonably briskly to the desired speed, changing up through the gears as soon as possible without making the engine labour.

Air conditioning
Air conditioning absorbs quite a bit of energy from the engine – typically 3 kW (4 hp) or so. The effect on fuel consumption is at its worst in slow traffic. Switch it off when not required.

Anticipation
Drive smoothly and try to read the traffic flow so as to avoid unnecessary acceleration and braking.

Automatic transmission
When accelerating in an automatic, avoid depressing the throttle so far as to make the transmission hold onto lower gears at higher speeds. Don't use the 'Sport' setting, if applicable.

When stationary with the engine running, select 'N' or 'P'. When moving, keep your left foot away from the brake.

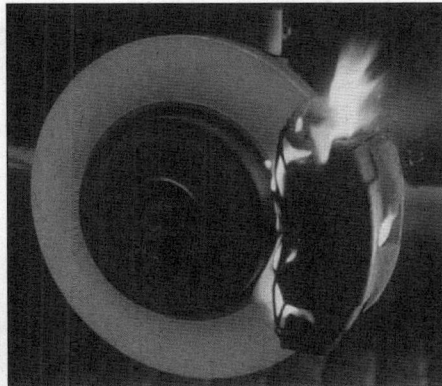

Braking
Braking converts the car's energy of motion into heat – essentially, it is wasted. Obviously some braking is always going to be necessary, but with good anticipation it is surprising how much can be avoided, especially on routes that you know well.

Carshare
Consider sharing lifts to work or to the shops. Even once a week will make a difference.

REF•4 Fuel economy

Electrical loads
Electricity is 'fuel' too; the alternator which charges the battery does so by converting some of the engine's energy of motion into electrical energy. The more electrical accessories are in use, the greater the load on the alternator. Switch off big consumers like the heated rear window when not required.

Freewheeling
Freewheeling (coasting) in neutral with the engine switched off is dangerous. The effort required to operate power-assisted brakes and steering increases when the engine is not running, with a potential lack of control in emergency situations.

In any case, modern fuel injection systems automatically cut off the engine's fuel supply on the overrun (moving and in gear, but with the accelerator pedal released).

Gadgets
Bolt-on devices claiming to save fuel have been around for nearly as long as the motor car itself. Those which worked were rapidly adopted as standard equipment by the vehicle manufacturers. Others worked only in certain situations, or saved fuel only at the expense of unacceptable effects on performance, driveability or the life of engine components.

The most effective fuel saving gadget is the driver's right foot.

Journey planning
Combine (eg) a trip to the supermarket with a visit to the recycling centre and the DIY store, rather than making separate journeys.

When possible choose a travelling time outside rush hours.

Load
The more heavily a car is laden, the greater the energy required to accelerate it to a given speed. Remove heavy items which you don't need to carry.

One load which is often overlooked is the contents of the fuel tank. A tankful of fuel (55 litres / 12 gallons) weighs 45 kg (100 lb) or so. Just half filling it may be worthwhile.

Lost?
At the risk of stating the obvious, if you're going somewhere new, have details of the route to hand. There's not much point in achieving record mpg if you also go miles out of your way.

Parking
If possible, carry out any reversing or turning manoeuvres when you arrive at a parking space so that you can drive straight out when you leave. Manoeuvering when the engine is cold uses a lot more fuel.

Driving around looking for free on-street parking may cost more in fuel than buying a car park ticket.

Premium fuel
Most major oil companies (and some supermarkets) have premium grades of fuel which are several pence a litre dearer than the standard grades. Reports vary, but the consensus seems to be that if these fuels improve economy at all, they do not do so by enough to justify their extra cost.

Roof rack
When loading a roof rack, try to produce a wedge shape with the narrow end at the front. Any cover should be securely fastened – if it flaps it's creating turbulence and absorbing energy.

Remove roof racks and boxes when not in use – they increase air resistance and can create a surprising amount of noise.

Fuel economy REF•5

Short journeys
The engine is at its least efficient, and wear is highest, during the first few miles after a cold start. Consider walking, cycling or using public transport.

Speed
The engine is at its most efficient when running at a steady speed and load at the rpm where it develops maximum torque. (You can find this figure in the car's handbook.) For most cars this corresponds to between 55 and 65 mph in top gear.

Above the optimum cruising speed, fuel consumption starts to rise quite sharply. A car travelling at 80 mph will typically be using 30% more fuel than at 60 mph.

Supermarket fuel
It may be cheap but is it any good? In the UK all supermarket fuel must meet the relevant British Standard. The major oil companies will say that their branded fuels have better additive packages which may stop carbon and other deposits building up. A reasonable compromise might be to use one tank of branded fuel to three or four from the supermarket.

Switch off when stationary
Switch off the engine if you look like being stationary for more than 30 seconds or so. This is good for the environment as well as for your pocket. Be aware though that frequent restarts are hard on the battery and the starter motor.

Windows
Driving with the windows open increases air turbulence around the vehicle. Closing the windows promotes smooth airflow and reduced resistance. The faster you go, the more significant this is.

And finally . . .
Driving techniques associated with good fuel economy tend to involve moderate acceleration and low top speeds. Be considerate to the needs of other road users who may need to make brisker progress; even if you do not agree with them this is not an excuse to be obstructive.

Safety must always take precedence over economy, whether it is a question of accelerating hard to complete an overtaking manoeuvre, killing your speed when confronted with a potential hazard or switching the lights on when it starts to get dark.

REF•6 Conversion factors

Length (distance)
Inches (in)	x 25.4	= Millimetres (mm)	x 0.0394	=	Inches (in)
Feet (ft)	x 0.305	= Metres (m)	x 3.281	=	Feet (ft)
Miles	x 1.609	= Kilometres (km)	x 0.621	=	Miles

Volume (capacity)
Cubic inches (cu in; in^3)	x 16.387	= Cubic centimetres (cc; cm^3)	x 0.061	=	Cubic inches (cu in; in^3)
Imperial pints (Imp pt)	x 0.568	= Litres (l)	x 1.76	=	Imperial pints (Imp pt)
Imperial quarts (Imp qt)	x 1.137	= Litres (l)	x 0.88	=	Imperial quarts (Imp qt)
Imperial quarts (Imp qt)	x 1.201	= US quarts (US qt)	x 0.833	=	Imperial quarts (Imp qt)
US quarts (US qt)	x 0.946	= Litres (l)	x 1.057	=	US quarts (US qt)
Imperial gallons (Imp gal)	x 4.546	= Litres (l)	x 0.22	=	Imperial gallons (Imp gal)
Imperial gallons (Imp gal)	x 1.201	= US gallons (US gal)	x 0.833	=	Imperial gallons (Imp gal)
US gallons (US gal)	x 3.785	= Litres (l)	x 0.264	=	US gallons (US gal)

Mass (weight)
Ounces (oz)	x 28.35	= Grams (g)	x 0.035	=	Ounces (oz)
Pounds (lb)	x 0.454	= Kilograms (kg)	x 2.205	=	Pounds (lb)

Force
Ounces-force (ozf; oz)	x 0.278	= Newtons (N)	x 3.6	=	Ounces-force (ozf; oz)
Pounds-force (lbf; lb)	x 4.448	= Newtons (N)	x 0.225	=	Pounds-force (lbf; lb)
Newtons (N)	x 0.1	= Kilograms-force (kgf; kg)	x 9.81	=	Newtons (N)

Pressure
Pounds-force per square inch (psi; lbf/in^2; lb/in^2)	x 0.070	= Kilograms-force per square centimetre (kgf/cm^2; kg/cm^2)	x 14.223	=	Pounds-force per square inch (psi; lbf/in^2; lb/in^2)
Pounds-force per square inch (psi; lbf/in^2; lb/in^2)	x 0.068	= Atmospheres (atm)	x 14.696	=	Pounds-force per square inch (psi; lbf/in^2; lb/in^2)
Pounds-force per square inch (psi; lbf/in^2; lb/in^2)	x 0.069	= Bars	x 14.5	=	Pounds-force per square inch (psi; lbf/in^2; lb/in^2)
Pounds-force per square inch (psi; lbf/in^2; lb/in^2)	x 6.895	= Kilopascals (kPa)	x 0.145	=	Pounds-force per square inch (psi; lbf/in^2; lb/in^2)
Kilopascals (kPa)	x 0.01	= Kilograms-force per square centimetre (kgf/cm^2; kg/cm^2)	x 98.1	=	Kilopascals (kPa)
Millibar (mbar)	x 100	= Pascals (Pa)	x 0.01	=	Millibar (mbar)
Millibar (mbar)	x 0.0145	= Pounds-force per square inch (psi; lbf/in^2; lb/in^2)	x 68.947	=	Millibar (mbar)
Millibar (mbar)	x 0.75	= Millimetres of mercury (mmHg)	x 1.333	=	Millibar (mbar)
Millibar (mbar)	x 0.401	= Inches of water (inH$_2$O)	x 2.491	=	Millibar (mbar)
Millimetres of mercury (mmHg)	x 0.535	= Inches of water (inH$_2$O)	x 1.868	=	Millimetres of mercury (mmHg)
Inches of water (inH$_2$O)	x 0.036	= Pounds-force per square inch (psi; lbf/in^2; lb/in^2)	x 27.68	=	Inches of water (inH$_2$O)

Torque (moment of force)
Pounds-force inches (lbf in; lb in)	x 1.152	= Kilograms-force centimetre (kgf cm; kg cm)	x 0.868	=	Pounds-force inches (lbf in; lb in)
Pounds-force inches (lbf in; lb in)	x 0.113	= Newton metres (Nm)	x 8.85	=	Pounds-force inches (lbf in; lb in)
Pounds-force inches (lbf in; lb in)	x 0.083	= Pounds-force feet (lbf ft; lb ft)	x 12	=	Pounds-force inches (lbf in; lb in)
Pounds-force feet (lbf ft; lb ft)	x 0.138	= Kilograms-force metres (kgf m; kg m)	x 7.233	=	Pounds-force feet (lbf ft; lb ft)
Pounds-force feet (lbf ft; lb ft)	x 1.356	= Newton metres (Nm)	x 0.738	=	Pounds-force feet (lbf ft; lb ft)
Newton metres (Nm)	x 0.102	= Kilograms-force metres (kgf m; kg m)	x 9.804	=	Newton metres (Nm)

Power
Horsepower (hp)	x 745.7	= Watts (W)	x 0.0013	=	Horsepower (hp)

Velocity (speed)
Miles per hour (miles/hr; mph)	x 1.609	= Kilometres per hour (km/hr; kph)	x 0.621	=	Miles per hour (miles/hr; mph)

Fuel consumption*
Miles per gallon, Imperial (mpg)	x 0.354	= Kilometres per litre (km/l)	x 2.825	=	Miles per gallon, Imperial (mpg)
Miles per gallon, US (mpg)	x 0.425	= Kilometres per litre (km/l)	x 2.352	=	Miles per gallon, US (mpg)

Temperature
Degrees Fahrenheit = (°C x 1.8) + 32   Degrees Celsius (Degrees Centigrade; °C) = (°F - 32) x 0.56

It is common practice to convert from miles per gallon (mpg) to litres/100 kilometres (l/100km), where mpg x l/100 km = 282

Buying spare parts

Spare parts are available from many sources, including maker's appointed garages, accessory shops, and motor factors. To be sure of obtaining the correct parts, it will sometimes be necessary to quote the vehicle identification number. If possible, it can also be useful to take the old parts along for positive identification. Items such as starter motors and alternators may be available under a service exchange scheme – any parts returned should be clean.

Our advice regarding spare parts is as follows.

Officially appointed garages

This is the best source of parts which are peculiar to your car, and which are not otherwise generally available (eg, badges, interior trim, certain body panels, etc). It is also the only place at which you should buy parts if the vehicle is still under warranty.

Accessory shops

These are very good places to buy materials and components needed for the maintenance of your car (oil, air and fuel filters, light bulbs, drivebelts, greases, brake pads, touch-up paint, etc). Components of this nature sold by a reputable shop are usually of the same standard as those used by the car manufacturer.

Besides components, these shops also sell tools and general accessories, usually have convenient opening hours, charge lower prices, and can often be found close to home. Some accessory shops have parts counters where components needed for almost any repair job can be purchased or ordered.

Motor factors

Good factors will stock all the more important components which wear out comparatively quickly, and can sometimes supply individual components needed for the overhaul of a larger assembly (eg, brake seals and hydraulic parts, bearing shells, pistons, valves). They may also handle work such as cylinder block reboring, crankshaft regrinding, etc.

Tyre and exhaust specialists

These outlets may be independent, or members of a local or national chain. They frequently offer competitive prices when compared with a main dealer or local garage, but it will pay to obtain several quotes before making a decision. When researching prices, also ask what extras may be added – for instance fitting a new valve and balancing the wheel are both commonly charged on top of the price of a new tyre.

Other sources

Beware of parts or materials obtained from market stalls, car boot sales or similar outlets. Such items are not invariably sub-standard, but there is little chance of compensation if they do prove unsatisfactory. in the case of safety-critical components such as brake pads, there is the risk not only of financial loss, but also of an accident causing injury or death.

Second-hand components or assemblies obtained from a car breaker can be a good buy in some circumstances, but this sort of purchase is best made by the experienced DIY mechanic.

Vehicle identification numbers

Modifications are a continuing and unpublicised process in vehicle manufacture, quite apart from major model changes. Spare parts manuals and lists are compiled upon a numerical basis, the individual vehicle identification numbers being essential to correct identification of the component concerned.

When ordering spare parts, always give as much information as possible. Quote the car model, year of manufacture, body and engine numbers as appropriate.

The *vehicle identification plate* is situated on the driver's side B-pillar **(see illustration)**. The *vehicle identification number* is also repeated in the form of plate visible through the windscreen on the passenger's side **(see illustration)**.

The *engine number* is located on the left-hand front side of the engine cylinder block (1.4 and 1.6 litre engines) or on the left-hand side rear of the engine cylinder block (1.8 and 2.0 litre engines).

Other identification numbers or codes are stamped on major items such as the gearbox, etc.

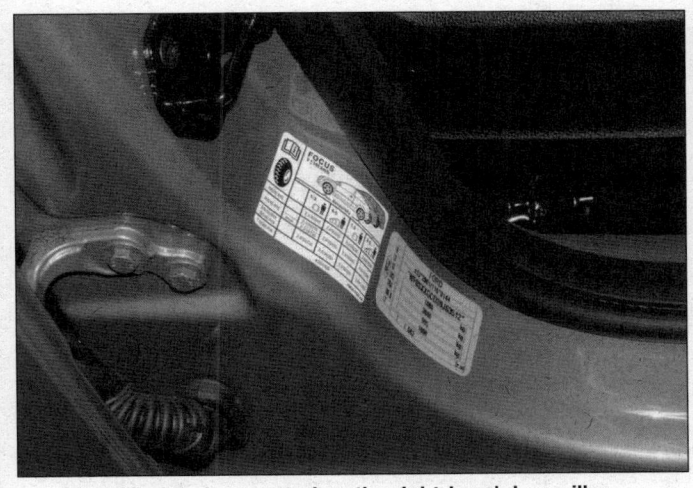

The VIN plate is mounted on the right-hand door pillar . . .

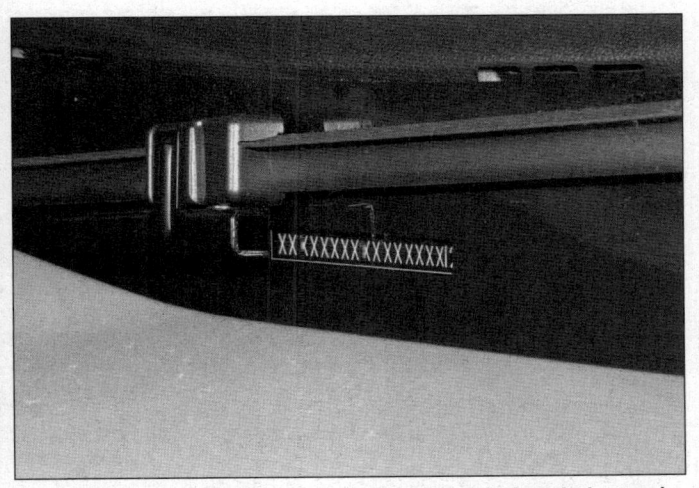

. . . and on a plate on the facia (visible through the windscreen)

General repair procedures

Whenever servicing, repair or overhaul work is carried out on the car or its components, observe the following procedures and instructions. This will assist in carrying out the operation efficiently and to a professional standard of workmanship.

Joint mating faces and gaskets

When separating components at their mating faces, never insert screwdrivers or similar implements into the joint between the faces in order to prise them apart. This can cause severe damage which results in oil leaks, coolant leaks, etc upon reassembly. Separation is usually achieved by tapping along the joint with a soft-faced hammer in order to break the seal. However, note that this method may not be suitable where dowels are used for component location.

Where a gasket is used between the mating faces of two components, a new one must be fitted on reassembly; fit it dry unless otherwise stated in the repair procedure. Make sure that the mating faces are clean and dry, with all traces of old gasket removed. When cleaning a joint face, use a tool which is unlikely to score or damage the face, and remove any burrs or nicks with an oilstone or fine file.

Make sure that tapped holes are cleaned with a pipe cleaner, and keep them free of jointing compound, if this is being used, unless specifically instructed otherwise.

Ensure that all orifices, channels or pipes are clear, and blow through them, preferably using compressed air.

Oil seals

Oil seals can be removed by levering them out with a wide flat-bladed screwdriver or similar implement. Alternatively, a number of self-tapping screws may be screwed into the seal, and these used as a purchase for pliers or some similar device in order to pull the seal free.

Whenever an oil seal is removed from its working location, either individually or as part of an assembly, it should be renewed.

The very fine sealing lip of the seal is easily damaged, and will not seal if the surface it contacts is not completely clean and free from scratches, nicks or grooves. If the original sealing surface of the component cannot be restored, and the manufacturer has not made provision for slight relocation of the seal relative to the sealing surface, the component should be renewed.

Protect the lips of the seal from any surface which may damage them in the course of fitting. Use tape or a conical sleeve where possible. Where indicated, lubricate the seal lips with oil before fitting and, on dual-lipped seals, fill the space between the lips with grease.

Unless otherwise stated, oil seals must be fitted with their sealing lips toward the lubricant to be sealed.

Use a tubular drift or block of wood of the appropriate size to install the seal and, if the seal housing is shouldered, drive the seal down to the shoulder. If the seal housing is unshouldered, the seal should be fitted with its face flush with the housing top face (unless otherwise instructed).

Screw threads and fastenings

Seized nuts, bolts and screws are quite a common occurrence where corrosion has set in, and the use of penetrating oil or releasing fluid will often overcome this problem if the offending item is soaked for a while before attempting to release it. The use of an impact driver may also provide a means of releasing such stubborn fastening devices, when used in conjunction with the appropriate screwdriver bit or socket. If none of these methods works, it may be necessary to resort to the careful application of heat, or the use of a hacksaw or nut splitter device. Before resorting to extreme methods, check that you are not dealing with a left-hand thread!

Studs are usually removed by locking two nuts together on the threaded part, and then using a spanner on the lower nut to unscrew the stud. Studs or bolts which have broken off below the surface of the component in which they are mounted can sometimes be removed using a stud extractor.

Always ensure that a blind tapped hole is completely free from oil, grease, water or other fluid before installing the bolt or stud. Failure to do this could cause the housing to crack due to the hydraulic action of the bolt or stud as it is screwed in.

For some screw fastenings, notably cylinder head bolts or nuts, torque wrench settings are no longer specified for the latter stages of tightening, "angle-tightening" being called up instead. Typically, a fairly low torque wrench setting will be applied to the bolts/nuts in the correct sequence, followed by one or more stages of tightening through specified angles.

When checking or retightening a nut or bolt to a specified torque setting, slacken the nut or bolt by a quarter of a turn, and then retighten to the specified setting. However, this should not be attempted where angular tightening has been used.

Locknuts, locktabs and washers

Any fastening which will rotate against a component or housing during tightening should always have a washer between it and the relevant component or housing.

Spring or split washers should always be renewed when they are used to lock a critical component such as a big-end bearing retaining bolt or nut. Locktabs which are folded over to retain a nut or bolt should always be renewed.

Self-locking nuts can be re-used in non-critical areas, providing resistance can be felt when the locking portion passes over the bolt or stud thread. However, it should be noted that self-locking stiffnuts tend to lose their effectiveness after long periods of use, and should then be renewed as a matter of course.

Split pins must always be replaced with new ones of the correct size for the hole.

When thread-locking compound is found on the threads of a fastener which is to be re-used, it should be cleaned off with a wire brush and solvent, and fresh compound applied on reassembly.

Special tools

Some repair procedures in this manual entail the use of special tools such as a press, two or three-legged pullers, spring compressors, etc. Wherever possible, suitable readily-available alternatives to the manufacturer's special tools are described, and are shown in use. In some instances, where no alternative is possible, it has been necessary to resort to the use of a manufacturer's tool, and this has been done for reasons of safety as well as the efficient completion of the repair operation. Unless you are highly-skilled and have a thorough understanding of the procedures described, never attempt to bypass the use of any special tool when the procedure described specifies its use. Not only is there a very great risk of personal injury, but expensive damage could be caused to the components involved.

Environmental considerations

When disposing of used engine oil, brake fluid, antifreeze, etc, give due consideration to any detrimental environmental effects. Do not, for instance, pour any of the above liquids down drains into the general sewage system, or onto the ground to soak away, as this is likely to pollute your local environment. Many local council refuse tips provide a facility for waste oil disposal, as do some garages. You can find your nearest disposal point by calling the Environment Agency on 03708 506 506 or by visiting www.oilbankline.org.uk.

OIL CARE

Note: It is illegal and anti-social to dump oil down the drain. To find the location of your local oil recycling bank, call 03708 506 506 or visit www.oilbankline.org.uk.

Jacking and vehicle support REF•9

The jack supplied with the vehicle tool kit should only be used for changing the roadwheels – see *Wheel changing* at the front of this manual. When carrying out any other kind of work, raise the vehicle using a hydraulic trolley jack, and always supplement the jack with axle stands positioned under the vehicle jacking points.

When using a trolley jack or axle stands, position the jack head or axle stand head adjacent to one of the relevant wheel changing jacking points under the sills **(see illustration)**. Use a block of wood between the jack or axle stand and the sill.

Do not attempt to jack the vehicle under the sump, or any of the suspension components.

The jack supplied with the vehicle locates in the jacking points on the underside of the sills – see *Wheel changing* at the front of this manual. Ensure that the jack head is correctly engaged before attempting to raise the vehicle.

Never work under, around, or near a raised vehicle, unless it is adequately supported in at least two places.

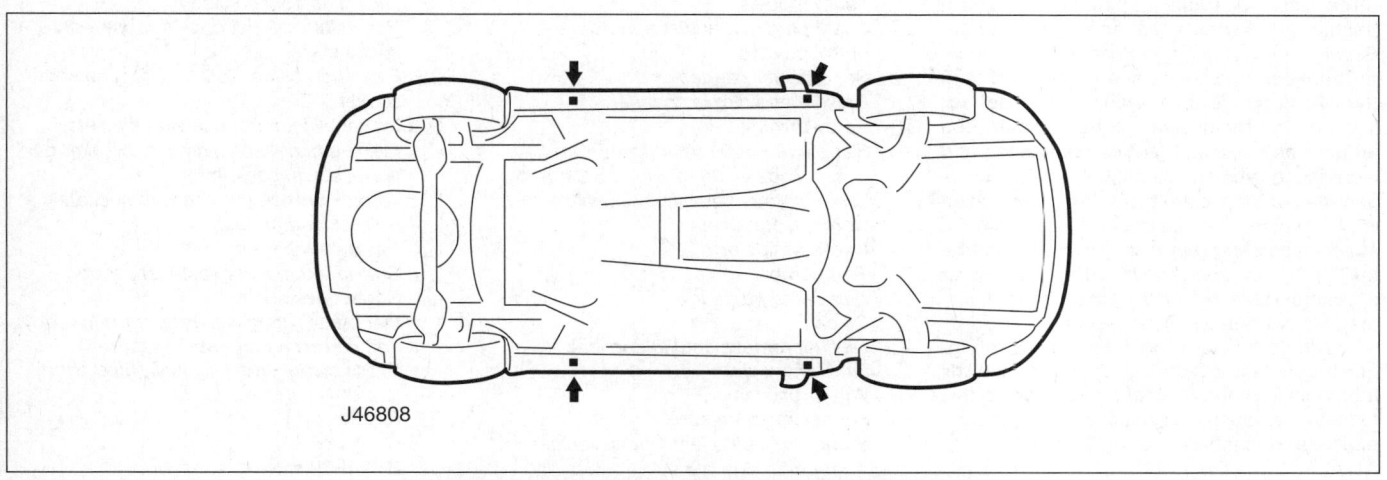

Use a workshop/trolley jack at the points indicated

Tools and working facilities

Introduction

A selection of good tools is a fundamental requirement for anyone contemplating the maintenance and repair of a motor vehicle. For the owner who does not possess any, their purchase will prove a considerable expense, offsetting some of the savings made by doing-it-yourself. However, provided that the tools purchased meet the relevant national safety standards and are of good quality, they will last for many years and prove an extremely worthwhile investment.

To help the average owner to decide which tools are needed to carry out the various tasks detailed in this manual, we have compiled three lists of tools under the following headings: *Maintenance and minor repair*, *Repair and overhaul*, and *Special*. Newcomers to practical mechanics should start off with the *Maintenance and minor repair* tool kit, and confine themselves to the simpler jobs around the vehicle. Then, as confidence and experience grow, more difficult tasks can be undertaken, with extra tools being purchased as, and when, they are needed. In this way, a *Maintenance and minor repair* tool kit can be built up into a *Repair and overhaul* tool kit over a considerable period of time, without any major cash outlays. The experienced do-it-yourselfer will have a tool kit good enough for most repair and overhaul procedures, and will add tools from the *Special* category when it is felt that the expense is justified by the amount of use to which these tools will be put.

Maintenance and minor repair tool kit

The tools given in this list should be considered as a minimum requirement if routine maintenance, servicing and minor repair operations are to be undertaken. We recommend the purchase of combination spanners (ring one end, open-ended the other); although more expensive than open-ended ones, they do give the advantages of both types of spanner.

- ☐ *Combination spanners:*
  Metric - 8 to 19 mm inclusive
- ☐ *Adjustable spanner - 35 mm jaw (approx.)*
- ☐ *Spark plug spanner (with rubber insert) - petrol models*
- ☐ *Spark plug gap adjustment tool - petrol models*
- ☐ *Set of feeler gauges*
- ☐ *Brake bleed nipple spanner*
- ☐ *Screwdrivers:*
  Flat blade - 100 mm long x 6 mm dia
  Cross blade - 100 mm long x 6 mm dia
  Torx - various sizes (not all vehicles)
- ☐ *Combination pliers*
- ☐ *Hacksaw (junior)*
- ☐ *Tyre pump*
- ☐ *Tyre pressure gauge*
- ☐ *Oil can*
- ☐ *Oil filter removal tool (if applicable)*
- ☐ *Fine emery cloth*
- ☐ *Wire brush (small)*
- ☐ *Funnel (medium size)*
- ☐ *Sump drain plug key (not all vehicles)*

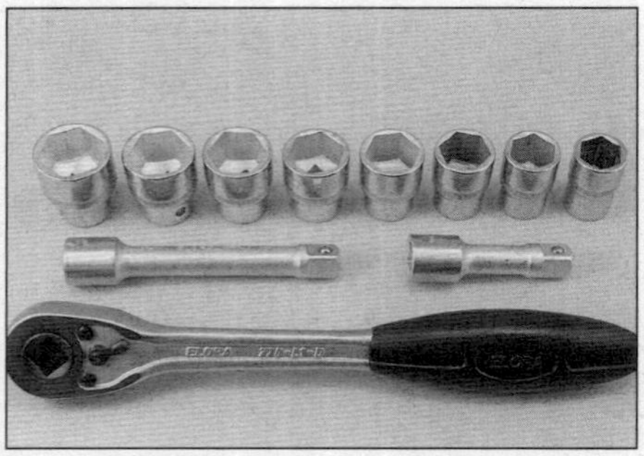

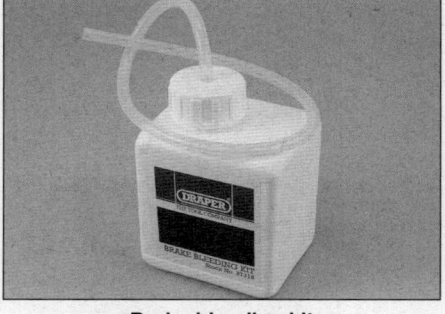

Repair and overhaul tool kit

These tools are virtually essential for anyone undertaking any major repairs to a motor vehicle, and are additional to those given in the *Maintenance and minor repair* list. Included in this list is a comprehensive set of sockets. Although these are expensive, they will be found invaluable as they are so versatile - particularly if various drives are included in the set. We recommend the half-inch square-drive type, as this can be used with most proprietary torque wrenches.

The tools in this list will sometimes need to be supplemented by tools from the *Special* list:

- ☐ *Sockets to cover range in previous list (including Torx sockets)*
- ☐ *Reversible ratchet drive (for use with sockets)*
- ☐ *Extension piece, 250 mm (for use with sockets)*
- ☐ *Universal joint (for use with sockets)*
- ☐ *Flexible handle or sliding T "breaker bar" (for use with sockets)*
- ☐ *Torque wrench (for use with sockets)*
- ☐ *Self-locking grips*
- ☐ *Ball pein hammer*
- ☐ *Soft-faced mallet (plastic or rubber)*
- ☐ *Screwdrivers:*
  Flat blade - long & sturdy, short (chubby), and narrow (electrician's) types
  Cross blade – long & sturdy, and short (chubby) types
- ☐ *Pliers:*
  Long-nosed
  Side cutters (electrician's)
  Circlip (internal and external)
- ☐ *Cold chisel - 25 mm*
- ☐ *Scriber*
- ☐ *Scraper*
- ☐ *Centre-punch*
- ☐ *Pin punch*
- ☐ *Hacksaw*
- ☐ *Brake hose clamp*
- ☐ *Brake/clutch bleeding kit*
- ☐ *Selection of twist drills*
- ☐ *Steel rule/straight-edge*
- ☐ *Allen keys (inc. splined/Torx type)*
- ☐ *Selection of files*
- ☐ *Wire brush*
- ☐ *Axle stands*
- ☐ *Jack (strong trolley or hydraulic type)*
- ☐ *Light with extension lead*
- ☐ *Universal electrical multi-meter*

Sockets and reversible ratchet drive

Brake bleeding kit

Torx key, socket and bit

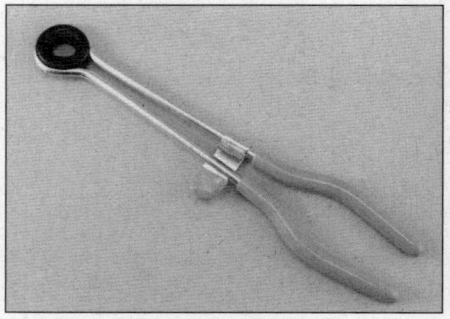

Hose clamp

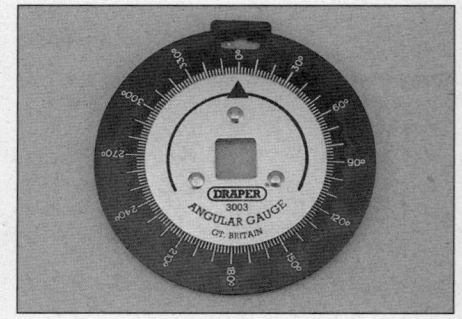

Angular-tightening gauge

Tools and working facilities REF•11

Special tools

The tools in this list are those which are not used regularly, are expensive to buy, or which need to be used in accordance with their manufacturers' instructions. Unless relatively difficult mechanical jobs are undertaken frequently, it will not be economic to buy many of these tools. Where this is the case, you could consider clubbing together with friends (or joining a motorists' club) to make a joint purchase, or borrowing the tools against a deposit from a local garage or tool hire specialist.

The following list contains only those tools and instruments freely available to the public, and not those special tools produced by the vehicle manufacturer specifically for its dealer network. You will find occasional references to these manufacturers' special tools in the text of this manual. Generally, an alternative method of doing the job without the vehicle manufacturers' special tool is given. However, sometimes there is no alternative to using them. Where this is the case and the relevant tool cannot be bought or borrowed, you will have to entrust the work to a dealer.

- ☐ *Angular-tightening gauge*
- ☐ *Valve spring compressor*
- ☐ *Valve grinding tool*
- ☐ *Piston ring compressor*
- ☐ *Piston ring removal/installation tool*
- ☐ *Cylinder bore hone*
- ☐ *Balljoint separator*
- ☐ *Coil spring compressors (where applicable)*
- ☐ *Two/three-legged hub and bearing puller*
- ☐ *Impact screwdriver*
- ☐ *Micrometer and/or vernier calipers*
- ☐ *Dial gauge*
- ☐ *Tachometer*
- ☐ *Fault code reader*
- ☐ *Cylinder compression gauge*
- ☐ *Hand-operated vacuum pump and gauge*
- ☐ *Clutch plate alignment set*
- ☐ *Brake shoe steady spring cup removal tool*
- ☐ *Bush and bearing removal/installation set*
- ☐ *Stud extractors*
- ☐ *Tap and die set*
- ☐ *Lifting tackle*

Buying tools

Reputable motor accessory shops and superstores often offer excellent quality tools at discount prices, so it pays to shop around.

Remember, you don't have to buy the most expensive items on the shelf, but it is always advisable to steer clear of the very cheap tools. Beware of 'bargains' offered on market stalls, on-line or at car boot sales. There are plenty of good tools around at reasonable prices, but always aim to purchase items which meet the relevant national safety standards. If in doubt, ask the proprietor or manager of the shop for advice before making a purchase.

Care and maintenance of tools

Having purchased a reasonable tool kit, it is necessary to keep the tools in a clean and serviceable condition. After use, always wipe off any dirt, grease and metal particles using a clean, dry cloth, before putting the tools away. Never leave them lying around after they have been used. A simple tool rack on the garage or workshop wall for items such as screwdrivers and pliers is a good idea. Store all normal spanners and sockets in a metal box. Any measuring instruments, gauges, meters, etc, must be carefully stored where they cannot be damaged or become rusty.

Take a little care when tools are used. Hammer heads inevitably become marked, and screwdrivers lose the keen edge on their blades from time to time. A little timely attention with emery cloth or a file will soon restore items like this to a good finish.

Working facilities

Not to be forgotten when discussing tools is the workshop itself. If anything more than routine maintenance is to be carried out, a suitable working area becomes essential.

It is appreciated that many an owner-mechanic is forced by circumstances to remove an engine or similar item without the benefit of a garage or workshop. Having done this, any repairs should always be done under the cover of a roof.

Wherever possible, any dismantling should be done on a clean, flat workbench or table at a suitable working height.

Any workbench needs a vice; one with a jaw opening of 100 mm is suitable for most jobs. As mentioned previously, some clean dry storage space is also required for tools, as well as for any lubricants, cleaning fluids, touch-up paints etc, which become necessary.

Another item which may be required, and which has a much more general usage, is an electric drill with a chuck capacity of at least 8 mm. This, together with a good range of twist drills, is virtually essential for fitting accessories.

Last, but not least, always keep a supply of old newspapers and clean, lint-free rags available, and try to keep any working area as clean as possible.

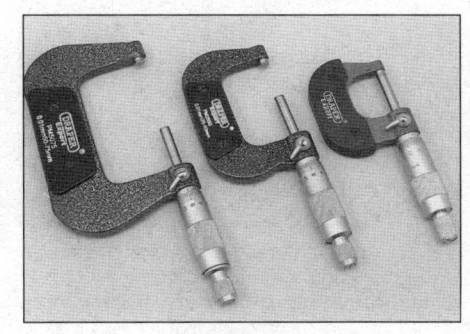

Micrometers

Dial test indicator ("dial gauge")

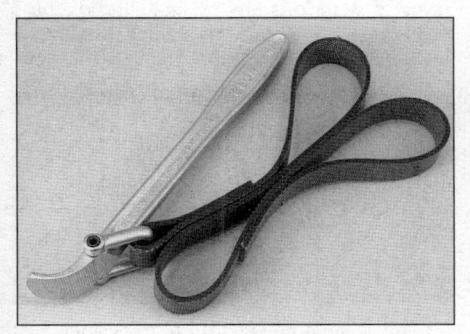

Oil filter removal tool (strap wrench type)

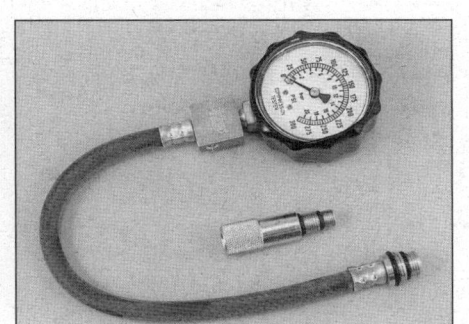

Compression tester

Bearing puller

REF•12 MOT test checks

This is a guide to getting your vehicle through the MOT test. Obviously it will not be possible to examine the vehicle to the same standard as the professional MOT tester. However, working through the following checks will enable you to identify any problem areas before submitting the vehicle for the test.

It has only been possible to summarise the test requirements here, based on the regulations in force at the time of printing. Test standards are becoming increasingly stringent, although there are some exemptions for older vehicles.

An assistant will be needed to help carry out some of these checks.

The checks have been sub-divided into four categories, as follows:

1 Checks carried out **FROM THE DRIVER'S SEAT**

2 Checks carried out **WITH THE VEHICLE ON THE GROUND**

3 Checks carried out **WITH THE VEHICLE RAISED AND THE WHEELS FREE TO TURN**

4 Checks carried out on **YOUR VEHICLE'S EXHAUST EMISSION SYSTEM**

---

1 Checks carried out **FROM THE DRIVER'S SEAT**

Handbrake (parking brake)

☐ Test the operation of the handbrake. Excessive travel (too many clicks) indicates incorrect brake or cable adjustment.

☐ Check that the handbrake cannot be released by tapping the lever sideways. Check the security of the lever mountings.

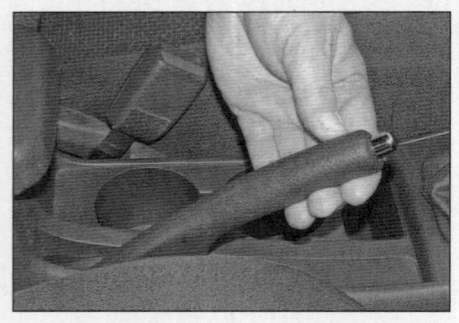

☐ If the parking brake is foot-operated, check that the pedal is secure and without excessive travel, and that the release mechanism operates correctly.

☐ Where applicable, test the operation of the electronic handbrake. The brake should engage and disengage without excessive delay. If the warning light does not extinguish when the brake is disengaged, this could indicate a fault which will need further investigation.

Footbrake

☐ Depress the brake pedal and check that it does not creep down to the floor, indicating a master cylinder fault. Release the pedal, wait a few seconds, then depress it again. If the pedal travels nearly to the floor before firm resistance is felt, brake adjustment or repair is necessary. If the pedal feels spongy, there is air in the hydraulic system which must be removed by bleeding.

☐ Check that the brake pedal is secure and in good condition. Check also for signs of fluid leaks on the pedal, floor or carpets, which would indicate failed seals in the brake master cylinder.

☐ Check the servo unit (when applicable) by operating the brake pedal several times, then keeping the pedal depressed and starting the engine. As the engine starts, the pedal will move down slightly. If not, the vacuum hose or the servo itself may be faulty.

Steering wheel and column

☐ Examine the steering wheel for fractures or looseness of the hub, spokes or rim.

☐ Move the steering wheel from side to side and then up and down. Check that the steering wheel is not loose on the column, indicating wear or a loose retaining nut. Continue moving the steering wheel as before, but also turn it slightly from left to right.

☐ Check that the steering wheel is not loose on the column, and that there is no abnormal movement of the steering wheel, indicating wear in the column support bearings or couplings.

☐ Check that the ignition lock (where fitted) engages and disengages correctly.

☐ Steering column adjustment mechanisms (where fitted) must be able to lock the column securely in place with no play evident.

Windscreen, mirrors and sunvisor

☐ The windscreen must be free of cracks or other significant damage within the driver's field of view. (Small stone chips are acceptable.) Rear view mirrors must be secure, intact, and capable of being adjusted.

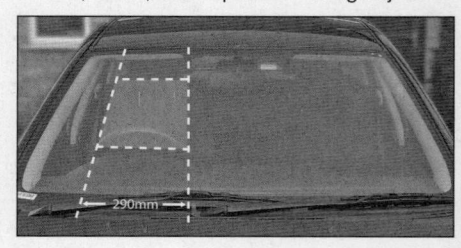

☐ The driver's sunvisor must be capable of being stored in the "up" position.

MOT test checks REF•13

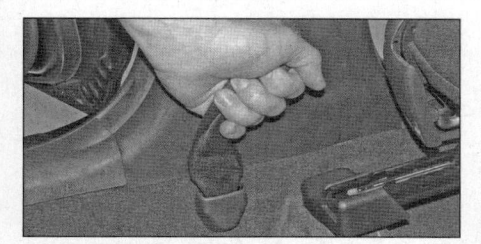

Seat belts and seats

Note: *The following checks are applicable to all seat belts, front and rear.*

☐ Examine the webbing of all the belts (including rear belts if fitted) for cuts, serious fraying or deterioration. Fasten and unfasten each belt to check the buckles. If applicable, check the retracting mechanism. Check the security of all seat belt mountings accessible from inside the vehicle, ensuring any height adjustable mountings lock securely in place.
☐ Seat belts with pre-tensioners, once activated, have a "flag" or similar showing on the seat belt stalk. This, in itself, is not a reason for test failure.
☐ The front seats themselves must be securely attached and the backrests must lock in the upright position.

Doors

☐ Both front doors must be able to be opened and closed from outside and inside, and must latch securely when closed.

Bonnet and boot/tailgate

☐ The bonnet and boot/tailgate must latch securely when closed.

2 Checks carried out WITH THE VEHICLE ON THE GROUND

Vehicle identification

☐ Number plates must be in good condition, secure and legible, with letters and numbers correctly spaced – spacing at (A) should be 33 mm and at (B) 11 mm. At the front, digits must be black on a white background and at the rear black on a yellow background. Other background designs (such as honeycomb) are not permitted.

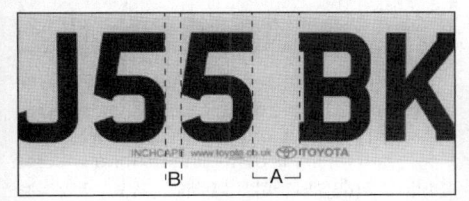

☐ The VIN plate and/or homologation plate must be permanently displayed and legible.

Electrical equipment

☐ Switch on the ignition and check the operation of the horn.
☐ Check the windscreen washers and wipers, examining the wiper blades; renew damaged or perished blades. Also check the operation of the stop-lights.

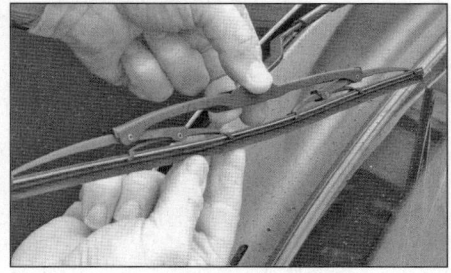

☐ Check the operation of the sidelights and number plate lights. The lenses and reflectors must be secure, clean and undamaged.
☐ Check the operation and alignment of the headlights. The headlight reflectors must not be tarnished and the lenses must be undamaged.
☐ Switch on the ignition and check the operation of the direction indicators (including the instrument panel tell-tale) and the hazard warning lights. Operation of the sidelights and stop-lights must not affect the indicators - if it does, the cause is usually a bad earth at the rear light cluster. Indicators should flash at a rate of between 60 and 120 times per minute – faster or slower than this could indicate a fault with the flasher unit or a bad earth at one of the light units.
☐ Check the operation of the rear foglight(s), including the warning light on the instrument panel or in the switch.
☐ The ABS warning light must illuminate in accordance with the manufacturers' design. For most vehicles, the ABS warning light should illuminate when the ignition is switched on, and (if the system is operating properly) extinguish after a few seconds. Refer to the owner's handbook.

Footbrake

☐ Examine the master cylinder, brake pipes and servo unit for leaks, loose mountings, corrosion or other damage. If ABS is fitted, this unit should also be examined for signs of leaks or corrosion.

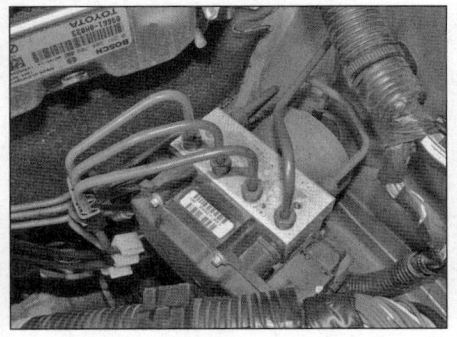

☐ The fluid reservoir must be secure and the fluid level must be between the upper (A) and lower (B) markings.

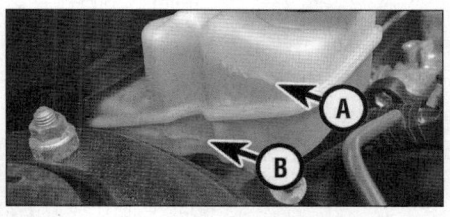

☐ Inspect both front brake flexible hoses for cracks or deterioration of the rubber. Turn the steering from lock to lock, and ensure that the hoses do not contact the wheel, tyre, or any part of the steering or suspension mechanism. With the brake pedal firmly depressed, check the hoses for bulges or leaks under pressure.

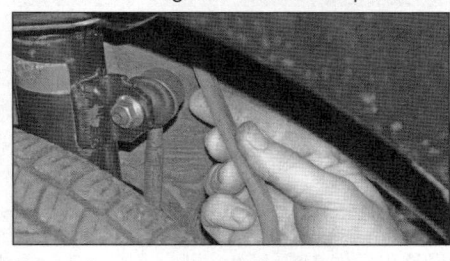

Steering and suspension

☐ Have your assistant turn the steering wheel from side to side slightly, up to the point where the steering gear just begins to transmit this movement to the roadwheels. Check for excessive free play between the steering wheel and the steering gear, indicating wear or insecurity of the steering column joints, the column-to-steering gear coupling, or the steering gear itself.
☐ Have your assistant turn the steering wheel more vigorously in each direction, so that the roadwheels just begin to turn. As this is done, examine all the steering joints, linkages, fittings and attachments. Renew any component that shows signs of wear or damage. On vehicles with power steering, check the security and condition of the steering pump, drivebelt and hoses.
☐ Check that the vehicle is standing level, and at approximately the correct ride height.

Shock absorbers

☐ Depress each corner of the vehicle in turn, then release it. The vehicle should rise and then settle in its normal position. If the vehicle continues to rise and fall, the shock absorber is defective. A shock absorber which has seized will also cause the vehicle to fail.

MOT test checks

Exhaust system

☐ Start the engine. With your assistant holding a rag over the tailpipe, check the entire system for leaks. Repair or renew leaking sections.

3 Checks carried out WITH THE VEHICLE RAISED AND THE WHEELS FREE TO TURN

Jack up the front and rear of the vehicle, and securely support it on axle stands. Position the stands clear of the suspension assemblies. Ensure that the wheels are clear of the ground and that the steering can be turned from lock to lock.

Steering mechanism

☐ Have your assistant turn the steering from lock to lock. Check that the steering turns smoothly, and that no part of the steering mechanism, including a wheel or tyre, fouls any brake hose or pipe or any part of the body structure.
☐ Examine the steering rack rubber gaiters for damage or insecurity of the retaining clips. If power steering is fitted, check for signs of damage or leakage of the fluid hoses, pipes or connections. Also check for excessive stiffness or binding of the steering, a missing split pin or locking device, or severe corrosion of the body structure within 30 cm of any steering component attachment point.

Front and rear suspension and wheel bearings

☐ Starting at the front right-hand side, grasp the roadwheel at the 3 o'clock and 9 o'clock positions and rock gently but firmly. Check for free play or insecurity at the wheel bearings, suspension balljoints, or suspension mount-ings, pivots and attachments.
☐ Now grasp the wheel at the 12 o'clock and 6 o'clock positions and repeat the previous inspection. Spin the wheel, and check for roughness or tightness of the front wheel bearing.

☐ If excess free play is suspected at a component pivot point, this can be confirmed by using a large screwdriver or similar tool and levering between the mounting and the component attachment. This will confirm whether the wear is in the pivot bush, its retaining bolt, or in the mounting itself (the bolt holes can often become elongated).

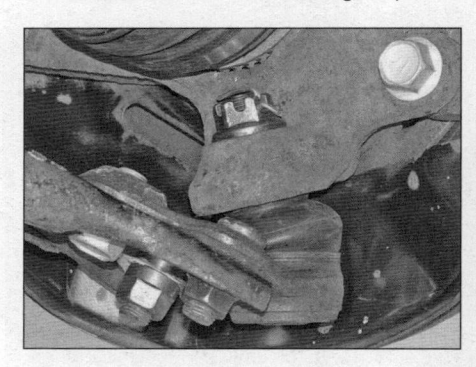

☐ Carry out all the above checks at the other front wheel, and then at both rear wheels.

Springs and shock absorbers

☐ Examine the suspension struts (when applicable) for serious fluid leakage, corrosion, or damage to the casing. Also check the security of the mounting points.
☐ If coil springs are fitted, check that the spring ends locate in their seats, and that the spring is not corroded, cracked or broken.
☐ If leaf springs are fitted, check that all leaves are intact, that the axle is securely attached to each spring, and that there is no deterioration of the spring eye mountings, bushes, and shackles.

☐ The same general checks apply to vehicles fitted with other suspension types, such as torsion bars, hydraulic displacer units, etc. Ensure that all mountings and attachments are secure, that there are no signs of excessive wear, corrosion or damage, and (on hydraulic types) that there are no fluid leaks or damaged pipes.
☐ Inspect the shock absorbers for signs of serious fluid leakage. Check for wear of the mounting bushes or attachments, or damage to the body of the unit.

Driveshafts (fwd vehicles only)

☐ Rotate each front wheel in turn and inspect the constant velocity joint gaiters for splits or damage. Also check that each driveshaft is straight and undamaged.

Braking system

☐ If possible without dismantling, check brake pad wear and disc condition. Ensure that the friction lining material has not worn excessively, (A) and that the discs are not fractured, pitted, scored or badly worn (B).

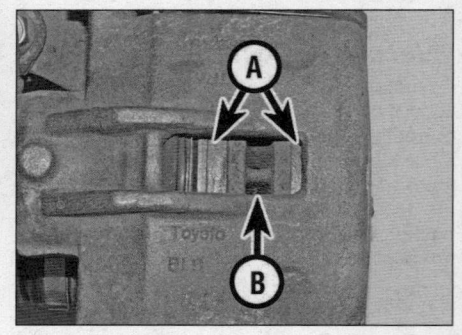

☐ Examine all the rigid brake pipes underneath the vehicle, and the flexible hose(s) at the rear. Look for corrosion, chafing or insecurity of the pipes, and for signs of bulging under pressure, chafing, splits or deterioration of the flexible hoses.
☐ Look for signs of fluid leaks at the brake calipers or on the brake backplates. Repair or renew leaking components.
☐ Slowly spin each wheel, while your assistant depresses and releases the footbrake. Ensure that each brake is operating and does not bind when the pedal is released.

MOT test checks REF•15

☐ Examine the handbrake mechanism, checking for frayed or broken cables, excessive corrosion, or wear or insecurity of the linkage. Check that the mechanism works on each relevant wheel, and releases fully, without binding.

☐ It is not possible to test brake efficiency without special equipment, but a road test can be carried out later to check that the vehicle pulls up in a straight line.

Fuel and exhaust systems

☐ Inspect the fuel tank (including the filler cap), fuel pipes, hoses and unions. All components must be secure and free from leaks. Locking fuel caps must lock securely and the key must be provided for the MOT test.

☐ Examine the exhaust system over its entire length, checking for any damaged, broken or missing mountings, security of the retaining clamps and rust or corrosion.

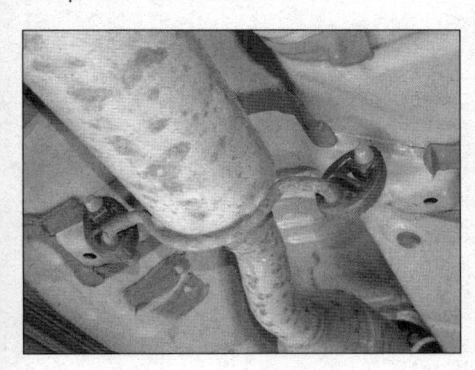

Wheels and tyres

☐ Examine the sidewalls and tread area of each tyre in turn. Check for cuts, tears, lumps, bulges, separation of the tread, and exposure of the ply or cord due to wear or damage. Check that the tyre bead is correctly seated on the wheel rim, that the valve is sound and properly seated, and that the wheel is not distorted or damaged.

☐ Check that the tyres are of the correct size for the vehicle, that they are of the same size and type on each axle, and that the pressures are correct.

☐ Check the tyre tread depth. The legal minimum at the time of writing is 1.6 mm over the central three-quarters of the tread width. Abnormal tread wear may indicate incorrect front wheel alignment or wear in steering or suspension components.

☐ If the spare wheel is fitted externally or in a separate carrier beneath the vehicle, check that mountings are secure and free of excessive corrosion.

Body corrosion

☐ Check the condition of the entire vehicle structure for signs of corrosion in load-bearing areas. (These include chassis box sections, side sills, cross-members, pillars, and all suspension, steering, braking system and seat belt mountings and anchorages.) Any corrosion which has seriously reduced the thickness of a load-bearing area (or is within 30 cm of safety-related components such as steering or suspension) is likely to cause the vehicle to fail. In this case professional repairs are likely to be needed.

☐ Damage or corrosion which causes sharp or otherwise dangerous edges to be exposed will also cause the vehicle to fail.

Towbars

☐ Check the condition of mounting points (both beneath the vehicle and within boot/hatchback areas) for signs of corrosion, ensuring that all fixings are secure and not worn or damaged. There must be no excessive play in detachable tow ball arms or quick-release mechanisms.

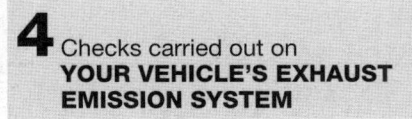

4 Checks carried out on YOUR VEHICLE'S EXHAUST EMISSION SYSTEM

Petrol models

☐ The engine should be warmed up, and running well (ignition system in good order, air filter element clean, etc).

☐ Before testing, run the engine at around 2500 rpm for 20 seconds. Let the engine drop to idle, and watch for smoke from the exhaust. If the idle speed is too high, or if dense blue or black smoke emerges for more than 5 seconds, the vehicle will fail. Typically, blue smoke signifies oil burning (engine wear); black smoke means unburnt fuel (dirty air cleaner element, or other fuel system fault).

☐ An exhaust gas analyser for measuring carbon monoxide (CO) and hydrocarbons (HC) is now needed. If one cannot be hired or borrowed, have a local garage perform the check.

CO emissions (mixture)

☐ The MOT tester has access to the CO limits for all vehicles. The CO level is measured at idle speed, and at 'fast idle' (2500 to 3000 rpm). The following limits are given as a general guide:
  At idle speed – Less than 0.5% CO
  At 'fast idle' – Less than 0.3% CO
  Lambda reading – 0.97 to 1.03

☐ If the CO level is too high, this may point to poor maintenance, a fuel injection system problem, faulty lambda (oxygen) sensor or catalytic converter. Try an injector cleaning treatment, and check the vehicle's ECU for fault codes.

HC emissions

☐ The MOT tester has access to HC limits for all vehicles. The HC level is measured at 'fast idle' (2500 to 3000 rpm). The following limits are given as a general guide:
  At 'fast idle' – Less then 200 ppm

☐ Excessive HC emissions are typically caused by oil being burnt (worn engine), or by a blocked crankcase ventilation system ('breather'). If the engine oil is old and thin, an oil change may help. If the engine is running badly, check the vehicle's ECU for fault codes.

Diesel models

☐ The only emission test for diesel engines is measuring exhaust smoke density, using a calibrated smoke meter. The test involves accelerating the engine at least 3 times to its maximum unloaded speed.

Note: *On engines with a timing belt, it is VITAL that the belt is in good condition before the test is carried out.*

☐ With the engine warmed up, it is first purged by running at around 2500 rpm for 20 seconds. A governor check is then carried out, by slowly accelerating the engine to its maximum speed. After this, the smoke meter is connected and the engine is accelerated quickly to maximum speed three times. If the smoke density is less than the limits given below, the vehicle will pass:
  Non-turbo vehicles: 2.5m-1
  Turbocharged vehicles: 3.0m-1

☐ If excess smoke is produced, try fitting a new air cleaner element, or using an injector cleaning treatment. If the engine is running badly, where applicable, check the vehicle's ECU for fault codes. Also check the vehicle's EGR system, where applicable. At high mileages, the injectors may require professional attention.

REF•16 Fault finding

Engine
☐ Engine fails to rotate when attempting to start
☐ Engine rotates, but will not start
☐ Engine difficult to start when cold
☐ Engine difficult to start when hot
☐ Starter motor noisy or excessively-rough in engagement
☐ Engine starts, but stops immediately
☐ Engine idles erratically
☐ Engine misfires at idle speed
☐ Engine misfires throughout the driving speed range
☐ Engine hesitates on acceleration
☐ Engine stalls
☐ Engine lacks power
☐ Engine backfires
☐ Oil pressure warning light illuminated with engine running
☐ Engine runs-on after switching off
☐ Engine noises

Cooling system
☐ Overheating
☐ Overcooling
☐ External coolant leakage
☐ Internal coolant leakage
☐ Corrosion

Fuel and exhaust systems
☐ Excessive fuel consumption
☐ Fuel leakage and/or fuel odour
☐ Excessive noise or fumes from exhaust system

Clutch
☐ Pedal travels to floor – no pressure or very little resistance
☐ Clutch fails to disengage (unable to select gears)
☐ Clutch slips (engine speed increases, with no increase in vehicle speed)
☐ Judder as clutch is engaged
☐ Noise when depressing or releasing clutch pedal

Manual transmission
☐ Noisy in neutral with engine running
☐ Noisy in one particular gear
☐ Difficulty engaging gears
☐ Jumps out of gear
☐ Vibration
☐ Lubricant leaks

Automatic transmission
☐ Fluid leakage
☐ General gear selection problems
☐ Transmission will not downshift (kickdown) with accelerator pedal fully depressed
☐ Engine will not start in any gear, or starts in gears other than Park or Neutral
☐ Transmission slips, shifts roughly, is noisy, or has no drive in forward or reverse gears

Driveshafts
☐ Vibration when accelerating or decelerating
☐ Clicking or knocking noise on turns (at slow speed on full-lock)

Braking system
☐ Vehicle pulls to one side under braking
☐ Noise (grinding or high-pitched squeal) when brakes applied
☐ Excessive brake pedal travel
☐ Brake pedal feels spongy when depressed
☐ Excessive brake pedal effort required to stop vehicle
☐ Judder felt through brake pedal or steering wheel when braking
☐ Pedal pulsates when braking hard
☐ Brakes binding
☐ Rear wheels locking under normal braking

Steering and suspension
☐ Vehicle pulls to one side
☐ Wheel wobble and vibration
☐ Excessive pitching and/or rolling around corners, or during braking
☐ Wandering or general instability
☐ Excessively-stiff steering
☐ Excessive play in steering
☐ Lack of power assistance
☐ Tyre wear excessive

Electrical system
☐ Battery will not hold a charge for more than a few days
☐ Ignition/no-charge warning light remains illuminated with engine running
☐ Ignition/no-charge warning light fails to come on
☐ Lights inoperative
☐ Instrument readings inaccurate or erratic
☐ Horn inoperative, or unsatisfactory in operation
☐ Windscreen/tailgate wipers inoperative, or unsatisfactory in operation
☐ Windscreen washers inoperative, or unsatisfactory in operation
☐ Electric windows inoperative, or unsatisfactory in operation

Introduction

The vehicle owner who does his or her own maintenance according to the recommended service schedules should not have to use this section of the manual very often. Modern component reliability is such that, provided those items subject to wear or deterioration are inspected or renewed at the specified intervals, sudden failure is comparatively rare. Faults do not usually just happen as a result of sudden failure, but develop over a period of time. Major mechanical failures in particular are usually preceded by characteristic symptoms over hundreds or even thousands of miles. Those components which do occasionally fail without warning are often small and easily carried in the vehicle.

With any fault-finding, the first step is to decide where to begin investigations. Sometimes this is obvious, but on other occasions, a little detective work will be necessary. The owner who makes half a dozen haphazard adjustments or replacements may be successful in curing a fault (or its symptoms), but will be none the wiser if the fault recurs, and ultimately may have spent more time and money than was necessary. A calm and logical approach will be found to be more satisfactory in the long run. Always take into account any warning signs or abnormalities that may have been noticed in the period preceding the fault – power loss, high or low gauge readings, unusual smells, etc – and remember that failure of components such as fuses or spark plugs may only be pointers to some underlying fault.

The pages which follow provide an easy-reference guide to the more common problems which may occur during the operation of the vehicle. These problems and their possible causes are grouped under headings denoting various components or systems, such as Engine, Cooling system, etc. The general

Fault finding REF•17

Chapter which deals with the problem is also shown in brackets; refer to the relevant part of that Chapter for system-specific information. Whatever the fault, certain basic principles apply. These are as follows:

Verify the fault. This is simply a matter of being sure that you know what the symptoms are before starting work. This is particularly important if you are investigating a fault for someone else, who may not have described it very accurately.

Don't overlook the obvious. For example, if the vehicle won't start, is there fuel in the tank? (Don't take anyone else's word on this particular point, and don't trust the fuel gauge either!) If an electrical fault is indicated, look for loose or broken wires before digging out the test gear.

Cure the disease, not the symptom. Substituting a flat battery with a fully-charged one will get you off the hard shoulder, but if the underlying cause is not attended to, the new battery will go the same way. Similarly, changing oil-fouled spark plugs for a new set will get you moving again, but remember that the reason for the fouling (if it wasn't simply an incorrect grade of plug) will have to be established and corrected.

Don't take anything for granted. Particularly, don't forget that a new component may itself be defective (especially if its been rattling around in the boot for months), and don't leave components out of a fault diagnosis sequence just because they are new or recently-fitted. When you do finally diagnose a difficult fault, you'll probably realise that all the evidence was there from the start.

Engine

Engine fails to rotate when attempting to start
☐ Battery terminal connections loose or corroded (see *Weekly checks*).
☐ Battery discharged or faulty (Chapter 5A).
☐ Broken, loose or disconnected wiring in the starting circuit (Chapter 5A).
☐ Defective starter solenoid or switch (Chapter 5A).
☐ Defective starter motor (Chapter 5A).
☐ Starter pinion or flywheel/driveplate ring gear teeth loose or broken (Chapter 2 and 5A).
☐ Engine earth strap broken or disconnected (Chapter 5A or 12).

Engine rotates, but will not start
☐ Fuel tank empty.
☐ Battery discharged (engine rotates slowly) (Chapter 5A).
☐ Battery terminal connections loose or corroded (see *Weekly checks*).
☐ Ignition components damp or damaged (Chapters 1 and 5B).
☐ Broken, loose or disconnected wiring in the ignition circuit (Chapters 1 and 5B).
☐ Worn, faulty or incorrectly-gapped spark plugs (Chapter 1).
☐ Fuel injection system fault (Chapter 4A).
☐ Major mechanical failure (eg, timing belt/chain) (Chapter 2).

Engine difficult to start when cold
☐ Battery discharged (Chapter 5A).
☐ Battery terminal connections loose or corroded (see *Weekly checks*).
☐ Worn, faulty or incorrectly-gapped spark plugs (Chapter 1).
☐ Fuel injection system fault (Chapter 4A).
☐ Other ignition system fault (Chapters 1 and 5B).
☐ Low cylinder compressions (Chapter 2).

Engine difficult to start when hot
☐ Air filter element dirty or clogged (Chapter 1).
☐ Fuel injection system fault (Chapter 4A).
☐ Low cylinder compressions (Chapter 2).

Starter motor noisy or excessively-rough in engagement
☐ Starter pinion or flywheel ring gear teeth loose or broken (Chapter 2 and 5A).
☐ Starter motor mounting bolts loose or missing (Chapter 5A).
☐ Starter motor internal components worn or damaged (Chapter 5A).

Engine starts, but stops immediately
☐ Loose or faulty electrical connections in the ignition circuit (Chapters 1 and 5B).
☐ Vacuum leak at the throttle body or intake manifold (Chapter 4A).
☐ Blocked injector/fuel injection system fault (Chapter 4A).

Engine idles erratically
☐ Air filter element clogged (Chapter 1).
☐ Vacuum leak at the throttle body, intake manifold or associated hoses (Chapter 4A).
☐ Worn, faulty or incorrectly-gapped spark plugs (Chapter 1).
☐ Uneven or low cylinder compressions (Chapter 2).
☐ Camshaft lobes worn (Chapter 2).
☐ Timing belt incorrectly fitted (Chapter 2).
☐ Blocked injector/fuel injection system fault (Chapter 4A).

Engine misfires at idle speed
☐ Worn, faulty or incorrectly-gapped spark plugs (Chapter 1).
☐ Vacuum leak at the throttle body, intake manifold or associated hoses (Chapter 4A).
☐ Blocked injector/fuel injection system fault (Chapter 4A).
☐ Uneven or low cylinder compressions (Chapter 2).
☐ Disconnected, leaking, or perished crankcase ventilation hoses (Chapter 4B).

Engine misfires throughout the driving speed range
☐ Fuel pump faulty, or delivery pressure low (Chapter 4A).
☐ Fuel tank vent blocked, or fuel pipes restricted (Chapter 4).
☐ Vacuum leak at the throttle body, intake manifold or associated hoses (Chapter 4A).
☐ Worn, faulty or incorrectly-gapped spark plugs (Chapter 1).
☐ Faulty ignition coil (Chapter 5B).
☐ Uneven or low cylinder compressions (Chapter 2).
☐ Blocked injector/fuel injection system fault (Chapter 4A).

Engine hesitates on acceleration
☐ Worn, faulty or incorrectly-gapped spark plugs (Chapter 1).
☐ Vacuum leak at the throttle body, intake manifold or associated hoses (Chapter 4A).
☐ Blocked injector/fuel injection system fault (Chapter 4A).

REF•18 Fault finding

Engine (continued)

Engine stalls
- [ ] Vacuum leak at the throttle body, intake manifold or associated hoses (Chapter 4A).
- [ ] Fuel pump faulty, or delivery pressure low (Chapter 4A).
- [ ] Fuel tank vent blocked, or fuel pipes restricted (Chapter 4).
- [ ] Blocked injector/fuel injection system fault (Chapter 4A).
- [ ] Faulty injector(s) (Chapter 4A).

Engine lacks power
- [ ] Timing belt incorrectly fitted or tensioned (Chapter 2).
- [ ] Fuel pump faulty, or delivery pressure low Chapter 4A).
- [ ] Uneven or low cylinder compressions (Chapter 2).
- [ ] Worn, faulty or incorrectly-gapped spark plugs – (Chapter 1).
- [ ] Vacuum leak at the throttle body, intake manifold or associated hoses (Chapter 4A).
- [ ] Blocked injector/fuel injection system fault (Chapter 4A).
- [ ] Brakes binding (Chapter 9).
- [ ] Clutch slipping (Chapter 6).
- [ ] Air filter element clogged (Chapter 1).

Engine backfires
- [ ] Timing belt incorrectly fitted or tensioned (Chapter 2).
- [ ] Vacuum leak at the throttle body, intake manifold or associated hoses (Chapter 4A).
- [ ] Blocked injector/fuel injection system fault (Chapter 4A).

Oil pressure warning light illuminated with engine running
- [ ] Low oil level, or incorrect oil grade (*Weekly checks*).
- [ ] Faulty oil pressure switch (Chapter 5A).
- [ ] Worn engine bearings and/or oil pump (Chapter 2).
- [ ] High engine operating temperature (Chapter 3).
- [ ] Oil pressure relief valve defective (Chapter 2).
- [ ] Oil pick-up strainer clogged (Chapter 2).

Engine runs-on after switching off
- [ ] Excessive carbon build-up in engine (Chapter 2).
- [ ] High engine operating temperature (Chapter 3).
- [ ] Fuel injection system fault (Chapter 4A).

Engine noises

Pre-ignition (pinking) or knocking during acceleration or under load
- [ ] Ignition system fault (Chapters 1 and 5B).
- [ ] Incorrect grade of spark plug (Chapter 1).
- [ ] Vacuum leak at the throttle body, intake manifold or associated hoses (Chapter 4A).
- [ ] Excessive carbon build-up in engine (Chapter 2).
- [ ] Blocked injector/fuel injection system fault (Chapter 4A).

Whistling or wheezing noises
- [ ] Leaking intake manifold or throttle body gasket (Chapter 4A).
- [ ] Leaking exhaust manifold gasket or pipe-to-manifold joint (Chapter 4).
- [ ] Leaking vacuum hose (Chapters 4 and 9).
- [ ] Blowing cylinder head gasket (Chapter 2).

Tapping or rattling noises
- [ ] Worn valve gear or camshaft (Chapter 2).
- [ ] Ancillary component fault (coolant pump, alternator, etc) (Chapters 3, 5, etc).

Knocking or thumping noises
- [ ] Worn big-end bearings (regular heavy knocking, perhaps less under load) (Chapter 2).
- [ ] Worn main bearings (rumbling and knocking, perhaps worsening under load) (Chapter 2).
- [ ] Piston slap (most noticeable when cold) (Chapter 2).
- [ ] Ancillary component fault (coolant pump, alternator, etc) (Chapters 3, 5, etc).

Cooling system

Overheating
- [ ] Insufficient coolant in system (*Weekly checks*).
- [ ] Thermostat faulty (Chapter 3).
- [ ] Radiator core blocked, or grille restricted (Chapter 3).
- [ ] Electric cooling fan or thermostatic switch faulty (Chapter 3).
- [ ] Inaccurate temperature gauge sender unit (Chapter 3).
- [ ] Airlock in cooling system.
- [ ] Expansion tank pressure cap faulty (Chapter 3).

Overcooling
- [ ] Thermostat faulty (Chapter 3).
- [ ] Inaccurate engine coolant temperature sensor (Chapter 3).

External coolant leakage
- [ ] Deteriorated or damaged hoses or hose clips (Chapter 1).
- [ ] Radiator core or heater matrix leaking (Chapter 3).
- [ ] Pressure cap faulty (Chapter 3).
- [ ] Coolant pump internal seal leaking (Chapter 3).
- [ ] Coolant pump-to-housing seal leaking (Chapter 3).
- [ ] Boiling due to overheating (Chapter 3).
- [ ] Core plug leaking (Chapter 2).

Internal coolant leakage
- [ ] Leaking cylinder head gasket (Chapter 2).
- [ ] Cracked cylinder head or cylinder block (Chapter 2).

Corrosion
- [ ] Infrequent draining and flushing (Chapter 1).
- [ ] Incorrect coolant mixture or inappropriate coolant type (see *Weekly checks*).

Fuel and exhaust systems

Excessive fuel consumption
- [ ] Air filter element dirty or clogged (Chapter 1).
- [ ] Fuel injection system fault (Chapter 4A).
- [ ] Ignition system fault (Chapters 1 and 5B).
- [ ] Tyres under-inflated (see *Weekly checks*).

Fuel leakage and/or fuel odour
- [ ] Damaged fuel tank, pipes or connections (Chapter 4).

Excessive noise or fumes from exhaust system
- [ ] Leaking exhaust system or manifold joints (Chapters 1 and 4).
- [ ] Leaking, corroded or damaged silencers or pipe (Chapters 1 and 4).
- [ ] Broken mountings causing body or suspension contact (Chapter 1).

Fault finding

Clutch

Pedal travels to floor – no pressure or very little resistance
- [ ] Faulty master or slave cylinder (Chapter 6).
- [ ] Faulty hydraulic release system (Chapter 6).
- [ ] Broken clutch release bearing or arm (Chapter 6).
- [ ] Broken diaphragm spring in clutch pressure plate (Chapter 6).

Clutch fails to disengage (unable to select gears)
- [ ] Faulty master or slave cylinder (Chapter 6).
- [ ] Faulty hydraulic release system (Chapter 6).
- [ ] Clutch disc sticking on gearbox input shaft splines (Chapter 6).
- [ ] Clutch disc sticking to flywheel or pressure plate (Chapter 6).
- [ ] Faulty pressure plate assembly (Chapter 6).
- [ ] Clutch release mechanism worn or incorrectly assembled (Chapter 6).

Clutch slips (engine speed increases, with no increase in vehicle speed)
- [ ] Faulty hydraulic release system (Chapter 6).
- [ ] Clutch disc linings excessively worn (Chapter 6).
- [ ] Clutch disc linings contaminated with oil or grease (Chapter 6).
- [ ] Faulty pressure plate or weak diaphragm spring (Chapter 6).

Judder as clutch is engaged
- [ ] Clutch disc linings contaminated with oil or grease (Chapter 6).
- [ ] Clutch disc linings excessively worn (Chapter 6).
- [ ] Faulty or distorted pressure plate or diaphragm spring (Chapter 6).
- [ ] Worn or loose engine or gearbox mountings (Chapter 2).
- [ ] Clutch disc hub or gearbox input shaft splines worn (Chapter 6).

Noise when depressing or releasing clutch pedal
- [ ] Worn clutch release bearing (Chapter 6).
- [ ] Worn or dry clutch pedal pivot (Chapter 6).
- [ ] Faulty pressure plate assembly (Chapter 6).
- [ ] Pressure plate diaphragm spring broken (Chapter 6).
- [ ] Broken clutch friction plate cushioning springs (Chapter 6).

Manual transmission

Noisy in neutral with engine running
- [ ] Input shaft bearings worn (noise apparent with clutch pedal released, but not when depressed) (Chapter 7A).*
- [ ] Clutch release bearing worn (noise apparent with clutch pedal depressed, possibly less when released) (Chapter 6).

Noisy in one particular gear
- [ ] Worn, damaged or chipped gear teeth (Chapter 7A).*

Difficulty engaging gears
- [ ] Clutch fault (Chapter 6).
- [ ] Worn or damaged gear linkage (Chapter 7A).
- [ ] Worn synchroniser units (Chapter 7A).*

Jumps out of gear
- [ ] Worn or damaged gear linkage (Chapter 7A).
- [ ] Worn synchroniser units (Chapter 7A).*
- [ ] Worn selector forks (Chapter 7A).*

Vibration
- [ ] Lack of oil (Chapter 1).
- [ ] Worn bearings (Chapter 7A).*

Lubricant leaks
- [ ] Leaking oil seal (Chapter 7A).
- [ ] Leaking housing joint (Chapter 7A).*
- [ ] Leaking input shaft oil seal (Chapter 7A).

*Although the corrective action necessary to remedy the symptoms described is beyond the scope of the home mechanic, the above information should be helpful in isolating the cause of the condition, so that the owner can communicate clearly with a professional mechanic.

Automatic transmission

Note: *Due to the complexity of the automatic transmission, it is difficult for the home mechanic to properly diagnose and service this unit. For problems other than the following, the vehicle should be taken to a dealer service department or automatic transmission specialist. Do not be too hasty in removing the transmission if a fault is suspected, as most of the testing is carried out with the unit still fitted.*

Fluid leakage
- [ ] Automatic transmission fluid is usually dark in colour. Fluid leaks should not be confused with engine oil, which can easily be blown onto the transmission by airflow.
- [ ] To determine the source of a leak, first remove all built-up dirt and grime from the transmission housing and surrounding areas using a degreasing agent, or by steam-cleaning. Drive the vehicle at low speed, so airflow will not blow the leak far from its source. Raise and support the vehicle, and determine where the leak is coming from.

General gear selection problems
- [ ] Chapter 7 deals with checking and adjusting the selector mechanism on automatic transmissions. The following are common problems which may be caused by a poorly-adjusted mechanism:
  a) Engine starting in gears other than Park or Neutral.
  b) Indicator panel indicating a gear other than the one actually being used.
  c) Vehicle moves when in Park or Neutral.
  d) Poor gear shift quality or erratic gear changes.
- [ ] Refer to Chapter 7B for the selector mechanism adjustment procedure.

Transmission will not downshift (kickdown) with accelerator pedal fully depressed
- [ ] Low transmission fluid level (Chapter 1).
- [ ] Incorrect selector mechanism adjustment (Chapter 7B).

Engine will not start in any gear, or starts in gears other than Park or Neutral
- [ ] Incorrect selector mechanism adjustment (Chapter 7B).

Transmission slips, shifts roughly, is noisy, or has no drive in forward or reverse gears
- [ ] There are many probable causes for the above problems, but unless there is a very obvious reason (such as a loose or corroded wiring plug connection on or near the transmission), the car should be taken to a franchise dealer or specialist for the fault to be diagnosed. The transmission control unit incorporates a self-diagnosis facility, and any fault codes can quickly be read and interpreted by a dealer with the proper diagnostic equipment.

REF•20 Fault finding

Driveshafts

Vibration when accelerating or decelerating
- [ ] Worn inner constant velocity joint (Chapter 8).
- [ ] Bent or distorted driveshaft (Chapter 8).

Clicking or knocking noise on turns (at slow speed on full-lock)
- [ ] Worn outer constant velocity joint (Chapter 8).
- [ ] Lack of constant velocity joint lubricant, possibly due to damaged gaiter (Chapter 8).

Braking system

Note: *Before assuming that a brake problem exists, make sure that the tyres are in good condition and correctly inflated, that the front wheel alignment is correct, and that the vehicle is not loaded with weight in an unequal manner. Apart from checking the condition of all pipe and hose connections, any faults occurring on the anti-lock braking system should be referred to a Ford dealer for diagnosis.*

Vehicle pulls to one side under braking
- [ ] Worn, defective, damaged or contaminated front or rear brake pads/shoes on one side (Chapters 1 and 9).
- [ ] Seized or partially-seized front or rear brake caliper or wheel cylinder (Chapter 9).
- [ ] A mixture of brake pad/shoe lining materials fitted between sides (Chapter 9).
- [ ] Brake caliper mounting bolts loose (Chapter 9).
- [ ] Worn or damaged steering or suspension components (Chapters 1 and 10).

Noise (grinding or high-pitched squeal) when brakes applied
- [ ] Brake pad/shoe friction lining material worn down to metal backing (Chapters 1 and 9).
- [ ] Excessive corrosion of brake disc/drum – may be apparent after the vehicle has been standing for some time (Chapters 1 and 9).
- [ ] Foreign object (stone chipping, etc) trapped between brake disc and shield (Chapters 1 and 9).

Excessive brake pedal travel
- [ ] Faulty master cylinder (Chapter 9).
- [ ] Air in hydraulic system (Chapter 9).
- [ ] Faulty vacuum servo unit (Chapter 9).
- [ ] Faulty vacuum pump, where fitted (Chapter 9).

Brake pedal feels spongy when depressed
- [ ] Air in hydraulic system (Chapter 9).

- [ ] Deteriorated flexible rubber brake hoses (Chapters 1 and 9).
- [ ] Master cylinder mountings loose (Chapter 9).
- [ ] Faulty master cylinder (Chapter 9).

Excessive brake pedal effort required to stop vehicle
- [ ] Faulty vacuum servo unit (Chapter 9).
- [ ] Disconnected, damaged or insecure brake servo vacuum hose (Chapters 1 and 9).
- [ ] Faulty vacuum pump, where fitted (Chapter 9).
- [ ] Primary or secondary hydraulic circuit failure (Chapter 9).
- [ ] Seized brake caliper/wheel cylinder (Chapter 9).
- [ ] Brake pads/shoes incorrectly fitted (Chapter 9).
- [ ] Incorrect grade of brake pads/shoes fitted (Chapter 9).
- [ ] Brake pads/shoes contaminated (Chapter 9).

Judder felt through brake pedal or steering wheel when braking
- [ ] Excessive run-out or distortion of brake disc(s)/drums (Chapter 9).
- [ ] Brake pad/shoe linings worn (Chapters 1 and 9).
- [ ] Brake caliper mounting bolts loose (Chapter 9).
- [ ] Wear in suspension or steering components or mountings (Chapters 1 and 10).

Pedal pulsates when braking hard
- [ ] Normal feature of ABS – no fault

Brakes binding
- [ ] Seized brake caliper piston(s)/wheel cylinder (Chapter 9).
- [ ] Incorrectly-adjusted handbrake mechanism (Chapter 9).
- [ ] Faulty master cylinder (Chapter 9).

Rear wheels locking under normal braking
- [ ] Rear brake pad/shoe linings contaminated (Chapters 1 and 9).
- [ ] Rear brake discs/drums warped (Chapters 1 and 9).

Fault finding REF•21

Steering and suspension

Note: *Before diagnosing suspension or steering faults, be sure that the trouble is not due to incorrect tyre pressures, mixtures of tyre types, or binding brakes.*

Vehicle pulls to one side
- [ ] Defective tyre (see *Weekly checks*).
- [ ] Excessive wear in suspension or steering components (Chapters 1 and 10).
- [ ] Incorrect front wheel alignment (Chapter 10).
- [ ] Accident damage to steering or suspension components (Chapters 1 and 10).

Wheel wobble and vibration
- [ ] Front roadwheels out of balance (vibration felt mainly through the steering wheel) (Chapter 10).
- [ ] Rear roadwheels out of balance (vibration felt throughout the vehicle) (Chapter 10).
- [ ] Roadwheels damaged or distorted (Chapter 10).
- [ ] Faulty or damaged tyre (*Weekly checks*).
- [ ] Worn steering or suspension joints, bushes or components (Chapters 1 and 10).
- [ ] Wheel nuts loose (Chapter 1 and 10).

Excessive pitching and/or rolling around corners, or during braking
- [ ] Defective shock absorbers (Chapters 1 and 10).
- [ ] Broken or weak coil spring and/or suspension component (Chapters 1 and 10).
- [ ] Worn or damaged anti-roll bar or mountings (Chapter 10).

Wandering or general instability
- [ ] Incorrect front wheel alignment (Chapter 10).
- [ ] Worn steering or suspension joints, bushes or components (Chapters 1 and 10).
- [ ] Roadwheels out of balance (Chapter 10).
- [ ] Faulty or damaged tyre (*Weekly checks*).
- [ ] Wheel nuts loose (Chapter 10).
- [ ] Defective shock absorbers (Chapters 1 and 10).

Excessively-stiff steering
- [ ] Seized track rod end balljoint or suspension balljoint (Chapters 1 and 10).
- [ ] Broken or incorrectly adjusted auxiliary drivebelt (Chapter 1).
- [ ] Incorrect front wheel alignment (Chapter 10).
- [ ] Steering gear damaged (Chapter 10).

Excessive play in steering
- [ ] Worn steering column universal joint(s) (Chapter 10).
- [ ] Worn steering track rod end balljoints (Chapters 1 and 10).
- [ ] Worn steering gear (Chapter 10).
- [ ] Worn steering or suspension joints, bushes or components (Chapters 1 and 10).

Lack of power assistance
- [ ] Broken or incorrectly-adjusted auxiliary drivebelt (Chapter 1).
- [ ] Incorrect power steering fluid level (*Weekly checks*).
- [ ] Restriction in power steering fluid hoses (Chapter 10).
- [ ] Faulty power steering pump (Chapter 10).
- [ ] Faulty steering gear (Chapter 10).

Tyre wear excessive

Tyres worn on inside or outside edges
- [ ] Incorrect camber or castor angles (Chapter 10).
- [ ] Worn steering or suspension joints, bushes or components (Chapters 1 and 10).
- [ ] Excessively-hard cornering.
- [ ] Accident damage.

Tyre treads exhibit feathered edges
- [ ] Incorrect toe setting (Chapter 10).

Tyres worn in centre of tread
- [ ] Tyres over-inflated (*Weekly checks*).

Tyres worn on inside and outside edges
- [ ] Tyres under-inflated (*Weekly checks*).
- [ ] Worn shock absorbers (Chapter 10).

Tyres worn unevenly
- [ ] Tyres/wheels out of balance (*Weekly checks*).
- [ ] Excessive wheel or tyre run-out (Chapter 10).
- [ ] Worn shock absorbers (Chapters 1 and 10).
- [ ] Faulty tyre (*Weekly checks*).

Electrical system

Note: *For problems associated with the starting system, refer to the faults listed under Engine earlier in this Section.*

Battery will not hold a charge more than a few days
- [ ] Battery defective internally (Chapter 5A).
- [ ] Battery electrolyte level low – where applicable (*Weekly checks*).
- [ ] Battery terminal connections loose or corroded (*Weekly checks*).
- [ ] Auxiliary drivebelt worn – or incorrectly adjusted, where applicable (Chapter 1).
- [ ] Alternator not charging at correct output (Chapter 5A).
- [ ] Alternator or voltage regulator faulty (Chapter 5A).
- [ ] Short-circuit causing continual battery drain (Chapters 5 and 12).

Ignition/no-charge warning light remains illuminated with engine running
- [ ] Auxiliary drivebelt broken, worn, or incorrectly adjusted (Chapter 1).
- [ ] Internal fault in alternator or voltage regulator (Chapter 5A).
- [ ] Broken, disconnected, or loose wiring in charging circuit (Chapter 5A).

Ignition/no-charge warning light fails to come on
- [ ] Broken, disconnected, or loose wiring in warning light circuit (Chapter 12).
- [ ] Alternator faulty (Chapter 5A).

REF•22 Fault finding

Electrical system (continued)

Lights inoperative
- [ ] Bulb blown (Chapter 12).
- [ ] Corrosion of bulb or bulbholder contacts (Chapter 12).
- [ ] Blown fuse (Chapter 12).
- [ ] Faulty relay (Chapter 12).
- [ ] Broken, loose, or disconnected wiring (Chapter 12).
- [ ] Faulty switch (Chapter 12).

Instrument readings inaccurate or erratic

Fuel or temperature gauges give no reading
- [ ] Faulty coolant temperature sensor (Chapter 3).
- [ ] Wiring open-circuit (Chapter 12).
- [ ] Faulty gauge (Chapter 12).

Fuel or temperature gauges give continuous maximum reading
- [ ] Faulty coolant temperature sensor (Chapters 3).
- [ ] Wiring short-circuit (Chapter 12).
- [ ] Faulty gauge (Chapter 12).

Horn inoperative, or unsatisfactory in operation

Horn operates all the time
- [ ] Horn contacts permanently bridged or horn push stuck down (Chapter 12).

Horn fails to operate
- [ ] Blown fuse (Chapter 12).
- [ ] Cable or cable connections loose, broken or disconnected (Chapter 12).
- [ ] Faulty horn (Chapter 12).

Horn emits intermittent or unsatisfactory sound
- [ ] Cable connections loose (Chapter 12).
- [ ] Horn mountings loose (Chapter 12).
- [ ] Faulty horn (Chapter 12).

Windscreen/tailgate wipers inoperative, or unsatisfactory in operation

Wipers fail to operate, or operate very slowly
- [ ] Wiper blades stuck to screen, or linkage seized or binding (*Weekly checks* and Chapter 12).
- [ ] Blown fuse (Chapter 12).
- [ ] Cable or cable connections loose, broken or disconnected (Chapter 12).
- [ ] Faulty relay (Chapter 12).
- [ ] Faulty wiper motor (Chapter 12).

Wiper blades sweep over too large or too small an area of the glass
- [ ] Wiper arms incorrectly positioned on spindles (Chapter 12).
- [ ] Excessive wear of wiper linkage (Chapter 12).
- [ ] Wiper motor or linkage mountings loose or insecure (Chapter 12).

Wiper blades fail to clean the glass effectively
- [ ] Wiper blade rubbers worn or perished (*Weekly checks*).
- [ ] Wiper arm tension springs broken, or arm pivots seized (Chapter 12).
- [ ] Insufficient windscreen washer additive to adequately remove road film (*Weekly checks*).

Windscreen washers inoperative, or unsatisfactory in operation

One or more washer jets inoperative
- [ ] Blocked washer jet (Chapter 12).
- [ ] Disconnected, kinked or restricted fluid hose (Chapter 12).
- [ ] Insufficient fluid in washer reservoir (*Weekly checks*).

Washer pump fails to operate
- [ ] Broken or disconnected wiring or connections (Chapter 12).
- [ ] Blown fuse (Chapter 12).
- [ ] Faulty washer switch (Chapter 12).
- [ ] Faulty washer pump (Chapter 12).

Electric windows inoperative, or unsatisfactory in operation

Window glass will only move in one direction
- [ ] Faulty switch (Chapter 12).

Window glass slow to move
- [ ] Regulator seized or damaged, or in need of lubrication (Chapter 11).
- [ ] Door internal components or trim fouling regulator (Chapter 11).
- [ ] Faulty motor (Chapter 11).

Window glass fails to move
- [ ] Blown fuse (Chapter 12).
- [ ] Faulty relay (Chapter 12).
- [ ] Broken or disconnected wiring or connections (Chapter 12).
- [ ] Faulty motor (Chapter 11).
- [ ] Faulty GEM (Chapter 12).

Central locking system inoperative, or unsatisfactory in operation

Complete system failure
- [ ] Blown fuse (Chapter 12).
- [ ] Faulty GEM (Chapter 12).
- [ ] Broken or disconnected wiring or connections (Chapter 12).

Latch locks but will not unlock, or unlocks but will not lock
- [ ] Faulty switch (Chapter 12).
- [ ] Broken or disconnected latch operating rods or levers (Chapter 11).
- [ ] Faulty GEM (Chapter 12).

One lock fails to operate
- [ ] Broken or disconnected wiring or connections (Chapter 12).
- [ ] Faulty motor (Chapter 11).
- [ ] Broken, binding or disconnected lock operating rods or levers (Chapter 11).
- [ ] Fault in door lock (Chapter 11).

Glossary of technical terms REF•23

A

ABS (Anti-lock brake system) A system, usually electronically controlled, that senses incipient wheel lockup during braking and relieves hydraulic pressure at wheels that are about to skid.

Air bag An inflatable bag hidden in the steering wheel (driver's side) or the dash or glovebox (passenger side). In a head-on collision, the bags inflate, preventing the driver and front passenger from being thrown forward into the steering wheel or windscreen.

Air cleaner A metal or plastic housing, containing a filter element, which removes dust and dirt from the air being drawn into the engine.

Air filter element The actual filter in an air cleaner system, usually manufactured from pleated paper and requiring renewal at regular intervals.

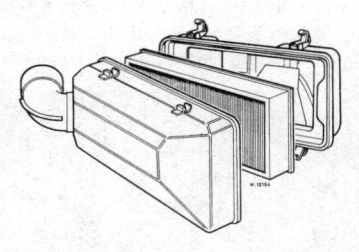

Air filter

Allen key A hexagonal wrench which fits into a recessed hexagonal hole.

Alligator clip A long-nosed spring-loaded metal clip with meshing teeth. Used to make temporary electrical connections.

Alternator A component in the electrical system which converts mechanical energy from a drivebelt into electrical energy to charge the battery and to operate the starting system, ignition system and electrical accessories.

Ampere (amp) A unit of measurement for the flow of electric current. One amp is the amount of current produced by one volt acting through a resistance of one ohm.

Anaerobic sealer A substance used to prevent bolts and screws from loosening. Anaerobic means that it does not require oxygen for activation. The Loctite brand is widely used.

Antifreeze A substance (usually ethylene glycol) mixed with water, and added to a vehicle's cooling system, to prevent freezing of the coolant in winter. Antifreeze also contains chemicals to inhibit corrosion and the formation of rust and other deposits that would tend to clog the radiator and coolant passages and reduce cooling efficiency.

Anti-seize compound A coating that reduces the risk of seizing on fasteners that are subjected to high temperatures, such as exhaust manifold bolts and nuts.

Asbestos A natural fibrous mineral with great heat resistance, commonly used in the composition of brake friction materials. Asbestos is a health hazard and the dust created by brake systems should never be inhaled or ingested.

Axle A shaft on which a wheel revolves, or which revolves with a wheel. Also, a solid beam that connects the two wheels at one end of the vehicle. An axle which also transmits power to the wheels is known as a live axle.

Axleshaft A single rotating shaft, on either side of the differential, which delivers power from the final drive assembly to the drive wheels. Also called a driveshaft or a halfshaft.

B

Ball bearing An anti-friction bearing consisting of a hardened inner and outer race with hardened steel balls between two races.

Bearing The curved surface on a shaft or in a bore, or the part assembled into either, that permits relative motion between them with minimum wear and friction.

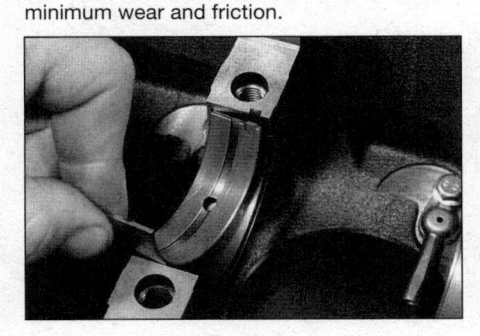

Bearing

Big-end bearing The bearing in the end of the connecting rod that's attached to the crankshaft.

Bleed nipple A valve on a brake wheel cylinder, caliper or other hydraulic component that is opened to purge the hydraulic system of air. Also called a bleed screw.

Brake bleeding Procedure for removing air from lines of a hydraulic brake system.

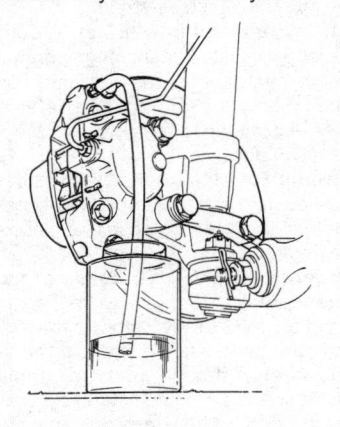

Brake bleeding

Brake disc The component of a disc brake that rotates with the wheels.

Brake drum The component of a drum brake that rotates with the wheels.

Brake linings The friction material which contacts the brake disc or drum to retard the vehicle's speed. The linings are bonded or riveted to the brake pads or shoes.

Brake pads The replaceable friction pads that pinch the brake disc when the brakes are applied. Brake pads consist of a friction material bonded or riveted to a rigid backing plate.

Brake shoe The crescent-shaped carrier to which the brake linings are mounted and which forces the lining against the rotating drum during braking.

Braking systems For more information on braking systems, consult the *Haynes Automotive Brake Manual*.

Breaker bar A long socket wrench handle providing greater leverage.

Bulkhead The insulated partition between the engine and the passenger compartment.

C

Caliper The non-rotating part of a disc-brake assembly that straddles the disc and carries the brake pads. The caliper also contains the hydraulic components that cause the pads to pinch the disc when the brakes are applied. A caliper is also a measuring tool that can be set to measure inside or outside dimensions of an object.

Camshaft A rotating shaft on which a series of cam lobes operate the valve mechanisms. The camshaft may be driven by gears, by sprockets and chain or by sprockets and a belt.

Canister A container in an evaporative emission control system; contains activated charcoal granules to trap vapours from the fuel system.

Canister

Carburettor A device which mixes fuel with air in the proper proportions to provide a desired power output from a spark ignition internal combustion engine.

Castellated Resembling the parapets along the top of a castle wall. For example, a castellated balljoint stud nut.

Castor In wheel alignment, the backward or forward tilt of the steering axis. Castor is positive when the steering axis is inclined rearward at the top.

Glossary of technical terms

Catalytic converter A silencer-like device in the exhaust system which converts certain pollutants in the exhaust gases into less harmful substances.

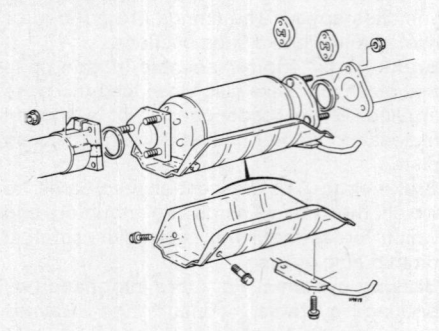

Catalytic converter

Circlip A ring-shaped clip used to prevent endwise movement of cylindrical parts and shafts. An internal circlip is installed in a groove in a housing; an external circlip fits into a groove on the outside of a cylindrical piece such as a shaft.

Clearance The amount of space between two parts. For example, between a piston and a cylinder, between a bearing and a journal, etc.

Coil spring A spiral of elastic steel found in various sizes throughout a vehicle, for example as a springing medium in the suspension and in the valve train.

Compression Reduction in volume, and increase in pressure and temperature, of a gas, caused by squeezing it into a smaller space.

Compression ratio The relationship between cylinder volume when the piston is at top dead centre and cylinder volume when the piston is at bottom dead centre.

Constant velocity (CV) joint A type of universal joint that cancels out vibrations caused by driving power being transmitted through an angle.

Core plug A disc or cup-shaped metal device inserted in a hole in a casting through which core was removed when the casting was formed. Also known as a freeze plug or expansion plug.

Crankcase The lower part of the engine block in which the crankshaft rotates.

Crankshaft The main rotating member, or shaft, running the length of the crankcase, with offset "throws" to which the connecting rods are attached.

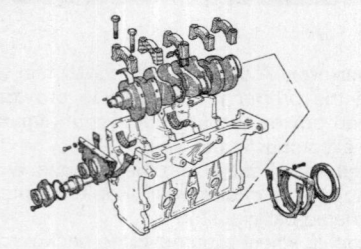

Crankshaft assembly

Crocodile clip See Alligator clip

D

Diagnostic code Code numbers obtained by accessing the diagnostic mode of an engine management computer. This code can be used to determine the area in the system where a malfunction may be located.

Disc brake A brake design incorporating a rotating disc onto which brake pads are squeezed. The resulting friction converts the energy of a moving vehicle into heat.

Double-overhead cam (DOHC) An engine that uses two overhead camshafts, usually one for the intake valves and one for the exhaust valves.

Drivebelt(s) The belt(s) used to drive accessories such as the alternator, water pump, power steering pump, air conditioning compressor, etc. off the crankshaft pulley.

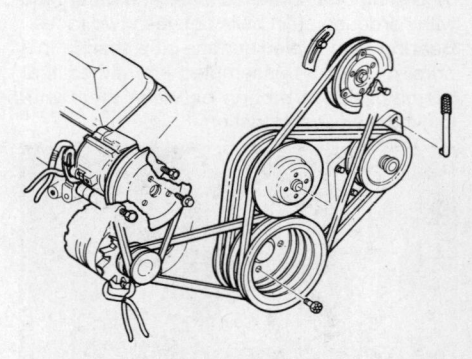

Accessory drivebelts

Driveshaft Any shaft used to transmit motion. Commonly used when referring to the axleshafts on a front wheel drive vehicle.

Drum brake A type of brake using a drum-shaped metal cylinder attached to the inner surface of the wheel. When the brake pedal is pressed, curved brake shoes with friction linings press against the inside of the drum to slow or stop the vehicle.

E

EGR valve A valve used to introduce exhaust gases into the intake air stream.

Electronic control unit (ECU) A computer which controls (for instance) ignition and fuel injection systems, or an anti-lock braking system. For more information refer to the *Haynes Automotive Electrical and Electronic Systems Manual*.

Electronic Fuel Injection (EFI) A computer controlled fuel system that distributes fuel through an injector located in each intake port of the engine.

Emergency brake A braking system, independent of the main hydraulic system, that can be used to slow or stop the vehicle if the primary brakes fail, or to hold the vehicle stationary even though the brake pedal isn't depressed. It usually consists of a hand lever that actuates either front or rear brakes mechanically through a series of cables and linkages. Also known as a handbrake or parking brake.

Endfloat The amount of lengthwise movement between two parts. As applied to a crankshaft, the distance that the crankshaft can move forward and back in the cylinder block.

Engine management system (EMS) A computer controlled system which manages the fuel injection and the ignition systems in an integrated fashion.

Exhaust manifold A part with several passages through which exhaust gases leave the engine combustion chambers and enter the exhaust pipe.

F

Fan clutch A viscous (fluid) drive coupling device which permits variable engine fan speeds in relation to engine speeds.

Feeler blade A thin strip or blade of hardened steel, ground to an exact thickness, used to check or measure clearances between parts.

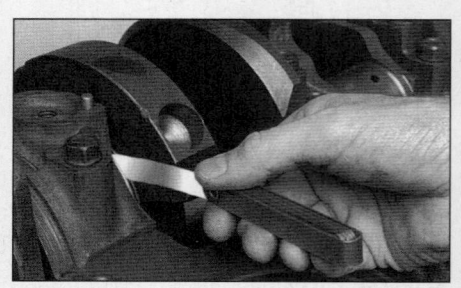

Feeler blade

Firing order The order in which the engine cylinders fire, or deliver their power strokes, beginning with the number one cylinder.

Flywheel A heavy spinning wheel in which energy is absorbed and stored by means of momentum. On cars, the flywheel is attached to the crankshaft to smooth out firing impulses.

Free play The amount of travel before any action takes place. The "looseness" in a linkage, or an assembly of parts, between the initial application of force and actual movement. For example, the distance the brake pedal moves before the pistons in the master cylinder are actuated.

Fuse An electrical device which protects a circuit against accidental overload. The typical fuse contains a soft piece of metal which is calibrated to melt at a predetermined current flow (expressed as amps) and break the circuit.

Fusible link A circuit protection device consisting of a conductor surrounded by heat-resistant insulation. The conductor is smaller than the wire it protects, so it acts as the weakest link in the circuit. Unlike a blown fuse, a failed fusible link must frequently be cut from the wire for replacement.

Glossary of technical terms REF•25

G

Gap The distance the spark must travel in jumping from the centre electrode to the side electrode in a spark plug. Also refers to the spacing between the points in a contact breaker assembly in a conventional points-type ignition, or to the distance between the reluctor or rotor and the pickup coil in an electronic ignition.

Adjusting spark plug gap

Gasket Any thin, soft material - usually cork, cardboard, asbestos or soft metal - installed between two metal surfaces to ensure a good seal. For instance, the cylinder head gasket seals the joint between the block and the cylinder head.

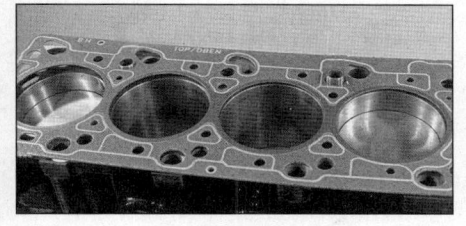

Gasket

Gauge An instrument panel display used to monitor engine conditions. A gauge with a movable pointer on a dial or a fixed scale is an analogue gauge. A gauge with a numerical readout is called a digital gauge.

H

Halfshaft A rotating shaft that transmits power from the final drive unit to a drive wheel, usually when referring to a live rear axle.
Harmonic balancer A device designed to reduce torsion or twisting vibration in the crankshaft. May be incorporated in the crankshaft pulley. Also known as a vibration damper.
Hone An abrasive tool for correcting small irregularities or differences in diameter in an engine cylinder, brake cylinder, etc.
Hydraulic tappet A tappet that utilises hydraulic pressure from the engine's lubrication system to maintain zero clearance (constant contact with both camshaft and valve stem). Automatically adjusts to variation in valve stem length. Hydraulic tappets also reduce valve noise.

I

Ignition timing The moment at which the spark plug fires, usually expressed in the number of crankshaft degrees before the piston reaches the top of its stroke.
Inlet manifold A tube or housing with passages through which flows the air-fuel mixture (carburettor vehicles and vehicles with throttle body injection) or air only (port fuel-injected vehicles) to the port openings in the cylinder head.

J

Jump start Starting the engine of a vehicle with a discharged or weak battery by attaching jump leads from the weak battery to a charged or helper battery.

L

Load Sensing Proportioning Valve (LSPV) A brake hydraulic system control valve that works like a proportioning valve, but also takes into consideration the amount of weight carried by the rear axle.
Locknut A nut used to lock an adjustment nut, or other threaded component, in place. For example, a locknut is employed to keep the adjusting nut on the rocker arm in position.
Lockwasher A form of washer designed to prevent an attaching nut from working loose.

M

MacPherson strut A type of front suspension system devised by Earle MacPherson at Ford of England. In its original form, a simple lateral link with the anti-roll bar creates the lower control arm. A long strut - an integral coil spring and shock absorber - is mounted between the body and the steering knuckle. Many modern so-called MacPherson strut systems use a conventional lower A-arm and don't rely on the anti-roll bar for location.
Multimeter An electrical test instrument with the capability to measure voltage, current and resistance.

N

NOx Oxides of Nitrogen. A common toxic pollutant emitted by petrol and diesel engines at higher temperatures.

O

Ohm The unit of electrical resistance. One volt applied to a resistance of one ohm will produce a current of one amp.
Ohmmeter An instrument for measuring electrical resistance.
O-ring A type of sealing ring made of a special rubber-like material; in use, the O-ring is compressed into a groove to provide the sealing action.
Overhead cam (ohc) engine An engine with the camshaft(s) located on top of the cylinder head(s).
Overhead valve (ohv) engine An engine with the valves located in the cylinder head, but with the camshaft located in the engine block.
Oxygen sensor A device installed in the engine exhaust manifold, which senses the oxygen content in the exhaust and converts this information into an electric current. Also called a Lambda sensor.

P

Phillips screw A type of screw head having a cross instead of a slot for a corresponding type of screwdriver.
Plastigage A thin strip of plastic thread, available in different sizes, used for measuring clearances. For example, a strip of Plastigage is laid across a bearing journal. The parts are assembled and dismantled; the width of the crushed strip indicates the clearance between journal and bearing.

Plastigage

Propeller shaft The long hollow tube with universal joints at both ends that carries power from the transmission to the differential on front-engined rear wheel drive vehicles.
Proportioning valve A hydraulic control valve which limits the amount of pressure to the rear brakes during panic stops to prevent wheel lock-up.

R

Rack-and-pinion steering A steering system with a pinion gear on the end of the steering shaft that mates with a rack (think of a geared wheel opened up and laid flat). When the steering wheel is turned, the pinion turns, moving the rack to the left or right. This movement is transmitted through the track rods to the steering arms at the wheels.
Radiator A liquid-to-air heat transfer device designed to reduce the temperature of the coolant in an internal combustion engine cooling system.
Refrigerant Any substance used as a heat transfer agent in an air-conditioning system. R-12 has been the principle refrigerant for many years; recently, however, manufacturers have begun using R-134a, a non-CFC substance that is considered less harmful to the ozone in the upper atmosphere.
Rocker arm A lever arm that rocks on a shaft or pivots on a stud. In an overhead valve engine, the rocker arm converts the upward movement of the pushrod into a downward movement to open a valve.

Glossary of technical terms

Rotor In a distributor, the rotating device inside the cap that connects the centre electrode and the outer terminals as it turns, distributing the high voltage from the coil secondary winding to the proper spark plug. Also, that part of an alternator which rotates inside the stator. Also, the rotating assembly of a turbocharger, including the compressor wheel, shaft and turbine wheel.

Runout The amount of wobble (in-and-out movement) of a gear or wheel as it's rotated. The amount a shaft rotates "out-of-true." The out-of-round condition of a rotating part.

S

Sealant A liquid or paste used to prevent leakage at a joint. Sometimes used in conjunction with a gasket.

Sealed beam lamp An older headlight design which integrates the reflector, lens and filaments into a hermetically-sealed one-piece unit. When a filament burns out or the lens cracks, the entire unit is simply replaced.

Serpentine drivebelt A single, long, wide accessory drivebelt that's used on some newer vehicles to drive all the accessories, instead of a series of smaller, shorter belts. Serpentine drivebelts are usually tensioned by an automatic tensioner.

Serpentine drivebelt

Shim Thin spacer, commonly used to adjust the clearance or relative positions between two parts. For example, shims inserted into or under bucket tappets control valve clearances. Clearance is adjusted by changing the thickness of the shim.

Slide hammer A special puller that screws into or hooks onto a component such as a shaft or bearing; a heavy sliding handle on the shaft bottoms against the end of the shaft to knock the component free.

Sprocket A tooth or projection on the periphery of a wheel, shaped to engage with a chain or drivebelt. Commonly used to refer to the sprocket wheel itself.

Starter inhibitor switch On vehicles with an automatic transmission, a switch that prevents starting if the vehicle is not in Neutral or Park.

Strut See MacPherson strut.

T

Tappet A cylindrical component which transmits motion from the cam to the valve stem, either directly or via a pushrod and rocker arm. Also called a cam follower.

Thermostat A heat-controlled valve that regulates the flow of coolant between the cylinder block and the radiator, so maintaining optimum engine operating temperature. A thermostat is also used in some air cleaners in which the temperature is regulated.

Thrust bearing The bearing in the clutch assembly that is moved in to the release levers by clutch pedal action to disengage the clutch. Also referred to as a release bearing.

Timing belt A toothed belt which drives the camshaft. Serious engine damage may result if it breaks in service.

Timing chain A chain which drives the camshaft.

Toe-in The amount the front wheels are closer together at the front than at the rear. On rear wheel drive vehicles, a slight amount of toe-in is usually specified to keep the front wheels running parallel on the road by offsetting other forces that tend to spread the wheels apart.

Toe-out The amount the front wheels are closer together at the rear than at the front. On front wheel drive vehicles, a slight amount of toe-out is usually specified.

Tools For full information on choosing and using tools, refer to the Haynes Automotive Tools Manual.

Tracer A stripe of a second colour applied to a wire insulator to distinguish that wire from another one with the same colour insulator.

Tune-up A process of accurate and careful adjustments and parts replacement to obtain the best possible engine performance.

Turbocharger A centrifugal device, driven by exhaust gases, that pressurises the intake air. Normally used to increase the power output from a given engine displacement, but can also be used primarily to reduce exhaust emissions (as on VW's "Umwelt" Diesel engine).

U

Universal joint or U-joint A double-pivoted connection for transmitting power from a driving to a driven shaft through an angle. A U-joint consists of two Y-shaped yokes and a cross-shaped member called the spider.

V

Valve A device through which the flow of liquid, gas, vacuum, or loose material in bulk may be started, stopped, or regulated by a movable part that opens, shuts, or partially obstructs one or more ports or passageways. A valve is also the movable part of such a device.

Valve clearance The clearance between the valve tip (the end of the valve stem) and the rocker arm or tappet. The valve clearance is measured when the valve is closed.

Vernier caliper A precision measuring instrument that measures inside and outside dimensions. Not quite as accurate as a micrometer, but more convenient.

Viscosity The thickness of a liquid or its resistance to flow.

Volt A unit for expressing electrical "pressure" in a circuit. One volt that will produce a current of one ampere through a resistance of one ohm.

W

Welding Various processes used to join metal items by heating the areas to be joined to a molten state and fusing them together. For more information refer to the Haynes Automotive Welding Manual.

Wiring diagram A drawing portraying the components and wires in a vehicle's electrical system, using standardised symbols. For more information refer to the Haynes Automotive Electrical and Electronic Systems Manual.

Index REF•27

Note: *References throughout this index are in the form "Chapter number" • "Page number". So, for example, 2C•15 refers to page 15 of Chapter 2C.*

A

A-pillar trim – 11•22
ABS
  hydraulic unit – 9•14
  wheel sensor – 9•15
Accelerator pedal – 4A•4
Accelerometer sensor – 9•15
Accumulator/dehydrator – 3•14
Aerial – 12•19
Air conditioning system – 3•11
  control panel illumination – 12•11
  controls – 3•10
Air filter – 1•13, 4A•3
Airbags – 0•5, 12•20
  crash/lateral acceleration sensors – 12•22
  restraint control module (RCM) – 12•22
  wiring contact unit – 12•21
Airflow sensor – 4A•10
Airlocks – 1•21
Alarm system – 12•22
Alternator – 5A•4
Antifreeze – 0•11, 0•17, 1•21, 3•3
Anti-roll bar – 10•7, 10•11
Approach light – 12•9
Audio unit – 12•18, 12•19
Auto-dimming mirror – 11•15
Automatic temperature control – 3•11
Automatic transmission – 7B•1 *et seq*
  control module – 7B•5
  fault finding – 7B•2, REF•19
  fluid – 0•17, 1•18
  fluid temperature sensor – 7B•5
Auxiliary drivebelt – 1•15

B

B-pillar trim – 11•22
Battery – 0•5, 0•15, 5A•2, 5A•3
  remote control – 1•19
Beam adjustment
  halogen headlight – 12•13
  Xenon gas discharge headlight – 12•15
Bleeding
  brakes – 9•13
  clutch – 6•3
  steering system – 10•13
Blower motor – 3•7, 3•8
  switch – 3•11
Body electrical system – 12•1 *et seq*
Bodywork and fittings – 11•1 *et seq*
  corrosion – REF•15
Bonnet – 11•8
  locks – 11•8
  strut – 11•17
Boot lid – 11•15
  lock – 11•16, 11•18
  strut – 11•17
Braking system – 1•12, 9•1 *et seq*, REF•12, REF•13, REF•14
  discs – 1•9, 9•5, 9•10
  drums – 1•10, 9•5
  fault finding – REF•20
  fluid – 0•12, 0•17, 1•19
  light – 9•15, 12•10, 12•13
  pads – 1•9, 9•2, 9•8
  pedal position switch – 7B•4, 9•15
  pedal shift interlock actuator – 7B•4
  pipes – 1•11
Bulbs – 0•16, 12•7, 12•10
Bumpers – 11•4
Buying spare parts – REF•7

C

C-pillar trim – 11•23
Cables
  gearchange – 7A•2, 7A•3
  handbrake – 9•16
  selector – 7B•2
Calipers – 9•4, 9•10
Camshafts – 2A•12, 2B•9
  oil seals – 2A•12
  position sensor – 4A•11
  sprockets – 2A•10
  timing oil control solenoids – 4A•12
Canister purge valve (EVAP) – 4B•3
Carbon canister – 4B•2
Carpets – 11•2
Catalytic converters – 4B•2
CD autochanger – 12•19
Central locking system – 11•18, •17
  switches – 12•6
Centre console – 11•27
  switches – 12•5
Charging – 5A•2, 5A•3
Clutch – 1•12, 6•1 *et seq*
  fault finding – REF•19
  fluid – 0•12, 0•17
  pedal position switch – 4A•12
Coil spring – 10•9
Coils (ignition) – 5B•2
Compression test – 2A•3, 2B•3
Compressor – 3•13
Condenser – 3•12
Connecting rods – 2C•6
Console – 11•27, 11•29
Control arm – 10•6, 10•10
Conversion factors – REF•6
Coolant – 0•11, 0•17, 1•20, 3•3
  pump – 3•7
  temperature sensor – 3•5
Cooling, heating & air conditioning systems – 3•1 *et seq*
Cooling system fault finding – REF•18
Courtesy lights – 12•11
  switches – 12•6
Crankcase emission control – 4B•1, 4B•2
Crankshaft – 2C•6
  oil seals – 2A•17, 2B•12
  position sensor – 4A•11
  pulley – 2A•6, 2B•6
  sprocket – 2A•11
Crash/lateral acceleration sensors – 12•22
Cylinder head – 2A•14, 2B•12, 2C•5
  cover – 2A•5, 2B•5

D

D-pillar trim – 11•24
Degas shut-off valve – 3•5
Dehydrator – 3•14
Depressurisation of fuel system – 4A•2
Dimensions – REF•1
Dipped beam
  halogen headlight – 12•7
  Xenon gas discharge headlight – 12•14
Direction indicators – 12•8, 12•9
Discs – 1•9, 9•5, 9•10
Distance sensor – 12•18
Doors – 11•14, REF•13
  handles – 11•12
  inner trim panel – 11•8
  locks – 11•12, 11•18
  mirror – 11•14, 12•5
  window glass – 11•10
  window regulator – 11•10
Drain tubes (sun roof) – 11•19
Drivebelt – 1•15
Driveplate – 2A•18, 2B•16
Driver's lower facia panel – 11•27
Driveshafts – 8•1 *et seq*, REF•14
  fault finding – REF•20
  gaiters – 1•11, 8•3,
  oil seals – 7A•4
Drivetrain – 1•12
Drums – 1•10, 9•5
DVD
  navigation system – 3•11
  player – 12•19

E

Earth fault – 12•3
EGR solenoid/valve – 4B•3
Electric shock – 0•5
Electric window switches – 12•6
Electrical system – 1•12, REF•13
  fault finding – 12•2, REF•21, REF•22
Electro-hydraulic power steering – 10•14
Electronic control modules
  generic electronic module (GEM) – 12•22
  lighting control module (LCM) – 12•23
Electronic stability control – 9•15
Emblems – 11•18
Emission control systems – 4B•1 *et seq*, REF•15
Engine fault finding – 5B•2, REF•17, REF•18
Engine oil – 0•11, 0•17, 1•6
Engine removal and overhaul procedures – 2C•1 *et seq*
Evaporative emission control – 4B•1, 4B•2
Evaporator – 3•12
Exhaust emission control – 4B•1, 4B•3
Exhaust gas recirculation (EGR) – 4B•2
Exhaust manifold – 4A•13
Exhaust specialists – REF•7
Exhaust system – 1•10, 4A•14, REF•14, REF•15
Expansion tank – 3•6
  pressure cap – 1•22

F

Facia – 11•27, 11•30
  switches – 12•5
Fans – 3•4
Fault finding – REF•16 *et seq*
  automatic transmission – 7B•2, REF•19
  braking system – REF•20
  clutch – REF•19

REF•28 Index

Note: *References throughout this index are in the form "**Chapter number**" • "**Page number**". So, for example, 2C•15 refers to page 15 of Chapter 2C.*

cooling system – REF•18
driveshafts – REF•20
electrical system – 12•2, •21, REF•22
engine – 5B•2, REF•17, REF•188
fuel and exhaust systems – REF•18
manual transmission – REF•19
steering and suspension – REF•21
Filler flap motor – 12•23
Filter
    air – 1•13, 4A•3
    oil – 1•6
    pollen – 1•12
Fixed windows – 11•18
Fluid
    cooler – 7B•6
    pan – 7B•5
    temperature sensor – 7B•5
Fluid leaks – 1•7
Fluids – 0•17
Flywheel – 2A•18, 2B•16
Foglamp – 12•8, 12•10, 12•12, 12•13
    switch – 12•6
Footwell lights – 12•11
Ford Focus manual – 0•4
Fuel & exhaust systems – 4A•1 *et seq*
    fault finding – REF•18
Fuel economy – REF•2
Fuel filler flap motor – 12•23
Fuel hoses – 1•8
Fuel line – 1•11, 4A•3
Fuel system – REF•15
Fuses – 0•16, 12•3

G

Gaiters
    driveshaft – 1•11, 8•3
    steering rack – 10•13
Gas discharge headlight system – 12•14
Gaskets – REF•8
Gear lever – 7A•3, 7B•3
Gearchange cables – 7A•2, 7A•3
General repair procedures – REF•8
Generic electronic module (GEM) – 11•18, 12•22
Glass (doors) – 11•10
Glossary of technical terms – REF•23 *et seq*
Glovebox – 11•30
    light – 12•11
    light switch – 12•5
Grab handle – 11•22
Grille – 11•7

H

Handbrake – 1•13, 9•15, 9•16, REF•12
    warning switch – 12•6
Handles
    doors – 11•12
    grab – 11•22
Hazard warning switch – 12•6
Headlight – 12•12
    control switch – 12•6
    halogen – 12•7
    Xenon gas discharge system – 12•14
Heating/ventilation system – 3•2, 3•7
    blower motor – 3•7

control panel illumination – 12•11
controls – 3•10
matrix – 3•8, 3•10
High- and low-pressure cut-off switches – 3•15
High-level brake light – 12•10, 12•13
Hinge lubrication – 1•11
Horn – 1•7, 12•17
Hoses – 3•3, 9•12
    condition – 1•7
HT coils – 5B•2
Hub carrier – 10•3, 10•8
Hydraulic unit (ABS) – 9•14

I

Identifying leaks – 0•9
Ignition system – 5B•1 *et seq*
    switch – 12•4
In-car repair procedures
    1.4 & 1.6 litre engines (Duratec 16V) – 2A•1 *et seq*
    1.8 & 2.0 litre engines (Duratec HE) – 2B•1 *et seq*
Indicators – 12•8, 12•9
Inertia switch – 4A•7
Injectors – 4A•8
Inlet manifold – 4A•12
Input shaft speed sensor – 7B•4
Instrument panel – 1•12, 12•15
    bulbs – 12•11
Interior lights – 12•11
    switches – 12•6
Intermediate section – 2C•6

J

Jacking and vehicle support – REF•9
Joint mating faces – REF•8
Jump starting – 0•7

K

Keyless entry system module – 11•18
Knock sensor – 5B•3

L

Lambda sensors – 4B•1, 4B•3
Lateral acceleration sensors – 12•22
Lateral link – 10•8
Leaks – 0•9, 1•7
Lights – 12•12
    check – 1•7
    switch – 12•5
Lighting control module (LCM) – 12•14, 12•23
Limited Operation Strategy (fuel system) – 4A•7
Link arms – 10•10
Locks
    bonnet – 11•8
    boot lid – 11•16, 11•18
    central locking – 11•18, 12•17
    central locking switches – 12•6
    doors – 11•12, 11•18
    lubrication – 1•11
    tailgate – 11•17, 11•18
Lower control arm – 10•10

Lower facia panel – 11•27
Low-pressure cut-off switch – 3•15
Lubricants and fluids – 0•17
Luggage compaartment
    light – 12•11
    side panel – 11•25

M

Main beam
    halogen headlight – 12•7
    Xenon gas discharge headlight – 12•14
Main bearing caps – 2C•6
Manifolds – 4A•12
Manual transmission – 7A•1 *et seq*
    fault finding – REF•19
    oil – 0•17, 1•19, 7A•5
Mass airflow sensor – 4A•10
Master cylinder
    brakes – 9•10
    clutch – 6•3
Matrix – 3•8, 3•10
Metal pipes – 1•8
Mirrors – 11•14, 11•15, REF•12
    adjuster – 12•5
    light – 12•11
Misfire – 5B•2
MOT test checks – REF•12 *et seq*
Mountings – 2A•18, 2B•17

N

Navigation system – 3•11
Number plate light – 12•10

O

Oil control solenoids – 4A•12
Oil
    engine – 0•11, 0•17, 1•6
    manual transmission – 0•17, 1•19, 7A•5
Oil filter – 1•6
Oil pressure switch – 2A•17, 2B•15
Oil pump – 2A•16, 2B•14
Oil seals – REF•8
    automatic transmission – 7B•5
    camshaft – 2A•12
    crankshaft – 2A•17, 2B•12
    manual transmission – 7A•4
Oil separator – 4B•2
Open-circuit – 12•2
Output shaft speed sensor – 7B•5
    oil seal – 7B•5
Overhead console – 11•29
Oxygen (lambda) sensors – 4B•1, 4B•3

P

Pads – 1•9, 9•2, 9•8
Parcel shelf – 11•27
Parking aid components – 12•18
Pedals
    accelerator – 4A•4
    brake – 9•12
    brake position switch – 7B•4, 9•15
    brake shift interlock actuator – 7B•4
    clutch – 6•1
    clutch position switch – 4A•12

Index REF•29

Note: *References throughout this index are in the form "**Chapter number** • "**Page number**". So, for example, 2C•15 refers to page 15 of Chapter 2C.*

Pipes – 1•8, 1•11, 4A•3, 9•12
Pistons – 2C•6
Pollen filter – 1•12
Power steering
　fluid – 0•12, 0•17
　pump – 10•14
Powertrain Control Module – 4A•10
Pressure cap – 1•22
Puncture repair – 0•8

Q
Quick-release couplings – 4A•3

R
Radiator – 3•5
　electric cooling fans – 3•4
　grille – 11•7
Range control positioning motor (Xenon gas discharge headlight) – 12•15
Range sensor (automatic transmission) – 7B•3
Range/distance sensor (parking) – 12•18
Reading lights – 12•10
Rear combination light – 12•9, 12•13
Rear side panel – 11•27
Regulator (door window) – 11•10
Relays – 12•4
Release bearing (clutch) – 6•4
Remote control battery – 1•19
Restraint control module (RCM) – 12•22
Reversing lights – 12•10, 12•13
　switch – 7A•4
Ride height sensor (Xenon gas discharge headlight) – 12•14, 12•15
Road test – 1•12
Roadside repairs – 0•6 *et seq*
Roadwheel nut tightness – 1•11
Roll restrictor – 2A•19, 2B•17
Roll-over valve – 4A•6
Routine maintenance –
　bodywork and underframe – 11•2
　upholstery and carpets – 11•2
Routine maintenance & servicing – 1•1 *et seq*

S
Safety first! – 0•5, 0•12
Scratches – 11•2
Seat belts – 1•13, 11•20
Seats – 11•19
　heating switches – 12•7
Selector – 7B•3
　cable – 7B•2
　lever shift interlock solenoid – 7B•5
　shaft oil seal – 7A•4
Servo unit – 9•13, 9•14
Shock absorbers – 10•9, REF•13, REF•14
Short-circuit – 12•2
Shut-off (inertia) switch – 4A•7
Sidelight
　halogen headlight – 12•8
　Xenon gas discharge headlight – 12•14
Slave cylinder (clutch) – 6•3
Spark plugs – 1•14
Speakers – 12•18, 12•19
Speed sensor – 7B•4, 7B•5

Springs – 10•9, REF•14
Sprockets – 2A•10
Starting and charging systems – 5A•1 *et seq*
Steering – 1•10, 1•12, REF•13, REF•14
　angles – 10•15
　column – 10•11, REF•12
　column shrouds – 11•25
　column switches – 12•5
　rack – 10•12
　rack gaiters – 10•13
　wheel – 10•11, REF•12
　wheel rotation sensor – 9•15
　wheel switches – 12•6
Strut
　suspension – 10•5
　tailgate, boot lid or bonnet – 11•17
Subframe – 10•16
Sump – 2A•15, 2B•14
Sun blind – 11•18
Sunroof – 11•18
　control switch – 12•6
　motor – 12•17
Sunvisor – 11•22
　light – 12•11
Support bearing (driveshaft) – 8•4
Suspension and steering – 1•10, 1•11, 1•12, 10•1 *et seq*, REF•13, REF•14
　fault finding – REF•21
Switches – 12•5
　blower motor – 3•11
　brake light – 9•15
　brake pedal position – 9•15
　clutch pedal position – 4A•12
　high- and low-pressure cut-off (air conditioning) – 3•15
　ignition – 12•4
　illumination – 12•11
　oil pressure – 2A•17, 2B•15
　reversing light – 7A•4

T
Tailgate – 11•16
　locks – 11•17, 11•18
　strut – 11•17
　wiper motor – 12•17
Tappets – 2A•12, 2B•9
Technical terms – REF•23 *et seq*
Temperature control – 3•11
Temperature sensor – 3•5, 7B•5
Tensioner – 2A•10, 2B•8
Thermostat – 3•3
Throttle body – 4A•7
Tie-rod – 10•10
Timing (ignition) – 5B•2
Timing belt – 2A•8
　covers – 2A•8
　tensioner and sprockets – 2A•10
Timing chain, tensioner and guides – 2B•8
　cover – 2B•6
TMAP sensor – 4A•9
Tools and working facilities – REF•8, REF•10 *et seq*
Top Dead Centre (TDC) for No 1 piston location – 2A•4, 2B•4
Towing – 0•9
Track rod end – 10•15

Traction control system – 9•15
Transmission
　control module – 7B•5
　range sensor – 7B•3
Trim mouldings – 11•18
Trim panels – 11•22
　doors – 11•8
Turbine (input) shaft speed sensor – 7B•4
Tyres – REF•15
　condition and pressure – 0•13
　pressures – 0•17
　specialists – REF•7

U
Underbonnet check points – 0•10
Upholstery – 11•2
Upper control arm – 10•10

V
Vacuum hoses – 1•8
Vacuum servo unit – 9•13, 9•14
Valve clearances – 2A•6, 2B•5
Valves – 2C•6
Vanity mirror light – 12•11
Variable camshaft timing oil control solenoids – 4A•12
Vehicle identification – REF•7, REF•13
Vehicle support – REF•9
Ventilation system – 3•2, 3•7
Vibration damper – 2A•6

W
Washer system – 12•16
　fluid – 0•14
Weekly checks – 0•10 *et seq*
Weights – REF•1
Wheels – 1•11, REF•15
　alignment – 10•15
　bearings – 10•3, 10•8, REF•14
　changing – 0•8
　nut tightness – 1•11
Wheel arch liner – 11•31
Wheel cylinder – 9•7
Wheel sensor (ABS) – 9•15
Windows – 11•10, 11•18
　regulator (doors) – 11•10
　switches – 12•6
Windscreen – 11•18, REF•12
　wipers – 12•15
Wiper arms – 12•15
Wiper blades – 0•14
Wiper motor
　tailgate – 12•17
　windscreen – 12•16
Wiring check – 1•8
Wiring diagrams – 12•24 *et seq*
Working facilities – REF•11

X
Xenon gas discharge headlight – 12•14

Y
Yaw rate sensor – 9•15

Notes

Notes

Preserving Our Motoring Heritage

The Model J Duesenberg Derham Tourster. Only eight of these magnificent cars were ever built – this is the only example to be found outside the United States of America

Almost every car you've ever loved, loathed or desired is gathered under one roof at the Haynes Motor Museum. Over 300 immaculately presented cars and motorbikes represent every aspect of our motoring heritage, from elegant reminders of bygone days, such as the superb Model J Duesenberg to curiosities like the bug-eyed BMW Isetta. There are also many old friends and flames. Perhaps you remember the 1959 Ford Popular that you did your courting in? The magnificent 'Red Collection' is a spectacle of classic sports cars including AC, Alfa Romeo, Austin Healey, Ferrari, Lamborghini, Maserati, MG, Riley, Porsche and Triumph.

A Perfect Day Out

Each and every vehicle at the Haynes Motor Museum has played its part in the history and culture of Motoring. Today, they make a wonderful spectacle and a great day out for all the family. Bring the kids, bring Mum and Dad, but above all bring your camera to capture those golden memories for ever. You will also find an impressive array of motoring memorabilia, a comfortable 70 seat video cinema and one of the most extensive transport book shops in Britain. The Pit Stop Cafe serves everything from a cup of tea to wholesome, home-made meals or, if you prefer, you can enjoy the large picnic area nestled in the beautiful rural surroundings of Somerset.

John Haynes O.B.E., Founder and Chairman of the museum at the wheel of a Haynes Light 12.

Graham Hill's Lola Cosworth Formula 1 car next to a 1934 Riley Sports.

The Museum is situated on the A359 Yeovil to Frome road at Sparkford, just off the A303 in Somerset. It is about 40 miles south of Bristol, and 25 minutes drive from the M5 intersection at Taunton.
Open 9.30am - 5.30pm (10.00am - 4.00pm Winter) 7 days a week, *except Christmas Day, Boxing Day and New Years Day*
Special rates available for schools, coach parties and outings Charitable Trust No. 292048